MICHIGAN

PAUL VACHON

Contents

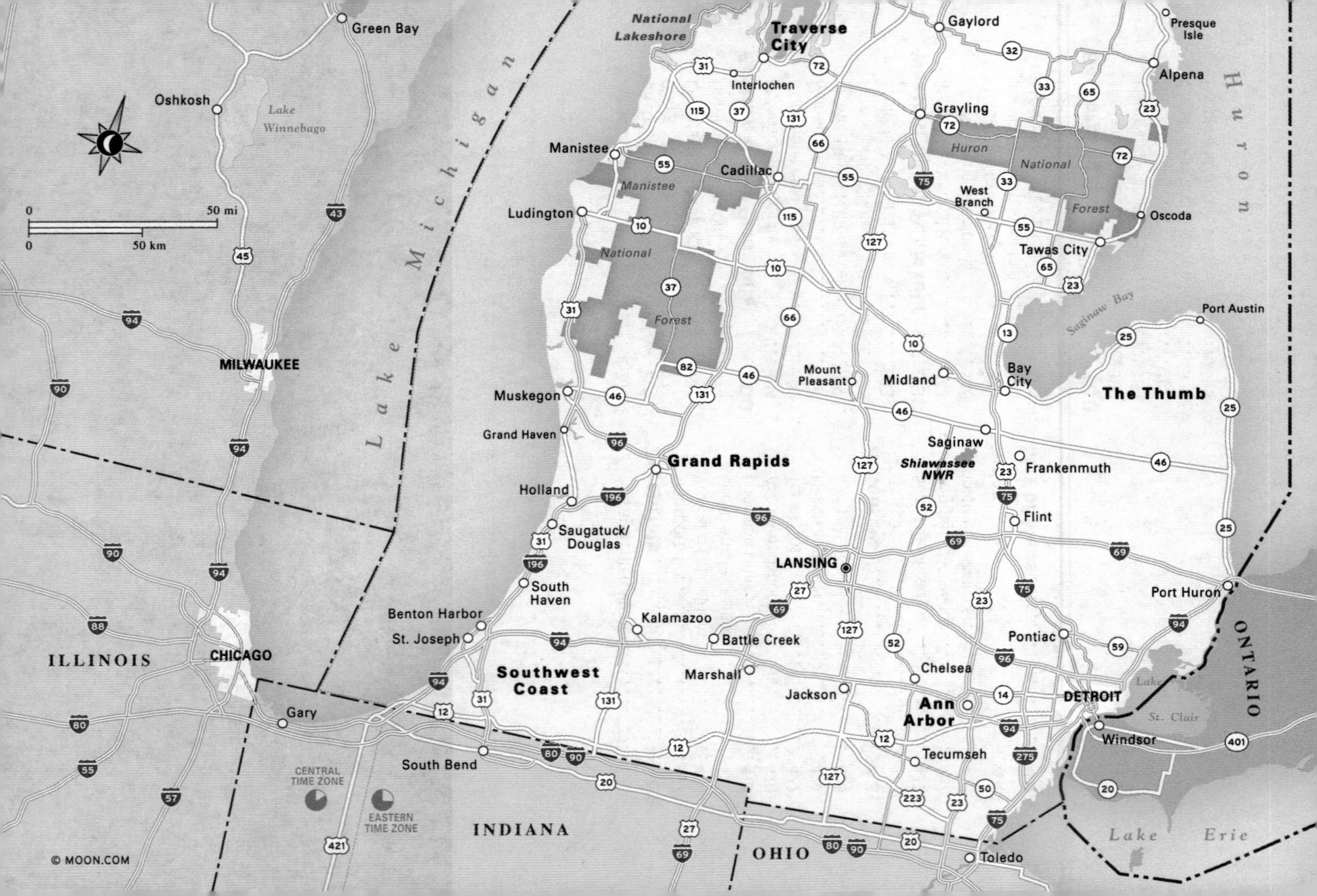
Green Bay
National Lakeshore
Traverse City
Gaylord
Presque Isle
Oshkosh
Lake Winnebago
Interlochen
Alpena
Grayling
Huron National Forest
Manistee
Cadillac
Manistee National Forest
Lake Michigan
Huron
Ludington
West Branch
Oscoda
Tawas City
Saginaw Bay
Port Austin
MILWAUKEE
Mount Pleasant
Midland
Bay City
The Thumb
Muskegon
Grand Haven
Saginaw
Grand Rapids
Shiawassee NWR
Frankenmuth
Holland
Flint
Saugatuck/Douglas
LANSING
South Haven
Port Huron
Benton Harbor
Kalamazoo
St. Joseph
Battle Creek
Pontiac
ILLINOIS
CHICAGO
Southwest Coast
Marshall
Chelsea
Jackson
Ann Arbor
DETROIT
Lake St. Clair
ONTARIO
Gary
Windsor
Tecumseh
South Bend
CENTRAL TIME ZONE
EASTERN TIME ZONE
INDIANA
Lake Erie
OHIO
Toledo
© MOON.COM
0
50 mi
0
50 km

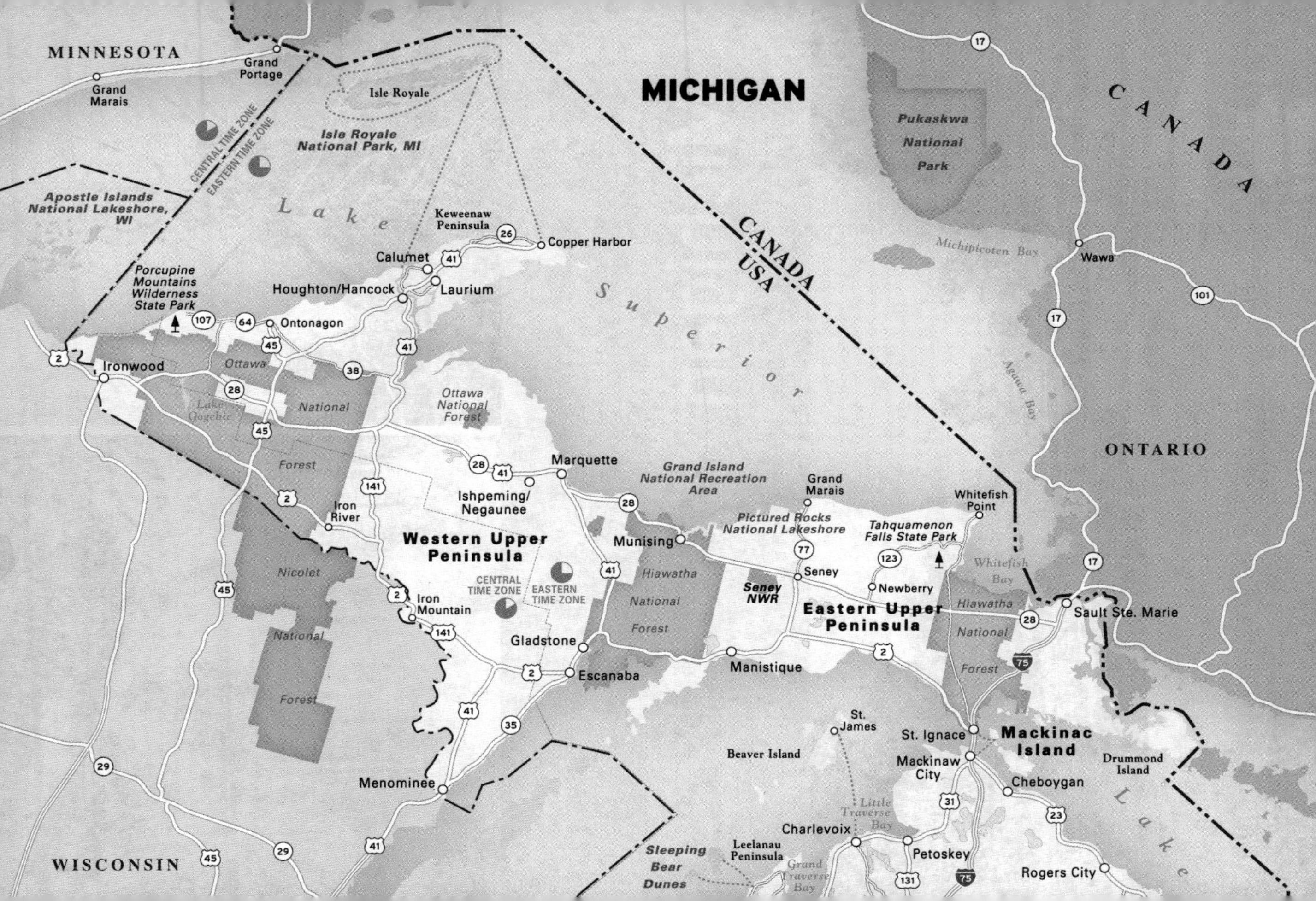
MICHIGAN
MINNESOTA
Grand Portage
Grand Marais
Isle Royale
Isle Royale National Park, MI
CENTRAL TIME ZONE
EASTERN TIME ZONE
Apostle Islands National Lakeshore, WI
Lake Superior
Keweenaw Peninsula
Copper Harbor
Calumet
Laurium
Houghton/Hancock
Porcupine Mountains Wilderness State Park
Ontonagon
Ironwood
Ottawa National Forest
Lake Gogebic
Marquette
Ishpeming/Negaunee
Iron River
Western Upper Peninsula
Nicolet National Forest
Iron Mountain
CENTRAL TIME ZONE
EASTERN TIME ZONE
Gladstone
Escanaba
Menominee
Munising
Grand Island National Recreation Area
Grand Marais
Pictured Rocks National Lakeshore
Tahquamenon Falls State Park
Whitefish Point
Seney
Seney NWR
Newberry
Hiawatha National Forest
Eastern Upper Peninsula
Whitefish Bay
Sault Ste. Marie
Manistique
St. James
Beaver Island
St. Ignace
Mackinac Island
Mackinaw City
Cheboygan
Drummond Island
Little Traverse Bay
Charlevoix
Petoskey
Leelanau Peninsula
Sleeping Bear Dunes
Grand Traverse Bay
Rogers City
Lake
WISCONSIN
CANADA
USA
Pukaskwa National Park
Michipicoten Bay
Wawa
Agawa Bay
ONTARIO
CANADA

DISCOVER

Michigan

Michigan may be known mainly for Motown, Madonna, and muscle cars. But beneath the surface, the Great Lakes State offers a great deal of diversity.

Divided into the mitten-shaped Lower Peninsula and the breathtaking Upper Peninsula, Michigan is the only U.S. state that is surrounded by four of the five Great Lakes—lakes so massive that scientists classify them as inland seas. The Lower Peninsula boasts a wealth of rural areas, nostalgic villages, resort towns, and urban centers like Detroit and Grand Rapids, plus a bevy of art galleries and wineries. North of the Mackinac Bridge, the Upper Peninsula is a vast tract of forests, beaches, mountains, and waterfalls.

Most tourists visit in spring and summer, yet the snowy winters have grown popular, too, for adventures like skating across frozen lakes or riding snowmobiles through glistening forests. Autumn invites drives along winding country roads flanked by apple orchards and crimson maple trees.

With so much to experience, you may begin a love affair with this remarkable state that will create lasting memories.

Clockwise from top left: sculpture by Roxy Paine in the Frederik Meijer Gardens and Sculpture Park in Grand Rapids; Wagner Falls in Munising; Michigan Capitol Dome interior; metal horse by Doug Melvin near Cross Village; windmill and tulips in Holland, Michigan; Anna Scripps Whitcomb Conservatory on Belle Isle.

9 TOP EXPERIENCES

1 **Cruise along the Pictured Rocks:** The calm lake waters and the remarkable mineral colors of the cliffs combine to create an unmatched experience (page 324).

2 **Romantic Getaway to Mackinac Island:** If you're looking for a long, romantic weekend, look no further. You'll find picturesque views and plenty of Victorian charm (page 19).

3 Go Museum Hopping: Ann Arbor (page 87) and Grand Rapids (page 137) are home to some of the finest museums in the Midwest. Whether your interests lie with natural sciences, art, or American history, there are lots of ways to let your imagination soar.

4 Hit the Trail: The Upper and Lower Peninsulas offer hundreds of miles of hiking trails, from easy paths to advanced backpacking routes (page 23).

5 Explore the Shore: Michigan is blessed with the most miles of shoreline among the contiguous 48 states. Lake Superior's shore offers hearty pine trees, stony beaches, and craggy rocks while soft, sandy beaches line Lake Michigan (page 20).

6 Raise a Glass: Explore the ever-expanding wine industry (page 24) or, if you prefer beer, follow the Traverse City Ale Trail to sample microbreweries one by one (page 220).

7 Experience Bavarian Culture in Frankenmuth: "Michigan's Little Bavaria" has grown from a quiet German farm town to the state's top tourist attraction (page 114).

8 Dine out in Detroit: What better way to experience Detroit's ongoing renaissance than eating your way through its restaurant scene? The possibilities are endless, from fried zucchini in Greektown or taquitos in Mexicantown and scaloppine *picante* at any of numerous the Italian restaurants (page 59).

9 See Wildlife: Invest in a good pair of binoculars, offer up a day of your time, and you'll be rewarded with sightings of moose, elk, and many varieties of avian life (page 27).

Planning Your Trip

Where to Go

Detroit

Michigan's densely populated southeast corner offers a huge variety of experiences in a tightly compact area. Known for its **Motown music,** rock-and-roll vibe, and legendary **sports** figures, **Detroit** is undergoing a renaissance, with the revitalizing of its downtown and Midtown areas and a vibrant **nightlife** scene.

Ann Arbor

Ann Arbor offers a unique blend of **big-city energy** and **college-town friendliness,** with galleries, gardens, and, of course, football. Visitors are often surprised by the cultural attractions that abound in this region, from impressive museums like **University of Michigan's Museum of Art** and **Museum of Natural History** to the **Purple Rose Theatre Company** in nearby Chelsea.

The Thumb

If you're looking for a secluded summer vacation spot, you've found it. Waterfront **resorts and cottages,** the warm waters of **Lake Huron,** and tranquil **beaches** will seduce any leisure seeker. As a bonus, a number of inviting lakeside communities offer welcoming **summer festivals and concerts.**

Grand Rapids and the Heartland

A wide swath of rolling **prairies,** scenic lakes, weathered barns, and abundant **farmland,** the Heartland is also home to some of the state's finest

covered bridge, Sleeping Bear Dunes National Lakeshore

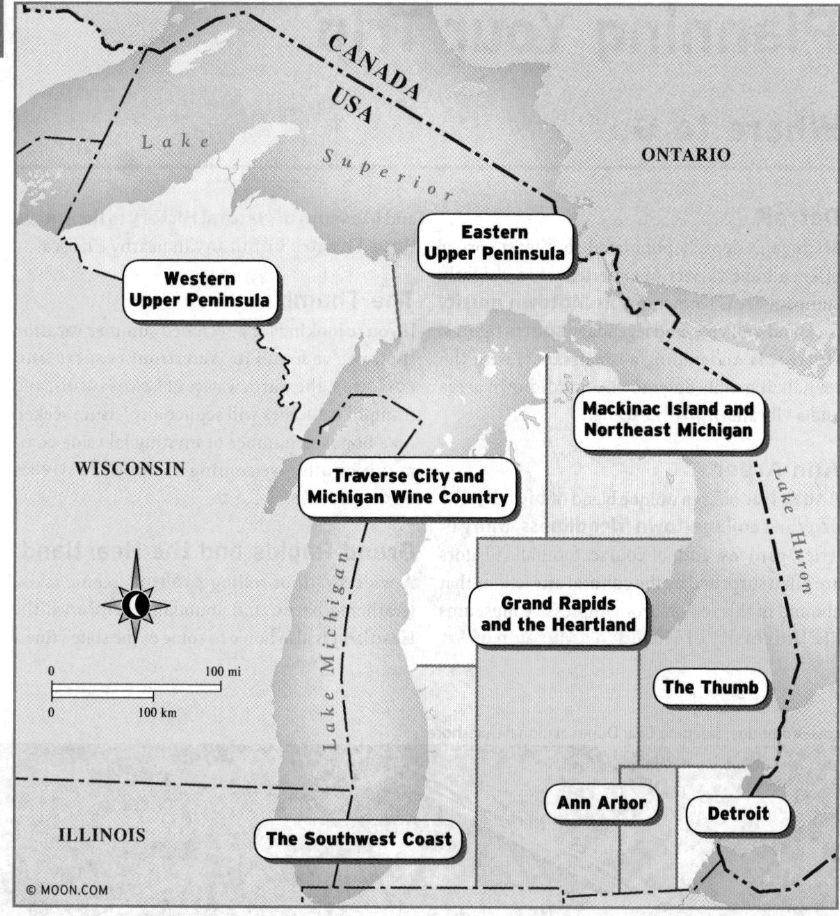

educational institutions and largest **cities,** including Grand Rapids, Kalamazoo, Midland, and Lansing. **Grand Rapids,** hometown of President Gerald Ford, offers a walkable downtown surrounded by the picturesque Grand River. Experience a flight simulator at the **Air Zoo** in Kalamazoo, or head to the **Michigan International Speedway** to watch a NASCAR race.

The Southwest Coast

Part resort, part artist colony, the Southwest Coast offers dramatic **sand dunes,** coastal state parks, and abundant **art galleries.** Home to the state's hospitable Dutch community and the annual **Tulip Time Festival,** this region also anchors the southern tier of Michigan's long arc of **wineries** and tasting rooms.

Traverse City and Michigan Wine Country

The crown jewel of northern lower Michigan, **Traverse City** offers fine restaurants, an inviting shopping district, out-of-the-way antiques shops, and **wineries**—lots of them. After exploring Traverse City, a visit to pleasant **Petoskey** and a journey through the **"tunnel of trees"** (M-119) will inspire anyone, especially in autumn. The majesty of nature is most evident at **Sleeping Bear Dunes.** Northwest Michigan is also known for its superb golf courses and **ski resorts.**

Mackinac Island and Northeast Michigan

The absence of automobiles makes **Mackinac Island** as close as you can get to 19th-century America. In this picturesque place, horse-drawn carriages ferry guests to the incomparable **Grand Hotel.** The **lighthouses** and small towns of the **Rogers City** area will awaken any visitor's sense of adventure. For lovers of all things touristy, the quirky shops of **Mackinaw City** will provide plenty of stimulation, as will the omnipresent **fudge** shops.

Eastern Upper Peninsula

Most travelers reach the UP by crossing the **Mackinac Bridge** to **St. Ignace.** From here, you can explore a bevy of noteworthy sights, including lighthouses, a shipwreck museum, and the Soo Locks near **Sault Ste. Marie.** You'll find terrific fishing spots like the **Manistique Lakes,** excellent **canoeing** rivers like the Two Hearted, incredible views at **Pictured Rocks National Lakeshore,** and acres of undisturbed forestland.

Western Upper Peninsula

Take a walk on the wild side. Hike through the **Porcupine Mountains** or descend to the depths of an abandoned copper mine in **Hancock.** Backpackers can lose themselves within expansive forests, and kayakers can explore the frigid waters of **Lake Superior. Isle Royale,** an island national park in **Lake Superior,** is for the truly daring who wish to enjoy nature as a totally immersive experience.

pumpkins for sale in autumn

Know Before You Go

When to Go

Summer is the most popular time to visit Michigan—people come for the beaches, inland lakes, and major events like the National Cherry Festival in Traverse City and African World Festival in Detroit. July is typically the warmest month. In northern Michigan, it's also the most bug-infested. Timing a camping trip before mid-June or after mid-August is smart, as the mosquitoes and blackflies are less bothersome.

Autumn may be the very best time to visit. Days are cool, night skies are clear, bugs are gone, and fall colors are outstanding. For peak color, the second week of September in the UP and the second week of October for the Lower Peninsula are usually the best times, but this can vary depending on weather conditions. Make sure to research this ahead of time.

Winter usually descends in November in the Upper Peninsula, in December in the Lower Peninsula, and can linger through March. For snow sports, February is the safest time to ensure good cover.

Spring emerges in southern Michigan in early May, working its way northward. With moderate temperatures and blossoming trees, this season is ideal for foliage lovers.

Reservations

Reservations may be necessary, especially for popular B&Bs during the summer. **Northern Michigan** is a **seasonal** place—some attractions and accommodations are only open late spring-early fall. If you come during the off-season, make sure to call ahead.

Getting Around

The best way to navigate this sprawling state is to bring your own vehicle or **rent a car.** All major airports have rental car services.

Recreation Passport

A Recreation Passport (www.michigan.gov/dnr) is **required** for all vehicles entering state parks and recreation areas, state boat launches, state forest campgrounds and state trail parking lots.

Michigan residents can purchase an **annual Recreation Passport** ($12 vehicles, $6 motorcycles) with their license plate registration renewal, or at the entrance to any state park for an additional $5 convenience fee.

Nonresidents have the option to buy an annual Recreation Passport ($34) or a **day pass** ($9). The annual Recreation Passport for nonresidents is valid until the end of the calendar year—a great deal if you plan on visiting multiple state parks. Both of these nonresident passes can be purchased at Michigan state parks or DNR customer service centers (the latter accepts cash or check only). Additionally, nonresidents can purchase the annual Recreation Passport online at a DNR e-store.

What to Pack

Be prepared for a variety of **weather** conditions—even in summer, **jackets** and **umbrellas** may be necessary. Attire is **casual,** though nicer restaurants and houses of worship appreciate business casual. If your plans include golfing and bird-watching, you might want to bring your **favorite clubs** and **binoculars.** Heavier, bulkier items such as canoes, bikes, fishing gear, and other such equipment are easy to rent once you arrive.

Foreign travelers will need passports and electric adapter plugs. Anyone planning to travel to and from Canada should have **proper identification** as well.

Romance on Mackinac Island

Situated between Michigan's Upper and Lower Peninsulas, Mackinac Island is an ideal spot for a **weekend getaway,** especially during the summer. Whether you reach this nostalgic place via ferry or plane, you and your sweetheart will surely have a memorable weekend.

Friday

Prior to your getaway, reserve a room at one of the island's more unique hotels, such as the **Chippewa Hotel Waterfront,** the **Hotel Iroquois,** or the **Mission Point Resort,** all of which feature luxurious suites and spectacular views. If cost is no issue, you might prefer the exquisite **Grand Hotel,** the setting (and filming location) for the 1980 romance *Somewhere in Time.*

After checking into your hotel, take a narrated horse-drawn **carriage tour** of the island, which will introduce you to some of its best landmarks and attractions. For a romantic dinner, consider the **Yankee Rebel Tavern,** which offers fireplace seating, an ample wine and beer selection, and a variety of winning selections, from slow-roasted ribs to pistachio-crusted whitefish.

Saturday

Start the day with breakfast at or near your hotel, then head to the bustling downtown area along Main and Market Streets, where you can browse shops, sample fudge, and visit historic homes, such as the **Biddle House** and the **Benjamin Blacksmith Shop,** both of which are included with admission to **Fort Mackinac.**

For lunch, head up to the **Fort Mackinac Tea Room,** where you can enjoy delicious soups, salads, and sandwiches from a picturesque terrace with a stunning view of the waterfront. Afterward, stroll amid the former barracks and other buildings that comprise the whitewashed fort. Observe the musket firings and cannon

carriage horses in front of a Victorian home on Mackinac Island

Top 10 Beaches

Michigan is blessed with the most miles of shoreline among the contiguous 48 states. Fortunately, a high percentage of that coastline is pristine, sandy beach. While locals do patronize them, most visitors are tourists, often venturing from landlocked environs. While inviting Michigan beaches number in the dozens, some of the very best are found along the Lake Michigan shore from St. Joseph to Grand Haven.

THE SOUTHWEST COAST

- **Saugatuck Dunes State Park:** Boasting a more hidden location than its counterparts, this 2.5-mile long beach includes costal dunes over 200 feet high.
- **Oval Beach:** Families flock to this popular Saugatuck-area beach, where swimmers can enjoy relatively warm waters in summer and adventurers can explore the nearby dunes.
- **Holland State Park:** One of Michigan's loveliest and most accessible beaches lures hundreds of swimmers and sunbathers on summer weekends. The park offers campgrounds, volleyball courts, amazing sunsets, a nearby boating lake, and terrific lighthouse views.
- **Grand Haven State Park:** Easy to reach from downtown Grand Haven, this sandy swimming beach is usually crowded with sun-seekers and metal-detecting enthusiasts in summer. Others come for the fishing pier, campground, picnic area, and photo-worthy lighthouses.
- **Muskegon State Park:** Part of a diverse 1,233-acre park, this two-mile stretch of sand attracts tons of swimmers, beachcombers, surfers, and picnickers every year. Head inland for hiking, fishing, and other recreational opportunities.

NORTHWEST MICHIGAN AND THE UPPER PENINSULA

- **North Beach:** Also known as Miller Beach, this serene beach with pristine sand is located just north of the town of Leland.
- **Sleeping Bear Dunes National Lakeshore:** It's a must that you visit this natural wonder during your trip to Michigan. Here, you'll find a curvy stretch of Lake Michigan shoreline, with some of the tallest dunes in the state, and ideal places to canoe, fish, hike, and, in winter, ski.

stairs to the beach on Lake Michigan

- **Pictured Rocks National Lakeshore:** Although the UP's Lake Superior coast isn't ideal for swimmers—given the lake's frigid temperatures year-round—the beaches here are perfect for beachcombers, bird-watchers, hikers, and sea kayakers with wetsuits. For relative solitude, venture toward Grand Sable Dunes.

NORTHEAST MICHIGAN AND THE THUMB

- **Tawas Point State Park:** East of Tawas City, this park is noted for its pure-white sandy beach, its warm waters, its well-preserved lighthouse, and its incredible view of the sunrise over Lake Huron.
- **Lakeport State Park:** Located on the more peaceful eastern shore of Michigan, this park offers a classic beach experience close to the urban centers in the southeast of the state.

salutes reenacted by costumed guides, then ride to the Grand Hotel and take a leisurely stroll through the landscaped grounds.

If you still have energy, venture across **Mackinac Island State Park,** which encompasses much of the island. Along the way, you'll see vibrant forests, limestone bluffs, lake vistas, and curious rock formations, such as **Skull Cave** and **Arch Rock.** If you're slightly more athletic, head over to the **Mackinac Island Bike Shop.** Here, you'll find a wide selection of rental bikes, ideal for exploring this 2,200-acre paradise. Pick up a free island map and explore as much as your desire and stamina will allow. If you're really ambitious, you may want to pedal the entire circumference of the island via Lake Shore Boulevard (M-185). When you're ready, head toward the marina, return your bikes, and opt for a casual dinner at the **Seabiscuit Café,** which stays open late and serves several delectable entrées, from steak burgers to curry chicken to French Creole jambalaya.

Sunday

Head to the Chippewa Hotel Waterfront—if you're not already staying here—and have breakfast at the **Pink Pony,** which offers omelets, pancakes, and fresh berry parfaits amid stunning marina views. Then, take one last stroll through the downtown area, and if there's time, visit the **Original Mackinac Island Butterfly House & Insect World,** where you'll spy hundreds of vibrant butterflies amid a tropical garden. Afterward, check out of your hotel and return to the mainland via ferry or plane.

Old Mackinac Point Light Station

Fall into the Upper Peninsula

The Upper Peninsula offers one of the nation's best yearly displays of **autumn colors.** Collectively, the area's assortment of flaming maples, oaks, and various other hardwoods reveal a truly stunning palette of reds, ambers, and yellows—balanced with a fair amount of aquamarine from the high number of evergreens.

It's essential to time your trip with precision. While fall colors in the Upper Peninsula typically peak between **late September** and **early October,** a given year's weather conditions can either accelerate or delay their appearance. During the weeks prior to your trip, monitor the fall color reports via the media and be prepared to change your plans as necessary.

Once you settle on your dates, the following itinerary will lead you to some of the UP's very best spots for fall color.

Day 1: Tahquamenon Falls

Begin your trip at **Tahquamenon Falls State Park,** one of the nation's most beautiful waterfalls west of Niagara. Take your time exploring the park while enjoying the rustic trails that link the upper and lower falls, which appear even more beautiful when set against the background of autumnal color. An excellent place to stay is the **Magnuson Grand Hotel** in Paradise.

Day 2: Pictured Rocks

After checking out Tahquamenon Falls, head west toward **Pictured Rocks National Lakeshore** via M-28 and M-77. Here you'll find **Miners Falls** and **Mosquito Falls,** nestled in a swath of fall color. Each requires a short hike from the parking area—but it's worth it. On your way toward Munising to spend the night, be sure to check out **Wagner Falls,** another gem. Stay at the **AmericInn by Wyndham** in Munising.

Day 3: Hiawatha National Forest

After departing Munising, get on M-28

the Pictured Rocks

Top 5 Hikes

The Great Lakes State is a haven for outdoor enthusiasts of all skill levels. The Upper and Lower Peninsulas offer hundreds of miles of hiking trails, from easy paths to advanced backpacking routes.

THE UPPER PENINSULA

- **Escarpment Trail:** This 4.3-mile well-maintained trail in Porcupine Mountains Wilderness State Park winds east along a sheer escarpment, crossing Cloud Peak and Cuyahoga Peak and offering a stunning view of the Lake of the Clouds. During the winter, this trail is also popular among cross-country skiers.
- **Tahquamenon River Trail:** Day hikers favor this four-mile family-friendly path in the 50,000-acre Tahquamenon Falls State Park. Passing through an old-growth forest, this scenic trail leads from the Lower Falls to the Upper Falls. Along the way, you can access several overlooks of the stunning waterfalls.

walkway at Tahquamenon Falls

THE LOWER PENINSULA

- **Dunes Trail:** Encompassing more than 71,000 acres, Sleeping Bear Dunes National Lakeshore provides lots of options for hikers. Of the more than 100 miles of designated trails on offer, the most popular choice is this strenuous 3.5-mile hike, which stretches across steep, rugged dunes. Along the way, enjoy a spectacular view of Glen Lake.
- **Kal-Haven Trail:** For a longer trek, consider this 34-mile route, which extends from Kalamazoo to South Haven. Tracing an abandoned railroad, this trail crosses various bridges and passes through several small towns. It's also popular among bikers, bird-watchers, cross-country skiers, and snowmobilers.
- **Highbanks Trail:** This seven-mile ungroomed trail about 14 miles west of Oscoda follows the Au Sable River Valley, offering picturesque views of this popular canoeing river from the bluffs on the south shore, not to mention terrific opportunities for wildlife lovers. You'll encounter photogenic sites like the Lumberman's Monument and the Canoers Memorial. Cross-country skiers also favor this trail, which is free to use year-round.

to Harvey, where you can pick up U.S. 41. Take U.S. 41 south through **Rapid River, Gladstone,** and **Escanaba.** The route will wind through **Hiawatha National Forest,** where you'll experience miles of uninterrupted nature. Stay the evening at the **Terrace Bay Hotel** in Gladstone.

Day 4: Garden Peninsula and U.S. 2

Take U.S. 41 north to U.S. 2. Head east toward St. Ignace (and possibly detour down the Garden Peninsula). Along the way you'll pass through **Manistique** while enjoying more color on your left and the crystal blue water of Lake Michigan on your right.

Wine Tasting Tour

In recent years, Michigan has gained a reputation for crafting award-winning wines. Wineries are scattered throughout the state, within Michigan's two principal winemaking regions in the Lower Peninsula—along the Southwest Coast and around Grand Traverse Bay—and a few in the Upper Peninsula near Escanaba and Manistique. The American Viticultural Association recognizes four distinct growing regions in Michigan: the Old Mission Peninsula and the Leelanau Peninsula in the north plus Fennville and the Lake Michigan Shore in the south. Collectively, the Great Lakes State is home to some 120 wineries and tasting rooms. In this region, the winter months produce lake-effect snow, which protects the vines and extends the growing season for up to a month.

Wine connoisseurs could easily spend over a week sampling the state's finest wineries, preferably during summer or fall. Here's an overview of the best for those with less time.

Days 1 and 2: Leelanau and Old Mission Peninsulas

The area surrounding **Traverse City** is the epicenter of Michigan wineries. Here is where you'll find the greatest density of established wineries, vineyards, and tasting rooms. Beginning at the northern tip of the **Old Mission Peninsula**, check out **2 Lads Winery**, which offers a sleek, modern tasting room to sample their northern sparkling varieties. It also conducts tours of its facility for groups large and small. For a more immersive experience, consider spending a night at **Chateau Chantal**, a winery and inn where you can enjoy a luxurious stay with a stunning view of Grand Traverse Bay, sample their offerings, and even attend a winemaking seminar.

The larger **Leelanau Peninsula** hosts a bevy of wineries as well. **Black Star Farms** offers a comprehensive selection of white, sparkling, fruit, and dessert wines. A distillery on the premises even produces spirits. They also operate an exquisite inn with different dining options. Continue up M-22 until you arrive at **Leelanau Cellars**, where you'll find a variety of creative wines, including Tall Ship Chardonnay and Witches Brew, a secret blend with cinnamon, cloves, and nutmeg added to enhance the flavor. Stay the night at the inn at **Black Star Farms**—a truly unforgettable experience.

Day 3: Petoskey, Harbor Springs, and the Tunnel of Trees

Heading farther north, you'll find an attractive cluster of wineries in the Petoskey-Harbor Springs area. Check out the **Mackinaw Trail Winery** in Petoskey, where you can imbibe their exclusive blanc de noir or blanc de blanc, or choose from a number of pinot noirs, merlots, or cabernets. Enjoy lunch at their stylish bistro before continuing north toward Mackinaw City along M-119, the Tunnel of Trees, where you'll enjoy one of the most scenic drives in the United States.

Day 4: Escanaba

Cross the Mackinac Bridge and head west toward Escanaba along U.S. 2. In Bark River, stop by the tasting room of the **Northern Sun Winery**, an out-of-the-way gem among Michigan's wineries. Northern Sun needs to take special precautions to grow quality grapes at such a northern latitude, but the effort pays off handsomely. Featured wines include the Leon Millot, described as a "smooth, smoky round wine with velvety notes of raspberry, cherry, and a bit of chocolate," and the LeCrescent, "an off-dry wine bursting with fruit aromas."

Michigan is known as America's summer golf mecca, the Gaylord area alone boasts nearly 20 courses, and the UP offers a number of seasonal choices. While there are several private clubs—such as Oakland Hills Country Club, which hosted the 2008 PGA Championship—there's also a wide array of public courses and resorts. Here are some of the best options in the northern half of the Lower Peninsula, the state's most popular region for golfers.

- **Arcadia Bluffs Golf Club:** Set along a gorgeous stretch of Lake Michigan shoreline, this world-class resort offers an 18-hole golf course that's long been considered the best public course in the state by golfing magazines.
- **Grand Traverse Resort and Spa:** With comfortable accommodations, excellent dining, a top-notch spa, an indoor water park, a 24-hour dog care facility, and three on-site golf courses (The Bear, The Wolverine, and Spruce Run), this 900-acre resort in Acme has easily become one of Michigan's finest golfing destinations.
- **A-Ga-Ming Golf Resort:** Overlooking lovely Torch Lake, not far north of Traverse City, this long-standing resort presents three 18-hole courses: Torch, Antrim Dells, and Sundance.
- **Shanty Creek Resorts:** Divided into three villages—Cedar River, Schuss, and Summit—this enormous Bellaire resort features several dining, lodging, and spa options, numerous downhill skiing runs, and four championship golf courses: Cedar River, Schuss Mountain, Summit, and Arnold Palmer's The Legend.
- **Boyne Highlands Resort:** Just north of Petoskey, this year-round resort offers superb lodging, four spectacular golf courses (The Heather, Arthur Hills, Donald Ross Memorial, and The Moor), a lighted par-3 course, and access to a wealth of seasonal activities, from fishing to dogsledding.
- **Hidden River Golf and Casting Club:** Between Petoskey and Mackinaw City you'll find this handsome resort that appeals to golfers as well as fly-fishing enthusiasts.
- **Black Lake Golf Club:** Operated by the United Auto Workers, this magnificent golf course is part of the union's 1,000-acre family center, which sits astride picturesque Black Lake near the town of Onaway.
- **Treetops Resort:** This year-round resort near Gaylord keeps visitors busy with downhill skiing in winter, horseback riding in summer, a full-service spa, and, of course, five stunning golf courses: Masterpiece, Premier, Signature, Tradition, and Threetops.
- **Garland Lodge & Resort:** Considered one of the state's most beautiful resorts, this rustic destination presents four magnificent golf courses (Fountains, Reflections, Swampfire, and Monarch) amid the woods of northeastern Michigan.

golfing in Michigan

Michigan Sampler

These short itineraries each highlight a section of the state. Explore a region at a time, or link them all together for a grand statewide road trip.

Detroit to Kalamazoo

SUGGESTED STAY: 2 DAYS

TOTAL DISTANCE: 120 MILES; 2 HOURS

If you've started your adventure in the Motor City, head about eight miles southwest of downtown to **Dearborn,** where you'll find **The Henry Ford,** a fascinating complex of historical attractions that includes the Henry Ford Museum, Greenfield Village, and the Ford Rouge Factory Tour.

From Dearborn, head west along I-94, through **Ann Arbor** and **Battle Creek.** Two notable sights are the **W. K. Kellogg Bird Sanctuary** near Augusta and the **Air Zoo,** an enormous complex devoted to the history of aviation in **Kalamazoo.**

Saugatuck to Traverse City

SUGGESTED STAY: 4 DAYS

TOTAL DISTANCE: 249 MILES; 4.5 HOURS

From Kalamazoo, head north on U.S. 131 for about 18 miles and continue on M-89 for roughly 33 miles, toward the **Art Coast,** a cluster of art galleries in and around the towns of **Saugatuck** and **Douglas.**

After spending some time amid the area's shops, restaurants, and inns, drive north on U.S. 31 to the incredible **Sleeping Bear Dunes National Lakeshore,** a marvelous 35-mile stretch of beaches, dunes, and lakes that lies alongside Lake Michigan and about 174 miles north of Saugatuck.

From the lakeshore headquarters in Empire, head east on M-72 for 24 miles to **Traverse City,** an ideal base from which to explore gorgeous **Grand Traverse Bay,** popular with boaters and surrounded by several scenic resort towns, golf resorts, and an abundance of wineries that rival California's Napa Valley.

Mackinac Bridge to Munising

SUGGESTED STAY: 5 DAYS

TOTAL DISTANCE: 353 MILES; 6 HOURS

Expect a 140-mile drive on U.S. 31 from Traverse City, through the towns of Charlevoix and Petoskey, to the amazing five-mile-long **Mackinac Bridge,** one of the world's longest suspension bridges. After crossing the bridge and passing through St. Ignace, head north for about 50 miles on I-75 to **Sault Ste. Marie,** Michigan's oldest city. Here, you'll glimpse another engineering marvel, the **Soo Locks,** through which massive freighters pass between Lakes Huron and Superior. For an up close view, take a **Soo Locks Boat Tour.**

Head west along M-28 for about 38 miles through the Hiawatha National Forest, then turn north on M-123 for another 26 miles until you arrive at **Tahquamenon Falls,** one of the largest waterfall systems east of the Mississippi. Afterward, continue north on M-123 to Paradise. Continue north on Whitefish Point Road for 11 miles to **Whitefish Point,** where you'll find the **Great Lakes Shipwreck Museum,** the only museum dedicated to the perils of maritime transportation on the Great Lakes. Roughly 115 miles farther west lies **Pictured Rocks National Lakeshore,** a fabulous stretch of sand dunes, desolate beaches, sandstone cliffs, and shady forests beside Lake Superior. To get there, take M-123 southwest to M-28 for 23 miles until you come to M-77. From there, head north along M-77 for 25 miles until you arrive at **Grand Marais,** which is the eastern terminus of Pictured Rocks. The national park spans more than 40 miles along the lake, from Grand Marais to **Munising.**

The Keweenaw Peninsula

SUGGESTED STAY: 2-3 DAYS

TOTAL DISTANCE: 145 MILES; 2.5 HOURS

If you want to venture farther into the wilds of the UP, head west from Munising on M-28/U.S. 41 for about 145 miles to the heart of the

Wildlife Watching

Observing wildlife is an immensely rewarding activity, especially in a fauna-rich state like Michigan. Watching the activities of other species helps one relate to nature in ways both inspiring and intimate. But viewing animals in their natural habitats requires knowledge, determination, and an abundance of patience.

ELK

While elk have been sighted elsewhere in Michigan, the highest concentration is in the **Pigeon River Country State Forest** just northeast of Gaylord. A population of about 1,000 roams the area between I-75 and M-33. Visit Michigan.org to find a printable map.

MOOSE

Moose can be more difficult to spot. While they often stay close to narrow rivers and small inland lakes, they can occasionally be seen strolling through the streets of small towns. The greater **Newberry** area bills itself as the Moose Capital of Michigan, but another (possibly larger) population occupies the area around **Marquette.**

BIRDS

Michigan's abundance of open space and low human population density provide rich habitats for hundreds of bird species. Examples range from the red-tailed hawks and eastern screech owls at the **W. K. Kellogg Bird Sanctuary** near Battle Creek to common loons and sandhill cranes at the **Seney National Wildlife Refuge** in the Upper Peninsula.

BEARS

Oswald's Bear Ranch, near Newberry in the Upper Peninsula, is the perfect place to see Michigan black bears. Here you can see 40 black bears up close and personal in secure enclosures surrounded by dense woods.

Moose can be dangerous; keep your distance.

OTHER WILDLIFE AREAS

Michigan's numerous **state parks**, besides offering peace and solitude, also host much of the state's wildlife. Wolves, coyotes, and the occasional black bear can be found in the better-known state properties, including **Tahquamenon Falls State Park** and **Porcupine Mountains Wilderness State Park.** Their web of trails offers opportunities to experience nature and wildlife.

Keweenaw Peninsula. History buffs will enjoy the **Keweenaw National Historical Park.** From nearby Houghton, adventurous hikers, backpackers, kayakers, and wildlife enthusiasts can take a ferry ride to **Isle Royale National Park,** a wild, isolated archipelago in the northern reaches of Lake Superior.

Straits of Mackinac to the Thumb

SUGGESTED STAY: 6 DAYS

TOTAL DISTANCE: 481 MILES; 8 HOURS

Once you're done exploring the Upper Peninsula, head south to Mackinaw City, which lies about 266 miles from Houghton. To get there, take U.S. 41 south through L'Anse and Ishpeming, and into **Marquette**—a distance of 128 miles. A college town with a sophisticated yet "up north" feel, Marquette is a worthy destination in its own right.

From Marquette, take M-28 through Munising, Shingleton, and Seney until you come to I-75. Take I-75 south, cross the Mackinac Bridge and you'll find yourself in **Mackinaw City.** Board a ferry for **Mackinac Island,** a charming vacation spot that has long banned automobiles in favor of bikes and horse-drawn carriages. Rife with Victorian mansions, this nostalgic island offers a true step back in time, anchored by the magnificent **Grand Hotel,** which prides itself as America's Summer Place.

Back on the mainland, drive south on I-75 for about 58 miles through a cluster of excellent golf courses in the greater Gaylord area, and continue south for roughly 27 miles to **Hartwick Pines State Park,** home to the largest stand of virgin white pines in the Lower Peninsula.

End your tour of Michigan on a festive note by heading south on I-75 for about 125 miles, toward the Bavarian-style town of **Frankenmuth,** site of German shops and festivals, all-you-can-eat chicken dinners, and a year-round Christmas store.

the Mackinac Bridge

Music and Motor Cars

Detroit's nicknames—Motown and the Motor City—underscore its rich musical and automotive heritage. Visitors will find an array of sites, activities, and annual festivals that celebrate the city's contributions to American music and industry.

a Motor City hot rod

MUSEUMS AND HISTORIC HOMES

In the Detroit area, tour the region's vintage car collections, musical heritage exhibits, and former auto baron homes. Begin in downtown Detroit, where the GM Renaissance Center presents the **GM Showroom,** a 40,000-square-foot, year-round display of vintage vehicles, concept cars, and new models.

Afterward, head to the Cultural Center and view an authentic auto assembly line at the **Detroit Historical Museum.** At the nearby **Charles H. Wright Museum of African American History,** music lovers can learn about great performers like John Lee Hooker and Aretha Franklin. Just a bit north, the **Motown Museum** is a small repository of costumes, records, photographs, and other memorabilia that celebrate icons such as Marvin Gaye, Diana Ross, Stevie Wonder, and The Temptations.

Head southwest to Dearborn, where you'll find **The Henry Ford,** a museum complex that explores U.S. history, industry, and innovation. Tour Ford's childhood home, a collection of presidential limousines and other vintage cars, and a Ford truck assembly line. History buffs may also enjoy visiting **Fair Lane,** Henry Ford's former Dearborn estate, and the **Edsel and Eleanor Ford House,** a Cotswold-style mansion in Grosse Pointe Shores.

DETROIT'S MUSICAL NIGHTLIFE

Detroit has been a favored city among musicians as varied as Smokey Robinson, Bob Seger, and Eminem. In the Theater District, the **Music Hall Center for the Performing Arts** has, for more than 85 years, hosted legendary musical acts. Detroit's lively nightclubs, including **Baker's Keyboard Lounge** and **Flood's Bar & Grille,** offer live jazz music and delicious soul food.

YEARLY CELEBRATIONS

In June, auto lovers can attend the **North American International Auto Show,** which promises a first look at the latest innovative vehicle designs. Two other car-related celebrations include the **Chevrolet Detroit Belle Isle Grand Prix,** a challenging race that usually takes place in the spring, and the **Woodward Dream Cruise,** a mid-August event that highlights vintage cars. On Labor Day weekend, meanwhile, the **Detroit Jazz Festival** presents open-air jazz concerts alongside the Detroit River.

Detroit

Almost any Michiganian knows the trick. Look at the back of your left hand and you'll find a handy "map" of Michigan's Lower Peninsula. When a visitor from out of state asks for the location of a particular destination, the knowledgeable native will point to the appropriate spot—near one of the knuckles, along the edge of the pinky finger, or when referencing the region surrounding the state's premier city, the area between the wrist and the base of the thumb.

Southeast Michigan is the end product of over a century of outgrowth from the city of Detroit—a military fort turned early industrial town turned economic behemoth. Detroit grew exponentially when Henry Ford's assembly line transformed the town—and the world—forever. A plethora of early competitors—names like Buick,

Highlights

Look for ★ to find recommended sights, activities, dining, and lodging.

★ **GM Renaissance Center:** Enjoy a vintage auto collection, a tropical atrium, and incredible views of the Detroit and Windsor skylines (page 38).

★ **Belle Isle Park:** This oasis in the Detroit River is a treasured spot, with biking paths, a zoo, a swimming beach, a conservatory, and numerous historic edifices (page 38).

★ **Greektown:** Experience Greek culture at its best at lively tavernas and the annual Detroit Greek Independence Day Parade (page 43).

★ **The Cultural Center:** Midtown boasts museums, a science center, art galleries, theaters, and several well-preserved Victorian structures (page 44).

★ **New Center:** This storied neighborhood is home to the stunning Fisher Building and the superb Motown Museum (page 47).

★ **Hamtramck:** Come to this culturally diverse enclave for Polish sausages, European baked goods, and traditional artwork (page 71).

★ **The Henry Ford:** See Ford's childhood home, Thomas Edison's Menlo Park laboratory, and the bus on which Rosa Parks refused to surrender her seat (page 73).

★ **Lake Erie Metropark:** This 1,607-acre recreation area has hiking, bird-watching, fishing, and stunning views of the Detroit River, Lake Erie, and North America's first international wildlife refuge (page 83).

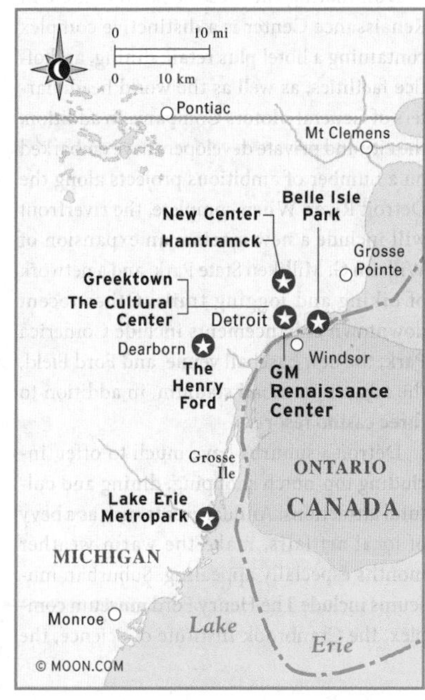

Dodge, Maxwell, Chevrolet, Chalmers, and Packard—joined Ford in the booming new industry, and gradually morphed into what we now know as the Detroit Three: Ford, General Motors, and Chrysler.

Throughout much of the 20th century, the Motor City, as Detroit came to be known, thrived and was largely responsible for the creation of the American middle class. Later economic problems combined with persistent racial segregation, however, left crime and unemployment in their wake. But today's Motor City is defined more by its innovation and fortitude than by its shortcomings. Nicknamed the "Renaissance City," Detroit has begun to shed its troubled past. Although still a work in progress, this tenacious town—also known for its Motown music, rock-and-roll vibe, and legendary sports figures—has polished its tarnished image.

Dominating the Detroit skyline, the GM Renaissance Center is a distinctive complex containing a hotel plus retail, dining, and office facilities, as well as the world headquarters of General Motors Company. In addition, the city and private developers have embarked on a number of ambitious projects along the Detroit River. When complete, the riverfront will include a new marina, an expansion of William G. Milliken State Park, and a network of biking and jogging trails. Other recent downtown enhancements include Comerica Park, the new baseball venue, and Ford Field, the adjacent football stadium, in addition to three casino resorts.

Detroit's suburbs have much to offer, including top-notch shopping, dining and cultural attractions. Annual events such as a bevy of local art fairs, make the warm-weather months especially appealing. Suburban museums include The Henry Ford museum complex, the Cranbrook Institute of Science, the Holocaust Memorial Center, and the Arab American National Museum.

PLANNING YOUR TIME

Southeast Michigan is a relatively small area, easy to traverse by car. Several major routes link Detroit and its suburbs to other parts of the state, including I-75 from Flint, I-96 from Lansing, or I-94 from Battle Creek. Detroit Metropolitan Airport (DTW) is a hub for Delta, and the main Amtrak line from Chicago, the *Wolverine*, serves Dearborn, Detroit, Royal Oak, Troy, and Pontiac. Greyhound also has regular bus service to Detroit, Southfield, and Pontiac.

Unlike in other parts of Michigan, museums, shops, and restaurants in Detroit and its suburbs generally operate year-round. You'll need at least three days to explore the region's key destinations, such as downtown Detroit and The Henry Ford complex in Dearborn. Five days is preferable, especially if you plan to make a trip across the border to Windsor, Ontario, in Canada.

Just remember that Detroit is a big unpredictable city, and crime can be a concern here. Areas frequented by visitors, such as greater downtown and Midtown, are well patrolled, but it's important to stay vigilant even in relatively safe areas. Always travel with someone else, hide your money and cards beneath your clothing, and leave valuable jewelry at home.

For more information about Detroit and its suburbs, consult the **Detroit Metro Convention & Visitors Bureau** (211 W. Fort St., Ste. 1000, 313/202-1800 or 800/338-7648, www.visitdetroit.com, 9am-5pm Mon.-Fri.) or **Travel Michigan** (Michigan Economic Development Corporation, 300 N. Washington Square, Lansing, 888/784-7328, www.michigan.org).

Previous: *The Spirit of Detroit* Statue by Marshall Fredericks; flag of the City of Detroit; the Detroit Institute of Arts.

Detroit Area

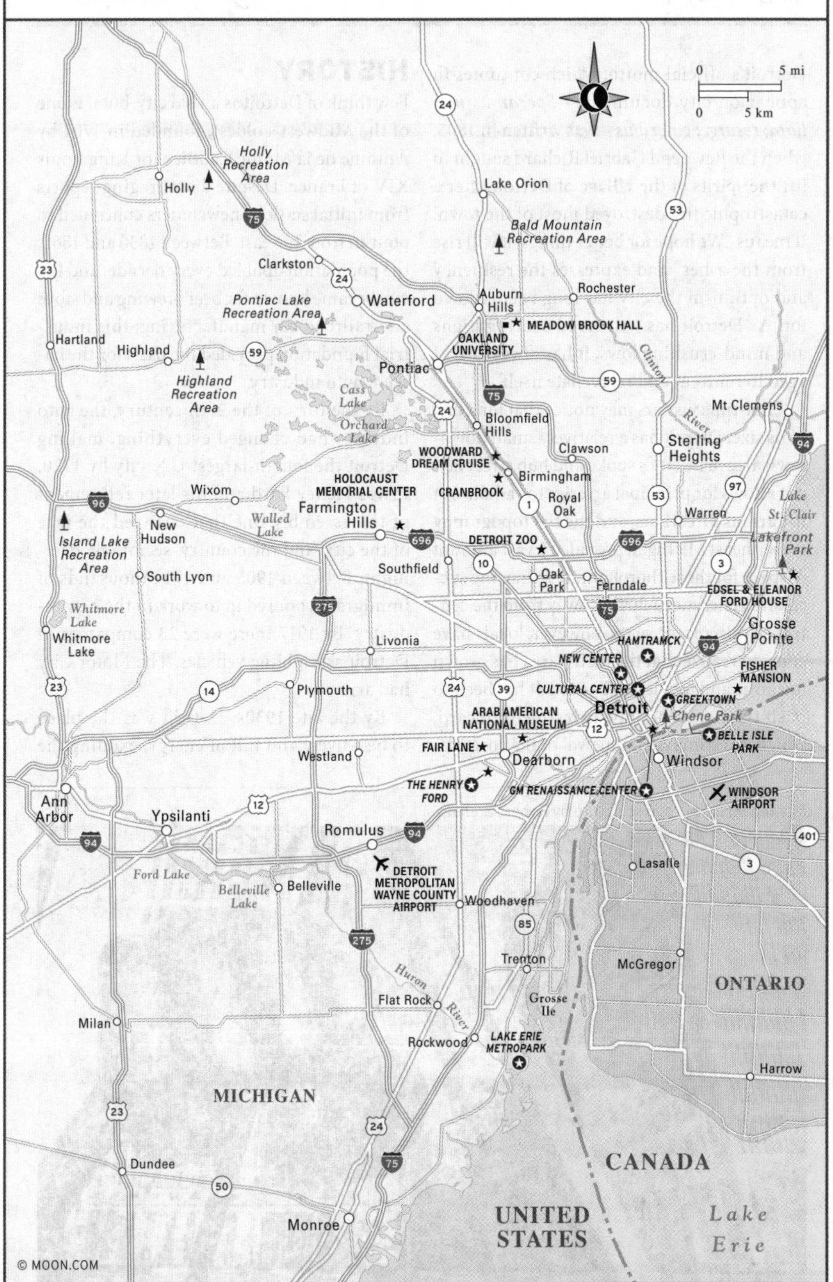

Detroit

Detroit's official motto, which continues to appear on city documents—*Speramus meliora; resurget cineribus*—was written in 1805, when the Reverend Gabriel Richard sought to lift the spirits of the village of Detroit after a catastrophic fire destroyed most of the town. It means "We hope for better things; it will rise from the ashes" and expresses the resiliency and optimism the city has long been known for. As Detroit has witnessed soaring highs and mind-crushing lows, it has always managed to reinvent and rejuvenate itself.

First-time visitors may notice that for a city of its size, Detroit has a relatively small downtown area. The city's spoke and hub street layout allows for principal arteries to radiate out in various directions, and the flat topography of southeast Michigan provided a vast amount of space for those thoroughfares, drawing successive generations farther away from the central city. In recent years, however, locals have come to realize that the metro area has grown too large and unwieldy. The result has been to push the new economic investment inward, which has stimulated renewal of the core city.

HISTORY

Few think of Detroit as an old city, but it is one of the Midwest's oldest, founded in 1701 by Antoine de la Mothe Cadillac for King Louis XIV of France. Despite discouraging reports from initial settlers, newcomers continued to pour in from the east. Between 1830 and 1860, the population doubled every decade, and the city became known for beer brewing and stove and railroad car manufacturing; this industrial foundation provided the basis for the nascent auto industry.

By the turn of the 20th century, the auto industry had changed everything, making Detroit the fourth-largest U.S. city by 1920. It was Henry Ford and his later refinement of the assembly line that changed the face of the city, and the country, seemingly overnight. Between 1905 and 1924 thousands of immigrants poured in to work in the new industry. By 1917 there were 23 companies in Detroit assembling vehicles. The Motor City had arrived.

By the late 1930s, Detroit was the place to be—lively and full of energy, exuding the

Monument to Joe Louis sculpture by Robert Graham

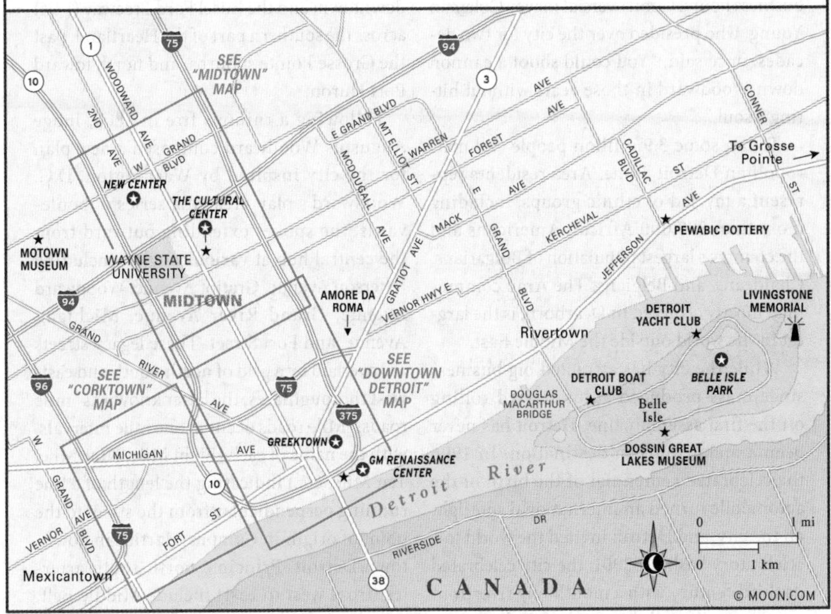

prosperity of the new middle class. First-class shopping, elegant hotels, and a multitude of entertainment options emerged, including bars known as "blind pigs" (Prohibition-era hideouts that served liquor) and "black and tan" clubs, where the unwritten rules of racial segregation were ignored and people of all races mingled.

During the 1940s, Detroit became known as the Arsenal of Democracy. In response to the outbreak of World War II, the city transformed its industrial might from civilian to military production. With just 2 percent of the U.S. population, Detroit produced 10 percent of the hardware to win the war. But by June 1943, the tension placed on the community combined with the poor state of race relations culminated in a race riot that lasted three days and resulted in 34 fatalities. Prosperity returned as the war ended, but soon the city began to experience losses from the movement of population and economic resources to the suburbs. As in other U.S. cities, freeways took people farther from the urban core, leaving behind vacant storefronts, abandoned houses, poverty, and crime.

In the 1960s one bright spot was the birth of the Motown Sound, which began in the tiny studio run by Berry Gordy Jr. on West Grand Boulevard. Like the city, Motown had a hard driving beat, and it quickly took over airwaves across the country. Hitsville USA, as the studio came to be known, churned out top-10 tunes by artists such as Marvin Gaye, Stevie Wonder, the Supremes, and Smokey Robinson and the Miracles.

The late 1960s brought massive unrest nationwide. In 1967, Detroit was the site of the worst of 59 incidents of urban violence throughout the country, a tragedy in which 43 people were killed and hundreds injured. The nightly news showed Detroit in flames, leaving a lasting impression nationwide and a deep scar on the city's psyche. The tragic incident only accelerated the "white flight" that was already underway, leaving Detroit with a black majority in less than 10 years. By the late 1970s, downtown had become deserted after business hours. Controversial mayor Coleman Young, who presided over the city for two decades, once said, "You could shoot a cannon down Woodward in those years without hitting a soul."

Today, some 3.9 million people call metropolitan Detroit home. Area residents represent a myriad of ethnic groups, including more than 880,000 African Americans and the country's largest population of Bulgarians, Chaldeans, and Belgians. The Arab community, mostly centered in Dearborn, is the largest in the world outside the Middle East.

While the city has attracted big business since mass-produced autos started rolling off the first assembly line, Detroit has never been a major tourism destination. In 1996 the celebrated centennial of the birth of the automobile turned an international spotlight on the city, and Detroit invited the world to a celebratory bash. In 2001, the city celebrated its third century with a monthlong riverfront party featuring tall ships and a full slate of entertainment. Stevie Wonder led the homecoming concert, which attracted a million people. While city boosters don't expect flashy events such as these to erase Detroit's considerable challenges, they hope that they'll help to heal the wounds that have long plagued the city—and perhaps ameliorate more recent troubles, such as Mayor Kwame Kilpatrick's 2008 resignation and subsequent felony conviction or Detroit's 2013 municipal bankruptcy.

ORIENTATION

Detroit isn't difficult to navigate. The extensive freeway system makes it easy to get around the sprawling tapestry of neighborhoods. The Chrysler Freeway (I-75) snakes through downtown, where it becomes the Fisher Freeway and links southern towns like Monroe to northern Royal Oak, Pontiac, and Holly. Other major routes include the Jeffries Freeway (I-96) from Lansing; the Walter Reuther Freeway (I-696) through Farmington Hills, Southfield, and Ferndale; the John Lodge Freeway (M-10), which links the northwestern suburbs and Detroit's west side to downtown; and the Edsel Ford Freeway (I-94) across the southern part of the Heartland, past the Grosse Pointe suburbs, and north toward Port Huron.

Following a ruinous fire in 1805, Judge Augustus Woodward composed a new plan for the city inspired by Washington, D.C. Woodward's plan created a series of boulevards, the spokes extending outward from the central hub at various angles, including Jefferson Avenue, Gratiot Avenue, Woodward Avenue, Grand River Avenue, Michigan Avenue, and Fort Street. These legacy streets are overlaid by a grid of north-south and east-west thoroughfares, the latter known as "mile roads." Mile roads occur at one mile intervals, with the name of each (Eight Mile, Nine Mile, Ten Mile, etc.) indicating the length of a line running perpendicular from the street to the point of origin in Campus Martius in downtown Detroit. Principle north-south arteries (from west to east) include Middle Belt, Telegraph, Lahser, Evergreen, Southfield, Greenfield, Livernois, Dequindre, Van Dyke, Mound, Ryan, Schoenherr, and Hoover Roads.

SIGHTS

On the Waterfront

Detroit's earliest history was made on its waterfront, which means it's a fitting start to exploring the city.

HART PLAZA

If it's a sunny day in any season, stroll the RiverWalk, near Hart Plaza, and watch for one of the thousands of hulking freighters that ply the Detroit River annually. With its active port, the waterfront was once the city's livelihood, but during much of its history, Detroit turned its sight inland, while erecting factories and mundane warehouses along its riverbank. Recent efforts have strived to

1: *Gateway to Freedom International Memorial to the Underground Railroad* by Ed Dwight **2:** GM Renaissance Center **3:** Hart Plaza

1
2
3

correct the mistake: When completed, the **Detroit International RiverWalk** (www.detroitriverfront.org) will include a network of biking and jogging trails and five miles of public parks and plazas linked by a continuous walkway hugging the water's edge.

For now, strollers can enjoy 3.5 miles of the RiverWalk, which integrates the expanded William G. Milliken State Park, Mt. Elliott Park, and 14-acre Hart Plaza, a popular venue for summertime festivals and concerts. Opened in 1975 and named after the late U.S. Senator Philip Hart, the plaza is the site of the breathtaking **Horace E. Dodge Fountain,** which was designed in 1978 by Isamu Noguchi and propels more than one million gallons of water per hour into the air via 300 nozzles and jets. Another key landmark in Hart Plaza is the **Gateway to Freedom International Memorial to the Underground Railroad,** which was sculpted by Ed Dwight and dedicated in October 2001 for Detroit's tricentennial, memorializing the city's pivotal role for thousands of former slaves seeking freedom in Canada in the 19th century. The sculpture depicts a family looking across the river in anticipation of their transit to freedom. A companion sculpture on the Windsor side, also by Dwight, depicts a family of new arrivals giving thanks and being welcomed by a Quaker woman.

★ GM RENAISSANCE CENTER

Next to Hart Plaza is the gleaming **GM Renaissance Center** (100 Renaissance Center, 313/567-3126, www.gmrencen.com). Soaring and fortresslike, the 73-story hotel, office, and retail complex dominates the skyline, with seven steel towers containing 5.5 million square feet of floor space, including a 1,300-room Marriott, the consulates of Canada and Japan, a fitness center, and dozens of restaurants and stores.

The road to the GM Renaissance Center's present incarnation was rocky. The project was originally proposed in 1973 by Henry Ford II as a way to revive the downtown following the 1967 uprising. A powerful name in Detroit, Ford used his influence to convince a group of investors to bankroll the complex. With big-name retailers, it was intended to draw suburbanites back downtown and catalyze additional development, but remained underutilized for many years after it opened in 1977. Designed by Atlanta architect John Portman, best known for building hotel atriums, it was a confusing maze of circles and elevators that made navigation difficult.

In 1996 General Motors purchased the landmark as its new world headquarters, and by 1999 had moved much of its white-collar staff in. It also embarked on a major renovation of the entire complex, making it much more inviting for the general public to shop or dine. Today, the GM Renaissance Center is living up to its original promise.

The GM Renaissance Center remains one of the largest privately financed developments in U.S. history, with more than $380 million ($1.8 billion in 2016 dollars) contributed by private investors. Representing a huge contribution toward the city's future, it is worth seeing on that basis alone. Once inside, you'll need a map to get around or you can take a free one-hour tour (313/568-5624, noon and 2pm Mon.-Fri.), offered on a first-come, first-served basis and departing from the Pure Detroit store on Level 1 of Tower 400. The tour includes sights like an outdoor world map carved in granite, a vintage auto collection, the world's tallest vertical glass sculpture, the Wintergarden atrium overlooking the Detroit River, and breathtaking views of Detroit and Windsor.

★ BELLE ISLE PARK

Belle Isle (844/235-5375, www.michigan.gov/dnr, 5am-10pm daily, annual Recreation Passport required: $12 Michigan residents, $34 nonresidents, $9 day pass available to nonresidents only), a tranquil oasis in the Detroit River, is where you can really feel the water's irresistible tug.

Accessible via the Douglas MacArthur Bridge at East Jefferson Avenue and East Grand Boulevard, the 982-acre, 2.5-mile-long urban sanctuary between Detroit and Windsor, Ontario, has been a recreational destination and public park since 1879. The island has variously been used as a dueling ground and a place for quartering troops, most recently during World War II.

Named after Isabelle Cass, the daughter of Governor Lewis Cass, Belle Isle was designed in 1883 by Frederick Law Olmsted, the famous landscape architect known for New York's Central Park. While some features of Olmsted's original concept were never built or later removed, his influence is still clear.

Until recent years Belle Isle was under the management of the Department of Parks and Recreation of the City of Detroit. As the city's finances deteriorated, maintenance of the park suffered. Since 2014 Michigan's Department of Natural Resources (DNR) has overseen the park and invested $15 million in infrastructure, including the planting of dozens of new cherry trees along the lagoon near Scott Fountain. Michigan State Police and DNR Conservation Officers have also taken over law enforcement, which has enhanced the sense of security and improved public safety.

Aside from being a haven for bird-watchers, Belle Isle attracts anglers to its north and south fishing piers. Visitors can also relax on Detroit's only swimming beach or tour the vintage glass **Anna Scripps Whitcomb Conservatory** (900 Inselruhe Ave., 313/821-5428, 10am-5pm Wed.-Sun., free), which features collections of ferns, orchids, cacti, and other plants. Nearby is the **Belle Isle Aquarium** (3 Inselruhe Ave., 313/402-0466, 10am-4pm, Fri.-Sun., free, but donations requested). Kids especially will appreciate the small playground, the giant slide ($1 pp), the **Belle Isle Nature Center** (176 Lakeside Dr., 313/852-4056, 10am-4pm Wed.-Sun. Nov.-Mar., 10am-4pm Wed.-Sun. Apr.-Oct., free), which oversees a one-acre deer enclosure, and the intriguing **Dossin Great Lakes Museum** (100 Strand Dr., 313/833-5538, www.detroithistorical.org, 10am-4pm Fri.-Sun., free), which traces the development of Great Lakes-area shipping, from sailing vessels to modern freighters, many of which can still be seen from the riverfront.

Other visitors come to jog, circle the island by bike, practice golf on the driving range and greens, or just set up a picnic lunch under one of the gazebos and watch the passing freighters. Boating enthusiasts can wander around the 80-foot-tall marble **Livingstone Memorial Lighthouse,** which operated from 1882 to 1930, or check out the pleasure craft docked at the 1922 **Detroit Yacht Club.** Other curious historic structures include the 1908 **Belle Isle Casino,** the 1923 **James Scott Memorial Fountain,** the 1940 **Nancy Brown Peace Carillon,** and numerous other monuments.

Since the early 1970s, four different groups—the Friends of Belle Isle, the Belle Isle Botanical Society, the Belle Isle Women's Committee, and the Friends of the Belle Isle Aquarium—have striven to preserve and promote the island. In 2009, the organizations joined forces to form the **Belle Isle Conservancy** (8109 E. Jefferson Ave., 313/331-7760, www.belleisleconservancy.org).

PEWABIC POTTERY

On Jefferson Avenue, not far from Belle Isle, is another worthwhile stop, **Pewabic Pottery** (10125 E. Jefferson Ave., at Cadillac Ave., 313/626-2000, www.pewabic.org, 10am-6pm Mon.-Sat., noon-4pm Sun.). Founded by Mary Chase Perry Stratton in 1903, this arts and crafts pottery center is housed within a picturesque Tudor Revival building, now a National Historic Landmark. Best known for their innovative and iridescent glazes, Pewabic tiles can be found throughout the nation, with the highest concentration in southeast Michigan, including at Detroit's Guardian and Fisher Buildings, the main Detroit Public Library, and the Detroit Institute of Arts. Examples outside Michigan include the Shedd Aquarium in Chicago and the Nebraska State Capitol in Lincoln. Due to their ubiquity, Pewabic vessels and tiles represent Detroit's contribution to the arts and crafts movement of the early 20th century.

Operating today as a museum and nonprofit ceramic arts center, Pewabic continues to produce the handcrafted vessels and architectural tiles that brought it fame. Visitors peer into huge fiery kilns on a self-guided tour during business hours. A landmark of Detroit's arts community, Pewabic is a pilgrimage for potters and ceramic artists from around the country as well as the site of popular classes, workshops, and lectures for all ages. But don't look for the secret to the pottery's lustrous glaze—Stratton took it to the grave, leaving her successors to carry on with only an approximation of her original formula.

RIVERBOAT TOURS

For a terrific view of Detroit's skyline, consider taking a ride on the Detroit River, the world's busiest international waterway. **Diamond Jack's River Tours** (313/843-9376, www.diamondjack.com, tours 1pm and 3:30pm Thurs.-Sun., $21 adults, $19 seniors, $16 age 5-12, age 4 and under free) offers two-hour narrated riverboat cruises June 10-September 1. There are two departure points for these informative tours: Detroit's Rivard Plaza and Wyandotte's Bishop Park. The tours are first-come, first-served, so arrive at least 30 minutes before departure time.

Downtown Detroit

The intersection of Woodward Avenue and I-75 (Fisher Freeway) marks the entrance to the city's official downtown business district. During the day it teems with office workers from banks, insurance companies, and high-tech businesses. Once quiet after business hours, the area now offers a growing nightlife scene, with new bars and restaurants operating along Woodward Avenue, plus sporting events and concerts at Little Caesars Arena.

An essential stop on any architectural tour is the **Wayne County Building** (600 Randolph St.) on the east end of Cadillac Square, an early example of the Roman Baroque Revival style in Michigan. Built between 1897 and 1902, it's one of the oldest extant buildings in the city. Look up to see its ornamental cornices—they depict General "Mad" Anthony Wayne conferring with local Native Americans. (General Wayne served during the Revolutionary War and negotiated a treaty that claimed all the land between the Ohio and Mississippi Rivers for the United States.) Not surprisingly, it was listed on the National Register of Historic Places in 1975. During the mid-1980s the building underwent a thorough restoration. Although the county no longer uses the building, its historical status assures that its beauty will be preserved.

History buffs may also appreciate the art deco **Guardian Building** (500 Griswold St., www.guardianbuilding.com), where Wayne County's offices are currently. The 40-story Aztec-inspired structure, designed by noteworthy architect Wirt Rowland, has been designated a National Historic Landmark. Friendly doormen at the 1929 structure are usually pleased to share trivia about this breathtaking building or point you in the right direction for a self-guided tour of its Pewabic-accented interior.

Among the rare and sumptuous architectural features of the Guardian Building is the **Tiffany clock** which sits atop the screen of Monel metal (a composite of copper, nickel and aluminum) that separates the lobby from the banking hall. One of only four such clocks in the world, the orange and yellow face of the Guardian's clock coordinates with the colors of the barrel-vaulted ceiling and marble floors to create a truly exquisite environment.

Meanwhile, the buildings of Woodward Avenue cast a long shadow over small triangular-shaped **Harmonie Park** (E. Grand River Ave., Centre St., and Randolph St.), and the intimate, charming neighborhood surrounding it. Originally populated with German immigrants, the area is now an emerging arts and entertainment district. Much of the credit for Harmonie Park's rejuvenation goes to local architectural firm Schervish Vogel Merz and dates to the 1980s, long before anyone else saw a future in its warehouse-style buildings and vintage

Downtown Detroit

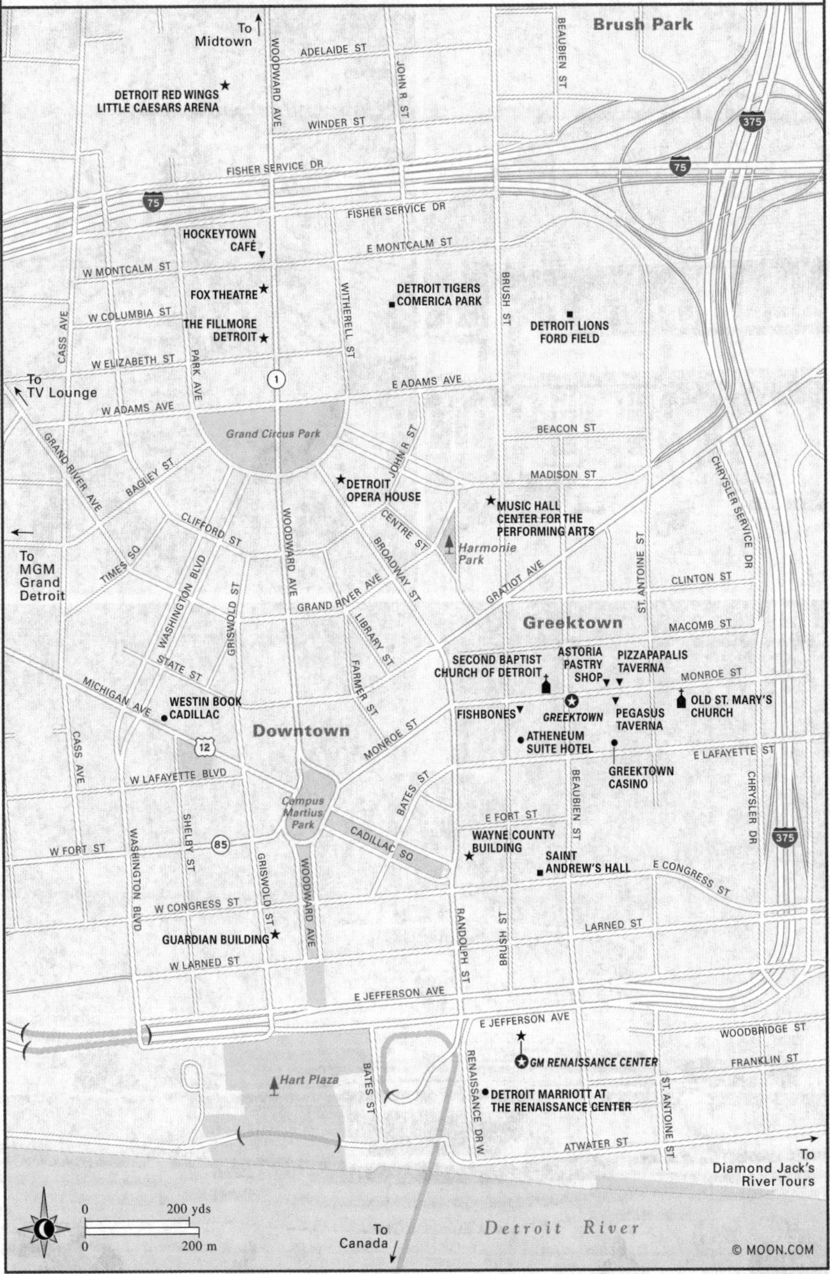

PEWABIC POTTERY
1
2
3

storefronts. Today, Harmonie Park is surrounded by pubs, galleries, and airy residential lofts. In recent years, the alternate name Paradise Valley has occasionally been used for the area as a tribute to a once thriving area nearby of African American nightlife up until the 1950s, demolished for construction of the Chrysler Freeway.

THEATER DISTRICT

At the northern end of downtown is Detroit's Theater District. This stretch of the Woodward corridor steadily deteriorated throughout the 1970s and into the mid-1980s until Mike Ilitch—owner of the nationwide Little Caesars Pizza chain and the Detroit Red Wings hockey team—stepped in and bought the aging **Fox Theatre** (2211 Woodward Ave., 313/471-7000, www.olympiaentertainment.com) in 1988.

What followed was a painstaking $8 million restoration that returned the gaudy yet glamorous structure to its original elegance. The 5,048-seat Fox is truly a marvel of 1920s architecture. Built in 1928 by William Fox and designed by noted theater architect C. Howard Crane, it was conceived in the style of an Arabian tent. The exotic style borrows motifs from a range of cultures, including Byzantine, Persian, Burmese, Indian, Thai, and Chinese. There are gold-leafed and hand-stenciled walls, marble-finish pillars, gold-tusked elephants, winged lions, a sunburst ceiling, and dreamlike decorative figures throughout. The lobby is six stories high, with 300,000 sparkling glass jewels, loads of brass, and a 13-foot two-ton stained-glass chandelier. The theater was listed on the National Register of Historic Places in 1985 and, following the successful restoration, designated a National Historic Landmark in 1989.

Today, the Fox is one of the nation's most successful theater operations, with almost nightly presentations, including touring Broadway musicals, big-name concerts, restored film epics, and other special events. You can't miss the 125-foot multicolored neon marquee, which stretches to the 10th floor of the Fox office building and was recently augmented with a high-tech digital display.

Luciano Pavarotti and Dame Joan Sutherland were among the notable names who traveled to the Motor City in 1996 to attend the opening of the restored **Detroit Opera House** (1526 Broadway St., 313/237-7464, www.michiganopera.org, tickets@motopera.org). Designed in 1922 by C. Howard Crane as a vaudeville stage, the 7,000-square-foot theater was reduced to running adult films by the 1970s. David DiChiera, the former university professor who founded the Michigan Opera Theatre in 1971 as a way to bring opera to kids, did the seemingly impossible when he raised $36 million for the opera's new 2,700-seat home. Today it acts as an important cultural resource, luring Broadway musicals as well as opera and ballet productions.

Other area theaters include **The Fillmore Detroit** (2115 Woodward Ave.), built in 1925, and the Music Hall Center for the Performing Arts (350 Madison St.), built in 1928. The Max M. Fisher Music Center (3711 Woodward Ave) houses the magnificently restored Orchestra Hall, built in 1919.

★ GREEKTOWN

Once a pioneer farm and now the city's best-known ethnic area, **Greektown** (www.greektowndetroit.org) has long been a center of downtown nightlife. Despite the unfortunate failure of the Trappers Alley shopping and entertainment complex during the 1980s, this famed stretch of Monroe Street attracts both locals and visitors. Parking rules are strictly enforced at the plentiful metered spots around Monroe Street.

Today's Greektown is a 21st-century rendering of an urban ethnic neighborhood that dates to 1915. The original families have long since moved away, and many of the restaurants and bakeries are upscale and not

---

1: Pewabic Pottery **2:** the Guardian Building's Tiffany glass clock **3:** the James Scott Memorial Fountain on Belle Isle

necessarily Greek, but you'll still find an occasional coffeehouse where old-timers gather to drink strong coffee or sip sweet retsina and play cards.

Other highlights of this charming neighborhood include two of Detroit's most notable churches. The ornate Roman Catholic **Old St. Mary's Church** (646 Monroe St., 313/961-8711, www.oldstmarysdetroit.com) was the city's first German Catholic congregation. Despite its address, the church actually faces St. Antoine Street. The **Second Baptist Church of Detroit** (441 Monroe St., 313/961-0920, www.secondbaptistdetroit.org, donation) was established in 1836 by several formerly enslaved people who had left the First Baptist Church due to discrimination against African Americans. Once a stop on the Underground Railroad, Second Baptist also established the first school for African American children. Members have included the country's first black schoolteacher, several presidents of the Detroit NAACP, and Ralph Bunche, the first African American to receive the Nobel Peace Prize. The basement houses a small museum explaining the church's role in aiding escaped slaves. Church docents are available for tours (donation).

Midtown

Head north along Woodward Avenue from downtown, and you'll come to the Cultural Center, part of Detroit's **Midtown** (www.midtowndetroit.org). Prior to the mid-1990s, the neighborhoods along the city's main drag north of downtown were commonly known as the Woodward Corridor, but for most Detroiters, the new name has been well received.

★ THE CULTURAL CENTER

Bookended by **Wayne State University** to the west and the **Detroit Medical Center** to the east, this is where you'll find a plethora of art galleries, performance venues, shops, and restaurants, plus most of the city's art and civic museums. It's also home to the **International Institute of Metropolitan Detroit** (111 E. Kirby St., 313/871-8600, www.iimd.org), which, besides offering citizenship classes and other educational programs, hosts the inexpensive International Cafe, the long-standing International Festival in early October, and the Ethel Averbach International Doll Collection, reportedly the world's largest collection of dolls dressed in native costumes. Roughly a block away from the International Institute is the main **Detroit Public Library** (5201 Woodward Ave., 313/481-1300, www.detroit.lib.mi.us, noon-8pm Tues.-Wed., 10am-6pm Thurs.-Sat.), which opened in 1921. With its 21 neighborhood branches, the DPL contains over 7.5 million items, the fourth-largest public library system in the United States. The Main Library hosts several special collections, including the Burton Historical Collection, covering the histories of Detroit and Michigan from the 1600s to the present, and the comprehensive E. Azalia Hackley Collection of African Americans in the Performing Arts, with books, manuscripts, photographs, recordings, and sheet music from the early 19th century through the Motown era.

You can wander the idealized "Streets of Old Detroit" in the basement of the **Detroit Historical Museum** (5401 Woodward Ave., 313/833-1805, www.detroithistorical.org, 9:30am-4pm Tues.-Fri., 10am-5pm Sat.-Sun., free, parking $7). You'll trudge along irregular cobblestones that once lined city streets past re-creations of barber shops, grocery stores, and other vintage businesses. The display, which opened in 1951 and has since been updated, traces several periods of Detroit history.

The permanent exhibit "Frontiers to Factories" traces the city's history from a trading post to an industrial giant, with a walk-in diorama from the 1750s, a railroad station, and a mock turn-of-the-20th-century exposition. Other highlights include the Glancy Train display, one of the world's largest; special exhibits about Detroit's leaders, symbols, and entertainment venues; and an exhibition named "America's Motor City," which traces

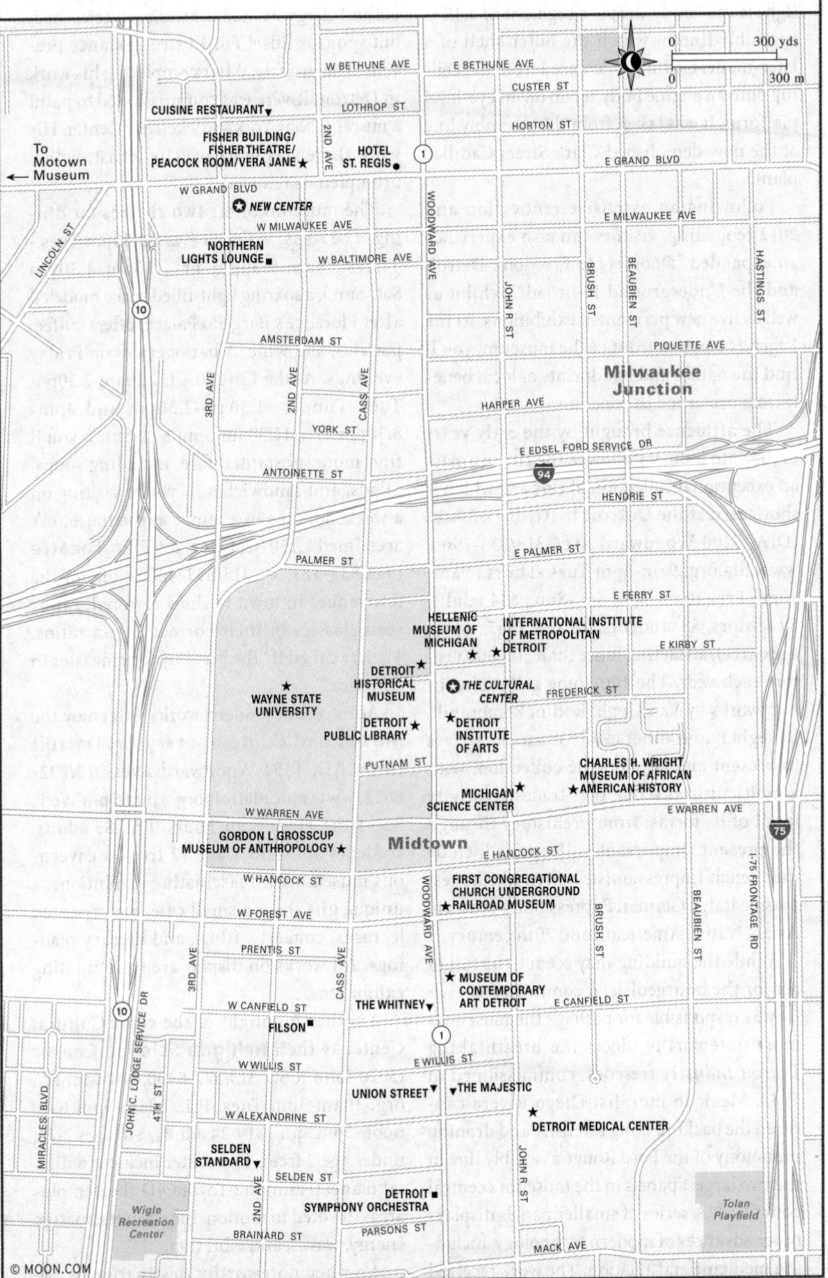
Midtown
0
300 yds
0
300 m
W BETHUNE AVE
E BETHUNE AVE
CUSTER ST
CUISINE RESTAURANT
LOTHROP ST
HORTON ST
FISHER BUILDING/
FISHER THEATRE/
PEACOCK ROOM/VERA JANE
HOTEL
ST. REGIS
To
Motown
Museum
1
E GRAND BLVD
W GRAND BLVD
NEW CENTER
W MILWAUKEE AVE
E MILWAUKEE AVE
LINCOLN ST
NORTHERN
LIGHTS LOUNGE
W BALTIMORE AVE
2ND AVE
WOODWARD AVE
BRUSH ST
BEAUBIEN ST
JOHN R ST
HASTINGS ST
10
AMSTERDAM ST
PIQUETTE AVE
Milwaukee
Junction
3RD AVE
2ND AVE
CASS AVE
HARPER AVE
YORK ST
E EDSEL FORD SERVICE DR
94
ANTOINETTE ST
HENDRIE ST
E PALMER ST
PALMER ST
E FERRY ST
HELLENIC
MUSEUM OF
MICHIGAN
INTERNATIONAL INSTITUTE
OF METROPOLITAN
DETROIT
E KIRBY ST
DETROIT
HISTORICAL
MUSEUM
THE CULTURAL
CENTER
WAYNE STATE
UNIVERSITY
FREDERICK ST
DETROIT
PUBLIC LIBRARY
DETROIT
INSTITUTE
OF ARTS
PUTNAM ST
CHARLES H. WRIGHT
MUSEUM OF AFRICAN
AMERICAN HISTORY
MICHIGAN
SCIENCE CENTER
E WARREN AVE
W WARREN AVE
75
GORDON L GROSSCUP
MUSEUM OF ANTHROPOLOGY
Midtown
E HANCOCK ST
W HANCOCK ST
FIRST CONGREGATIONAL
CHURCH UNDERGROUND
RAILROAD MUSEUM
W FOREST AVE
I-75 FRONTAGE RD
PRENTIS ST
MUSEUM OF
CONTEMPORARY
ART DETROIT
3RD AVE
CASS AVE
10
JOHN C. LODGE SERVICE DR
THE WHITNEY
W CANFIELD ST
E CANFIELD ST
FILSON
1
W WILLIS ST
E WILLIS ST
UNION STREET
THE MAJESTIC
MIRACLES BLVD
4TH ST
W ALEXANDRINE ST
DETROIT MEDICAL CENTER
SELDEN
STANDARD
SELDEN ST
2ND AVE
JOHN R ST
DETROIT
SYMPHONY ORCHESTRA
Wigle
Recreation
Center
Tolan
Playfield
BRAINARD ST
PARSONS ST
MACK AVE
© MOON.COM

the history of the car, the city, and the people who came to work here. The exhibit's highlight is the "body drop," a segment of a 1953 assembly line in which the outer shell of a later-model Cadillac is lowered from the ceiling onto an engine body set up on an eye-level platform. It was taken from the assembly line at the now-demolished Clark Street Cadillac plant.

Following an extensive renovation and 2012 reopening, visitors can also experience an expanded "Doorway to Freedom: Detroit and the Underground Railroad" exhibit as well as five new permanent exhibitions. At the Legends Plaza in front of the museum, you'll find the names and handprints of local benefactors preserved in concrete.

The affluence brought by the early years of the auto industry allowed the city to amass an exceptional collection of fine art, which is showcased at the **Detroit Institute of Arts** (DIA, 5200 Woodward Ave., 313/833-7900, www.dia.org, 9am-4pm Tues.-Thurs., 9am-10pm Fri., 10am-5pm Sat.-Sun., $14 adults, $9 seniors, $8 students, $6 ages 6-17, under age 6 free), attracting more than 500,000 visitors each year. The 100-some galleries contain works by Van Gogh, Rodin, Rembrandt, Brueghel, and others. The museum strives to present an encyclopedic collection, with a multicultural scope that traces creativity in all of its forms, from prehistory through the present. Important collections include the French Impressionist, Italian (the largest outside Italy), German Expressionist, African, Asian, Native American, and 20th century.

While the building may seem to be full of art for the bourgeoisie, a committed socialist was responsible for perhaps the museum's most noteworthy piece: the breathtaking *Detroit Industry* frescoes, commissioned in 1932. Mexican muralist Diego Rivera captured the backbreaking intensity and droning monotony of the Ford Rouge assembly line in the two largest panels in the museum's central courtyard. A series of smaller panels displays other advances of modern technology, including medicine and aviation. The work received a torrent of criticism for its damning commentary on capitalism. Numerous city leaders and clergy wanted the walls whitewashed, but sponsor Edsel Ford's strong stance prevented such a fate. After completing his work in Detroit, Rivera was commissioned to paint a mural at New York's Rockefeller Center. His work there was more overtly leftist, which prompted its removal.

The museum offers two choices for dining. The **Kresge Court** (9am-3:30pm Tues.-Thurs., 9am-9:30pm Fri., 10am-4:30pm Sat.-Sun.), a soaring light-filled space modeled after Florence's Bargello Palace, offers coffee, pastries, and wine. A bar operates on Friday evenings. At the **CaféDIA** (11:30am-2:30pm Tues.-Thurs., 11:30am-2:30pm and 4pm-8:30pm Fri., 11:30am-3pm Sat.-Sun.), you'll find more substantial fare, including soups, salads, and sandwiches. If you're visiting on a weekend, take in a movie at the museum's acclaimed 1,150-seat **Detroit Film Theatre** (313/833-3237 or 313/833-4005), one of the few venues in town to show restored, rarely seen classics in their correct aspect ratios. *Variety* called it "the best buy for cineastes in America."

Admirers of modern works will enjoy the **Museum of Contemporary Art Detroit** (MOCAD, 4454 Woodward Ave., 313/832-6622, www.mocadetroit.org, 11am-5pm Wed., Sat.-Sun., 11am-8pm Thurs.-Fri., $5 adults, students and under age 12 free), a cavernous museum with fascinating exhibitions, a unique gift shop, a small café, and assorted lectures, concerts, films, and literary readings. All works on display are from rotating exhibitions.

Another highlight of the city's Cultural Center is the **Michigan Science Center** (5020 John R St., 313/577-8400, www.mi-sci.org, 10am-3pm Tues.-Fri., 10am-5pm Sat., noon-5pm Sun., $19-24 adults, $16 ages 2-12, under age 2 free). The center includes a digital planetarium, the Toyota 4D theater, plus areas devoted to motion, life sciences, matter, energy, waves, and vibration.

Another noteworthy destination is the

Charles H. Wright Museum of African American History (315 E. Warren Ave., 313/494-5800, www.thewright.org, 9am-5pm Tues.-Sat., 1pm-5pm Sun., $8 adults, $5 over age 61 and ages 3-12, under age 3 free), which hosts the annual African World Festival and serves as the world's largest institution devoted to exploring the African American experience. Meanwhile, Wayne State University's recently renamed **Gordon L. Grosscup Museum of Anthropology** (4841 Cass Ave., Old Main, 1st fl., 313/577-2598, http://clasweb.clas.wayne.edu/anthromuseum, hours vary, free), which was established in 1958, houses both permanent and temporary exhibits, many of which feature artifacts from various sites throughout Detroit, from Fort Wayne to Belle Isle to the GM Renaissance Center.

Another intriguing site is the **First Congregational Underground Railroad Living Museum** (33 E. Forest Ave., 313/831-4080, www.friendsoffirst.com, 9am-5pm daily, free), housed in the First Congregational Church of Detroit and its Albert Kahn-designed Angels' Wing Community House. Visitors may appreciate strolling among the ornate religious paintings that line the walls of the 120-year-old sanctuary, but be advised that this is an active church, so it's best to visit weekday afternoons, 2pm-4pm Tuesday-Friday. The church offers an Underground Railroad Flight to Freedom Tour (hours vary Tues.-Sat., $12 adults, $10 ages 3-17, $8 over age 61, under age 3 free), a reenactment during which participants are shackled and led to liberation by a "conductor." Because this experience involves volunteer actors, however, the church staff require a minimum of 20 participants for each tour.

For a different aspect of Detroit's history, head to the **Hellenic Museum of Michigan** (67 E. Kirby St., 313/871-4100, www.hellenicmi.org, 1-5pm Sun., donation), which opened in 2010 in the hopes of becoming a modern-day version of the Mouseion (House of the Muses) of ancient Alexandria. Through the use of artifacts, photographs, oral histories, and personal documents, the museum presents the numerous artistic and intellectual achievements of Hellenic culture from ancient times to the present. It also aims to chronicle the considerable struggles, triumphs, and contributions of the Greek immigrants that settled in Michigan, including Detroit.

★ NEW CENTER

Situated about a mile north of the Cultural Center is the commercial district known as **New Center** (www.newcenterplace.com), developed during the 1920s as an alternate area of auto-related commerce, close to the factories, to complement downtown. The New Center was once best known for its most famous resident, General Motors. The enormous GM corporate headquarters housed thousands of workers. For decades its lavish 1st-floor showrooms, known as the General Motors Exhibit Hall, displayed the automaker's newest models.

By the 1980s, the residential neighborhood just north of the corporate headquarters, an area of once fine homes, had become seedy and derelict. Working to revive these blocks, GM invested heavily in buying, rehabbing, and reselling homes and renamed the neighborhood the New Center Commons. The idea was to beautify the company's surroundings, while making the neighborhood attractive for its employees and other middle- and upper-income families.

While the New Center neighborhood slowly began to improve, in 1999 GM moved its headquarters downtown to the Renaissance Center. Since then, the GM building has been acquired by the state of Michigan and renamed Cadillac Place. The building now serves as the seat of state government functions in Detroit.

The **Fisher Building** (3011 W. Grand Blvd.) is worth seeing for the dazzling ceiling murals alone. In 1927 the seven original Fisher brothers financed construction of the building from the proceeds of the sale of their Fisher Body Works company to General

Motors. The brothers wanted to build the finest office tower anywhere and gave architect Albert Kahn a blank check to do it. He didn't disappoint. Kahn made lavish use of expensive materials, including 420 tons of bronze, marble, Minnesota granite, and 24-karat gold. Today, the building's 30-story central tower and two 11-story wings house the Fisher Theatre, shops, restaurants, and office space. Detroiters often refer to the Fisher Building as the city's largest art object. In 1929 the Architectural League of New York recognized the Fisher Building as the world's most beautiful commercial structure.

Dwarfed by the Fisher Building and Cadillac Place is the diminutive **Motown Museum** (2648 W. Grand Blvd., 313/875-2264, www.motownmuseum.org, 10am-6pm Tues.-Sat. Sept.-Apr., 10am-6pm Tues.-Fri., 10am-8pm Sat. 10am-6pm Sun. May-Sept., $15 adults, $10 over age 61, $10 ages 5-17, age 4 and under, free; admission by guided tour only). Known across the country as Hitsville USA, this is where the Motown Sound exploded from the now legendary Studio A and soon had teenagers around the country "Dancin' in the Streets."

Berry Gordy Jr. bought the unremarkable two-story flat in 1959 as a fledgling songwriter with a dream of developing new talent. Today, portions of the state historic site look much as they did in the early 1960s, with an office and a tape library filled with reel-to-reel tape machines, company manuals, and newspaper clippings. The 2nd floor recreates Gordy's apartment, where he and his staff would spend nights packing records to ship to radio stations around the country. The museum's most prized display, however, is the original Studio A, where top tunes such as "Stop in the Name of Love" and "My Girl" were recorded. Diana Ross and the Supremes, Smokey Robinson and the Miracles, Martha Reeves and the Vandellas, Gladys Knight and the Pips, Lionel Richie and the Commodores, The Temptations, the Four Tops, the Marvelettes, Marvin Gaye, Stevie Wonder, and the Jackson Five all recorded in this studio during their early careers. Other artifacts on display in the two museum buildings (at its zenith, the company owned seven buildings along West Grand Boulevard and an office building downtown on Woodward Avenue) include rare photos, gold records, period costumes, and other memorabilia. The museum is closed on major holidays, and cameras and cell phones are strictly prohibited.

Mexicantown

You'll find a colorful Mexican mercado and you may see elderly Mexican women, heads covered with an old-fashioned lace mantilla, praying with their rosaries in one of the historic churches in this neighborhood, including **Ste. Anne de Detroit Catholic Church** (1000 Ste. Anne St., 313/496-1701, www.ste-anne.org, free). Ste. Anne's is the second-oldest continuously operating Catholic parish in the United States, established two days after King Louis XIV's emissary, Cadillac, landed in July 1701. The current church is the parish's eighth, constructed in 1886.

RECREATION

Spectator Sports

While Michigan boasts a variety of semi-professional teams—including minor league baseball teams like the Traverse City Beach Bums and the Lansing Lugnuts—most sports lovers flock to Detroit to watch the state's top-tier clubs in action. September to December, American football fans head to Ford Field (2000 Brush St., 313/262-2013) to cheer on the **Detroit Lions** (www.detroitlions.com). April to October, baseball fans can watch the **Detroit Tigers** (http://detroit.tigers.mlb.com) at Comerica Park (2100 Woodward Ave., 313/962-4000 or 866/668-4437). October to April, ice hockey fans can catch the **Detroit Red Wings** (http://redwings.nhl.com) at Little Caesar's Arena (2645 Woodward Ave, 313/471-7000, www.313presents.com). Basketball fans, meanwhile, can support the NBA's **Detroit Pistons** (www.nba.com/pistons) at The Palace of Auburn Hills (6

Championship Dr., Auburn Hills, 248/377-0100, www.palacenet.com) during the November-April season.

Biking

For a leisurely bike ride, head to **William G. Milliken State Park and Harbor** (1900 Atwater St., 313/396-0217, www.michigan.gov/dnr, 6am-10pm daily, free), formerly known as Tri-Centennial Park and now offering a bike path not far from the Detroit River. Experienced mountain bikers can head beyond the city limits, where the **Highland Recreation Area** (5200 E. Highland Rd., White Lake, 248/889-3750, www.michigan.gov/dnr, 8am-10pm daily) provides 16 miles of some of the area's most challenging mountain biking routes.

Another option is **Pinckney State Recreation Area** (8555 Silver Hill Rd., Pinckney, 734/426-4913, www.michigan.gov/dnr), home to the 17-mile Potawatomi Trail, recognized among the nation's top 10 routes and also catering to hikers and cross-country skiers. To enter the two recreation areas, an annual Recreation Passport ($12 Michigan residents, $34 nonresidents, $9 day pass available to nonresidents only) is required; the passport allows you access to all of the Michigan state parks and recreation areas that charge a fee.

Boating and Fishing

Given Detroit's proximity to the Detroit River, Lake Erie, and Lake St. Clair, boating and fishing are popular activities. If you don't have a boat, contact the **Michigan Charter Boat Association** (MCBA, 800/622-2971, www.michigancharterboats.com), which can help you locate and join sailing excursions and fishing charters. **William G. Milliken State Park and Harbor** (1900 Atwater St., 313/396-0217, free) offers easy access to shore fishing alongside the Detroit River. You'll also find pier fishing on the south side of Belle Isle Park (East Jefferson Ave. at East Grand River Ave., free). Fishing in any Michigan waters requires a valid **Michigan fishing license;** get one at www.mdnr-elicense.com.

Winter Activities

Detroit gets plenty of snow and ice during the winter months, although not nearly as much as northern Michigan. If you enjoy cold-weather diversions, ice-skating, ice fishing, sledding, tobogganing, cross-country skiing, and downhill skiing are all popular in and around the city.

Ice-skaters can head to the skating rink at **Campus Martius Park** (800 Woodward Ave., www.campusmartiuspark.org, mid Nov.-early Mar., 11am-6pm Mon.-Tues., 11am-9pm Wed.-Thurs., 11am-11pm, Fri., 10am-11pm Sat., noon-8pm Sun.), a 2.5-acre public square that also offers year-round entertainment. National and Olympic ice-skating champions have performed here, but the rink is also open for public skating ($10 adults, $8 under age 13 and over age 49). Skate rental is $5 or bring your own.

Another option for wintertime recreationists is **Lake Erie Metropark** (32481 W. Jefferson Ave., Brownstown, 734/379-5020, www.metroparks.com, 7am-10pm daily, $10 per vehicle, $35 per vehicle annually), a 1,607-acre recreation area that lies about 27 miles south of downtown Detroit. Cross-country skiers can embrace 4.25 miles of marked, groomed trails; ice-fishing enthusiasts can search for perch, bass, and other species on Lake Erie; and sledders can plummet down a large hill near the wave-pool complex.

ENTERTAINMENT AND EVENTS

Nightlife

No matter what your taste is, Detroit offers an abundance of places to listen to good music, from alternative sounds at **Saint Andrew's Hall** (431 E. Congress St., 313/961-8961, www.saintandrewsdetroit.com) to smooth jazz at the long-standing **Baker's Keyboard Lounge** (20510 Livernois Ave., 313/345-6300, www.theofficialbakerskeyboardlounge.com, 11am-1am Tues.-Fri., 4pm-12am Sat.,

1
2
3
THE BREWERY ON BROADWAY
Detroit
BEER Co.
EST. 2003 • DETROIT, MICHIGAN
CREDIT
SIMMONS
AND
CLARK
JEWELERS
BULOVA WATCHES
BULOVA

1pm-12:30am Sun.), the world's oldest continuously operating jazz club. Another popular spot is **Flood's Bar & Grille** (731 St. Antoine St., 313/963-1090, www.floodsdetroit.com, 4pm-11pm Mon., 4pm-1am Tues.-Thurs., 4pm-2am Fri., 7pm-2am Sat.-Sun., cover $10 Wed-Sun. after 8pm), which features jazz, R&B, sweet soul, or karaoke nightly.

For a throwback to the era of art deco elegance, make a visit to **Cliff Bell's** (2030 Park Ave., 313/961-2543, www.cliffbells.com, 5pm-midnight Tues.-Fri., 5pm-12:30am Sat., 11am-10pm Sun., entrées $23-44) to take in a pure jazz experience. Originally opened in 1935 and bearing its founder's name, the club offers a delectable menu (think pan-roasted pheasant and Chilean sea bass) plus a talented roster of musical artists representing different currents within the jazz tradition. Cover charge starts at $10, but for some performers the admission is free.

At the **Axis Lounge** (1117 3rd St., 313/465-1650, www.mgmgranddetroit.com, 10am-2am daily, no cover), inside the MGM Grand Detroit, the music ranges from jazz to Top 40 to classic rock performed by local bands. A stylish interior completes the scene. There are nightly drink specials.

Management at the **Delux Lounge** (350 Monroe St., 313/962-4200, www.deluxlounge.com, 7pm-2am Wed.-Thurs., 6pm-2am Fri.-Sat. no cover), one of the growing number of non-Greek establishments in Greektown, likes to think of the venue really as two bars. During the week it's more sedate, but on the weekends, the place attracts a younger crowd with a DJ spinning a succession of Top 40 hits. Inexpensive beer (from $3) and friendly staff make the Delux a great place to stop after a game at Comerica Park or Ford Field.

The Majestic (4140 Woodward Ave., at Willis St., 313/833-9700, www.majesticdetroit.com, 11am-2am daily) is Detroit's, and possibly one of America's, most eclectic entertainment destinations. Under one roof you'll find the 600-seat Majestic Theatre, featuring a full schedule of rock-and-roll acts; the Alley Deck, a rooftop bar and grill that's open during the warm-weather months; the Magic Stick, a dance club featuring LED lights and a newly expanded stage with enhanced sound; and the Garden Bowl, the oldest continuously operating bowling alley in the United States. Visit the website for more details about the many offerings.

When it opened in 2002, **Bleu Detroit** (1540 Woodward Ave., between Witherell St. and Clifford St., 313/974-7799, www.bleudetroit.com, 10pm-2am Fri.-Sat. but varying by show) was one of the first new nightclubs in years. And since that time it's grown even more exclusive and has become the personification of cool. A recent renovation included the addition of a high-tech LED lighting rig. The main bar area is adjacent to a huge dance floor with plenty of table space nearby. Here you'll find the leading performers of techno, a musical genre that originated in Detroit.

Northern Lights Lounge (660 W. Baltimore St., between 2nd Ave. and 3rd Ave., 313/873-1739, www.northernlightslounge.com, 11am-2am daily), tucked away in an unassuming corner of the New Center, prides itself as being Detroit's most diverse club. It's not surprising, considering the eclectic lineup of bands spanning the musical spectrum from R&B, Motown, and punk rock. On nights a band isn't playing, you'll find diversions like trivia contests and karaoke. A robust bar menu of burgers, chicken wings, and salads is available daily (11am-11pm), and brunch is served 11am-3pm on Sunday.

The **TV Lounge** (2548 Grand River Ave., at 4th St., 313/965-4789, 5pm-2am Wed.-Fri., 9pm-2am Sat., 5pm-midnight Sun., drinks average $6) considers itself "the Cheers of Detroit," where everybody knows your name. A fully stocked bar accompanies a steady mix of live music, with bands representing techno, hip-hop, and R&B. By their own admission, food is little more than an afterthought here,

1: statues honoring the Detroit Tigers at Comerica Park **2:** the Fisher Building at New Center **3:** neon signs in the theater district along Broadway

More Than Motown

Detroit has always been a complex town. Its many facets have spawned numerous monikers—not the least of which honors it as the birthplace of a groundbreaking musical style. But there's more to Detroit's musical heritage than the famous Motown story. Southeastern Michigan has also nurtured a brood of well-known rock and rollers and hip-hop stars, including:

- Alice Cooper
- Eminem
- Glenn Frey
- Bill Haley
- Madonna
- Iggy Pop
- Bob Seger

In addition, Detroit's great ethnic diversity has been responsible for the growth of numerous other genres, including jazz, gospel, and blues. The Paradise Valley entertainment district was home to several clubs that would often host performers representing these traditions, including Duke Ellington, Ella Fitzgerald, Pearl Bailey, and Count Basie.

but a quick bite is available. There is outdoor seating during the warmer months.

Corktown, Detroit's oldest neighborhood, is just west of downtown and is perhaps paradoxically also one of the most up-and-coming neighborhoods in the city. An array of new dining and drinking options is evolving, but an old classic bar is perhaps the best way to get a glimpse of the area's rich heritage. **Nancy Whiskey** (2644 Harrison St., 313/962-4247, www.nancywhiskeydetroit.com, 11am-2am daily) fits the bill perfectly. Occupying an old house-like space, this venerable watering hole dates to 1902—it survived Prohibition by operating a speakeasy in the basement. Live music is featured on Friday and Saturday nights, and on Wednesday the jukebox is free!

Casinos

In a controversial referendum in 1996, Michigan voters approved casino gambling within Detroit city limits. More than 20 years later, three casinos are now running—and remain controversial. Whether gambling helps or harms the struggling city is still undecided in the court of public opinion.

For those who enjoy rolling the dice, options include **MGM Grand Detroit** (1777 3rd St., 877/888-2121, www.mgmgranddetroit.com, 24/7), a flashy art deco palace that draws its inspiration from the Hollywood of yesteryear and offers nearly 4,000 slot and video poker machines, 100 table games, and a nonsmoking poker room. Beyond gaming activities, MGM Grand also features a full-service hotel, a sports pub, a Wolfgang Puck restaurant plus other dining options, a luxurious spa, four unique bars, a pulsating nightclub, and plenty of live entertainment.

Motown in all its glory provides the theme for the locally owned **MotorCity Casino Hotel** (2901 Grand River Ave., 866/752-9622, www.motorcitycasino.com, 24/7). The gaming area is in a former Wonder Bread warehouse and connected by skywalks to the hotel tower and parking structure. In addition to a smoke-free poker room, 59 table games, and more than 2,900 slot and video poker machines, the MotorCity Casino offers a comfortable hotel, a relaxing spa, a spacious concert hall, and several dining options, from award-winning Iridescence to the Assembly Line Buffet.

The recently renovated **Greektown Casino-Hotel** (555 E. Lafayette Ave., 313/223-2999, www.greektowncasino.com, 24/7) is the city's most spacious, with Las Vegas-style gaming and easy access to one of the city's liveliest neighborhoods. Dining options include Prism, voted in 2015 as Detroit's Best Steakhouse by *Hour Detroit* magazine, and Bistro 555, a buffet offering quality after-hours dining. As with its competitors, Greektown Casino also offers a stylish hotel, live entertainment, and various nightlife options.

Performing Arts

Productions at the 5,048-seat **Fox Theatre** (2211 Woodward Ave., 313/471-3200 or 313/471-6611, www.olympiaentertainment.com) include touring Broadway musicals, big-name concerts, restored film epics, and other special events. The restored **Detroit Opera House** (1526 Broadway St., 313/237-7464, www.michiganopera.org), home of the Michigan Opera Theatre, attracts full-scale productions of opera, ballet, and Broadway musicals.

Other area theaters include **The Fillmore Detroit** (2115 Woodward Ave., 313/961-5451, www.thefillmoredetroit.com), a live music venue built in 1925, and the **State Theatre and the Music Hall Center for the Performing Arts** (350 Madison St., 313/887-8500, www.musichall.org), which features contemporary ballet, live concerts, music festivals, and more. The music hall was built in 1928 by auto heiress Matilda Dodge Wilson for the production of "legitimate" theatrical productions. Its stage has been graced by luminaries such as Lucille Ball, W. C. Fields, Martha Graham, Ella Fitzgerald, Lillian Hellman, and Elaine Stritch. The **Fisher Theatre** (3011 W. Grand Blvd., 313/879-5433 or 313/872-1000, www.broadwayindetroit.com) opened as a movie and vaudeville house in 1928. In 1961 the theater was remodeled in midcentury modern style and converted to a venue for live entertainment. For over 50 years, the Fisher has featured both modern and classic Broadway shows. Fans of classical music make their way to the **Max M. Fisher Music Center** (3711 Woodward Ave., 313/576-5100 or 313/576-5111, www.dso.org), since 2003 home of the magnificently restored and acoustically perfect **Orchestra Hall,** originally built in 1919 for the Detroit Symphony Orchestra, as well as **The Cube** (an acronym for Curated, Urban, and Boundless Experience), a 450-seat performance hall that features an eclectic array of programming.

Festivals and Events

Detroit hosts numerous events and celebrations throughout the year, including the **North American International Auto Show** (Cobo Center, 1 Washington Blvd., 248/643-0250 or 313/877-8777, www.naias.com, $13 adults, $7 over age 64 and ages 7-12, under age 7 free). The world's second-largest show of its kind, the NAIAS offers the world a firsthand look at what cars will look like in the near and distant future. Traditionally held in January, the show will move to June for the first time in 2020. The new version of the event will include a number of outdoor displays and demonstrations.

In mid-April, Greektown comes alive with the annual **Detroit Greek Independence Day Parade** (http://detroitgreekparade.blogspot.com, free), held on Monroe Street, the main thoroughfare of this historic neighborhood.

In early June, the weekend-long **Chevrolet Detroit Belle Isle Grand Prix** (313/748-1800 or 866/464-7749, www.detroitgp.com) has races featuring Indy cars and off-road trucks on Belle Isle's 2.3-mile road course, considered one of the most challenging in the world. One-day general admission tickets are $40; two-day tickets are $75. Various VIP tickets, allowing access to the paddock and pit areas, are available at additional cost.

Taking over Woodward Avenue on the third Saturday of August is the annual **Woodward Dream Cruise** (www.

Elmore Leonard's Motor City

Born in New Orleans, Elmore John Leonard Jr. (1925-2013), the son of a General Motors employee, spent the bulk of his adolescent and teenage years in Detroit. Following high school, he served in the U.S. Navy for three years. After graduating from the University of Detroit with an English and philosophy degree, he began a career in advertising, writing copy for Chevrolet while working for a major Detroit ad agency.

While maintaining his advertising job, he also began to pen Western stories, which were popular in the 1950s. Leonard decided a decade later to focus on a full-time writing career. Soon he'd crafted his first crime novel, *The Big Bounce* (1969). Over the ensuing years, he continued to write crime novels, often set in Detroit, gradually gaining a loyal cult following. Adapting several of his stories into screenplays helped to fund his fiction career—until the publication of two best sellers propelled *Time* magazine to name him the "Dickens from Detroit" in 1984.

Leonard would continue to write best-selling crime novels and short stories from his Detroit suburb home until his death. Some of these became popular films and television shows, including *Get Shorty* (1995), *Jackie Brown* (1997), *Out of Sight* (1998), *Killshot* (2008), *Justified* (2010-2015), and *Freaky Deaky* (2012). Even his Western tales have made a resurgence: In 2007, Russell Crowe and Christian Bale starred in *3:10 to Yuma,* the second adaptation of his breakout short story.

If you're curious about Leonard's sharp-tongued take on gritty Detroit, visit the author's official website (www.elmoreleonard.com) or consider perusing the following titles:

- ***Unknown Man No. 89*** (1977): When a skillful Detroit process server is hired to search for a missing stockholder, he becomes the unwitting target of a lethal triple-cross.
- ***The Switch*** (1978): Hoping to make some easy ransom money, two ex-cons kidnap the wife of a Detroit developer who, unfortunately for them, has no desire to get her back.
- ***City Primeval*** (1980): A dedicated homicide detective strives to stop a psychopathic murderer in the Motor City.
- ***Touch*** (1987): A former Franciscan monk with faith-healing powers finds it difficult to be a saint in the city.
- ***Freaky Deaky*** (1988): After his fishy suspension from the Detroit Police Department, a determined sergeant must uncover a web of scams perpetrated by an ex-con, a former Black Panther, a movie dynamite expert, and an alcoholic auto industry heir.
- ***Out of Sight*** (1996): A career thief forms an unlikely relationship with a sexy U.S. marshal, which leads them from sunny Florida to the gritty streets and upscale suburbs of Detroit.
- ***Mr. Paradise*** (2004): When two roommates—a lingerie model and an escort—get involved with a retired Detroit lawyer, murder, greed, and pandemonium ensue.
- ***Up in Honey's Room*** (2007): In World War II-era Detroit, a young U.S. marshal befriends a free-spirited American woman in the hopes that she'll lead him to her husband—a German-born butcher who's giving shelter to German prisoners of war.

woodwarddreamcruise.com). Owners of classic cars parade their prized vehicles along Detroit's main street in both directions from Eight Mile Road north to Pontiac. The traffic moves rather slowly, which allows for great views of the cars.

Over the last weekend in June, the St. Nicholas Greek Orthodox Church holds the annual **Opa! Fest** (760 W. Wattles Rd., Troy, 248/362-9575, www.opafest.org, $2 pp, under age 12 free), filled with Greek music, traditional Greek folk dancing, Greek arts and crafts, cooking demonstrations, and, of course, Greek cuisine, from kebabs and gyros to pastries and wine. Another popular summertime event is the **African World Festival**

(313/494-5824, free), which has been hosted by the **Charles H. Wright Museum of African American History** (315 E. Warren Ave., 313/494-5800, www.thewright.org) for the past three decades. Usually held in mid-August, this beloved festival features world music, jazz and blues, a folk village, an international marketplace, ethnic cuisine, traditional dances, and other tantalizing diversions.

Over Labor Day weekend, there are two celebratory events worth attending. From Hart Plaza to Campus Martius, the **Detroit Jazz Festival** (313/447-1248, www.detroitjazzfest.com, free) presents a wide array of open-air concerts and a world-class selection of music masters—the largest free jam in the world. Festival attendees can also experience lively interviews, panel discussions, and presentations by musicians, journalists, and jazz radio hosts.

Just north of Detroit proper, downtown Royal Oak is the venue for the annual festival **Ford Arts, Beat and Eats** (248/541-7550, www.artsbeatseats.com, $3, $5 after 3pm, under age 3 free). This unique event offers something for everyone, including local and national musical acts performing on nine separate stages, a juried fine art show drawing talent from around the nation, and food offerings from kiosks operated by some of Detroit's signature restaurants. Proceeds benefit 13 local charities.

SHOPPING

GM Renaissance Center

Downtown shoppers can browse the boutiques inside the **GM Renaissance Center** (100 Renaissance Center, 313/567-3126, www.gmrencen.com). Options run the gamut from **The Runway** (313/568-7977, 10am-6pm Mon.-Fri., 11am-4pm Sat.-Sun.), which sells high-end men's and women's apparel, to the charming **Renaissance 500 Shoppe** (313/259-6510, 7am-5:30pm Mon.-Fri.), where the friendly staff sell fine tobacco products and other specialty items. For finding that unique item exclusive to the Motor City, be sure to check out **Pure Detroit** (313/259-5100, www.puredetroit.com, 10:30am-5:30pm Mon.-Sat.), where you'll uncover a bevy of items, all reminiscent of Detroit, including books, clothing, jewelry, coffee mugs, and messenger bags. Particularly noteworthy are the Pewabic tiles, some featuring etchings of local landmarks, Detroit's official crest, or maps of Michigan.

Woodward Avenue and Environs

Throughout the 20th century, Woodward Avenue offered some of the finest shopping available in the Midwest. Three major department stores (the largest, J. L. Hudson, was over two million square feet) complemented dozens of specialty shops lining the avenue and the adjacent streets, offering everything from clothing, shoes, and jewelry to furniture and other items for the home. Regrettably, the combined impact of suburban shopping malls and a shifting population decimated the area's customer base, resulted in once proud Woodward Avenue becoming abandoned and blighted.

But beginning around 2005, eyesore buildings were cleaned up and repaired in preparation for the flood of visitors for Super Bowl XL in 2006. Slowly but consistently investors began to respond to the growing number of new downtown residents and convention visitors. As a result, Woodward has seen the beginnings of a retail rebirth. The shops opening up do not come close to rivaling their historic predecessors, but this welcome change has inspired hope—and some good bargains to boot.

John Varvatos (1500 Woodward Ave., 313/437-8095, www.johnvarvatos.com, 11am-7pm Mon.-Sat., noon-6pm Sun.) is a place where the name says it all. The internationally acclaimed menswear designer, a Detroit-area native, proudly opened his Detroit location in 2013, offering high-end men's dress and casual wear plus a full line of shoes and outerwear. The store is pricey but worth a visit.

Moosejaw (1275 Woodward Ave., 2 blocks north of Campus Martius, 313/338-3661,

The Heidelberg Project

the Heidelberg Project

Buses full of Japanese tourists may be an unexpected sight in the run-down McDougall-Hunt neighborhood on the city's near east side. But in reality, visitors from all parts of the world are anything but unusual. This was the childhood home of artist Tyree Guyton, and today it's the location of his unique creation: **The Heidelberg Project** (3600 Heidelberg St. Detroit, www.heidelberg.org), a remarkable piece of urban environmental art.

As a child, Guyton lived in the neighborhood in poverty. In addition, he suffered from abuse and harassment for developing his interest in art. Only his grandfather encouraged him. Despite the odds, Guyton went on to study at Detroit's highly respected College for Creative Studies (CCS), but he never forgot his roots. His first work was *Fun House,* created in 1986 from an abandoned house next to his grandfather's duplex. He transformed the dilapidated frame structure by adding bright patches of color and covered it with old toys, dollhouses, picture frames, shoes, signs, and other assorted discards.

The Heidelberg Project grew to envelop most of Heidelberg Street between Mt. Elliott Avenue and Ellery Street. The site is easily accessible from downtown Detroit by taking Gratiot Avenue northeast to Mt. Elliott Avenue, making a right turn, and then another right onto Heidelberg Street.

From early on, the compelling outdoor exhibit drew acclaim from the media and the art community, including curators form the Detroit Institute of Arts. But despite this, it failed to win over neighbors, and then-mayor Coleman Young, who viewed the project as trash, periodically had it demolished by city crews—only for it to be rebuilt.

Young's successor, Dennis Archer, was more enlightened, but only took a neutral stance. He neither encouraged nor discouraged Guyton's work. In recent years, the Heidelberg Project has achieved mainstream acceptance.

Guyton's grandfather, who served as a tour guide of the project, passed away in 1992. His duplex, now known as the *Dotty Wotty House,* has since been integrated into the project. Guyton dedicated the house to his memory and to that of Martin Luther King Jr. Despite sporadic acts of vandalism and a recent streak of arson, the Heidelberg Project has endured. Improvements are on the horizon, including a grant-funded plan to transform the House That Makes Sense into the project's official center, with administrative offices, exhibition space, a library, and a children's workshop. Though admission is free, please keep in mind that the block is still home to full-time residents. Remember to respect their privacy and never enter individual structures without permission. Guided tours are available, but must be booked in advance.

www.moosejaw.com, 11am-7pm Mon.-Wed., 11am-8pm Thurs.-Sat., noon-5pm Sun.) is a locally owned purveyor of quality casual clothing plus outdoor gear, shoes, and apparel. Brands include Patagonia, The North Face, Black Diamond, and icebreaker. The staff like to create a friendly, informal atmosphere.

House of Vin (1433 Woodward Ave., between Grand River Ave. and Clifford St., 313/638-2501, www.houseofpurevin.com, noon-9pm Mon.-Thurs., noon-11pm Fri.-Sat., noon-7pm Sun.) is a wine and champagne retailer and tasting room that offers hundreds of varieties of wines from Michigan, California, and France, among others. The store relies on the expertise of master sommelier Claudia Tyagi, one of only three in Michigan, to select offerings and conduct frequent special events. Check the store's website for the schedule.

Nike Community Store (1261 Woodward Ave., between State St. and Grand River Ave., 313/965-3319, www.nike.com, 10am-8pm Mon.-Sat., 10am-6pm Sun.) is where you'll find well-stocked racks of top-quality athletic gear—shoes, workout clothing, outerwear, and accessories on two levels. **Lululemon** (1459 Woodward Ave., between Grand River Ave. and Clifford St., 313/965-0806, www.info.lululemon.com, 11am-7pm Mon.-Sat., noon-5pm Sun.) features premium clothing for yoga, aerobics, and other active pursuits. **Madewell** (1426 Woodward Ave., between E. Grand River Ave. and John R St., 313/965-4469, www.madewell.com, 10am-7pm Mon.-Sat., 11am-6pm Sun.) offers a wide array of women's apparel and accessories.

H & M (1505 Woodward Ave. at Clifford, 855-466-747, www.hm.com, 10am-9pm Mon.-Sat., 11am-7pm Sun.) is a worldwide retailer of affordable yet fashionable clothing, shoes, and accessories for men, women, and children. If your city doesn't have an H & M location, be sure to stop in.

Off Woodward Avenue, downtown offers several other specialty retailers. **Spectacles** (230 E. Grand River Ave. at Centre St., 313/963-6886, www.spectaclesdetroit.com, noon-6pm Mon.-Sat.) features funky, casual clothing and accessories for both men and women. **Sports Mania Detroit** (400 Monroe in Greektown, 313/962-0391, www.sportsmaniausa.com, 11am-8pm Mon.-Thurs., 11:30am-10pm Fri.-Sat., noon-6pm Sun.) is the quintessential source for Detroit-themed sports merchandise. As everyone knows, Detroit sports fans are the most passionate in the world!

Midtown

The Midtown area, the neighborhood straddling Woodward Avenue north of the downtown core, is a noteworthy destination for shopping as well as dining and entertainment.

Vera Jane (3011 W. Grand Blvd., Fisher Bldg., 313/875-4588, 11am-6pm Tues.-Sat.) is a cutting-edge boutique that offers women's handbags, accessories, cosmetics, and intimate apparel. Also in the Fisher Building, be sure to visit **Yama** (313/315-3060, 10am-6pm, Mon-Sat., noon-5pm Sun.), which sells contemporary women's ready-to-wear by up-and-coming designers.

The **Peacock Room** (15 E. Kirby, 313/559-5000, and in the Fisher Building, 313/315-3061, 10am-6pm Mon.-Sat., noon-5pm

Woodward Avenue looking south

Sun.—both locations) offers bright, imaginative dresses and suits for the "women of yesterday, today, and tomorrow."

Filson (441 W. Canfield, 313/285-1880, 10am-7pm Mon.-Sat., 11am-5pm Sun.) specializes in tough, rugged clothing and gear for the outdoors. Here's where you'll come to get outfitted for fishing, hunting, and backpacking before you head to northern Michigan.

At the same address is the flagship location of **Shinola** (313/285-2390, www.shinola.com, 10am-7pm Mon.-Sat., 11am-5pm Sun.). A gem among locally based companies, Shinola represents true Detroit pride. It showcases the very best of its eclectic products line, consisting of quality watches, bicycles, and small leather goods.

Also at the same West Canfield address is **Third Man Records** (313/209-5205, 10am-7pm Mon.-Sat., 11am-5pm Sun.). Begun in 2001 by rock musician and Detroit native Jack White, Third Man offers vinyl records produced at its in-house pressing plant. Featured are recordings by cutting-edge artists such as The White Stripes, The Raconteurs, and The Stools.

In the Cultural Center, the **DIA Museum Shop** (5200 Woodward Ave., in the Detroit Institute of Arts, 9am-4:30pm Tues.-Thurs., 9am-10:30pm Fri., 10am-5:30pm Sat.-Sun.) is a different sort of shopping destination. Most of its offerings are inspired by the vast collection of the DIA. Examples include apparel, jewelry, accessories, custom reproductions, etc. There's also a great selection of books covering art history and local lore.

The museum shop at the **Detroit Historical Museum** (5401 Woodward, 313/833-1805, www.detroithistorical.org, 9:30am-4pm Tues-Fri., 10am-5pm Sat.-Sun.), also in the Cultural Center, offers an array of items related to its collection. While not as complete as its counterpart at the DIA, this delightful little store's offerings include books and novelty items that draw from Detroit's rich past.

Eastern Market

There is one place in the city where old and young, eastsider and westsider, black and white meet. Bring your wagon or grocery bag to the historic **Eastern Market** (2934 Russell St., 313/833-9300, www.detroiteasternmarket.com), between Mack and Gratiot Avenues, on a Saturday morning to participate in a Detroit tradition and take in the colorful cornucopia of smells, sights, street musicians, mimes, and a few open bars. In a city that has known great cycles of boom and bust, the Eastern Market is as perennial as the fruit and flowers it sells.

Built on the site of an early hay and wood market, this bustling six-block area northeast of downtown has lured Detroiters since 1891. Shoppers come to buy meat, cheese, produce, fruit, and flowers from large, open-air stalls and wholesale-retail specialty shops. Many wholesalers are the descendants of the Belgian, German, and Polish farmers who frequented the market generations ago, or the Italian and Lebanese merchants who began catering to the booming city in the 1920s.

Saturdays are busiest, when the farmers market runs 6am-4pm and thousands of shoppers pour into the area among goods that range from fresh chitterlings to cilantro. Highlights include the flower stalls (the market is the largest bedding center in the world) and the aromas at **Germack's,** the oldest pistachio importer in the United States.

The market also operates on a more limited scale from 9am-3pm on Tuesday, June-October. Many of the merchants are full-time farmers and can only come into the city on weekends. During the same months, you'll find the Sunday Street Market (10am-4pm Sun.), featuring vendors selling clothing, jewelry, and gift items.

Henry the Hatter (2472 Riopelle, 313/962-0970, www.henrythehatterdetroit.com, 9:30am-6pm Mon.-Sat. year-round, 11am-4pm Sun. June-Sept.) has been a fixture in Detroit since 1893, despite its recent relocation to the Eastern Market area. Here you'll find every conceivable style of dress and casual hats for men, for any season, plus

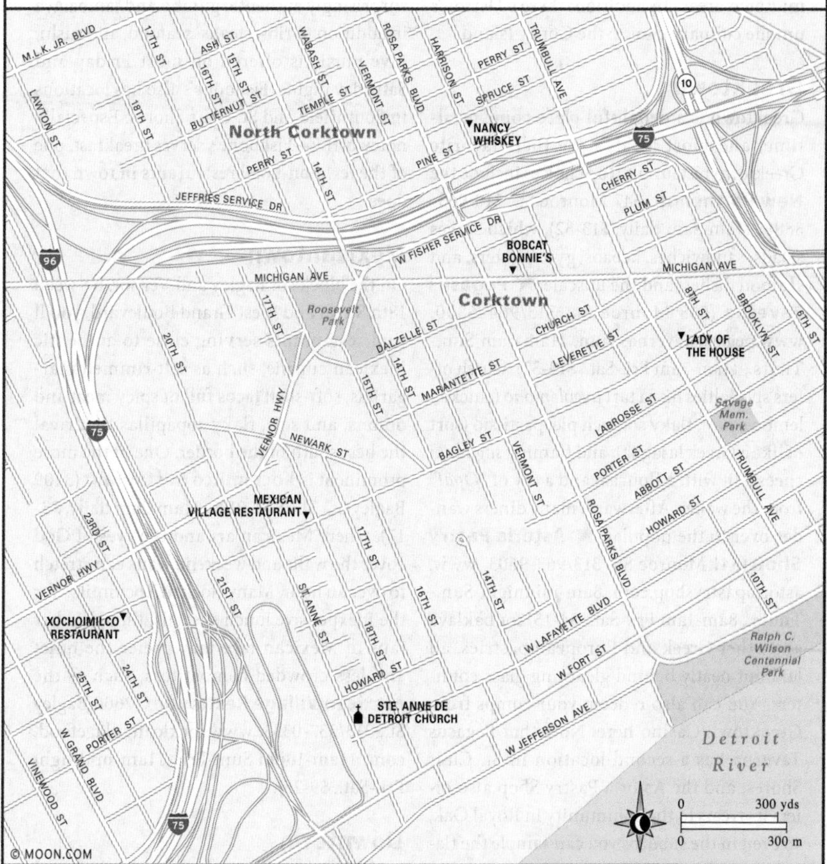

accessories like walking sticks and hat storage boxes.

Corktown

If you're looking for something with more of a bohemian influence, head to **Mama Coo's Boutique** (1701 Trumbull, 313/404-2543, www.mamacoosboutique.com, noon-6pm Mon.-Sat., noon-5pm Sun.). The unique vintage and resale shop is a noteworthy destination for handmade jewelry and home furnishings.

Another interesting Corktown emporium is the **Eldorado General Store** (1700 Michigan Ave., 313/784-9220, www.eldoradogeneralstore.com, noon-6pm Sun.-Fri., 11am-7pm Sat.). Here you'll find vintage clothing for men and women, handcrafted accessories, and household items. Everything is presented in a warm, intimate setting.

TOP EXPERIENCE

FOOD

Detroit's cosmopolitan nature is reflected in its cuisine. The city offers a variety of dining options geared to every level of price and formality. Bistros, cafes, and fine dining venues are plentiful throughout the city, with the highest concentration in the downtown and midtown areas. In addition, there's Detroit's unique culinary choice: the Coney Island.

Greektown

Greektown is a delightful place come mealtime, and most locals have their favorite Greektown restaurant. Top choices include the **New Parthenon** (547 Monroe St., 313/963-8888, 11am-3am daily, $13-32), which serves salads, sandwiches, kebabs, gyro platters, and seafood dishes, and the upscale ★ **Pegasus Taverna** (558 Monroe St., 313/964-6800, www.pegasustavernas.com, 11am-1am Sun.-Thurs., 11am-3am Fri.-Sat., $13-32), which offers specialties like a tart *avgolemono* (chicken lemon soup), flaky spinach pie, pastitsio (sort of like a Greek lasagna), and flaming *saganaki* cheese, lit with a flourish and a cry of "*Opa!*" from the waiter. Afterward, many diners wander over to the popular ★ **Astoria Pastry Shop** (541 Monroe St., 313/963-9603, www.astoriapastryshop.com, 8am-midnight Sun.-Thurs., 8am-1am Fri.-Sat., $4-15) for baklava and other Greek and European pastries, all laid out neatly behind gleaming glass counters. You can also redeem your comps from Greektown Casino here. Note that Pegasus Taverna has a second location in St. Clair Shores, and the Astoria Pastry Shop also offers its treats to the community in Royal Oak, so even in the suburbs you can sample the flavors of Greektown.

Of course, not everything worth seeing (and eating) in Greektown is Greek. **PizzaPapalis Taverna** (553 Monroe St., 313/961-8020, www.pizzapapalis.com, 11am-midnight Sun.-Thurs., 11am-1am Fri.-Sat. $10-36) is perhaps the only place in Detroit where you can get Chicago-style pizza. Only the name is Greek: Very deep-dish pies are the specialty. In addition, calzones, strombolis, and flatbread sandwiches round out the menu. Meanwhile, ★ **Fishbone's** (400 Monroe St., 313/965-4600, www.fishbonesusa.com, 6:30am-midnight Sun.-Thurs., 6:30am-1am Fri.-Sat., $9-65) is a New Orleans-inspired eatery that opened in the mid-1980s and has been hugely popular ever since. It serves up surprisingly authentic gumbo and jambalaya in addition to ribs, steaks, seafood, and sushi. Live music is offered on most Friday and Saturday nights. Fishbone's also has locations in Southfield and St. Clair Shores. Especially noteworthy—Fishbone's serves breakfast, one of the few non-hotel restaurants in town that does.

Mexicantown

On the blocks of Bagley and Vernor, between 18th Street and West Grand Boulevard, you'll find restaurants serving close to authentic Mexican cuisine, such as salt-rimmed margaritas, soft-shell tacos full of spicy meat and onions, and soft, flaky sopapillas that rival the best south of the border. One of the more prominent is **Xochimilco Restaurant** (3409 Bagley St., 313/843-0179, 11am-2am daily, $8-17), where Mexican art and the eyes of God cover the walls and weekend waits can stretch to over an hour. Many flock to Xochimilco for the inexpensive lunch specials, though other fans of Mexican fare may prefer the quiet and less crowded competitors, such as the **Mexican Village Restaurant** (2600 Bagley St., 313/237-0333, www.mexicanvillagefood.com, 11am-10pm Sun.-Fri., 11am-midnight Fri.-Sat., $9-25).

Downtown

In the heart of downtown is the **Townhouse** (500 Woodward Ave. at Congress St., 313/723-1000, www.eatattownhouse.com, 10am-midnight Sun.-Thurs., 10am-2am Sat., $20-35), a newer addition to downtown's restaurant scene. Patterned after the original location in suburban Birmingham, the Townhouse is a great place for a hearty but reasonably priced brunch, lunch, or dinner featuring good American comfort food. A variety of burgers, chicken, and fish dishes are featured, either portioned for the individual or as a sharable dish. The real treat here is the dramatic view. The restaurant was built as a glass structure that resembles a greenhouse

Coney Cuisine

Coney Island dogs, Detroit style

Philly has the cheesesteak and Chicago its deep-dish pie, but Detroit has the Coney Island. No, not the amusement park—the hot dog. Detroiters take their Coneys very seriously, downing thousands of these hot dogs annually. Curiously, the name Coney Island serves simultaneously as both a destination and a dish.

Family-owned and operated since 1917, **American Coney Island** (114 W. Lafayette Blvd., 313/961-7758, www.americanconeyisland.com, open 24 hours daily) is the place where a wiener with skin, beanless chili, onions, and mustard was first called "one with everything." Although this beloved 24-hour eatery now also serves soups, salads, desserts, and spinach pie, it's the dogs that lure a clientele ranging from cops on the beat to suburbanites grabbing a bite after the theater or before a game. American Coney Island has garnered the respect of a long list of celebrities, including Michigan governors, famous musicians and athletes, and well-known actors like Tim Allen and Jeff Daniels. In recent years, a second location has opened in Las Vegas at the D Hotel.

Right next door is **Lafayette Coney Island** (118 W. Lafayette Blvd., 313/964-8198, 8:30am-3am Mon.-Thurs., 8:30am-4am Fri.-Sat., 9:30am-3am Sun.), originally started by the brother of the founder of American Coney Island. The founder's heirs, however, eventually sold the business.

Today, Coney Island restaurants are ubiquitous throughout southeast Michigan. In some suburbs you can find one at almost every major intersection. Almost every Coney Island in Michigan today can trace its history to someone who once worked at one of the two original locations at the intersection of Lafayette Boulevard, Griswold Street, and Michigan Avenue.

grafted onto the corner of the Ally Detroit Center. The result is a wide, uninterrupted view of the skyscrapers of lower downtown. The roof is partially retractable, allowing it to be opened during warm weather. There is also outdoor seating, providing an excellent opportunity for people-watching.

Just down Congress Street in the Financial District is the **London Chop House** (155 W. Congress, 313/962-0277, www.thelondonchophouse.com, lunch 11am-3pm Mon.-Fri., dinner 5pm-10pm Mon.-Thurs., 5pm-11pm Fri.-Sat., $55-160). The Chop represents the pinnacle of old Detroit money and power. Long a destination for the elite of the auto industry, the restaurant enjoyed a heyday from the 1940s through the mid-1980s. Sagging fortunes forced it to close in 1991, but in 2012 it reopened to rave reviews and has been going strong ever since. The menu explains the upper-tier pricing: 35-day dry-aged rib-eye steaks, seared Faroe Island salmon, whole two-pound lobster, and the like.

Nothing speaks of big-city elegance more than a fine restaurant atop a high-rise offering a panoramic view. Beginning in the 1970s, Detroit's GM Renaissance Center has offered such an establishment atop its central hotel tower, at an altitude of 72 stories. In 2017 the restaurant closed, but as of this writing, owner General Motors promises that a new, exciting eatery will be opening in early 2020.

Detroit's impressive Theater District is home to more than just gorgeously restored entertainment venues; it also boasts an excellent array of restaurants, which, depending on the hours, might be ideal for a postgame or preshow meal. Behind the Comerica Park scoreboard, the **Elwood Bar & Grill** (300 Adams Ave., 313/962-2337, www.elwoodgrill.com, 11am-8pm Mon.-Sat., $11-14) might just be Detroit's most recognizable art deco diner. Built in 1936 by local architect Charles Noble, relocated in 1997 (its name is an allusion to its former location—Elizabeth and Woodward), and subsequently renovated, the Elwood is a popular spot for sports fans, with menu items that range from chicken wings and Coney-style hot dogs to patty melts and club sandwiches. Another equally casual option is the ★ **Hockeytown Cafe** (2301 Woodward Ave., 313/471-3454, www.hockeytowncafe.com, 11am-midnight Tues.-Sat., hours vary Sun. and Mon. depending on scheduled games and events, $12-23). Though not far from the Fox Theatre, this bustling sports bar is more popular with sports fans headed to or from Little Caesars Arena, Comerica Park, or Ford Field. Diners here can expect frequent drink specials; tasty treats like chicken wings, salads, pizza, ribs, and burgers; and lots of high-definition TVs broadcasting a variety of sporting events. There are also gluten-free options on the menu, from nachos to breadless sandwiches.

Corktown

No visit to Detroit is complete without a stop in Corktown, the city's oldest extant neighborhood, just west of downtown. During the last several years Corktown has redefined itself, and now ranks as one of the coolest urban enclaves in America. Dining options include **Lady of the House** (1426 Bagley Ave., 313/818-0218, www.ladyofthehousedetroit.com, 5pm-midnight Tues.-Sun., brunch 10am-2pm Sat.-Sun., moderate to expensive). The creation of local chef Kate Williams, the restaurant bills itself as "Modern American" with an emphasis on "freshness and creativity." The locally sourced menu varies by season, but examples of dishes include carrot steak, king prawns, and mushroom fettucine.

Another choice is **Bobcat Bonnie's** (1800 Michigan Ave., www.bobcatbonnies.com 313/962-1383, 11am-10pm Mon.-Wed., 11am-11pm Thurs., 11am-midnight Fri., 10am-midnight Sat., 10am-9pm Sun, $11-14). This is a friendly, down-to-earth eatery in a historic setting. Here you'll find comfort food like mac and cheese, barbecue bacon meat loaf, and salmon pasta. There's also a terrific brunch on the weekends.

Eastern Market

After shopping in the Eastern Market, head over to the ★ **Amore da Roma** (3401 Riopelle St., 313/831-5940, www.romacafe.com, 11am-10pm Mon.-Thurs., 11am-11pm Fri.-Sat., 11am-8pm Sun., $18-34). Established in 1890 as Roma Café, this venerable Detroit institution was renovated and reopened by a new owner in 2017. While classic dishes such as gnocchi, lasagna, and eggplant parmigiana are mainstays, you'll also find treats like breaded frog legs, filet mignon, and broiled whitefish. Don't miss their Monday-night buffet (5pm-9pm), an all-you-can-eat spread of veal parmigiana, various pastas with meat sauce, chicken, and Italian sausage, with fresh fruit and cannoli for dessert.

Midtown

If you get hungry while exploring the

Cultural Center, stop by ★ **Union Street** (4145 Woodward Ave., 313/831-3965, www.unionstreetdetroit.com, 11:30am-10pm Tues.-Thurs., 11:30am-midnight Fri.-Sat., 11am-8pm Sun., $19-33), an eclectic eatery offering dishes like lobster carbonara, Scooby Doo pasta, and a 14 oz. hickory grilled New York strip. Lunchtime tends to get crowded with people from Wayne State University and the Detroit Medical Center.

A new and promising Midtown bistro is **Selden Standard** (3921 2nd Ave., at Selden St., 313/438-5055, www.seldenstandard.com, 11am-2:30pm and 4:30pm-11pm Mon.-Fri., 10am-2pm and 4:30pm-11pm Sat.-Sun., dinner entrées $12-28). It prides itself on serving "delicious, rustic, fun food" with seasonal, locally sourced ingredients, so the menu changes often. Dishes include lamb ragù, grilled quail, and Thai mussels. The portions are served according to the small plates model.

For a decidedly more upscale experience, make a reservation at ★ **The Whitney** (4421 Woodward Ave., 313/832-5700, www.thewhitney.com, dinner 4:30pm-9pm Mon.-Thurs.,4:30pm-10pm Fri.-Sat., 4pm-9pm Sun., brunch 10am-1:30pm Sat.-Sun., high tea 2pm daily by 48-hour advanced reservation only, entrées $28-79). Arguably Detroit's grandest restaurant, The Whitney is housed in an ornate 120-year-old mansion built by 19th-century lumber baron David Whitney. The menu is decidedly upscale, featuring exquisite dishes such as beef Wellington, stuffed lobster, roasted lamb rack, and bourbon-glazed salmon. A prix fixe theater menu is also available. If you'd like to enjoy a libation, or if you still have room for dessert after a sumptuous dinner, or if you dine elsewhere and want to enjoy an extra special treat, check out the **Ghostbar** on the third floor (4:30pm-10pm Mon.-Thurs., 4:30pm-midnight Fri.-Sat., 4pm-9pm Sun.). The bar earns its name from reported sightings of the ghost of David Whitney.

The New Center district has its own dining gem: ★ **Cuisine Restaurant** (670 Lothrop Rd., 313/872-5110, www.cuisinerestaurant.com, 5pm-10pm Tues.-Thurs., 5pm-11pm Fri.-Sat., 5pm-9pm Sun, $50-80), behind the Fisher Building. Cuisine specializes in modern European dining. If you're willing to spend a fair amount, treat yourself to one of chef Paul Grosz's progression menus ($50-80 pp), which might include dishes like white and green asparagus, creamed Maine lobster with leeks and tapioca, almond-crusted soft-shell crabs, roasted Alaskan halibut, wild sturgeon with potato gnocchi, and strawberry Charlotte. The restaurant also offers vegetarian options and a superb wine list.

ACCOMMODATIONS

Detroit offers hotels, motels, and inns to suit all budgets. Although most downtown accommodations are of the business-class hotel-chain variety, you'll also find a few Victorian-style inns and casino resorts.

Under $150

A bargain in the heart of downtown, the newly renovated **Hotel Indigo Detroit** (1020 Washington Blvd., 313/887-7000, $136-160 d) offers clean, attractive accommodation within walking distance to many of downtown's most noteworthy attractions.

$150-300

The ★ **Atheneum Suite Hotel** (1000 Brush Ave., 313/962-2323 or 800/772-2323, www.atheneumsuites.com, $159-259 d) is downtown's best all-suite hotel, located in the heart of Greektown. It borrows classical motifs from the surrounding neighborhood in its 174 luxury suites, all with separate living rooms, marble baths, free wireless Internet access, and other amenities. Wheelchair-accessible suites are also available.

Close to downtown attractions, the **Hotel St. Regis** (3071 W. Grand Blvd., 313/873-3000 or 855/408-7738, www.hotelstregisdetroit.com, $129-188 d) provides 124 renovated rooms and suites, free wireless Internet access, valet parking ($20 per day), a 24-hour business center, and an on-site restaurant, La

Musique (6am-10pm Mon.-Wed., 6am-11pm Thurs.-Fri., 8am-11pm Sat., 8am-9pm Sun., $13-29).

West of Detroit's stadiums and theaters, the 144-room **Trumbull & Porter Hotel** (1331 Trumbull St., 313/496-1400, www.trumbullandporterhotel.com, $135-239 d) has recently been refurbished and boasts a new fitness center, spacious rooms, and an exquisite art collection in the common areas. The Red Dunn Kitchen (7am-10pm daily, Sunday brunch 8am-3pm, $15-36) offers breakfast, lunch and dinner daily.

If you really travel in style, consider **The Westin Book Cadillac Detroit** (1114 Washington Blvd., at Michigan Ave., 313/442-1600, www.bookcadillacwestin.com, $200-1,500 d). As you step into the luxurious lobby, consider that this grand hotel was once a candidate for the wrecking ball. Opened in 1924, the Book was the premier Detroit hotel for decades until its fortunes began to decline in the 1960s. It finally closed in 1984 and stood as an abandoned hulk for over 20 years. In the early 2000s a group of investors did a top-to-bottom restoration and it reopened in 2008. Nowhere is Detroit's revival more tangible than here. The stylishly appointed rooms each offer a flat-screen TV, a luxury bath, a stunning view of either Washington Boulevard or the Detroit River, and high-speed Internet access for a fee. The Westin Book Cadillac also offers five dining options, including Iron Chef Michael Symon's Roast, plus banquet and meeting facilities, the Spa Book Cadillac, a business center, and a large fitness and workout room.

Another solid option is the **Detroit Marriott at the Renaissance Center** (GM Renaissance Center, 400 Renaissance Dr., 313/568-8000 or 888/236-2427, www.marriott.com, $205-469 d), which provides stunning views of the Detroit River as well as easy access to the Renaissance Center's shops and restaurants, Detroit's three casinos, and the Detroit-Windsor Tunnel. Enjoy high-speed Internet access, a fitness center, a business center, and an on-site restaurant.

For traditional chain lodgings, consider the **Hilton Garden Inn Detroit Downtown** (351 Gratiot Ave., 313/967-0900, www.hiltongardeninn.com, $159-229 d), set within the Harmonie Park neighborhood only a block from Comerica Park and Ford Field. Housing 198 rooms and suites, the Hilton also offers free wireless Internet access, a business center, two on-site restaurants, a fitness center, an indoor pool, and plenty of wheelchair-accessible features. Another mid-range option is the **Holiday Inn Express Hotel & Suites Detroit Downtown** (1020 Washington Blvd., 313/887-7000 or 888/233-0353, www.ihg.com, $150-199 d), halfway between the MGM Grand Detroit and the Jack Detroit Casino-Hotel Greektown and within walking distance of Campus Martius Park. Besides affordable guest rooms, the Holiday Inn Express also features suites with fully equipped kitchens, plus a fitness center, an indoor heated pool, a 24-hour business center, valet parking ($27 per day), free high-speed Internet access, and a complimentary breakfast bar. You might also try **Courtyard Detroit Downtown** (333 E. Jefferson Ave., 313/222-7700 or 888/236-2427, www.marriott.com, $166-219 d), with 260 oversize rooms, free wireless Internet access, an extensive health club, an enormous indoor pool, and an outdoor aboveground tennis court and running track that offers terrific views of the city's surrounding vintage architecture.

The **Crown Plaza Detroit Downtown Convention Center** (2 Washington Blvd., 313/965-4457, www.ihg.com, $139-315), despite its all-business name, is equally friendly to both leisure and business travelers. Reopened in 2012 after an extensive renovation, this classic of midcentury architecture offers close proximity to downtown attractions (most notably Cobo Exhibition Center, just across Washington Blvd.) and some of the best hotel dining anywhere. The building is constructed in an innovative faceted style, which means every room enjoys a view of the Detroit River. You may hear locals refer to the hotel as the Pontchartrain—the establishment's original name. A shortened version of the legacy name lives on in the title of the restaurant on the 25th floor, the Top of the Pontch.

A newcomer on the Detroit lodging scene is the **Aloft Hotel** (1 Park Ave., 313/237-1700, www.aloftdetroit.com, $161-225), an elegant boutique hotel in the newly restored David Whitney Building. Here the familiar elegance of the building's neo-Renaissance architecture blends seamlessly with contemporary appointments, evident in the soaring lobby atrium, the WXYZ Bar (named after one of Detroit's premier TV stations), and the tastefully decorated rooms. Self-serve 24/7 dining is available at Re-fuel, the in-house snack bar. At this writing, plans are underway for a fine dining restaurant on the main floor facing Woodward.

Another recent arrival is the **DoubleTree Suites** (525 W. Lafayette Blvd., 313/963-5600, http://doubletree3.hilton.com, $96-429). The Double Tree represents another Detroit success story, as it is the rebirth of the old Pick Ft. Shelby Hotel (the original moniker is still visible). Its 2008 reopening was the culmination of a top-to-bottom renovation of this tarnished Detroit gem, originally built in 1917. The all-suite facility has a prime downtown location close to the theater district and fine dining spots. You'll also find free Wi-Fi access, a fitness center, and valet parking ($28 per day). Casual dining is available at the Motor City Kitchen restaurant.

Just east of greater downtown is the **Roberts RiverWalk Hotel** (1000 River Place Dr., 313/259-9500, www.detroitriverwalkhotel.com, $149-450), an intimate boutique inn. Given its classic architecture (it was once the headquarters of a pharmaceutical firm) and charming location right at the water's edge, staying at the Roberts RiverWalk almost makes you feel like you're at an out-of-the-way country estate. Aimed largely at the business traveler, the hotel offers free Internet access, executive workspace, room service, and a fitness center. There's also an on-site bar and restaurant. While you're there, take time to enjoy the breathtaking view of the Detroit River and Canada.

There are a number of other hotels either proposed or under construction downtown. Obtain the latest information by visiting the Detroit Metro Convention & Visitors Bureau (www.visitdetroit.com).

Casino Resorts

For even more amenities, consider staying at one of Detroit's three downtown casino resorts. The shimmering ★ **MGM Grand Detroit** (1777 3rd St., 888/646-3387 or 877/888-2121, www.mgmgranddetroit.com, $249-499 d) houses an enormous gaming space, a full-service spa, über-luxurious hotel rooms, live entertainment, four unique bars, a lively nightclub, and several dining options, including the Wolfgang Puck Pizzeria and Cucina as well as Wolfgang Puck Steak. The **MotorCity Casino Hotel** (2901 Grand River Ave., 866/752-9622, www.motorcitycasino.com, $205-899 d) also promises more than Las Vegas-style games, including a 24-hour fitness center, a luxurious spa, live concerts, varied dining options, and 400 stylish state-of-the-art rooms and suites. Even Greektown has its own resort, the **Greektown Casino-Hotel** (1200 St. Antoine St., 313/223-2999 or 877/424-5554, www.greektowncasino.com, $159-109 d), which offers several restaurants, a video poker lounge, a wide range of gaming tables and slot machines, and amenities like ergonomic desks, plush bedding, and free parking. As a bonus, the building's distinctive blue color will make it easy for a lost pedestrian to identify.

INFORMATION AND SERVICES

Information

For information about Detroit, consult the **Detroit Metro Convention & Visitors Bureau** (211 W. Fort St., Ste. 1000, 313/202-1800 or 800/338-7648, www.visitdetroit.com, 9am-5pm Mon.-Fri.). The two daily newspapers, the ***Detroit News*** (www.detnews.com) and the ***Detroit Free Press*** (www.freep.

com), are supplemented by a wide variety of suburban dailies and weeklies, as well as the **Detroit Metro Times** (www.metrotimes.com). The *Metro Times* is the city's first—and most successful—alternative paper, with thoughtful reporting on a variety of civic and social issues, extensive entertainment listings, and consciousness-raising (if not eyebrow-raising) classifieds. It's distributed freely at bins throughout the city and suburbs. Another good read is **Hour Detroit** (www.hourdetroit.com), a tabloid-size full-color glossy magazine that's a tribute to quality journalism and photography, offering thought-provoking pieces on topics of local interest.

Local radio and television stations are also excellent sources for regional information, including Detroit's ABC affiliate WXYZ-TV (www.wxyz.com), NBC affiliate WDIV-TV (www.wdiv.com), and CBS affiliate WWJ-TV (www.detroit.cbslocal.com).

Services

As a major urban center, Detroit has no shortage of services, including banks, mailing centers, and grocery stores. In nonemergency situations, contact the **Detroit Police Department** (1301 3rd St., 313/596-2200 or 313/596-1300, www.detroitmi.gov); you can also dial 311 within city limits. For medical assistance, you'll find several hospitals in the metropolitan area; one option is the **Detroit Medical Center** (DMC, 888/362-2500, www.dmc.org), which has a number of facilities.

GETTING THERE AND AROUND

Most international travelers arrive by air (except those coming from Ontario, Canada), while U.S. visitors also come by train, bus, or car.

Getting There

AIR

The **Detroit Metropolitan-Wayne County Airport** (DTW, I-94 and Merriman Rd., 734/247-7678, www.metroairport.com), also known as the Detroit Metro Airport, spreads over some 7,000 acres, 21 miles southwest of the city in Romulus, just off I-94 and Merriman Road. Delta, United, and American, among a dozen other airlines, including four foreign carriers, offer nonstop flights from 160 cities.

Limo service ($31-98) from the airport to downtown hotels and area suburbs is available by reservation from **Detroit Metro Airport Taxi** (248/214-6823, www.metrotaxidetroit.com), **Metro Airport Taxi** (800/745-5191, www.metro-airport-taxi.com), **Metro Airport Limo** (800/906-9030 or 800/591-8370, www.airportmetrolimo.com), or **Metroride** (248/666-0222 or 800/320-1683, www.detroitmetroairport.com).

Detroit Metro also has many car rental services on-site and others accessible via shuttle. For details, consult **Alamo** (800/327-9633, www.alamo.com), **Avis** (800/331-1212, www.avis.com), **Budget** (800/527-0700, www.budget.com), **Dollar** (800/421-6878, www.dollar.com), **Enterprise** (800/325-8007, www.enterprise.com), **Hertz** (800/654-3131, www.hertz.com), **National** (800/227-7368, www.nationalcar.com), or **Thrifty** (800/367-2277, www.thrifty.com).

TRAIN

Via the Michigan Services route from Chicago, the *Wolverine* line of **Amtrak** (800/872-7245, www.amtrak.com) offers daily service to five Detroit-area stops: Dearborn (16121 Michigan Ave.), Detroit (11 W. Baltimore Ave.), Royal Oak, Birmingham, and Pontiac.

BUS

Greyhound (800/231-2222, www.greyhound.com) serves downtown Detroit (1001 Howard St., 313/961-8011, 6am-1:30am daily). Be careful at this station; it's not in the safest part of town, and daytime arrivals and departures are advised.

1: QLINE streetcar **2:** light tunnel at the Detroit Metropolitan Airport

1

2

CAR

The interstate highways make it easy to navigate Detroit. From Flint, take I-75 to downtown Detroit. Without traffic, the 69-mile trip usually takes about an hour. From Toledo, head north on I-75 for 61 miles; a one-hour trip without traffic. From Lansing, take I-96, I-696, and M-10 to downtown Detroit, a 90-mile trip that requires 80-90 minutes. I-94 runs to Detroit from Ann Arbor and points west. It's roughly 45 miles and 45 minutes from Ann Arbor to Detroit. From Port Huron, take I-94 west to Detroit for 63 miles. From Chicago, use I-94, a 283-mile trip that takes four hours.

Getting Around

While the car is still king for mobility in the greater Detroit area, newer modes of transit are gradually becoming available. The best method(s) depends upon your point of origin and your destination. Generally, the closer to Detroit's urban core, the more varied the options.

CAR

Detroit is laced with freeways. The Chrysler Freeway (I-75) is the major north-south thoroughfare on the east side, with the John Lodge Freeway (M-10) serving as its west-side counterpart. The Jeffries Freeway (I-96), Reuther Freeway (I-696), and Edsel Ford Freeway (I-94) run east-west. If you're traveling any of these routes during rush hours (generally 6am-10am and 3pm-7pm weekdays), allow plenty of extra time. It's wise to seek out alternate routes such as I-275, which splits off from I-696, and to pick up a map of the area.

Various rental car agencies operate at Detroit Metro Airport, and **Checker Cab** (313/963-5005, www.checkercab-det.com, $2.50 pickup, $1.60 per mile), for instance, has been driving passengers around the greater Detroit area since 1921. From the airport to downtown hotels, it typically costs about $40 per trip, while it's roughly $10 from downtown Detroit to the New Center district.

Seat belts are required by law; all drivers, front-seat passengers, and children over age 7 must wear seat belts while in a moving vehicle. Law enforcement often tickets motorists for not being buckled up.

MASS TRANSIT

Detroit has not traditionally emphasized mass transit. The **Detroit Department of Transportation** (DDOT, 313/933-1300 or 888/336-8287, www.detroitmi.gov/ddot) operates buses (one-way $1.50 adults, $0.75 students, $0.50 seniors, $0.10 transfers) from 6am until 1am along most of the city's major arteries, and in a few inner suburban communities; 14 of the most popular routes operate 24 hours daily. DDOT buses and bus stops are recognizable by their trademark green and yellow.

Streetcars made a return to Detroit in 2018 with the completion of the **QLINE** (www.qlinedetroit.com, 6am-midnight Mon.-Thurs., 8am-2am Sat., 8am-11pm Sun.), a grade-level line that runs along Woodward Avenue (mostly at curbside) from Congress Street to Grand Boulevard, a distance of approximately 3.3 miles. Since its rollout the system has improved service and is now adhering to its schedule of fifteen-minute intervals. Fare is $1.50 for unlimited rides within a three-hour window or $3 for an entire day.

Detroit's suburbs are served by the **Suburban Mobility Authority for Regional Transportation** (SMART, www.smartbus.org) bus service ($2.50, transfers $0.50) along most major arteries in Wayne, Oakland, and Macomb Counties. Look for the bus stops identified with the stylized "Smart Ride" logo in black and red. Some SMART routes extend into Detroit, but SMART buses don't pick up passengers on inbound routes.

Downtown, you can take advantage of the **Detroit People Mover** (313/224-2160 or 800/541-7245, www.thepeoplemover.com, 6:30am-midnight Mon.-Thurs., 6:30am-2am Fri., 9am-2am Sat., noon-midnight Sun.), which never quite lived up to expectations, although it does offer a convenient way to get around downtown. For $0.75, you'll get a 15-minute ride along a three-mile track that passes the Civic Center, Greektown, and the Theater and Financial Districts and offers easy access to major attractions, such as the GM Renaissance Center and the Joe Louis Arena in the heart of the business district. Check out the 13 People Mover stations tastefully decorated with works by local artists.

Windsor, Ontario

A city of 211,000, Windsor sits along the southern banks of the Detroit River, just across from the Motor City. Crossing the river, the first-time visitor will immediately notice the cultural differences from the United States. Windsor has a very low crime rate, a roster of excellent restaurants, and a friendly and civic-minded populace happy to welcome visitors. Detroiters have long shuttled back and forth to enjoy Windsor's restaurants, casinos, European-style shops, terrific riverfront views, and, yes, strip clubs.

SIGHTS

The **Canadian Transportation Museum** (6155 Arner Town Line, County Rd. 23, Kingsville, 519/776-6909, www.ctmhv.com, 9am-4pm Tues.-Sun. May-Oct., 9am-4pm Wed.-Fri. Nov.-Apr., C$6 adults, C$2 ages 6-12, under age 6 free), which charts the history of transportation in Canada, both pre- and post-automobile. Here you'll find horse- and oxen-drawn wagons, Ford Model Ts, and several examples from the golden age of the sports car.

The **Park House Museum** (King's Navy Yard Park, 214 Dalhousie St., Amherstburg, 519/736-2511, www.parkhousemuseum.com, 11am-4pm daily June-Aug., 11am-4pm Mon.-Fri. Sept.-May, C$4 adults, C$3 seniors, $2.50 children 5-16, under age 5 free) has the unique distinction of being the oldest house in Windsor and the oldest house from Detroit. The house was built near the mouth of the Rouge River in Detroit in the 1790s, but when the city was turned over to the Americans with the signing of the Jay Treaty, Alexander Mackintosh, a loyalist to the crown, moved the house to Amherstburg in 1796.

SHOPPING

Wander Ouellette Avenue, the main drag, and the narrow streets surrounding it. Shops are full of imported clothing and books, both new and used, many from British publishers, and the T-shirt stands are ubiquitous. One standout is **Shanfields-Meyers** (188 Ouellette Ave., 519/253-6098, www.shanfields.com, 11am-4:30pm Mon.-Fri.), a family-owned business that opened in 1946 and now houses a sparkling array of crystal, including a whole room devoted to Waterford, and a wide selection of discounted china and gifts.

FOOD

While the shopping is good in Windsor, it doesn't compare to the eating. Top restaurants include **The Cook's Shop Restaurant** (683 Ouellette Ave., 519/254-3377, http://cooksshoprestaurant.wordpress.com, 5pm-8pm Tues.-Thurs. and Sun., 5pm-9:30pm Fri.-Sat., C$18-33), a tiny basement eatery where everything is homemade, including the melt-in-your-mouth gnocchi, tortellini, and other pastas prepared table-side on a rolling cart. The menu also features a wide assortment of dishes popular with both Canadians and Americans, including spring chicken *diable* and Angus beef scaloppine. Restaurants in Detroit generally do not have such an eclectic menu.

Another option, **The Mini** (475 W. University Ave., 519/254-2221, www.themini.doestakeout.com, 11:30am-10pm Tues.-Fri., 5pm-10pm Sat., 4pm-8pm Sun.-Mon. and holidays, C$7-14) now operates as only a takeout establishment. But the menu's hard-to-find Vietnamese selections make the trip from Detroit worthwhile. Specialties like grilled chicken over papaya or cabbage salad and seafood in congee (rice soup) will tempt the more adventurous diner.

★ **Mezzo Ristorante & Lounge** (804 Erie St. E, 519/252-4055, www.mezzo.ca, 11:30am-9pm Mon.-Wed., 11:30am-10pm Thurs.-Fri., 11:30am-11pm Sat., 4pm-9pm Sun., C$24-52), located in Windsor's Little Italy, is a modern yet intimate bistro that does Italian cuisine differently than its Detroit counterparts. Here you'll find classic recipes prepared more elaborately, such as *provimi* veal—pan-seared veal scaloppine in a wild mushroom, white truffle cream sauce.

Fourteen Restaurant and Sky Lounge (100 Ouellette Ave., 14th fl., 226/526-7214, www.fourteenrestaurantandskylounge.com, 4pm-10pm Tues.-Thurs., 4pm-11pm Fri.-Sat., 4pm-9pm Sun., C$19-45). Classic Canadian/American food with a bit of a French twist is the highlight of the menu. Think Lake Erie perch, braised beef short ribs, and surf and turf poutine. Add in the excitement of dining fourteen floors above street level with a stunning view of the Detroit skyline, something you can't do from the other side!

ACCOMMODATIONS

For a bit of luxury, consider staying at **Caesars Windsor** (377 E. Riverside Dr., 800/991-7777, www.caesars.com, C$199-269 d), the city's premier gambling resort, boasting 758 luxurious rooms and suites in two towers that overlook the Detroit River. Amenities include full concierge service and complimentary valet parking as well as various table games and slot machines, a world-class poker room, live concerts and comedy shows, several stylish bars, upscale shops, a soothing spa, an indoor pool, a fully equipped gym with incredible views, and several restaurants, including Neros, a superb steakhouse, and the Artist Cafe.

INFORMATION

For more information about Windsor, consult **Tourism Windsor, Essex, Pelee Island** (333 W. Riverside Dr., Ste. 103, Windsor, 519/255-6530 or 800/265-3633, www.tourismwindsoressex.com, 8:30am-4:30pm Mon.-Fri.).

GETTING THERE AND AROUND

Windsor has its own airport, the **Windsor International Airport** (YQG, 3200 CR-42, 519/969-2430, www.yqg.ca), but most visitors from Michigan take day trips from Detroit by car. Two routes connect Detroit and Windsor: the **Ambassador Bridge** (www.ambassadorbridge.com, one-way C$6.25/US$5 passenger vehicles and motorcycles) and the **Detroit-Windsor Tunnel** (www.dwtunnel.com, passenger vehicles Windsor to Detroit C$4.75-5/US$4.50-4.75, Detroit to Windsor C$6.25/US$5). The bridge offers quicker access to Highway 401 to Toronto, but the tunnel is a more direct route to downtown Windsor.

The tunnel can be accessed from the corner of Jefferson Avenue and Randolph Street, immediately west of the GM Renaissance Center. Tolls are paid on whichever side you're exiting. Transit to the Canadian side takes approximately five minutes, although delays can develop for various reasons, such as traffic accidents or stricter customs enforcement. After clearing customs, you're right in downtown Windsor.

The bridge can be accessed by heading south from downtown along Fort Street (M-3). Turn right at W. Grand Boulevard, go one block before coming to the Fisher Freeway (I-75) service drive, make another right turn, and follow the road to the bridge on-ramps. Tolls are paid on the American side for both directions of traffic. Transit to the Canadian side takes approximately 10 minutes. After clearing customs, you can get to downtown Windsor via Wyandotte Street West, which should take an additional 10 minutes.

You can always rent a vehicle or hire a taxi or limo at the Detroit Metro Airport. **Checker Cab** (313/963-7000, www.checkerdetroit.com, US$2.50 pickup, US$2.00 per mile), for instance, charges about US$46 for a one-way trip from the airport to Windsor. **Detroit Metro Airport Taxi** (248/214-6823, www.metrotaxidetroit.com) and **Metro Airport Taxi** (800/745-5191, www.metro-airport-taxi.com) are also good options.

Since you're traveling across an international border, you'll need to have your **passport**. An alternative for U.S. citizens traveling in either direction is an Enhanced Driver's License (an acceptable form of identification under the REAL ID Act) issued by Michigan, Connecticut, Minnesota, New Jersey, New York, South Dakota, Vermont, and Washington. They also work for land and sea crossings to Canada, Mexico, and the Caribbean.

The Suburbs

The invention that built the Motor City also spawned its seemingly limitless swaths of suburbs. Bigger and better cars and an expanding network of freeways took Detroiters farther and farther from the urban core. The result was a chain of cookie-cutter suburbs lacking in personality—now bedroom communities that bear little interest for the visitor. Some exceptions include Hamtramck, a historically Polish and now multicultural neighborhood north of downtown Detroit; Dearborn, where Henry Ford was born and established Greenfield Village and his eponymous museum, now one of the state's largest attractions; Royal Oak, home to the nationally recognized Detroit Zoo; Birmingham, an enclave of chic boutiques and fine art galleries; and Grosse Pointe, where Lake Shore Drive boasts some of the area's finest homes—and offers one of best scenic drives anywhere.

★ HAMTRAMCK

"A Touch of Europe in America," reads the sign at **Hamtramck** (www.hamtramck.com), a small city surrounded by Detroit that emerged as a Polish community after World War I. Given that its residents have stubbornly withstood annexation, this curious community has survived as a city within a city.

Named for John Francis Hamtramck, a French Canadian colonel who served during the post-Revolutionary Indian Wars, the village was at first mostly German farms in 1901. In 1910 the enterprising Dodge brothers began work on their mammoth new factory Dodge Main. Its promise of jobs swelled the population from 3,589 to 45,615 over the next decade—the largest increase anywhere in the United States. Many were Polish immigrants, earning Hamtramck the nickname "Little Poland." The plant closed in 1981, with the site becoming part of the much larger GM Detroit-Hamtramck Assembly Plant. By 2000, the Polish community represented just 11 percent of the population, the balance comprising people with Arab, African American, Bangladeshi, and other Eastern European heritage. Nevertheless, the Polish legacy is still evidenced by many of the street names and several Polish-owned shops and restaurants.

Sights and Shopping

Drive along Joseph Campau Street, Hamtramck's main drag, and you'll find Polish bakeries, Polish bookstores, Polish clubs, and shops selling Polish sausage. There's even a tribute at the corner of Belmont and Joseph Campau Streets to the first Polish pope, John Paul II, who visited Hamtramck in 1987. Stop at the **Polish Art Center** (9539 Joseph Campau St., 313/874-2242 or 888/619-9771, www.polartcenter.com, 9:30am-6pm Mon.-Sat., 11am-3pm Sun.) for unusual goods such as folk art rugs, leaded glass, Ukrainian-decorated eggs, and *szopkas,* intricate Nativity scenes made of tinfoil. Afterward, stop in the **Saint Florian Roman Catholic Church** (2626 Poland St., 313/871-2778, www.stflorianparish.org), one of the remaining Polish parishes in the area. Founded in 1907 and completed in 1926, this stately sanctuary now serves hundreds of faithful parishioners, including Polish, Albanian, and Asian residents.

Detroiters have long known about the old-world charms of Hamtramck. The glass storefronts along Joseph Campau Street have a vintage 1930s feel, full of Polish imports, discount clothing, and baked goods and meats. Hamtramck's retro appearance and low rents have attracted artists such as potter and jeweler Marcia Hovland and filmmakers Chuck Cirgenski and Janine Menlove. Hollywood-backed *Polish Wedding* (1998), a movie starring Claire Danes, Lena Olin, and Gabriel Byrne, was filmed here. With the new wave of artists and filmmakers have come corner coffeehouses, late-night alternative music cafés, and colorful studios and shops that add a new hipness to the otherwise baroque surroundings.

Food

Many Polish suburbanites return to Hamtramck with their families on weekends to sip *czarnina* (duck's blood soup), linger over *nalesniki* (crepes), and dine on pierogi (filled dumplings) before heading home with loaves of fresh pumpernickel or rye and a few Polish pastries, such as *paczki* (plump jelly doughnuts), to enjoy later. Highlights of Polish Hamtramck include the **New Palace Bakery** (9833 Joseph Campau St., 313/875-1334, www.newpalacebakery.com, 6am-6pm Mon.-Sat.), the most popular of the many bakeries, and the **Polonia Restaurant** (2934 Yemans St., 313/873-8432, www.polonia-restaurant.net, 11am-8pm Mon.-Thurs., 11am-9pm Fri.-Sat., noon-7pm Sun., $10-13), housed in a former 1930s food co-op.

Getting There

Well known locally, Hamtramck can be hard to find. From downtown Detroit, follow I-375 north to I-75 (the Chrysler Freeway), take the Holbrook Street exit, turn right onto Holbrook, and then turn left onto Joseph Campau Street. In light traffic, this six-mile trip from downtown takes about 15 minutes.

DEARBORN

Home to the world headquarters of Ford Motor Company and the largest population of Arabic-speaking people in the United States, Dearborn is known as "the town that Ford built." There was little here but farmland when Henry Ford was born in a small white farmhouse at the corner of Ford Road and Greenfield Avenue. In 1944 the house was moved to Greenfield Village, where it is currently on display.

Sights

ARAB AMERICAN NATIONAL MUSEUM

While in Dearborn, make time for at least a taste of its Arab culture. Most of Dearborn's Arab residents live in the neighborhoods that line Ford Road, Warren Avenue, and Michigan Avenue east of the Southfield Freeway (M-39), and in Dearborn's south end, straddling the intersection of Dix Road and Vernor Highway. The mostly working-class population is more than 90 percent Arab, primarily from Yemen. You'll frequently see signs in both English and Arabic, headscarves on women, and men with traditional skullcaps. The restaurants and shops along Dix offer sights and sounds of the Middle East, including a call to prayer broadcast five times daily from a local mosque. The fascinating **Arab American National Museum** (13624 Michigan Ave., 313/582-2266, www.arabamericanmuseum.org, 10am-6pm Wed.-Sat., noon-5pm Sun., $8 adults, $4 seniors, students, and ages 6-12, under age 6 free), the only museum in the United States dedicated to the preservation of Arab American history and culture, has several permanent exhibits that explore Arab culture, the experiences of Arab immigrants, and the influence of Arab Americans and their organizations on American life. Rotating exhibits range from student art displays to immersive multimedia exhibitions that illustrate the Arab Spring uprisings.

★ THE HENRY FORD

The Henry Ford (20900 Oakwood Blvd., 313/982-6001 or 800/835-5237, www.thehenryford.org) is the collective name for the Henry Ford Museum of American Innovation, Greenfield Village, and the Ford Rouge Factory Tour. Local residents, area schoolchildren, and a steady stream of visitors make it one of Michigan's most popular destinations.

Henry Ford was quoted by the *Chicago Tribune* in 1916 as saying that "history is more or less bunk." He filed a lawsuit against the paper claiming he had been misquoted, and during his testimony claimed he meant to say that history as he had learned it was bunk—that it emphasized kings and their military ventures instead of stories about common people. Seeking to rectify this, Ford began to create a museum and an outdoor village that told history from a different perspective.

Ford sent his assistants across the Midwest and New England to assemble enough artifacts to fill the 12-acre **Henry Ford Museum of American Innovation** (9:30am-5pm daily, $24 adults, $22 over age 61, $18 ages 5-12, under age 5 free), an impressive and enormous colonial-style building featuring a landmark tower that is a precise duplication of Independence Hall in Philadelphia. Inside is one vast collection after another, including an encyclopedic assemblage of historic American autos, several presidential limousines (including Dwight Eisenhower's, John Kennedy's, and Ronald Reagan's), the world's greatest holdings of 19th-century farm and kitchen tools, a fine grouping of American furniture, iconic early aircraft (including some produced by Ford Motor Company), and many other artifacts that trace the evolution of modern American technologies.

Worth the price of admission alone is the excellent exhibit known as "The Automobile in American Life," which nostalgically shows the car's effect on the American landscape. There's a 1950s McDonald's sign, complete with oversize golden arches; a 1946 diner from Marlboro, Massachusetts, where an egg salad sandwich cost 15 cents; a VW camper van, complete with a handy awning; and a Holiday Inn guest room, circa 1960. The evolution of the auto industry is explained using TV monitors and restored automobiles from each period.

Also worth a look is the permanent "Made in America" exhibit, which traces the evolution of American manufacturing. Far from dull, it explains technology in an entertaining manner, accented by film clips, including one from the *I Love Lucy* show in which Lucy joins a candy-making assembly line with disastrous results. One exhibit, "With Liberty & Justice for All," presents the highlights of four U.S. revolutions—the American Revolution, the Civil War, the women's suffragist movement, and the civil rights era—and features such iconic artifacts as Abraham Lincoln's chair and the bus that Rosa Parks famously rode, restored to pristine condition.

In the adjacent **Greenfield Village** (9:30am-5pm daily mid-Apr.-Oct., 9:30am-5pm Fri.-Sun. Nov., $28 adults, $25.25 over age 61, $21 ages 5-12, under age 5 free), Ford gathered historic buildings and reproduced a few others that together chart how the United States grew from an agrarian to an industrial society. Many of the displays are working exhibits—you can see docents engaged in glassblowing at the Sandwich Glass Plant, machinists crafting parts in a reproduction of the original Ford factory on Mack Avenue, and farmers tending the fields at the working 19th-century Firestone Farm.

The village can be a bit disconcerting in that it lacks continuity. It is a patchwork quilt of unrelated people and places, where a 16th-century English Cotswold cottage sits a few hundred yards from an 18th-century New England saltbox. Other features include Ford's childhood home and Thomas Edison's Menlo Park laboratory, plus actors offering monologues detailing life in the early United States.

Homes of the Auto Barons

As Detroit grew to become the motor capital of the world, great fortunes were amassed. The automotive royalty that emerged took on an opulent lifestyle befitting their status and built great estates full of art and intricate craftsmanship. While some have unfortunately met the wrecking ball, a few survive. Today, these four estates offer visitors the chance to see firsthand how the auto pioneers lived during the golden age of the auto industry.

FISHER MANSION

The **Fisher Mansion** (383 Lenox Ave., 313/331-6740, www.detroitiskconlive.com) was built by Lawrence P. Fisher, one of the seven Fisher brothers, of the Fisher Body Company. A talented playboy who once courted actress Jean Harlow, Fisher spent millions constructing this magnificent riverfront estate, which has been described as "glitz bordering on garish." Constructed in the Mediterranean style and completed in 1928, the home is most noted for its ornate stone and marble work, exquisite European handcrafted stained-glass windows, doors and arches carved from woods imported from India and Africa, and rare black walnut and rosewood parquet floors. More than 200 ounces of gold and silver leaf highlight the decorative ceilings and moldings. Fisher was close friends with publisher William Randolph Hearst, and it's been speculated that his grand designs for the mansion were driven by a friendly rivalry after Hearst built the San Simeon estate in California.

The mansion fell into neglect after Fisher's death and was purchased for $300,000 in 1975 by Alfred Brush Ford, great-grandson of Henry Ford, and by Elisabeth Reuther Dickmeyer, daughter of legendary United Auto Workers chief Walter Reuther, who together spent $2 million to restore it before donating it to the International Society for Krishna Consciousness, of which they are members. Today, the mansion serves as the Bhaktivedanta Cultural Center, which welcomes the public to daily worship services and special cultural events. Tours are available on Sunday only, 4pm to 7pm, by appointment only. In addition, visitors are welcome 4:45am to 9pm Monday through Saturday to view the fine art gallery and an exhibit about India's colorful heritage.

EDSEL AND ELEANOR FORD HOUSE

Tucked far back from Lake Shore Drive stands the **Edsel and Eleanor Ford House** (1100 Lake Shore Dr., Grosse Pointe Shores, 313/884-4222, www.fordhouse.org, 11am-4pm Tues.-Fri., 10am-4pm Sat., noon-4pm Sun., closed major holidays, grounds $5 pp, under age 6 free, tours $12 adults, $11 seniors, $8 ages 6-12, under age 6 free) at Gaukler Pointe. The Cotswold-style mansion, designed by noted local architect Albert Kahn, was built in 1929 for Henry Ford's only son, who raised his four children in this house. Much of the interior paneling and furniture was salvaged from distinguished old English manors; even the roof is of imported English stones expertly laid by imported Cotswold roofers. Throughout the home is evidence of the Fords' love of art; copies of masterpieces now replace the originals, which were donated to the Detroit Institute of Arts. One especially unusual feature: the dining room is without electricity, as Eleanor wanted all meals by candlelight.

What makes the house especially interesting is that it remains much as it did when the Fords lived here. Edsel died in 1943, but his wife, Eleanor Clay Ford, left the estate virtually untouched. It represents a style of living and quality of craftsmanship virtually nonexistent today. Eleanor passed away in 1976, and per her will, the house is used for the benefit of the greater community. Today the mansion is the site of outdoor concerts, classic auto shows, and a host of other community functions.

Visitors can watch a 13-minute video about the Fords and take an hour-long guided tour that leads them through the distinctive dwelling and/or a self-guided tour of the grounds and outer buildings. Highlights include a stylish art deco recreation room by famed industrial designer Walter Dorwin Teague, Edsel's personal study lined with framed family photos and images of luminaries like Thomas Edison, and the Tudor-style playhouse created in 1930 for daughter Josephine's seventh birthday. Premium tours (10am Tues.-Fri.) cost an additional $3 and take visitors to more rooms than the general tours. Those who decide not to tour the house can simply wander the grounds.

FAIR LANE

Of the auto baron estates, Henry Ford's **Fair Lane** (1 Fair Lane Dr., Dearborn, 313/668-3200, www.henryfordfairlane.org, grounds 8am-6pm Mon.-Fri. Oct. 1-Apr. 30; daily May 1-Sept. 30, admission to the grounds and parking free) may seem the least regal. By the time it was completed in 1915, Ford had hired four different architects to work on the project, three of whom he fired. The result is an unusual home hewing closely to the Prairie style, but including several details common to English manor homes. Today Fair Lane is listed as a National Historic Landmark. At the time of writing, the mansion is undergoing restoration and is closed for tours, but the public is free to explore the grounds.

Meadow Brook Hall

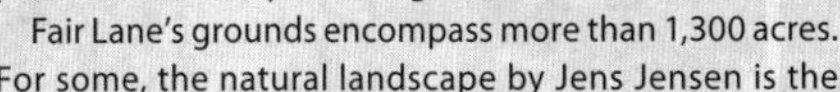

Fair Lane's grounds encompass more than 1,300 acres. For some, the natural landscape by Jens Jensen is the highlight of a visit. Others may find the estate's technical features, including the extensive six-level hydroelectric power plant, more fascinating. The plant, which harnessed electricity from the Rouge River, was created by Ford and Thomas Edison and supplied power not only to the estate but also much of Dearborn.

Ford entertained some of the world's most influential people here, including Charles Lindbergh (also a Detroit native), President Herbert Hoover, and the Duke of Windsor. Ford himself died in the mansion during a storm in April 1947. On that night, the storm knocked out the power, leaving the estate illuminated only by candlelight.

In 2013, stewardship of the historic estate passed to the nonprofit that also operates the Edsel and Eleanor Ford Mansion. In 2016 an extensive restoration began. While the work is ongoing, there is no public access to the house. Visitors, however, can explore the grounds.

MEADOW BROOK HALL

John Dodge and his brother Horace were among the car makers responsible for Detroit's meteoric rise to prominence in the auto business. John died suddenly in 1920, leaving a vast fortune to his widow, Matilda, his former secretary. In 1925 Matilda remarried a wealthy lumberman, Alfred Wilson. The couple toured Europe and dreamed of a grand estate, building the 110-room Tudor-style **Meadow Brook Hall** (480 S. Adams Rd., Rochester, 248/364-6200, www.meadowbrookhall.org, tours 11am-3pm daily May 28-Sept. 1, tour schedule during off-season on website, $15 adults, $12 over age 61, $10 active military with ID, $7.50 age 6-12, 11 and under free) in the late 1920s for the then astonishing sum of $4 million. Interiors were copied from drawings of English estates.

Matilda Wilson left the estate to Oakland University, which administers the property. The mansion's rooms—including a two-story ballroom, a game room copied from old English pubs, and Matilda's bathroom accented with locally sourced Pewabic tile—still house original family collections and furnishings. A walk in the surrounding woods reveals a six-room playhouse known as **Knole Cottage** (noon-5pm daily during the Holiday Walk, house tours 11am-5pm daily, $20 adults, $7.50 ages 6-12, under age 6 free), built at three-quarters scale for their daughter Frances Wilson.

The Holiday Walk is an annual celebration here from late November to December 23.

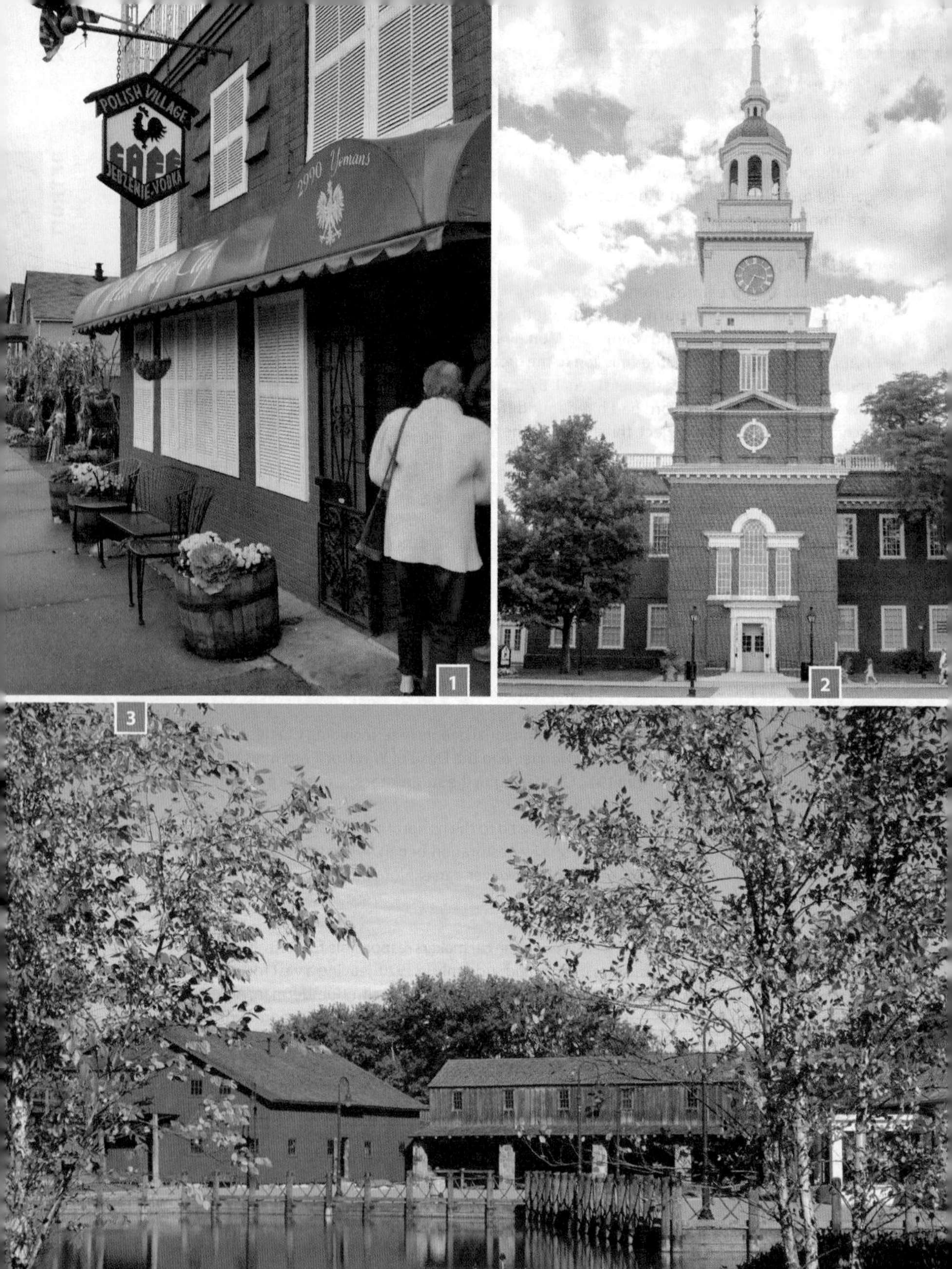
POLISH VILLAGE
CAFE
JEDZENIE·VODKA
2990 Yemans
1
2
3

But despite the lack of cohesion, the village is truly a fascinating place to visit.

With thousands of items, the entire complex is more than a bit overwhelming, especially since the museum has a somewhat confusing layout. A good idea is to split a visit into two days, with one day to explore each attraction. You might need even more time if you plan to take in other on-site features like the **Giant Screen Experience** ($10 adults, $9 over age 61, $7.50 under age 12). Tour buses regularly leave for the **Ford Rouge Factory Tour** (9:30am-5pm Mon.-Sat., $18 adults, $16.25 over age 61, $13.50 ages 5-11, under age 5 free), a five-part excursion that culminates with a stroll through the Ford F-150 truck assembly plant.

Food

Dearborn offers its share of quality dining. ★ **Ford's Garage** (21367 Michigan Ave., 313/752-3673, www.fordsgarageusa.com, 10:30am-10pm Sun.-Thurs., 10:30am-11pm Fri.-Sat., $9-25), pays tribute to Dearborn's signature company through the use of the Ford name. Quotes from Henry Ford adorn the walls, and even the hamburger buns are branded with the famous Ford logo. A wide array of burger options is complemented by several chicken and seafood choices, plus a selection of salads.

Accommodations

The Dearborn Inn, A Marriot Hotel (20301 Oakwood Blvd., 313/271-2700, www.marriott.com, $218-349 d) has a terrific location on 23 lush acres, with 229 refined guest rooms and five colonial-style homes that make this a unique hotel experience. Dining options include the higher-end Edison's, open for breakfast, lunch, and dinner, or the Ten Eyck Tavern for lunch and dinner, featuring more moderate selections. Amenities added during a recent renovation include plush bedding, flat-screen TVs, high-speed Internet access, a fitness center, a business center, and an outdoor swimming pool. These are truly historic lodgings: Just across Oakwood Boulevard, Ford Motor Company once operated a small airport with scheduled flights. To accommodate passengers, the Dearborn Inn was built in 1931 as the world's first airport hotel.

Nearby, **The Henry** (300 Town Center Dr., 313/441-2000, www.behenry.com, $227-389 d), attracts power brokers from across the country as well as visiting rock stars and celebrities. The award-winning TRIA Restaurant is known for its excellent, if pricey, American cuisine, and the elegant rooms feature contemporary artwork, custom furnishings, and include high-speed Internet access. Other on-site amenities include a fitness center, an indoor swimming pool, and massage treatment rooms.

Information

For more information about Dearborn, consult the **Dearborn Area Chamber of Commerce** (22100 Michigan Ave., Dearborn, 313/584-6100, www.dearbornchamber.org, 9am-5pm Mon.-Fri.).

Getting There

Amtrak (800/872-7245, www.amtrak.com) offers regular service to Dearborn Station (21201 Michigan Ave.). If you're driving from downtown Detroit, take Lodge Freeway (M-10) and the Edsel Ford Freeway (I-94) to Dearborn, a 10-mile trip that takes about 15 minutes.

FARMINGTON HILLS

Holocaust Memorial Center

America's first freestanding **Holocaust Memorial Center** (28123 Orchard Lake Rd., 248/553-2400, www.holocaustcenter.org, 9:30am-8:30pm Mon., 9:30am-5pm Tues., Thurs., and Sun. 9:30am-3pm Fri., $8 adults, $6 over age 61, $5-6 students) provides a vivid portrayal of the Holocaust. Features include extensive material and state-of-the-art display techniques that explain this dark period in modern history. Docent-led tours

1: a Polish cafe in Hamtramck **2:** clock tower at the Henry Ford Museum **3:** campus of The Henry Ford

(available between 9am and 3pm daily, last tour at 1:30pm Fri.) often conclude with a visit by a Holocaust survivor.

Information

For more information about Farmington Hills, consult the **Greater Farmington Area Chamber of Commerce** (32780 Grand River Ave., Ste. 207, 248/919-6917, www.gfachamber.com, 9am-5pm Mon.-Fri.).

Getting There

From downtown Detroit, take the Lodge Freeway (M-10) to the Reuther Freeway (I-696) and exit 5 (Orchard Lake Rd.) to Farmington Hills. This 29-mile trip should take about 30 minutes.

ROYAL OAK AND FERNDALE

Heading north on Woodward from downtown Detroit, Ferndale and Royal Oak are the first suburbs you'll encounter after you cross 8 Mile Road and the city limits.

Until the 1970s **Royal Oak** was seen as a sleepy community a few miles north of Detroit's city limits. Since then it's taken on a more cutting-edge personality, and today ranks as an eclectic destination, offering something for just about everyone.

Perhaps the city's most noteworthy claim to fame is the 125-acre **Detroit Zoo** (8450 W. 10 Mile Rd., 248/541-5717, www.detroitzoo.org, 9am-5pm daily Apr.-Labor Day, 10am-5pm daily Sept.-Oct., 10am-4pm daily Nov.-Mar., $18 adults, $15 over age 61 and ages 2-15, under age 2 free), home to 1,300 animals from flamingos and trumpeter swans to wolverines and gorillas. Three of the favorite exhibits are the Wildlife Interpretive Gallery, site of a popular hummingbird/butterfly garden; the Arctic Ring of Life, which features polar bears and Arctic species; and the new Polk Penguin Conservation Center and the Holden Museum of Living Reptiles.

Ferndale, immediately to Royal Oak's south, was blue-collar and conservative until the mid-1980s, when it emerged as a center of progressive politics and bohemian living, observed in its commercial streets, filled with vintage clothing and record shops, antiques emporiums, and funky coffeehouses. In Royal Oak, by contrast, a few of the original boutiques remain, with most having been replaced by high-rent glitzy shops and restaurants.

Ferndale remains a community in the strong embrace of alternative cultures and lifestyles. By the early 1990s, much of metro Detroit's gay population was concentrated here. In 1992, Affirmations, a community center for LGBT people, opened on 9 Mile Road, and it underwent a significant expansion in 2007. The neighborhood is also home to numerous bars, clubs, and restaurants.

The major streets—Main Street and Washington Avenue in Royal Oak, and Woodward and 9 Mile Road in Ferndale—are all great spots for window-shopping and people-watching.

Shopping

Shopping in Royal Oak and Ferndale is far removed from a typical mall. **Dos Manos** (210 W. 6th St., Royal Oak, 248/542-5856 or 800/572-4957, www.dosmanos.com, 10am-6pm daily) is where you'll find Latin American handicrafts.

Royal Oak is also home to **Noir Leather** (124 W. 4th St., Royal Oak, 248/541-3979, www.noirleather.com, noon-9pm Mon.-Thurs., 11am-10pm Fri.-Sat., noon-6pm Sun.), a fetish fashion boutique founded in 1983.

In Ferndale a great place to peruse is the **Rust Belt Market** (22801 Woodward Ave., Ferndale, 810/441-0956, www.rustbeltmarket.com, noon-7pm Fri., 11am-7pm Sat., 11am-6pm Sun.), a common marketplace where various merchants rent space and offer their wares for sale each weekend. Examples are purveyors of jewelry, art, clothing, and custom framing.

Food

Tom's Oyster Bar (318 S. Main St., Royal Oak, 248/541-1186, www.tomsoysterbar.

com, noon-2am Mon.-Fri., noon-midnight Sat.-Sun. $9-48) features the area's most extensive selection of oysters, as well as tasty steaks and innovative fresh seafood. **BD's Mongolian Barbecue** (430 S. Main St., Royal Oak, 248/398-7755, www.gomongo.com, 11am-10pm Sun.-Thurs., 11am-11pm Fri.-Sat., $8-23) lets you watch as chefs prepare your stir-fry creation on a huge central grill. Since opening in Royal Oak in 1992, it's expanded to other Detroit suburbs and to other states, from Illinois to Florida.

A few of the choicer locations in Ferndale include **Rosie O'Grady's** (279 W. 9 Mile Rd., Ferndale, 249/591-9163, www.rosieogradysirishpub.com, 11am-2am Tues.-Sat., noon-2am Sun., $10-20), a welcoming bar and grill. The food is anything but an afterthought, with creative dishes like chicken Rockefeller, blackened salmon, Cajun shrimp pasta, and artisan-style pizza. Best of all, everything is made from scratch.

For a vegetarian option, try **Greenspace Café** (215 W. 9 Mile Rd., Ferndale, 248/206-7510, www.greenspacecafe.com, 11am-9pm Mon.-Thurs., 11am-10:30pm Fri.-Sat., 10am-3pm Sun., $10-20). Menu offerings change often, but a few recent examples are pesto rigatoni, forest mushroom tacos, and a farro lentil burger. You'll also find a number of mixed drink offerings.

Detroit Bubble Tea (22821 Woodward Ave., Ferndale, 248/239-1131, www.detroitbubbletea.com, 11am-10pm Mon.-Sun.) offers variations of that delicious beverage, as well as tempting gluten-free French macarons and vegan cupcakes.

Information

For more information about Royal Oak, consult the **Royal Oak Downtown Development Authority** (211 Williams St., Royal Oak, 248/246-3280, www.downtownroyaloak.org, 8am-4:30pm Mon.-Thurs., 8am-noon Fri.). For details about Ferndale, get in touch with the **Ferndale Downtown Development Authority** (149 W. 9 Mile Rd., 248/546-1632, www.downtownferndale.com, 9am-5pm Mon.-Fri.).

Getting There

You can access the Royal Oak-Ferndale area via **Amtrak** (800/872-7245, www.amtrak.com), which offers train service at a sheltered platform (201 S. Sherman Dr., Royal Oak). From downtown Detroit by car, take the Chrysler Freeway (I-75) and exit at 9 Mile Road for Ferndale or 11 Mile Road for Royal Oak. This 14-mile drive takes less than 30 minutes.

BIRMINGHAM

In 1996 naysayers were concerned that downtown Birmingham—a chic enclave of expensive shops and galleries—would shrivel and die when the nearby Somerset Collection, a gleaming upscale shopping complex, expanded to double its previous size. While the character of downtown Birmingham certainly did change, the city diversified its offerings to include even more unique shops and restaurants. In doing so, Birmingham has demonstrated its remarkable resiliency and remains a tony suburb with a thriving downtown area. Shoppers from all over the metro area come here to see and be seen, linger in cafés and restaurants, and exercise their credit cards.

Shopping

Even if you're not a shopper, Birmingham is worth a trip for its art galleries, one of the most impressive concentrations in the Midwest. You'll find cutting-edge contemporary art at places like the **Robert Kidd Gallery** (107 Townsend St., 248/642-3909, www.robertkiddgallery.com, 11am-8pm Mon.-Sat.), in business since 1976. This and more than a dozen other influential art outlets are scattered around downtown Birmingham.

Accommodations

In Birmingham, ★ **The Townsend Hotel** (100 Townsend St., 248/642-7900, www.townsendhotel.com, $325-479 d) is the upscale—if relatively unpretentious—European-style hostelry where famous celebrities and sports figures are frequent guests. Nothing but the best is good enough here—Belgian linens, pillows of the fluffiest down, yards of marble in the baths, and a restaurant staffed with world-class chefs who cater to the guests' every desire. Located near the fashionable shops and galleries, it's also a favorite stop for afternoon tea, served daily.

Information

For more information about Birmingham, consult the **Birmingham Principal Shopping District** (151 Martin St., Birmingham, 248/530-1200, www.enjoybirmingham.com, 8am-5pm Mon.-Fri.).

Getting There

You can access Birmingham via **Amtrak** (800/872-7245, www.amtrak.com), which offers train service to the nearby Troy Transit Center (1201 Doyle Dr., Troy). By car from downtown Detroit, take the Chrysler Freeway (I-75) to 14 Mile Road, proceed west, and turn right at Woodward Avenue. Without traffic, this 20-mile trip takes 30 minutes.

BLOOMFIELD HILLS

For a look at how the top 1 percent lives, head north to Bloomfield Hills. Long the suburb of choice for automotive executives and other members of the city's power establishment, it ranks among the wealthiest communities in the United States. Past and present residents have included Detroit Pistons captain Isaiah Thomas and the queen of soul, Aretha Franklin. Unlike Grosse Pointe, which still struggles with vestiges of its Waspy heritage, ethnicity and race don't matter in Bloomfield Hills; money is the key here.

If Grosse Pointe epitomizes old money, Bloomfield Hills attracts its newer, shinier counterpart. Huge houses are spread throughout its rolling hills—a geographic anomaly in southeastern Michigan. Most were built in the late 20th century, although older residences can be found near Cranbrook, the former home of newspaper magnate George Booth, whose father-in-law James Scripps founded the *Detroit News*. Drive the winding lanes and you'll find Old Tudor, Georgian, and other 1920s-era mansions. One notable exception is the Smith House (5045 Pon Valley Rd.), designed by Frank Lloyd Wright and constructed in 1946.

Cranbrook

Despite its celebrities, Bloomfield Hills remains best-known as home to **Cranbrook** (39221 N. Woodward Ave., 877/462-7262, www.cranbrook.edu), a renowned 315-acre arts and educational complex. Here, famed Finnish architect Eliel Saarinen created a lush and lovely refuge for artists and students.

Cranbrook is known throughout the world for the integrated aesthetics of its environment. All buildings, gardens, sculptures, and interiors are treated as an integral and important part of a whole. This creative cohesion is the work of patron George Booth and Saarinen. Booth purchased the land in Bloomfield Hills in 1904 and commissioned noted Detroit architect Albert Kahn to build him a large Tudor-style mansion. Booth and his wife decided to name the house Cranbrook, after the family's ancestral hometown in England. Booth was a noted proponent of the arts and crafts movement, which advocated a reunification of ordinary life and art. After a 1922 trip to Rome, where he visited the American Academy, the Booths decided to create something that would be a lasting legacy for the community. Over the next several decades, they established three schools, a science museum, and an academy of art, design, and architecture. Saarinen was the principal architect for the new campus.

While the academy enjoys a stellar reputation worldwide, equal acclaim is drawn by the **Cranbrook Art Museum** (248/645-3319, www.cranbrookartmuseum.org, 11am-5pm Tues.-Sun., closed major holidays, $10 adults, $8 over age 64, $6 students, under age 13 free), operated by the **Cranbrook Academy of Art**

(248/645-3300, www.cranbrookart.edu) and the largest museum in southeast Michigan devoted to modern and contemporary art, architecture, and design. It presents exhibits by students and faculty members. Another popular attraction is the **Cranbrook Institute of Science** (248/645-3200 or 877/462-7262, http://science.cranbrook.edu, 10am-5pm Mon.-Thurs., 10am-10pm Fri.-Sat., noon-4pm Sun., $13 adults, $9.50 over age 64 and ages 2-12, under age 2 free; admission half off after 5pm Fri.-Sat.), a family-friendly science and natural history museum with a collection of more than 200,000 objects and artifacts. In addition to galleries devoted to geology, anthropology, astronomy, Native Americans, and other absorbing subjects, popular diversions here include a planetarium ($5, $1 under age 2), a live bat program ($5, $1 under age 2), and an observatory (included with museum admission) that's open on Friday and Saturday evenings, weather permitting.

Accommodations

To stay overnight in Bloomfield Hills, head to the **DoubleTree by Hilton** (39475 Woodward Ave., 248/644-1400, www.doubletree3hilton.com, $165-365 d), a comfortable property in a prime location. In addition to more than 150 rooms and suites, the DoubleTree offers a fitness center, an indoor saltwater pool, a business center, three on-site dining options, included Wi-Fi, and shuttle service within a 10-mile radius.

Information

For more information, consult the **City of Bloomfield Hills** (45 E. Long Lake Rd., Bloomfield Hills, 248/644-1520, www.bloomfieldhillsmi.net).

Getting There

Driving from downtown Detroit, take the Chrysler Freeway (I-75) to the I-75 Business Loop, which becomes Square Lake Road, and continue to Woodward Avenue. In light traffic, this 26-mile trip should take 30 minutes.

GROSSE POINTE

Five individual cities make up the area collectively known as Grosse Pointe, wedged between the east side of Detroit and Lake St. Clair. As a whole, Grosse Pointe Shores, Grosse Pointe Farms, Grosse Pointe Woods, the city of Grosse Pointe, and Grosse Pointe Park are among the metro area's wealthiest communities—a land of landscaped estates, tree-lined streets, and large homes.

A summer community through much of the 19th century, Grosse Pointe began to change in about 1910, when wealthy Detroiters sought to separate themselves from the increasing number of immigrants arriving in the city. The wealthiest built mansions that imitated the elegant country houses of England, France, and Italy, importing stone fireplaces and entire rooms that were later incorporated into new construction. Some even brought in European artisans for their craftsmanship.

Grosse Pointe is where some of the city's most prominent families settled, and where many of their descendants still live. Until the 1950s, prospective home buyers were screened by an infamous point system to perpetuate WASP homogeneity. Today you'll find a much more diverse population, although the area is still overwhelmingly white. Grosse Pointe Park reflects a more middle-class population, with a number of smaller homes and modest 1920s housing. An especially densely populated neighborhood, sometimes referred to as the Cabbage Patch because its early Belgian residents grew the vegetable in their yards, was developed to house servants for the nearby estates.

Sights

Virtually all of the large mansions housed only one generation of the families that built them. In subsequent decades most were razed, although a few remain along Lake Shore Drive. It's a beautiful drive in any season, with the view of Lake St. Clair attracting joggers, freighter watchers, and others just to look at the architecture. To get a peek inside one of the area's original estates, stop at the former **Russell Alger House,** now known as the **Grosse Pointe War Memorial** (32 Lake Shore Dr., Grosse Pointe Farms, 313/881-7511, www.warmemorial.org, 9am-8pm Mon.-Sat., free). Built in 1910, this roomy Italian Renaissance-style mansion was originally the home of Russell Alger Jr., heir to a lumber fortune and an early investor in the Packard Motor Company. For a time it served as a satellite to the Detroit Institute of Arts, and today it functions as a community center, hosting private parties and weddings, as well as offering occasional concerts.

Information

For more information, consult the **Grosse Pointe Chamber of Commerce** (63 Kercheval Ave., Ste. 16, Grosse Pointe, 313/881-4722, www.grossepointechamber.com, 10am-5pm Mon.-Fri.).

Getting There

If you're driving from downtown Detroit, take East Jefferson Avenue to Grosse Pointe. In light traffic, this eight-mile trip takes 20 minutes.

MOUNT CLEMENS

Directly northeast of Detroit is the picturesque community of Mount Clemens. With a history dating to the early 19th century, Mount Clemens is an example of an independent community that was later surrounded by Detroit's suburban sprawl.

Mount Clemens's big claim to fame dates to the mid-19th century, when the area's wells were thought to have medicinal properties; by 1900 several mineral bathhouses were operating. Notable people from around the nation, including Babe Ruth, William Randolph Hearst, and Mae West, traveled to Mount Clemens to seek relief from ailments such as aching muscles and skin problems. This influx stimulated the development of hotels and dining establishments. The last bathhouse closed in 1974.

Mount Clemens's charming downtown, parts of which are closed to vehicular traffic, invites leisurely strolls and window-shopping. The **Anton Art Center** (125 Macomb Place, 586/469-8666, www.theartcenter.org, 10am-5pm Tues.-Sat., by donation) provides exhibit space for local and emerging artists and offers adults and youth classes in drawing, painting, and sculpture. The center is housed in a building endowed by Andrew Carnegie, originally the Mount Clemens Public Library.

The **Recreation Bowl** (40 Crocker Blvd., 586/468-7746, www.therecreationbowl.com, 10am-2am Mon.-Sat., 10am-10pm Sun) might look like just a bowling alley, but you'll also find nightly darts and billiards competitions and a full-service restaurant offering a wide variety of inexpensive burgers, salads, and sandwiches. During the warm-weather months, you'll find a full schedule of big band, jazz, and rock-and-roll acts.

Information

For more information, consult the **Mount Clemens Downtown Development Authority** (1 Crocker Blvd., 586/469-4168, www.downtownmountclemens.com, 9am-5pm Mon.-Fri.).

Getting There

From downtown Detroit, the quicker, more efficient route is Gratiot Avenue (M-3), a 25-mile, 40-minute trip. The alternative is to take the Edsel Ford Freeway (I-94) approximately 22 miles to exit 236 (16 Mile Rd.), turn right, and continue to Crocker Boulevard. Turn left on Crocker and go three miles to Mount Clemens. In light traffic, this route should take about 50 minutes.

GROSSE ILE

Not far from the Detroit River International Wildlife Refuge, Grosse Ile is a lengthy bottle-shaped island in the Detroit River just upstream from the beginning of Lake Erie. Virtually all of the island is residential, but taking a leisurely drive to look at the palatial homes can be a wonderful way to spend an afternoon.

Sights

LIGHTHOUSES

While Grosse Ile isn't a huge destination, there are two nearby lighthouses worth a look: the **Grosse Ile North Channel Range Front Light,** a white, 50-foot-tall octagonal tower lit in 1906 and deactivated in 1963, and the **Detroit River Light** in Lake Erie, only accessible via boat. Although the **Grosse Ile Historical Society** (734/675-1250, www.gihistory.org) offers an annual one-day tour of the Grosse Ile lighthouse, the Detroit River Light, built in 1885 and still an active navigational aid operated by the U.S. Coast Guard, can only be viewed from outside. The Detroit River Light has also been known as the Bar Point Shoal Light.

★ LAKE ERIE METROPARK

Southeastern Michigan boasts several parks and natural areas ideal for outdoor enthusiasts weary of Detroit's downtown bustle. Detroit is the site of North America's first international wildlife refuge, established in 2001, the **Detroit River International Wildlife Refuge** (Brownstown Charter Township, 734/365-0219, www.fws.gov/midwest/detroitriver), which comprises islands, marshes, coastal wetlands, and waterfront terrain along the lower Detroit River and western shoreline of Lake Erie. Though public access is limited, you can appreciate at least part of the refuge by visiting the **Lake Erie Metropark** (32481 W. Jefferson Ave., Brownstown Township, 734/379-5020, www.metroparks.com, 6am-10pm daily summer, 7am-8pm daily winter, $10/vehicle daily, $35/vehicle annually), a well-preserved 1,607-acre recreation area situated south of Grosse Ile and offering stunning views of the nearby river, lake, and islands. Popular among outdoor enthusiasts, the Metropark features three miles of shoreline, an 18-hole golf course (734/379-0048), hiking and biking trails, a swimming pool, a marina and boat launches (7am-9pm daily Memorial Day-Labor Day, $10 daily, $70 annually), and the **Marshlands Museum and Nature Center** (1pm-5pm Mon.-Fri., 10am-5pm Sat.-Sun. included in park admission). While anglers, kayakers, and bird-watchers enjoy this peaceful place spring through fall, during the winter months cross-country skiers can explore 4.25 miles of flat groomed trails.

Food

You'll find several eateries on the island. One tasty option is **Kathy's Cafe** (9105 Macomb St., 734/671-0059, 7am-4pm daily, $10-20), with typical American fare offered in a warm, family-friendly atmosphere.

Information

For more information, consult the **Township of Grosse Ile** (9601 Groh Rd., Grosse Ile, 734/676-4422, www.grosseile.com, 8am-5pm Mon.-Fri.).

Getting There

There are two bridges that lead to the island. A toll bridge (one-way $2.50) connects to the mainland near the island's northern end at Jefferson Avenue and Sibley Road in Riverview. A free bridge links the island to the mainland farther south, near Jefferson Avenue and Van Horn Road in Trenton.

To reach Grosse Ile Township from downtown Detroit, take M-10 and I-75 to West Road, turn right onto Allen Road, left onto Van Horn Road, left onto West Jefferson Avenue, and then right onto Grosse Ile Parkway, which connects the mainland to Grosse Ile. In light traffic, this 27-mile trip takes about 40 minutes.

Ann Arbor

The quintessential university town of Ann Arbor offers a slate of cultural opportunities large enough to rival Detroit's—the Ann Arbor Symphony, the University of Michigan Museum of Art, and the Matthaei Botanical Gardens are just a few examples. And, of course, there's University of Michigan Big 10 Conference football: Each fall the Wolverines take the field against some of the nation's top powerhouse schools in the quest for a trip to the Rose Bowl.

Nearby Chelsea seems the ideal setting for a small, intimate theater—and the Purple Rose, owned by actor Jeff Daniels, supplies the need beautifully. The theater presents dramas and comedies year-round. Operating on an apprentice model where the actors and students both stage the shows and maintain the building, Daniels based

Highlights

Look for ★ to find recommended sights, activities, dining, and lodging.

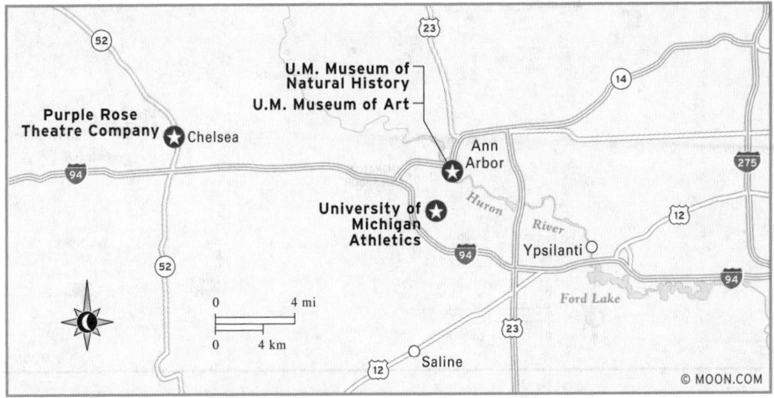

★ **University of Michigan Museum of Natural History:** Learn the fascinating story of life on Earth and how it continues to evolve (page 89).

★ **University of Michigan Museum of Art:** Perhaps the finest university art museum in the nation, the recently expanded facility is home to world-class artwork (page 89).

★ **University of Michigan Athletics:** To get a real appreciation of the Ann Arbor spirit, there's nothing like attending a Wolverines game (page 90).

★ **Purple Rose Theatre Company:** Audiences travel from far and wide to catch the latest play at this renowned theater, founded by actor Jeff Daniels (page 98).

Ann Arbor

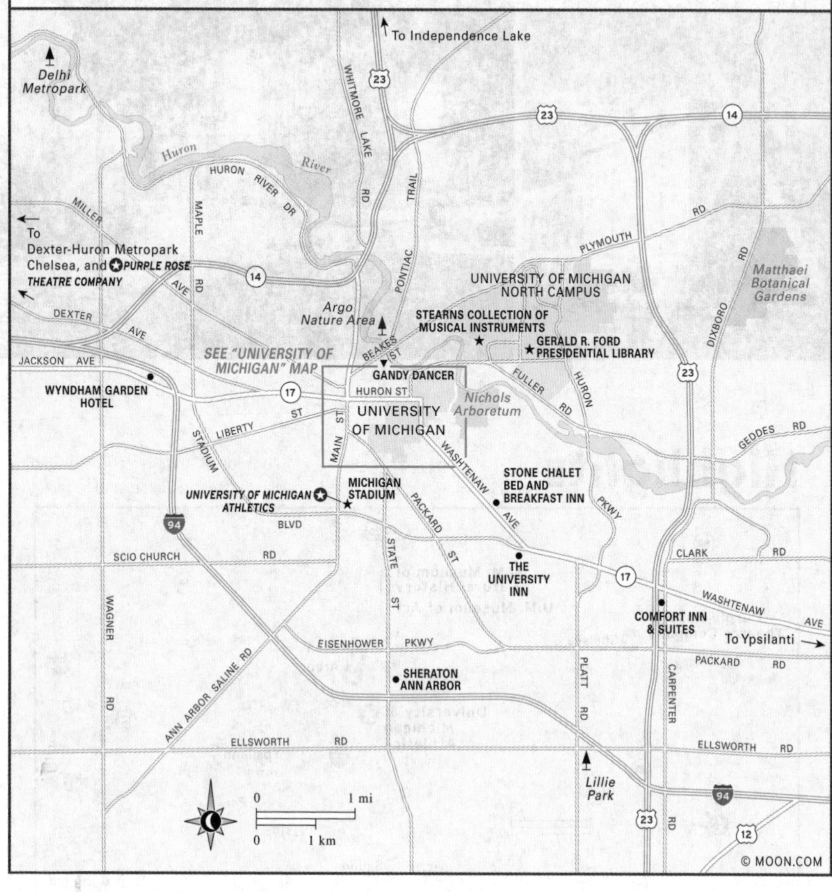

the program on his experience with the Circle Repertory Company in New York.

Few would dispute the claim that Ann Arbor, with its population of roughly 116,000, is one of Michigan's most interesting cities. Ann Arbor has a unique blend of big-city energy and college-town informality. About 40 miles west of Detroit, Ann Arbor is the suburb of choice for Detroit's intelligentsia, a choice driven by the presence of one of the nation's finest research institutions and a community that places a high value on learning, evidenced by numerous bookstores, art galleries, and museums.

Ann Arbor is dominated by the university, which occupies most of the blocks just east of downtown. Founded in Detroit in 1817, the University of Michigan moved to Ann Arbor in 1837 and has a long reputation for excellence in academics and athletics, with the

Previous: the historic Michigan Theater in Ann Arbor; the University of Michigan's *Orion* sculpture by Mark di Suvero; University of Michigan Museum of Art.

country's largest premed and nursing programs. Graduates include eight Nobel laureates, 30 Pulitzer Prize winners, one U.S. president, eight astronauts, and numerous actors and filmmakers.

PLANNING YOUR TIME

Ann Arbor is only about an hour's drive from downtown Detroit and offers scores of educational and cultural opportunities. For the typical tourist, one to two days here should be adequate. For more information about Ann Arbor, consult **Destination Ann Arbor** (315 W. Huron St., #340, Ann Arbor, 734/995-7281, www.visitannarbor.org, 8:30am-5pm Mon.-Fri.).

HISTORY

Ann Arbor started back in 1824 as a simple farming community. The wives of the hamlet's founders, John Allen and Elisha Rumsey, both had the first name of Ann. Their husbands purchased a nearby plot of bur oaks. Thus, they gave the town its original name of "Annarbour." In 1836 when Michigan was working toward statehood, Allen and Rumsey offered forty acres to serve as the site of the permanent capital (the first constitution mandated that Detroit serve as capital for 10 years, after which it would be relocated). When Lansing was chosen instead, the land was offered to the University of Michigan. Over the years the city and the university have grown in tandem. Today the university's central campus is intertwined with non-university buildings, making for an engaging urban environment.

TOP EXPERIENCE

SIGHTS

University of Michigan

The heart of the **University of Michigan** (www.umich.edu) is the **"Diag,"** the diagonal walkway crossing the original 40-acre campus between State Street, North University Avenue, and South University Avenue. Many of the nearby buildings house classrooms and laboratories. The Diag is frequently the site of outdoor concerts and student demonstrations, although the university is no longer the hotbed of activism it was during the Vietnam era, when in 1965 it was the site of a "teach in" organized by students and faculty opposed to the war.

For a terrific view, climb the eight floors to the map room in the **Harlan Hatcher Graduate Library.** Afterward, cross State Street, where you'll find the venerable **Michigan Union** (530 S. State St., 734/763-5750, 7am-2am Mon.-Sat., 9am-2am Sun. fall-winter, 7am-midnight Mon.-Sat., 9am-midnight Sun. spring-summer), built in the 1920s and the site of President Kennedy's announcement of the Peace Corps—a plaque commemorating the event is embedded in the front steps. Closed for renovation at the time of writing, the Union is slated for a late winter reopening in 2020. Just north of the Diag, you'll find another historic student union, the **Michigan League** (911 N. University Ave., 734/764-0446, 7am-11pm daily), opened in 1929 as a center for women's social and cultural activities on campus; today it houses a gift shop, information center, 640-seat theater, and small inn for visitors.

Across from the League is the **Burton Memorial Tower,** a campus landmark capped by the **Charles Baird Carillon,** one of the world's heaviest, containing 53 bells weighing 43 tons. Another campus favorite is the **Law Quadrangle,** home of U of M's highly respected law school. Built between 1923 and 1933, the picturesque quad was modeled after Cambridge and Oxford Universities, with the massive library patterned after King's College Chapel at Cambridge. The level of workmanship in the Gothic building was rare even by standards of the 1920s. Rest your feet in the library's hushed reading room, where maize and blue plaster medallions decorate the ceiling and the crests of other American law schools adorn the windows.

No visit to Wolverine territory would be complete without a stop at **Michigan**

University of Michigan

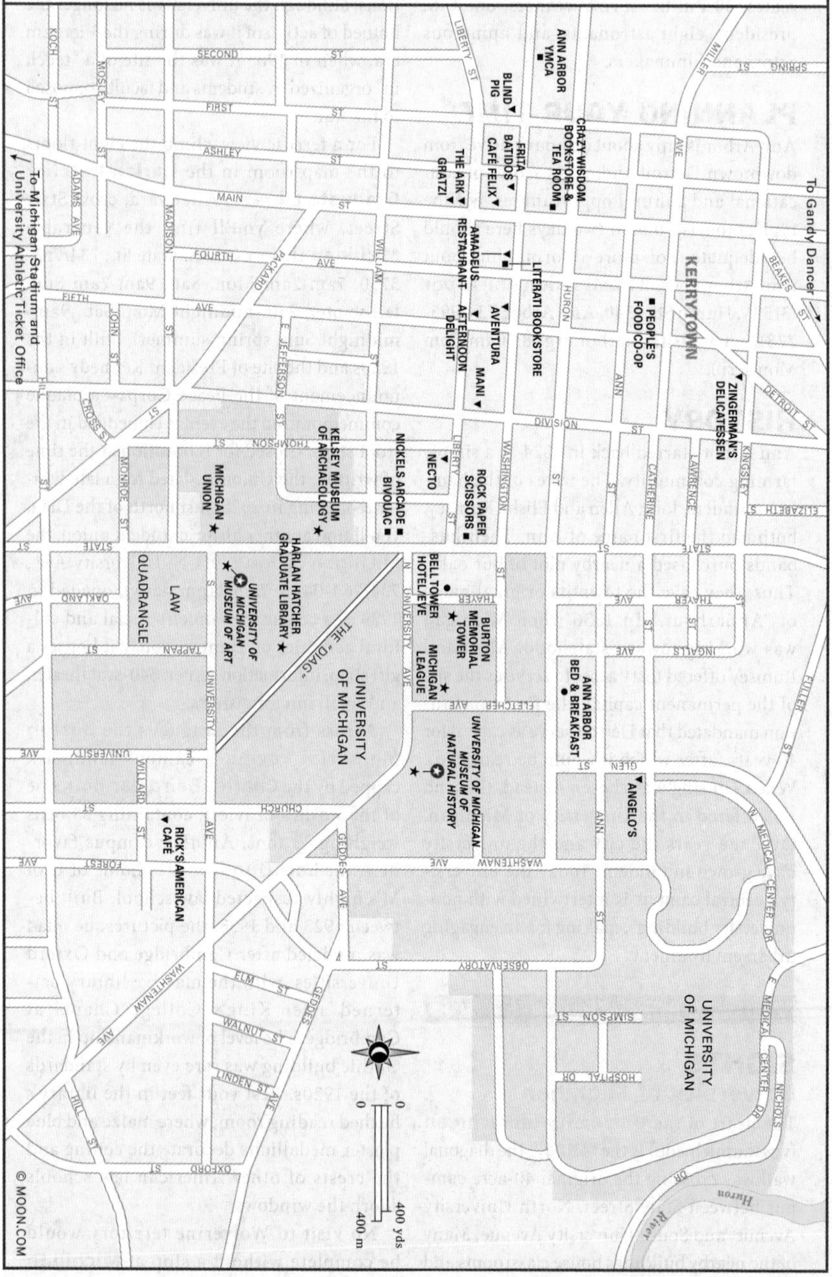
ANN ARBOR YMCA
BLIND PIG
CRAZY WISDOM BOOKSTORE & TEA ROOM
FRITA BATIDOS
CAFÉ FELIX
THE ARK
GRATZI
AMADEUS RESTAURANT
LITERATI BOOKSTORE
AFTERNOON DELIGHT
AVENTURA
MANI
PEOPLE'S FOOD CO-OP
KERRYTOWN
ZINGERMAN'S DELICATESSEN
To Gandy Dancer
To Michigan Stadium and University Athletic Ticket Office
KELSEY MUSEUM OF ARCHAEOLOGY
MICHIGAN UNION
NICKELS ARCADE
BIVOUAC
NECTO
ROCK PAPER SCISSORS
HARLAN HATCHER GRADUATE LIBRARY
UNIVERSITY OF MICHIGAN MUSEUM OF ART
LAW QUADRANGLE
THE "DIAG"
UNIVERSITY OF MICHIGAN
BELL TOWER HOTEL/EVE
BURTON MEMORIAL TOWER
MICHIGAN LEAGUE
UNIVERSITY OF MICHIGAN MUSEUM OF NATURAL HISTORY
ANN ARBOR BED & BREAKFAST
ANGELO'S
RICK'S AMERICAN CAFÉ
UNIVERSITY OF MICHIGAN
Huron River
SECOND ST
FIRST ST
ASHLEY ST
MAIN ST
FOURTH AVE
FIFTH AVE
DIVISION ST
STATE
THAYER
INGALLS
FLETCHER AVE
GLEN ST
WASHTENAW AVE
OBSERVATORY ST
SIMPSON ST
HOSPITAL DR
ELIZABETH ST
THOMPSON ST
MONROE ST
OAKLAND AVE
TAPPAN ST
E UNIVERSITY AVE
CHURCH ST
FOREST AVE
GEDDES AVE
ELM ST
WALNUT ST
LINDEN ST
OXFORD ST
HILL ST
WILLARD
N UNIVERSITY AVE
LIBERTY ST
WILLIAM
PACKARD
E JEFFERSON
MADISON
JOHN ST
CROSS ST
KOCH
MOSLEY ST
ADAMS AVE
HURON
WASHINGTON
CATHERINE
LAWRENCE
KINGSLEY
ANN
DETROIT ST
BEAKES ST
MILLER AVE
SPRING ST
FULLER ST
W MEDICAL CENTER DR
E MEDICAL CENTER DR
NICHOLS
0 400 yds
0 400 m
© MOON.COM

Stadium on Stadium Boulevard and South Main Street. The largest collegiate stadium in the United States, it draws more than 105,000 fans for home games and post-game tailgating parties. Constructed in 1927, this historic stadium has remained open and active ever since, even during a much-needed renovation that was completed in 2010.

★ University of Michigan Museum of Natural History

U of M has long been a leading research institution, and over the years has accumulated several extensive collections housed in the university's exceptional museums. The **University of Michigan Museum of Natural History** (Biological Sciences Bldg., 1105 N. University Ave., 734/764-0478, www.lsa.umich.edu, 9am-5pm Fri.-Wed., 9am-8pm Thurs., free, but donations accepted) is one of the best natural science museums in the country, with displays on prehistoric life, dinosaurs, anthropology, evolution, Native Americans, Michigan wildlife, and geology. In 2019 the museum relocated to its present site featuring a number of interactive exhibits plus a Planetarium and Dome Theatre.

★ University of Michigan Museum of Art

Among the top 10 U.S. university art museums, the **University of Michigan Museum of Art** (525 S. State St., 734/764-0395, www.umma.umich.edu, 11am-5pm Tues.-Sat., noon-5pm Sun., free, $10 suggested donation) has a permanent collection of more than 15,000 regularly rotated pieces, including works by major names like Picasso, Miró, and Cézanne. Masterpieces include Max Beckmann's *Begin the Beguine,* Monet's *The Break-up of the Ice,* and an especially strong collection of Whistler prints. The knowledgeable staff work hard to make art more accessible and relevant, with a high-caliber museum shop, enthusiastic docents, and a weekly series of gallery talks, art videos, and slide lectures. In March 2009, the museum completed a massive renovation of its historic home, Alumni Memorial Hall, and unveiled a 53,000-square-foot expansion dedicated to its lead benefactors Maxine and Stuart Frankel.

University Gardens

For collections of a more natural kind, stroll through the University of Michigan's lovely gardens. The **Matthaei Botanical Gardens** (1800 N. Dixboro Rd., 734/647-7600, www.lsa.

Angel Hall, University of Michigan

umich.edu/mbg, grounds 10am-8pm daily, conservatory 10am-4:30pm Mon.-Tues. and Thurs.-Sun., 10am-8pm Wed., free) is an ideal place for a nature walk. In addition to an expansive conservatory of tropical, warm-temperate, and desert plants, you'll find picturesque gardens, several nature trails, and a recreated prairie.

The **Nichols Arboretum** (1610 Washington Heights Rd., 734/647-7600, www.lsa.umich.edu/mbg, 8am-6pm daily, free) offers some of the area's best hiking trails and a natural area that serves as an education and research facility for the university. It's located next to the central campus and offers more than 400 identified tree species, a variety of plant collections, and a lush peony garden which blooms in early summer.

Other Sights

The **Ann Arbor Hands-On Museum** (220 E. Ann St., 734/995-5439, www.aahom.org, 10am-5pm Mon., Wed., Fri.-Sat., 9am-5pm Tues., 10am-8pm Thurs., noon-5pm Sun., $12.50, under age 2 free) is a wonderful place for kids to learn and have fun. A host of interactive exhibits covering nature, evolution, and human biology will keep youngsters entertained while they learn.

WSG Gallery (306 S. Main St., 734/761-2287, noon-6pm Tues.-Thurs., noon-9pm Fri.-Sat., noon-5pm Sun, free) offers monthly rotating exhibits from a roster of talented artists representing various media: paintings (abstract, landscape, watercolor), sculpture (ceramic, cast bronze), plus paper arts, jewelry, photography, and more.

The **Gerald R. Ford Presidential Library** (1000 Beal Ave., 734/205-0555, www.ford.utexas.edu, 8:45am-4:45pm Mon.-Fri., free) is an enormous collection of letters, reports, photographs, televised campaign commercials, audiotapes of speeches, and other archival materials. The library and the Gerald R. Ford Museum in Grand Rapids are one institution under the management of the National Archives and Records Administration, not the University of Michigan.

RECREATION

★ College Sports

If you're a sports fan visiting Ann Arbor during the fall football season, you might want to catch a U of M Wolverines game, which can be a rousing all-day affair. For information about tickets and schedules—or for details about any university sporting event, from baseball to ice hockey—contact the **University of**

Nichols Arboretum, University of Michigan

Michigan Athletics Ticket Office (1000 S. State St., 734/764-0247, www.mgoblue.com, 8:30am-5pm Mon.-Fri.). Although the Wolverines have posted disappointing results of late, the ironclad commitment of their loyal fan base assures that every home game is a loud, boisterous affair. In winter, the basketball team playing at nearby Crisler Arena enjoys a similar following.

Biking

Ann Arbor prides itself on being a bike- and pedestrian-friendly city. In fact, besides being a means of recreation, biking has evolved into a bona fide alternate mode of transportation. Dedicated bike lanes are clearly marked in urban areas, but if you're looking for a long ride in an idyllic setting, check out the **Border-to-Border Trail** (www.washtenaw.org), a 40-mile (and growing) nonmotorized path that runs along the east perimeter of Ann Arbor and continues southeasterly toward Ypsilanti. The route begins at Bandemer Park near the junction of M-14 and U.S. 23. From there, the rider is treated to stunning views of the Huron River while pedaling through shady woods. For use of a bicycle, check out **ArborBike** (www.arborbike.net), a network of convenient bike rental stations near the U of M central campus. A one-day rental pass is only $8.

Golf

Want to hit the links while in Ann Arbor? Head to the conveniently located **Leslie Park** (2120 Traver Rd., www.a2gov.org, daily, May 1-mid-Nov., $25 or $41 with cart). Designed in the 1960s by golf course architect E. Lawrence Packard, this 18-hole facility was named the number one municipal course in Michigan in 2009 by *Golf Digest*. *Michigan Golfer* has commented that Leslie Park is "a must play in Southeast Michigan." **Huron Hills** (3465 E. Huron River Dr.) is Leslie Park's sister course. It offers a terrific view of the Huron River.

ENTERTAINMENT AND EVENTS

Nightlife

Like many college towns, Ann Arbor offers eclectic nightlife. The **Blind Pig** (208 S. 1st St., 734/996-8555, www.blindpigmusic.com) was one of the first clubs outside Seattle to give Nirvana a boost; besides rock-and-roll the cool space features reggae and blues artists. The city's gay community convenes weekly for Pride Friday at the New York-style **Necto** (516 E. Liberty, 734/994-5436, www.necto.com, 9pm-2am Thurs.-Mon.), a dance club that features a different theme each night, including industrial and top 40.

One of the best known of Ann Arbor's clubs is **The Ark** (316 S. Main St., 734/761-1818, www.a2ark.org), a 400-seat venue that has been hosting local, national, and international acoustic performers since 1965, including Pete Seeger, Arlo Guthrie, and Michigan's own Jeff Daniels. The club moved to larger digs on South Main Street in the former Kline's Department Store in 1996, but the number one priority of attracting the very best folk talent remains unchanged.

No college town is complete without a good brewpub. The **Grizzly Peak Brewing Company** (120 W. Washington St., 734/741-7325, www.grizzlypeak.net, 11am-11pm Sun.-Thurs., 11am-midnight Fri.-Sat., dinner entrées $10-14) does both beer and food equally well, which is not universal among brewpubs. Creatively named libations such as Annie's Spring Elixir and Final Repose Ale complement a menu that goes beyond the normal bar fare to include chicken bruschetta pizza, a vegetable hummus wrap, and a smoked turkey sandwich with gouda. There's also an extensive menu of gluten-free options.

Looking for that perfect place to catch the game and hang out? Try **The Haymaker Public House** (203 E. Washington St., 734/997-5399, www.haymakerpublichouse.com, 11am-2am Fri.-Sat., noon-10am Sun., 11:30pm-midnight Mon.-Thurs., $11-22). This friendly watering hole offers 15 TVs showing the action, and 24 rotating craft beers on tap. The food menu includes some unusual finds, like brisket and waffle poutine and caprese chicken. Weeknights are variously dedicated to trivia, poker, and karaoke.

If you're looking for a watering hole that takes an especially sophisticated approach to the mixing of potent potables, stop by the **Alley Bar** (112 W. Liberty St., 734/662-8757, www.alleybarannarbor.com, 7pm-2am daily, drinks $10-12). The location has been functioning as a bar for over 130 years. While the beer selection is impressive, it's in the cocktail department where their expertise really shines. Innovative drinks such as the Kentucky Mule (bourbon, mint, lemon, and ginger beer) share menu space with 19 variations of scotch and numerous varieties of whiskey (rye, Tennessee, bourbon, and Irish). There's a DJ spinning the latest tunes.

Another good brewpub choice is the **Jolly Pumpkin Café and Brewery** (311 S. Main St., 734/913-2730, www.jollypumpkin.com, 11am-midnight Mon.-Thurs., 11am-2am Fri., 10am-2am Sat., 10am-midnight Sun., dinner entrées $14-16). The Jolly Pumpkin serves up some tempting craft beers, the names of which have a quasi-Halloween theme: Jolly Pumpkin Barn Biere, Jolly Pumpkin Oro De Calabaza, and Jolly Pumpkin Sour Ale. They also offer their in-house beers in bottles, something unusual for a brewpub. Full lunch and dinner menus feature salads, sandwiches, and granite-baked pizza.

The Arts

The University of Michigan's School of Music, Theater and Dance offers numerous productions. Contact the **University Musical Society** (UMS, 734/764-2538, www.ums.org), which oversees a wide assortment of choral and chamber concerts, dance and theatrical performances, jazz and piano series, and family-friendly shows. Performances take place at venues throughout the campus, including the **Lydia Mendelssohn Theatre** (911 N. University Ave.), the **Hill Auditorium** (825 N. University Ave.), and the **Power Center for the Performing Arts** (121 Fletcher St.).

Festivals and Events

For three weeks each summer, usually mid-June-early July, the **Ann Arbor Summer Festival** (734/764-2538, www.a2sf.org) presents a diverse array of concerts, dance performances, comedy routines, films, exhibitions, parties, and other activities throughout town. The festival, a beloved community tradition for over 35 years, features an eclectic mix of performers, which has included Aretha Franklin, Garrison Keillor, Willie Nelson, and Bonnie Raitt.

Another longtime summer event is the **Ann Arbor Art Fair** (https://www.annarbor.org, 10am-9pm Thurs.-Sat., noon-6pm Sun.), usually the third week of July. The annual event is actually four separate fairs that go on simultaneously: the Ann Arbor Street Art Fair, the Ann Arbor Summer Art Fair, the State Street Art Fair, and Ann Arbor's South University Art Fair. Each has its own traditions but observe the same hours and policies. The oldest of the four fairs dates to 1960, with the others debuting soon after. The fairs lure an impressive collective of painters, photographers, sculptors, woodworkers, jewelry makers, and other artists from around the world to the streets of downtown Ann Arbor.

SHOPPING

Downtown

The area along **State Street** serves as the commercial strip for the main campus, with a diverse mix of coffeehouses, bookstores, and urbane boutiques. A standout is the historic 1915 **Nickels Arcade,** a small European-style arcade filled with ever-changing boutiques and galleries between State and Maynard Streets. One longtime favorite is **Bivouac** (336 S. State St., 734/761-6207, www.bivouacannarbor.com, 10am-9pm Mon.-Fri., 10am-7pm Sat., noon-5pm Sun.), the resource for Ann Arbor-area campers, hikers, climbers, and skiers.

More shopping is concentrated on and around **Main Street** (www.mainstreetannarbor.org) in the city's traditional downtown. Once a mainstay of longtime German businesses, it has since become a stylish place for browsing, people-watching, and noshing.

Independent bookstores, while still rare, are enjoying a comeback. Few stores fulfill their mission better than **Literati Bookstore** (124 E. Washington St., 734/585-5567, https://literatibookstore.com, 10am-9pm Mon.-Thurs., 10am-10pm Fri.-Sat., 10am-7pm Sun.). In their shop, owners Mike and Hilary Gustafson seek to revive the passion for books for which independent bookstores were traditionally known. They take their goal seriously, hosting book clubs, poetry nights, and other special events.

A less mainstream shop is **Crazy Wisdom Bookstore and Tearoom** (114 S. Main St., 734/665-2757, www.crazywisdom.net, 11am-9pm Mon.-Thurs., 11am-11pm Fri., 10am-11pm Sat., noon-8pm Sun.). This store specializes in New Age titles and complements its offerings with Tea and Tunes (8:30pm Fri.-Sat., no cover charge). You'll also find art, jewelry, and crystals.

A great place to find that quirky gift is **Rock Paper Scissors** (216 S. Main St., 734/531-6264, www.rockpaperscissorsshop.com, 11am-6pm Sun.-Mon., 11am-8pm Tues.-Thurs., 10am-10pm Fri.-Sat.). Here is where you'll find a universe of cool and creative gifts, including items for the home and kitchen, exquisite paper goods, and more.

Kerrytown District

Once forlorn and forgotten, this old commercial strip north of downtown is enjoying its second go-round as a retail district, boasting the impressive **Peoples Food Co-op** (216 N. 4th Ave., 734/994-9174, www.peoplesfood.coop, 7am-9pm Mon.-Sat., 8am-9pm Sun.), Ann Arbor's only community-owned grocery store. Two other popular shopping options are the colorful if pricey open-air **Ann Arbor Farmers Market** (315 Detroit St., 734/994-6255, www.a2gov.org/market, 7am-3pm Wed. and Sat. May-Dec., 8am-3pm Sat. Jan.-Apr.), where early risers will find the finest flowers and produce, and, at the same location, the **Ann Arbor Artisan Market** (315 Detroit St., 734/913-9622, www.artisanmarket.org, 11am-4pm Sun. Apr.-late Dec.), a great place for arts and crafts lovers.

Top restaurants and interesting indoor shops also lure visitors into the **Kerrytown**

Nickels Arcade

Market & Shops (415 N. 5th Ave., 734/662-5008, www.kerrytown.com), where you can browse through boutiques such as **Mudpuddles Toys,** a kids' store featuring puppets, wildlife mobiles, award-winning games, and other delights; the destination for the wine aficionado, **Everyday Wines** offering wines from around the world; the 5,000-square-foot **Hollander's,** the premier place for decorative paper and bookbinding supplies; and **V2V,** offering a unique selection of contemporary women's apparel and home items. For more information about this one-of-a-kind shopping district, contact the **Kerrytown District Association** (www.kerrytown.org).

FOOD

Along with surrounding Washtenaw County, Ann Arbor is home to more than 275 restaurants, a number seldom found in comparably sized cities.

Downtown

Reliable choices in downtown Ann Arbor include **Afternoon Delight** (251 E. Liberty St., 734/665-7513, www.afternoondelightcafe.com, 8am-3pm Mon.-Sat., 8:30am-3pm Sun., $4-10), an ideal spot for homemade soups, deli sandwiches, and tempting desserts, and **Amadeus Restaurant** (122 E. Washington St., 734/665-8767, www.amadeusrestaurant.com, 11:30am-2:30pm and 5pm-10pm Tues.-Thurs., 11:30am-2:30pm and 5pm-11pm Fri., 11:30am-11pm Sat., 11am-3pm Sun., $15-24), a cozy European-inspired café and patisserie that features hearty Polish, central European, and vegetarian entrées.

Aventura (216 E. Washington St., 734/369-3153, www.aventuraannarbor.com, 3pm-midnight daily, $10-45) offers Spanish cuisine, traditionally underrepresented in the United States. Here you'll find a complete array of food from the Iberian Peninsula, such as *cochinillo* (suckling pig with black lentils and apricot) and *setas* (mushrooms, spiced goat cheese, olive oil and arugula).

A Cuban establishment is another Michigan rarity. **Frita Batidos** (117 W. Washington St., 734/761-2882, www.fritabatidos.com, 11am-11pm Sun.-Wed., 11am-midnight Thurs.-Sat., $15-30) is such a place. The menu here is à la carte: pick your *frita* (a Cuban-style burger made of chicken, beef, or fish), then your batidos (a tropical milkshake), such as hibiscus or coconut cream, and finally your sides, with choices such as garlic-cilantro fries or crisped plantains.

artists from around the nation exhibit their work at the Ann Arbor Art Fair

Another nearby favorite is ★ **Gratzi** (326 S. Main St., 734/663-6387, www.gratzirestaurant.com, 4pm-10pm Mon.-Thurs., noon-11pm Fri.-Sat., noon-9pm Sun., $9-30), serving up northern Italian fare in a vintage 1920s theater. For the best view of the large Bacchanalian murals, sit in the balcony. Another noteworthy Italian option is **Mani** (341 E. Liberty St., 734/769-6700, www.maniosteria, 11:30am-10pm Tues.-Thurs., 11:30am-11pm Fri., noon-11pm Sat., 11am-9pm Sun., $9-20). The menu features wood fired pizza and handcrafted pasta.

North of Downtown

Ann Arbor has a strong affinity for dedicated breakfast restaurants. If you're an early riser, be sure to check out **The Broken Egg** (221 N. Main St., 734/662-5340, 7am-3pm Mon.-Sat., 8am-3 pm Sun., $7-12). Hearty breakfast fare such as oatmeal, Canadian bacon, and honey cured ham are among the offerings.

Kerrytown District

Head a few blocks into the Kerrytown District, where you shouldn't miss ★ **Zingerman's Delicatessen** (422 Detroit St., 734/663-3354, www.zingermansdeli.com, 7am-9pm daily, $12-21), a story in itself. Gastronomes and food critics alike consider this New York-style deli the best in the Midwest. Most head for the deli counter, offering more than 100 sandwiches, side salads, and fragrant imported cheeses. The grocery side of the store has homemade breads and surrounding shelves stocked with the best of everything, from jams to olive oils. The grocery counter is busiest on weekday mornings, after work, and all day on weekends; the sandwich area is mobbed for lunch and dinner. Consider calling ahead to have your order waiting, and plan on eating at the relaxed Zingerman's Next Door, where you can linger over a meal.

Around the University of Michigan

If you're looking for a more-than-decent breakfast spot near campus, consider **Angelo's** (1100 E. Catherine St., 734/761-8996, www.angelosa2.com, 6am-3pm Mon.-Sat., 7am-2pm Sun. fall-spring, 6am-2pm Mon.-Sat., 7am-2pm Sun. summer, $8-15), the hands-down favorite for their famous deep-fried French toast, made with homemade raisin bread and loaded with fresh berries. Since 1956, Angelo's has been an Ann Arbor mainstay and was even immortalized by local folk singer Dick Siegel in his song "Angelo's."

A sophisticated dining experience awaits at the ★ **Gandy Dancer** (401 Depot St., 734/769-0592, www.muer.com, 11am-10pm Mon.-Thurs., 11am-11pm Fri., 3:30pm-11pm Sat., 10am-9pm Sun., $25-50), part of the Muer seafood restaurant chain. Housed inside the restored 1886 Michigan Central Depot, this elegant restaurant showcases creative seafood dishes like grilled Tuscan swordfish and grilled halibut panzanella. The delectable Sunday brunch features live jazz.

ACCOMMODATIONS

Under $150

Lodgings in Ann Arbor aren't as varied as the entertainment or dining options. Most are very visible chain hotels on your way into town. The 223-room **Holiday Inn** (3600 Plymouth Rd., 734/769-9800, www.ichotelsgroup.com, $124-220 d) has an indoor pool, a fitness center, a beauty salon, laundry facilities, and high-speed Internet access, plus convenient in-room coffeemakers and irons. A more affordable option is the **Comfort Inn & Suites** (3501 S. State St., 844/491-7949, www.comfortinn.com, $80-157 d), which offers 50 comfortable rooms, an indoor pool and exercise room, free wireless Internet access, and other basic amenities. You'll also find two more Holiday Inn Express locations and one additional Comfort Inn in the Ann Arbor Area.

On the eastern edge of town, the **Wyndham Garden Hotel** (2900 Jackson Ave., 734/249-6157, www.wyndham.com, $80-130 d), a full-service hotel, provides an indoor-outdoor pool, a sauna, a fitness center, a restaurant and lounge, cable TV, Internet access, and abundant free parking.

Budget-conscious travelers will appreciate the **University Inn** (2424 E. Stadium Blvd., 734/971-8000 or 877/971-8001, www.universityinnannarbor.com, $49-89 d), which offers included continental breakfast, comfortable rooms with wireless Internet access, and convenient shopping at the adjacent Lamp Post Plaza.

$150-300

For a unique option, consider the intimate ★ **Bell Tower Hotel** (300 S. Thayer St., 734/769-3010, www.belltowerhotel.com, $197-247 d), with 66 rooms and suites right in the middle of campus. It's a surprisingly elegant place, with accommodations decorated in a crisp, traditional English style.

There's also the elegant ★ **Sheraton Ann Arbor** (3200 Boardwalk Dr., 734/996-0600, www.marriott.com, $165-250 d), with a fitness center, a sauna, a heated pool, a gift shop, a small plates restaurant, and 197 tasteful guest rooms.

For history buffs, the restored ★ **Stone Chalet Bed & Breakfast Inn** (1917 Washtenaw Ave., 734/417-7223, www.stonechalet.com, $189-269 d) promises more than just 10 old-fashioned rooms. Each has its own bath, Internet access, and included deluxe breakfast. The stone chalet was built by Dean Meyer in 1917 and was a Unitarian parsonage before becoming a sophisticated cultural retreat, a favorite among artists and scholars.

Another bed-and-breakfast option is the **Ann Arbor Bed & Breakfast** (921 E. Huron St., 734/994-9100, www.annarborbedandbreakfast.com, $149-199 d). Just steps from some of the university's finest entertainment venues, the inn features hearty breakfasts, wireless Internet access, and free parking. Two of the guest studios even come with kitchenettes.

INFORMATION AND SERVICES

For more information about Ann Arbor, contact the **Ann Arbor Area Convention & Visitors Bureau** (315 W. Huron St., Ste. 340, 734/995-7281, www.annarbor.org, 8:30am-5pm Mon.-Fri.) or the **Ann Arbor Ypsilanti Regional Chamber of Commerce** (2010 Hogback Rd., Ste. 4, Ann Arbor, 734-665-4433, www.a2ychamber.org, 9am-5pm Mon.-Fri.). For local news and entertainment, consult ***mlive*** (www.mlive.com) or **WCBN** (88.3 FM, www.wcbn.org), the University of Michigan's student-run radio station.

Ann Arbor is of sufficient size to offer all the services required by travelers, from grocery stores to banks to pharmacies. Ann Arbor is also a terrific place for free wireless Internet access, so find a coffee shop, such as **Café Verde** (216 N. 4th Ave., 734/302-7032, www.peoplesfood.coop, 8am-10pm daily) for your online needs.

For medical assistance, consult the **University of Michigan Health System** (1500 E. Medical Center Dr., 734/936-4000, www.med.umich.edu).

GETTING THERE AND AROUND

Reaching Ann Arbor is easy due to its central location. Both **Amtrak** (325 Depot St., 800/872-7245, www.amtrak.com) and **Greyhound** (116 W. Huron St., 734/662-5511 or 800/231-2222, www.greyhound.com) serve the city. You can fly into **Detroit Metropolitan-Wayne County Airport** (DTW, I-94 and Merriman Rd., Detroit, 734/247-7678, www.metroairport.com), rent a vehicle from one of the national car rental agencies, and head west on I-94 to Ann Arbor, a 26-mile trip that, in light traffic, will take about 30 minutes. **Metro Airport Taxi** (800/745-5191, www.metro-airport-taxi.com) costs $52-69 for a trip between the airport and Ann Arbor. **Detroit Metro Airport Taxi** (248/214-6823, www.metrotaxidetroit.com) is another good option.

The best way to reach Ann Arbor from downtown Detroit is via I-94 (the Edsel Ford Expressway). Enter the freeway westbound and exit at State Street. Turn right and proceed north for five miles to downtown Ann Arbor.

Driving from Flint, take I-69 to I-75, continue onto U.S. 23 and M-14, and follow the U.S. 23 Business Route to Ann Arbor, a 55-mile trip that will take about an hour. From Chicago, take I-90 and I-94, passing through Kalamazoo, Battle Creek, Marshall, and Jackson, a 240-mile trip that requires 3.5 hours. Part of I-90 serves as the Indiana Toll Road.

Unlike most cities, the freeways don't enter Ann Arbor but rather circle its perimeter. The payoff is the beautiful and unscarred city and campus that so many enjoy. Ann Arbor is a walking town, and there's a reliable public bus system, the **Ann Arbor Transportation Authority** (734/996-0400 or 734/973-6500, www.theride.org, $1.50 adults, $0.75 ages 6-18, seniors and under age 6 free), which delivers passengers around the main campus as well as farther afield. **Amazing Blue Taxi** (734/846-0007, www.amazingbluetaxi.com) offers service around the greater Ann Arbor area.

Driving, watch for the easy-access parking garages throughout the city. There's also plenty of street parking available, but note that the city strictly enforces its parking ordinances. Bring plenty of change for the parking meters and read the signs carefully.

Ypsilanti

Not far from Ann Arbor is the community of Ypsilanti (Ip-sil-AN-ti). Besides being the home of **Eastern Michigan University** (EMU, 734/487-1849, www.emich.edu), Ypsilanti features two unique museums. The **Michigan Firehouse Museum** (110 W. Cross St., 734/547-0663, www.michiganfirehousemuseum.org, noon-4pm Thurs.-Sun., $5 adults, $3 ages 5-16, under age 5 free) offers a look at Michigan's firefighting history while also promoting fire safety and prevention. The **Ypsilanti Historical Museum** (220 N. Huron St., 734/482-4990, www.ypsilantihistoricalsociety.org, 2pm-5pm Tues.-Sun., free) provides a glimpse of Ypsilanti's history since its founding in 1832.

But without question the most significant point of interest in Ypsilanti is the **Yankee Air Museum** (47884 D St., Belleville, 734/483-5076, www.yankeeairmuseum.org, 10am-4pm Tues.-Sat., 11am-4pm Sun., $12 adults, $8 ages 3-17, over age 64, military, and veterans, under age 2 free). On the grounds of Willow Run Airport, the museum documents the history of U.S. military aviation from World War II through the Vietnam War. Fascinating exhibits and authentic military memorabilia tell the story of how the "Arsenal of Democracy," as Detroit was once known, proved essential to the Allied victory in World War II. The museum even maintains a working fleet of vintage military aircraft that can be hired for a personal flight.

The museum's location is significant: During World War II, Willow Run was the site of a mammoth plant operated by Ford Motor Company that mass-produced the B-24 Liberator Bomber for the war effort in Europe. The plant, which was on the opposite side of the airport, was recently demolished—except for the small portion from which the finished planes would exit. Museum officials raised the funds necessary to purchase the building and are now working to restore it as a new home for the museum.

Also in Ypsilanti, you'll find the **Riverside Arts Center** (76 N. Huron St., 734/480-2787, www.riversidearts.org, program times vary, gallery hours 3pm-8pm Thurs.-Fri., noon-5pm Sat.), a venue for cultural events, principally different styles of dance and the visual arts. For a bite to eat, visit **Aubree's Pizzeria & Tavern** (39 E. Cross St., 734/483-1870, www.aubrees.com, 11am-2am Mon.-Sat., noon-2am Sun., $7-17), which offers a variety of pizzas and calzones.

For more information about the Ypsilanti area, consult the **Ypsilanti Area Convention & Visitors Bureau** (106 W. Michigan Ave., 734/483-4444, www.ypsireal.com). To reach the town, take Washtenaw Avenue from Ann Arbor; the eight-mile trip takes about 18 minutes.

Chelsea

Considered by many to be little more than a trendy suburb of neighboring Ann Arbor, Chelsea has begun to make a name for itself thanks to a big-name Hollywood star who still resides in this picturesque little town.

★ PURPLE ROSE THEATRE COMPANY

When he's not appearing on Broadway or making a film, actor Jeff Daniels eschews Hollywood glitz for his hometown of Chelsea. Despite an exhausting work schedule, Daniels keeps busy with the **Purple Rose Theatre Company** (137 Park St., 734/433-7673, www.purplerosetheatre.org, $25-43), which he founded in 1991, naming it after the Woody Allen film *The Purple Rose of Cairo,* in which he'd starred six years earlier. This critically acclaimed regional playhouse features original plays, some written by Daniels himself, as well as American classics such as *The Odd Couple* and *Morning's at Seven.*

After catching a show at this landmark theater, head to the town's other big attraction: **The Common Grill** (112 S. Main St., 734/475-0470, www.commongrill.com, 11am-10pm Tues.-Thurs., 11am-11pm Fri.-Sat., 11am-9pm Sun., $10-36), a superb restaurant founded in 1991 by former employees of Detroit's Chuck Muer restaurant chain. Seafood dominates the menu, but there are a few meat options as well. The Grill helped put Chelsea on the map, and wait times easily reach two hours on weekends. Folks come for the signature fish dishes and the chic yet comfortable atmosphere, which includes painted Hopperesque scenes

the Purple Rose Theatre in Chelsea, founded by Jeff Daniels

of old Chelsea (including the Jiffy Baking Company's tower) on the exposed brick walls.

WATERLOO RECREATION AREA

Sprawling across two counties and some 20,000 acres, the **Waterloo Recreation Area** (16345 McClure Rd., 734/475-8307, www.michigan.gov/dnr, hours vary, annual Recreation Passport required: $12 Michigan residents, $34 nonresidents, $9 day pass available to nonresidents only) is the largest state park in the Lower Peninsula. The park's landscape clearly shows evidence of the glaciers that once blanketed this part of the state. Waterloo is at the intersection of the Kalamazoo and the Missaukee moraine systems, where two glaciers collided thousands of years ago. The ice sheets ripped apart massive mountains of rock from the Canadian Shield to the north, carrying fragments with them as they moved across this part of the state—a journey one park interpreter has described as "the movement of pancake batter on a hot griddle."

The area is a pleasing patchwork of field, forest, and lake. Pick up a map at park headquarters to help you navigate around this expansive place, which contains 11 fishing lakes, several beaches and picnic areas, and miles of hiking, biking, equestrian, and cross-country skiing trails. You'll also find the year-round **Gerald E. Eddy Discovery Center,** which offers engaging exhibits about Michigan's geologic features, and the 1,000-acre **Haehnle Audubon Sanctuary,** a fall habitat for sandhill cranes.

Waterloo maintains four campgrounds ($14-28). Equestrian (for campers with horses) and Green Lake are rustic areas, with nice wooded sites. Portage Lake and Sugarloaf are large, modern campgrounds, with sites near, but not on, their namesake lakes.

INFORMATION

For more information about Chelsea, consult the **Chelsea Area Chamber of Commerce** (310 N. Main St., Ste. 120, 734/475-1145, www.chelseamichamber.org, 10am-4pm Mon.-Fri.).

GETTING THERE AND AROUND

Chelsea is about halfway between Ann Arbor and Jackson, so it's easily accessible via car. From Ann Arbor, head west on I-94 to exit 159 and follow M-52 north to Chelsea; the 17-mile trip should take 23 minutes. From Jackson, take I-94 to M-52, which leads directly to Chelsea. This 24-mile trip takes about 29 minutes. Once here, park your car and take a stroll or ride a bike through the central area of town.

The Thumb

Michigan's Lower Peninsula is hard to miss on any U.S. map. It unmistakably resembles a mitten, an apt metaphor for a state that endures such long cold winters. As with any mitten, there's a thumb-like protrusion—here, the large rural peninsula along Michigan's southeastern shore, sandwiched between Lake Huron and Saginaw Bay. Called "the Thumb" by locals and visitors alike, this flat, isolated region offers a quiet alternative to bustling Detroit.

Save for peripheral destinations like Port Huron, Frankenmuth, and the cities along I-75, much of this fertile area has been overlooked by contemporary travelers, just as many of Michigan's 19th-century settlers bypassed it in favor of seemingly better farmland elsewhere. The European immigrants who did establish the Thumb's earliest

Highlights

Look for ★ to find recommended sights, activities, dining, and lodging.

★ **Flint Cultural Center:** This impressive collection of museums and theaters presents enough options, from auto exhibits to comedy shows, to fill several days (page 106).

★ **Crossroads Village & Huckleberry Railroad:** This authentic 19th-century community offers a snapshot of long-ago rural life (page 108).

★ **Bronner's CHRISTmas Wonderland:** It doesn't matter if it's the height of summer. Stop at this enormous, eye-popping repository of holiday goodies, open year-round (page 114).

★ **Bird-Watching near Saginaw:** The Saginaw River abounds with excellent bird-watching sites, including the 9,700-acre Shiawassee National Wildlife Refuge (page 121).

★ **Diving in Lake Huron's Underwater Preserves:** Scuba divers will find over 30 major shipwrecks (page 127).

★ **Port Huron Museum:** See exhibits on arts, history, and the local marine heritage (page 129).

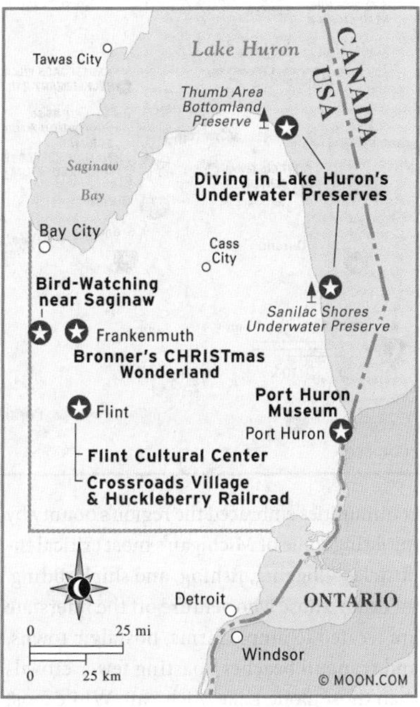

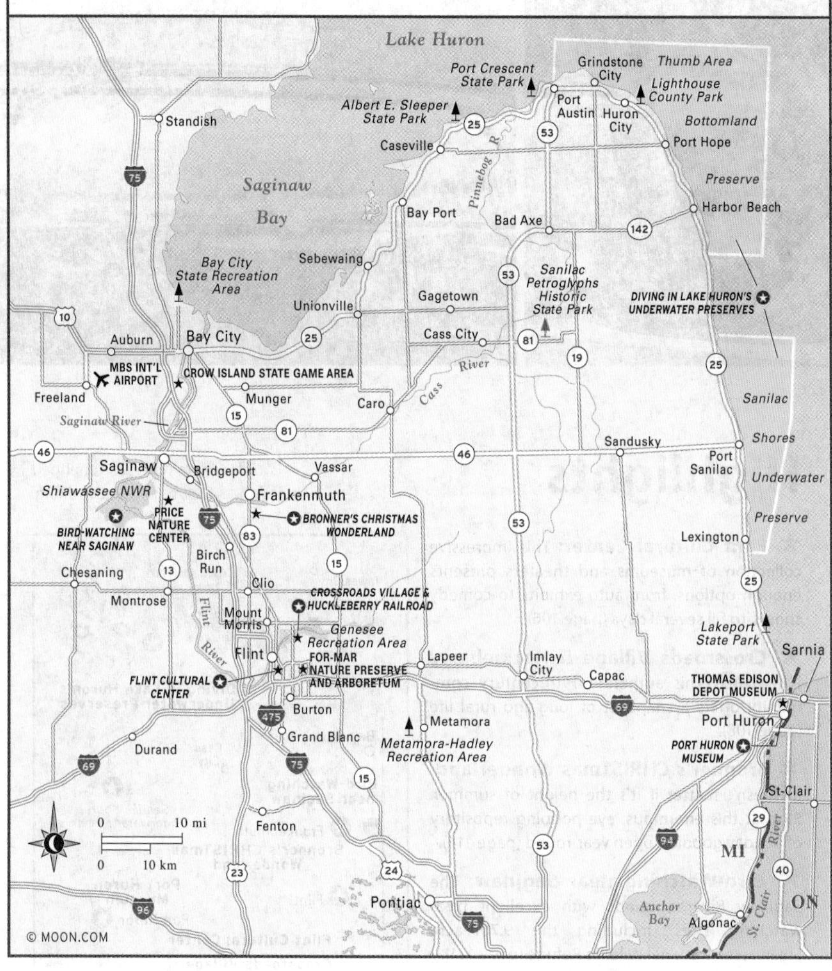

communities embraced the region's bounty by initiating some of Michigan's most critical industries—logging, fishing, and shipbuilding.

Today, those who venture off the interstate are treated to ample farms, nostalgic towns, and tranquil beaches boasting fewer crowds than those along Lake Michigan. While most visitors aim for the Bavarian-style attractions of Frankenmuth or the cultural diversions of Saginaw, the Thumb offers a wealth of other curiosities, many of which relate to the region's diverse history.

Along the Lake Huron shore lie a variety of nautical sights, including Port Huron's stunning Fort Gratiot Lighthouse, Michigan's oldest, and numerous shipwrecks that make up

Previous: the fishing pier in Harbor Beach; *Boy and Bear* sculpture by Marshall Fredericks at Saginaw Valley State University; the Blue Water Bridge linking Port Huron with Sarnia, Ontario.

the Thumb Area Bottomland Preserve. Also intriguing is Flint's Crossroads Village, a community of restored 19th-century buildings that transport visitors to a time when hoop skirts and hard work prevailed. In the Thumb's rarely visited interior is Sanilac Petroglyphs Historic State Park, south of Bad Axe, with its mysterious Native American rock carvings that were chipped into exposed sandstone up to 1,000 years ago.

Outdoor enthusiasts may especially appreciate this quiet region, where bicyclists can explore the Genesee Recreation Area, birdwatchers can view ducks and eagles at the Shiawassee National Wildlife Refuge, and anglers can board fishing charters and head out onto Lake Huron. Various annual events—from car shows to county fairs—make the Thumb an even more enticing stopover before exploring the rest of the Great Lakes State.

PLANNING YOUR TIME

Except for the communities along the I-75 corridor, the Thumb is no doubt the least visited region in Michigan's Lower Peninsula. The potential for fewer crowds, even in summer, is perhaps the area's biggest advantage.

At minimum, you should reserve three days, although a full week allows more time to experience urban hot spots, interior sites, and the Lake Huron shoreline. You could spend at least two days in each of the destinations along I-75, particularly if you plan to visit museums as well as nearby nature preserves and golf courses. Frankenmuth alone could fill a solid day with its quaint shops, historic structures, Bavarian cuisine, and year-round Christmas store. Depending on your interests, the coastal towns and interior villages can each be explored in a half day. Cultural sites are usually concentrated along the shore or within historic downtown districts, and most towns only offer one main recreation area. In fact, only one coastal locale requires multiple days—Port Huron.

Bear in mind that only the major cities, such as Saginaw, have public transit, so reaching the rest of the Thumb will require a vehicle—either your own or a rental car from one of several agencies at an airport or along I-75. Since the bulk of the Thumb's attractions lie around its perimeter, it's relatively easy to get to them via car. From Flint, I-75 leads to Bay City, from which M-25 traces the coast to Port Huron, where I-69 returns to Flint, roughly forming a 270-mile loop. This circuitous route makes it difficult to have one home base while visiting the Thumb.

view from Lake Huron shore near Port Austin

Like many regions of Michigan, the Thumb is a seasonal place. While a wintertime visit can be fun in a year-round town like Frankenmuth, many of the more isolated inns, restaurants, and attractions are only open during the summer. In addition, although most of the Thumb's towns and rural areas are relatively safe to visit, caution is advised when visiting cities like Flint. As in other urban areas, be certain to secure your belongings, avoid walking alone at night, and consult residents about other safety concerns.

For more information about the Thumb area, consult the **Thumb Area Tourism Council** (TATC, Millington, 989/673-2849, www.thumbtourism.org), **ThumbTravels.com** (P.O. Box 340, Port Austin, MI 48467, www.thumbtravels.com), **Visit Michigan's Thumb** (Harbor Beach, http://michigan-thumb.com), the **Tip of The Thumb Heritage Water Trail** (P.O. Box 92, Caseville, MI 48725, www.thumbtrails.com), and the **Huron County Economic Development Corporation** (250 E. Huron Ave., Ste. 303, Bad Axe, 989/269-6431 or 800/358-4862, www.huroncounty.ca).

HISTORY

The Thumb's original inhabitants were Native American communities, some of whom left ancient rock carvings in Sanilac County. While many European settlers had bypassed this region for the center of the Lower Peninsula, by the early 1800s some pioneers had decided to take advantage of the Thumb's resources of timber, fisheries, and fertile land, and began to establish towns like Flint, today the Thumb's largest city. Once an important river crossing on the Pontiac Trail—a link to several Native American routes crossing the wilderness—Flint owes its existence to Detroit fur trader Jacob Smith, who in 1819 persuaded the Ojibwa and Potawatomi people to surrender the lands of Saginaw County. Not long after Smith settled on the site, other colonists followed, establishing a post office, a bank, a factory, and other necessary establishments; by 1855, Flint was an incorporated city.

The Thumb's sleepy personality belies its past as one of the most productive lumber centers in the United States. During the mid-1800s, millions of logs were sent down the Saginaw River to be processed at Saginaw and Bay City. The explosion of the logging business created the need for log-hauling carts and wagons—all produced in Flint. As the timber industry prospered, profits were reinvested into the local coach-building trade, which provided the foundation for Flint's earliest automotive companies. Saginaw Bay, meanwhile, developed the state's largest commercial fishing industry as well as some of the largest shipyards ever established on the Great Lakes, industries that gradually faded away to be replaced by automotive-related concerns.

Travel by ship and by rail eventually gave way to the age of the automobile, igniting southeastern Michigan's most significant 20th-century industry. By the 1890s, Flint became known for producing road carts, followed by carriage manufacturers. Buick Motor Company was incorporated in Detroit in 1903, moved to Flint the following year, and soon began offering its first vehicles for sale.

By that time, the Thumb's timber stock was virtually depleted, forcing residents to turn to agriculture as a new source of livelihood. Today, the region's crops include fish, sugar beets, navy beans, grains, corn, and various fruits.

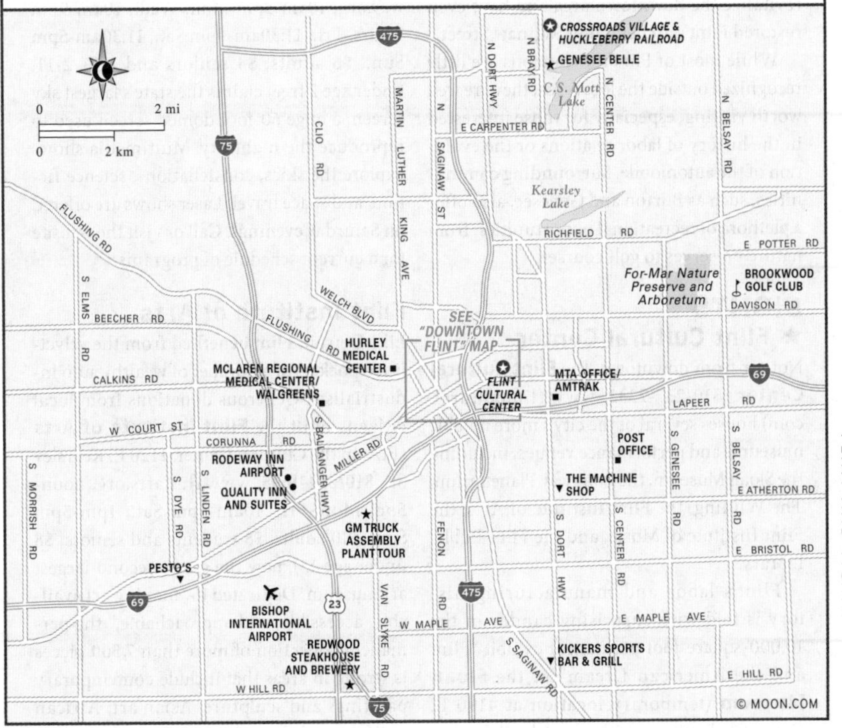

Flint and Vicinity

Flint is now, and has long been, a worker's town. For decades the city's economy was intimately linked to several local General Motors plants. As long as the factories were booming, the city did well. In this respect the city reflects the state of Michigan in microcosm. By the mid-1980s, however, increased global competition resulted in an array of plant closings, bringing mass unemployment and permanently altering the city's economic underpinnings. Independent filmmaker and native son Michael Moore documented the city and its relationship with GM in the biting satire *Roger & Me,* showing Americans images likely to haunt this weary town forever.

Despite its blue-collar image, however, Flint possesses a rich cultural life. In addition to Moore, the city boasts a long line of native artists and activists. Others include assembly-line author Ben Hamper, whose book *Rivethead* topped the *New York Times* best-seller list for several weeks in 1991; writer Edmund G. Love, author of the book *Subways Are for Sleeping;* comedienne Sandra Bernhard, perhaps best known for her stint on the sitcom *Roseanne;* actor Seamus Dever, whose most famous role has been that of Detective Kevin Ryan on *Castle;* and 1960s activist and White Panther Party founder John Sinclair. The Flint Cultural Center offers an impressive array of exhibits and live performances. Dedicated locals have also worked to revitalize the downtown area and have even restored Flint's arches along Saginaw Street.

While most of Flint's attractions are little recognized outside the local area, they are well worth visiting, especially for those interested in the history of labor relations or the evolution of the automobile. Surrounding communities, such as Burton and Genesee, also offer a plethora of recreational opportunities, from nature preserves to golf courses.

SIGHTS

★ Flint Cultural Center

Not far from downtown, the **Flint Cultural Center** (810/237-7333, www.flintcultural.com) houses several of the city's more notable museums and performance venues, including the Sloan Museum, the Longway Planetarium, The Whiting, the Flint Institute of Arts, the Flint Institute of Music, and the Flint Public Library.

Flint's labor and manufacturing history is told with surprising candor in the 10,000-square-foot permanent exhibit "Flint and the American Dream" at the **Sloan Museum** (temporary location at 4190 E. Court St., Burton, inside Courtland Center. 810/237-3450, www.sloanlongway.org, 10am-5pm Mon.-Fri., noon-5pm Sat.-Sun., $8 adults, $7 over age 59, $6 ages 2-11, under age 2 free). The museum, which focuses on local history and culture, has an impressive collection of neon signs, period clothing, classic motorcycles, and antique automobiles, including the oldest production-model Chevrolet in existence, which is worth a look even if you're not a car buff. Exhibits trace the city from Native American hunting and gathering (check out the life-size tepee), through commercial fur trapping and logging, and finally to its identity as an auto manufacturing center. A 1912 pennant promotes Good Roads Day with the slogan "No More Mud!" Currently the museum's principal location is closed for renovations. It is scheduled to reopen sometime in 2021.

The **Longway Planetarium** (1310 E. Kearsley St., 810/237-3400, www.sloanlongway.org, 10am-5pm Mon.-Wed., 10am-9pm Thurs.-Fri., 11:30am-9pm Sat., 11:30am-5pm Sun., $6 adults, $4 seniors and ages 2-11, under age 2 free) claims the state's largest sky screen, a huge 60-foot domed screen used to reproduce the night sky. Multimedia shows explore the skies, constellations, science fiction, and space travel. Laser shows are offered on Saturday evenings. Call or visit the website for a current schedule of programs.

Flint Institute of Arts

Like Detroit, Flint benefited from the velvet-lined pockets of a number of wealthy auto industrialists. Generous donations from local citizens built the **Flint Institute of Arts** (FIA, in the Cultural Center, 1120 E. Kearsley St., 810/234-1695, www.flintarts.org, noon-5pm Mon.-Fri., 10am-5pm Sat., 1pm-5pm Sun., $10 adults, $8 students and seniors, $8 under age 13), now the state's second-largest art museum. Dedicated to "making art available, accessible, and approachable," the permanent collection of more than 7,500 pieces is strong in areas that include contemporary paintings and sculpture, Asian art, African artifacts, glass paperweights, and 19th-century French paintings (predominantly landscapes), including ever-popular works by the French Impressionists. The Bray Gallery houses a fine array of European paintings, furniture, and tapestries that range from the 15th to the 18th centuries.

Buckham Gallery

In downtown Flint, the alternative artist-run **Buckham Gallery** (121 W. 2nd St., 810/239-6233, www.buckhamgallery.org, 11am-6pm Wed.-Fri., free, special event prices vary) is dedicated to showing "contemporary cutting-edge art, with no censorship or interference," making for some interesting shows. Established in 1984, the space is also often used for performance art and poetry readings.

1: the Flint Institute of the Arts **2:** downtown Flint

1
INSTITUTE OF ARTS
2
FERRIS BROS
FURS
Ladies Ready-to-Wear

Downtown Flint

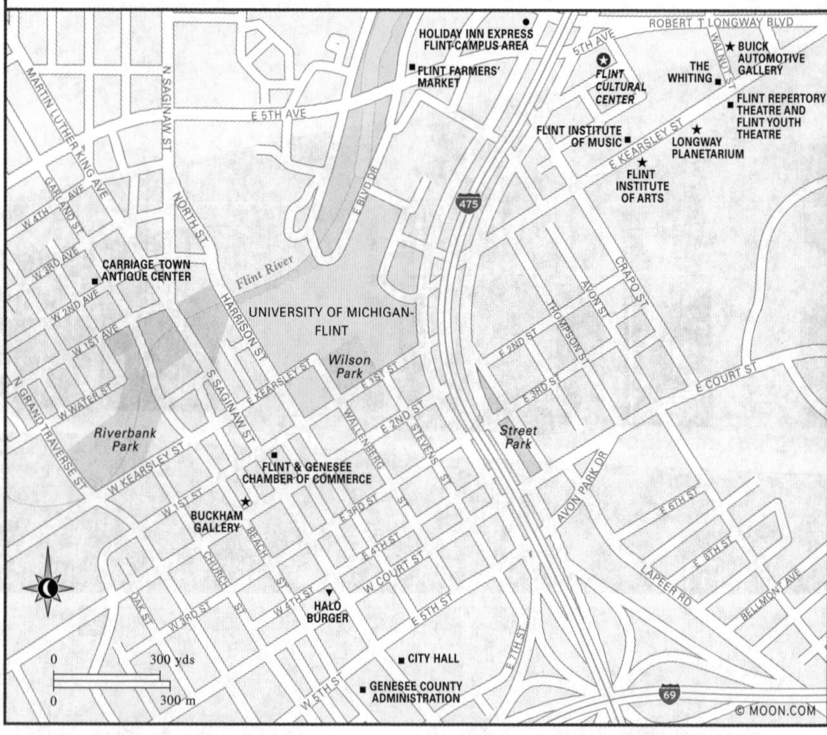

★ Crossroads Village & Huckleberry Railroad

Despite the well-documented plant closures of recent decades, the city of Flint remains a key element in GM's global manufacturing system, with several plants still operating—including a few built within the last 20 years. After seeing the city's modern factories and learning about its historic ones, you'll gain a renewed appreciation for the hardships of the early industrial age. The often hazardous working habits of the preindustrial 19th century are the focus at the **Crossroads Village & Huckleberry Railroad** (6140 Bray Rd., 800/648-7275, www.geneseecountyparks.org, 10am-5pm Wed.-Sun., village admission $10 adults, $8 ages 2-12, $9 seniors; village, train, and boat $18 adults, $14.50 ages 2-12, $17 seniors). This restored village has 35 vintage buildings that show a variety of industries, complete with the era's authentic grit, noise, and pervasive smoke. An 1836 gristmill, a sawmill, a cider mill, a print shop, a blacksmith shop, and more give visitors an idea of Genesee County in the mid-1800s. Numerous special weekend events are held throughout the year, especially during holidays. The village operates as a nonprofit and, outside of the summer months, offers themed celebrations at Halloween and Christmas.

The 40-minute ride on the Huckleberry Railroad is a treat. The narrow-gauge train, a collection of vintage wooden coaches and steam locomotives, leads guests through scenic woods and alongside lovely Mott Lake. Also nearby is the ***Genesee Belle,*** a paddle-wheel riverboat offering scenic 45-minute

The Second Motor City: Origin of the Labor Movement

While Detroit is considered the birthplace of automobile manufacturing, Flint is credited with the start of the American labor movement. As the auto industry grew during the early 20th century, workers from across the country flocked to factories in Detroit and its neighboring cities, including Flint, Saginaw, and Bay City.

By the 1920s, the industry was booming—until the Great Depression descended on the nation, causing massive job losses. In order to conserve cash, automakers demanded higher productivity while cutting wages. Autoworkers soon became disgusted with the poor working conditions, high-speed assembly lines, and the lack of job security. Using solidarity to garner more control, they began to organize.

UAW members on strike

In 1935, autoworkers established the United Automobile Workers of America (UAW), which General Motors refused to recognize as the bargaining agent for its workforce. When Flint-area workers heard about GM's plan to move production to factories where the UAW had a weaker hold, they initiated Michigan's first large-scale sit-down strike on December 30, 1936.

Continuing into the next year, the sit-down was an effective form of protest: As long as workers remained in the plant, management was unable to bring in replacements. As the weeks wore on, however, the strike resulted in severe riots that ultimately injured 16 workers and 11 police officers.

On February 11, 1937, the strike finally ended with an agreement under which GM recognized the UAW as their workers' bargaining representative. The success of the UAW inspired the birth of unions across the country, jump-starting the modern labor movement and ushering in the era of the American middle class, made possible by good wages and extensive benefits for workers throughout Michigan and the rest of the country.

It can be argued that unions today have grown as powerful, if not more so, than the car companies themselves. This fragile balance has led to new financial problems, such as the controversial government bailout of GM and Chrysler in 2009. For many, the bailout was only necessary because car companies were forced to maintain high union wages despite falling profits. Other circumstances, however, were undoubtedly contributing factors—including the slow development of alternative energy vehicles, an unsustainable number of brands and dealerships, and the launch of no-interest consumer financing plans.

cruises on Mott Lake during the summer months.

RECREATION

Parks and Preserves

The **Genesee Recreation Area** (Branch Rd., Flint, 810/736-7100, www.geneseecountyparks.org, 8am-sunset daily, free) provides a pleasant contrast to Flint's urban environment. Covering more than 4,500 acres along the Flint River off I-475, the park offers beaches, biking paths, a boat launch, a campground, fishing sites, plus hiking and horse trails.

Southeast of Flint, the 380-acre **For-Mar Nature Preserve and Arboretum** (2142 N. Genesee Rd., Burton, 810/736-7100, www.geneseecountyparks.org, 8am-sunset Wed.-Sun., buildings close at 5pm, free) includes a patchwork of woodlands, restored prairies, open fields, meadows, ponds, and Kearsley Creek as well as an arboretum planted with specimen trees, shrubs, and vines. Seven miles of up-and-down hiking trails weave through a diverse habitat. Two trails are accessible to wheelchairs. An interpretive center has a live bird-viewing area and several animal and reptile displays, including the Foote Bird Museum, which contains more than 600 stuffed and mounted specimens.

Golf

Every summer, golfers flock to Michigan for its numerous well-groomed courses, and the Flint area is no exception. Just a short drive from the city are three public 18-hole golf courses: **Brookwood Golf Club** (6045 Davison Rd., Burton, 810/742-4930, www.imarecreation.org, daily Apr.-mid-Nov., $18-30 with cart); **Captain's Club at Woodfield** (10200 Woodfield Dr., Grand Blanc, 810/695-4653, www.captainsclubatwoodfield.com, daily Apr.-Oct., $24-40 with cart); and **Fenton Farms Golf Club** (12312 Torrey Rd., Fenton, 810/629-1212, www.fentonfarms.com, daily Apr.-Oct., $31 with cart).

ENTERTAINMENT AND EVENTS

Nightlife

Though Flint isn't known for its nightlife scene, those seeking respite will find a few bars and music clubs in town. If you're looking for a casual hangout, **Kickers Sports Bar & Grill** (5577 S. Saginaw Rd., 810/695-2060, www.kickerssportsbar.com, 11am-2am Mon.-Sat., no cover) can keep you busy all night. Besides watching football, basketball, and countless other televised sports, you can play pool, darts, or video games and choose from a wide selection of draft and bottled beers, wines, and cocktails. The food's not bad either and includes bar favorites like fried pickles, loaded potato skins, and battered mushrooms as well as an assortment of salads, sandwiches, burgers, pastas, pizzas, and even ribs and fajitas. The joint also offers plenty of specials, from $0.55 chicken wings on Monday to $0.89 tacos on Tuesday, and happy-hour specials 11am-9pm daily.

If your musical tastes run a bit more hardcore, never fear. Since 2002, **The Machine Shop** (3539 S. Dort Hwy., 810/715-2650, www.themachineshop.info, 7pm-2am Mon.-Sat., 7pm-midnight Sun.) has hosted a variety of rock performers, from Blind Melon to Kid Rock.

The Arts

The **Flint Cultural Center,** a refreshing creative corner in the heart of an industrial town, houses several winning performance venues. For concerts, operas, dance shows, and Broadway musicals, reserve your seat at **The Whiting** (1241 E. Kearsley St., 810/237-7337, www.thewhiting.com), where recent programs have included *Into the Woods* as well as presentations by artists as varied as Itzhak Perlman, Jeff Daniels, and Amy Grant. Other plays and musicals are featured at the **Flint Repertory Theatre** (1220 E. Kearsley St., 810/237-1530, www.flintrep.org), and the nearby **Flint Institute of Music** (FIM, 1025 E. Kearsley St., 810/238-1350, www.thefim.com) presents concerts by the Flint Symphony Orchestra.

Fairs and Festivals

Flint-area residents don't need much of an excuse to hold an annual event, especially during the pleasant summer season. During the third weekend of June, the Flint Institute of Arts hosts the **Flint Art Fair** (810/234-1695, www.flintarts.org, adults, $5, age 12 and under free), presented on the front lawn. The fair showcases the work of over 150 contemporary artists and craftspeople from the United States, Canada, and places as far away as Bermuda. Art lovers will appreciate the chance to peruse sculpture, glasswork, photography, textiles, and fine jewelry, among other impressive treasures.

In mid-August, the five-day **Back to the Bricks Cruise Weekend** (810/232-8903, www.backtothebricks.org, free) celebrates the region's industrial roots with a parade of classic vehicles, hot rods, sports cars, vintage trucks, and customized motorcycles through downtown Flint. Also in mid-August, the **Genesee County Fair** (2188 W. Mount Morris Rd., Mount Morris, 810/687-0953, www.gcf.org, free) offers a countrified change of pace to Flint's auto-related attractions and events. For a solid week, you'll be treated to livestock shows, agricultural exhibits, pig races, pie-eating contests, and demolition derbies.

One of the area's most eagerly anticipated events is the annual **Michigan Renaissance Festival** (12600 Dixie Hwy., Holly, 248/634-5552, www.michrenfest.com, 10am-7pm Sat.-Sun. late Aug.-early Oct., $23.95 adults, $21.95 students, $21.95 over age 64, $14.95 ages 5-12), which has brought revelry and pageantry to southeastern Michigan since 1979. Over the course of seven weekends, this popular family-friendly event typically lures more than 220,000 visitors to its permanent home, a 312-acre property just 12 miles south of Flint. You'll encounter authentic costumes, roving minstrels, live performances, staged jousts, archery competitions, and human chess matches. Many attendees also appreciate the property's centerpiece: an 18-acre replica of a 16th-century village, a collection of open-air cottages featuring a variety of old-fashioned food and drinks from sugary mead to smoked turkey legs, as well as handcrafted Renaissance-style wares from pewter dishes and musical instruments to elegant capes and menacing swords. In addition to the admission charge, performers often pass a hat after their presentations; donating is at your discretion.

SHOPPING

While the Flint area is not known as an exceptional shopper's destination, there are a few stops worth a look. In a region that's well-known for its bountiful farms and orchards, it's hard to pass up a produce market. Luckily, the **Flint Farmers' Market** (300 E. 1st St., 810/232-1399, www.flintfarmersmarket.com, 9am-6pm Tues. and Thurs., 8am-5pm Sat.) is open three days a week. This storied institution returned to downtown Flint in 2014 after an absence of 70 years. Its new home is a building once occupied by a printer. In addition to produce vendors, you'll also find a bakery and a popular eatery known as Steady Eddy's, which offers a surprising number of vegetarian dishes.

For more fresh fruit and veggies, take a side trip to **Montrose Orchards** (12473 Seymour Rd., Montrose, 810/639-6971, www.montroseorchards.com, 10am-5pm Mon.-Sun., mid-May-Dec.), a family-owned farm. Besides seasonal blueberry fields, pumpkin patches, a bakery, and other market goodies, the farm offers several family-friendly activities, including hayrides.

FOOD

According to the *Flint Journal,* **Halo Burger** (810/238-4607, www.haloburger.com, hours vary, $7-12) serves up the best burgers in town, with 6 locations in the Flint area. For a livelier atmosphere, head to the ★ **Redwood Steakhouse and Brewery** (5304 Gateway Center Dr., 810/233-8000, www.redwoodsteakhouseandbrewery.com, 11am-10:30pm Mon.-Thurs., 11am-11:30pm Fri., noon-11:30pm Sat., noon-9pm Sun., $13-31), a rustic eatery that offers a fine wine selection, excellent cuisine such as seafood pasta, signature steaks, and sushi, and a lounge featuring live music.

A good choice for Italian dishes is **Pesto's** (5275 Miller Rd., 810/732-4390, www.pestos.com, 10:30am-9pm Mon.-Thurs., 10:30pm-10pm Fri.-Sat., noon-8pm Sun., $11-30), where you'll find homemade dressings, classic and creative entrées like blackened chicken Alfredo and hurricane shrimp, and desserts big enough for two.

ACCOMMODATIONS

Although most travelers tend to make day trips to the Flint area, it's possible to stay overnight, with a number of chain hotels, including the **Quality Inn and Suites** (2361 Austin Pkwy., 810/232-4222, www.comfortinn.com,

The Flint Water Crisis

Today, the tap water in Flint is safe to drink. But getting to that point has been a long, arduous road.

The water crises began in the spring of 2014, when government officials in Flint undertook a variety of efforts to deal with its persistent financial troubles. One measure included terminating its long-standing contact with the Detroit Water and Sewage Department as the source for the city's tap water. As an alternative, the city decided to draw water from the Flint River, treat it in its own filtration plant, and distribute it to residents and businesses. However, the new procedure failed to add corrosion inhibitors. The result was that the unprotected water absorbed lead leached from the interiors of the aging service lines throughout the city.

Flint Water Plant

Within a few months, the effects became evident, as tap water began emitting a foul odor and showing signs of discoloration. Medical experts cited the ill effects of consuming water with elevated levels of lead. Children were especially vulnerable to these dangers. As a stop-gap measure, the state of Michigan and various private charities shipped in truckloads of bottled water for months.

Years of investigation followed, involving the state and federal governments, and extensive litigation ensued. Meanwhile, the laborious task of replacing the lead service lines progressed. At this writing, the task is nearly complete, and Flint has resumed sourcing its water from the Detroit system.

$55-65 d) and **Holiday Inn Express Flint-Campus Area** (1150 Robert T. Longway Blvd., 810/238-7744, www.ihg.com, $100-170 d). For especially economical lodgings, try **Rodeway Inn Airport** (2325 Austin Pkwy., 810/232-7777, www.choicehotels.com, $50-80 d).

Camping

Within the Genesee Recreation Area, Genesee County operates the **Wolverine Campground** ($18-26). Located in the 2,000-acre Holloway Reservoir Regional Park, this summer-only spot has a nice setting in a pine forest, with 195 tent sites, several shower and restroom buildings, a boat launch, and a guarded swimming beach. Reservations are recommended. Contact the **Genesee County Parks and Recreation Commission** (5045 Stanley Rd., 810/736-7100 or 800/648-7275, www.geneseecountyparks.org). Lakefront sites require a minimum three-night stay.

INFORMATION AND SERVICES

Flint offers all the services that a traveler might need or want, from tourism bureaus to pharmacies. For more information about the Flint area, contact the **Flint & Genesee Chamber of Commerce** (519 S. Saginaw St., Ste. 200, 810/600-1404, www.flintandgenesee.org, 8am-5pm Mon.-Fri.). For local news and events, pick up a copy of the daily ***Flint Journal*** (www.mlive.com/flint).

For medical assistance, contact the **Hurley Medical Center** (1 Hurley Plaza, 810/262-9000, www.hurleymc.com) or the **McLaren Flint Emergency Room** (401 S. Ballenger Hwy., 810/342-2000, www.mclarenregional.org). There are several pharmacies, including a **Walgreens** (502 S. Ballenger Hwy.,

810/424-9270, www.walgreens.com, 6am-midnight daily) with extended hours. Another **Walgreens** (901 S. State Rd., Davison, 810/653-4020, www.walgreens.com, 9am-9pm) has the same pharmacy hours as the store.

Many banks have 24-hour ATMs, including **Chase** (www.chase.com) at the Hurley Medical Center, the McLaren Regional Medical Center, and the Genesee Towers (210 W. 1st St.).

GETTING THERE AND AROUND

Getting There

Bishop International Airport (FNT, G-3425 W. Bristol Rd., 810/235-6560, www.bishopairport.org) has daily scheduled flights on Delta and American from Atlanta, Chicago, Dallas, and other cities. Get a ride to your hotel or another destination with **Chippewa Cab** (989/892-2227).

Amtrak (800/872-7245, www.amtrak.com) trains arrive from Chicago, with stops across Michigan, including Kalamazoo, Battle Creek, East Lansing, Flint, and Detroit. Trains stop at **Flint Station** (1407 S. Dort Hwy.), also home to **Greyhound** (810/232-1114 or 800/231-2222, www.greyhound.com) and **Indian Trails** (800/292-3831, www.indiantrails.com), both of which provide regular bus service.

Given Genesee County's well-designed expressway system, travel by car is easy. From Detroit, drive northwest on I-75 and connect to I-475, which crosses I-69 and runs directly through Flint; in light traffic, this 68-mile trip takes just over an hour. From Saginaw, head southeast on I-75/U.S. 23 and I-475 to downtown Flint; this 37-mile trip should take about 38 minutes. Flint is also accessible from Port Huron or Lansing via I-69, an east-west interstate; from Port Huron, the 67-mile trip will take about an hour, while the 56-mile trip from Lansing will require at least 55 minutes. If you're coming from Chicago, take I-90, I-94, and I-69 to Flint; in light traffic, the 274-mile trip will take about four hours. From Chicago, parts of I-90 and I-94 are the Indiana Toll Road.

Getting Around

If you arrive in Flint via air or train, you can easily rent a vehicle from various rental agencies, such as **Alamo** (810/239-4341 or 800/462-5266), **Avis** (810/234-7847 or 800/331-1212), **Budget** (810/238-8300 or 800/527-0700), **Enterprise** (810/235-1101 or 800/261-7331), **Hertz** (810/234-2041 or 800/654-3131), or **National** (810/239-4341 or 800/227-7368). Flint's public bus system (one-way $2.25-3.50 pp) can get you around town. For information on routes and schedules, contact the **Mass Transportation Authority** (MTA, 1401 S. Dort Hwy., 810/767-0100, www.mtaflint.org). You might also consider joining a bus tour of the area; for more information, contact **Blue Lakes Charters & Tours** (12154 N. Saginaw Rd., Clio, 800/282-4287, www.bluelakes.com).

Frankenmuth

TOP EXPERIENCE

Today, it's easy to dismiss Frankenmuth as too commercialized and overdone. Charming as it appears, "Michigan's Little Bavaria" was, until recent decades, a quiet and undistinguished German farm town of 4,000, but has since grown to become the state's top tourist attraction, with an estimated three million visitors each year.

Frankenmuth houses the world's largest Christmas store, which began as a side business by sign-maker Wally Bronner. The city also boasts a two-mile-long street of pseudo-Bavarian shops with a template set by the Zehnder family in the 1920s, and three restaurants that serve all-you-can-eat family-style chicken dinners. Frankenmuth's chicken dinners started as an attraction for traveling salesmen, but later became a staple of the Detroit Sunday-drive set in the 1920s and '30s. Buoyed by the seemingly endless flow of visitors, the area has expanded over the years to include an 18-hole public golf course and the Midwest's largest outlet mall.

Despite the neo-Bavarian image it relentlessly pushes today, much of Frankenmuth's history resembles other Saginaw Valley towns. A group of 15 young Lutherans from an area near Nuremberg, Germany, founded the city in 1845 (*Frankenmuth* means "courage of the Franconians"). This optimistic group followed the call to become missionaries in the United States, with hopes of tending to the growing Saginaw Valley German community and while converting the local Ojibwa people to Christianity. German remained the community's principal language well into the 1920s.

SIGHTS

Old Frankenmuth

Beneath the commercialism is a genuine German community where people are old-world friendly. This side of Frankenmuth can be found in a number of places in town, which are, not surprisingly, the places most tourists skip.

The 1880 **St. Lorenz Lutheran Church** (140 Churchgrove Rd., 989/652-6141, www.stlorenz.org, 9am-noon Mon.-Sat. June-Sept., free) is home to the largest congregation east of the Mississippi of the conservative Missouri Synod of the Lutheran Church. Self-guided tours reveal scenes of Lutheran and Frankenmuth history, an early cemetery, a small museum, and a reconstruction of the first settlers' original log church and parsonage.

Frankenmuth Historical Museum

The **Frankenmuth Historical Museum** (613 S. Main St., 989/652-9701, www.frankenmuthmuseum.org, 10am-5pm Mon.-Thurs., 10am-7pm Fri.-Sat., noon-5pm Sun., $2 adults, $1 children, $5 family pass—2 adults plus 4 students) traces the city's rich past through possessions and letters from the original settlers. Displays explore the city's connections to logging, Prohibition, the rise of the chicken-dinner phenomenon, and the Frankenmuth brewery. The museum shop is a pleasant surprise among the cookie-cutter shops along Main Street, with vintage-style toys, sophisticated crafts, and an excellent selection of books relating to the city and surrounding area. Separate tours in German are available on request.

★ Bronner's CHRISTmas Wonderland

Check any cynicism at the door when visiting **Bronner's CHRISTmas Wonderland** (25 Christmas Ln., 989/652-9931 or 800/255-9327, www.bronners.com, 9am-9pm Mon.-Sat., noon-7pm Sun. June-Dec., shorter hours Jan.-May). Prepare yourself for a building that encompasses almost 100,000 square

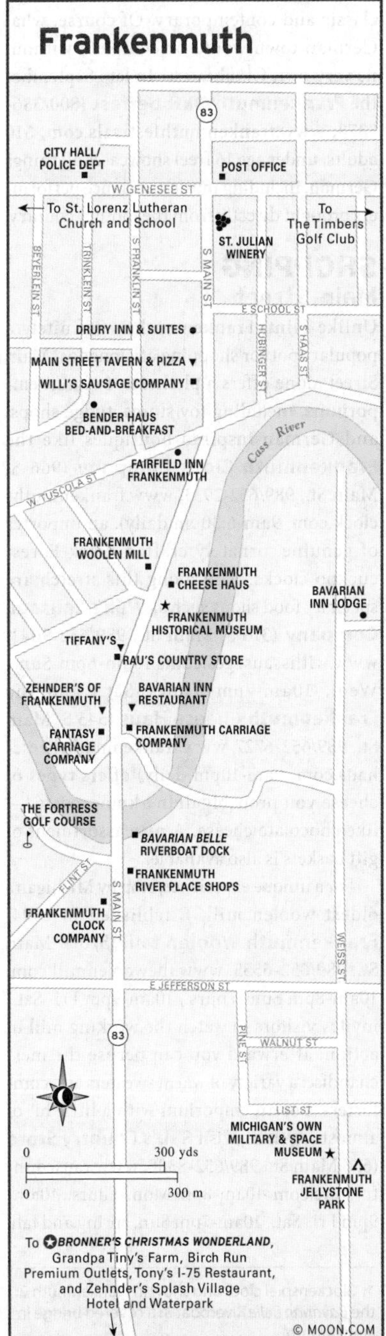

feet filled with more than 350 decorated Christmas trees, 800 animated figures, 500 styles of Nativity scenes from 75 countries, 6,000 glass ornaments, Bibles in more than 30 languages, Advent calendars, lighted villages, and nutcrackers. Many of the offerings are from Eastern Europe, but the staff have worked hard in recent years to add diversity to the store's offerings. These days, you can find books on Hanukkah and Kwanzaa, as well as non-Caucasian Santas and Nativity characters. The complex, which encompasses 27 acres, also houses the Silent Night Memorial Chapel, a replica of the Austrian church built where "Silent Night" was first sung in 1818. The store is closed New Year's Day, Easter, Thanksgiving, and Christmas. Even if you're not an avid shopper, a stop at Bronner's will thoroughly amaze you.

Grandpa Tiny's Farm

A historical 45-acre working farm founded by William "Tiny" Zehnder, **Grandpa Tiny's Farm** (7775 Weiss St., 989/652-5437 or 989/871-2937 www.grandpatinysfarm.com, 10am-5pm Sat.-Sun. April, noon-4pm Memorial Day, 10am-5pm Tues.-Sun. May-Oct., noon-6pm, Sat.-Sun. third week of Nov.-third week of Dec., $5 pp, under age 2 free) invites visitors, especially children, to interact with bunnies, lambs, goats, and other farm animals. Guides give personal tours through the farm, where plowing and wool-spinning demonstrations, narrated horse-drawn wagon rides, and other activities highlight the area's agricultural history.

Other Attractions

St. Julian Winery (127 S. Main St., 989/652-3281, www.stjulian.com, 11am-7pm Sun.-Thurs., 10am-7pm Fri.-Sat., free tours), is the state's largest, with several Michigan locations. The Frankenmuth site has a tasting room offering up to six complimentary tastings. The facility showcases 80 wines and sparkling juices. There's also a small winery on-site where solera cream sherry is aged.

Michigan's Heroes Museum (1250

Weiss St., 989/652-8005, www.michigansmilitarymuseum.com, 10am-5pm daily, $7 adults, $6 seniors, $5 students, $3 ages 6-18) features exhibits about Michigan governors, astronauts, and veterans of several foreign wars.

GOLF

For golfers, there are three options near Frankenmuth. Zehnder's, probably the town's most famous restaurant and hotel, offers **The Fortress Golf Course** (950 Flint St., 800/863-7999, www.zehnders.com, daily May-Oct., $45-70 with cart), an 18-hole championship course not far from Main Street. If you're looking for a more tranquil setting, head five miles west of town to the **Green Acres Golf Course** (7323 Dixie Hwy., Bridgeport, 989/777-3510, www.greenacresgc.net, daily Apr.-Oct., $25-29 with cart). An alternative is **The Timbers Golf Club** (7300 Bray Rd., Vassar, 989/871-4884, www.timbersgolfclub.com, daily Apr.-Oct., $37-41 with cart), a wooded course about five miles east of Frankenmuth.

FESTIVALS

As one of Michigan's top tourism destinations, Frankenmuth hosts its share of annual events, including a music festival in August and a holiday celebration in November. In late January, **Zehnder's Snowfest** (800/863-7999, www.zehnders.com, outdoor events free) honors winter with fireworks, live entertainment, ice-carving competitions, and delicious treats.

In May, the **World Expo of Beer** (www.worldexpoofbeer.com, $10 adults, 21 or over only), Michigan's largest beer-sampling event, brings together over 150 beers from breweries around the world. During the two-day event, visitors can enjoy live bands, watch brewing demonstrations, and vote for their favorite beer. The following month, the four-day **Frankenmuth Bavarian Festival** in mid-June (877/879-8919, www.bavarianfestival.com, $10 adults, under age 16 free) highlights German culture with traditional music and food—plus a car show featuring various German vehicles, both classic and contemporary. Of course, what German town would be complete without its very own Oktoberfest? In late September the **Frankenmuth Oktoberfest** (800/386-3378, www.frankenmuthfestivals.com, $10 adults, under age 16 free) showcases all things German, including music and dance performers brought directly from the mother country.

SHOPPING

Main Street

Unlike Flint, Frankenmuth is definitely a popular spot for shopping aficionados. Main Street alone offers a plethora of quaint emporiums, including toy stores, fudge shops, and German-inspired boutiques like the **Frankenmuth Clock Company** (966 S. Main St., 989/652-2933, www.frankenmuthclock.com, 9am-6:30pm daily), an importer of genuine, ornately crafted Black Forest cuckoo clocks. Also along this stretch are specialty food shops such as **Willi's Sausage Company** (316 S. Main St., 989/652-9041, www.willissausages.com, 10am-6pm Sun.-Wed., 10am-7pm Thurs.-Sat.) and the **Frankenmuth Cheese Haus** (545 S. Main St., 989/652-6727, www.frankenmuthcheesehaus.com, 9am-10pm daily) offers types of cheese you probably didn't know existed—like chocolate cheese. A nice assortment of gift baskets is also available.

For a unique experience, stop by Michigan's oldest woolen mill. Established in 1894, **Frankenmuth Woolen Mill** (570 S. Main St., 989/652-6555, www.thewoolenmill.com, 10am-8pm Sun.-Thurs., 10am-9pm Fri.-Sat.) invites visitors to watch the working mill in action; afterward you can peruse the merchandise: a variety of warm sweaters and comforters. For an emporium with a little bit of almost anything, visit **Rau's Country Store** (656 Main St., 989/652-8388, www.rauscountrystore.com, 10am-8pm Mon.-Thurs., 10am-9pm Fri.-Sat., 10am-7pm Sun. spring and fall;

1: Glockenspiel clock and show in Frankenmuth **2:** the *Bavarian Belle* Riverboat **3:** a covered bridge in Frankemuth

1

Bavarian Belle

2

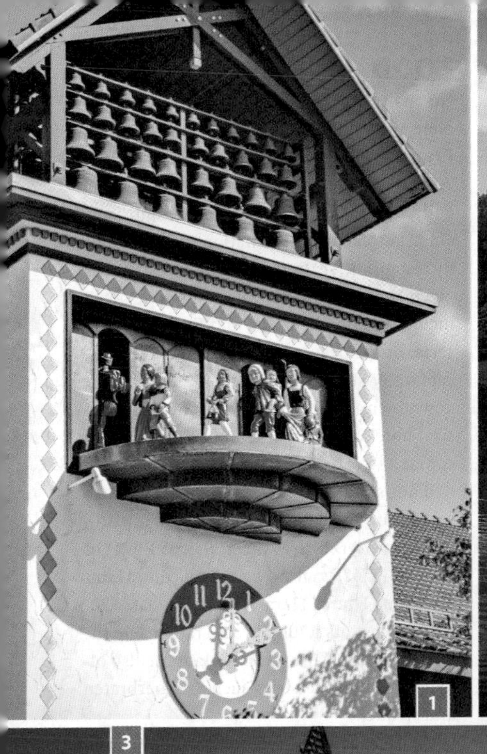

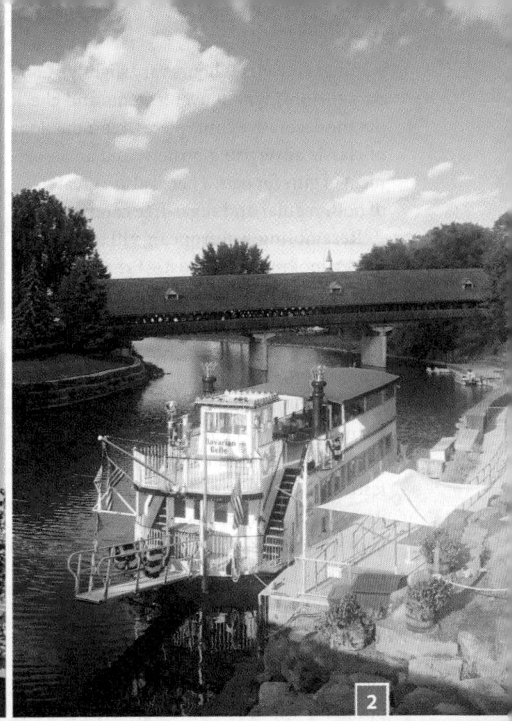

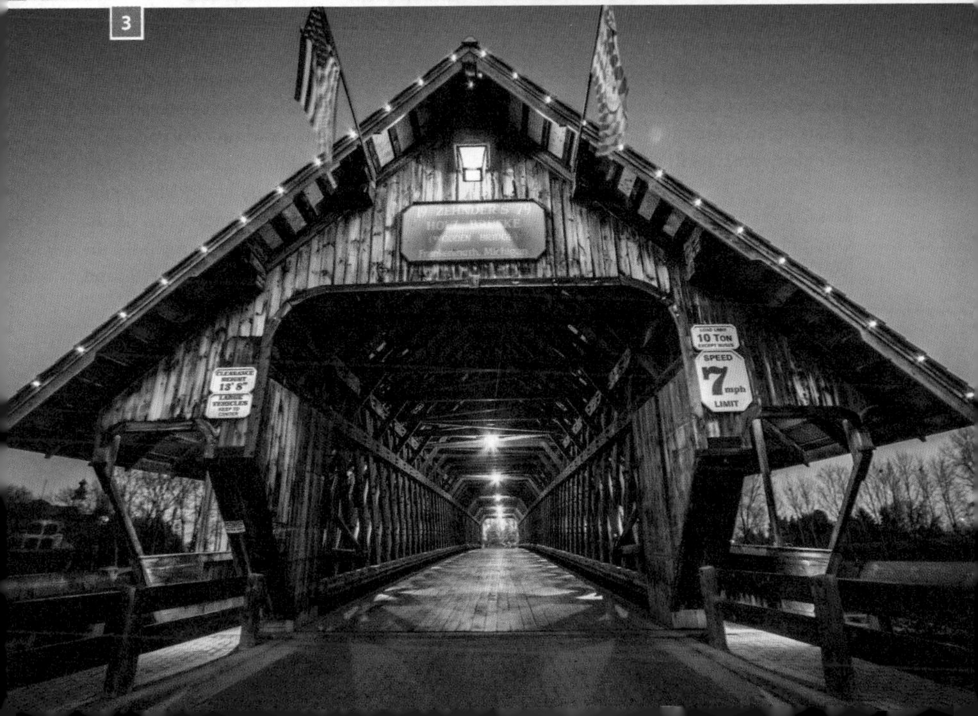
Frankenmuth, Michigan
LOAD LIMIT
10 TON
EXCEPT BUSES
SPEED
7 mph
LIMIT
CLEARANCE HEIGHT
13' 5"
LARGE VEHICLES
KEEP TO CENTER

3

summer and winter hours vary slightly). Look past the ordinary souvenir items and check out the decorative china pieces, reproductions of classic advertising posters, and an assortment of gifts for pets. There's also a great stock of both regular and sugar-free candy.

Resembling a European village—albeit newer-looking than most—**Frankenmuth River Place Shops** (925 S. Main St., 800/600-0105, www.frankenmuthriverplace.com, 10am-6pm Sun.-Thurs., 10am-8pm Fri.-Sat. Jan.-May, 10am-8pm Sun.-Thurs., 10am-9pm Fri.-Sat. June, 10am-9pm daily July-Aug., 10am-7pm Sun.-Thurs., 10am-9pm Fri.-Sat. Sept.-Dec.—special extended hours during festivals) is Frankenmuth's only mall. Among its more than 30 shops and attractions are a quilt store, a glass-art gallery, a day spa, a shop featuring Michigan-themed items, and the state's largest bead store. There are also spots for children, including Mother Earth's Toy Jungle and Dino Land. From May through October, River Place is also the launching point for the ***Bavarian Belle* Riverboat** (866/808-2628, www.bavarianbelle.com, departure times posted daily, $12 adults, $4 ages 5-12, under age 5 free); departures can vary due to weather conditions. The cruise takes guests on an informative one-hour narrated tour along the Cass River.

Birch Run

Once just an obscure village eight miles southwest of Frankenmuth, Birch Run is now the state's discount shopping capital, with more than 140 stores within its famed outlet mall, **Birch Run Premium Outlets** (12240 S. Beyer Rd., 989/624-6226, www.premiumoutlets.com, 10am-9pm Mon.-Sat., 11am-7pm Sun.), the second largest in the world. Plunder the offerings of Nike, Ann Taylor, Calvin Klein, and many more. Located at the second-busiest exit on I-75 (the first is at Orlando, Florida), Birch Run now contains a movie palace and a motor speedway—improvements designed to make the town a true weekend destination for the shopping set.

FOOD

No visit to Frankenmuth would be complete without a meal at ★ **Zehnder's of Frankenmuth** (730 S. Main St., 800/863-7999, www.zehnders.com, 11am-9:30pm daily, $21-35), a historic complex comprising a marketplace and the nation's largest family restaurant, seating over 1,500 guests at any given time in nine dining rooms. The menu includes seafood, steaks, and European desserts, but is best known for its all-you-can-eat family-style chicken dinners. South of the downtown area, Zehnder's also offers a whimsical hotel, a water park, and an 18-hole golf course.

Thousands of chicken dinners are also served annually at the vast **Bavarian Inn Restaurant** (713 S. Main St., 989/652-9941 or 800/228-2742, www.bavarianinn.com, 11am-9pm Sun.-Thurs., 11am-9:30pm Fri.-Sat., $22-30), which seats 1,200. If you'd rather skip the poultry, the Bavarian Inn Restaurant also offers German specialties such as sauerbraten and strudel.

A nice alternative to Zehnder's and Bavarian Inn is **Tiffany's** (656 S. Main St., 989/652-6881, www.tiffanysfoodandspirits.com, 11am-11pm daily, $10-18). In the historic Hotel Goetz, the elaborate carved wooden bar, original to the building, exudes charm and nostalgia as soon as you enter. The casual menu features an array of sandwiches, salads, and specialties with an Italian emphasis, including seafood Alfredo, linguine pesto, and gluten-free penne pasta.

The **Main Street Tavern & Pizza** (310 S. Main St., 989/652-2222, 3pm-2am daily, $8-18) is owned by a former baker from Zehnder's, who makes all the fragrant bread and buns on the premises. His cheeseburger is made from local beef and cheese; a house specialty is the pizza with Italian sausage from Willi's Sausage Company next door. Wash it down with a Carling's or a Frankenmuth Pilsner for a delicious meal filled with old-world flair at a reasonable price.

Like any good tourist destination, Frankenmuth and Birch Run have a number of smaller restaurants, including the all-too-common chains and fast-food locations. Across from Birch Run's discount mall, **Tony's I-75** (8781 Main St., 989/624-5860, 6am-10pm Sun.-Thurs., 6am-11pm Fri.-Sat., $10-16) is a long-standing local eatery that began life as a truck stop and is still known for its overstuffed sandwiches and thick shakes. Beware—portions are exceptionally large; two adults can easily satisfy their appetites on one dish. For example, if you order off their breakfast menu, you'll get a whole pound of bacon with your scrambled eggs. Lines can be long, so plan to wait or visit during off-hours.

ACCOMMODATIONS

Frankenmuth has several bed-and-breakfast inns, such as the **Bender Haus Bed-and-Breakfast** (337 Trinklein St., 989/652-8897, $110-130 d). There is no shortage of chain hotels in the area, including **Drury Inn & Suites** (260 S. Main St., 989/652-2800, www.druryhotels.com, $130-160 d) and **Fairfield Inn Frankenmuth** (430 S. Main St., 989/652-5000, www.marriott.com, $125-160 d).

In downtown Frankenmuth, you can also opt for the ★ **Bavarian Inn Lodge** (1 Covered Bridge Ln., 888/775-6343, www.bavarianinn.com, $125-315 d), set behind the restaurant and shops along the Cass River. The 360 rooms are clean and bright, with balconies and Bavarian touches. Each is named in honor of one of the town's early inhabitants, complete with family pictures. The lodge is especially popular with kids, who flock here to hang out at the indoor water park, minigolf course, and Family Fun Center, which includes video games and other entertainment.

Families may also appreciate **Zehnder's Splash Village Hotel and Waterpark** (1365 S. Main St., 800/863-7999, www.zehnders.com, $209-250 d, $220-469 suites). Situated near the southern edge of Frankenmuth, beside Bronner's CHRISTmas Wonderland, Zehnder's features 146 rooms and suites, a video arcade, a 30,000-square-foot indoor water park, and complimentary shuttle service to the Zehnder's restaurant and the Fortress Golf Course.

Camping

Despite the plethora of tourist-oriented hotels and inns in Frankenmuth, there is an option for those who enjoy sleeping outdoors. Not far from Bronner's, the year-round **Frankenmuth Jellystone Park** (1339 Weiss St., 989/652-6668, www.frankenmuthjellystone.com, $55-178) offers tent sites, small cottages and cabins, full RV hookups, a laundry, heated restrooms, an indoor pool, a playground and minigolf course, along with free wireless Internet access.

INFORMATION AND SERVICES

For more information about Frankenmuth, contact the **Frankenmuth Chamber of Commerce and Convention & Visitors Bureau** (635 S. Main St., 800/386-8696, www.frankenmuth.org, 8am-5pm Mon.-Fri., 10am-5pm Sat., noon-5pm Sun.). For local news, pick up a copy of ***Frankenmuth News*** (www.frankenmuthnews.com).

In emergencies, contact the **Frankenmuth Police Department** (240 W. Genesee St., 989/652-8371) or **Mobile Medical Response** (989/758-2900, www.mobilemedical.org).

GETTING THERE AND AROUND

You won't be able to take a plane, train, or bus to Frankenmuth, but getting there by car is very simple. From Detroit, take I-75 north to exit 136 (Frankenmuth/Birch Run), drive two miles east on Birch Run Road, and head north on M-83 for 5.7 miles, where the road becomes Main Street; the 93-mile trip will take about 90 minutes. From Saginaw, take southbound I-75/U.S. 23 to exit 144 (Frankenmuth/Bridgeport), drive two miles southeast on Dixie Highway, head east on Junction Road for four miles to where the road becomes Genesee Street, and continue on Genesee Street for about a mile to Main Street; in light traffic, this 15-mile trip takes 25 minutes. Once within the city limits, you can drive, walk the downtown area, or take a carriage ride with the **Fantasy Carriage Company** (780 S. Mill St., 989/777-4757 or 989/245-1891, noon-8pm Mon.-Thurs., noon-9pm Fri., 11am-9:30pm Sat., 11am-9pm Sun.) or the **Frankenmuth Carriage Company** (713 S Main St., 989/652-3101, 1pm-8pm daily).

Saginaw

Saginaw, the industrial heart of east-central Michigan, stretches for four miles along both banks of the Saginaw River.

Saginaw Bay appears variously on 17th- and 18th-century French maps as "Sikonam," "Sakonam," "Saaguinam," and "Saquinam." Southeastern Michigan was generally described as "Saquinam Country" as early as 1688. Later, when lumber camp raconteurs told of Paul Bunyan's legendary feat of "logging off the Saginaw Country," the reference referred to the entire Lower Peninsula.

Native Americans lived peacefully on these lands for centuries. The earliest nonnatives to penetrate the Saginaw Valley were Canadians; in 1816 Louis Campau built a fur trading post near present-day downtown, followed by the stationing of troops at Fort Saginaw in 1822. To the delight of the area's indigenous people, the post was abandoned in 1823. But settlers didn't stay away long. By the 1850s, lumberjacks moved in and constructed 14 sawmills by 1857. Their prey on the heavily forested land around the city lasted until the late 1880s, when timber was replaced by coal as the city's principal industry. Remnants of those years can still be seen, as in the stunning Montague Inn, an elegant inn and restaurant in the Georgian-style mansion of a former sugar beet magnate.

SIGHTS

Museums and Cultural Sights

Easily dismissed as an aging industrial center, Saginaw is a city of surprises. One of the most delightful is the **Japanese Cultural Center, Tea House, and Gardens of Saginaw** (527 Ezra Rust Dr., 989/759-1648, www.japaneseculturalcenter.org, noon-4pm Tues.-Sat. Apr.-Oct., free, tour and tea ceremony $5 pp, cash only; ceremony at 2pm on the second Sat. of each month), an authentic Japanese teahouse and garden. The 16th-century-style teahouse was built in 1985 to resemble a Zen monastery. It is one of the few places in the United States where visitors can see a formal Japanese tea ceremony designed to promote inner tranquility in an authentic setting. Admission includes a cup of tea and a traditional Japanese sweet.

At other times, visitors can tour the teahouse and garden, learn more about the ancient ritual of tea, and contemplate its importance in Japanese architecture, politics, and religion.

Behind the teahouse, the Friendship Garden is a variation of a traditional Japanese garden, with delicate plantings and an arched footbridge over a stream. Many of the garden's trees, bridges, and stones came directly from Japan. Saginaw was chosen as the center's unlikely site because of its relationship with sister city Tokushima.

Another surprise is the **Marshall M. Fredericks Sculpture Museum** at Saginaw Valley State University (SVSU, 7400 Bay Rd., 989/964-7125, www.marshallfredericks.org, 11am-5pm Mon.-Fri., noon-5pm Sat., free). The Scandinavian American artist and one of the state's most renowned sculptors studied under famous Swedish sculptor Carl Milles and is best known for his *Spirit of Detroit* statue in front of the Coleman A. Young Municipal Center. The gallery features original works, more than 200 original plaster models, photos of pieces installed around

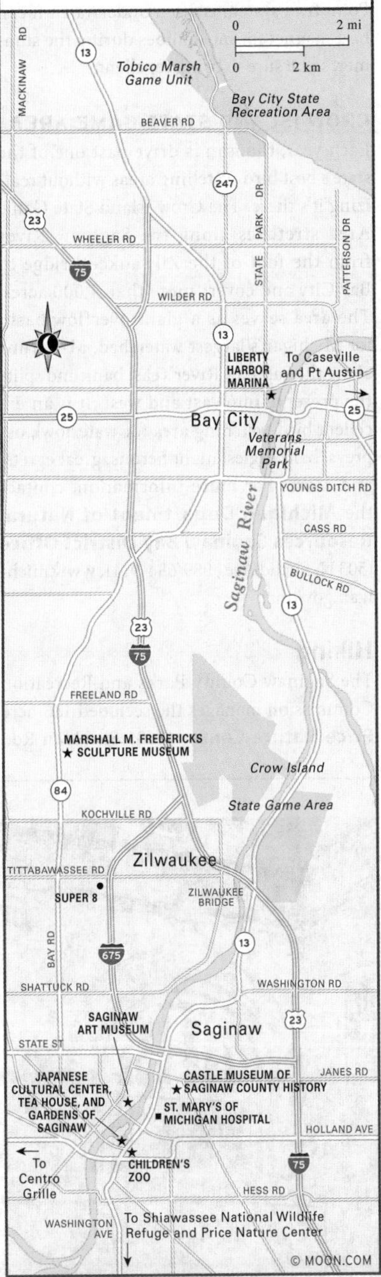

the world, a collection of bronze casts in the nearby outdoor sculpture garden, and original sketches. The Sculptor's Studio, a space created in 2003 to showcase the casting process, contains over 300 of Fredericks's clay models, molds, tools, and sculptures.

The **Saginaw Art Museum** (1126 N. Michigan Ave., 989/754-2491, www.saginawartmuseum.org, noon-5pm Tues.-Sat., $5 adults, $3 students with valid ID and seniors over 61, under age 16 free) features the work of local and international artists in a 1904 Georgian Revival mansion. Highlights include a research library, fine collections of 19th- and 20th-century American art, a sculpture solarium, and a garden restored to reflect the home's original plantings.

The **Castle Museum of Saginaw County History** (500 Federal Ave., 989/752-2861, www.castlemuseum.org, 10am-4:30pm Tues.-Sat., 1pm-4:30pm Sun., $1 adults, $0.50 children) is one of the city's most recognizable landmarks. Constructed in 1898 by architect William Aiken, the limestone building, originally a post office, was intended to replicate a French château. Today, the museum chronicles the region's rich heritage, with artifacts and dioramas that explore the area's former fur trading, logging, farming, and manufacturing industries.

Saginaw Children's Zoo

The **Children's Zoo** (Celebration Square, 1730 S. Washington Ave., 989/759-1408, www.saginawzoo.com, 10am-5pm daily, late Apr.-late Oct., $5 pp, $3.50 on Tues. and for active duty military and veterans) is a bargain-priced zoo at a manageable size. It features more than 130 animals, most native to the region. The timber wolves and bald eagles are especially popular with kids.

RECREATION

★ Bird-Watching

SHIAWASSEE NATIONAL WILDLIFE REFUGE

Nature takes center stage at the **Shiawassee National Wildlife Refuge** (6975 Mower Rd.,

989/777-5930, www.fws.gov/midwest/shiawassee, 7:30am-4pm Mon.-Fri.), just southwest of Saginaw. The refuge and the nearby **Green Point Environmental Learning Center** (3010 Maple St., 989/759-1669) share a region near the confluence of four rivers—the Flint, the Tittabawassee, the Cass, and the Shiawassee—that form the Saginaw River.

Covering more than 9,700 acres, the refuge was established in 1953 as a wetland for migrating waterfowl and is now widely regarded as one of the top birding sites in the United States. A checklist, available at the headquarters, lists more than 270 species that frequent the refuge. In October some 30,000 ducks and 25,000 geese converge on the area, along with songbirds, wading birds, owls, hawks, and an occasional bald eagle. About 500 tundra swans migrate through annually.

An observation deck and a wheelchair-accessible blind are strategically placed for prime viewing. The refuge has more than 13 miles of hiking trails (sunrise-sunset daily), including the 4.5-mile Woodland Trail that loops through bottomland hardwoods and skirts the Tittabawassee River. The adjacent Green Point is operated under a co-op agreement with the U.S. Fish and Wildlife Service and has 76 acres of diverse habitat and an interpretive center. Because it lies in the floodplain of the Tittabawassee River, the Green Point trail system is often underwater. It can be a magnet for mosquitoes during the summer, so be sure to bring repellent.

CROW ISLAND STATE GAME AREA

Each year, thousands drive past one of the state's best bird-watching areas without realizing it's there. The Crow Island State Game Area stretches along the Saginaw River from the foot of the Zilwaukee Bridge to Bay City and covers more than 1,000 acres. The area serves as a giant overflow basin for Michigan's largest watershed. M-13 runs along the Saginaw River's east bank and splits the preserve into east and west. It is an excellent bird-watching area for waterfowl, ospreys, bald eagles, night herons, great egrets, and more. For more information, contact the **Michigan Department of Natural Resources Saginaw Bay District Office** (503 N. Euclid Ave., 989/684-9141, www.michigan.gov/dnr).

Hiking

The Saginaw County Parks and Recreation Commission manages the secluded 186-acre **Price Nature Center** (6685 Sheridan Rd.,

Castle Museum in downtown Saginaw

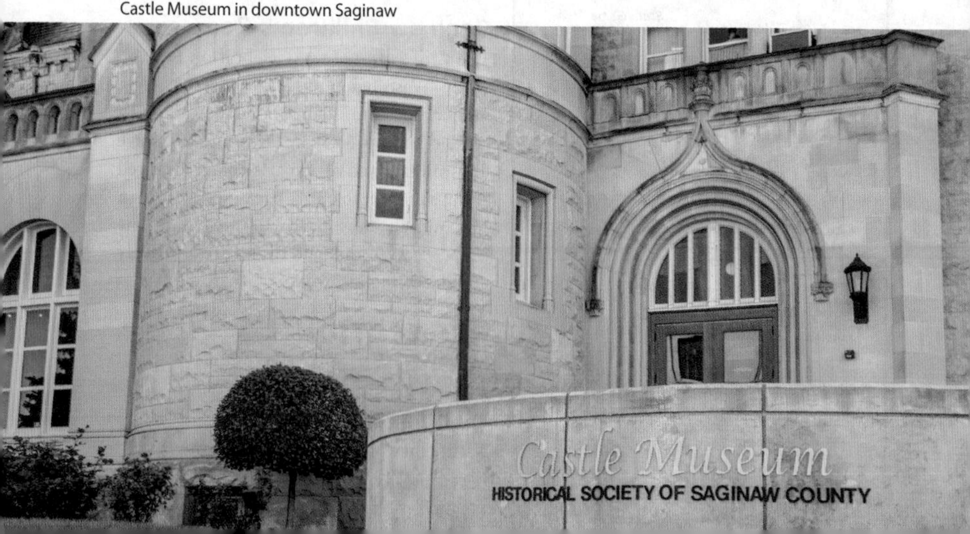

989/790-5280, www.michigan.org/property/price-nature-center, 8am-5pm Mon.-Fri., 10am-6pm Sat., 9am-10pm Sun.) five miles south of Saginaw, near the I-75 Bridgeport exit. A good spot for day hikes, the center features a 200-year-old beech and maple forest, three miles of hiking and cross-country skiing trails, a picnic pavilion, and a rustic campground.

ENTERTAINMENT AND EVENTS

The Arts

The Dow Event Center (303 Johnson St., 833/215-5121, www.doweventcenter.com), home to the Saginaw Spirit Hockey Club, hosts various concerts and Broadway musicals year-round. In addition to classic films, the **Temple Theatre** (203 N. Washington Ave., 877/754-7469, www.templetheatre.com), a grand 1927 performance venue, presents performances by the **Saginaw Choral Society** (www.saginawchoralsociety.com) and **Saginaw Bay Symphony Orchestra** (www.saginawbayorchestra.com).

Early August welcomes the **Saginaw Old Town Art Fair** (www.facebook.com/pg/saginawart). Held in the 400 block of Court Street, the event includes fine art vendors, plus art demonstrations.

Festivals

Saginaw is home to a large Hispanic community, many of whom initially settled here to work on the construction of the state's railroads. Many of their descendants stayed on to work at area sugar beet refineries. Saginaw and Bay City's sugar beet industry makes Michigan the fifth-largest sugar beet producer in the country. In May, the Saginaw area is home to the state's largest **Cinco de Mayo** festival and parade, held on Ojibway Island behind the teahouse in Rust Park.

Southwest of Saginaw, the community of Chesaning hosts the annual **Saginaw County Fair** (989/845-2143, www.saginawcountyfair.org). Usually held in early August, this family-friendly event stages everything from rodeos to scavenger hunts.

SHOPPING

While not a shoppers' paradise like Frankenmuth and Birch Run, Saginaw is an ideal place to look for antiques. Situated within the historic district, you'll find **Adomaitis Antiques & Theatrics** (412 Court St., 989/790-7469, www.adomaitis.com, 11am-4pm Wed.-Sat.), a repository of vintage clothing and costumes. Watch for its occasional estate sales, too. If you can't find what you need at Adomaitis, head to **The Antique Warehouse** (1122 Tittabawassee, 989/755-4343, www.theaw.net, 10am-6pm Mon.-Sat., noon-6pm Sun. and holidays), one of Michigan's largest antiques malls, housing 70 antiques dealers, 12 specialty shops, and a café. You could conceivably spend an entire day perusing its inventory, including toys, jewelry, furniture, and more.

The Saginaw area also boasts Michigan's largest village of country shops, the **Pride and Country Village** (5965 Holland Rd., 989/754-5807, www.prideandcountry.com, 10am-5:30pm Mon.-Fri., 10am-6pm Sat., 11am-5pm Sun.). Comprising several renovated historic structures with over 40,000 square feet of shopping, this unique complex offers a variety of country-style treasures, from candles in the 1899 schoolhouse to handcrafted furnishings in the five-level 1904 farmhouse.

FOOD AND ACCOMMODATIONS

Saginaw has a number of excellent dining options. One standout for lunch is **Fralias** (422 Hancock St., 989/799-0111, www.fralias.com, 10:30am-3:30pm Mon.-Fri., 11am-3pm Sat., $7-10). Generous deli sandwiches dominate the menu, including the croque monsieur (turkey, swiss cheese, and coleslaw on rye), plus a creative variety of soups and salads. A slightly more upscale choice is the **Artisan Urban Bistro**

(417 Hancock, 989/401-6019, www.artisanurbanbistro.com, 4pm-9pm Wed.-Sat., 10am-3pm Sun. brunch, $12-30). The menu concentrates on French and Italian dishes and is vegetarian-friendly.

Plenty of chain hotels can be found along I-75 and I-675, including the **Super 8** (4848 Towne Centre Rd., 989/791-3003, www.super8.com, $55-70 d) and the **Hampton Inn and Suites** (2695 Tittabawassee Rd., 989/797-2220, $129-185d).

INFORMATION AND SERVICES

For more information about Saginaw, contact the **Saginaw County Chamber of Commerce** (515 N. Washington Ave., 3rd fl., 989/752-7161, www.saginawchamber.org, 8am-4:30pm Mon.-Fri.) or the **Go Great Lakes Bay** (515 N. Washington Ave., 2nd fl., 989/752-7164 or 800/444-9979, www.gogreat.com, 8am-4:30pm Mon.-Fri.). For local news, pick up a copy of the ***Saginaw News*** (www.saginaw-news.com or www.mlive.com).

For nonemergencies, contact the **Police Department** (612 Federal St., 989/759-1229) or the **Fire Department** (801 Federal St., 989/759-1376). For medical treatment, contact **Ascension St. Mary's Emergency Care** (800 S. Washington Ave., 989/907-8733, www.healthcare.ascension.org). Prescriptions can be filled at any one of several pharmacies, including a 24-hour **Walgreens** (4989 State St., 989/791-3088, www.walgreens.com).

GETTING THERE AND AROUND

The closest airport to Saginaw is the **MBS International Airport** (MBS, 8500 Garfield Rd., Freeland, 989/695-5555, www.mbsairport.org), which also serves Bay City and Midland. You can access Saginaw via **Greyhound** (989/753-5454 or 800/231-2222, www.greyhound.com) or **Indian Trails** (800/292-3831, www.indiantrails.com) bus services to the **Saginaw Bus Station** (511 Johnson St.).

Most travelers, however, reach Saginaw via I-75. North from Flint, take exit 149 to M-46 west or exit 150 to I-675. In light traffic it takes about 40 minutes to cover the 38-mile distance. From Bay City, take M-25 west, followed by I-75/U.S. 23 to exit 155, where the I-675 bypass leads to the northern edge of Saginaw; the 17-mile trip takes about 24 minutes.

In Saginaw, you can drive or take the bus (one-way $1.25 adults, $0.60 over age 61 and children shorter than the fare box) run by the **Saginaw Transit Authority Regional Services** (STARS, 615 Johnson St., 989/907-4000, www.saginaw-stars.com).

Grindstone City to Lakeport

Lining Michigan's eastern shore is a string of coastal villages, including Harbor Beach and Port Sanilac. While some are little more than ghost towns, they're nonetheless rich in history, culture, and natural delights, including several well-preserved 19th-century buildings and two underwater preserves.

GRINDSTONE CITY

For more than a century, this village took advantage of its plentiful supply of abrasive rock and produced some of the finest grindstones in the world, exporting them to England and other markets around the globe. Two factories operated until World War I, when the development of Carborundum quickly made grindstone quarrying unprofitable. Almost overnight, the town's greatest asset became virtually worthless. Huge stones, many up to six feet in diameter, were left behind to litter the beach. Also left behind were old docks, stores, houses, mills, and office buildings. Today, grindstones are popular as local lawn art.

Petroglyphs Shrouded in Controversy

Sanilac petroglyph

In the center of Michigan's Thumb area, about 13 miles south of Bad Axe via M-53 and Germania Road, the ancient sandstone carvings of **Sanilac Petroglyphs Historic State Park** (8251 Germania Rd., Cass City, 989/856-4411, www.michigan.gov/dnr, 10am-5pm Wed.-Sun. Memorial Day-Labor Day, annual Recreation Passport required: $12 Michigan residents, $34 nonresidents, $9 day pass available to nonresidents only) have been the subject of controversy since their discovery in the late 19th century. Although most scientists agree that the petroglyphs provide a glimpse into the lives of ancient Native American artists, the meaning of the images is unclear, even after years of intense study.

For instance, one of the faded etchings depicts the legendary "underwater panther," a spiny, horned mountain lion that supposedly inhabited lakes and was thought to cause storms. Some insist that this creature resembles the long-extinct stegosaurus, lending credence to their belief that dinosaurs might have lived long enough to interact with ancient people.

Equally strange are the religious symbols that appear amid these ancient carvings, such as Christian crosses and Jewish menorahs. Along with the presence of Roman numerals and letters, they provide evidence that Christopher Columbus was not the first European to visit the Americas and make a lasting impression.

While the religious have embraced the validity of such interpretations, scientists attribute the petroglyphs to indigenous mythology or the human imagination, which could transform an elk into a dinosaur-like creature. The wonder lies in the possibilities.

HURON CITY

Just four miles south of Grindstone City is Huron City. Though not quite a ghost town, it is close. Langdon Hubbard had big plans for Huron City when he arrived from Connecticut in the 1870s, buying up thousands of acres of woodland and building sawmills that churned out lumber. In 1881 a huge fire—not uncommon in regions where clear-cut land is easily ignited—roared across the Thumb and destroyed his empire.

Huron City was partially rebuilt—Hubbard even contributed a public roller rink—but the area's water had been contaminated by salt-making, a secondary industry. By 1884, the population had dwindled from 1,500 to about 15.

Huron City's quick demise makes its most dominant building all the more fascinating. The Italianate **House of Seven Gables** (989/428-4123, www.huroncitymuseums.org/sevengables.htm, hours and fees vary; call ahead) was rebuilt by Langdon Hubbard after the 1881 fire. It later became the summer residence of his son-in-law, William Lyon Phelps, a popular Yale English teacher dubbed "America's favorite college professor" by *Life* magazine in the 1930s. The Hubbard family lived in the house from 1881 until 1987, when it was turned into an informal museum.

The house offers an almost unparalleled authentic glimpse into a bygone era. The family's books lie piled on tables, the ornate 1886 pool table looks ready for a game, the walls are lined with family portraits of the beloved Hubbard dogs and cats, and the state-of-the-art 1915 kitchen even shows off its strange-looking fancy dishwasher. Along with the

House of Seven Gables, you can visit the other buildings remaining in Historic Huron City, including the general store, an inn, a church, and barns.

Port Hope

From Huron City, M-25 curves south along Lake Huron about seven miles to the lakeshore town of Port Hope, where the 1857 Pointe aux Barques Lighthouse guards the coastline. It's surrounded by the pleasant **Lighthouse County Park** (7320 Lighthouse Rd., 989/269-6404, www.huroncountyparks.com, May-Oct., free). The park includes a 110-site campground, a picnic area, a beach, and a small lighthouse museum.

HARBOR BEACH

From Port Hope, M-25 continues south toward Harbor Beach, home to the largest artificial freshwater harbor in the world. Michigan's busy logging industry in the 1870s meant more ships were plying the waters up and down the Lake Huron shore and across Saginaw Bay needing a safe refuge from strong currents and heavy seas. The federal government began work on a harbor in 1873, a gargantuan project dragging on for more than two decades. When completed, the break wall stretched 8,000 feet. It continues to serve its original function today, along with the 1881 Coast Guard Station and 1885 lighthouse.

Originally named Sand Beach, Harbor Beach was once notorious as the site of an illegal money factory. In the mid-19th century, counterfeit U.S. and Mexican currency were made here and distributed throughout the Americas.

Frank Murphy ranks as Harbor Beach's most famous son—the Michigan governor best known for collective bargaining during the 1937 Flint sit-down strike, paving the way for the rise of the United Auto Workers (UAW). He went on to become U.S. attorney general and a U.S. Supreme Court justice. The 1910 **Frank Murphy Birthplace** (142 S. Huron Ave., 989/479-3363, http://harborbeach.com/ParksRecreation/Museums.aspx 8am-4pm Wed.-Sat., noon-4pm Sun., and by appointment, Memorial Day-Labor Day, $2 adults, $1 children) serves as a repository for Murphy's personal memorabilia. While the contents prove interesting, the house itself is plain in comparison with the Hubbard mansion in Huron City.

PORT SANILAC

Until the mid-1850s the Port Sanilac area was known as Bark Shanty Point, a name heatedly defended in an issue of the village's alternative newspaper, the *Bark Shanty Times*. The *Times* was produced by placing a sheet of newsprint on the counter of the town's general store; townsfolk simply wrote news or commentary down until it was filled up.

Port Sanilac's past is preserved at the **Sanilac County Historical Museum** (228 S. Ridge St., 810/622-9946, www.sanilaccountymuseum.org, 11am-5pm Wed.-Sun. Memorial Day-Labor Day, by appointment May-Dec., $8 adults, $5 ages 5-12). Housed in a nicely restored Victorian mansion, the 1872 Loop-Harrison House, the museum contains most of its original furnishings as well as old-fashioned medical instruments, antique glassware, military and Native American artifacts, and an original Bark Shanty post office stamp. The grounds also include a dairy museum, a restored late-19th-century cabin, a general store, and a barn with exhibits relating to the fishing, logging, and blacksmithing trades.

LAKEPORT STATE PARK

About 20 miles south of Port Sanilac on M-25, **Lakeport State Park** (7605 Lakeshore Rd., 810/327-6224, 8am-10pm daily, annual Recreation Passport required: $12 Michigan residents, $34 nonresidents, $9 day pass available to nonresidents only) preserves more than a mile of fine sand beach on southern Lake Huron. The 556-acre facility was established in 1936, making it one of Michigan's oldest state parks. A couple of miles to the north, in a separate unit of the park, a popular campground ($31-43 per night) offers 315 modern sites that are just a short walk from another beach. From the park's low bluffs, you can see distant views of freighter traffic heading to the upper Great Lakes. Other park amenities include a picnic shelter, a beach house, and a playground. For campground reservations (which are strongly recommended), contact the **Michigan Department of Natural Resources** (800/447-2757, www.michigan.gov/dnr).

RECREATION

Boating and Fishing

Lake Huron is a wonderful place to explore via boat, whether you're a pleasure cruiser or a die-hard angler. Grindstone City has an artificially constructed harbor and a state-owned boat launch, ideal for private boaters and anglers who want to experience this quiet coast on their own.

Charter boats operate out of many Thumb communities; contact the **Thumb Area Charter Boat Association** (www.thumbareacharterboats.com) for accredited boat captains and fishing guides. Before heading out, purchase a valid state fishing license (www.mdnr-elicense.com) for anyone over 17.

★ Diving

Two of Michigan's excellent underwater preserves are off this stretch of Lake Huron shoreline. Between Port Austin and Harbor Beach, 19 major shipwrecks lie within the 276-square-mile **Thumb Area Bottomland Preserve.** Most sites are 100 feet down or deeper, accessible only to advanced divers. An exception is the popular *Chickamauga,* a 322-foot turn-of-the-20th-century schooner—it was built in the late 1890s and foundered in 1919. Resting in just 35 feet of water, it's in a relatively protected area about 0.5 miles east of Harbor Beach.

Farther south, the **Sanilac Shores Underwater Preserve** between Port Sanilac and Lexington contains some recent shipwreck finds, including the 250-foot *Regina,* a freighter that sank in 1913 but wasn't discovered until 1986. Sanilac Shores shipwrecks tend to be in shallower water, and many are in excellent condition. For information on both preserves and a listing of dive shops and charters, contact the **Huron County Economic Development Corporation** (989/269-6431 or 800/358-4862, www.huroncounty.com) or the **Michigan Underwater Preserve Council** (MUPC, 800/970-8717, www.michiganpreserves.org).

the public marina in Lexington

FESTIVALS

The towns alongside Lake Huron celebrate with a variety of annual events. In mid-July, the **Maritime Festival** (www.themaritimefestival.com) presents activities throughout Harbor Beach, including historical tours and fireworks displays. Also in late July, the **Summer Festival** (www.portsanilac.net) lights up downtown Port Sanilac with an array of competitions from horseshoe tournaments to sandcastle contests. In mid-September, Lexington offers its own dose of culture with the **Bach and Friends Festival** (https://huroniaheights.com/event/lexington-bach-fest), a three-day musical extravaganza.

SHOPPING

While the Lake Huron shore isn't a noted shopping destination, there's at least one worthwhile stop. **Angel's Garden** (7260 Huron Ave., Lexington, 810/359-2496, www.angelsgardengifts.com, daily Apr.-Dec.), a former harness shop built in the 1840s, now houses a massive collection of angel sculptures, garden accessories, and other unique gifts produced by local artists.

FOOD AND ACCOMMODATIONS

A great place to grab a meal while traveling along M-25 is the **Williams Inn** (1724 S. Lakeshore Rd., Harbor Beach, 989/479-3361, 8am-9pm daily, $12-23). Enjoy their fresh lake perch, steaks, chicken, and seafood—plus a good selection of sandwiches. There's also a full bar.

Perched just 500 feet from Lake Huron, the **Raymond House Inn** (111 S. Ridge St., Port Sanilac, 810/622-8800, $76-130 d) is an impressive 1871 home that's been converted to an inn. The inn has seven bedrooms on the second floor, an on-site art gallery and gift shop, and free wireless Internet access.

INFORMATION AND SERVICES

For more information about Grindstone City and Huron City, contact the **Greater Port Austin Area Chamber of Commerce** (2 W. Spring St., Port Austin, 989/738-7600, www.portaustinarea.com, 9am-1pm Mon., Wed., and Fri.-Sat.). For more information about the Lake Huron shore, contact the **Harbor Beach Chamber of Commerce** (989/479-6477, www.harborbeachchamber.com), the **Village of Port Sanilac** (56 N. Ridge St., Port Sanilac, 810/622-9963, www.portsanilac.net), and the **Lexington Business Association** (810/359-7774, www.lexingtonmichigan.org).

For local and regional news, consult the ***Huron Daily Tribune*** (www.michiganstthumb.com), the ***Lakeshore Guardian*** (www.lakeshoreguardian.com), or the ***Sanilac County News*** (www.thepaperboy.com/newspaper).

Despite the small size of these coastal towns, travelers will still find many essential services. Contact the **police** (810/622-9131) in Port Sanilac.

GETTING THERE AND AROUND

Grindstone City, Huron City, Harbor Beach, Port Sanilac, and Lakeport are easy to reach via car. Follow M-25 along the shore; the route from Grindstone City to Lakeport is roughly 73 miles and takes at least 90 minutes. Given the relatively small size of these coastal towns, you can drive or walk around each locale. For bus route information, contact the **Thumb Area Transit** (TAT, 1513 Bad Axe Rd., Bad Axe, 989/269-2121 or 800/322-1125, www.tatbus.com), which services Huron County.

Port Huron

At the southern end of M-25, Port Huron is at the juncture of Lake Huron and the St. Clair River, part of a vital shipping route that links Lake Huron to Lake Erie. Port Huron stretches eight miles along the lake and this international river boundary, opposite Sarnia, Ontario. On any given day, visitors can watch as a steady procession of pleasure craft, oil tankers, and bulk freighters file past.

Due to its strategic geographical position, Port Huron is one of the oldest settlements in Michigan and one of the earliest outposts in the American interior. The French built Fort St. Joseph here in 1686, mainly to seal off the entrance to the upper Great Lakes from the rival English. The first permanent settlement was established in 1790. In 1814 the Americans built Fort Gratiot on the site, also an attempt to repel the British. The fort was occupied off and on after the Civil War, when it served as a recruiting station.

In the late 1800s, four local villages—Peru, Desmond, Huron, and Gratiot—united to form Port Huron and helped develop the area into a lumber center. When the big trees ran out, Port Huron weathered the industry's demise better than most Michigan cities, since it had already diversified. When the city rejected the bids of chemical companies to build plants here, fearing environmental and safety problems, they instead found a home on the Canadian side of the river, and today make up the 20-mile-long "chemical valley"—Canada's greatest concentration of chemical companies, which are responsible for most of the pollution in the lower St. Clair River.

SIGHTS

★ Port Huron Museum

You can experience a slew of nautical history at the **Port Huron Museum** (1115 6th St., 810/982-0891, www.phmuseum.org, 11am-4pm Tues.-Sat., $10 adults, $8 seniors and students). Housed in a former library that dates to 1904, the two-story museum includes a restored freighter pilothouse where you can work the wheel, signal the alarm horn, and ring the engine bell; marine-related items; objects recovered from Lake Huron shipwrecks; Native American artifacts; and contemporary paintings by local artists. One of the most interesting exhibits displays objects recovered from digs on the site of Thomas Edison's boyhood home, which include evidence of an early laboratory. The museum also oversees three other sites: the Thomas Edison Depot Museum, the Fort Gratiot Lighthouse, and the *Huron* Lightship.

THOMAS EDISON DEPOT MUSEUM

Port Huron's most famous resident was native son Thomas Alva Edison (1847-1931). He is honored at **Thomas Edison Park,** located under the enormous Blue Water Bridge. In the bridge's shadow is the restored **1858 Grand Trunk Depot** (810/982-0891, www.phmuseum.org, 10am-5pm Sat.-Sun. May-Oct., $10 adults, $8 seniors and students, included in Port Huron Museum admission), where Edison boarded the Detroit-bound train daily to sell fruit, nuts, magazines, and newspapers. He used much of his earnings to buy chemicals for the small laboratory he had set up in the train's baggage car. The depot now houses a museum dedicated to Edison with historical photos and displays, including artifacts excavated from the site of Edison's boyhood home.

LIGHTHOUSES

Just north of the Blue Water Bridge, the **Fort Gratiot Lighthouse** (800/852-4242, 11am-5pm Fri.-Mon. May-Oct., $10 adults, $8 seniors and students, included in Port Huron Museum admission), Michigan's oldest, stands 86 feet tall over **Lighthouse Park.** The original tower was poorly constructed in 1825 and crumbled just four years later. It was replaced in 1829 by the sturdier brick structure that stands today. The light is older than Michigan itself, admitted to the Union in 1837. The lighthouse was automated in 1933, and it continues to flash a warning to mariners coming south from Lake Huron. Tours are available; call for information.

At nearby Pine Grove Park, you can take a self-guided tour of the 1921 ***Huron* Lightship** (810/982-0891, www.phmuseum.org, 10am-5pm daily June-Aug., 11am-5pm Sat.-Sun. Sept.-Oct., $10 adults, $8 seniors and students, included in Port Huron Museum admission), operated by the Port Huron Museum. This 97-foot vessel served as a floating lighthouse visible from 14 miles away. Retired in 1970, the *Huron* Lightship was the last to operate on the Great Lakes. The park also offers a view of the bridge and passing boat traffic on the St. Clair River, and it is an interesting place to watch anglers catch walleye and steelhead.

CRUISES

For a closer look at the St. Clair River, sign on for a two-hour trip aboard the ***Huron Lady II*** (810/984-1500, $23 adults, $12 ages 5-12, $21 over age 59, mid-June-early Sept.), a 65-foot excursion boat that cruises under the Blue Water Bridge and heads out onto Lake Huron, where it treats passengers to views of giant freighters as they load and unload their cargo. A number of special cruises area also offered, including a fireworks cruise, a Sturgeon viewing cruise, and a three-hour cruise on Lake Huron to view the start of the Port Huron to Mackinac sailboat race.

TOURS

The **USGS Cutter *Bramble***, (2336 Military St., https://bramblereborn.com) is a World War II vessel once used as a Great Lakes icebreaker until it was decommissioned in 2003. Unlike most decommissioned ships, the *Bramble* still sails to some of the same destinations she did while active, principally the Northwest Passage. However, when in Port Huron, it is occasionally open for tours. Watch the website for details.

GOLF

The Port Huron area boasts a dozen golf courses, including the **Holly Meadows Golf Course** (4855 Capac Rd., Capac, 810/395-4653, www.hollymeadows.com, daily Mar.-Nov., $29-33 with cart), **Rattle Run Golf Course** (7163 St. Clair Hwy., St. Clair, 810/329-2070, www.rattlerun.com, daily Mar.-Nov., $29-43 with cart), and **Black River Country Club** (3300 Country Club Dr., Port

A former library houses the Port Huron Museum.

Huron, 810/982-9595, www.blackrivergolfclub.com, daily Apr.-Oct., $36-42 with cart), an 18-hole championship course founded in 1926 that offers stunning views of the Black River.

EVENTS

Port Huron and its surrounding communities hold a variety of events throughout the year, from fishing tournaments to arts and crafts shows. One intriguing option is the **St. Clair Flats Historical Encampment** (Algonac State Park, Algonac, 810/765-5605) in mid-September. During the two-day event, historical interpreters demonstrate the crafts, skills, and games of the different peoples, both Native Americans and Europeans, who inhabited the Great Lakes region during the mid-1700s.

The Blue Water Area hosts its biggest annual event in mid-July: The **Port Huron to Mackinac Race** attracts some 300 sailboats for the trip up the Huron shore to Mackinac Island; in preceding days, sailors and spectators pack the area's restaurants and hotels—don't show up without room reservations. Contact the **Bayview Yacht Club in Detroit** (www.byc.com) for more information.

SHOPPING

For crafters, a visit to **Mary Maxim** (2001 Holland Ave., 810/987-2000, www.marymaxim.com, 10am-6pm Mon.-Sat., 11am-5pm Sun.), an enormous emporium of needlework and home decor, is a must. Others will relish Port Huron's downtown district, where you'll find jewelry boutiques, furniture stores, and more.

FOOD AND ACCOMMODATIONS

Just south of the Grand Trunk Depot and near the former Fort Gratiot site, the ★ **DoubleTree by Hilton Hotel Port Huron** (500 Thomas Edison Pkwy., 810/984-8000, www.hilton.com, $164-214 d) is the city's nicest and largest hotel. You can enjoy wonderful bridge and water views from **Freighters Eatery and Taproom** (800 Harker St., 810/941-6010, www.freightersph.com, $8-22), with a menu that includes a barbecue pulled pork sandwich and eastern shore crab cakes.

For a more down-to-earth choice, consider **Lynch's Irish Tavern** (210 Huron Blvd., 810/824-4021, www.lynchsirishtavern.com, 10:45am-2am Mon-Sat., 11am-midnight Sun., $10-18), a warm and welcoming watering hole with good food, such as chipotle chicken, shepherd's pie, or pork banger and mash.

INFORMATION AND SERVICES

For more information about the Port Huron area, contact the **Blue Water Area Convention & Visitors Bureau** (520 Thomas Edison Pkwy., 800/852-4242, www.bluewater.org, 8am-5pm Mon.-Fri., 10am-3pm Sat.) and the **Blue Water Area Chamber of Commerce** (512 McMorran Blvd., 810/985-7101, www.bluewaterchamber.com, 8:30am-4:30pm Mon.-Fri.). For local news, pick up a copy of the daily ***Times Herald*** (www.thetimesherald.com).

As one of the largest cities in the Thumb, Port Huron provides travelers with everything they might need. For medical emergencies, contact the **McLaren Port Huron Hospital** (1221 Pine Grove Ave., 810/987-5000, www.mclaren.org). **Rite Aid** (2910 Pine Grove Ave., 810/987-3663, www.riteaid.com) has pharmacy hours from 8am to midnight daily. You can contact the **Port Huron Police Department** (810/984-8415) for emergencies.

GETTING THERE AND AROUND

Although the closest major airport is in Detroit, a few hours to the southwest, travelers can get to Port Huron via train. **Amtrak** (800/872-7245, www.amtrak.com) trains run from Chicago, with stops across Michigan, including East Lansing, Flint, and the **Port Huron Station** (2223 16th St.).

By car, there are three major routes to Port

Huron. From Detroit, take I-94 and the I-69 Business Loop, a 64-mile route that takes about an hour. From Flint, I-69 and the I-69 Business Loop make up a 67-mile trip that takes a little over an hour. The 154-mile scenic route along the Thumb's coastline via M-25 takes you from Bay City to Port Austin to Port Huron in about three hours. The town can also be reached from Sarnia, Ontario, Canada, across the **Blue Water Bridge** (www.michigan.gov/mdot, $3 [C$4] passenger vehicles); motorists often experience a delay when traversing the international border crossing. U.S. citizens need a passport to enter Canada. Returning to the United States requires a passport or an enhanced driver's license.

Grand Rapids and the Heartland

From any point in Michigan, at least one of the five Great Lakes is never more than 85 miles away. That's auspicious news for Michigan's Heartland—also known as central Michigan—the region with the least coastal frontage. Stretching from the southern state line to the middle of the Lower Peninsula, this wide swath of rolling prairies, scenic lakes, weathered barns, and abundant farmland is also home to some of Michigan's finest educational institutions and largest cities, including Grand Rapids, Kalamazoo, Midland, and Lansing, the state capital since 1847.

As with the Thumb, modern travelers often overlook much of Michigan's Heartland. Early settlers of the 19th century, however, recognized the appeal of this central region. A surge of eager

Highlights

Look for ★ to find recommended sights, activities, dining, and lodging.

★ **Gerald R. Ford Presidential Museum:** In addition to celebrating the life of President Ford and his wife, this museum offers temporary exhibits from the Smithsonian Institution and the National Archives (page 138).

★ **Frederik Meijer Gardens and Sculpture Park:** This impressive collection of gardens also boasts sculptures by Auguste Rodin, Claes Oldenburg, and Henry Moore (page 140).

★ **Michigan State University:** Stroll lovely gardens, attend Big 10 football games, view an assortment of art and science exhibits, and catch a wide array of live performances at the Wharton Center (page 145).

★ **Bird-Watching at the W. K. Kellogg Bird Sanctuary:** Hike amid 180 acres of diverse habitats that nurture hundreds of bird species (page 157).

★ **Air Zoo:** Devoted to aviation and space exploration, this enormous complex features flight simulators, World War II-era bombers, astronaut artifacts, and a pseudo-paratrooper jump (page 164).

★ **Soaring Eagle Casino and Resort:** One of the Midwest's largest casinos offers thousands of slot machines and table games, a soothing spa, and live entertainment (page 166).

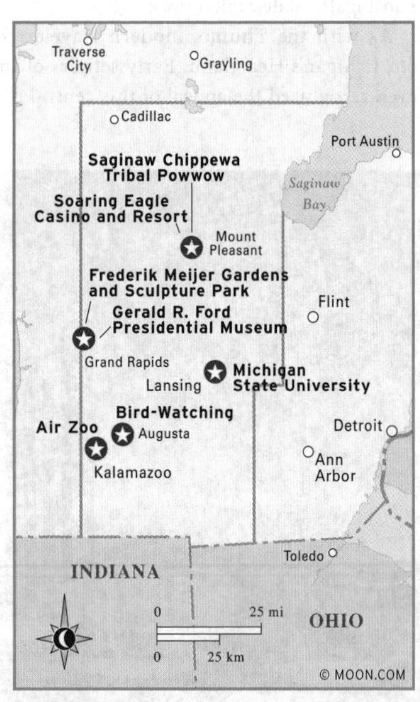

★ **Saginaw Chippewa Tribal Powwow:** This gathering of the clans showcases traditional dancing, drumming, chanting, and cuisine (page 166).

frontier-bound settlers resulted in the establishment of some of Michigan's most historic towns, including Battle Creek, which was a major stopping point on the Underground Railroad prior to the Civil War and later the home of abolitionist pioneer Sojourner Truth. Migrating Easterners were also responsible for the establishment of many of the Heartland's private colleges in towns such as Hillsdale, Albion, Alma, and Olivet. The Heartland is also home to major universities—Michigan State University in East Lansing, Western Michigan University in Kalamazoo, and Central Michigan University in Mount Pleasant.

Besides strolling through well-groomed campuses and well-preserved villages, travelers will find a myriad of other outdoor and cultural pursuits as well. And whether exploring the Gerald R. Ford Presidential Museum in Grand Rapids, marveling at Kalamazoo's Air Zoo, or hiking through the W. K. Kellogg Bird Sanctuary, cost-conscious visitors will be grateful for the moderate prices of Michigan's interior.

PLANNING YOUR TIME

The Heartland (sometimes referred to as "mid-Michigan") is an enormous place, extending from the Indiana border to M-20, near the center of the Lower Peninsula; it's bordered on the eastern side by Ann Arbor and Midland and on the western side by Kalamazoo and Grand Rapids. Given its size, what you're able to see depends on your schedule; likewise, your interests will determine how long to plan your stay. If you only intend to visit the area's major cities, you should put aside about five days. You'll need at least 10, however, if you also want to explore the region's outdoor attractions and smaller towns like Jackson and Mount Pleasant.

Reaching the Heartland is easy. With several major towns and cities, it's possible to get here by plane, train, or bus. The region has several commercial airports in or near Kalamazoo, Grand Rapids, Lansing, and Midland, as well as in nearby Flint and Detroit. Amtrak and Greyhound both offer routes to Kalamazoo, Battle Creek, East Lansing, Jackson, and Grand Rapids. Needless to say, the Heartland is not a compact region, so despite the presence of several public transit systems, having a car is a must—whether you bring your own or rent one. Major highways and interstates—such as U.S. 23, U.S. 127, U.S. 131, I-69, I-75, I-94, and I-96—make it convenient to get from one end of the region to the other.

For more information about Michigan's Heartland, consult **Pure Michigan** (Michigan Economic Development Corporation, 300 N. Washington Sq., Lansing, 888/784-7328, www.michigan.org) or the **West Michigan Tourist Association** (WMTA, 741 Kenmoor Ave., Ste. E, Grand Rapids, 616/245-2217, www.wmta.org).

HISTORY

By the 1830s, Michigan had become attractive to settlers coming from the East via the newly completed Erie Canal and passing through Detroit and along the new Detroit-Chicago Road (today's Michigan Avenue), which cut across the southern half of the Lower Peninsula. Their destination was Michigan's rolling prairies, with rich soil and fertile land that the federal government was selling at the bargain price of $1.25 an acre.

A rush of settlement between 1825 and 1855 spurred some of Michigan's largest towns, including Battle Creek and Jackson. By 1849 the Michigan Central Railroad had begun making regular state crossings, delivering thousands of optimistic settlers. The most visible evidence of these early settlers can be found in the Greek Revival homes that dominate the cities and villages they built.

Previous: Grand Rapids skyline hugging the Grand River; *Light of the Moon* by Igor Mitoraj at Frederick Meijer Gardens and Sculpture Park; the Blue Bridge across the Grand River in Grand Rapids.

Grand Rapids and the Heartland

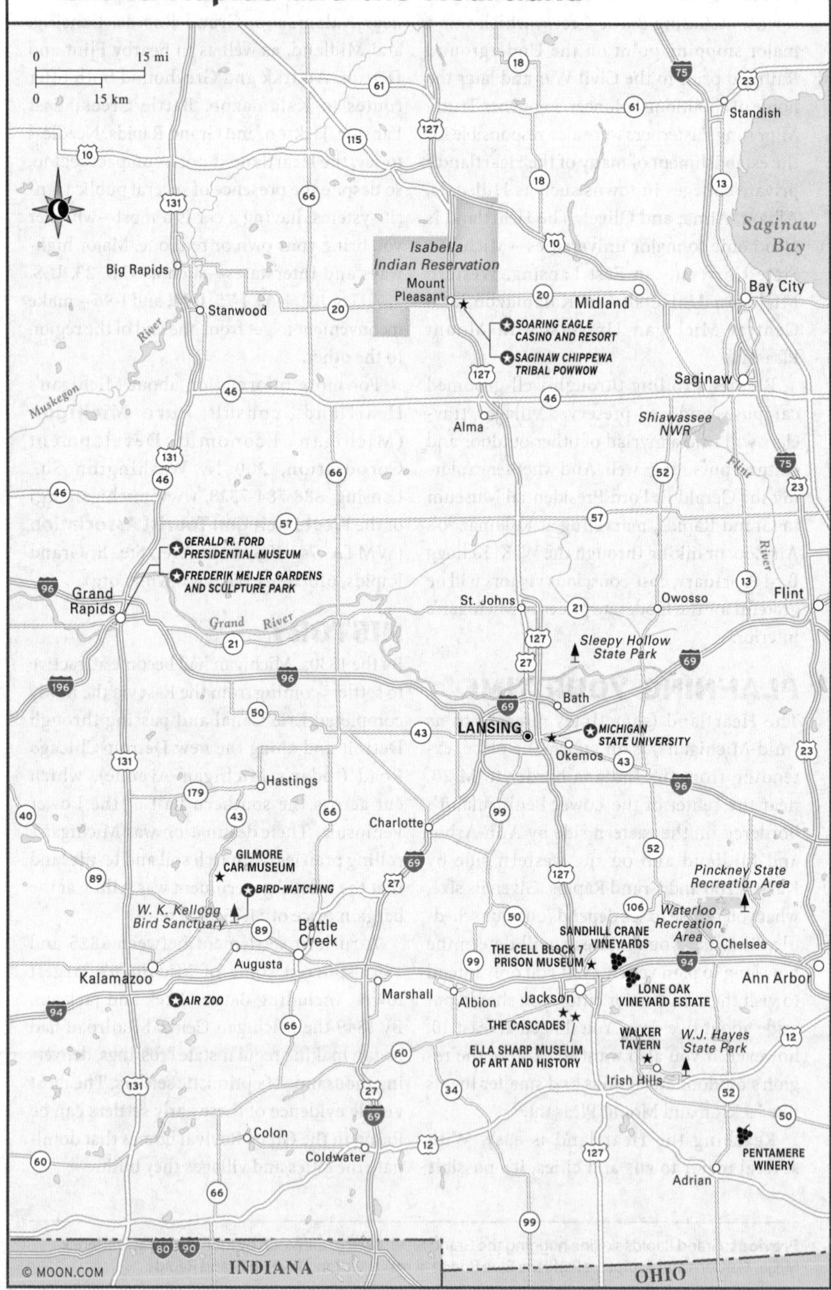

Grand Rapids

Grand Rapids—the state's second-largest city, with a population of 192,300—owes its development and name to the rapids of the free-flowing Grand River, a place of gathering and exchange since Louis Campau established a trading post here in 1826. The power and transportation afforded by the river, coupled with the abundance of wood from the neighboring forests, spurred the city's furniture industry. By 1854, logging had become the local economic cornerstone, and Grand Rapids entered the most vigorous phase of its development.

During the 1860s, Campau Square was notorious for its brothels, gambling houses, and basement saloons. It became better known for its furniture-making in 1876 through a display at the nation's centennial celebration in Philadelphia. In 1880, the incorporation of the Wolverine Chair and Furniture Company solidified that reputation, and by 1900, Grand Rapids had earned the nicknamed "Furniture City." And the moniker endures, as the area still serves as headquarters for Herman Miller and Steelcase, two of the largest office furniture companies in the country.

Grand Rapids went through a period of decline in the early 1980s, but has managed to reinvent itself as a thriving showcase for the arts, local history, and business. Today, the downtown sparkles with busy hotels, shopping districts, pedestrian malls, and public artworks. One of the most striking downtown sights is Alexander Calder's dramatic sculpture, *La Grande Vitesse,* a 42-ton strawberry-red piece that pays homage to the rapids that built the city. More recent city improvements include a new ecofriendly Grand Rapids Public Museum and the addition of one of the nation's largest lion exhibits at the John Ball Zoo.

Much of the redevelopment can be attributed to the area's loyal and exceedingly generous business leaders, including the Meijer Corporation and direct marketing firm Amway. Grand Rapids is also a center of religious publishing, home to both Zondervan (now a division of HarperCollins) and William B. Eardmans. And while industrious Grand Rapids may be known for its Protestant work ethic, a surprising amount of diversity hides beneath the city's Calvinist veneer. While still a Republican stronghold, Grand Rapids is also home to an active alternative press and one of the state's largest Native American populations. The city's older neighborhoods celebrate a diverse mix of cultures.

TOP EXPERIENCE

SIGHTS

Heritage Hill Historic District

As a manufacturing city with many locally owned businesses, early residents weren't shy about displaying their wealth, building mansions on the city's hillside. **Heritage Hill** (616/459-8950, www.heritagehillweb.org) was their neighborhood of choice from roughly 1840 through 1920. Just east of downtown, more than 60 architectural styles are reflected in its 1,300 residences. Heritage Hill is now one of the largest urban historic districts in the country. Today's Heritage Hill residents are more economically and racially diverse.

The highlight is the **Meyer May House** (450 Madison Ave., 616/246-4821, www.meyermayhouse.steelcase.com, 10am-1pm Tues. and Thurs., 1pm-4pm Sun., free), an anomaly in this predominantly Victorian neighborhood. It was designed in 1906 by Frank Lloyd Wright for the founder of the May's clothing stores. Vincent Scully, an architectural historian, has called the Meyer May House the most beautifully and completely restored of Wright's Prairie houses. Through generous funding from office furniture maker Steelcase, the house has since been restored to reflect Wright's original

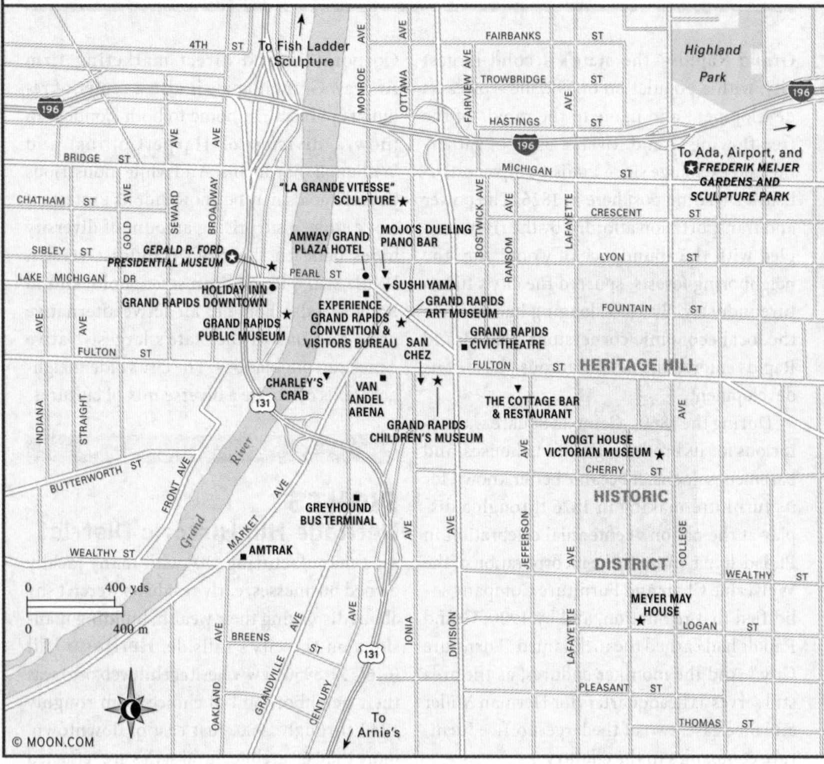

organic building concept, with custom-made furniture, art glass, carpets, light fixtures, and even linens.

★ Gerald R. Ford Presidential Museum

The **Gerald R. Ford Presidential Museum** (303 Pearl St. NW, 616/254-0400, www.fordlibrarymuseum.gov, 9am-5pm Mon.-Sat., noon-5pm Sun., $10 adults, $8 seniors, $7 college students with ID, $4 ages 6-18) honors the nation's 38th president and the only one from Michigan, in this triangular building on the west bank of the Grand River. Ford grew up in Grand Rapids and was in Congress from 1948 to 1973, when he became the nation's first vice president appointed under the 25th Amendment.

Recently renovated, the museum portrays both the private life and public challenges that Ford dealt with, president for less than three years. The most popular exhibits are the full-size replicas of the Oval Office and the Cabinet Room as they looked while Ford was president. Other exhibits include a surprisingly moving section on Nixon's resignation and his subsequent pardon by Ford, the events surrounding the fall of Saigon, and a multimedia re-creation of 1970s pop culture. Visitors can also view Gerald and Betty Ford's burial site.

1: the Gerald R. Ford Presidential Museum **2:** Frank Lloyd Wright's Meyer May House

1

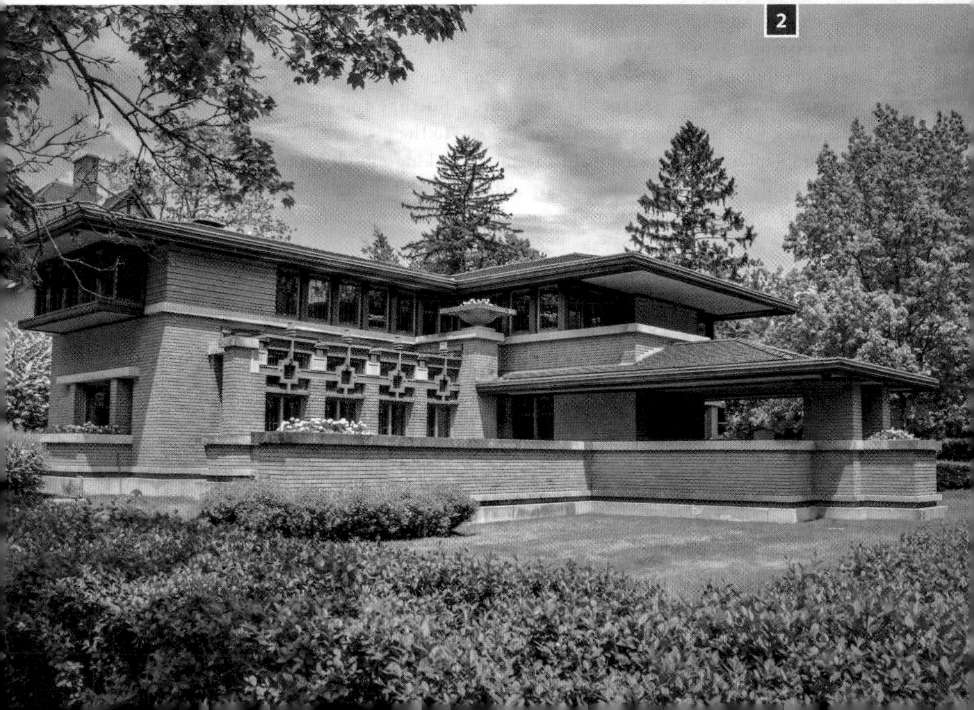

2

Other Museums

In 2007 the long-standing **Grand Rapids Art Museum** (GRAM, 101 Monroe Center, 616/831-1000, www.artmuseumgr.org, 10am-5pm Tues.-Wed. and Fri.-Sat., 10am-9pm Thurs., noon-5pm Sun., $10 adults, $8 seniors and students with ID, $6 ages 6-17) was moved to an environmentally friendly building praised by architecture critics. Inside, extensive collections include fine 19th- and 20th-century prints, paintings, photographs, sculptures, and decorative arts, with an emphasis on furniture.

The art museum's major competition is the **Grand Rapids Public Museum** (272 Pearl St. NW, 616/456-3977, www.grmuseum.org, 9am-5pm Mon.-Fri., 10am-5pm Sat.-Sun., $8 adults, $7 over age 61, $3 students and children ages 3-17). Arguably the city's best museum, it is housed in a spectacular structure and ranks as the largest general museum in the state. Built in 1995, the museum was largely financed through a gift from Amway cofounder Jay Van Andel.

The Grand Rapids Public Museum holds an outstanding permanent collection. See the massive flywheel of a 1905 Corliss-type steam engine that once powered the city's furniture factories; walk through a re-creation of 1890s Grand Rapids; take a turn aboard a restored 1928 Spillman carousel; or see stars at the Roger B. Chaffee Planetarium. The groundbreaking exhibit "Anishinabek: The People of This Place" explores the culture and artifacts of the Anishinabe people, the first residents of western Michigan. An illuminating explanation of the state's indigenous Ottawa, Chippewa, and Potawatomi peoples, it includes video interviews that trace the modern challenges of Native Americans. The museum also hosts temporary exhibits.

Grand Rapids has a special museum for the young: The **Grand Rapids Children's Museum** (11 Sheldon Ave., 616/235-4726, www.grcm.org, 9:30am-5pm Tues.-Wed. and Fri.-Sat., 9:30am-8pm Thurs., noon-5pm Sun., $8.50 adults, $7.50 over age 64, school faculty, and active military with ID, $7 children, under age 1 free) is dedicated to the value of play. A bevy of permanent exhibits, including Lego, Lite-Brite, and the Spin Table, complement programs in the humanities, math, and science as the museum seeks to nurture developing minds.

★ Frederik Meijer Gardens and Sculpture Park

Another local benefactor, Fred Meijer, owner and founder of the Meijer grocery stores, has given back to his hometown with the spectacular **Frederik Meijer Gardens and Sculpture Park** (1000 E. Beltline Ave. NE, 616/957-1580, www.meijergardens.org, 9am-5pm Mon.-Sat., 11am-5pm Sun., $14.50 adults, $11 seniors and students, $7 ages 5-13, $4 ages 3-4), established in 1995. Its 125 acres encompass a 15,000-square-foot tropical conservatory, the state's largest; an outdoor area of colorful flower gardens complemented by ponds, woods, and wetlands; and an extensive collection of sculpture—including works by Auguste Rodin, Henry Moore, Claes Oldenburg, and Coosje van Bruggen. Quotations displayed throughout the gardens by Michigan poets, such as Theodore Roethke and Jim Harrison, connect people to the plants. Given the size of the facility, taking a guided tram tour ($4 adults, $2 age 12 and younger—in addition to basic admission) is recommended. The docents provide a wealth of knowledge about the artwork and plantings.

PERFORMING ARTS

Grand Rapids' performing arts scene is rich and diverse, offering everything from Michigan's only professional ballet company to summertime concerts at the outdoor amphitheater in Frederik Meijer Gardens. One must-see is the **Grand Rapids Civic Theatre** (30 Division Ave., 616/222-6650, www.grct.org), a grand piece of the city's architecture. The largest community theater in Grand Rapids and one of the biggest in the United States, this impressive landmark offers six main-stage and two children's productions annually in a restored 1903 theater once known as The Majestic. Recent productions include *Steel Magnolias*, *Mamma Mia!*, and *James and the Giant Peach*.

Another destination for quality drama is the **Jewish Theatre Grand Rapids** (2727 Michigan NE, 616/234-3946, www.jtgr.org). In addition to familiar classics, the JTGR also presents a slate of thought-provoking plays touching on themes related to the intersection of politics and religion. All will appreciate the significance and timeliness of many of the productions.

FOOD AND ACCOMMODATIONS

The city's oldest operating bar and restaurant, **The Cottage Bar & Restaurant** (18 LaGrave Ave., 616/454-9088, www.cottagebar.biz, 11am-1am Mon.-Thurs., 11am-2am Fri.-Sat., $8-14), concocts Grand Rapids' best burgers and three different styles of chili. The outside café is a popular meeting place in good weather.

Tapas, paella, and other specialties of the Iberian Peninsula draw crowds tired of prime rib and pasta to ★ **San Chez A Tapas Bistro** (38 W. Fulton, 616/774-8272, www.sanchezbistro.com, 8am-10pm Mon.-Thurs., 8am-11pm Fri., noon-11pm Sat., 4pm-10pm Sun., $4-20). Lively and fun, it draws an eclectic crowd with entrées such as spiced Moroccan meatballs and lamb ribs with raspberry chili sauce. Also open for breakfast, you'll also find familiar favorites like omelets made to order and vanilla maple oatmeal.

Charley's Crab (63 Market Ave. SW, 616/459-2500, www.muer.com, 11:30am-10pm Mon.-Thurs., 11:30am-11pm Fri., 4pm-11pm Sat., 10am-9pm Sun., $12-48) is part of Chuck Muer's well-loved chain of seafood restaurants. Try one of the fresh catches or tasty pastas, or load up on carbs at Sunday brunch. The signature rolls have been copied by a number of restaurants across the state. In good weather, ask for an outside table overlooking the Grand River.

At **Sushi Yama** (166 Monroe Center, Ste. 102, 616/233-9881, www.sushiyama.com, 11am-7:30pm Mon.-Sat., $5-12) on the lower level of the McKay Tower, you'll find an assortment of favorites, including the Pacific roll (tuna, salmon, and avocado) or the crispy snapper (fried snapper, avocado, and cucumber).

A great place to experience some quality entertainment while enjoying dinner is **Mojo's Dueling Piano Bar and Restaurant** (180 Monroe Ave., 616/776-9000, www.mojospianobar.com, 5pm-1:30am Wed., Fri.-Sat., 5pm-11:30pm Thurs., $8-11). Each evening the main floor features live entertainment while a DJ offers music on the second level. A dueling piano show is featured nightly. The menu offers various burgers, salads, panini, and flatbread pizzas.

For one of the best values downtown, consider the **Holiday Inn Grand Rapids Downtown** (310 Pearl St. NW, 616/235-7611, www.holidayinn.com, $115-200 d), centrally located near the Gerald Ford and other public museums, with high-speed Internet access, a pool, a fitness center, a restaurant, and clean, attractive rooms. Pets are welcome.

At the other end of the spectrum, the ★ **Amway Grand Plaza Hotel** (187 Monroe NW, 616/774-2000, www.amwaygrand.com, $200-395 d) ranks as the finest lodging in Grand Rapids and one of Michigan's top hotels. Two hotels actually make up the complex: the original 1913 structure, once known as the Pantlind Hotel, and the newer Glass Tower, completed in 1981. Choose from a lush traditional or cool contemporary room. In all, the two house more than 680 rooms, nine restaurants (including The Kitchen Counter, a Wolfgang Puck establishment) and coffee shops, several elegant boutiques, and a state-of-the-art fitness center.

INFORMATION AND SERVICES

For more information about the Grand Rapids area, contact the **Experience Grand Rapids Convention & Visitors Bureau** (171 Monroe Ave. NW, Ste. 545,

The Making of a President

Born in Omaha, Nebraska, as Leslie Lynch King Jr., the man who would eventually be known as **Gerald R. Ford Jr.** (1913-2006), actually spent the first few years of his life, along with his mother Dorothy Ayer Gardner, at the home of his maternal grandparents in Grand Rapids, Michigan. Before he'd reached the age of three, Ford's mother, who had divorced his abusive father in 1913, married a paint salesman named Gerald Rudolff Ford. Never formally adopted, the future president eventually changed his legal name to Gerald Rudolph Ford Jr. in 1935.

Raised in Grand Rapids with three half-brothers from his mother's second marriage, Ford enjoyed close relationships with his mother and stepfather. As a child, he was involved in the Boy Scouts, earning the highest rank of Eagle Scout—the only U.S. president to have done so.

Ford attended Grand Rapids South High School, where he became a star athlete and the captain of his football team. He eventually enrolled at the University of Michigan, where, as center and linebacker, he helped the Wolverines achieve undefeated seasons and national titles in both 1932 and 1933. Following his graduation in 1935 with a Bachelor of Arts in economics, he accepted an assistant coaching job for the football and boxing teams at Yale University. Later, Ford enrolled in and graduated from Yale Law School.

Over the following decades, Ford opened a law practice with a friend, enlisted in the Navy during World War II, married a department store fashion consultant with whom he had four children, and spent 25 years in the U.S. House of Representatives. In 1973 he was selected by President Richard Nixon to replace Spiro Agnew, who had resigned following federal indictment on a variety of charges, as vice president. Following the Watergate scandal and Nixon's resignation, Ford became the nation's 38th president. Shortly after taking office, he made the controversial decision to pardon Nixon for any crimes that he might have committed during his presidency. Ford also tried to combat rising inflation, confronted a potential swine flu epidemic, supported the Equal Rights Amendment, officially ended U.S. involvement in the Vietnam War, and survived two assassination attempts, before ultimately losing his reelection bid to Jimmy Carter.

616/258-7388, www.experiencegr.com, 8:30am-5pm Mon.-Fri.) or the **Grand Rapids Area Chamber of Commerce** (250 Monroe NW, 616/771-0300, www.grandrapids.org, 8:30am-5pm Mon.-Fri.). For local news, entertainment, and sports, consult the ***Grand Rapids Press*** (www.mlive.com/grpress) or watch **WOOD** (www.woodtv.com), the local NBC affiliate.

Grand Rapids offers all the services you might require, including gas stations, laundry, and banks. For groceries, prescriptions, and other supplies, stop by a **Meijer Superstore** (www.meijer.com); there are several in the area.

For medical assistance, consult **Spectrum Health** (866/989-7999, www.spectrum-health.org), which oversees several hospitals and medical centers in the region.

GETTING THERE AND AROUND

As with several other towns in the Heartland, Grand Rapids is accessible via plane, train, bus, and car, of course. **Gerald R. Ford International Airport** (GRR, 5500 44th St. SE, 616/233-6000, www.grr.org) is southeast of town and has rentals from several national car chains, or opt for a luxury sedan from **Metro Cars** (616/827-6500 or 800/456-1701, www.metrocars.com), which offers 24-hour service from the airport. A ride from the Ford airport to downtown Grand Rapids costs about $40. **Amtrak** (431 Wealthy St. SW, 800/872-7245, www.amtrak.com) serves the city, as does **Greyhound** (616/456-1700 or 800/231-2222, www.greyhound.com) and **Indian Trails** (800/292-3831, www.indiantrails.com); both provide service at the

In the years following his presidency, Ford remained active. He and his wife moved to Denver and ultimately Rancho Mirage, California. In 1977 he established the Gerald R. Ford Institute of Public Policy at Michigan's Albion College. In 1981 he opened the Gerald R. Ford Presidential Library on the North Campus of the University of Michigan and established the Gerald R. Ford Presidential Museum in Grand Rapids. In 1999 the university renamed its Schools of Public Policy the Gerald R. Ford School of Public Policy. By 1988 Ford had become a member of several corporate boards, and in 2001, received the John F. Kennedy Profiles in Courage Award for his decision to pardon Nixon. That year he also broke from the Republican Party by supporting equal treatment of gay and lesbian couples.

bronze statue of President Ford by J. Brett Grill

Five years later, at the age of 93, President Ford died at his California home, having just become the longest-lived U.S. president of that time, outliving Ronald Reagan by just 45 days. He also had the distinction of being the only person to hold the presidency and vice presidency without being elected to either office. Despite his rocky tenure as president, Ford was considered by many to be an honest, kindhearted, and likable man—no doubt a characteristic of his Midwestern roots. Today, Grand Rapids is proud of its native son, and several sites in the Grand Rapids area bear his name, including the Gerald R. Ford Middle School, the Gerald R. Ford International Airport, and the Gerald R. Ford Freeway.

Grand Rapids bus station (250 Grandville Ave. SW).

By car, you can reach Grand Rapids from downtown Detroit north via M-10, I-696, and I-96; without traffic, the 158-mile trip should take around 2.25 hours. From Chicago, I-90, I-94, and I-196 make up a 178-mile trip that usually requires about 2.75 hours. From Chicago, parts of I-90 and I-94 serve as the Indiana Toll Road.

Once in Grand Rapids you'll probably want to use your car to get around. An alternative is **The Rapid** (616/776-1100, www.ridetherapid.org, one-way $1.75 adults or a 10-ride ticket is $13.50, $0.85 seniors and disabled, children under 42 inches tall free with a paying adult), an outstanding public transit system that links Grand Rapids to surrounding towns.

1

2

3

Lansing and East Lansing

The Works Progress Administration *Guide to Michigan,* published in 1941, described Lansing as a place where "the political activity of a state capital, the rumbling tempo of an industrial city, and the even temper of a farming community are curiously blended." Over 75 years later, it's still an apt description.

Michigan's 1835 constitution mandated that Detroit remain the state's capital until 1847, after which time it was to be relocated to a city chosen by the legislature. Detroit's proximity to the international border made it vulnerable to British attack; moving the capital near the center of the state would encourage economic development and make it more accessible to all citizens, a pattern repeated by a number of other states. Parochial loyalties, however, made the selection process laborious. After months of wrangling and debate, Lansing, a tiny village too small to be an initial contender, was chosen to break the stalemate. The state's seat of government moved to Lansing in 1847.

When the tiny town, named after Lansing, New York, became the new capital, many wanted to rename it Michigan or Michigamme, but the legislature once again became bogged down; Lansing it remained. Once the new capital was established, it began to grow. By the time the city was incorporated in 1859, it had 4,000 residents, a new capitol, and two newspapers. In 1897 R. E. Olds founded what was originally named the Olds Motor Vehicle Company.

Today, Lansing is also headquarters for many trade and professional associations and heavy industry. East Lansing, a neighboring community, is the home of Michigan State University, part of the Big 10 collegiate athletic conference. Urban decay and rampant freeway construction have bruised downtown Lansing, and the city is often all but empty after 5pm. While it has been described as a city in search of a center, it actually has a surprising amount to offer: a beautifully restored state capitol, excellent museums, a full plate of university events, and some of the state's loveliest and most accessible gardens. The city also hosts a minor league baseball team, the Lansing Lugnuts.

1: Japanese Garden at Frederik Meijer Gardens and Sculpture Park **2:** one man band performing by the Grand River **3:** Grand Rapids Public Museum

SIGHTS

★ Michigan State University

Michigan's 1850 constitution mandated the establishment of an agricultural school. The high concentration of farming in the area led the Michigan State Agricultural Society to locate this school in Lansing, in 1855, the forerunner of the nationwide land grant university system. Now called Michigan State University (MSU), it has an excellent reputation.

The MSU campus has grown to more than 5,000 beautifully landscaped acres, home to more than 7,000 different species and varieties of trees, shrubs, and vines. Curving drives and Gothic buildings create a parklike setting, shaded by huge beeches and gnarled white oaks that date back more than 200 years. Students walk to class through what has become an arboretum.

The campus has long been regarded as one giant outdoor laboratory. Very few planted environments in the Midwest have enjoyed such sustained commitment. School policy once demanded three hours of manual labor per day from all students, part of the hands-on approach that helped the university maintain the campus and enabled poor students to afford a college education. Today, both students and professional landscapers maintain the university's impressive collection of gardens.

Campus Gardens

Among MSU's extensive plantings are the

Lansing

Horticulture Gardens (B-110 Plant and Soil Sciences Bldg., 517/353-3770, www.hrt.msu.edu, sunrise-sunset daily, free). Once as flat and bare as a new suburban subdivision, the 14-acre area is now full of pergolas, gazebos, arbors, and topiary. The entrance is off Bogue Street, south of Wilson Road, not far from the Wharton Center. Before venturing into the gardens, pick up a map at the Plant and Soil Sciences Building.

South of the Horticulture Gardens is the year-round **Clarence E. Lewis Landscape Arboretum** (517/355-5191, www.canr.msu.edu, sunrise-sunset daily, free), dedicated in 1984 as an instructional arboretum for students interested in landscape development. The ever-growing collection of demonstration gardens experiments with vegetables, fruit, herbs, conifers, and native plants. You can walk through a water garden, a sculpture garden, a Japanese garden, and a topiary garden, among other displays.

Another campus area worth a special stop is the **W. J. Beal Botanical Garden** (www.cpa.msu.edu, sunrise-sunset daily, free), founded in 1873 and believed to be the oldest continuously operated garden of its type in the country. Situated between the Red Cedar River and West Circle Drive, this outdoor museum of living plants includes more than 2,000 species arranged by family and economic use, as well as exotic flowering landscape specimens and an enlightening section on endangered plants.

Campus Museums

With a collection of more than one million items, the 150-year-old **Michigan State University Museum** (W. Circle Dr., 517/355-7474, www.museum.msu.edu, 9am-5pm

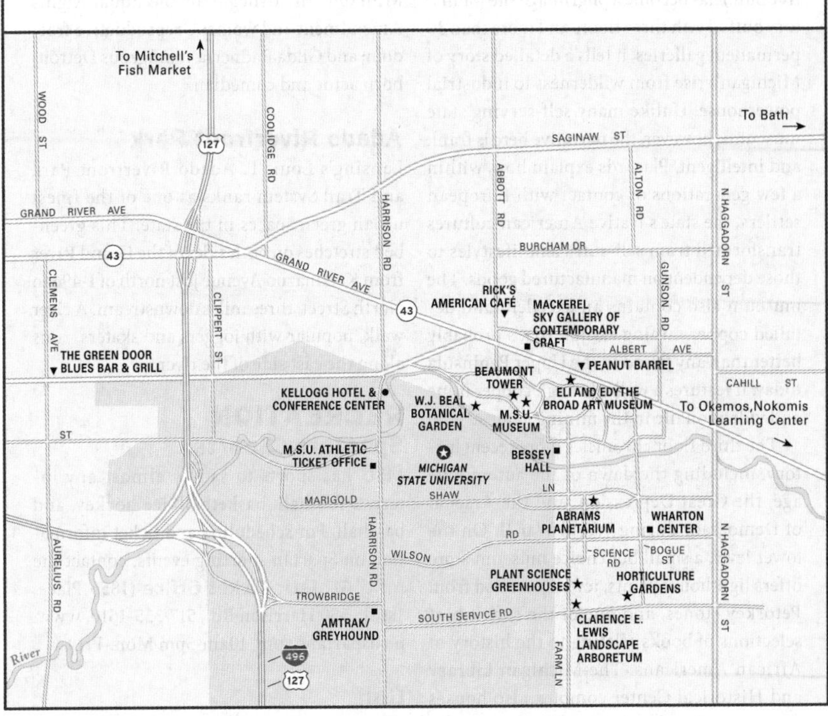

Mon., Wed.-Fri., 9am-8pm Tues., 10am-5pm Sat., $5 donation suggested), situated east of Beaumont Tower, has been called one of the Midwest's best-kept secrets. In 2001, Michigan's leading public natural and cultural history museum also became the state's first museum to receive Smithsonian affiliate status. Three floors of exhibits concentrate on the history of the Great Lakes region; on display are numerous tools, quilts, folk art pieces, and other archaeological artifacts. Popular stops include the fur trader's cabin and the life-size dinosaur dioramas.

Also on campus, at the intersection of Auditorium and Physics Roads, the new **Eli and Edythe Broad Art Museum** (547 E. Circle Dr., 517/884-3900, www.broadmuseum.msu.edu, noon-7pm Tues.-Sun., free) has inherited an impressive array of artwork from Kresge Art Museum, which closed in 2012. Designed by award-winning architect Zaha Hadid, the dynamic glass and steel edifice contains thousands of works, from Greek and Roman antiquities to Renaissance illuminations to 20th-century sculptures by Alexander Calder and Jenny Holzer. Wide-ranging highlights include a dramatic *Vision of St. Anthony of Padua* by Francisco Zurburán and a solid collection of art from the 1960s and '70s, an era often overlooked by other museums. In keeping with the mission of the museum, future acquisitions will focus on works from 1945 to the present.

Other Museums

Part of the huge Michigan Library and Historical Center, the **Michigan Historical Museum** (702 W. Kalamazoo St., 517/373-3559, www.michigan.gov/museum, 9am-4:30pm Mon.-Fri., 10am-4pm Sat., 1pm-5pm

Sun., $6 adults, $4 over age 64, $2 ages 6-17, free Sun.) has become a pilgrimage site for history buffs. With three floors and more than 30 permanent galleries, it tells a detailed story of Michigan's rise from wilderness to industrial powerhouse. Unlike many self-serving state museums, however, the narrative here is frank and intelligent. Placards explain how, within a few generations of contact with European settlers, the state's Native American cultures transformed from self-sufficient lifestyles to those dependent on manufactured goods. The museum also contains an excellent and detailed copper mining exhibit that's probably better than any found in the Upper Peninsula today. It features a walk-through copper mine and videos on life in the mining camps.

The third floor chronicles more recent history, including the dawn of the automobile age, the Great Depression, and the Arsenal of Democracy during World War II. On the lower level, a small but choice museum store offers lighthouse prints, jewelry crafted from Petoskey stones, and one of the state's best selections of books relating to the history of African Americans. The Michigan Library and Historical Center complex also houses the state archives and state library, a popular pilgrimage spot for genealogists from around the country. The building itself is of interest, too, designed by prominent Detroit architect William Kessler, and relying largely on local building materials.

Not far from downtown Lansing, **The Michigan Women's Historical Center and Hall of Fame** (213 W. Main St., 517/484-1880, www.michiganwomenshalloffame.org, noon-5pm Mon.-Fri., free, $5 donation requested) honors the mostly unsung achievements of the state's native daughters through changing and permanent exhibitions. It celebrates the lives and contributions of Michigan women such as Sojourner Truth, a former slave and crusader for human rights; Laura Smith Haviland, an organizer of one of the state's first Underground Railroad stations; Anne Howard Shaw, a minister and physician whose dynamic leadership resulted in the passage of the 19th Amendment; former first lady Helen Milliken, an advocate for the Equal Rights Amendment and women's reproductive freedom; and Gilda Radner, a courageous Detroit-born actor and comedian.

Adado Riverfront Park

Lansing's Louis F. Adado Riverfront Park and Trail System ranks as one of the finest urban green spaces in the state. This greenbelt stretches on both sides of the Grand River from Kalamazoo Avenue just north of I-496 to North Street, three miles downstream. A river walk, popular with joggers and skaters, runs along the east side of the river.

RECREATION

Spectator Sports

MSU has sports to satisfy almost any interest: football, basketball, ice hockey, and baseball. For scheduling and ticket information on Spartan sporting events, contact the **MSU Athletic Ticket Office** (1855 Place, 1st fl., 550 Harrison Rd., 517/355-1610, www.msuspartans.com, 10am-5pm Mon.-Fri.).

Golf

Although northern Michigan boasts more award-winning golf courses, the Heartland has its share of eye-catchers. **Eagle Eye Golf Club** (15500 Chandler Rd., Bath, 517/903-8064, https://eagleeyegolfclub.com, daily Apr.-Oct., $25-95 pp) is one such place about 10 miles northeast of Lansing along I-69. Even better, this exceptional course is part of a spread that includes three others: the 9-hole Falcon, the 27-hole Hawk Hollow, and the Little Hawk putting course.

ENTERTAINMENT

Nightlife

East Lansing's best club is arguably **Rick's American Café** (224 Abbot Rd., East Lansing, 517/351-2285, www.ricksamericancafe.com,

1: costumed football fan at Michigan State University game **2:** clock tower at Michigan State University **3:** Michigan's Capitol in downtown Lansing

1
MICHIGAN
2
3
Comerica
ONLY
ONLY

6pm-2am Mon.-Sat., cover charge varies), with great live acts, top-notch DJs, and drink specials every night. Rick's was named one of the top 25 college bars in the nation by The Daily Meal, a website devoted to all things related to food and drink. Caution: this place tends to get loud. **The Green Door Blues Bar & Grill** (2005 E. Michigan Ave., 517/482-6376, www.greendoorlive.com, 3pm-2am Mon.-Fri., 6pm-2am Sat., no cover) features some top-notch jazz and blues acts and dynamite drink specials, while offering the kind of moody lounge atmosphere you might find in a bigger city.

The Arts

Lovers of Broadway musicals, dance, comedy routines, and other special events can get their fill at the **Wharton Center** (800/942-7866, www.whartoncenter.com) on the MSU campus. This renowned venue boasts four unique stages—the Pasant Theatre, the MSU Concert Auditorium, the Fairchild Theatre, and Cobb Great Hall, where the Lansing Symphony Orchestra regularly performs.

SHOPPING

Not far from Adado Riverfront Park is the **Lansing City Market** (333 N. Cedar St., 517/483-7460, www.michigan.org/property/lansing-city-market, generally 10am-6pm Tues.-Fri., 10am-6pm Sat.). Established in 1909 and relocated to its current spot in 1938, this year-round market attracts plenty of vendors offering fruit, vegetables, sandwiches, baked goods, and more. After making your purchases, you can enjoy the picnic area near the river.

In nearby Okemos, **Meridian Mall** (1982 W. Grand River Ave., 517/349-2031, www.meridianmall.com, 10am-9pm Mon.-Sat., noon-6pm Sun.) is a favorite local destination for bargain hunters. Familiar department stores like Macy's and JCPenney anchor the property, which sports a wide swath of specialty stores, including Bath and Body Works, Foot Locker, H & M, and Schuler Books and Music.

FOOD AND ACCOMMODATIONS

If you're in the mood for seafood, check out **Mitchell's Fish Market** (2975 Preyde Blvd., 517/482-3474, www.mitchellsfishmarket.com, 11am-10pm Sun.-Thurs., 11am-11pm Fri.-Sat., $18-38), where you'll find everything from exotic seafood to local catches.

You can't beat the combination of good burgers, friendly service, inexpensive prices, and cold beer at ★ **Peanut Barrel** (521 E. Grand River, East Lansing, 517/351-0608, www.peanutbarrel.com, 10am-midnight daily, $6-9). The olive burger is exquisite.

For something a bit more upscale, try **Knight Cap** (320 E. Michigan Ave., 517/484-7676, www.theknightcap.com, 4pm-10pm Mon.-Thurs., 4pm-11pm Fri.-Sat., $30-60). A community mainstay since 1969, this is where you can find items like oysters Rockefeller, caprese salad, and duck confit—plus a number of other familiar classics.

A newcomer on the Lansing dining scene is **Bowdie's Chophouse** (320 E. Michigan, 517/580-4792, www.bowdieschophouse.com, 5pm-10pm Sun.-Thurs., 5pm-11pm Fri.-Sat. $15-89). Bowdie's is where you go when you have a very hearty appetite. The à la carte menu offers an amazing selection for each course of a full meal: smoked duck ravioli as an appetizer, massive steaks for a main course, like an 18oz bone-in Kansas City, and seared broccoli or lobster mac as a shareable side dish.

There's no lack of lodgings in the Lansing area, thanks to Big 10 fans and business travelers. You'll find a long list of reliable franchise options, including the **Hampton Inn** (525 N. Canal Rd., 517/627-8381, www.hamptoninn.com, $69-129 d), with well-maintained rooms and a free breakfast bar—an affordable spot for your football-weekend accommodations. For a bit more luxury, try the **Kellogg Hotel & Conference Center** (55 S. Harrison Rd., East Lansing, 517/432-4000, www.kelloggcenter.com, $114-369 d), the only four-star hotel on MSU's campus.

INFORMATION AND SERVICES

For more information about Lansing and East Lansing, contact the **Greater Lansing Michigan Convention & Visitors Bureau** (1223 Turner St., Ste. 200, 888/252-6746, www.lansing.org, 8:30am-5pm Mon.-Fri.). For local news, entertainment, and sports, consult the ***Lansing State Journal*** (www.lansingstatejournal.com) or watch **WLNS** (www.wlns.com), the local CBS affiliate.

For groceries, prescriptions, and other supplies, stop by a **Meijer Superstore** (www.meijer.com); there are several in the area.

For medical services, go to **Sparrow Hospital** (1215 E. Michigan Ave., 517/364-1000, www.sparrow.org).

GETTING THERE AND AROUND

To reach Lansing, travelers can fly into the **Capital Region International Airport** (LAN, 4100 Capital City Blvd., 517/321-6121, www.flylansing.com), where it's possible to take a taxi or rent a car from one of several rental agencies. You can also take the train with **Amtrak** (800/872-7245, www.amtrak.com) or the bus with **Greyhound** (517/332-2595 or 800/231-2222, www.greyhound.com) or **Indian Trails** (800/292-3831, www.indiantrails.com) to **Lansing Bus Station** (420 S. Grand Ave.). There's also the **East Lansing Station** (1240 S. Harrison Rd.).

From downtown Detroit, take M-10, I-696, I-96, and I-496 to downtown Lansing; in light traffic, the 91-mile trip should take around 80 minutes. From Chicago, take I-90, I-94, I-69, and I-496, a 218-mile trip that usually requires about 3.25 hours. En route from Chicago, parts of I-90 and I-94 serve as the Indiana Toll Road.

It's easiest to explore Lansing by car, but if you're tired of driving, catch a bus operated by the **Capital Area Transportation Authority** (CATA, 517/394-1000, www.cata.org, one-way $1.25 adults, children under 42 inches free). Lansing and East Lansing also have several reliable taxi companies, including **New Skool Taxi** (517/348-9335, m.me/NewSkoolTaxi).

Jackson and Vicinity

Jackson's biggest claim to fame is its role in U.S. political history. The Republican Party was founded in this small city of 33,400 back in 1854. More than 1,000 Free Soilers, Whigs, and northern Democrats gathered here to adopt the Republican name, issue a platform, and nominate candidates for state office. A Michigan Historical Marker (titled "Under the Oak Tree") identifies the spot at the corner of Franklin and 2nd Streets. Jackson is also the hometown of U.S. astronauts Alfred Worden and James McDivitt, and former Michigan governor Austin Blair, who led the state during the Civil War. Each August, Jackson holds the Midwest's largest and oldest Civil War muster, attracting more than 1,200 costumed reenactors who gather for battle, balls, and ballistics.

Like many once-booming industrial cities in mid-Michigan, downtown Jackson was hit hard by unemployment and "mallification." Few shops still occupy the city's stately Victorian and art deco storefronts. Even Jacobson's—the upscale department store chain founded and based in Jackson, with stores that once stretched to Florida—eventually filed for bankruptcy in 2002.

But even a flat economy can't affect the wealth of freshwater in surrounding Jackson County. Hundreds of natural lakes dot the countryside, making it an easy weekend getaway for recreation. An abundance of golf courses, museums, antiques shops, and vineyards also entice vacationers.

SIGHTS

Ella Sharp Museum

A great place to trace the development of the Jackson area is at the **Ella Sharp Museum** (3225 4th St., 517/787-2320, www.ellasharpmuseum.org, 10am-5pm Tues.-Wed. and Fri.-Sat., 10am-7pm Thurs., noon-5pm Sun., galleries $5 adults, $3 ages 6-17, under age 6 free, house tours $3 adults, $2 ages 6-12, under age 6 free). Sharp's mother was a rich expatriate who had invested in western Michigan land in the 1800s and later came to live on it—a rarity, since most investors were absentee landlords. Ella, born in Jackson, grew up to be a successful reformer who worked to improve rural life through good government, women's associations, and conservation. She was also a keen collector, so plenty of 19th-century artifacts and memorabilia fill this museum complex, which includes Ella Sharp's 1857 farmhouse, an 1840 log cabin, a one-room schoolhouse, and perhaps the Midwest's finest wildlife art collection.

An extension of the Ella Sharp Museum operates just outside town. **The Cell Block 7 Prison Museum** (4000 Cooper St., 517/745-6813, 10am-5pm Wed.-Sun. Mar.-Oct., 10am-5pm Fri.-Sun. early Nov.-Feb., $15 adults, $10 seniors, military, and Ella Sharp Museum members, $8 ages 5-17) showcases the dank, gritty environment of inmate life in the world's largest walled prison. Part of the museum is still an active correctional facility, so be sure to follow the rules laid out for your safety.

The Cascades

Perhaps in response to the awe-inspiring waterfalls of the Upper Peninsula, Jackson has one of the largest artificial waterfalls in North America. Better known as **The Cascades** (1401 S. Brown St., 517/768-2901, www.jacksonmich.com/cascades2.html, 8pm-11pm Thurs.-Sun., 7pm-11pm Wed. late May-early Sept., $5 adults, $4 seniors 65 and up, $3 children age 4-12, under age 4 free), they were a creation of "Captain" William Sparks, a well-known area industrialist, philanthropist, and mayor. This is truly an amazing slice of Americana: 18 separate falls up to 500 feet high, six fountains of various heights and patterns, 1,200 colored lights, and choreographed show tunes. Kids especially love it. The falls and surrounding 465-acre Sparks County Park date back to the early 1930s, when Sparks, a three-term mayor and chamber of commerce president, developed the whole park and presented it as a gift to his beloved city. You can make a day of it here, since the falls are augmented by a golf course, a picnic area, fishing ponds, tennis courts, and paddleboats available to rent.

Southeast Michigan Pioneer Wine Trail

While the winemaking region of southeastern Michigan is small compared to the wineries of the Southwest Coast and the Grand Traverse Bay regions, connoisseurs will still appreciate the selections that constitute the **Southeast Michigan Pioneer Wine Trail** (www.pioneerwinetrail.com). In Jackson, you'll find **Sandhill Crane Vineyards** (4724 Walz Rd., 517/764-0679, www.sandhillcranevineyards.com, tasting room 11am-7pm Wed.-Sat., 6pm-9pm Thurs., noon-6pm Sun.), an award-winning family-owned winery with a year-round tasting room in addition to a small restaurant. Other area wineries include the **Lone Oak Vineyard Estate** (8400 Ann Arbor Rd., Grass Lake, 517/522-8167, www.loneoakvineyards.com, 11am-5:30pm Mon.-Sat., noon-5:30pm Sun.), established in 1997 and offering complimentary tastings; and the **Pentamere Winery** (131 E. Chicago Blvd., Tecumseh, 517/423-9000, www.pentamerewinery.com, 11am-6pm Mon.-Sat., noon-5pm Sun.), where you can even take classes on the techniques of tasting and evaluating wines.

RECREATION

Michigan International Speedway

The **Michigan International Speedway** (12626 U.S. 12, Brooklyn, 517/592-6666 or tickets 888/905-7223, www.mispeedway.com), which opened in 1968, offers one of the country's premier auto-racing facilities, with 80,000 seats, a large RV campground, and NASCAR races mid-June through mid-August. The speedway often hosts official race-driving schools during the warmer months, so you can try a bit of legal speeding.

Golf

Two good local courses are the **Arbor Hills Golf Club** (1426 Arbor Hills Rd., 517/750-2290, www.arborhillsgolf.com, daily Apr.-Oct., $20-30 pp with cart), a private club for over 80 years but now open to anyone, and the **Cascades Golf Course** (1992 Warren Ave., 517/788-4323, www.cascadesgolfcourse.com, daily Apr.-Oct., $21-38 pp with cart), a beautiful venue established in 1929.

FESTIVALS AND EVENTS

The **Ella Sharp Museum** (3225 4th St., 517/787-2320, www.ellasharpmuseum.org) holds three interesting annual events: the **Sugar & Shearing Festival,** observed on the last weekend of March, which celebrates the arrival of springtime with sheepshearing and maple sugar demonstrations; the **Art, Beer, and Wine Festival,** which invites visitors to the museum grounds in early June for the chance to sample area wines and peruse regional artwork; and the **Fall Harvest Festival,** an October event that celebrates autumn with pumpkin painting, a farmers market, and an antique tractor trade.

For something completely different, plan a trip around the annual **Hot Air Jubilee** (Ella Sharp Park, 2800 4th St., 517/782-1515, www.hotairjubilee.com, free) in mid-July. Watching nearly 70 colorful hot-air balloons take to the sky at once is quite a dazzling sight. Besides the balloons, the weekend features an arts and crafts show, stunt kite demonstrations, carnival rides, aircraft and antique military displays, and live entertainment. Stay until sunset for the Balloon Night Glow, a spectacular light show of tethered balloons.

FOOD AND ACCOMMODATIONS

Jackson is very much a meat-and-potatoes type of place, a trend so dominant that it's difficult to escape. To embrace it, try **Steve's Ranch** (311 Louis Glick Hwy., 517/787-4367, www.stevesranch.com, 6am-10pm Mon.-Sat., 6am-8pm Sun., $10-25), a longtime favorite for omelets, burgers, and, of course, steaks.

Michigan International Speedway

You'll find a range of reasonably priced chain hotels clustered near the I-94 interchange in Jackson. Three include the **Hampton Inn** (2225 Shirley Dr., 517/789-5151, www.hamptoninn3.com, $105-200 d) and the **Fairfield Inn** (2395 Shirley Dr., 517/784-7877, www.marriott.com, $79-169 d).

INFORMATION AND SERVICES

For more information, contact **Experience Jackson** (134 W. Michigan Ave., 517/764-4440, www.experiencejackson.com, 8am-5pm Mon.-Fri.) or the **Jackson County Chamber of Commerce** (134 W. Michigan Ave., 517/782-8221, www.jacksonchamber.org, 8am-5pm Mon.-Fri.). For local news and events, consult the ***Jackson Citizen Patriot*** (www.mlive.com/jackson).

For groceries and prescriptions, stop by **Meijer** (3333 E. Michigan Ave., 517/787-8722, www.meijer.com), part of a large regional chain. For banking assistance, find a **Flagstar** (www.flagstar.com), which has several branches in town.

For medical services, go to **Henry Ford Allegiance Health** (205 N. East Ave., 517/205-5971, www.henryford.com).

GETTING THERE AND AROUND

Both **Amtrak** (501 E. Michigan Ave., 800/872-7245, www.amtrak.com) and **Greyhound** (127 W. Cortland, 517/789-6148 or 800/231-2222, www.greyhound.com) serve Jackson. The city is situated halfway between the **Detroit Metropolitan-Wayne County Airport** (DTW, I-94 and Merriman Rd., Detroit, 734/247-7678, www.metroairport.com) and the **Kalamazoo/Battle Creek International Airport** (AZO, 5235 Portage Rd., Kalamazoo, 269/388-3668, www.flyazo.com). From the Detroit airport you can easily rent a vehicle and head to Jackson via I-94, a 61-mile trip that will take you about an hour. From the Kalamazoo airport, take I-94 to M-50/U.S. 127; in light traffic, this 64-mile trip will take about an hour.

By car from Lansing, follow I-496 to M-50/U.S. 127; without traffic, the 39-mile trip will normally take about 40 minutes. Once you reach Jackson, you can drive, bike, or even walk around town. It's also possible to rely on the **Jackson Area Transportation Authority** (JATA, 517/787-8363, www.jacksontransit.com, one-way $1.50 adults, $1 students, $0.75 seniors and children) bus service.

THE IRISH HILLS AND LENAWEE COUNTY

Southeast of Jackson via U.S. 127 and U.S. 12, the lovely Irish Hills have long been a popular family getaway, dotted with summer cottages. The geography formed during the last ice age, when huge ice chunks swept across the land, leaving behind a varied landscape of round kettle-hole lakes, steep valleys, and picturesque sweeping meadows. Its name derives from early Irish settlers who thought the region resembled their homeland.

You can enjoy the area's natural state at 654-acre **W. J. Hayes State Park** (1220 Wamplers Lake Rd., Onsted, 517/467-7401, www.michigan.gov/dnr, hours vary, annual Recreation Passport required: $12 Michigan residents, $34 nonresidents, $9 day pass available to nonresidents only), 23 miles southeast of Jackson, with two popular fishing lakes amid gentle rolling hills. Facilities include a sandy swimming beach, a boat launch, a picnic area, and 185 modern campsites.

Nearby, the **Cambridge Junction Historic State Park** (13220 M-50, Brooklyn, 517/467-4414, hours vary, free) features the 1832 **Walker Tavern,** which tells the story of the spine-crunching Chicago Road (present-day Michigan Ave.), the chief route of settlement during the 1830s settlement boom. Now a small state historical museum, it illustrates how travelers once piled into the tavern's few sleeping rooms, shared beds, and passed much of their time in the first-floor bar and dining room. Daniel Webster and James Fenimore Cooper stayed here on westward expeditions. Note that the nearby Brick Walker Tavern is privately owned and not part of the state park.

Information

For more information about the Irish Hills, contact the **Lenawee County Conference & Visitors Bureau** (230 W. Maumee St., Adrian, 517/263-7747, www.visitlenawee.com 8am-5pm Mon.-Fri.).

Battle Creek

To generations of American youngsters, Battle Creek was the home of Tony the Tiger, that gr-r-reat and magical place where they sent their cereal box tops in exchange for free gifts and toys. For decades before that, however, Battle Creek was known as the home of the Church of Seventh Day Adventists and the church's sanitarium, the Western Health Reform Institute, which opened in 1866. John Harvey Kellogg joined the founders in 1876 and spent the next 25 years developing the sanitarium into an institution recognized worldwide for its regimen of hydrotherapy, exercise, and a vegetarian diet.

Part of that regimen was a healthy new grain-based flaked breakfast that Kellogg developed in 1894. An alternative to traditional breakfast foods such as grits, bacon, and eggs, Kellogg's creation revolutionized the breakfast-foods industry and fueled the economy of this former settlement. From 1901 to 1905, more than 1,500 new homes were built to house those hoping to capitalize on the renown of "Health City." This story was the basis for *The Road to Wellville,* a 1994 Hollywood film starring Anthony Hopkins, which paints a less than flattering portrait of the Kellogg family.

Today, Battle Creek is still the headquarters of the Kellogg Company as well as Post Cereals (recently transferred from Kraft Foods to Ralcorp). It's also home to the World's Longest Breakfast Table, a downtown event held as part of the annual Battle Creek Cereal Festival in June.

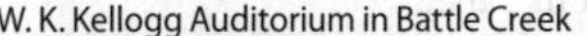

W. K. Kellogg Auditorium in Battle Creek

SIGHTS

Museums and Historic Sites

If you're curious about the Kelloggs, you can visit the sanitarium, now the **Hart-Dole-Inouye Federal Center** (74 N. Washington Ave., 269/961-7015, www.gsa.gov/hdifedctr, free). Recognized on the National Register of Historic Places, the building now houses governmental and military offices, though there are still artifacts and other items on display about the Kellogg era.

If you're looking for an engaging place to take the kids, try the newly renovated **Kingman Museum** (175 Limit St., 269/965-5117, www.kingmanmuseum.org, noon-4pm Sat.-Sun., museum admission free; planetarium shows 11:15am, 12:15pm, 1:15pm, 2:15pm, and 3:15pm $2 pp). The museum offers a wide array of paleontological and anthropological artifacts, from fossils and skulls to Native American war shields. Visitors can also catch a star show in the modern planetarium.

Binder Park Zoo

More modern species can be found at the **Binder Park Zoo** (7400 Division Dr., 269/979-1351, www.binderparkzoo.org, 9am-5pm Mon.-Fri., 9am-6pm Sat., 11am-6pm Sun. May 1-Sept. 2., 10am-4pm daily Apr. 17-30, Sept.-Oct., $14.25 adults, $13.25 seniors, $12.25 ages 2-10, under age 2 free), a small but choice zoo that houses exotic and domestic animals in natural settings. Highlights include the **Swamp Adventure,** a boardwalk that takes you over bird-filled bogs, marshes, and swamps; and **Wild Africa,** a replica of a savanna, with giraffes, zebras, ostriches, antelopes, and other animals of the region.

Parks and Gardens

The Kelloggs preached plenty of fresh air as part of their health regimen. Battle Creek, therefore, excels in parks and recreational opportunities. Among the most unusual is the **Battle Creek Linear Park** (269/966-3431, www.bcparks.org, sunrise-sunset daily), a 17-mile system that links wooded areas, open fields, and parks with a continuous paved pathway. It's a favorite of local cyclists, skaters, and joggers. Walkers and other nature lovers, in particular, head to the **Leila Arboretum** (928 W. Michigan Ave., 269/969-0270, http://lasgarden.org, sunrise-sunset daily, free), part of Linear Park. This excellent 72-acre botanical garden is one of the best reasons to visit Battle Creek. The gift of Leila Post Montgomery, it contains more than 3,000 species of trees and shrubs, many planted in the 1920s, laid out in the manner of famous European gardens. Highlights include a rhododendron garden, a breathtaking flowering tree collection, and a magical children's garden.

RECREATION

Golf

During the warmer months, drive out to **Gull Lake View Golf Club & Resort** (7417 N. 38th St., Augusta, 269/731-4149 or 800/432-7971, www.gulllakeview.com, daily Apr.-Oct., $46-65 pp), the oldest and largest golf resort in southwestern Michigan. En route from Battle Creek to Kalamazoo, this long-standing family-operated resort offers top-notch lodging and dining plus five championship golf courses: Gull Lake View East, Gull Lake View West, Stonehedge North, Stonehedge South, and Bedford Valley.

Hiking and Skiing

Naturalists will appreciate the **W. K. Kellogg Experimental Forest** (7060 N. 42nd St., Augusta, 269/731-4597 www.canr.msu.edu/kelloggforest, 8am-8pm daily summer, 8am-sunset daily winter, free), begun by the cereal king as a demonstration project for reforesting abandoned farms. Michigan State University maintains the 716-acre property as an experimental forest, which includes more than 200 species of trees, 2.5 miles of roads, and 35 miles of hiking and cross-country skiing trails. Hikers, picnickers, and skiers also use the forest's 25 miles of ungroomed firebreaks separating experimental stands of trees.

Sojourner Truth

Sojourner Truth Memorial statue by Tina Allen

Described by one biographer as a "riveting preacher and spellbinding singer who dazzled listeners with her wit and originality," Sojourner Truth was born around 1797 as Isabella Baumfree in Swartekill, New York. She spent her childhood and early adulthood as an enslaved person, suffering abuse at the hands of her owners and giving birth to several children. Towering more than six feet, she gained her freedom in the late 1820s, when New York State abolished slavery. She decided to change her given name and moved west on a "sojourn to preach truth." Her antislavery crusade took her into both small rural churches and the office of President Abraham Lincoln.

In 1857 Truth settled in Battle Creek, an abolitionist stronghold, and continued to help people escape enslavement along the Underground Railroad to Canada. While revisionist history has claimed that she never physically assisted runaway slaves, she no doubt inspired many of them with her fiery oratories, which preached economic competence, self-improvement, and social tolerance. A few days before she died in 1883, she said, "I isn't goin' to die, honey, I'se goin' home like a shootin' star." Her funeral was described as the largest Battle Creek had ever seen. She is buried in Oak Hill Cemetery by a simple old-fashioned square monument—still a popular pilgrimage spot—just steps away from the ornate marble mausoleum of cereal pioneer C. W. Post.

★ Bird-Watching

Ornithologists and other bird lovers flock to the experimental **W. K. Kellogg Bird Sanctuary** (12685 E. C Ave., Augusta, 269/671-2510, https://birdsanctuary.kbs.msu.edu, 9am-7pm Mon.-Fri., 9am-5pm Sat.-Sun., $5 adults, $4 seniors, $3 ages 2-17), one of North America's pioneer wildlife conservation centers. W. K. Kellogg started the sanctuary in 1928 as a refuge for Canada geese, which were then threatened by a loss of habitat to agriculture and urbanization. Today, Canada geese thrive at the 180-acre sanctuary, now part of MSU's W. K. Kellogg Biological Station, along with other native waterfowl, including ducks and swans that stay year-round. Also present are several species of raptors and game birds, including red-tailed hawks and pheasants, which you can view from several observation areas on the grounds. Many other species migrate through the region in spring and fall.

Situated along the waterfront of Wintergreen Lake, the grounds can be explored year-round on self-guided trails. A bookstore on-site carries information on how to transform your backyard into a bird sanctuary following the same principles and planting guidelines used in the refuge.

FESTIVALS AND EVENTS

Battle Creek hosts several celebrations throughout the year. For over five decades, the **Battle Creek Cereal Festival** (www.bcfestivals.com/cerealfest) has celebrated the city's most famous industry in mid-June with a parade, live entertainment, and the world's longest breakfast table, offering complimentary cereals, fruit juice, and other Kellogg's breakfast foods. Started in 1956 as part of the Kellogg Company's Golden Jubilee, it has become a beloved annual tradition in downtown. Another popular event

Return of the Trumpeter Swan

trumpeter swans

The trumpeter swan, the world's largest waterfowl, can weigh up to 35 pounds when fully grown, with a wingspan of nearly eight feet. Similar in appearance to other white swans, its distinguishing characteristic is its all-black bill. Trumpeter swans typically create large nests in marshy areas among cattails and other aquatic plants.

Centuries ago, trumpeter swans were abundant throughout the Great Lakes region, even in southern Michigan. Antoine de la Mothe Cadillac, founder of Detroit, noted their presence along the Detroit River in 1701. As European settlers spread throughout the state, however, the swan population plummeted. During the late 19th century, hunters captured swans for their fine down, while settlers drained crucial marsh habitat. By 1933, only an estimated 66 trumpeter swans remained in the continental United States, mostly in remote parts of Alaska and the Rocky Mountains.

In the mid-1980s, Michigan initiated a reintroduction program, intended to establish three self-sustaining populations of at least 200 swans by 2000. Despite early failures, biologists were eventually able to incubate eggs collected from zoos and rear the cygnets for two years before releasing them into prime wetland habitat. In 1989, biologists from the Michigan Department of Natural Resources and the W. K. Kellogg Bird Sanctuary traveled to Alaska to collect eggs from wild populations as well.

By 2000, the program was considered a success, with more than 400 trumpeter swans thought to be living in Michigan: in the southwestern and northeastern parts of the Lower Peninsula and in the Upper Peninsula's Seney National Wildlife Refuge.

In recent years, the W. K. Kellogg Bird Sanctuary, which today nurtures over 20 year-round trumpeter swans, has continued reintroduction efforts. Since 2003, the sanctuary has released 28 swans in order to establish breeding populations elsewhere, including six that were transported to Sleeping Bear Dunes in 2007. In 2004, Michigan State University conducted a state population survey, revealing that 655 trumpeter swans were then living in Michigan: roughly 45 percent in the UP and 26 percent in the Lower Peninsula's northwestern region, with the remaining 29 percent downstate.

For more information about conservation efforts, consult the **Michigan Department of Natural Resources** (www.michigan.gov/dnr) or the **W. K. Kellogg Bird Sanctuary** (www.kbs.msu.edu).

is the **International Festival of Lights** (www.bcfestivals.com/international-festival-of-lights) during which Linear Park is decorated with lighted holiday displays from late November to New Year's Eve.

FOOD AND ACCOMMODATIONS

Battle Creek offers plenty of dining options, from fast-food establishments to fancier fare. One solid choice is the **Arcadia Brewing Company** (103 W. Michigan Ave., 269/963-9520, www.arcadiaales.com, 11am-11pm Mon.-Fri., noon-midnight Sat., 10am-2pm Sun., $7-18), a microbrewery that specializes in British-style ales and offers an adjacent restaurant and tavern called TC's Wood Fired Fare. For hearty all-American cuisine, consider **Finley's Grill and Smokehouse** (140 E. Columbia, 269/968-3938, www.finleysamericangrill.com, 11am-10pm Sun.-Thurs., 11am-11pm Fri.-Sat., $6-22), part of

The Kellogg Capital

The history of American business contains several examples of innovators turned entrepreneurs who started their companies on a shoestring, achieved considerable prosperity, and left a lasting legacy, all while never leaving their hometown. The community and the company essentially grow up together, both sharing in the benefits the other offers.

Since its founding by William Kellogg in 1906, the Kellogg Company has been synonymous with its home city of Battle Creek. Despite opening plants around the world, Battle Creek remains the company's corporate headquarters and home to some manufacturing operations, with a collective staff of over 2,000, making it Battle Creek's largest employer.

Over the decades the Kellogg Company has diversified, acquiring or introducing brands such as Eggo waffles, Pringles potato chips, and Chips Deluxe. It has also purchased entire companies, such as Keebler, Morningstar Farms, and Kashi.

When large corporate mergers occur, Michigan cities, as a general rule, often find themselves on the losing end, with jobs moving to distant cities. Kellogg has proven to be an exception and continues to be a real source of Michigan pride.

a popular southern Michigan chain, with locations in Jackson, Kalamazoo, and Lansing. If you're in the mood for Italian dishes, stop by **Fazoli's** (5445 Beckley Rd., 269/979-8662, www.fazolis.com, 11am-9pm daily, $8-19), part of a nationwide chain that offers pasta bowls, panini, pizzas, and tasty favorites like pizza-baked spaghetti.

Situated amid rolling meadows, ★ **Greencrest Manor** (6174 Halbert Rd., 269/962-8633, www.greencrestmanor.com, $150-280 d, 2 night min.) is an unexpected discovery—a French château in the middle of the Midwestern prairie. Eight rooms, including six suites, are decorated with lots of art and antiques. For something less expensive, try the **Baymont Inn & Suites** (4725 Beckley Rd., 269/979-5400, www.baymontinns.com, $113-149 d), which includes free breakfast, Internet access, and use of the pool.

INFORMATION AND SERVICES

For more information, contact the **Calhoun County Visitors Bureau** (1 Riverwalk Centre, 34 Jackson St., Battle Creek, 800/397-2240 www.battlecreekvisitors.org, 8am-5:30pm Mon.-Fri., 10am-3pm Sat.). For local news, entertainment, and sports, consult the ***Battle Creek Enquirer*** (www.battlecreekenquirer.com) or watch **WWMT** (www.wwmt.com), the CBS affiliate that serves Battle Creek, Kalamazoo, and Grand Rapids.

Battle Creek offers all the services necessary for travelers, including groceries, pharmacies, gas stations, laundries, and banks. For medical assistance, visit the **Bronson Battle Creek Hospital** (300 North Ave., 269/245-8446, www.bronsonhealth.com).

GETTING THERE AND AROUND

Battle Creek is accessible via plane, train, bus, and, naturally, car. The **Kalamazoo/Battle Creek International Airport** (AZO, 5235 Portage Rd., Kalamazoo, 269/388-3668, www.flyazo.com) is situated 25 miles southwest, while the **Capital Region International Airport** (LAN, 4100 Capital City Blvd., Lansing, 517/321-6121, www.flylansing.com) is 59 miles northeast. You can rent a vehicle at either airport. By car it will take about 24 minutes from Kalamazoo and an hour from Lansing to reach Battle Creek. In addition, **Amtrak** (800/872-7245, www.amtrak.com), **Greyhound** (269/964-1768 or 800/231-2222, www.greyhound.com), and **Indian Trails** (800/292-3831, www.indiantrails.com) all serve the same **Battle Creek Station** (119 S. McCamly St.).

By car, you can reach Battle Creek via I-94

and I-69. From downtown Detroit, take M-10, I-75, I-96, M-14, and I-94, and follow M-66 north to downtown Battle Creek. In light traffic, the trip should take about two hours. Use **Battle Creek Transit** (269/966-3474, www.battlecreekmi.gov, one-way $1.25 adults, $0.60 seniors, free children shorter than fare box), which offers bus service in and around town.

Kalamazoo and Vicinity

The original name of Kalamazoo, Kikanamaso, is from the Potawatomi language and may either mean "bubbling water"—a reference to the area's natural springs—or "the mirage" or "reflecting river." Its modern notoriety came later, when the city's name inspired the Glenn Miller song "(I've Got a Gal in) Kalamazoo," followed by numerous other musical mentions, in addition to a Carl Sandburg's poem, "The Sins of Kalamazoo."

Due south of Grand Rapids, Kalamazoo is the center for produce from the nearby vegetable-growing region, and home to several papermaking plants and top pharmaceutical companies. Academia provides steady employment too: Kalamazoo is home to Western Michigan University and a number of respected private schools, including the academically renowned Kalamazoo College, site of a popular annual Bach festival and internationally known for its K-Plan, which includes international study and internships.

Kalamazoo's population of approximately 75,000 includes a sizable gay community, a substantial African American population, a burgeoning alternative music scene, a number of big-city refugees, and an almost even split between liberals and conservatives.

While Carl Sandburg didn't think much of Kalamazoo, its downtown streets reveal pleasures of life characteristic of a midsize city: quaint paths perfect for walking, a gracious downtown park, vintage architecture, interesting shops including a number of antiques outlets, and several luxurious bed-and-breakfasts. There's a great sense of civic pride and an active population that gets intimately involved in civic affairs. Although it may not be your final destination, Kalamazoo makes a great stop en route to Harbor Country to the south or Lake Michigan's well-known resort communities in the north.

SIGHTS

Built in 1927, the opulent Spanish-style **Kalamazoo State Theatre** (404 S. Burdick St., 269/345-6500, www.kazoostate.com) now showcases rock, blues, country, and folk concerts. The interior is a rare example of the work of famed architect John Eberson, who replicated an exotic Mediterranean town with a working cloud machine and stars that really twinkle.

The **Kalamazoo Valley Museum** (230 N. Rose St., 269/373-7990, www.kalamazoomuseum.org, 9am-5pm Mon.-Sat., 1pm-5pm Sun. and holidays, free) is a frequently overlooked cultural treasure. The collection of some 57,000 objects including photographs, documents, and artifacts examine the complex history of the central Michigan region. The A.M. Todd Collection includes books, decorative objects, and works of art. Also, the Civil War collection displays memorabilia and documents that actually belonged to veterans from the Kalamazoo area.

Unlike many other Michigan towns, Kalamazoo was largely immune to the boom-and-bust cycles in the last century, thanks to its diversified economy. Houses are well maintained, and many have stayed in families for generations. You can see the results of that care in the **South Street Historic District.** Impressive houses went up here between 1839 and World War I in varied architectural styles including Greek Revival, Georgian, and Italianate. Just north of Kalamazoo College,

Kalamazoo and Vicinity

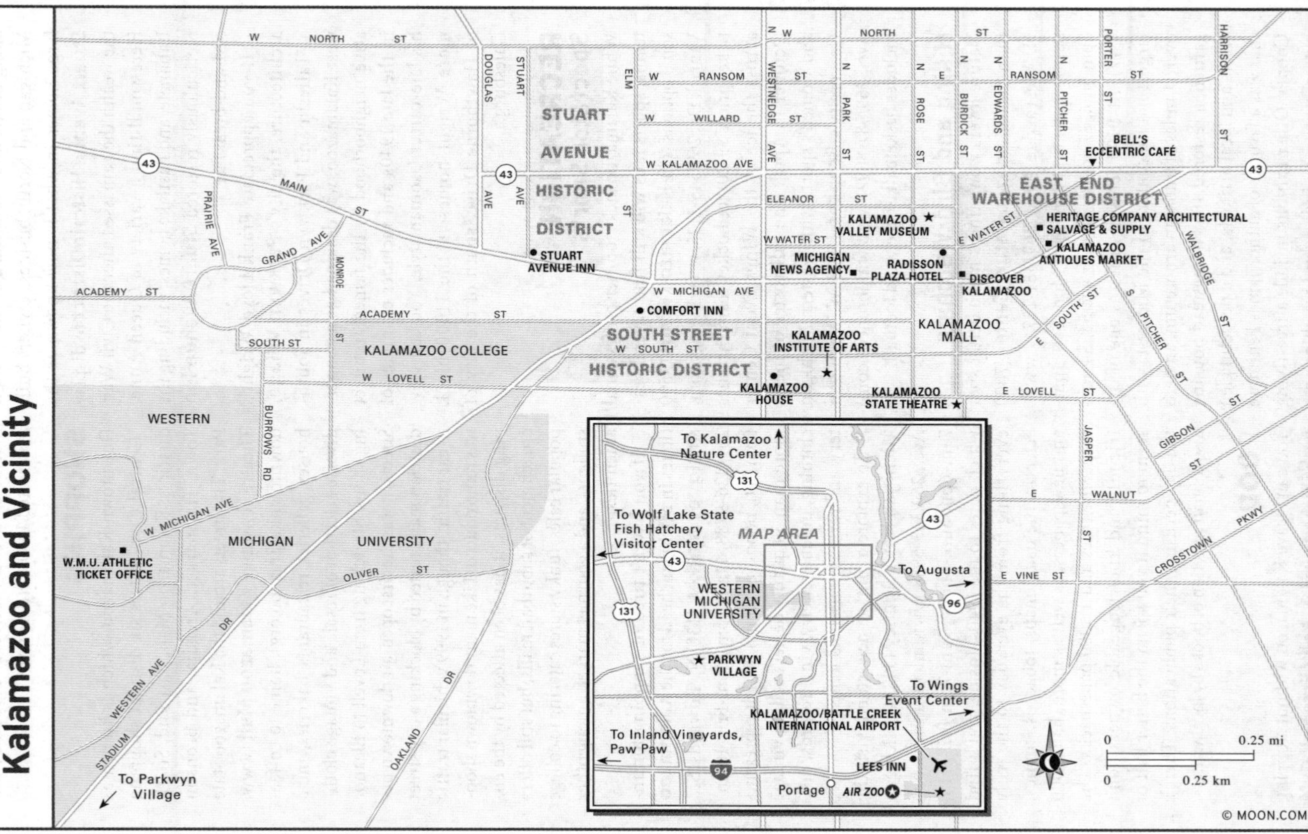

along Stuart and Woodward between West Michigan and North, business owners built large homes in what is now known as the **Stuart Avenue Historic District** to display the wealth they amassed after the Civil War. Here you'll find a variety of Queen Anne, Italianate, and Eastlake homes, including the meticulously restored **Stuart Avenue Inn** bed-and-breakfast.

If you appreciate Frank Lloyd Wright's architecture, the city's **Parkwyn Village,** at Taliesin and Parkwyn Drives in southwest Kalamazoo, was designed as a cooperative neighborhood by the famed architect in the late 1940s and includes examples of his late-career Usonian style. You can view more Wright homes in the 11000 block of Hawthorne Drive, south of the city of Galesburg.

RECREATION

Spectator Sports

While Kalamazoo lacks top-tier professional teams, sports fans will still find several seasonal options. The **Kalamazoo Wings** (3600 Vanrick Dr., 269/345-1125, www.kwings.com, ticket prices $9-20) ice hockey team thrashes across the ice of the Wings Event Center October to April. The full roster of men's and women's sports with Western Michigan University's **Broncos** (1903 W. Michigan Ave., 269/387-8092, www.wmubroncos.com) includes basketball, soccer, and football.

Hiking and Bird-Watching

Nature lovers won't find a much better spot than the **Kalamazoo Nature Center** (7000 N. Westnedge Ave., 269/381-1574, www.naturecenter.org, 9am-5pm Mon.-Sat., 1pm-5pm Sun., $7 adults, $6 over age 54, $4 ages 4-17). At 1,100 acres, it ranks as one of the largest nature centers in the Midwest, with over 11 miles of trails, an arboretum, an herb garden, a restored 1858 homestead housing crafts and local artifacts, and a peaceful glen that was a favorite of author James Fenimore Cooper. Other exhibits include a free-flying butterfly zone, an indoor bird-watching area that looks out over the trees and grounds, and a recreated 1830s settlers farm.

SHOPPING

Downtown Kalamazoo, which is known as "Central City," offers six distinct shopping districts: Kalamazoo Mall, East End, South Town, Haymarket, Arcadia, and Bronson Park. The streets around the Kalamazoo State Theatre constitute **Kalamazoo Mall** (www.downtownkalamazoo.org), home to coffeehouses, galleries, restaurants, bakeries, and a diverse selection of resale and vintage clothing shops. Stretching from Lovell to Eleanor Streets, it was the first open-air downtown pedestrian mall created by blocking a city street to car traffic, though in 1999 vehicular traffic was reintroduced. Like many downtown shopping districts, it has been affected by the encroachment of suburban malls, but still offers popular cafés, funky stores catering to college students, and a gourmet market, among other amenities.

If you haven't tired of shopping for antiques in Michigan, head for the **Kalamazoo Antiques Market** (130 N. Edwards St., 269/226-9788, 11am-5pm Mon.-Fri., 10am-5pm Sat., noon-4pm Sun.), which represents more than 30 quality dealers selling vintage clothing, unique jewelry, vinyl records, pottery, and various household items.

To explore a vintage newsstand, visit the **Michigan News Agency** (308 W. Michigan Ave., 269/343-5958, www.michigannews.biz, 7am-6pm Sun.-Thurs., 7am-7pm Fri.-Sat.), which dates to the 1940s. Inside, you'll find everything from the everyday to the truly eclectic: the usual maps, tobaccos, comics, and newspapers, as well as more than 6,000 magazine titles and 15,000 paperbacks. The friendly and knowledgeable owners don't seem to mind if you spend the better half of the day perusing their publications. There's also a small selection of books by local writers.

FOOD

You can't leave Kalamazoo without stopping by the highly touted ★ **Bell's Eccentric Café**

(355 E. Kalamazoo Ave., 269/382-2332, www.bellsbeer.com, 11am-midnight Mon.-Wed., 11am-2am Thurs.-Sat., noon-midnight Sun., $5-15), part of Bell's Brewery, a forerunner of the Kalamazoo Brewing Company. Owner Larry Bell's more than 20 acclaimed brews, including Amber Ale, Kalamazoo Stout, and Cherry Stout, have won a loyal following in Chicago, where much of his output is sold. While you're downing a few pints, enjoy snacks in the smoke-free eatery. This appealing spot has board games scattered around the tables, table tennis, and live acoustic music on Friday and Saturday nights. In warm weather, casual crowds congregate on the outdoor beer garden patio.

If you're visiting Kalamazoo around the third week of January, you may want to join the fun during **Kalamazoo Beer Week** (www.kalamazoobeerweek.com). This annual event celebrates the tradition of the local craft breweries and consists of a pub crawl, beer tastings, food pairings, and more. Visit the website for details and ticket information.

ACCOMMODATIONS

Kalamazoo offers a wide assortment of chain hotels and motels, including **Comfort Inn** (739 W. Michigan Ave., 269/743-4466, www.chociehotels.com, $100-145 d), an ideal location for exploring the downtown area. Another excellent, more upscale choice is the **Radisson Plaza Hotel** (100 W. Michigan Ave., 269/343-3333, www.radisson.com, $155-320 d). Nestled in the heart of everything, it's within an easy walk of downtown attractions.

For a more distinctive experience, consider the ★ **Stuart Avenue Inn** (229 Stuart Ave., 269/342-0230, www.stuartavenueinn.com, $119-179 d), widely regarded as the city's best bed-and-breakfast. It comprises three adjacent 19th-century homes (including the Bartlett-Upjohn House, once owned by the Upjohn pharmaceutical family) and lovely perennial gardens. The present owners furnished the inn's well-appointed rooms with many of their own antiques plus others collected on shopping sprees around the state. **The Kalamazoo House** (447 W. South St., 269/382-0880, $159-219 d), built in 1878, resembles a boutique hotel more than a traditional B&B. All rooms have amenities like flat-screen TVs, hair dryers, private baths or showers, and individually controlled heat and air-conditioning. You'll also find some special touches, like cookies and milk before bed.

South Kalamazoo Mall

INFORMATION AND SERVICES

For more information about the area, contact **Discover Kalamazoo** (240 W. Michigan Ave., 269/488-9000, www.discoverkalamazoo.com, 8am-5pm Mon.-Fri.). For local news, entertainment, and sports, check out the ***Kalamazoo Gazette*** (www.mlive.com/kalamazoo) or watch **WWMT,** the local CBS affiliate.

With its assortment of groceries, pharmacies, gas stations, laundries, banks, and other helpful establishments, Kalamazoo can fulfill most travelers' needs. For medical assistance, there is the **Ascension Borgess Hospital** (1521 Gull Rd., 269/226-7000, https://healthcare.ascension.org).

GETTING THERE AND AROUND

Kalamazoo is accessible via plane, train, bus, and, of course, car. The **Kalamazoo/Battle Creek International Airport** (AZO, 5235 Portage Rd., 269/388-3668, www.flyazo.com) is just south of town; once here, you can catch a taxi or hire a rental car. In addition, **Amtrak** (800/872-7245, www.amtrak.com), **Greyhound** (269/337-8201 or 800/231-2222, www.greyhound.com), and **Indian Trails** (800/292-3831, www.indiantrails.com) all serve the **Kalamazoo Station** (459 N. Burdick St.).

By car, reach Kalamazoo via I-94 or U.S. 131. From downtown Detroit, take M-10 north and then I-75 south, I-96 west, M-14 west, and I-94 west to Kalamazoo; in light traffic, the 143-mile trip should take less than 2.25 hours. From Chicago, take I-90, I-94, and U.S. 131 to Kalamazoo, a 147-mile trip that usually requires about 2.25 hours. En route from Chicago, parts of I-90 and I-94 serve as the Indiana Toll Road. From Grand Rapids, take U.S. 131; in light traffic, this 51-mile journey should take about 49 minutes.

Public transportation in and around town is provided by **Kalamazoo Metro Transit** (269/337-8222, www.kmetro.com, one-way $1.50 adults, $0.75 seniors and children under 48 inches tall).

GREATER KALAMAZOO

★ Air Zoo

Just south of the Kalamazoo/Battle Creek International Airport, you'll spy the excellent **Air Zoo** (6151 Portage Rd., 269/382-6555, www.airzoo.org, 9am-5pm Mon.-Sat., noon-5pm Sun., $15.95 adults, $12.95 over age 59, $14.95 ages 5-18). Considered the nation's premier museum of military aircraft, the three-campus Air Zoo stands out because of its emphasis on education. Not only can visitors examine vintage planes, like the Curtiss P-40 Warhawk or Grumman F-14A Tomcat, they can also sit at the controls of state-of-the-art flight simulators and get a small taste of what fighter pilots experience.

This enormous museum also features educational flight-related displays, such as a 2,000-square-foot exhibit chronicling the history of aircraft carriers (complete with over 400 archival photographs and three large models). The Air Zoo's original facility (now called the East Campus) houses the **Michigan Space Science Center,** a 17,000-square-foot repository of space artifacts, from a Gemini crew training simulator to a replica of a Mercury space capsule. This impressive facility, much of which was once near Jackson, offers an interactive exhibit as well. The International Space Station Exhibit uses hands-on demonstrations, simulations, models, theaters, and other experiences to illustrate the history and everyday operations of the largest international peacetime project in the world.

Gilmore Car Museum

Put aside a few hours for the **Gilmore Car Museum** (6865 Hickory Rd., Hickory Corners, 269/671-5089, www.gilmorecarmuseum.org, 9am-5pm Mon.-Fri., 9am-6pm Sat.-Sun., $15 adults, $10 ages 7-17, free for active military with ID), considered one of the top five car museums in the United States. On 90 landscaped acres northeast of Kalamazoo, not far from Gull Lake are housed 200 vintage automobiles in several restored historic barns, including an 1899 locomotive, the infamous 1948 Tucker, and muscle cars of the 1970s. Other curiosities include a new miniature museum and an authentic 1941 diner, a great place for an afternoon snack. All buildings are wheelchair accessible.

Mount Pleasant

As exemplified by the city seal, Mount Pleasant's history was indelibly shaped by four elements—its Native American heritage as well as agriculture, education, and the discovery of oil. Native Americans, promised lands in an 1855 treaty, began settling in Isabella County the following year. When a timber scout named David Ward purchased the land on the southern side of the Chippewa River, directly opposite what is today the Isabella Indian Reservation, he decided to call the fledgling village Mount Pleasant. Soon merchants, artisans, and farmers flocked to the area.

The town gradually expanded, and by 1892, there was even a community college which would eventually become Central Michigan University. The discovery of oil in 1928 changed the fortunes of the burgeoning town, which soon boasted hotels, restaurants, and scores of new residents. During the oil boom other commerce left the area, making Mount Pleasant a one-industry town.

Today, Mount Pleasant (population 26,000) is a typical Midwestern college town that continues to celebrate its Chippewa heritage. Its two biggest attractions, in fact, are a Chippewa-owned casino and an annual powwow. The area's numerous golf courses, military memorials, recreational parks, and CMU football games also attract visitors.

ZIIBIWING CENTER

The Midwest's premier Native American museum, the **Ziibiwing Center of Anishinabe Culture and Lifeways** (6650 E. Broadway, 989/775-4750, www.sagchip.org/ziibiwing, 10am-6pm Mon.-Sat., $6.50 adults, $3.75 over age 59, ages 5-17, and active military with ID, $4.50 college students with ID) demonstrates the rich culture and history of the Great Lakes' Anishinabe people. The permanent "Diba Jimooyung" exhibit illustrates the amazing history of the original inhabitants of the Great Lakes, including their prophecies and their struggle to preserve their land, language, and culture. The museum hosts traveling exhibits about indigenous people from other parts of Michigan and elsewhere in the United States.

RECREATION

College Sports

Throughout the year, the Central Michigan University Chippewas host a wide range of sporting events, from men's football to women's basketball. To catch a game, contact the **CMU Athletics Ticket Office** (989/774-3045, www.cmuchippewas.com).

Golf

The Mount Pleasant area offers several quality golf courses. Two options include **Bucks Run Golf Club** (1559 S. Chippewa Rd., 989/773-6830, www.bucksrun.com, daily Apr.-Nov., $40-88 pp with cart), situated on 290 gorgeous acres with wetlands, three lakes, and the Chippewa River; and **Riverwood Resort** (1313 E. Broomfield Rd., 989/772-5726, www.riverwoodresort.com, daily Apr.-Oct., $39-49 pp), which offers 27 classic holes, a spacious clubhouse, several deluxe villas, and two dozen bowling lanes.

ENTERTAINMENT AND EVENTS

★ Soaring Eagle Casino and Resort

The **Soaring Eagle Casino and Resort** (6800 Soaring Eagle Blvd., 888/732-4537, www.soaringeaglecasino.com, 24 hours daily) is next to the Isabella Indian Reservation, the state's largest, and home to the Saginaw Chippewa people. Featuring an enormous gaming area, six restaurants, and more than 500 well-appointed rooms, the resort has something for everyone. Even if you don't like gaming, you can still relax in one of the on-site pools or spend the day at the spa. After dining in one of the resort's eateries or fine restaurants, catch a show at the concert hall, where big-name entertainment often takes to the stage.

★ Saginaw Chippewa Tribal Powwow

For over 20 years, the annual **Saginaw Chippewa Tribal Powwow** (7070 E. Broadway, 989/775-4000, www.sagchip.org, free) has offered visitors the opportunity to observe and experience traditional Native American dress, dancing, drumming, chanting, cuisine, and crafts. The competition, held in late July, attracts performers from all over the United States, making it one of the biggest local events and a terrific place for outsiders to learn about Native American culture.

FOOD AND ACCOMMODATIONS

The Soaring Eagle Casino isn't the only food option in town. **The Brass Cafe and Saloon** (128 S. Main St., 989/772-0864, 11am-3pm, 5pm-10pm Tues.-Sat., $11-29) offers a wide range of menu choices, featuring innovative American and global cuisine. Housed within two turn-of-the-20th-century shopfronts, this popular eatery offers an intimate setting for relaxing after a hard day of golf or gambling.

Aside from the Soaring Eagle, there are also a number of chain hotels scattered around Mount Pleasant. The newest is the **Courtyard Marriott** (2400 E. Campus Dr., 989/773-1444, www.marriott.com, $210-279 d) adjacent to Central Michigan University's sports stadium. The rooms boast the latest technological amenities: high-speed internet, USB charging stations for mobile devices, and large desks.

INFORMATION AND SERVICES

For more information, consult the **Mount Pleasant Area Convention & Visitors Bureau** (113 E. Broadway, Ste. 180, 888/772-2022, www.mountpleasantwow.com, 8am-5pm Mon.-Fri.). For local and regional news, review the ***Morning Sun*** (www.themorningsun.com).

Although not as large as other mid-Michigan cities, Mount Pleasant still has plentiful banks, gas stations, and groceries, including a **Meijer Superstore** (1015 E. Pickard St., 989/772-4700, www.meijer.com).

For medical services, head to **McLaren Central Michigan Hospital** (1221 South Dr., 800/671-1453, www.mclaren.org).

GETTING THERE AND AROUND

To reach Mount Pleasant, situated in the middle of the Lower Peninsula, you can fly into **MBS International Airport** (MBS, 8500 Garfield Rd., Freeland, 989/695-5555, www.mbsairport.org), where it's possible to rent a car from one of five national rental agencies. Take U.S. 10 and M-20 west to Mount Pleasant; the 39-mile trip will take about 50 minutes. **Greyhound** (989/772-4246 or 800/231-2222, www.greyhound.com) and **Indian Trails** (800/292-3831, www.indiantrails.com) offer bus service from the **bus station** (300 E. Broomfield St.) at CMU.

M-20 and U.S. 127 pass through Mount Pleasant. From Lansing, take I-496 and U.S. 127, a 70-mile trip that normally takes a little over an hour. From downtown Detroit, take I-375, I-75, U.S. 10, and M-20; in light traffic, this 155-mile trip should require less than 2.5 hours. From Traverse City, take South

Garfield Avenue, Voice Road, and Clark Road to M-113, then turn right onto U.S. 131 and follow M-115, U.S. 10, and U.S. 127; in light traffic, the 112-mile trip will take roughly two hours.

In Mount Pleasant, buses are operated by the **Isabella County Transportation Commission** (ICTC, 2100 E. Transportation Dr., 989/772-9441 or 989/773-2913, one-way $2 adults, $1 over age 59, $1.50 under age 18), on which CMU students and faculty members greatly depend.

Midland

When the lumber industry withdrew from Midland to pursue the green frontier to the north, the city might have become just another ghost town if it weren't for Herbert H. Dow. In 1890, Dow began a series of experiments to extract chemicals from the salt brine below the surface of much of central Michigan, eventually establishing Dow Chemical Company.

Although the 24-year-old was called "Crazy Dow" by the locals when he arrived in town, he was a surprisingly farsighted inventor and humanitarian who founded a well-planned city of neat streets and pleasing architecture. Today, this city of 42,000 continues to benefit from Dow's influence, and many of its attractions—from sports to cultural activities—bear his imprint.

SIGHTS

If your schedule allows for only one attraction in Midland, make it the **Dow Gardens** (1809 Eastman Ave., 800/362-4874, www.dowgardens.org, 9am-8:30pm daily mid-Apr.-Labor Day, 9am-6:30pm daily Labor Day-Oct., 9am-4:15pm daily Nov.-mid-Apr., $10 adults, $2 ages 6-17 and students with ID) and the buildings designed by Alden B. Dow, Herbert's son. Alden Dow was one of Frank Lloyd Wright's original Taliesin fellows and had a long and distinguished architectural career. Like Wright, he tried to merge architecture and nature, insisting that "gardens never end and buildings never begin."

Developed by Herbert and Alden Dow over the course of 70 years, the garden's lovely landscape began as Herbert Dow's

the Tridge near downtown Midland

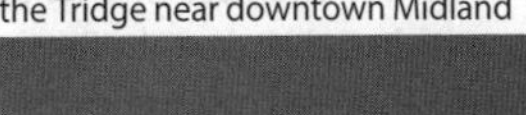

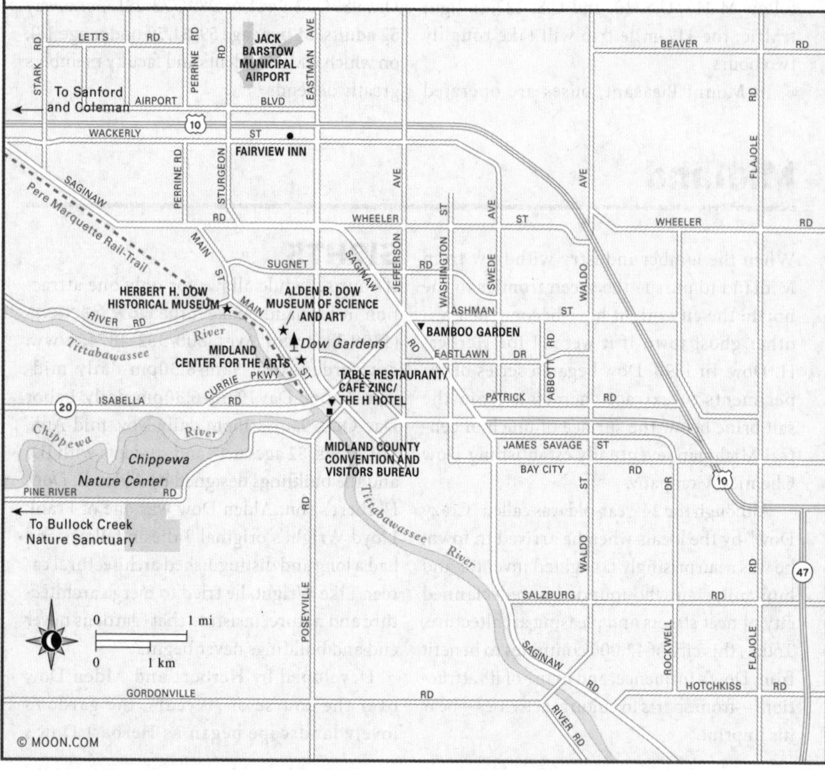

extended 10-acre backyard. When he arrived in Midland, the town was a barren land of stumps left behind by the lumber industry. In 1899, Dow began to landscape the space around his house to show his fellow townsfolk what they could do with their yards. He took his hobby seriously and corresponded with Luther Burbank and other leading horticulturists of the era. Over the subsequent years, Dow planted 5,000 fruit trees, including 40 varieties of plums.

Unlike other historic American gardens, which owe a design debt to the formal gardens of Europe, the Dow Gardens are original, an unusual place of unfolding environments often likened to Japanese or other Asian styles. Always an enthusiastic traveler, Dow visited Japan frequently and became friends with the designer of the public parks in Tokyo.

Texture, form, and contrast are as important as the more obvious displays of blooms. The gardens were renovated in the 1970s by Alden Dow as a retirement project, and more than a thousand trees and shrubs were added. Fantasy environments, including a jungle walk and a yew maze, reveal Dow's gentle, playful spirit. Don't miss the wheelchair-accessible sensory trail, the herb garden, and the extensive garden of perennials.

The **Midland Center for the Arts** (MCFTA, 1801 W. St. Andrews Rd., 989/631-5930, www.mcfta.org) is housed in another Alden Dow building. Inside the midcentury modern structure are two museums, two performance venues, several art studios and lecture halls, and the Saints & Sinners Lounge, a popular hangout before and after concerts and plays. Families favor the adjacent **Alden B. Dow Museum of Science and Art** (9am-4pm Mon.-Wed. and Fri., 10am-8pm Thurs., 9am-7pm Sat., noon-5pm Sun June-Aug., 10am-4pm Mon.-Wed. and Fri., 10am-8pm Thurs., 10am-7pm Sat., 1pm-5pm Sun. Sept.-May, $10 adults, $9 seniors and military with ID, $7 ages 4-14, under age 4 free), which features rotating art and science exhibits, a hands-on Hall of Ideas, and a ferocious-looking mastodon that's especially popular with kids.

RECREATION

In Midland, cyclists enjoy the **Pere Marquette Rail-Trail** (989/832-6870), a 30-mile-long asphalt trail that's also a hit for those on foot, skates, wheelchairs, or strollers. It begins in downtown Midland near the **Tridge,** a three-way pedestrian footbridge spanning the confluence of the Tittabawassee and Chippewa Rivers. The Tridge is a local landmark and gathering spot for picnics, concerts, festivals, and more. From there, the rail trail follows Saginaw Road to Coleman, passing by the Dow Historical Museum and Bradley Home before reaching the towns of Averill and Sanford.

After a visit in the 1970s, the vice president of the National Audubon Society called the **Chippewa Nature Center** (400 S. Badour Rd., 989/631-0830, www.chippewanaturecenter.org, visitors center 8am-5pm Mon.-Sat., noon-5pm Sun. and select holidays, free) "one of the finest—if not *the* finest—private nature centers in the world." More recently, the National Park Service cited the center for its outstanding educational accomplishments and designated it a National Environmental Study Area. The 1,200-acre center along the Pine River was designed by Frank Lloyd Wright student Alden Dow to merge with the living world around it. Its most striking feature is the River Overlook, a 60-foot-long glass-enclosed room cantilevered over the Pine, with stunning views of the center's birdlife and wildlife.

The center offers a comprehensive mix of things to see, including an authentic log homestead, items discovered from on-site archaeological digs, and a display that's a good all-around introduction to the area's natural history. Other highlights include well executed dioramas that show Michigan geology and scenes from the Saginaw Valley Native Americans. Despite the wide range of attractions, the center's hallmark is the seclusion, peace, and beauty of its surroundings. A map available at the visitors center guides visitors through the 13-mile trail system that parallels the Chippewa River. Popular with hikers and cross-country skiers, the trails include artificial wetlands, begun in 1990 to compensate for a wetlands destroyed to build a nearby shopping mall.

FOOD AND ACCOMMODATIONS

For a special dinner, head over to the **Table Restaurant** at the H Hotel (111 Main St., 800/282-7778, www.thehhotel.com, 5:30pm-9pm Tues.-Thurs., 5:30pm-10pm Fri.-Sat., $15-68). The à la carte menu offers basic meat and seafood done in upscale fashion, featuring side dishes like brick doe shrimp or crab and sweet corn flatbread. Also in the H Hotel is **Café Zinc** (800/282-7778, 6:30am-10pm daily, $9-36), an excellent choice for breakfast, lunch, or dinner. Breakfast offerings include such appealing dishes as eggs Benedict or the tomato spinach caprese tartine. Dinner entrées include ginger bourbon roasted half chicken and kurobuta pork chop. Hungry yet?

For a more moderate option, consider the **Bamboo Garden** (721 S. Saginaw Rd., 989/832-7967, 10:30am-9:30pm Mon.-Sat., noon-9pm Sun., $9-16), a classy Chinese restaurant with a relaxing atmosphere and reliably good food, including sizzling steak, Buddha duck, and moo shu pork with Mandarin pancakes.

The H Hotel (111 W. Main St., 866/611-5231, www.thehhotel.com, $191-239) brings an unparalleled level of class and sophistication to town. Built primarily to serve business travelers, the H is a AAA Four Diamond property with two fine dining options and airport shuttle service.

You'll also find a variety of dependable chain motels clustered near the intersection of Wackerly Street and Eastman Avenue. Try the 90-room **Fairview Inn** (2200 W. Wackerly St., 989/631-0070, $79-109 d).

Camping

For campers, **Black Creek State Forest Campground** (W. Saginaw Rd. and NW River Rd., Sanford, 989/539-3021, daily mid-Apr.-Nov., $15) offers 23 sites with no electricity or showers that can accommodate tents or RVs. Sites are available on a first-come, first-served basis. Campers can enjoy nearby hiking trails, bird-watching opportunities, a boat launch, and access to several lakes and rivers ideal for anglers.

INFORMATION AND SERVICES

For more information about the Midland area, contact the **Midland County Convention & Visitors Bureau** (128 Main St., 989/839-9775, www.macc.org). You'll have no trouble finding groceries, banks, and the like. For medical assistance, head to the **MidMichigan Medical Center** (4005 Orchard Dr., 989/839-3100, www.midmichigan.org).

GETTING THERE AND AROUND

Travelers can fly to the **MBS International Airport** (MBS, 8500 Garfield Rd., Freeland, 989/695-5555, www.mbsairport.org), where it's possible to rent a car from one of five major rental agencies. From here, head to Midland via Garfield Road, U.S. 10, and M-20; in light traffic, the 13-mile trip should take about 20 minutes.

From Mount Pleasant, take M-20 to downtown Midland, a 27-mile trip that usually takes about 33 minutes. From downtown Bay City, take M-25, continue onto U.S. 10, and follow M-20 to downtown Midland; in light traffic the 19-mile trip takes roughly 23 minutes.

The Southwest Coast

Celebrated for its dramatic sand dunes and glorious sunsets, Michigan's Southwest Coast attracts thousands of visitors annually. The westerly winds that blow across Lake Michigan are responsible for pushing the sun-warmed waters closer to shore, making the beaches perfect for swimming in summer. Over the last century, wealthy visitors from Detroit, Grand Rapids, and Chicago have flocked to the sunny shores of southwestern Michigan and helped to transform a string of coastal villages into the upscale resort towns of today. This 130-mile stretch of picturesque coastline, extending from the Indiana border to just north of Muskegon, offers a wide array of diversions, including golf courses, bike paths, fishing and boating charters, several state parks, art galleries, picturesque lighthouses, and annual festivals

Highlights

Look for ★ to find recommended sights, activities, dining, and lodging.

★ **Lake Michigan Shore Wine Country:** Wineries and tasting rooms lure connoisseurs to the southwestern corner (page 178).

★ **Blossomtime Festival:** This annual celebration spotlights the local agricultural splendor (page 184).

★ **Art Galleries in Saugatuck and Douglas:** Together, the adjacent coastal villages of Saugatuck and Douglas are known as the Art Coast of Michigan, boasting roughly 20 fine art, studio, craft, and specialty galleries (page 190).

★ **Tulip Time Festival:** Holland honors its Dutch heritage in this annual springtime event with colorful tulip displays and carnival rides (page 199).

★ **Michigan's Adventure:** Children, teenagers, and even parents are fond of this amusement and water park, where you'll find one of the nation's highest and longest wooden roller coasters (page 209).

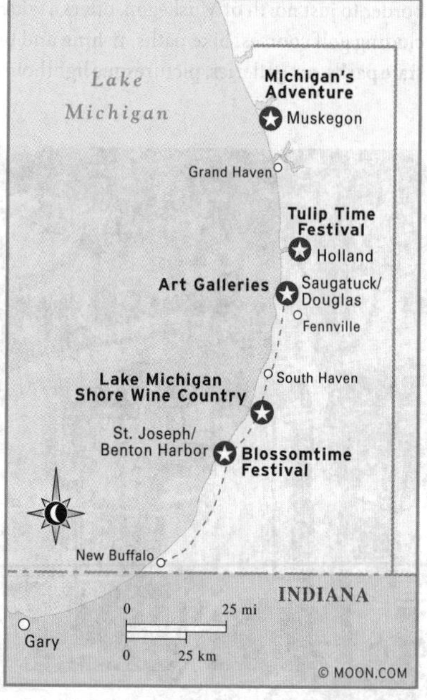

celebrating tulips in Holland and the Coast Guard in Grand Haven.

The same temperate climate that lures beach-loving visitors is also responsible for the inland abundance of flourishing fields, orchards, and vineyards. Popular mild-weather pastimes include touring one of the Midwest's finest wine-growing regions and plucking bushels of fresh produce at several self-pick farms. Here, visitors are welcome to sample gourmet delicacies, like homemade jams, honey, maple syrup, salsa, and baked goods.

Such diversity has earned the Southwest Coast a variety of monikers over the years, including Michigan's Gold Coast, the Art Coast of Michigan, and the Riviera of the Midwest. Whatever it's called, the Southwest Coast is an understandably popular destination for vacationers, especially in the summertime, when the vibrant blue waters of Lake Michigan, formed by enormous glaciers during the last ice age, entice travelers to contemplate the magnificence of nature.

PLANNING YOUR TIME

Practically the entire western coast of Michigan's Lower Peninsula—including the resort towns and incredible beaches that dot the southern half—is a major tourist draw, especially during the state's traditionally mild summers. If you're not fond of crowds, you might want to avoid places like Saugatuck and Grand Haven during July and August. But even in the off-season, the area holds appeal for art lovers, golfing enthusiasts, beachcombers, wine connoisseurs, and cross-country skiers.

Save for a few inland vineyards and villages, the area's most popular destinations lie close to the coast, accessible via I-94, I-196, and U.S. 31. The three-hour drive from Michiana to Montague is a journey that does not require GPS. To make the most of this coastal trip, allow at least five days, making sure to see South Haven, Saugatuck, Holland, Grand Haven, and Muskegon along the way. In twice that amount of time you'll also be able to linger in Saugatuck's art galleries, catch a few annual events, play a few rounds of award-winning golf, take a bike ride on the Kal-Haven Trail, and explore some of the vineyards and self-pick farms in the region's interior.

Options for traveling along the coast are numerous. Amtrak offers train service to New Buffalo, Niles, Dowagiac, St. Joseph, Bangor, and Holland. Muskegon, the largest town on the Southwest Coast, has superb public transit. A car, however, offers the greatest level of convenience. Bring warm clothes in winter, swimsuits in summer, and always be prepared for surprises—even in August, rain and cool temperatures are possible.

For more information about the Southwest Coast, consult the **Michigan Beachtowns Association** (www.beachtowns.org), the **Southwestern Michigan Tourist Council** (2300 Pipestone Rd., Benton Harbor, 269/925-6301, www.swmichigan.org), or the **West Michigan Tourist Association** (WMTA, 741 Kenmoor Ave., Ste. E, Grand Rapids, 616/245-2217, www.wmta.org).

HISTORY

The history of the Southwest Coast is steeped in stories of Native Americans, French explorers, lumber, and agriculture. Many area towns, like Paw Paw and Muskegon, still bear names derived from Native American languages. Several rivers, such as the Grand River near what is today Grand Haven, flow into Lake Michigan, creating the perfect transportation system for logs, which allowed southwestern Michigan to prosper during the golden age of the timber industry. After the Civil War, a growing number of sawmills operated along the shoreline, helping to make southwest Michigan one of the leading lumber-producing regions in the country.

Previous: shopping district in St. Joseph; the Black River in South Haven; a windmill in Holland, Michigan.

The Southwest Coast

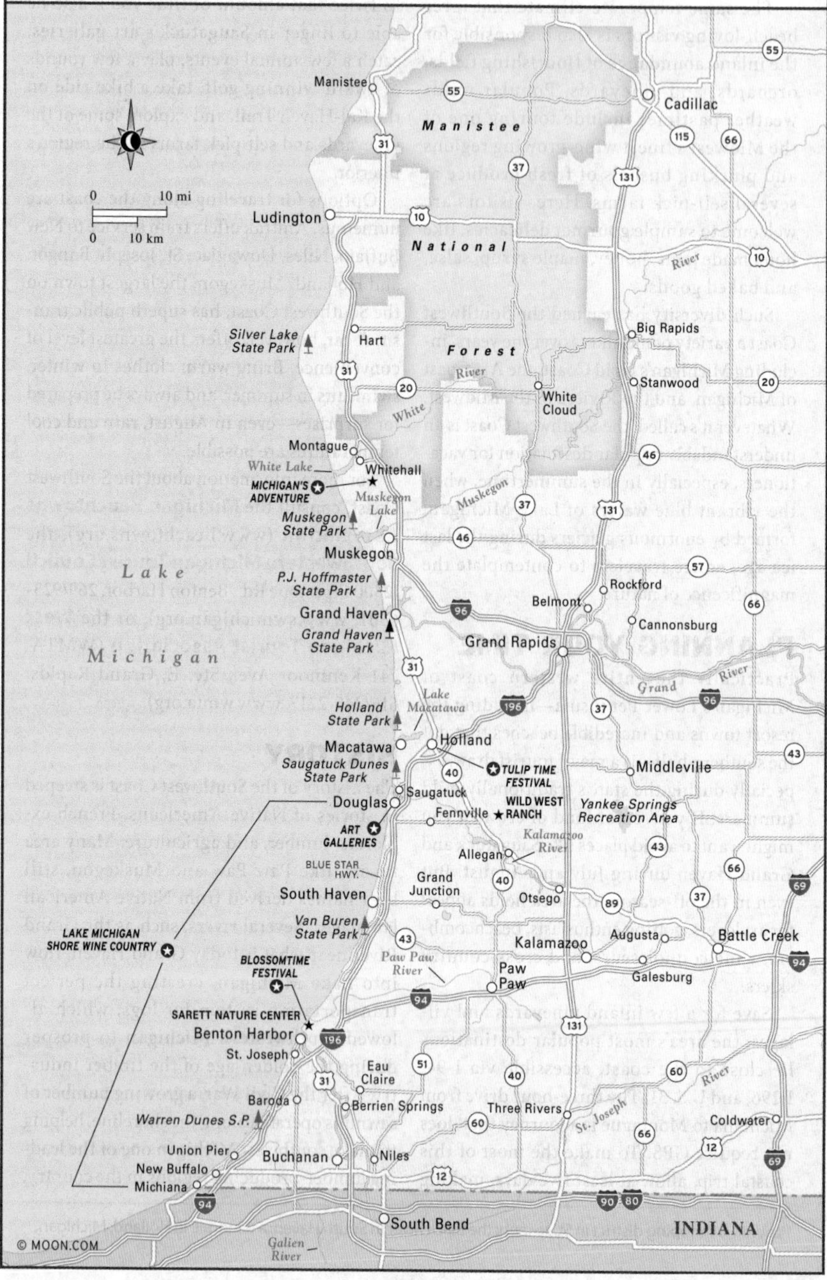

Most of the lumber used to rebuild Chicago after the Great Fire in 1871 was felled from its forests.

Once the forests were stripped, the region became known for its shipping ports and bountiful produce, luring settlers from places as far afield as the East Coast and the Netherlands. By the late-19th century, the main mode of transportation shifted from rivers to railroads and then to roads built for automobiles. With the car came tourists and one of southwestern Michigan's popular nicknames, Michigan's Gold Coast. Today a string of resort towns stretching north from the Indiana border serve as base camps for exploring the region's wealth of hiking trails, antiques shops, wineries, self-pick farms, and history, such as the Morton House, built by one of the founding families of Benton Harbor.

St. Joseph Wine Country

Once called Newburyport, the area now known as **St. Joseph** grew as a rest stop for travelers between Detroit and Chicago. Set on a bluff overlooking Lake Michigan, "St. Joe" is a pleasant city of 8,300 with attractive historic buildings and a vibrant downtown shopping district lined with art galleries, trendy boutiques, and charming coffeehouses. Ship captains and lumber barons built many of the town's 19th-century Victorian structures; today, vacationers and second-home owners enjoy the bluff-top views of the area's lovely beaches and parks.

Home to the Whirlpool company headquarters and one of the country's oldest Christian communities, **Benton Harbor,** St. Joseph's slightly larger northern neighbor, has a burgeoning arts community of its own. Together, the two towns present the well-attended Blossomtime Festival, the state's oldest multiple-community festival, every spring. Nearby is a string of wineries that make up the Lake Michigan Shore Wine Trail.

SIGHTS

Beaches

Many visitors need no more entertainment than the **Silver Beach County Park,** the

vineyard in Michigan wine country

lovely municipal beach that skirts downtown St. Joseph, a favorite spot for anglers and anyone wishing for a front-row seat for the sunset. From here—and from **Tiscornia Beach,** on the northern bank of the St. Joseph River—you can spot the North Pier, a long cement breakwater jutting 1,000 feet into the lake, leading to twin lighthouses that guard the harbor. The farther light is cylindrical, while its nearer counterpart is perched atop an octagonal red-roofed structure, a replica of the 1859 lighthouse that once stood on the bluff. The much-photographed **St. Joseph North Pier Lighthouse** was once featured on a U.S. postal stamp commemorating Great Lakes lighthouses. The two remain as one of only two range-light systems on the Great Lakes; the other is in Grand Haven, farther north.

Besides lighthouses, other worthy attractions abound. Just steps from family-friendly Silver Beach, kids will relish a ride on the **Silver Beach Carousel** (333 Broad St., 269/982-8500, www.silverbeachcarousel.com, 4pm-8:30pm Thurs., 11am-5pm Fri.-Sat., noon-5pm Sun. Jan.-Mar., 10am-5pm Thurs.-Sat., noon-5pm Sun. Apr.-May, 10am-10pm Mon.-Sat., noon-10pm Sun. June-Aug., 4pm-8:30pm Thurs., 11am-8pm Fri.-Sat., noon-5pm Sun. Sept.-Dec., $3 per ride), which contains 48 unique hand-carved carousel figures, including horses, tigers, and clown fish, and two chariots, including one that's wheelchair accessible. Open year-round, the lighted, music-enhanced carousel also features historical photographs chronicling St. Joseph's past.

Silver Beach boasts **Michigan's tallest kaleidoscope,** the **Whirlpool Compass Fountain** (5pm-9pm daily May, 10am-9pm daily Memorial Day-Labor Day, noon-2pm and 5pm-9pm daily Sept., free), where kids can cool off in the summer, and the **Curious Kids' Discovery Zone** (333 Broad St., 269/982-8500, www.curiouskidsmuseum.org, 10am-5pm Mon.-Sat., noon-5pm Sun. June-Labor Day, 4pm-8:30pm Thurs., 11am-5pm Fri.-Sat., noon-5pm Sun. Sept.-May, $6 pp, under age 3 free), which presents water-related exhibits as well as a climbing wall.

Museums and Historic Sites

Housed in an old brick four-square house above Lake Michigan, St. Joseph's clever **Curious Kids' Museum** (415 Lake Blvd., 269/983-2543, www.curiouskidsmuseum.org, 10am-5pm Mon.-Sat., 10am-4pm Sun. June-Aug., 10am-5pm Wed.-Sat., 10am-4pm Sun. Sept.-May, $6-10 pp) ranks as one of the best museums of its kind in the state. From the minute they walk in the door, visitors are treated to bright, colorful displays—including the lobby murals by eccentric Niles cartoonist and artist Nancy Drew—that are both engaging and playful. Excellent exhibits teach but don't preach. Kids can explore a rainforest, navigate a ship through the Great Lakes, experience what it's like to be disabled, or follow an apple crop through autumn processing and sell the results at a farm stand.

Down the street at the **Krasl Art Center** (707 Lake Blvd., 269/983-0271, www.krasl.org, 11am-8pm Mon.-Thurs., 11am-5pm Fri.-Sun., closed Tues. Jan.-Mar., free, $5 donation requested), visitors find both energetic volunteers and a schedule of well-chosen changing exhibits. Four galleries display fine art, contemporary works, folk arts and crafts, creations by regional artists, and occasional traveling exhibitions. A gallery shop offers art-related gifts and other interesting items, and the center encourages patrons to take a SculpTour, a self-guided tour of outdoor sculptures in St. Joseph and Benton Harbor.

The Heritage Museum and Cultural Center (601 Main St., 269/983-1191, www.theheritagemcc.org, 10am-4pm Tues.-Wed. and Fri.-Sat., 10am-8pm Thurs., free) explores the area's culture and history with exhibits, lectures, walking tours, and extensive archives. Recent exhibits have explored St. Joseph's lighthouses and southwestern Michigan's fruit belt.

While St. Joseph's history extends as far back as the 1670s, Benton Harbor's story

The Potawatomi Nation

Michigan's earliest inhabitants were, of course, Native Americans, and while some of their descendants still dwell here, many others departed, including the Potawatomi people, one of several Algonquian-speaking groups who occupied the Great Lakes region from prehistoric times through the early 19th century. Once part of a larger group that included the Chippewa and Ottawa, the autonomous Potawatomi lived in southwestern Michigan over 500 years ago.

Following the Beaver Wars of the mid-1600s, many Potawatomi moved to Wisconsin and became trappers for French fur traders. Soon the Potawatomi began hiring other indigenous people to collect and trap furs, which they would sell or trade to the French, thus expanding their control over a five-million-acre territory comprising Wisconsin, Illinois, Michigan, Indiana, and part of Ohio.

For most of the 1700s, the Potawatomi thrived. Adapted well to their environs, they traveled by canoe, fished in area lakes and streams, hunted waterfowl and larger game, harvested wild rice and berries, and cultivated an assortment of crops. The Potawatomi wore distinctive clothing, dwelled in birchbark wigwams, and celebrated communal events like the springtime tapping of sugar maple trees.

Unfortunately, the Potawatomi did not escape the fate of so many Native Americans; by 1800, European settlements had begun to displace indigenous villages. In the fall of 1838, one group of the Potawatomi, the Mission Band, was forced to leave Indiana and march over 660 miles to a reserve in Kansas on the Potawatomi Trail of Death.

For over 20 years, the Mission Potawatomi remained in Kansas, eventually settling small farms, many of which were later taken by European settlers and traders. In 1867, Mission Potawatomi members signed a treaty that allowed them to sell their Kansas lands and purchase new lands in present-day Oklahoma. After adopting U.S. citizenship, the Mission Band became known as the Citizen Potawatomi people.

By the 1870s, the Citizen Potawatomi had formed several communities near present day Shawnee. The Dawes Act of 1887, however, forced them to accept individual allotments again, and half of their reservation was lost during the 1891 government-sanctioned land run. Although some community members left for places such as California and Texas, many remained in Oklahoma. Now the ninth-largest Native American group in the United States, the Citizen Potawatomi Nation (www.potawatomi.org) owns several grocery stores, banks, and a casino resort.

This was not the end of the Potawatomi story in Michigan, however. In 1994, President Clinton restored recognition to the **Pokagon Band of Potawatomi Indians** (www.pokagon.com), which currently has over 4,500 citizens in a 10-county area, including four counties in southwestern Michigan. The Pokagon Band has three casinos, the **Four Winds Casinos** (866/494-6371, www.fourwindscasino.com), with locations in New Buffalo (11111 Wilson Rd.), Hartford (68600 Red Arrow Hwy.), and Dowagiac (58700 M-51 S.).

began in 1835, when Eleazar Morton and his family became the first nonnative settlers on the northern side of the St. Joseph River. By 1849 they owned 500 acres of farmland, including a peach orchard and a hilltop house overlooking what would become town, founded in part by Eleazar's son Henry. Today, the **Morton House Museum** (501 Territorial Rd., 269/925-7011, www.mortonhousemuseum.org, tours 1pm-3pm first Sat. June-Aug.; 10am-1pm Wed. May-Oct. $5 adults, $3 children), the oldest standing home in Benton Harbor, educates visitors about life in the 19th century.

Box Factory for the Arts

Until 1989, the Williams Brothers Box Factory, built near the turn of the 20th century, served as a manufacturing plant for various decorative and specialty boxes. Since 1995, the historic building has been used as an arts facility for local artists and residents. Today, the **Box Factory for the Arts** (1101 Broad St., St. Joseph, 269/983-3688, www.

boxfactoryforthearts.org, 10am-4pm Mon.-Sat., free) houses a gift shop, a café, three art galleries, and 37 artists' studios. The center also offers art classes and workshops, presents films on Friday nights, and holds concerts every Saturday evening.

★ Lake Michigan Shore Wine Country

Thanks to the moderating effects of nearby Lake Michigan, a pocket of southwestern Michigan from Buchanan to Fennville basks in a microclimate surprisingly conducive to growing grapes. With its sandy soils, gently rolling terrain, and dependable snow cover needed to protect the fragile vines, the area has been compared to the wine-producing areas of northern Europe, including France's renowned Champagne region.

While this may contain a bit of hyperbole, the state is indeed becoming more recognized for its winemaking. Early on, wineries experimented with hardy but overly sweet grapes such as concord and catawba. As tastes grew more sophisticated and drier wines came in vogue, French hybrids were introduced, including vidal blanc white grapes and red chancellor and chambourcin. In recent years, Michigan's award-winning wines have become genuine competition for those produced in California, and the industry works aggressively to promote the picturesque vineyards as an attraction.

Each of the wineries, vineyards, and tasting rooms makes a pleasant warm-weather pilgrimage. You may want to plan your visit for the weekend after Labor Day, when the three-day **Paw Paw Wine & Harvest Festival** (www.wineandharvestfestival.com) features free wine tastings. For more information about Michigan wines, contact the **Lake Michigan Shore Wine Trail** (www.lakemichiganshorewinetrail.com) or the **Michigan Grape and Wine Industry Council** (517/284-5733, www.michiganwines.com).

DOMAINE BERRIEN CELLARS AND WINERY

Established in 2001 on part of a family-owned 80-acre fruit farm six miles east of Lake Michigan, **Domaine Berrien Cellars and Winery** (398 E. Lemon Creek Rd., Berrien Springs, 269/473-9463, www.domaineberrien.com, noon-5pm daily Apr.-Dec., noon-5pm Fri.-Sun. Jan.-March) is one of the first vineyards you'll encounter on the road from St. Joseph. Although relatively new, Domaine

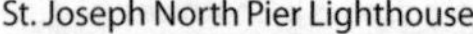

St. Joseph North Pier Lighthouse

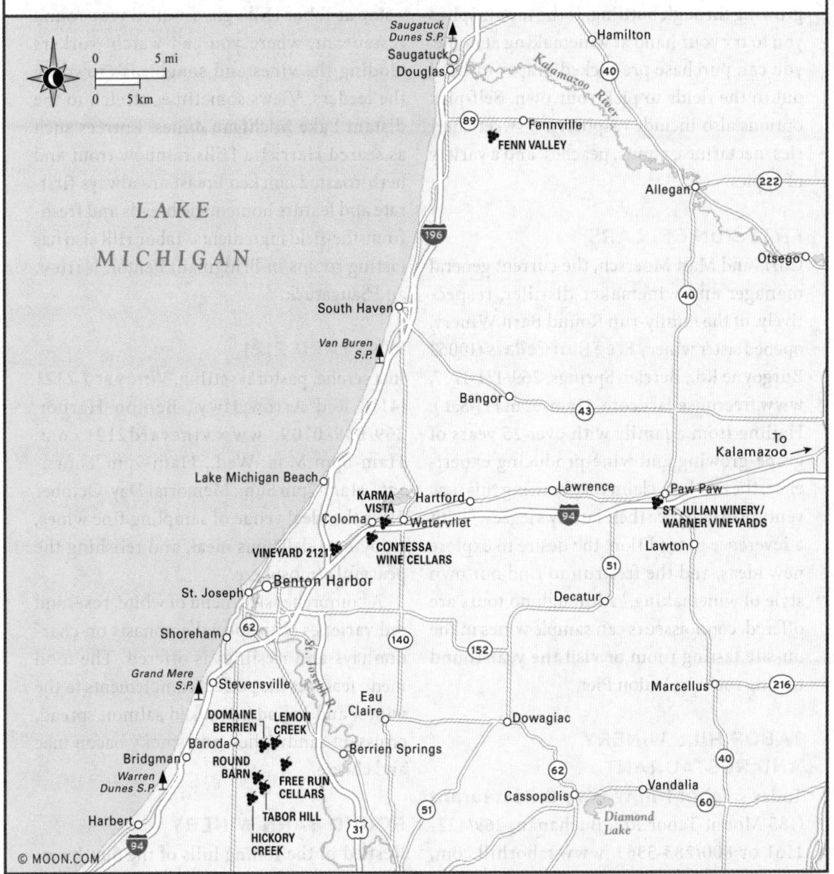

Berrien has already garnered a reputation for excellent handcrafted wines, including award-winning selections like pinot noir, cabernet franc, syrah, pinot grigio, and traminette. Visitors can tour the winemaking area and enjoy a glass with locally made cheeses and sausages on an outside patio overlooking the scenic vineyards.

LEMON CREEK WINERY AND FRUIT FARM

Just down the road from Domaine Berrien lies the **Lemon Creek Winery and Fruit Farm** (533 E. Lemon Creek Rd., Berrien Springs, 269/471-1321, www.lemoncreekwinery.com, 10am-6pm Mon.-Sat., noon-6pm Sun. May-Nov., noon-5pm Sun.-Thurs., noon-6pm Fri., 11am-6pm Sat. Dec.-Apr.). The vineyards are part of a 150-acre fruit farm that has been in the Lemon family for over 160 years. The farm began growing grapes in the early 1980s as a way of diversifying crops. The winery opened in 1984, eventually earning more than 100 awards. Well-known varietals include ruby rose and the full-bodied meritage.

Visitors are welcome to wander among the neatly labeled vines outside the tasting room and picnic at the nearby tables. Afterward, join one of the informal tours that give an overview of wine production from grape growing through bottling. If the tour inspires you to try your hand at winemaking at home, you can purchase pre-picked grapes or head out to the fields to pick your own. Self-pick options also include raspberries, sweet cherries, nectarines, plums, peaches, and a variety of apples.

FREE RUN CELLARS

Chris and Matt Moersch, the current general manager and winemaker-distiller, respectively, of the family-run Round Barn Winery, opened sister winery **Free Run Cellars** (10062 Burgoyne Rd., Berrien Springs, 269/471-1737, www.freeruncellars.com, 11am-6pm Fri-Sat.). Hailing from a family with over 25 years of grape-growing and wine-producing experience, the brothers claim they're using this new venture to enhance their family's legacy, "with a reverence to tradition, the desire to explore new ideas, and the free run to find our own style of winemaking." Although no tours are offered, connoisseurs can sample wines in the on-site tasting room or visit the year-round tasting room in Union Pier.

TABOR HILL WINERY AND RESTAURANT

Today's **Tabor Hill Winery & Restaurant** (185 Mount Tabor Rd., Buchanan, 269/422-1161 or 800/283-3363, www.taborhill.com, 11am-6pm Mon.-Tues., 11am-8pm Wed.-Sun., tours noon-4:30pm daily May-Oct. and noon-4:30pm Sat.-Sun. Nov.-Apr., tasting $9) is a far cry from the winery's early commune-like days under visionary founder and salesman Len Olson. David Upton, an heir to the Whirlpool fortune, rescued the ailing operation in the late 1970s, eventually turning it into one of the state's largest producing wineries. It's best known for its midpriced wines made from French hybrid grapes, including the classic demi-sec (known as the "president's wine" because it has been served at the White House), the dry riesling, and the grand mark—all award-winners.

If you're lucky, you might catch the winemaker's tour. After a tour or tasting, consider a stop at Tabor Hill's glass-walled year-round restaurant, where you can watch workers tending the vines and songbirds crowding the feeders. Views sometimes stretch to the distant Lake Michigan dunes. Entrées such as seared Harrietta Hills rainbow trout and herb-roasted chicken breast are always first-rate and feature homemade breads and fresh-from-the-field ingredients. Tabor Hill also has tasting rooms in Bridgman, Benton Harbor, and Saugatuck.

VINEYARD 2121

In a serene, pastoral setting, **Vineyard 2121** (4110 Red Arrow Hwy., Benton Harbor, 269/849-0109, www.vineyard2121.com, 11am-6pm Mon.-Wed., 11am-9pm Thurs.-Sat., 11am-7pm Sun., Memorial Day-October 31) is the ideal venue of sampling fine wines, enjoying a delicious meal, and relishing the peaceful atmosphere.

A comprehensive menu of white, rosé, and red varieties with special emphasis on chardonnays and rieslings is offered. The food menu features the perfect complements to the wines, and includes smoked salmon spread, croissant sandwiches, and smoky bacon mac and cheese.

ROUND BARN WINERY

Nestled in the rolling hills of the Southwest Coast's countryside, the **Round Barn Winery** (10983 Hills Rd., Baroda, 800/716-9463, www.roundbarn.com, 11am-6pm Sun.-Thurs., 11am-7pm Fri.-Sat.) is a family-owned winery, distillery, and brewery. It was opened in 1992 by former Tabor Hill winemaker Rick Moersch and specializes in handcrafted wines, fruit brandies, vodka, and microbrews. There's an additional tasting room in Union Pier.

An 1880s post-and-beam farmhouse serves as the tasting room, where you can learn about the winery's unique winemaking style, which incorporates techniques pioneered at Michigan State University. The staff are more than willing to explain the winery's unique characteristics, including its choice of the Alsatian style of winemaking and the unusual vine trellising system introduced by MSU.

During the warm-weather months, the winery hosts an array of fun events, including a concert series called "Jammin' in The Vineyard," an art fair, and a classic car show. Families are welcome.

HICKORY CREEK WINERY

The southernmost winery in the Lake Michigan Shore Wine Country, **Hickory Creek** (750 Browntown Rd., Buchanan, 269/422-1100, www.hickorycreekwinery.com, noon-5pm Mon.-Thurs., noon-6pm Fri., 11am-7pm Sat., noon-6pm Sun., tasting $10 for 5 wines, fee waived with purchase of two or more bottles) is the product of three distinct perspectives. The winery's trio of owners, all of whom share a lifelong passion for winemaking, originate from three premier wine-growing nations: the United States, Australia, and Germany. Hickory Creek specializes in crafting world-class wines from grapes grown exclusively along Lake Michigan's eastern shore. Current selections include riesling, chardonnay, pinot noir, gewürztraminer, and apple wine.

CONTESSA WINE CELLARS

Between Benton Harbor and Paw Paw, you'll find **Contessa Wine Cellars** (3235 Friday Rd., Coloma, 269/468-5534, www.contessawinecellars.com, noon-5pm daily, tasting fee $5 for 5 wines), the brainchild of third-generation winemaker Tony Peterson, who longed to blend traditional winemaking practices with old-world ambience. Here, visitors are treated to an enormous selection of wines, from a full-bodied merlot to a dry white divino to two varieties of fruit wine—blueberry and cherry—served in an elegant tasting room reminiscent of an Italian villa. The building also sits at an especially high spot; from the winery's European-style terrace, you can look across acres of stunning orchards nestled in the verdant Coloma Valley.

KARMA VISTA VINEYARDS AND WINERY

Just a little farther east, on the road to Paw Paw, you'll encounter **Karma Vista** (6991 Ryno Rd., Coloma, 269/468-9463, www.karmavista.com, 11am-5pm Mon., Wed.-Sat., noon-5pm Sun.), which prides itself on being "one of Michigan's newest wineries from one of the state's oldest farm families." Situated on a serene hillside above the town of Coloma, Karma Vista promises a relaxing experience for wine connoisseurs. Those with a sense of humor will also appreciate this quirky winery, where the colorful labels will elicit a chuckle with selections like Cha Cha Chardonnay, Watusi Red, Stone Temple Pinot, and Moondance Merlot.

ST. JULIAN WINERY

Family-owned **St. Julian** (716 S. Kalamazoo St., Paw Paw, 269/657-5568, www.stjulian.com, 9am-6pm Mon.-Thurs., 9am-8pm Fri.-Sat., 11am-6pm Sun.) has always prided itself on making good wines that are accessible to a wide variety of tastes and budgets. The winery is located on a busy commercial strip and heavily marketed to tour buses and groups, and thus provides less personalized attention than the boutique wineries. What the oldest and largest winery in the state does well is wine education and wine-related tourism: Its year-round tours include an informative audiovisual show and a visit to the bottling line and fermenting room. Visitors in late August and September can watch grapes being delivered and crushed. The winery and its tasting rooms in Union Pier, Dundee, and Frankenmuth are open year-round.

WARNER VINEYARDS

Next to St. Julian, **Warner Vineyards** (706 S. Kalamazoo St., Paw Paw, 269/657-3165 or 800/756-5357, www.warnerwines.com, 10am-6pm Mon.-Thurs., 10am-7pm Fri., 10am-8pm Sat., noon-5pm Sun.) operates the state's second-oldest winery out of an appealing 1898 waterworks building. Founded in 1938, Warner boasts one of the Midwest's few sparkling wine cellars, which realistically simulates the chalk storage vaults of the Champagne region of France. Visitors can take a short self-guided tour, then relax afterward over a refreshing glass on the charming wine deck. Warner's specialties include their award-winning dry sparkling wine and the popular liebestrauben and holiberry. Warner also has tasting rooms in Holland, Marshall, New Buffalo, and South Haven.

FENN VALLEY VINEYARDS AND WINE CELLAR

The northernmost winery in Lake Michigan Shore Wine Country, **Fenn Valley** (6130 122nd Ave., Fennville, 269/561-2396, www.fennvalley.com, 11am-5pm Sun.-Wed., 11am-7:30pm Thurs., 11am-7pm Fri.-Sat.) is conveniently close to the art galleries of Saugatuck and Douglas. Since 1973, this family-operated winery has been producing award-winning handcrafted wines that benefit from the combination of a favorable climate, traditional winemaking techniques, and modern technology. Vineyard tours are offered on weekends August-October. The tours go into considerable detail, run close to two hours, and include samplings along the way to illustrate the winemaking process. Cellar tours and special events are also offered year-round. Fenn Valley has a tasting room in nearby downtown Saugatuck.

RECREATION

Golf

Near the junction of I-94 and I-196, **Lake Michigan Hills Golf Club** (2520 Kerlikowske Rd., Benton Harbor, 269/849-2722, www.lakemichiganhills.com, daily Apr.-Oct., $45-69 pp with cart) has been voted one of the best public golf courses in southwestern Michigan by *Michigan Golfer* magazine. Farther inland, you'll find several other well-favored courses, including **Paw Paw Lake Golf Course** (4548 Forest Beach Rd., Watervliet, 269/463-3831, www.pplgcgolf.com, daily Apr.-Oct., $26-46 pp with cart) and **Indian Lake Hills Golf Course** (55321 Brush Lake Rd., Eau Claire, 269/782-2540, www.indianlakehills.com, daily Apr.-Oct., $24-39 pp with cart).

Bird-Watching

Nature lovers can find what they seek at the **Sarett Nature Center** (2300 Benton Center Rd., Benton Harbor, 269/927-4832, www.sarett.com, 9am-5pm Tues.-Fri., 10am-5pm Sat., 1pm-5pm Sun., by donation). These 800 acres along the Paw Paw River northeast of Benton Harbor encompass upland meadows, swamp forests, and lowland marshes. As an accommodation to bird-watchers, the property contains many benches, elevated towers, and five miles of trails open daily sunrise to sunset. A naturalist is usually on hand to answer questions. Ask about the full schedule of demonstrations, nature walks, workshops, and classes.

Boating and Fishing

Like most of the towns along the Southwest Coast, St. Joseph and Benton Harbor share both a shipping past and a modern-day boating fever, as evidenced by the 30 colorful boat sculptures throughout downtown St. Joseph and by the full-service **Pier 1000 Marina** (1000 Riverview Dr., 269/927-4471, www.pier1000.com) in adjacent Benton Harbor. There's nothing quite like sailing off across the blue expanse of Lake Michigan on a cloudless summer day.

If you don't own a boat but still want to explore the lake, check out **Headhunter Charters** (10034 Painter School Rd., Berrien Center, 269/921-6997, www.headhuntersportfishing.com), which specializes in year-round open-water sportfishing charters on Lake Michigan and guided river trips for salmon and steelhead on the St. Joseph River.

1: a street chalk artist in St. Joseph **2:** a Northern Cardinal at Sarett Nature Center **3:** tasting room at Vineyard 2121

1

2

3

FESTIVALS AND EVENTS

★ Blossomtime Festival

Among southwestern Michigan's many warm-weather events, one highlight is the Blossomtime Festival, held in early May in the neighboring communities of St. Joseph and Benton Harbor. Begun in 1923 to promote the area's agricultural industry, the **Blossomtime Festival** (269/982-8016, www.blossomtimefestival.org) celebrates the coming of spring with a Grand Floral Parade featuring more than 125 floats, tractors, antique cars, bands, and costumed performers from several surrounding communities. As the oldest and largest multiple-community festival in Michigan, Blossomtime also fills the weeklong celebration with children's events, food tents, pageants, and more.

Other Festivals

Given the Southwest Coast's notoriety as a significant wine-producing region, it's no surprise that the **Paw Paw Wine & Harvest Festival** (269/655-1111, www.wineandharvestfestival.com) takes place every September, the weekend after Labor Day. During the three-day event, festivalgoers can enjoy live music, carnival rides, car shows, turtle derbies, classic movies, and grape-stomping contests. Meanwhile, wine connoisseurs are treated to free winery tours and tastings at St. Julian Winery and Warner Vineyards all weekend long.

To the southeast, in nearby Cass County, you'll find at least two other fun-filled events. In mid-May, the **Dogwood Fine Arts Festival** (Dowagiac, 269/782-1115, http://dogwoodfinearts.org, donation) entices lovers of art, music, dance, and literature with two weeks of lectures, concerts, performances, and readings from regional artists.

In late July or early August, the six-day **Cass County Fair** (Cassopolis, 269/445-8265, www.mycasscountyfair.com, $6 adults, $1 ages 6-12) invites revelers to enjoy traditional small-town fun—dog shows, livestock competitions, demolition derbies, tractor pulls, parades, and other farm-related activities.

SHOPPING

While St. Joseph's State Street shopping district houses numerous bookstores, gift shops, clothing boutiques, and jewelry emporiums, perhaps the highlight of this region is its bountiful produce. Nature's fruits can be enjoyed at two of the area's largest growers: **Fruit Acres Farm Market & U-Pick** (2789 Friday Rd., Coloma, 269/208-3591, www.fruitacresfarms.com, 10am-4:30pm daily June-Oct., weather permitting) and **Tree-Mendus Fruit Farm** (9351 E. Eureka Rd., Eau Claire, 269/782-7101, 10am-6pm Wed.-Mon. June-Aug., 10am-6pm Fri.-Mon. Sept.-Oct.).

Since 1964, family-operated Fruit Acres has provided area communities with a wide range of fresh produce and products. Today, the 230-acre orchard boasts seasonal crops of plums, peaches, black cherries, tree-ripened apricots, and apples. The market also sells apple cider; flowers, fruit, and vegetables from other area farmers; and locally made jams, jellies, salsas, and other condiments. During the season, visitors can pick their own fruit every Saturday and Sunday. Leashed dogs are welcome.

Tree-Mendus is one of the area's best self-pick farms, with acres of apples, pears, cherries, nectarines, peaches, plums, and more. Don't miss the chance to bite into one of the special heritage apples, a hobby of Tree-Mendus's curator. Besides the full fields, there's also a packed roster of special events, such as pony rides, harvesttime activities, and the International Cherry Pit-Spitting Championship.

FOOD AND ACCOMMODATIONS

Area dining choices include **Schu's Grill & Bar** (501 Pleasant St., 269/983-7248, www.schus.com, 11am-10pm Sun.-Thurs., 11am-11pm Fri.-Sat., $14-31), a St. Joseph institution with great sandwiches, soups, and beers in a pub-style setting above the waterfront.

For morning coffee, baked goods, and some great breakfast choices, head for **Caffe Tosi** (516 Pleasant St., St. Joseph, 269/983-3354, www.caffetosi.com, 7am-7:30pm Mon., 7am-8pm Tues.-Fri., 8am-8pm Sat., 8am-4pm Sun., $5-16).

Overlooking Lake Michigan, ★ **The Boulevard Inn & Bistro** (521 Lake Blvd., St. Joseph, 269/983-6600, www.theboulevardinn.com, $125-275 d) provides spacious suites, a genteel decor, and a super restaurant, **Bistro on the Boulevard** (269/983-3882, 6:30am-9:30am, 11:30am-2pm, and 5pm-9pm Mon.-Thurs., 6:30am-9:30am, 11:30am-2pm, and 5pm-10pm Fri., 7:30am-10am and 5pm-10pm Sat., 7:30am-10am, 11am-2pm, and 5pm-9pm Sun., $12-43) that offers breakfast, lunch, and dinner daily. Dinner can be especially wonderful here; take a seat on the lovely outdoor terrace, order the chef's three-course special, select from an outstanding wine list, and enjoy the incredible lake views below. The Boulevard is within easy walking distance of shops, restaurants, and beaches.

The **South Cliff Inn** (1900 Lakeshore Dr., St. Joseph, 269/983-4881, www.southcliffinnsj.com, $150-275 d) is a gracious English-inspired bed-and-breakfast with seven sun-filled rooms that also overlook the big lake. It's run by charming Bill Swisher, who left behind a 10-year career as director of a probate court to open the inn.

If you'd feel more comfortable in a chain hotel, you'll find several in the area. Benton Harbor has at least two options: **Americas Best Value Inn** (798 Ferguson Dr., 269/927-1172, www.americasbestvalueinn.com, $75-150 d) and **Best Western Benton Harbor/St. Joseph** (1592 Mall Dr., 269/925-3000, http://bestwesternmichigan.com, $139-210 d). **Comfort Inn & Suites** (153 Ampey Rd., Paw Paw, 269/655-0303, www.comfortinnpawpaw.com, $125-185 d) is in the heart of southwestern Michigan's wine country.

Camping

For a real bargain, there are two excellent campgrounds in the vicinity. The **Dune Lake Campground** (80855 County Rd. 376, Coloma, 269/764-8941, www.dunelakecampground.com, $27-30) welcomes RVs and tents to a picturesque area not far from Lake Michigan. Farther inland, **Shamrock Park** (9385 Old U.S. 31 S., Berrien Springs, 269/473-5691, www.shamrockpark.net, $25-55), a year-round camping and fishing park in the heart of wine country, provides easy access to several of the wineries. Both campgrounds also offer rental cabins.

INFORMATION AND SERVICES

For more information about St. Joseph, Benton Harbor, and the surrounding area, contact the **Southwestern Michigan Tourist Council** (2300 Pipestone Rd., Benton Harbor, 269/925-6301, www.swmichigan.org, 8:30am-5pm Mon.-Fri.), the **Coloma-Watervliet Area Chamber of Commerce** (142 Badt Dr., Coloma, 269/468-4430, www.coloma-watervliet.org, 8:30am-2:30pm Mon.-Fri.), or the **Four Flags Area Council on Tourism** (321 E. Main St., Niles, 269/684-7444, 10am-3pm Tues. and Thurs.). For local news and weather, consult the ***Herald-Palladium*** (www.heraldpalladium.com).

Both St. Joseph and Benton Harbor have all the essential services such as groceries and banks, including a few branches of **Fifth Third Bank** (www.53.com).

For medical services, visit the **Lakeland Medical Center** (1234 Napier Ave., St. Joseph, 269/983-8300, www.spectrumhealthlakeland.org). If necessary, you can fill prescriptions in Benton Harbor at **Rite Aid** (1701 S. M-139, Benton Harbor, 269/927-3101, www.riteaid.com, 9am-9pm Mon.-Sat., 10am-7pm Sun.).

GETTING THERE AND AROUND

Amtrak (800/872-7245, www.amtrak.com) offers rail service between Chicago and **St. Joseph Station** (410 Vine St.), both **Greyhound** (2412 S. M-139, Benton Harbor, 269/925-1121 or 800/231-2222, www.greyhound.com) and **Indian Trails** (2413 S.

M-139, Benton Harbor, 800/292-3831, www.indiantrails.com) provide bus service at neighboring stops in Benton Harbor, and the **Kalamazoo/Battle Creek International Airport** (AZO, 5235 Portage Rd., Kalamazoo, 269/388-3668, www.flyazo.com) is fairly close via I-94. Exploring St. Joseph, Benton Harbor, and the surrounding wine country is infinitely easier with a vehicle.

I-94 leads directly to St. Joseph and Benton Harbor. From downtown Detroit, take M-10, I-75, I-96, M-14, and I-94 toward the coast; in light traffic, the 186-mile trip usually requires 2.75 hours. From Chicago, follow I-90 and I-94 through Illinois and Indiana, taking exit 28 for M-139/Scottdale Road, then Pipestone Road into Benton Harbor; in light traffic, the 100-mile trip will take about 1.75 hours. En route from Chicago, parts of I-90 East and I-94 East serve as the Indiana Toll Road. Once you reach the St. Joseph and Benton Harbor area, you can access the wineries and tasting rooms along the Lake Michigan Shore Wine Trail via I-94, I-196, U.S. 31, and U.S. 12.

South Haven

Once the center of Michigan's fruit belt, the South Haven area is still a leading producer of blueberries and peaches. Lake Michigan can take credit for the area's well-drained soil and the moderating temperature effects of the prevailing west winds. Southwest Michigan's fruit belt had its origins in the 1850s, when farmers in St. Joseph and Benton Harbor noticed that their peaches survived the severe winters that killed off crops in the rest of the state. Fresh fruit was in high demand in bustling Chicago, and by the 1860s, crops were being shipped across the lake almost as fast as they could be picked.

Eventually, fruit farming and fruit-related industries spread throughout much of Van Buren and Berrien Counties. South Haven became famous for its peach crop; at the turn of the 20th century, some 144,000 acres were devoted to peaches, but freezes during the 1920s led many farmers to abandon peaches in favor of heartier apples. More recently, blueberries have gained popularity, with the area around South Haven emerging as the world's leading

South Haven shopping district

producer of blueberries. In July, National Blueberry Month, blueberry stands along rural roadsides are a common sight.

South Haven proper is known for its beautiful beaches and scenic fishing port, which prompted the *Financial Times* to call it "one of the most picturesque and charming small fishing ports you could hope to find." In summer, the population swells from roughly 4,400 to nearly 20,000, as visitors fill the historic inns lining North Shore Drive, stroll along the walks and shops that parallel the Black River near its mouth, and sunbathe on the long arc of sand that rims the town's northwestern edge. The town also offers its share of museums, festivals, golf courses, and various outdoor diversions, including the trailhead of the Kal-Haven Trail, popular among hikers and bikers.

SIGHTS

Beaches

Seven lovely beaches line the Lake Michigan shore, north and south of where the Black River opens into the great lake. **North Beach,** situated on the northern bank of the river, is popular for summertime beachgoers, with its volleyball courts and concession stand. For swimmers who enjoy a slower, quieter place, **Packard Park Beach** farther north might be a better choice. For those eager to sunbathe, watch passing boats, and take a stroll toward the vibrant red and black **South Haven South Pier Lighthouse Light** (www.southhaven.com), **South Beach** is the preferred spot. Established in 1903 at the end of the South Pier and accessible via a sturdy catwalk, the cylindrical lighthouse is still active today—attracting visitors to walk along the picturesque pier for an up close glimpse.

Museums

The **Michigan Maritime Museum** (260 Dyckman Ave., 269/637-8078, www.michiganmaritimemuseum.org, 10am-5pm daily, $8 adults, $7 seniors, $5 students, under age 4 free) features a variety of maritime displays, some of which chronicle the U.S. Coast Guard and the commercial fishers who have plied the local waters. Another intriguing attraction is the **Michigan Flywheelers Museum** (06285 68th St., 269/639-2010, www.michiganflywheelers.org, 10am-3pm Wed. and Sat.-Sun. Memorial Day-Labor Day, by donation), dedicated to the preservation of antique gas engines, steam engines, and tractors. In early September the museum hosts its annual Antique Engine and Tractor Show, which includes historical demonstrations and a flea market as well as the usual parades, games, and crafts.

Van Buren State Park

South of South Haven, **Van Buren State Park** (23960 Ruggles Rd., 269/637-2788, daily, annual Recreation Passport required: $12 Michigan residents, $34 nonresidents, $9 day pass available to nonresidents only) boasts some of the best water views in this part of the state. The high, wooded sand dunes of the 400-acre park hide a narrow opening that leads to the property's main attraction: the limitless blue waters of Lake Michigan, edged by a broad sweep of fine black-speckled sand. "No Trespassing" signs on the huge barrier dunes will hopefully prevent human erosion of the fragile sand mountains.

RECREATION

Golf

Golfers shouldn't miss playing a round at **HawksHead** (523 HawksNest Dr., 269/639-2121, www.hawksheadlinks.com, daily Apr.-Oct., $40-85 pp), once an asparagus farm that has now become one of the state's highest-ranked resorts, with a fine restaurant, a luxurious inn, and a championship course overlooking Lake Michigan. Another excellent choice is **Beeches Golf Club** (09601 68th St., 269/637-2600, www.beechesgolfclub.com, daily Apr.-Oct., $40-65 pp with cart), offering five sets of tee boxes, sandy waste areas on the front nine holes, and water hazards on the back nine—a challenge for almost any player.

Hiking and Biking

The **Kal-Haven Trail** (www.kalhavenbiketrail.com), open to hiking and biking, stretches from South Haven to Kalamazoo along the abandoned Kalamazoo & South Haven Railroad. There are several access points along the 34-mile route, which passes through the towns of Grand Junction, Bloomingdale, Gobles, and Kendall. The trail is also popular among bird-watchers, cross-country skiers, and snowmobilers.

Diving

Given the shipping histories of the towns along the Southwest Coast, including St. Joseph, South Haven, Saugatuck, Holland, and Grand Haven, it's no surprise that underwater shipwrecks line the Lake Michigan shore. Established in 1999, the **Southwest Michigan Underwater Preserve** comprises at least 15 shipwrecks and geological formations between New Buffalo and Holland, with the greatest concentration of sites near South Haven. Some of the most popular include the *Rockaway*, a 107-foot schooner lost in a storm while transporting lumber from Ludington to Benton Harbor, and the *Havana*, a 92-foot yacht that sank in heavy seas en route from Chicago to Holland. Divers are welcome to explore these and other fascinating relics, though it's strongly advised that they bring along a compass, tow a warning flag, and watch out for obstacles that could cause entanglement. For more information, contact the **Michigan Underwater Preserve Council** (MUPC, 800/970-8717, www.michiganpreserves.org/southwest.htm).

ENTERTAINMENT AND EVENTS

The Arts

In addition to displaying a wide array of visual arts, the **South Haven Center for the Arts** (600 Phoenix St., 269/637-1041, www.southhavenarts.org, 10am-4pm Tues.-Wed., Fri.-Sat., 10am-7pm Thurs.) hosts numerous concerts each year, showcasing styles as varied as Brazilian jazz, Celtic, and classical music as well as blues and folk.

National Blueberry Festival

South Haven hosts several different events during the year, but the town is probably best known for its long-standing **National Blueberry Festival** (www.blueberryfestival.com), which takes place during the second week in August. Besides standard fare like raffles, pageants, parades, and the like, this four-day event celebrates the blessed fruit with blueberry-pie-eating contests, blueberry pancake breakfasts, and blueberry-related cooking demonstrations.

SHOPPING

South Haven has a few whimsical shops, such as **Decadent Dogs** (505 Phoenix Rd., 269/639-0716, www.decadentdogs.com, 9am-9pm daily May-Sept., 10am-5:30pm Sun.-Thurs., 10am-7pm Fri.-Sat. Oct.-Apr.), a terrific place to pamper your best friend with glitzy collars, fancy treat jars, and the like. For blueberries and blueberry products—including everything from jellies to plush toys—check out **The Blueberry Store** (525 Phoenix Rd., 269/637-6322 or 877/654-2400, www.theblueberrystore.com, 10am-7pm Mon.-Sat., 10am-6pm Sun. spring-summer, shorter hours fall-winter).

Farms, markets, and orchards in the vicinity sell their produce at the **South Haven Farm Market** (546 Phoenix St., 269/206-0324, www.southhavenfarmmarket.com, 8am-2pm Sat. mid-May-mid-Oct., 8am-2pm Wed., early June-late Sept.), a smorgasbord of locally grown seasonal items behind Dyckman Park. Northeast of South Haven, you'll find **McIntosh Apple Orchards** (6431 107th Ave., 708/878-3734, www.mcintoshorchards.com, 11am-5pm, Mon.-Thurs., 11am-7pm Fri., 10am-6pm Sat.-Sun., mid-June-late Oct.), a 76-acre orchard and winery that's home to 26 different apple varieties. You can purchase a myriad of homegrown products, including traditional hard cider.

FOOD AND ACCOMMODATIONS

★ **Clementine's** (500 Phoenix St., 269/637-4755, www.ohmydarling.com, 11am-10pm Sun.-Thurs., 11am-11pm Fri.-Sat., $8-24), originally a bank, is now a beloved family-owned restaurant. Don't miss the old pictures of Lake Michigan steamers and their captains and crews on the walls. The magnificently carved bar spent its first life on one of the many steamboats that once frequented the city. Almost everything on the menu has a clever, countrified moniker. Examples include Tin Pan Walleye (potato-crusted pan-fried Canadian walleye) and the Tugboat Annie (charbroiled steak smothered with mushrooms, crab, shrimp, and mozzarella).

South Haven has no shortage of lodgings, from campgrounds to luxurious resorts. The **Old Harbor Inn** (515 Williams St., 269/637-8480, www.oldharborinn.com, $189-410 d) is part of a New England-style waterfront shopping village on the banks of the Black River—a great location with extras like a friendly bar.

For a break from shopping on Phoenix Street, stop in at **The Living Room Community Café** (520 Phoenix, 269/872-3465, 8am-6pm Mon.-Fri., 8am-10pm Sat.). Coffee, treats, and a warm welcome are all available in abundance.

★ **The Last Resort B&B Inn** (86 N. Shore Dr., 269/637-8943, www.lastresortinn.com, early May-Oct., $135-295 d) was, despite its name, South Haven's first resort. A few rooms have been updated with whirlpool tubs, but the place has a real down-home feel to it, largely due to its artist-owner, Mary Hammer. All rooms and suites offer views of Lake Michigan or the garden.

Lake Bluff Inn & Suites (76648 11th Ave., 269/637-8531, www.lakebluffinnandsuites.com, May-Oct., $129-299 d) is a well-kept waterfront resort that has been expanded over the years. It sits on a lovely bluff-top site south of South Haven, with outdoor pools, an indoor hot tub, a playground, and wireless Internet access.

Camping

Like the area's other waterfront state parks, **Van Buren State Park** (23960 Ruggles Rd., 269/637-2788, daily, annual Recreation Passport required: $12 Michigan residents, $34 nonresidents, $9 day pass available to nonresidents only) draws visitors with a beach as well as the wooded dunes of Lake Michigan. Its 220 modern campsites ($16-25) are a five-minute walk from the beach and frequently fill up on summer weekends. Reservations (800/447-2757, www.michigan.gov/dnr) are strongly advised.

For fancier environs, you can opt for the **Sunny Brook RV Resort** (68300 County Rd. 388, 888/499-5253, www.sunnybrookrvresort.com, mid-Apr.-Oct., $72-84), which includes a pool, a laundry and bathhouse, hiking trails, and a fishing lake.

INFORMATION AND SERVICES

For more information, contact the **South Haven Van Buren Co. & Visitors Bureau** (546 Phoenix St., 800/764-2836, www.southhaven.org, 9am-5pm Mon.-Fri., 10am-5pm Sat., June-Labor Day, shorter winter hours) or the **Greater South Haven Chamber of Commerce** (606 Phillips St., 269/637-5171, www.southhavenmi.com, 9am-5pm Mon.-Fri.).

If you need an ATM, you'll find several branches of **Fifth Third Bank** (www.53.com) in the area, including one in South Haven (601 Phoenix St.) and another in nearby Bangor (101 W. Monroe St.).

For medical services, visit the main hospital of the **Bronson South Haven Hospital** (955 S. Bailey Ave., 269/637-5271, www.bronsonhealth.com); prescriptions can be filled at the **Walmart Supercenter** (201 73rd St., 269/637-7802, www.walmart.com).

GETTING THERE AND AROUND

Although there are no direct flights to South Haven, you can get fairly close by flying into

Kalamazoo/Battle Creek International Airport (AZO, 5235 Portage Rd., Kalamazoo, 269/388-3668, www.flyazo.com) and then renting a car. **Amtrak** (800/872-7245, www.amtrak.com) offers rail service between Chicago and **Bangor Station** (541 Railroad St., Bangor), about 11 miles (19 minutes) southeast of South Haven via M-3. You can travel via **Greyhound** (269/637-2944 or 800/231-2222, www.greyhound.com) or **Indian Trails** (800/292-3831, www.indiantrails.com) to South Haven's **Bus Center** (1210 Phoenix St.).

Driving from elsewhere along the coast or from the towns in Michigan's Heartland, the optimal route is via U.S. 31, I-196, I-94, or M-43. From Grand Rapids, follow I-196 and Phoenix Street to South Haven, a 58-mile trip that usually takes about 54 minutes. From Kalamazoo, M-43 offers direct access to downtown South Haven, a 39-mile trip that normally takes about 55 minutes. From Chicago, follow I-90 and I-94 east through Illinois and Indiana onto I-196/U.S. 31, and take Phoenix Street into South Haven; in light traffic, the 123-mile trip should take about two hours. En route from Chicago, parts of I-90 and I-94 serve as the Indiana Toll Road.

Saugatuck and Douglas

Some claim success has spoiled Saugatuck. You may be inclined to agree if you visit on a summer weekend, when the city's narrow streets fill with much of what urban refugees are looking to escape: long lines in restaurants, shops overstuffed with designer clothes, and beaches clogged with humanity. But during any other season, Saugatuck reveals its true charm in quiet streets, excellent local cuisine, and exceptional art galleries.

Saugatuck (meaning "river's mouth" in the language of the Potawatomi people who settled the area) grew up in a fine natural setting—near the mouth of the wide Kalamazoo River, tucked between steep, rolling Lake Michigan dunes immediately west and lush green orchards immediately east. Lumber interests discovered the region in the mid-1800s. Prolific Saugatuck produced the majority of the lumber used to rebuild Chicago after the Great Fire in 1871. When the trees inevitably disappeared, so did much of the city. The absence of trees left the town unprotected from wind and sand blowing in from Lake Michigan, eventually burying a neighboring village known as Singapore.

Saugatuck, however, found new life as an art colony. In 1911 artists from the Art Institute of Chicago began sponsoring a summer art camp here. Lured by the warm breezes and picturesque location, other creative types soon followed, earning Saugatuck an early reputation as Michigan's Art Coast. Today the Ox-Bow School of Art is still open to the public June to August and includes galleries, demonstrations, and changing exhibitions.

Douglas, Saugatuck's nearest neighbor, has also evolved over the years. Established in 1851 as a port for ships carrying lumber and produce to Chicago and other cities in the Great Lakes area, this small village by the sea is now a popular vacation spot. Together, Saugatuck and Douglas have become two of the state's premier resort towns, boasting historic homes, quaint eateries, unique shops, and a bevy of art galleries.

SIGHTS

★ Art Galleries

The area's reputation as the **Art Coast** has attracted over 20 galleries within Saugatuck, Douglas, and Fennville. Notable stops include the **Button Gallery** (33-35 Center St., Douglas, 269/857-2175, www.buttonartgallery.com, 11am-5pm Mon.-Wed., 11am-7pm Thurs.-Fri., 11am-9pm Sat., 11am-5pm Sun. June-Aug.), which offers a wide array of

Saugatuck and Douglas

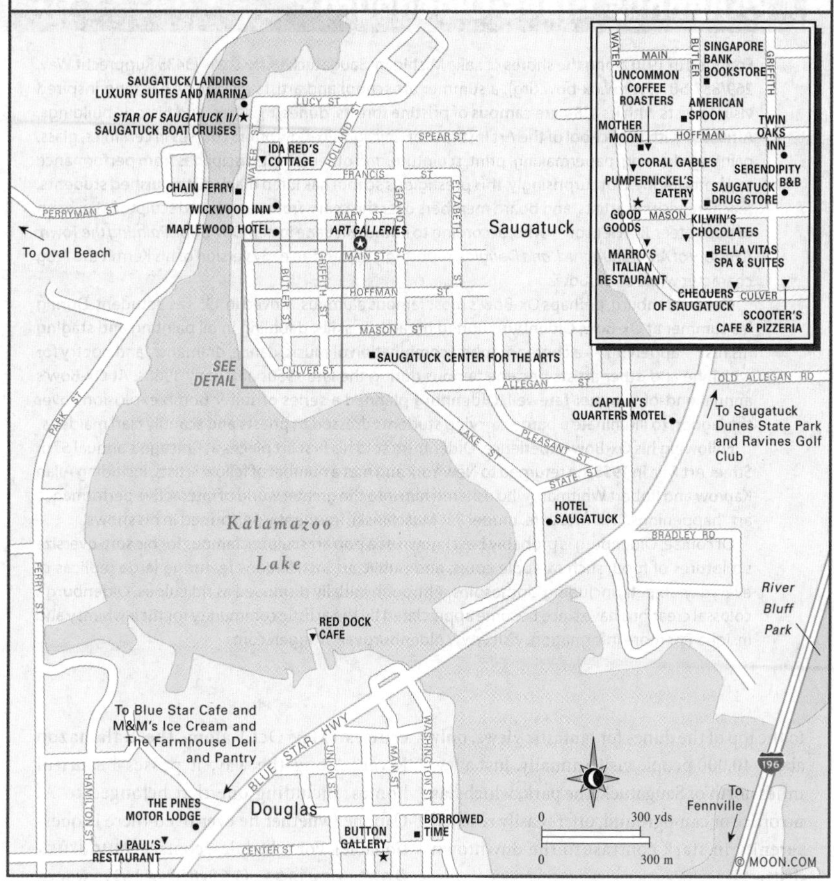

paintings, ceramics, sculptures, glasswork, and prints, and the eclectic **Good Goods** (106 Mason St., Saugatuck, 269/857-1557, www.goodgoods.com 10am-10pm daily), housed in a restored Victorian boardinghouse. Good Goods is the only place in town where you can pick up a one-of-a-kind piece by one of the area's founding artists, Sylvia Randolph, who was amazingly prolific into her 90s. Between South Haven and Saugatuck, you'll also encounter the **Blue Coast Artists** (6322 113th Ave., Fennville, 269/686-6343, www.bluecoastartists.net), a group of 12 artists who allow visitors a behind-the-scenes look into their studios and galleries every spring, summer, and fall; some are open year-round by appointment.

Beaches and Parks

For solitude, head for 1,000-acre **Saugatuck Dunes State Park** (269/637-2788, daily, annual Recreation Passport required: $12 Michigan residents, $34 nonresidents, $9 day pass available to nonresidents only). Despite 2.5 miles of undeveloped beach and dunes and 14 miles of well-marked trails, some winding

The Ox-Bow School and Alumnus Claes Oldenburg

Founded in 1910 along the shores of Lake Michigan, Saugatuck's **Ox-Bow** (3435 Rupprecht Way, 269/857-5811, www.ox-bow.org), a summer art school and artists residency, has long inspired visual artists with its 115-acre campus of pristine forests, dunes, marshes, and historic buildings. Affiliated with the School of the Art Institute of Chicago, Ox-Bow offers courses in ceramics, glass, painting, drawing, papermaking, print, sculpture, and other artistic disciplines from performance to photography. Not surprisingly, this prestigious school has lured many distinguished students, teachers, visiting artists, and board members over the years, from painter and sculptor Max Kahn to puppeteer Jim Henson—who, according to author Kit Lane in her 1997 book *Painting the Town: A History of Art in Saugatuck and Douglas,* reportedly created an early version of his Kermit the Frog character while at Ox-Bow.

Claes Oldenburg, perhaps Ox-Bow's most famous alumnus, arrived in 1953 as a student. During his summer at Ox-Bow, Oldenburg honed his artistic skills, dabbling in oil painting and staging his first "happening"—a choreographed combination of music, dance, dramatics, and poetry for which he and other artists became famous during the late 1950s and early 1960s. At Ox-Bow's annual end-of-summer farewell, Oldenburg planned a series of sulfur bomb explosions over the lagoon to illuminate a barge carrying students dressed as priests and scantily clad maidens.

Following his Ox-Bow experience, Oldenburg sold his first art pieces at Chicago's annual 57th Street Art Fair. In 1956, he returned to New York and met a number of fellow artists, including Allan Kaprow and Robert Whitman, who ushered him into the greater world of interactive performance art "happenings." His first wife, model Pat Muschinski, frequently performed in his shows.

Of course, Oldenburg is probably best known as a pop art sculptor, famous for his soft, oversize sculptures of food, such as apple cores, and public art installations featuring large replicas of everyday objects, including clothespins. Although initially dismissed as ridiculous, Oldenburg's colossal creations have since become appreciated by the artistic community for their whimsy and insight. For more information, visit www.oldenburgvanbruggen.com.

to the top of the dunes for fantastic views, only about 40,000 people visit annually. Just a few miles north of Saugatuck, the park, which has no office or campground, offers easily reached serenity in stark contrast to the downtown district.

Just a few steps from the shop-lined streets of Saugatuck, the frilly gingerbread **Chain Ferry** (528 Water St., 269/857-1701, www.saugatuck.com, Memorial Day-Labor Day, $2) shuttles visitors across the Kalamazoo River to the sandy Lake Michigan shore at **Oval Beach.** Families flock to this popular beach, filling the broad ribbon of sand and scaling Mount Baldhead, the steep dune that rises between town and the beach.

Tours

The two-level stern-wheeler docked on the riverfront, the ***Star of Saugatuck II,*** offers cruises (May-Oct.) along the Kalamazoo River. Along the way, it passes beautiful homes, including one that belonged to Al Capone (whether he ever lived there is questionable). For schedules, contact **Saugatuck Boat Cruises** (269/857-4261, www.saugatuckboatcruises.com, $27 adults, $15 ages 3-12, under age 3 free).

If you prefer land-based tours, consider **Saugatuck Dune Rides** (269/857-2253, www.saugatuckduneride.com, $22 adults, $12 ages 3-10). Expert guides lead small groups on 40-minute rides through the area's impressive dunes, sharing tales of the lost town of Singapore and educating visitors about local vegetation and wildlife.

RECREATION

Golf

For golfers, there are few nicer courses

than the **Ravines Golf Club** (3520 Palmer Dr., Saugatuck, 269/857-1616, www.ravinesgolfclub.com, daily Apr.-Oct., $59-69 pp with cart). In 2008, *Golf Digest* rated this Arnold Palmer-designed signature golf course as one of the "Best Places to Play" and as having "The Best Conditioned Course in the State."

Horseback Riding

You might enjoy a pleasant horseback ride at the **Wild West Ranch** (2855 36th St., Allegan, 269/673-3539, www.4horserides.com, daily by reservation only, $25-100 adults, $20-40 children), which offers a 1-hour trip past a natural wetland, a 1.5-hour trip through the woods, a 2-hour trip across scenic hills, a 3-hour ride to a horse campground or even a 4-hour ride to the horseman's campground, followed by a brief picnic, then a ride along a lovely creek trail. If you or your children need something a little tamer, you can always opt for a pony ride, a hayride, or, in winter, a sleigh ride.

ENTERTAINMENT AND EVENTS

Nightlife

Despite its small size, Saugatuck offers a number of after-hours diversions. A good place to stop at is **Borrowed Time** (329 Water St., 269/455-5256, www.borrowedtimesaugatuck.com, noon-10pm Mon.-Thurs., noon-11pm Fri.-Sat., noon-10pm Sun.), where you can sample craft beer, Michigan wines, small-plate entrées, and homemade desserts. Local bands perform almost every night during the summer, and many of the performances are held outdoors.

The Mermaid Bar and Grill (340 Water St., 269/857-8208, www.mermaidofsaugatuck.com 11:30am-9pm daily) offers one of the widest selections of libations anywhere: bottled and draft beer from points worldwide, rum, vodka, Kentucky bourbon, and some highly imaginative cocktails. There's also a food menu with a seaside theme, with offerings such as mahi-mahi tacos and ahi tuna.

In Douglas, the **Red Dock** (219 N Union St., 269/857-2185, noon-sundown daily May-Sept., cash only), sporting a Caribbean theme, is also a great evening choice. Regular features include reggae and creative cocktails. It also offers a good selection of salads and sandwiches.

The Arts

Visual arts are not Saugatuck's only creative claim to fame. The **Saugatuck Center for the Arts** (400 Culver St., 269/857-2399, www.sc4a.org) has, in addition to paintings and other artistic exhibitions, two theater spaces that present concerts, films, and comedy.

SHOPPING

Saugatuck and Douglas offer some of the best shopping in western Michigan, with an eclectic mix of more than 70 stores and 30 art galleries, most housed in well-kept 19th-century storefronts. The stylish merchandise ranges from highbrow antiques and trendy housewares to more commonplace touristy items.

Most of Saugatuck's shops are clustered along Butler Street, the main avenue. Two highlights include **American Spoon** (308 Butler St., 269/857-3084, www.spoon.com, 10am-8pm Mon.-Sat., 10am-6pm Sun.), a Petoskey-based company that specializes in fruit spreads and other gourmet foodstuffs, and the **Singapore Bank Bookstore** (317 Butler St., 269/857-3785, 10am-6pm daily, sometimes closes early), saved from the sands when it was moved here. Incense, jewelry, and metaphysical books are the specialty at **Mother Moon** (127 Hoffman St., 269/857-4407, www.magicalmothermoon.com, 11am-9pm Mon.-Sat., noon-5pm Sun.).

If trendiness threatens to overwhelm you, head for a breather at the **Saugatuck Drug Store and The Village Store** (201 Butler St., 269/857-2300, 9am-6pm Mon.-Fri., 9am-5pm Sat.), which has lured parched travelers and locals since 1913 with phosphates and other authentic treats.

For fresh produce, head to nearby Fennville, where family-operated **Crane Orchards** (6054 124th Ave., 269/561-8651,

JAMES BRANDESS
STUDIOS & GALLERY, INC.
238
BUTLER ST.
OPEN
OPEN
1

WHITE DOG
OX BOW
TOON
TAMAICA
2

3

Holiday Hill

www.craneorchards.com, 10am-6pm daily summer-fall) offers an outstanding self-pick orchard, boasting sweet cherries in June, peaches in July or August, and apples in the fall. On-site diversions include hayrides and a 20-acre corn maze. Almost more popular is **Crane's Pie Pantry Restaurant and Winery** (6054 124th Ave., 269/561-2297, www.cranespiepantry.com, 11am-4pm Tues.-Sun. Jan.-Mar., 11am-5pm daily Apr., 9am-8pm Sun.-Thurs., 9am-9pm Fri.-Sat., May-Oct., 10am-6pm Tues.-Sat., 11am-6pm Sun. Nov.-Dec., $4-10), which serves up thick sandwiches on homemade bread and Lue Crane's signature pies. There's a great winery on-site as well.

FOOD

Locals flock to **IDA Red's Cottage** (631 Water St., Saugatuck, 269/455-9834, 8am-2pm Thurs.-Sun., $10-16) for the best breakfast and lunch fare in town. Specialties include dishes with a Greek or Italian flair, like the delectable Italian sausage omelets.

Pick up an overstuffed sandwich and a few pastries for a carryout picnic at **Pumpernickel's Eatery** (202 Butler St., Saugatuck, 269/857-1196, www.pumpernickelssaugatuck.com, 9am-10pm Sun., Wed.-Thurs., 9am-midnight Fri.-Sat., $6-26), though you may want to eat here when you spot the restaurant's great patio and sundeck. The restaurant came under new ownership in 2018 and underwent several changes, including the addition of dinner hours.

★ **Chequers of Saugatuck** (220 Culver St., Saugatuck, 269/857-1868, 11:30am-9pm Mon.-Thurs., 11:30am-10pm Fri.-Sat., noon-9pm Sun., $12-24) is a bit of London in western Michigan, with a pub-like atmosphere of dark paneled walls, stained glass, and lots of leather. Classic Brit-inspired grub includes shepherd's pie, fish-and-chips, and bangers and mash. There's also a good variety of ales and beer. Reservations are not accepted, so expect a wait at peak hours.

The **Restaurant Toulouse** (248 Culver St., Saugatuck, 269/857-1561, 5pm-10pm Thurs.-Fri., 11am-10pm Sat.-Sun., $16-26) features French country cuisine in a Provence-inspired setting, complete with tableside fireplaces and live jazz on Saturday. Specialties include escargot, cassoulet, rack of lamb, and a killer chocolate fondue. At times the service can be slow; prepare for a leisurely meal.

Bowdie's Chophouse (230 Culver St., Saugatuck, 269/455-5481, www.bowdieschophouse.com, 5pm-10pm daily, $26-51) is the archetypal modern steakhouse, featuring classic red-meat dishes—bone-in filet and the Cowboy Ribeye—and balances the menu with several seafood and poultry dishes; all served in an über-contemporary setting.

Marro's Italian Restaurant (147 Water St., Saugatuck, 269/857-4248, www.marrosrestaurant.com, 5pm-10pm Tues.-Thurs. and Sun., 5pm-11pm Fri.-Sat., 5pm-10pm holiday Mon., closed Tues. in May and Sept., $10-40) takes its Italian name seriously and reflects it in its menu, with dishes like spicy penne ala vodka con salsiccia and chicken cancellara. There's also seafood options, like caramelized walnut salmon and lobster tails.

Phil's Bar and Grille (215 Butler St., Saugatuck, 269/857-1555, www.philsbarandgrille.com, 11am-10:30pm Sun.-Thurs., 11am-11pm Fri.-Sat., $19-42) takes bar food up a notch. Besides the expected burgers and tacos, you'll also find scallop pad thai, lamb lollipops, and a 10-ounce New York strip.

Coral Gables Restaurant (220 Water St., Saugatuck, 269/857-2162, www.coralgablessaugatuck.com, 11:30am-2am daily, $12-29) has it all—a waterfront location, an eclectic menu, and a well-stocked bar—in a 111-year-old building that's stood the test of time. Try one of the hearty pasta bowls or something off the "Real Meal" menu, like Great Lakes whitefish or baby back ribs.

J. Paul's Restaurant & Wine Bar at

1: shops and galleries in downtown Saugatuck **2:** colorful signpost by the water **3:** *Star of Saugatuck II* paddlewheeler

the Kirby (294 Center St., Douglas, 269/857-5472, www.thekirbyhotel.com, dinner 5pm-10pm Wed.-Sun., brunch 10am-2pm Sun., $10-33) is a place where the wine takes center stage. Here you can enjoy a wide swath of Michigan wines, along with artisanal spirits, craft cocktails, local beers, and hard cider. For food, there are small and large plate selections, including mushroom risotto, crispy-skin salmon, and house-made tagliatelle—topped off with a menu of dessert wines.

Scooter's Café & Pizzeria (322 Culver St., Saugatuck, 269/857-1041, www.scooterscafeandpizzeria.com, 11am-10pm Mon.-Thurs., 11am-midnight Fri.-Sat., 11am-9pm Sun., $5-25) is a great place for family dining. Salads and some standard dinner entrées complement the extensive pizza offerings, which include taco, Greek, vegetarian, and barbecue chicken. There's also a kids' menu, and the outdoor seating is pet-friendly.

The Farmhouse Deli and Pantry (100 Blue Star Hwy., Douglas, 269/455-5274, www.thefarmhousedeli.com, 9am-7pm daily, $8-12) is a place that does the deli tradition proud—turkey clubs, BLTs, and smoked ham sandwiches along with a number of hot sandwich options.

Blue Star Café and M&M's Ice Cream (121 Washington St., Douglas, 269/857-1030, 8am-10pm daily, $10-17) is a lunch place extraordinaire, with burgers, pitas, omelets, and a robust number of ice cream offerings.

At **Kilwin's Chocolates** (152 Butler St., Saugatuck, 269/857-1195, www.kilwins.com, 10am-10pm Sun.-Thurs., 10am-11pm Fri.-Sat., shorter winter hours; 121 Butler St., Saugatuck, 269/857-1195, 11am-6pm Sun.-Thurs., 10am-9pm Fri.-Sat., shorter winter hours, $5-10), just the names of the items on the menu say it all: chocolates, fudge, ice cream.

Uncommon Coffee Roasters (127 Hoffman St., Saugatuck, 269/857-3333, www.uncommoncoffeeroasters.com, 7am-9pm Sun.-Thurs., 7am-10pm Fri.-Sat., $3-12) is an ecologically sensitive coffee importer that takes pride in working with small growers and cooperatives. But ecological awareness doesn't diminish taste—choose from blends like Organic Costa Rica or Gera Estate from Ethiopia.

ACCOMMODATIONS

With at least 30 bed-and-breakfasts in the area, Saugatuck has fast become one of the B&B capitals of the Midwest. The 1860 Victorian-style **Twin Oaks Inn** (227 Griffith St., Saugatuck, 269/857-1600, $110-150 d) is among the friendliest of the inns, with spacious rooms, portable cribs, and pullout beds for families.

An 1860s Greek Revival building adjacent to the Saugatuck village square has served as a luxury resort hotel for more than 135 years. Today, it does business as the **Maplewood Hotel** (428 Butler St., Saugatuck, 269/857-1771, www.maplewoodhotel.com, $169-319 d), with 15 antiques-filled bedrooms in the heart of the city's shops, galleries, and restaurants. Some suites have amenities like double whirlpool tubs and fireplaces. Breakfast is served in the Burr Tillstrom Dining Room, named for the former Saugatuck resident, who was also the creator of *Kukla, Fran, and Ollie,* a once-popular children's puppet show.

The **Wickwood Inn** (510 Butler St., Saugatuck, 269/857-1465, www.wickwoodinn.com, $189-489 d) is owned by Julee Rosso, co-author of *The Silver Palate* cookbook series, who treats guests at her bed-and-breakfast with seasonal menus she creates herself. But that's not the only special touch at this art-filled inn, recognized by numerous magazines. The 11 guest rooms are lavishly decorated with English and French country antiques, feather beds, and antique linens.

Other local choices for lodging include the **Hotel Saugatuck** (900 Lake St., Saugatuck, 269/416-0731, www.thehotelsaugatuck.com, $259-541 d). Housed in an 1865 historical landmark, it bills itself as a "luxury bed-and-breakfast." Features include views of the Kalamazoo River, spacious suites, and hydrotherapy tubs. In a 100-year-old building in the heart of downtown Saugatuck, **Bella Vitas**

Spa & Suites (119 Butler St., Saugatuck, 269/857-8482, www.bellavitaspa.biz, $199-239 d) features six stylish suites that, despite their location, sport an amazingly tranquil atmosphere. The luxurious spa is in the same building and offers a complete range of spa services.

Saugatuck Landings Luxury Suites and Marina (726 Water St., Saugatuck, 269/686-6422, www.saugatucklandings.com, $290-345 d) is a tiny establishment offering two suites, upper and lower, right on the banks of the Kalamazoo River. Each offers a generous amount of living space, an updated kitchen with granite countertops, and a king bed. **The Serendipity B&B** (203 Griffith St., Saugatuck, 269/857-3400, www.serendipitybandbsaugatuck.com, $320-540 for two nights, 2 nights minimum required) offers both standard rooms and suites, all in the elegant Victorian tradition. A good hot breakfast is included. The **Lake Shore Resort** (2885 Lakeshore Dr., Saugatuck, 269/857-7121, www.lakeshoreresortsaugatuck.com, $165-340 d) offers a dramatic view from a bluff overlooking Lake Michigan. The 30 rooms all offer cable TV, coffeemakers, and refrigerators.

For more economical options, head away from the water and toward the Blue Star Highway, where you'll find simple motels like the **Captain's Quarters Motel** (3242 Blue Star Hwy., Saugatuck, https://captainsmotel.com, 269/857-2525, $120-150 d) or **The Pines Motor Lodge** (56 Blue Star Hwy., Douglas, 269/857-5211, www.thepinesmotorlodge.com, $149-205 d).

INFORMATION AND SERVICES

For more information about Saugatuck, Douglas, and surrounding towns, contact the **Saugatuck/Douglas Convention & Visitors Bureau** (95 Blue Star Hwy., Douglas, 269/857-1701, www.saugatuck.com, 9am-5pm Mon.-Fri.), the **Saugatuck/Douglas Area Business Association** (269/857-1620, www.saugatuckdouglas.com), the **West Michigan Blue Star Chamber of Commerce** (www.westmichiganbluestarchamber.com/), or the **Allegan County Tourist Council** (888/425-5342, www.visitallegancounty.com). For local or county news, refer to the ***Allegan County News*** (www.allegannews.com). For LGBTQ community-related events and businesses in the area, visit www.gaysaugatuckdouglas.com.

Despite their small size, Saugatuck and Douglas offer all essential services, from pharmacies to banks, including **Chemical Bank** (249 Mason St., Saugatuck, 269/857-2116, www.chemicalbankmi.com).

For medical services, head 10 miles north to the **Holland Hospital** (602 Michigan Ave., Holland, 616/392-5141, www.hollandhospital.org).

GETTING THERE AND AROUND

There are three major airports near Saugatuck and Douglas: the **Kalamazoo/Battle Creek International Airport** (AZO, 5235 Portage Rd., Kalamazoo, 269/388-3668, www.flyazo.com), the **Gerald R. Ford International Airport** (GRR, 5500 44th St. SE, Grand Rapids, 616/233-6000, www.grr.org), and the **Muskegon County Airport** (MKG, 99 Sinclair Dr., Muskegon, 231/798-4596, www.muskegonairport.com). All offer rental car services, so reaching the Art Coast is easy.

From Kalamazoo, which also has an **Amtrak train station** (459 N. Burdick St., Kalamazoo, 800/872-7245, www.amtrak.com), take U.S. 131, M-89, and County Road A2 (Blue Star Hwy.) to Saugatuck; in light traffic, the 52-mile trip should take little more than an hour. From Grand Rapids, which also has an **Amtrak train station** (431 Wealthy St. SW, Grand Rapids, 800/872-7245, www.amtrak.com), follow I-196 west to County Road A2 (Blue Star Hwy.), a 40-mile trip that usually takes about 39 minutes. From Muskegon, head south on U.S. 31, through Grand Haven and Holland, to Saugatuck and Douglas; in light traffic, the 47-mile trip should take less than an hour.

From Chicago, follow I-90 and I-94 through Illinois and Indiana onto I-196/U.S.

31 and take County Road A2 (Blue Star Hwy.) into Saugatuck; in light traffic, the 141-mile trip should take roughly 2.25 hours. En route from Chicago, parts of I-90 and I-94 serve as the Indiana Toll Road. The adjacent town of Douglas lies about a mile south of Saugatuck on County Road A2 (Blue Star Hwy.), just across Kalamazoo Lake.

Holland

For years, people of Dutch ancestry dominated the city of Holland, just north of Saugatuck. In fact, the city remained 90 percent Dutch for more than a century. While the ethnic makeup is now a bit more varied, many local families can still trace their roots back to the 1840s, when Dutch separatists settled in this part of the Midwest. Whatever their heritage, however, Holland's residents know it's the Dutch touch that brings thousands of visitors each year, and they are quick to roll out the "Welkom" mat for out-of-towners.

The city hits its stride in early May, when the annual Tulip Time Festival is in full bloom. The quaint downtown streets display a rainbow of flowers, while costumed *klompen* dancers, local bands, and parades provide entertainment.

SIGHTS

Dutch Experience

Holland clings proudly to its Dutch heritage at spots like **Veldheer Tulip Gardens** (12755 Quincy St., 616/399-1900, www.veldheer.com, 10am-5:30pm Mon.-Sat., 10am-4pm Sun. spring-summer, 10am-5pm Mon.-Fri. fall-winter, $12 adults, $6 ages 3-13, under age 3 free). While parts of Holland can appear overly commercial, you'll be charmed by the sheer spectacle of this rainbow of blooms in the spring, followed by more perennials such as lilies, then annuals from June to October. Beds are numbered to correspond with mail-order catalogs, so visitors can place orders for bulbs and flowering plants after seeing the flowers. Locals recommend visiting the gardens at sunset, when the tour buses are gone and a warm glow lingers on the thousands of beautiful blooms.

Adjacent to the gardens, the **De Klomp Wooden Shoe & Delftware Factory** (12755 Quincy St., 616/399-1803, www.dutchvillage.com, 9am-5pm daily spring-summer, 9am-5pm Mon.-Sat. fall-winter, free) remains the only working Delft production factory in the United States. Strategically placed windows allow visitors to watch the crisp blue-and-white china being made by hand and see craftspeople carve wooden shoes on well-worn Dutch machinery. A gift shop sells the goods produced here.

Head north on U.S. 31 to **Nelis' Dutch Village** (12350 James St., 616/396-1475, www.dutchvillage.com, shops 10am-6pm daily mid-Apr.-Oct., 10am-5pm Mon.-Sat. Nov.-mid-Apr., park 10am-5:30pm daily mid-Apr.-Oct., $12 adults, $11 over age 64, $10 ages 3-15, children under age 3 free), a theme park that's essentially a replica of a typical 19th-century community in the Netherlands. Here, you'll encounter Dutch dancing; wooden-shoe-carving demonstrations; Dutch products like pottery, lace, and cheese; and a museum dedicated to Dutch culture, including tulip farming.

Holland's treasure presides over Windmill Island on the east end of town. The 240-year-old **De Zwaan** (The Swan) was shipped to Michigan in 1964, the last authentic windmill the Dutch government allowed to leave the Netherlands. Guides give careful and thorough tours of the wooden windmill, lovingly reconstructed and still operating, its massive 40-foot blades spinning in the wind and grinding wheat into flour.

De Zwaan serves as the centerpiece of a variety of Dutch displays in **Windmill Island Gardens** (1 Lincoln Ave., 616/355-1030, www.windmillisland.org, 9:30am-6pm daily mid-Apr.-early Oct., $10 adults, $5 ages 5-15), including reconstructed buildings like the tile-roofed 14th-century Posthouse, an authentic Dutch carousel, and **Little Netherlands,** a 50-foot-long miniature model village complete with canals, farms, a cheese market, and, naturally, windmills.

Museums

City residents take great pride in three local museums: **The Holland Museum** (31 W. 10th St., 616/392-9084, www.hollandmuseum.org, 11am-4pm Wed.-Sat., noon-4pm Sun., $7 adults, $6 seniors, $4 students, under age 6 free), **Cappon House** (228 W. 9th St., 616/392-6740, www.hollandmuseum.org, 11am-4pm Fri.-Sat., guided tours on the hour, $5 pp), and the **Settlers House** (190 W. 9th St. 616/392-6740, www.hollandmuseum.org, 11am-4pm Fri.-Sat., $7 adults, $6 seniors, $4 students). Together, they contain more than 400 years of Dutch and American heritage, with displays that cover the city's 160-year history.

Beaches and Parks

The long, broad beach at **Holland State Park** (2215 Ottawa Beach Rd., 616/399-9390, daily, annual Recreation Passport required: $12 Michigan residents, $34 nonresidents, $9 day pass available to nonresidents only) is one of the most accessible and beautiful in the Lower Peninsula. Like the other state parks along this stretch of Lake Michigan, it attracts sunbathers by the hundreds on weekends. Facilities include a bathhouse, several beach volleyball courts, and two campgrounds. Lake Michigan fishing can be quite good from shore. As a bonus, the Holland State Park offers a clear view of a vibrant red lighthouse. Originally established in 1872, the **Holland Harbor Light** (called "Big Red" by the locals) was erected in 1907 on the southern pier, which partially separates Lake Michigan from Lake Macatawa.

If you'd like to do more than swim, sunbathe, and sightsee, other options are available. A few miles away on Lake Macatawa, **Holland Water Sports** (1810 Ottawa Beach Rd., 616/399-6672, www.hollandwatersports.com) rents a variety of watercraft ($95-495) for up to three hours: Jet Skis, powerboats, pontoon boats, and sailboats.

FESTIVALS AND EVENTS

★ Tulip Time Festival

A great time to visit Holland is during the spring and early summer—its season for festivals and art fairs. In early May, Holland's world-famous **Tulip Time Festival** (800/822-2770, www.tuliptime.com) is a weeklong celebration of Dutch heritage and culture, where visitors enjoy traditional arts and *klompen* dancing, free concerts, fireworks displays, carnival rides, and three rousing parades. Embracing it all are millions of vivid tulip bulbs in full bloom—a thrilling sight.

Other Festivals

One that you should definitely not miss is the **Waterfront Film Festival** (various venues, 269/767-8765, www.waterfrontfilm.org, $10/film). In mid-June, this well-respected fest brings a bit of Hollywood to Saugatuck. For one weekend, filmgoers, actors, producers, and directors converge for outstanding independent films from around the country, all screened in a casual setting.

Downtown Holland also hosts several other festivals and observances throughout the entire year. **Concerts in the Park** take place noon-1pm each Wednesday during the summer months at GDK Park. The **Street Performer Series** is offered 6:30pm-8:30pm each Thursday mid-June through late August at various points in the downtown area. On the fourth Saturday of June, Holland honors the LGBTQ community at the **Holland Pride Festival.**

SHOPPING

Like many other towns along the coast, Holland has its share of shopping options. Besides two malls and plenty of retail centers

VanRaalte's Detour

VanRaalte Passage

The founding of Holland, one of Michigan's most popular sightseeing destinations, was essentially a fluke. In 1846, Reverend Albertus Christiaan VanRaalte (1811-1876), seeking religious freedom and economic opportunity, led a group of 60 Dutch Calvinists on a seven-week trip from the Netherlands to New York. Despite a plan to head west and purchase land in Wisconsin, travel delays and early winter weather forced the group to stop in Detroit. When VanRaalte heard about available lands in southwestern Michigan, he decided to scout the territory. By January 1847, he'd reached the banks of present-day Lake Macatawa, and the initial group of settlers arrived about a month later.

While subsequent Dutch immigrants were dismayed to find a dense forest, an insect-infested swamp, and scarce food supplies, the settlers persevered, recognizing the value of the surrounding woods and lakes. Without government aid, they dug a channel to Lake Michigan and created a centralized market square. In 1851, VanRaalte helped to establish the Pioneer School, which gradually evolved into Hope College.

When two railroads extended spurs to Holland in the early 1870s, it seemed that the town was poised for a booming future. But in October 1871 disaster struck when a fire swept through town, bankrupting its citizens. Luckily, with the aid of surrounding communities, the villagers began a steady revival, and by the end of the 19th century, Holland had utility systems, paved streets, mail delivery, transportation facilities, manufacturing plants, a thriving agricultural market, and several resort hotels.

As the 20th century dawned, Holland continued to prosper—as both a manufacturing center and a tourist destination. During the 1920s, thousands of vacationers flocked to its gorgeous beaches, burgeoning resorts, Tulip Time Festival, and other attractions. The Great Depression caused the closure of many of Holland's furniture factories, and yet the town survived. Farmers worked together, and new businesses replaced old ones, especially during and after World War II.

Newcomers from different backgrounds eventually arrived—Latino farmworkers in the 1940s and Southeast Asian refugees in the 1960s. But Holland continued to retain its Dutch persona. The 1947 centennial celebration included an exhibition of Dutch artwork and a play about the Dutch pioneers. In 1961 a local businesses successfully transplanted an authentic windmill from the Netherlands.

During the 1980s, greater Holland became more suburbanized with the arrival of fast-food restaurants, outlet stores, and shopping malls, but preservation efforts prevailed in the years following. The historic Tower Clock building was saved, three downtown parks were added, the old post office became The Holland Museum, and Hope College expanded.

Today, Holland continues to thrive, with Dutch-inspired sites, outdoor concerts, holiday festivities, and joyous annual events like the ever-popular Tulip Time Festival. In 2002, Holland was named a Distinctive Destination by the National Trust for Historic Preservation, and in 2009, the city was recognized as one of the 25 Best Places to Retire by *Money* magazine. Visitors and residents alike are no doubt grateful for VanRaalte's accidental detour.

along U.S. 31, the downtown area offers unique establishments, including several art galleries. Inspired by its coastal environment, the **Lake Effect Gallery** (16 W. 8th St., Ste. 100, 616/395-3025, www.lakeeffectgallery.com, 10am-5pm Mon.-Wed., 10am-8pm Thurs.-Fri., 10am-6pm Sun.) presents paintings, jewelry, and crafts from more than 20 of western Michigan's finest artists. **The Nines Gallery and Framing Studio** (196 W. 29th St., 616/392-3239, www.theninesgallery.com, 10am-5pm Mon. and Wed.-Fri., 10am-1pm Sat.) is one of Holland's most adventuresome galleries, specializing in emerging painters, sculptors, and printmakers. They also have an in-house framing studio.

FOOD

In downtown Holland, the **New Holland Brewing** (66 E. 8th St., 616/355-6422, www.newhollandbrew.com, 11am-midnight Mon.-Thurs., 11am-1am Fri.-Sat., 11am-10pm Sun., $8-18) is the perfect integration of a microbrewery, distillery, and lively restaurant and pub. In addition to handcrafted beers and other spirits, the menu includes soups, salads, sandwiches, pizza, and enormous desserts. **Butch's Dry Dock** (44 E. 8th St., 616/396-8227, www.butchs.net, 11am-9pm Mon.-Thurs., 11am-10pm Fri.-Sat., $13-50) serves up great New York-style deli sandwiches to eat on-site or pack for a picnic, along with specialty cheeses, wines, and more. There's also an extensive dinner menu featuring many classic favorites.

The ★ **Alpenrose Restaurant & Café** (4 E. 8th St., 616/393-2111, www.alpenroserestaurant.com, 8am-9pm Mon.-Sat., 10am-2pm Sun., $7-32) specializes in Wiener schnitzel, bratwurst, and other German and Austrian dishes in an authentic old-world atmosphere, complete with carvings by master German woodworkers adorning the ceilings and walls. The menu also features a few Italian selections and delicious dessert options including homemade European pastries. Takeout boxed lunches area also available. For a delectable sandwich, stop at **City Delicatessen** (52 E. 8th St., 616/396-9602, www.thecitydelicatessen.com, 11am-8pm Mon.-Sat., $6-9), where you'll find an array of traditional deli favorites.

ACCOMMODATIONS

The **Dutch Colonial Inn Bed-and-Breakfast** (560 Central Ave., 616/396-3664, www.dutchcolonialinn.com, $139-195 d) has five nonsmoking rooms and a complimentary full

a profusion of tulips in Holland, Michigan

breakfast in a restored 1928 home. Whirlpools, free wireless Internet access, and warm Dutch hospitality make this inn a great choice. **Bonnie's Parsonage 1908** (6 E. 24th St., 616/396-1316, www.bonniesparsonage.com, $130-160 d) is housed in a former Dutch parsonage built in 1908. It offers four guest rooms, a conservatory-porch, and an outdoor patio.

Away from downtown but near Nelis' Dutch Village, try **Country Inn and Suites by Radisson** (12260 James St., 616/396-6677, www.countryinns.com, $199-375 d). Like many places in town, it's decorated with Delft tiles and country decor. Of its 116 guest rooms, 24 have in-room whirlpools.

Camping

Holland State Park (2215 Ottawa Beach Rd., 616/399-9390, daily, annual Recreation Passport required: $12 Michigan residents, $34 nonresidents, $9 day pass available to nonresidents only) has 309 RV and tent sites ($31-33) in two units: one near Lake Michigan, the other near inland Lake Macatawa. The two campgrounds are within easy walking distance of each other. Most sites are quite close together with little shade. Of course, chances are you'll be spending most of your time by the water anyway.

INFORMATION AND SERVICES

For more information about the area, contact the **Holland Area Convention & Visitors Bureau** (76 E. 8th St., 616/394-0000, www.holland.org, 8am-5:30pm Mon.-Fri. year-round, 10am-5pm Sat. mid-Apr.-Nov.). For local news, pick up a copy of the ***Holland Sentinel*** (www.hollandsentinel.com).

To get supplies or fill a prescription, stop by **Meijer** (746 E. 16th St., 616/355-4864, www.meijer.com), part of a statewide superstore chain that sells groceries, pharmaceuticals, electronics, and other necessities.

For medical services, visit **Holland Hospital** (602 Michigan Ave., Holland, 616/392-5141, www.hollandhospital.org).

GETTING THERE AND AROUND

Travelers can reach Holland directly via bus or train. **Greyhound** (616/355-1010 or 800/231-2222, www.greyhound.com), **Indian Trails** (800/292-3831, www.indiantrails.com), and **Amtrak** (800/872-7245, www.amtrak.com) all offer service at **Holland Station** (171 Lincoln Ave.).

Two airports are situated in nearby cities: the **Gerald R. Ford International Airport** (GRR, 5500 44th St. SE, Grand Rapids, 616/233-6000, www.grr.org) and the **Muskegon County Airport** (MKG, 99 Sinclair Dr., Muskegon, 231/798-4596, www.muskegonairport.com); both have cars available from the national rental agencies.

From Grand Rapids, take I-196, a 30-mile trip that takes about 34 minutes; from Muskegon, take U.S. 31, a 37-mile trip that usually takes about 45 minutes. From Chicago, follow I-90 and I-94 through Illinois and Indiana onto I-196/U.S. 31 toward Holland; in light traffic, the 151-mile trip should take 2.25 hours. En route from Chicago, parts of I-90 and I-94 serve as the Indiana Toll Road. Once you reach Holland, it's easy to get around via car, bike, or on foot—the preferred method since the area is so compact.

Grand Haven

Just a few miles south of Muskegon is the lakeside town of Grand Haven, whose history dates back to 1833, when fur trapper and trader Rix Robinson purchased the area from the U.S. government and established a trading post at the mouth of the Grand River. By the spring of 1835, Grand Haven's first nonnative settlers—Reverend William Montague Ferry and his family and friends—had erected permanent dwellings and the town's first sawmill. Before the state's white pine forests had been depleted, Grand Haven had begun evolving into an important manufacturing town and shipping port, facilitated by the arrival of the railroad in 1858.

During the mid-19th century, Grand Haven also became a place of respite for affluent middle-class families seeking rest and recreation along the shores of the Grand River, Spring Lake, and Lake Michigan. Today this town of 10,650 residents continues to be a vacation destination, offering a variety of diversions such as art galleries, a historic shopping district, well-favored beaches, and the world's largest musical fountain. Adjacent Lake Michigan is popular among deepwater anglers, and the surrounding countryside is ideal for long-distance hikers and bikers.

SIGHTS

Tri-Cities Historical Museum

Grand Haven focuses its attention on the waterfront—in particular, the boardwalk that traces the Grand River's south bank from downtown to its mouth at Lake Michigan. The 2.5-mile stretch is full of places to shop, eat, and stroll. The walk wanders past the city's vintage railroad station, now the **Tri-Cities Historical Museum** (200 Washington Ave., 616/842-0700, www.tri-citiesmuseum.org, 10am-8pm Tues.-Sat., noon-5pm Sun. Memorial Day-Labor Day, 10am-5pm Tues.-Fri., noon-5pm Sat.-Sun. early Sept.-late May, free), where a puffer-belly steam locomotive and three railcars sit idle. It ends at Chinook Pier, where many of the area's Great Lakes fishing boats dock and display the day's catch.

Musical Fountain

Across the street, shops fill the **Harbourfront**

pier and lighthouse in Grand Haven

Place, a renovated Story & Clark Piano Company factory. Linger around the harbor at sunset, and you'll be treated to a burst of music and a revolving blast of colored lights, as Grand Haven's musical fountain begins to spray and dance in a choreographed half-hour show. The fountain is a beloved tradition in this resort town and plays every summer evening.

Beaches and Parks

Because it's connected to downtown by the city's popular boardwalk, you won't find solitude at **Grand Haven State Park** (1001 Harbor Ave., 616/847-1309, annual Recreation Passport required: $12 Michigan residents, $34 nonresidents, $9 day pass available to nonresidents only), but you will get a sandy swimming beach, a convenient campground, a fishing pier, and, of course, the **Grand Haven South Pier Lighthouses.** These two vivid red lighthouses—the outer light built in 1875 and moved to the end of the breakwater in 1905, and the inner 51-foot light fabricated in 1905—are still operational and constitute one of only two range light systems in the Great Lakes region; the other is farther south in St. Joseph. It's no surprise that Grand Haven's lighthouses are popular among photographers and sightseers. Just be careful on the breakwater when the winds blow across Lake Michigan.

Coopersville & Marne Railway

About 17 miles east of Grand Haven lies Coopersville, a small town that celebrates its agricultural heritage and friendly atmosphere with a number of annual events and historic sites, including the **Coopersville Farm Museum & Event Center** (375 Main St., 616/997-8555, www.coopersvillefarmmuseum.org, 10am-4pm Tues.-Sat. July-Sept., 10am-2pm Tues., Thurs., and 10am-1pm Sat. Oct.-June, $4 adults, $2 ages 4-12, under age 4 free), which showcases a tractor exhibit, a feed sack collection, and more. Of course, one of the most popular area attractions is the **Coopersville & Marne Railway** (306 E. Main St., Coopersville, 616/997-7000, www.coopersvilleandmarne.org, 9:30am and 1:30pm Wed. and Sat. May-Oct., 11am and 1pm Sat. Apr. and Nov.-Dec., $14 adults, $11.50 over age 59, $10.50 ages 2-12), a train of antique passenger cars that travels over farmlands, creeks, and bridges from Coopersville to Marne and back again for 14 miles and well over an hour. Throughout the year, the railway also offers thematic rides, including The Great Train Robbery and the Santa Train.

RECREATION

Golf

With all that Grand Haven has to offer, you still might want to set aside some time to play a round of golf on what *Golf Digest* considers one of the best public courses in the country. The **American Dunes Golf Club** (17000 Lincoln St., 616/842-4040, www.americandunesgolfclub.com) originally designed in 1965 by legendary golf course architect Bruce Matthews Sr., is currently being rebuilt and rebranded as a Jack Nicklaus Signature Gold Course. Completion and re-opening are projected for 2020.

Biking

Grand Haven and surrounding Ottawa County claim more than 100 miles of biking paths. (Most are also open to inline skates, roller skis, and other recreational uses.) The 15-mile **Lakeside Trail** circles inland Spring Lake, a lovely ride. The **Lakeshore Connector Path** links Grand Haven to Holland, 30 miles south, occasionally utilizing sidewalks but mostly a paved off-road route near the Lake Michigan shore. For more information about bike trails, contact the **Grand Haven Area Convention & Visitors Bureau** (225 Franklin Ave. 616/842-4499, www.visitgrandhaven.com, 9am-5pm Mon.-Fri. year-round, 10am-4pm Sat. summer).

FESTIVALS AND EVENTS

For two decades, Grand Haven has hosted the annual **Great Lakes Kite Festival** (106 Washington Ave., 616/846-7501, www.mackite.com), the state's biggest kite festival. During the mid-May event, experts from across the country display a wide array of giant kites. The impressive festival, the proceeds of which benefit the Children's Leukemia Foundation of Michigan, features everything from free kite seminars to nighttime flying. For more information, contact **Mackinaw Kites & Toys** (866/428-2335, www.mackite.com).

To honor the men and women of the U.S. Coast Guard, Grand Haven also holds an annual **Grand Haven Coast Guard Festival** (113 N. 2nd St., 616/846-5940, www.coastguardfest.org, most events free). The festival usually runs from the last week of July through early August. Highlights include a grand parade, a downtown carnival, and ship tours on two USCGC icebreaker vessels, the *Mackinaw* and the *Biscayne Bay*.

SHOPPING

If you do plan to attend Grand Haven's kite festival, there's no better place to pick up your own highflier than **Mackinaw Kites & Toys** (106 Washington Ave., 616/846-7501 or 866/428-2335, www.mackite.com, 9am-9pm daily). This whimsical store, a sponsor of the festival, has a wide assortment of amazing kites, as well as kiteboarding and kitesurfing gear.

For some gourmet Italian delicacies, look no further than **Fortino's** (114 Washington Ave., 616/842-0880, www.fortinosgeneralstore.com, 10am-8pm Mon.-Thurs., 10am-9pm Fri.-Sat., noon-7pm Sun.), not far from the kite shop, where you'll find a superb selection of fine wines, gourmet meats, and excellent cheeses. Take your pick, then head to the beach for a stylish picnic.

FOOD AND ACCOMMODATIONS

For dining, try ★ **The Kirby House** (2 Washington St., 616/846-3299, www.thegilmorecollection.com/kirbyhouse, 11:30am-10pm Mon.-Thurs., 11:30am-2am Fri.-Sat., 11:30am-10pm Sun., $13-32), situated within a historic 1873 building in the heart of downtown. It's actually three restaurants in one: The Kirby Grill, a casual eatery; The Grill Room, a stylish chophouse; and K2, an authentic pizzeria with a wood-fired oven.

While the accommodations options in Grand Haven used to be a bit slim, that's changed in recent years. You'll find a few chain hotels along U.S. 31, such as the **Best Western Beacon Inn** (1525 S. Beacon Blvd., 616/842-4720, www.bestwesternmichigan.com, $159-199 d) for basic motel rooms with coffeemakers and free movies. On the waterfront, you'll spy the charming **Harbor House Inn** (114 S. Harbor Dr., 616/846-0610, www.new.harborhousegh.com, $130-300 d), a spacious Victorian-style manor offering both comfortable guest rooms as well as the quaint Harbor Cottage for even more privacy.

Camping

Grand Haven State Park (1001 Harbor Ave., 616/847-1309, annual Recreation Passport required: $12 Michigan residents, $34 nonresidents, $9 day pass available to nonresidents only) offers a spacious campground with 174 modern sites ($31-33), mostly in an open area near the water, as well as clean restrooms. Reservations (800/447-2757, www.michigan.gov/dnr) are strongly advised.

INFORMATION AND SERVICES

For more information about the area, contact the **Grand Haven Area Convention & Visitors Bureau** (225 Franklin Ave., 616/842-4499, www.visitgrandhaven.com, 9am-5pm Mon.-Fri. year-round, 10am-4pm Sat. summer) or the **Grand Haven Chamber of Commerce** (1 S. Harbor Dr., 616/842-4910, www.grandhavenchamber.

org, 9:30am-5pm Mon., 8:30am-5pm Tues.-Fri.). For local news and events, pick up a copy of the ***Grand Haven Tribune*** (www.grandhaventribune.com).

The Grand Haven area offers a wide range of services necessary to travelers, including groceries, pharmacies, and banks. For medical services, consult the **North Ottawa Community Health System** (1309 Sheldon Rd., 616/842-3600, www.noch.org).

GETTING THERE AND AROUND

As with Benton Harbor and South Haven, Grand Haven is situated on the Lake Michigan coast, which means that it's easily accessible via private boat. Visitors can also reach the town by flying into one of two nearby airports—**Gerald R. Ford International Airport** (GRR, 5500 44th St. SE, Grand Rapids, 616/233-6000, www.grr.org) or **Muskegon County Airport** (MKG, 99 Sinclair Dr., Muskegon, 231/798-4596, www.muskegonairport.com). At either airport you can then rent a vehicle from one of several national rental agencies. From the Grand Rapids airport, drive to I-96, M-104, and U.S. 31 to Grand Haven, a 47-mile trip that will take about 52 minutes. From the Muskegon airport, take surface streets to U.S. 31, which leads to Grand Haven, a nine-mile trip that will normally take 14 minutes.

It's easy to reach Grand Haven via U.S. 31, a route that traces the entire western coast of the Lower Peninsula from the Indiana border to just north of Petoskey. A similar route leads to Grand Haven from Chicago; follow I-90 and I-94 through Illinois and Indiana, onto I-196/U.S. 31, to Grand Haven; in light traffic, the 172-mile trip will require less than three hours. En route from Chicago, parts of I-90 and I-94 serve as the Indiana Toll Road.

Muskegon and Vicinity

The largest city along this stretch of Lake Michigan shoreline, with more than 37,000 year-round residents, Muskegon has its roots in white pine. The deep Muskegon River, which flows through town, into Lake Muskegon and toward Lake Michigan, provided the perfect route for transporting timber from the rich inland pine forests to the city's sawmills. Muskegon's first sawmill went up in 1837. By the 1880s, it was known throughout the world as a lumber metropolis, home to 47 sawmills and at least as many saloons, dance halls, and gambling parlors—earning the city nicknames that ranged from Lumber Queen of the North to the more unsavory Red Light Queen.

Muskegon was unprepared for the day just a decade later when the area's timber supply was exhausted. Mills soon closed or were mysteriously torched. By the 1950s, the city teetered on the brink of ruin—until tourism took the place of logging. Muskegon has finally risen from the sawdust of its past. While many parts of the city still have a tattered feel, visitors to Muskegon are quick to notice its benefits, including more than 26 miles of Lake Michigan shoreline, western Michigan's most extensive lakeshore park system, outstanding cultural and historical resources, a popular amusement park, and an ethnically diverse population.

SIGHTS

Historic Sites

The lumber barons in Muskegon left behind grand homes—since lovingly restored—that preservationists point to as some of the finest Queen Annes in North America. The **Hackley & Hume Historic Site** (484 W. Webster Ave. and 6th St., 231/722-7578, www.lakeshoremuseum.org, 10am-4pm Mon. and Thurs.-Sat. May-Oct., $10 adults, $8 seniors 65 and up, $5 ages 3-12, children 2 and under free) includes two mansions built by lumber magnates Charles Hackley and Thomas Hume in the late 1800s. These colorful, historically faithful homes, administered by the Lakeshore Museum Center, feature some 28 shades of paint, lavish wood carving, stained glass, and high Victorian furnishings.

The **USS *Silversides* Submarine Museum** (1346 Bluff St., 231/755-1230, www.glnmm.org, www.silversidesmuseum.org, 10am-5:30pm daily May-Sept., 10am-4pm Mon.-Thurs., 10am-5:30pm Fri.-Sat. Oct.-Apr., $15 adults, $12.50 over age 61, $10.50 ages 5-18, active-duty military and under age 5 free) houses an array of exhibits and displays about World War II, the Pearl Harbor attack, submarines, the Cold War, marine technology, and Great Lakes shipping. In addition, it oversees two historic vessels, the USS *Silversides* and the USCGC *McLane*, which commemorate life at sea during World War II. Completed just after the attack on Pearl Harbor in 1941, *Silversides* went on to sink 23 ships, the third-highest total of all U.S. submarines that served in World War II. Now a national historic landmark, *Silversides* remains in excellent condition, with original furnishings that include bunks, sonar equipment, radios, and furniture. The tour offers a good idea of what it was like to venture out on a 45-day tour deep into hostile waters.

Just a short distance away resides another piece of American naval heritage. **The USS LST-393** (560 Mart St., 231/730-1477, www.lst393.org, 10am-5pm daily May-Sept., $8 adults, $5 students, free under age 5), which served during World War II as a Landing Ship Tank. The ship delivered tanks and other armored equipment to the battlefield during amphibious landings, including the Allied invasions of Salerno in 1943 and Normandy in 1944. Remarkably, the vessel sustained very little damage during her long tenure. Today the first deck of the ship is maintained as a museum honoring U.S. service personnel from all conflicts and tells its story through a remarkable collection of war memorabilia. Visitors can also explore the balance of the ship and see both the sailors' and officers' quarters and even descend into the engine room, which looks exactly as it did during the war.

Museums

Charles Hackley also donated to Muskegon one of the finest art museums in the state. The **Muskegon Museum of Art** (296

USS *Silversides* submarine museum

Michigan's Maple Syrup

tapped maple trees producing syrup

Centuries before European settlers discovered the undeniable sweetness of maple syrup, Native Americans were using it to flavor their meat and fish. Several legends exist about how various Native American communities first embraced distilled maple sap as a cooking ingredient. In one such tale—as recounted by the Chippewa and Ottawa people of Michigan—a god named Nenawbozhoo cast a spell on the sugar maple tree, turning the sweet pure syrup into colorless sap. His justification? Apparently, he feared his people would become lazy and ungrateful if nature's gifts were so readily available.

Though the legends varied, the original freezing and boiling methods of turning sap into syrup were pretty universal—and fairly time-consuming. As early 17th-century settlers discovered, 40 gallons of sap might be required to produce one gallon of syrup. Following the invention of the tin can during the mid-1800s, however, maple syrup production—the nation's oldest agricultural enterprise—became easier for the self-sufficient farmers in the burgeoning industry.

By the 1970s, large companies had taken over the maple syrup industry, using advancements like tubing systems, vacuum pumps, preheaters, reverse-osmosis filters, desalinization machines, and improved storage containers to increase production. Today, Michigan ranks fifth in the nation for maple syrup production; each year, roughly 2,500 commercial and home-use producers throughout the state utilize a mere 1 percent of Michigan's maple forests to yield an estimated 90,000 gallons of syrup. Harvested from February through April, Michigan's maple syrup is used to enhance everything from popcorn to pork ribs to ice cream. There's even a maple cocktail that blends maple syrup with gin, bourbon, and lemon juice.

For maple-related recipes and statistics, as well as information about seasonal events, consult the **Michigan Maple Syrup Association** (www.mi-maplesyrup.com). To purchase pure Michigan maple syrup, stop by one of the Southwest Coast's many roadside markets and farms.

W. Webster Ave., 231/720-2570, www.muskegonartmuseum.org, 10am-5pm Tues.-Wed. and Fri.-Sat., 10am-8pm Thurs., noon-5pm Sun., $10 adults, $8 seniors 65 and over, $6 students 17 and up, ages 16 and under free) is a surprise for a city of this size, with a permanent collection that includes the well-known *Tornado over Kansas* by John Steuart Curry and works by Winslow Homer, Edward Hopper, and Andrew Wyeth. Also among the museum's holdings is the largest collection of works by painter Françoise Gilot, best known as Picasso's mistress and mother to their daughter Paloma.

The **Lakeshore Museum Center** (430 W. Clay Ave., 231/722-0278, www.lakeshoremuseum.org, 9:30am-4pm Mon.-Fri., 10am-4pm Sat., noon-4pm Sun., $5 adults, children 2 and under free) recounts the city's colorful logging past, including details about the dangers of living in the city's lumber camps. Don't miss the murals of Muskegon's history, done for the National Lumberman's Bank in 1929. Other exhibits explore the area's geology, early Native Americans, and the wildlife of various habitats.

Beaches and Parks

Almost half a million swimmers, beachcombers, surfers, sailboarders, boaters, campers, and picnickers descend each year on **Muskegon State Park** (3560 Memorial Dr., North Muskegon, 231/744-3480, annual Recreation Passport required: $12 Michigan residents, $34 nonresidents, $9 day pass available to nonresidents only). Despite the large numbers, most visitors head for the beach, leaving the rest of the park almost unused. Its 1,165 acres feel more like several small parks, divided into swimming, fishing, and hiking areas. From the coast, you may spot the 53-foot-tall **Muskegon South Pierhead Lighthouse,** established in 1903. Still active today, the structure is often called the Pere Marquette Lighthouse, given its position on the south side of the Muskegon Lake Channel, near Pere Marquette Beach.

In winter, Muskegon State Park is best known for its **Muskegon Winter Sports Complex** (877/879-5843, www.msports.org, see website for price schedule, 10am-10pm daily winter), which offers ski and snowshoe rentals, houses an ice-skating rink, and includes one of the few luge runs in the nation. You can reserve a spot for a quick lesson and try it yourself. Speeds reach up to 40 mph careening down the ice-covered wooden chute—and seem terribly faster when traveling on a sled made only of wood, metal, and canvas. The luge course is open only on weekends, beginning in mid-December. A day's pass includes a sled, helmet, and coach. First-timers are fully supervised. The park is also a favorite among cross-country skiers, who find some of the longest lighted trails in the state. The area usually enjoys a long season thanks to reliable lake-effect snows.

The **Gillette Sand Dune Visitor Center** at **P. J. Hoffmaster State Park** (6585 Lake Harbor Rd., 231/798-3711, annual Recreation Passport required: $12 Michigan residents, $34 nonresidents, $9 day pass available to nonresidents only) gives an excellent introduction to dune history and ecology. Slideshows, dioramas, and colorful displays demonstrate the natural forces that shaped and continue to shape the face of these majestic mountains of sand. Besides the center, the 1,200-acre park contains 2 miles of shoreline, towering dunes that stand guard over a sandy beach, deep forests, interdunal valleys, 10 miles of hiking and cross-country trails (also popular with snowshoers in winter), and a nice campground.

★ Michigan's Adventure

Muskegon also has plenty to offer for those looking for more commercial amusements. Together, **Michigan's Adventure Amusement Park** and **Wild Water Adventure Water Park** (4750 Whitehall Rd., 231/766-3377, www.miadventure.com, 11am-9pm daily summer, other seasons vary, $36 pp, plus parking) make up the state's largest amusement and water park, with more than 60 rides and attractions, including seven roller coasters and several pools and waterslides. The newest roller coaster, Thunderhawk, is the state's first and only suspended coaster; it's the steel complement to the park's longtime favorite, Shivering Timbers, a 125-foot-tall wooden coaster that's routinely considered one of the best in the country.

RECREATION

Golf

If you're hankering to play a casual round of golf in a gorgeous setting, visit the **Stonegate Golf Club** (4100 Sweeter

Rd., Twin Lake, 231/744-7200, www.stonegategolfclub.com, daily Apr.-Oct., $30-57 pp without cart). In addition to the course, Stonegate provides golf training and a beautiful bar and grill, popular for its famous fish fry every Friday night.

Hiking and Biking

The 25-mile-long **Musketawa Trail** (www.musketawatrail.com) is a multiuse recreational pathway that links Marne in eastern Ottawa County to Muskegon. Passing amid a myriad of farmlands, wetlands, creeks, and villages, it offers hikers and biking enthusiasts a marvelous scenic tour of the area. Horseback riders, inline skaters, and nature lovers frequent the Musketawa as well. In winter, it's especially popular among cross-country skiers and snowmobilers.

FESTIVALS

In late June, the **Taste of Muskegon** (Western Ave., www.tasteofmuskegon.org, 4pm-10pm Fri., 11am-9pm Sat., free, food items $3-10), a relatively new diversion, offers a two-day celebration of the region's cuisine, with the area's best restaurants and bakeries serving their specialties to crowds of willing gourmands. Since all the proceeds benefit the Muskegon Main Street organization and Make a Wish Foundation of Michigan, you can enjoy a hearty meal while knowing you're helping two good causes.

FOOD

Adjacent to Muskegon's Shoreline Inn along the verge of Muskegon Lake, **The Lakehouse Waterfront Grille** (730 Terrace Point Blvd., 231/722-4461, www.thelakehousemi.com, 11am-11pm Mon.-Thurs., 11am-midnight Fri.-Sat., 10am-midnight, Sat., 10am-11pm Sun., $17-44) offers casual dining paired with gorgeous views. Given its extensive wine list, amazing house specials, and outdoor deck, you'll be hard-pressed to find a better dining experience in the area.

ACCOMMODATIONS

Overlooking Muskegon Lake, the ★ **Port City Victorian Inn** (1259 Lakeshore Dr., 231/759-0205, www.portcityinn.com, $180-235 d), a Queen Anne-style bed-and-breakfast built in 1877, has five guest rooms and a rooftop balcony with terrific views of the lake. It's open year-round. The **Delta Hotel by Marriott Muskegon** (939 3rd St., 231/722-0100 or 877/863-4780, www.marriott.com, $126-204 d) offers a convenient location in the heart of Muskegon. Amenities include an indoor pool and sauna.

Camping

Muskegon State Park (3560 Memorial Dr., North Muskegon, 231/744-3480, annual Recreation Passport required: $12 Michigan residents, $34 nonresidents, $9 day pass available to nonresidents only) has three campgrounds with a total of 247 sites ($23-36). Tents and RV campers are welcome; the campsites are equipped with 50-amp electricity, and there are modern restrooms available. The Lake Michigan Campground is especially amenity-rich. Despite not being on the water, it's protected by tall maples, beeches, and sand dunes, with an easy walk to the beach. Reservations (800/447-2757, www.michigan.gov/dnr) are definitely advised in summer.

INFORMATION AND SERVICES

For more information about the area, contact the **Muskegon County Convention & Visitors Bureau** (610 W. Western Ave., 231/724-3100, www.visitmuskegon.org, 8am-5pm Mon.-Fri.) or the **Muskegon Area Chamber of Commerce** (380 W. Western Ave., 231/722-3751, www.muskegon.org, 8:30am-5pm Mon.-Fri.). For local news, check out the ***Muskegon Chronicle*** (www.mlive.com/news/muskegon).

As the Southwest Coast's largest city, Muskegon has no shortage of services for travelers. **Meijer** (www.meijer.com), a Midwestern superstore chain, has three locations in the Muskegon area; fill prescriptions and purchase all manner of supplies. If you're looking for an ATM, you'll find plenty, including **Comerica Bank** (www.comerica.com) and **PNC** (www.pnc.com).

For medical services, consult the **Mercy Health Muskegon** (1500 E. Sherman Blvd., 231/672-2000, www.mercyhealth.com).

GETTING THERE AND AROUND

Travelers can reach Muskegon via boat, bus, plane, or car. The pet-friendly ***Lake Express*** (1918 Lakeshore Dr., 866/914-1010, www.lake-express.com, one-way $95.50 adults, $87 students, military personnel, and over age 64, $31 ages 5-17, under age 5 free), the first high-speed ferry to operate on the Great Lakes, has transported passengers and vehicles across Lake Michigan between Milwaukee and Muskegon since 2004. Private boats can also access Muskegon Lake.

Greyhound (351 Morris Ave., 231/722-6048 or 800/231-2222, www.greyhound.com) provides bus service to Muskegon, and United Airlines offers flights from Chicago to **Muskegon County Airport** (MKG, 99 Sinclair Dr., 231/798-4596, www.muskegonairport.com), where you can rent a vehicle from one of six major rental car agencies. From the airport, you can also get a ride from **Express Transportation** (231/571-0741), which charges about $19 for a trip to downtown Muskegon, $67 to Holland, and $92 to Grand Rapids.

U.S. 31 is the most convenient route to Muskegon. From Lansing and Grand Rapids take I-96 to Muskegon. From downtown Detroit, you'll have to cross almost the entire width of the Lower Peninsula; in light traffic, the 197-mile trip should take less than three hours. From Chicago, follow I-90 and I-94 through Illinois and Indiana onto I-196/U.S. 31; in light traffic, the 187-mile trip will require less than three hours. En route from Chicago, parts of I-90 and I-94 serve as the Indiana Toll Road.

Within Muskegon, public transportation is provided by the **Muskegon Area Transit System** (MATS, 231/724-6420, www.matsbus.com, one-way $1.25 pp, $0.60 seniors and disabled, under age 6 free).

Traverse City and Michigan Wine Country

Although all of Michigan is defined by the Great

Lakes, perhaps no region is more dramatically contoured by lakes, bays, and rivers than the northwestern corner of the Lower Peninsula, especially the coast surrounding Traverse City, the area's largest town and the self-proclaimed Cherry Capital of the World. The aquamarine waters of Lake Michigan mingle with two stunning coastal bays: Grand Traverse Bay, a majestic 32-mile-long inlet partially bisected by the slender Old Mission Peninsula, and Little Traverse Bay, situated farther north near Petoskey, a town famous for its high concentration of Petoskey stones, the fossilized coral rock that was named Michigan's state stone in 1965.

On summer weekends, the populations of the lakeside towns of

Highlights

Look for ★ to find recommended sights, activities, dining, and lodging.

★ **Wineries of Grand Traverse Bay:** Wineries and tasting rooms pepper the Leelanau and Old Mission Peninsulas, the destinations of choice for grape connoisseurs (pages 217 and 235).

★ **National Cherry Festival:** This annual celebration attracts over 500,000 participants every July with cherry-pie-eating contests, a grand buffet, a golf tournament, and a farmers market (page 223).

★ **Traverse City Film Festival:** Michigan's premier film festival—cofounded by filmmaker Michael Moore—lures thousands of filmmakers and fans of the cinema (page 223).

★ **Interlochen Center for the Arts:** Interlochen cultivates a passion for the performing and visual arts with dance performances, film screenings, and art exhibitions (page 228).

★ **Sleeping Bear Dunes National Lakeshore:** Climb the largest freshwater dunes in the world, then get in the water for kayaking or scuba diving (page 229).

★ **Tunnel of Trees:** Along this scenic stretch of M-119, trees arch to form a sun-dappled tunnel—to spectacular effect in autumn (page 255).

Traverse City, Charlevoix, and Petoskey grow exponentially. While some fear the development that's encroached in recent years, visitors continue to flock in, embracing a wide array of diversions—windsurfing, fishing charters, bike trails, upscale restaurants and galleries, golf and ski resorts, and traditional downtown shopping districts. Visitors can also admire a number of historic lighthouses.

Meanwhile, other attractions have drawn visitors inland. Legions of designer golf resorts, blue-ribbon rivers for fly-fishing, backroad biking routes, and some of the Midwest's largest ski resorts have become commonplace. This breathtaking area is also home to many state parks, several state forests, and the expansive Manistee National Forest. Along the western edge of the Leelanau Peninsula, known for scenic vistas and award-winning wineries, lies another natural wonder: Sleeping Bear Dunes National Lakeshore, one of the Midwest's finest natural escapes and a popular destination for anglers, hikers, bikers, skiers, kayakers, and amateur geologists. The most visually compelling features are the pyramidal dunes themselves, some of which rise over 400 feet high, constituting the largest freshwater dunes in the world and offering an unparalleled view of Glen Lake and the surrounding hills.

PLANNING YOUR TIME

Extending from the southern edge of Manistee National Forest to the Mackinac Bridge, northwestern Michigan is a sprawling region. If your time is limited, plan a weekend getaway to Traverse City. A two-week experience, however, will ensure the opportunity to explore the Cherry Capital plus Sleeping Bear Dunes, the Leelanau Peninsula, Manistee National Forest, Beaver Island, and several coastal towns, beaches, and golf resorts.

Summer is exceedingly popular in the resort towns of northwestern Michigan, especially during the area's annual festivals. If you're uncomfortable with crowds, it's probably best to come in spring, fall, or winter. Even during the off-season, the region will appeal to art lovers, golfing enthusiasts, beachcombers, wine connoisseurs, cross-country skiers, and assorted other fun seekers.

Although you can reach the area via boat, bus, or plane, the easiest method is by car. A network of highways allows easy access—U.S. 31 from Muskegon, U.S. 131 from Grand Rapids, U.S. 10 from Midland, and I-75 from Detroit and the Upper Peninsula. For more details about northwestern Michigan, contact the **West Michigan Tourist Association** (WMTA, 741 Kenmoor Ave., Ste. E, Grand Rapids, 616/245-2217, www.wmta.org).

HISTORY

Traverse City has been hosting visitors since the French explorers and fur traders first passed through the area in the 1600s, soon spreading word of the treacherous canoe passage across the gaping mouth of the bay, *la grande traversée.* Since then, the Traverse region has attracted people like the Hemingway family, who summered for decades on the shores of Walloon Lake. But it was the Victorian resort dwellers who left an indelible mark. The first summer visitors began arriving in the 1860s, escaping hot and humid Midwestern cities for the lake's crisp breezes and gentle shores. Old money from Detroit, Chicago, and Cleveland built exclusive summer homes. Those of lesser means stayed in grand pastel-painted hotels. Church-run camps soon evolved from canvas tents to Victorian cottages that remain well preserved today. Decade after decade, summer people attended Sousa concerts in the park, sailed dinghies across the harbor, and enjoyed lemonade on verandas overlooking the beautiful blue-green bays.

Today Grand Traverse Bay and Little Traverse Bay anchor one of the state's most popular vacation areas, where the air is still

Previous: vineyard in Michigan; beach at Sleeping Bear Dunes; Mission Point Lighthouse.

Traverse City and Michigan Wine Country

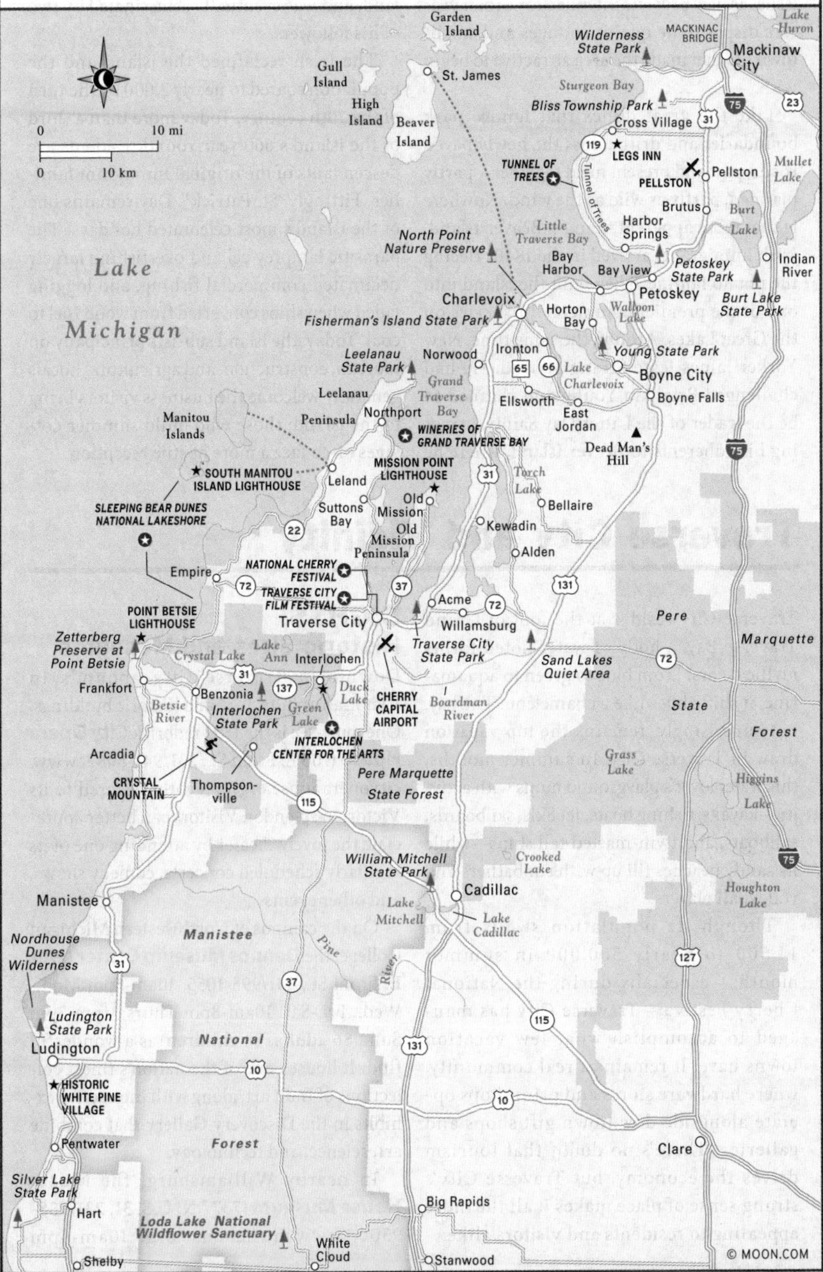

crisp and clean and the waters remain clear and accessible. Development is a controversial issue, as new projects intended for urban visitors displace the quaint cottages and small-town life that made the area attractive to begin with.

Like the great dunes that ignore park boundaries and drift across the newly paved roads, past and present meld together—partly planned, partly as wild as the wind. Nowhere is that more apparent than on Beaver Island. Irish immigrants arrived in the 1840s fleeing the potato famine. They built the island into one of the premier commercial fisheries on the Great Lakes. Around the same time, New Yorker James Jesse Strang arrived. He had challenged Brigham Young and claimed to be the leader of the Latter Day Saints, bringing his adherents to Beaver Island, where he proclaimed himself king, took five wives, began a newspaper, pushed the Irish off the land, and was eventually assassinated by two of his followers.

The Irish reclaimed the island and the population soared to nearly 2,000 by the turn of the 20th century. Today more than a third of the island's 660 year-round residents are descendants of the original immigrant families. Fittingly, St. Patrick's Day remains one of the island's most celebrated holidays. The parasitic lamprey eel and overfishing largely decimated commercial fishing, and logging faded when ships converted from wood fuel to coal. Today, the island subsists principally on tourism, construction, and agriculture. Locals generally welcome the business visitors bring to the island; those who build summer cottages often face a more hostile reception.

Traverse City and Vicinity

Traverse City resides at the foot of Grand Traverse Bay, a body of water noted for its idyllic colors. From blue to green to aquamarine, it shifts hues like a chameleon. The bay, not surprisingly, remains the top vacation draw in Traverse City. In summer months, this water lover's playground hums with activity—kayaks, fishing boats, Jet Skis, sailboards, sailboats, and twin-masted tall ships—while its sandy beaches fill up with sunbathers and volleyball players.

Though its population swells from 14,500 to nearly 300,000 in summer months—especially during the National Cherry Festival—Traverse City has managed to accomplish what few vacation towns have: It remains a real community, where hardware stores and print shops operate alongside downtown gift shops and galleries. There's no doubt that tourism drives the economy, but Traverse City's strong sense of place makes it all the more appealing to residents and visitors alike.

SIGHTS

Historic Sites and Museums

Downtown Traverse City abounds in Victorian architecture and historic buildings. One must-see is the 1892 redbrick **City Opera House** (106 E. Front St., 231/941-8082, www.cityoperahouse.org), recently restored to its Victorian splendor. Visitors can better appreciate the lovely theater by attending one of its regularly scheduled concerts, comedy shows, and other events.

On the campus of Northwestern Michigan College, the **Dennos Museum Center** (1701 E. Front St., 231/995-1055, 10am-5pm Mon.-Wed., Fri.-Sat. 10am-8pm Thurs., 1pm-5pm Sun., $6 adults, $4 children) is a wonderful find. It houses one of the nation's finest collections of Inuit art, along with interactive exhibits in the Discovery Gallery that combine art, science, and technology.

In nearby Williamsburg, the **Music House Museum** (7377 N. U.S. 31, 231/938-9300, www.musichouse.org, 10am-4pm

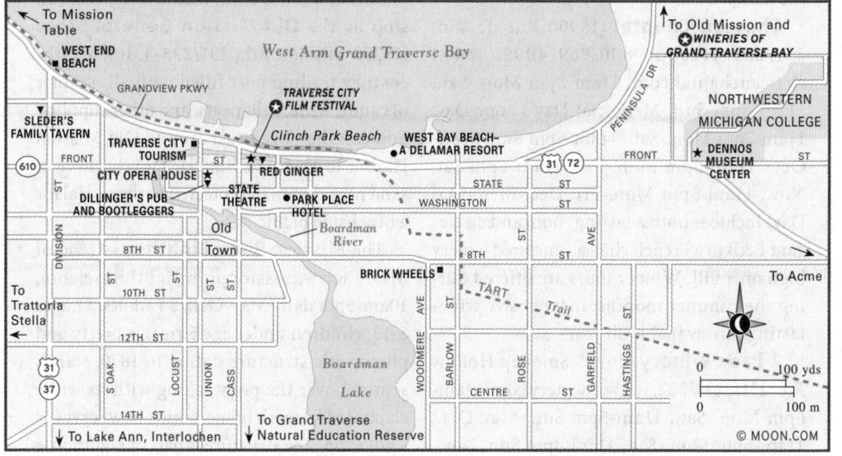

Mon.-Sat., noon-4pm Sun. May-Oct., 10am-4pm Sat., noon-4pm Sun. Nov.-Dec., $10 adults, $3 ages 6-15) is another surprise, showcasing a vast array of rare antique musical instruments from 1870 to 1930. Its collection includes music boxes, jukeboxes, nickelodeons, pipe organs, and a hand-carved Belgian dance organ.

Old Mission Peninsula

The Old Mission Peninsula pierces the waters north from Traverse City, a narrow sliver of land that neatly divides Grand Traverse Bay in two. This ridge stretches for 22 miles, a quiet agrarian landscape marked with a patchwork of cherry orchards and grape vineyards. Nowhere else on earth do more cherries grow per acre than the Old Mission Peninsula, where the surrounding waters, insulating snows, and cool summer air form the perfect microclimate for raising fruit. Veer off M-37 onto almost any country road to wander past the pretty peaceful orchards.

Grapes also thrive on the Old Mission Peninsula, creating a burgeoning **winemaking industry** (www.wineriesofoldmission.com). Most of the eight wineries here offer tours and tastings, and visiting them brings an extra benefit: The ridgetop roads of the Old Mission Peninsula come with incredible views that, in clear weather, take in both arms of Grand Traverse Bay.

★ WINERIES

Chateau Grand Traverse (12239 Center Rd., 231/223-7355 or 800/283-0247, www.cgtwines.com, 10am-7pm Mon.-Sat., 10am-6pm Sun. Memorial Day-Labor Day, 10am-6pm Mon.-Sat., 10am-5pm Sun., Labor Day-Oct., 10am-5pm daily, Nov.-Apr.), nine miles north of Traverse City on M-37, was a pioneer in bringing European viniferous wines to the Midwest. It has a spacious tasting room that offers understated elegance with wonderful bay views for sampling its award-winning rieslings and ice wines. The winery offers tours as well as luxurious accommodations in its hilltop inn.

Just east of Bowers Harbor, **Bowers Harbor Vineyards** (2896 Bowers Harbor Rd., 231/223-7615 or 800/616-7615, www.bowersharbor.com, 10:30am-6pm Sun.-Thurs., 10:30am-7pm Fri.-Sat. May-Oct., 10:30am-5pm Sun.-Thurs., 10:30am-6pm Fri.-Sat. Nov.-Apr.) is a small, friendly family-run winery with a year-round tasting room. Friendly, non-barking dogs are welcome on the patio.

Chateau Chantal (15900 Rue de Vin, 231/223-4110 or 800/969-4009, www.chateauchantal.com, 11am-8pm Mon.-Sat., 11am-6pm Sun. Memorial Day-Labor Day, 11am-7pm Mon.-Sat., 11am-6pm Sun. Sept.-Oct., 11am-5pm Mon.-Fri., 11am-6pm Sat. Nov., 11am-5pm Mon.-Fri. Dec.-Memorial Day) includes both a tasting room and an elegant B&B in a French château-inspired winery high on a hill. Winery tours are offered during the summer months; inexpensive wine-tastings are available all year.

2 Lads Winery (16985 Smokey Hollow Rd., 231/223-7722, www.2lwinery.com, 11am-6pm Mon.-Sat., 11am-5pm Sun. May-Oct., 11am-5pm Mon.-Sat., 11am-4pm Sun. Nov.-Apr.) offers tastings, winery tours, and a dramatic view of the east arm of Grand Traverse Bay—all housed in a cutting-edge modern building.

Peninsula Cellars (11480 Center Rd., 231/933-9787, www.peninsulacellars.com, 10am-6pm daily April-Oct., 10am-5pm daily Nov.-Mar.) is one of the peninsula's newer wineries, with a tasting room in a converted 1896 schoolhouse.

OLD MISSION SIGHTS

The peninsula was named for the mission first built near its tip in 1829 by a Presbyterian minister who came from Mackinac to convert the Ojibwa and Ottawa people to Christianity. The **Mission Church** on M-37 in Old Mission is a replica, but it houses the original bell. A few displays tell the peninsula's early history and evolution into a fruit-growing region. Nearby, the 1842 **Dougherty House,** the region's first frame building, is original. Once home to Reverend Peter Dougherty and his family, the homestead began undergoing restoration in late 2019, after which the house and surrounding acreage will be open to the public. For more information about the Dougherty Homestead, consult the Old Mission Peninsula Historical Society (www.omphistoricalsociety.org) or the Dougherty House's dedicated site: www.oldmissionhouse.com. Meanwhile, you can stop by the **Old Mission General Store** (18250 Mission Rd., 231/223-4310), a 19th-century trading post filled with all manner of candy, wine, deli meats, and other supplies. You can then head east around Old Mission Harbor to **Haserot Beach,** a lovely curve of sand near the small protected harbor, ideal for a beachside picnic.

The **Mission Point Lighthouse** (end of M-37, www.missionpointlighthouse.com, 10am-5pm daily May-Oct., $4 adults, $2 ages 5-12, children under age 5 free), a pretty and photogenic structure dating to 1870, stands sentinel over the point, along with its white clapboard keeper's home, which now serves as a gift shop. The structure is part of Lighthouse Park, operated by Peninsula Township.

Beaches and Tours

Grand Traverse Bay has two "arms." The West Arm is larger and deeper, home to marinas, the bay's tall ship cruises, and a few commercial enterprises. The East Arm is shallower, warmer, and ringed with sugary sand at its south end—home to hotels and water-sports ventures.

There are a number of excellent beaches on both the Leelanau Peninsula and in downtown Traverse City. Most popular is **Clinch Park Beach** on West Bay, east of Union Street. Farther west, at the foot of Division Street, **West End Beach** is a popular place for volleyball. Just off U.S. 31 near the Acme turnoff on East Bay is **Bayside Park,** which has 600 feet of sand beach and a bathhouse.

The ***Nauti-Cat*** (231/947-1730, www.nauti-cat.com) offers cruises on West Bay aboard a 47-foot catamaran, including a kids' cruise (90 minutes, $15) and a champagne sunset cruise ($35). The open-deck arrangement allows for up to 43 guests. Reservations are recommended, but walk-ons are accepted if space allows.

An authentic replica of an 18th-century wooden schooner, the ***Tall Ship Manitou***

(Dockside Plaza, 13390 S. West Bay Shore Dr., 231/941-2000, www.tallshipsailing.com, $42-49 adults, $20-28 children) sets sail three times daily in July and August, cruising the West Bay. They also offer a B&B option ($129-150 for singles, $228-270 for couples). From Tuesday through Saturdays during the summer months an evening cruise is followed by an overnight stay in the ship's staterooms. A sumptuous breakfast is served in the morning.

RECREATION

Golf

Award-winning golf courses abound just a few minutes away from Traverse City. About three miles from town, **Elmbrook Golf Course** (1750 Townline Rd., 231/946-9180, www.elmbrookgolf.com, daily Apr.-Oct., $47 pp with cart) is an older, unpretentious course, with lots of hills, valleys, and views of Grand Traverse Bay.

In Acme, about five minutes east of Traverse City on U.S. 31, you'll find one of the state's most challenging golfing destinations. The 900-acre **Grand Traverse Resort and Spa** (100 Grand Traverse Village Blvd., 231/534-6000, www.grandtraverseresort.com, daily Apr.-Oct., $45-150 pp) features two signature courses: the Bear, an exceptionally tough course designed by Jack Nicklaus, with tiered greens and deep bunkers, and the Wolverine, designed by South African golf legend Gary Player. The Wolverine is a watery course with dramatic views of Grand Traverse Bay. Both tend to overshadow Spruce Run, the resort's third championship course, equally stunning, though less challenging. Set amid an evergreen forest where ducks, swans, and blue herons abound, Spruce Run can also be appreciated by bird-watchers. In addition to the courses, the resort provides comfortable accommodations, fine dining, a luxurious day spa, an indoor water park, and a 24-hour dog care facility.

The picturesque views of Torch Lake add an extra challenge to keeping your head down at the **A-Ga-Ming Golf Resort** (627 Agaming Dr., Kewadin, 231/264-5081, www.a-ga-ming.com, daily Apr.-Oct., $25-90 pp), north of Acme via U.S. 31 and offering three 18-hole courses: Antrim Dells, Torch, and the relatively new Sundance.

Situated alongside a gorgeous stretch of the Lake Michigan shoreline is what is perhaps one of the finest public courses in Michigan. The 18-hole **Arcadia Bluffs Golf Club** (14710 Northwood Hwy., Arcadia, 231/889-3001, www.arcadiabluffs.com, daily Apr.-Nov., $80-215 pp) promises incredible views of the glistening lake, plus a pro shop and seasonal restaurant in the Nantucket-style clubhouse.

For a somewhat less challenging golf game, stop by **Pirate's Cove Adventure Park** (1710 N. U.S. 31, 231/938-9599, www.piratescove.net, 10am-11pm daily Apr.-Oct., $9.50 adults, $8.50 children), where families can play at one of the finest miniature golf chains in the country. At this award-winning theme park, players can learn about infamous pirates while navigating their way through caves, over footbridges, beneath cascading waterfalls, and alongside wrecked pirate ships. The complex offers two 18-hole courses in addition to bumper boats, racing go-karts, and a water coaster.

Hiking and Biking

Here's the happy general rule about the Traverse Bay region: In summer, downhill ski resorts morph into golf resorts, and cross-country skiing trails often become mountain biking trails.

As proof, the **Pere Marquette State Forest** has a couple of hiking paths in the Traverse City area that double as cross-country and mountain biking trails. Most widely known is the 15.6-mile **North American Vasa Trail** (www.vasa.org). The Vasa, named after Swedish king Gustav Vasa, has challenging climbs and descents. Take U.S. 31 toward Acme, turn right onto Bunker Hill Road, drive 1.5 miles, then turn right again onto Bartlett to reach the trailhead.

The **Sand Lakes Quiet Area** is a classic north woods area of small lakes, forest, and

TOP EXPERIENCE

Traverse City Ale Trail

Traverse City has become quite an oasis for beer lovers. Even the Travel Channel has taken note and included the city on its list of the Top Seven Beer Destinations. To celebrate the city's booming craft beer scene, the **Traverse City Ale Trail** (www.tcbrewbus.com), also known as the TC Ale Trail, is a fun way to experience eight different microbreweries in the area. Pick up a free TC Ale Trail passport at any of the participating breweries, most hotels and restaurants, or the **Traverse City Visitors Bureau** (101 W. Grandview Pkwy., 231/947-1120, www.visittraversecity.com). As you visit each of the featured breweries, collect a unique stamp with any purchase, and when you've visited all eight, return your completed passport to **The Filling Station Microbrewery** for a free commemorative silicone pint glass. For an extra kick, make a pit stop at the **Grand Traverse Distillery** (781 Industrial Cir., Ste. 5, 231/947-8635, www.grandtraversedistillery.com, 11:30am-5:30pm Mon.-Sat., noon-4pm Sun.), Michigan's oldest and largest vodka and whiskey distillery. Given the distance between these breweries, you'll need to go by car, so be sure to drink and drive responsibly.

Here are the breweries of the TC Ale Trail:

- **Brewery Ferment** (511 S. Union St., 231/735-8113, www.breweryferment.com, 3pm-10pm Mon.-Thurs., 3pm-midnight Fri., noon-midnight Sat.): Housed within a century-old building, this casual neighborhood spot offers a handful of flagship and specialty taps, such as the Old Town Brown, plus tasty bar snacks.
- **The Filling Station Microbrewery** (642 Railroad Place, 231/946-8168, http://thefillingstationmicrobrewery.com, 11:30am-11pm Mon.-Thurs., 11:30am-midnight Fri.-Sat., noon-10pm Sun.): Situated in the city's historic railroad district, this casual pub provides handcrafted ales, wood-fired flatbreads, fresh salads, and pleasant views of adjacent Boardman Lake.
- **Jolly Pumpkin** (13512 Peninsula Dr., 231/223-4333, www.jollypumpkin.com, 11:30am-9pm Sun.-Thurs., 11:30am-10pm Fri.-Sat.): Set in a cottage-like spot on the Old Mission Peninsula, this popular restaurant, microbrewery, and distillery serves local artisanal fare as well as spirits distilled on-site, wines from area vineyards, and craft beers.
- **North Peak Brewing Company** (400 W. Front St., 231/941-7325, www.northpeak.net, 11am-11pm Mon.-Thurs., 11am-midnight Fri.-Sat., noon-10pm Sun.): Established in 1995, North Peak prepares handcrafted beers, including Mission Point Porter and Shirley's Irish Stout, in

meadow about 10 miles east of Traverse City. Ten miles of trails loop through the 2,500 acres of terrain, which is moderately hilly—pleasant, but not extreme. For more information on biking, hiking, and camping in the Pere Marquette State Forest, call or stop by the **Michigan DNR district office** (970 Emerson Rd., 231/922-5280).

For getting around Traverse City and reaching various trailheads on your bike, you can avoid busy U.S. 31 by using the 10.5-mile **Traverse Area Recreation Trail** (TART, www.traversetrails.org). This off-road path shares a railroad right-of-way. It currently extends from U.S. 72 at the West Bay beach to the Acme area, with plans to continue expanding it eastward.

The entire Traverse region offers exceptional back-road cycling. The **Cherry Capital Cycling Club** (www.cherrycapitalcyclingclub.org) has mapped out dozens of options on its *Bicycle Map of Northwest Michigan,* printed on coated stock that can take a lot of abuse. It's available for $10 at local bike shops like **Brick Wheels** (736 E. 8th St., 231/947-4274, www.brickwheels.com). This full-service shop has knowledgeable employees and rents road bikes, mountain bikes, and inline skates.

an on-site brewery. It also offers a full menu of soups, salads, sandwiches, hearth-baked pizzas, steaks, ribs, pasta dishes, and well-prepared local fish.

fresh Michigan microbrew

- **Right Brain Brewery** (225 E. 16th St., 231/944-1239, www.rightbrainbrewery.com, noon-11pm Mon.-Thurs., 11am-midnight Fri.-Sat., noon-9pm Sun.): Recently named one of the "Top Five Local Breweries in the Nation," Right Brain definitely has an unpretentious atmosphere. This popular brewery is known for making award-winning, culinary-inspired beers, such as the creamy Smooth Operator and the CEO Stout, not to mention rotating signature, Belgian, and premium taps. While here, you can also sample hefty waffle sandwiches.
- **The Workshop Brewing Company** (221 Garland St., Ste. A, 231/421-8977, www.traversecityworkshop.com, 11am-10pm Sun.-Thurs., 11am-midnight Fri.-Sat.): Relatively new to Traverse City, this innovative, ecofriendly brewery offers a welcoming atmosphere; a wide array of traditional, seasonal, and oak-aged beers; and several tasty one-hander sandwiches that complement the brews.
- **Rare Bird Brewpub** (229 Lake Ave., 231/943-2053, www.rarebirdbrewpub.com, 3pm-midnight Mon.-Thurs., noon-2am Fri.-Sat., noon-10pm Sun.): Housed in a spacious, restored downtown building, this brewpub offers a bevy of both craft and branded beers and a hearty food menu to boot.
- **Brewery Terra Firma** (2959 Hartman Rd., 231/929-1600, www.breweryterrafirma.com, 10am-10pm Mon.-Sat., noon-9pm Sun.): This sophisticated brewery and taproom prides itself on being more of a tasting room than a pub. However, there are a few gourmet sandwich offerings. Parking is very limited, so it's a good idea to arrive via cab or public transit.

Bird-Watching

A few miles south of Traverse City on Cass Road, the **Grand Traverse Nature Education Reserve** maintains 435 acres along the Boardman River and the Sabin and Boardman Ponds. Though just outside town, this surprisingly peaceful area includes five miles of self-guided nature trails for walking (bicycles are not allowed) that wind along the river and cross through marshes and grasslands. The Traverse Bay region attracts particularly large populations of mute swans, and pairs frequently nest here and can be seen gliding gracefully across the glassy ponds. Farther upstream on the Boardman, large stands of oak crown a steep bluff climbing up from the river and another small flowage, **Brown Bridge Pond.** Stairs and trails lead out to observation platforms and down to the water's edge.

Canoeing and Fishing

Situated in the West Arm of Grand Traverse Bay is **Power Island,** a 200-acre nature preserve owned by the city, with beaches and five miles of hiking trails. For paddlers and other boaters, it's a fun destination for an afternoon

Loda Lake National Wildflower Sanctuary

Nestled within the Manistee National Forest, between the towns of Brohman and White Cloud, the **Loda Lake National Wildflower Sanctuary** (800/821-6263, www.fs.fed.us, 24 hours daily, $5 daily, $15 weekly) is the only sanctuary of its kind established in a national forest. Supported by the Federated Garden Clubs of Michigan for more than seven decades, the sanctuary welcomes visitors all year long, though it's particularly popular May to August. Nature lovers can take a self-guided tour through oak-maple woodlands, old pine plantations, and a shrub swamp, boasting a slew of wildflowers and other plant species, including columbine, witch hazel, and huckleberries. A detailed brochure is available from the **Baldwin/White Cloud Ranger District** (650 N. Michigan Ave., Baldwin, 231/745-4631, 8am-4:30pm daily mid-May-mid-Sept.). To reach Loda Lake, head north from White Cloud on M-37 for 6.8 miles; the sanctuary is on the left.

THE RULES OF LODA LAKE

While several diversions are allowed here, including hiking, hunting, boating, snowshoeing, and cross-country skiing, certain restrictions apply:

- Bicycles, llamas, pack and saddle animals, snowmobiles, and other motorized vehicles are not allowed into the sanctuary.
- Dogs must be leashed at all times.
- Hiking and foot travel are only permitted on official trails.
- Picking or removing wildflowers is prohibited.
- Only dead and down wood may be used for fires.
- Fires are limited to grills and fire rings only.
- Overnight camping is prohibited in the sanctuary.

For more information about Loda Lake National Wildflower Sanctuary, contact the **Baldwin/White Cloud Ranger Station** (231/745-4631).

picnic, but on weekends, it's popular with local revelers.

The beautiful **Boardman River** twists gently through Grand Traverse County before melting into the West Arm at Traverse City. The Boardman offers excellent fly-fishing and canoeing. Generally, its upper stretches run deeper and are better for paddling.

Skiing

West of Thompsonville on M-115, **Crystal Mountain** (12500 Crystal Mountain Dr., 855/995-5146, www.crystalmountain.com) began as a downhill skiing destination but has evolved into much more. While it still offers downhill—45 runs on two camel-humped slopes—it really shines as a cross-country venue. Nordic skiers ride a chairlift from the Nordic Center to the top of the downhill slopes, where a trailhead leads to 25 miles of impeccably groomed cross-country terrain—a combination of gentle pathways and roller-coaster rides that weave all over the resort's 1,500 acres. The network is truly one of the Midwest's finest.

Crystal Mountain offers attractive villas and tasteful condos scattered around its property. Rates begin at about $170 but vary widely depending on the unit and time of visit. Ski or golf packages are usually the best deal. In summer, Crystal's 36 holes of golf are the main draw, but it also offers clay tennis courts, indoor and outdoor pools, and other resort amenities. Some of the cross-country trails are accessible to mountain bikes in spring—more than 10 miles of intermediate and advanced terrain overlooking the Betsie River Valley, along with 13 more miles in the nearby state forest.

NIGHTLIFE

Dillinger's Pub and Bootleggers (121 and 119 S. Union St., 231/941-2276 or 231/922-7742, http://dillingerspubtc.com, 11am-2am daily, $9-16) proudly sports its outlaw image while doubling as a classic sports bar, with almost every major game on overhead TVs, daily food and drink specials, and 11 rotating varieties of beer. Let the fun begin!

Recently opened in the InsideOut art gallery, **Outre Lounge** (229 Garland at the InsideOut Gallery, 231/929-3254, noon-9pm Tues., noon-10pm Wed., noon-11pm Thurs., noon-midnight Fri.-Sat., $11-24) is the best place in Traverse City to hear classic rock and jazz while enjoying a cocktail and taking in the art on display.

The **Beacon Lounge** (Park Place Hotel, 300 E. State St., 231/948-5000, http://park-place-hotel.com, 5pm-11pm Mon.-Thurs., 4pm-midnight Fri.-Sat., 5pm-10pm Sun., $8-19) is a great place to relax with a mixed libation while taking in classic standards performed on the piano. There's also a delicious menu of flatbread pizza, appetizers, and desserts.

Little Bohemia (540 Front St., 231/946-6925, www.littlebohemia-tc.com, 11am-9pm Tues.-Sat., $8-20) offers a well-stocked bar, including 10 wine and 27 beer varieties, along with a comprehensive food menu. There's also live local music on Tuesday evenings.

Bubba's Restaurant and Bar (428 E. Front St., 231/995-0570, www.tcbubbas.com, 8am-11pm Mon.-Thurs., 8am-midnight Fri.-Sat., 8am-10pm Sun., $8-25) has daily specials, including Burger and Beer ($8) 4pm-close Tuesday and half off all alcohol and starters 3pm-5:30pm Monday-Friday.

FESTIVALS

★ National Cherry Festival

Without question, Traverse City's largest event is the **National Cherry Festival** (231/947-4230 or 800/968-3380, www.cherryfestival.org), running the first week of July in various locations in downtown Traverse City. First held in 1925, this annual celebration of Michigan's cherry industry attracts over 500,000 participants for the parades and fireworks, live entertainment, turtle races, cherry-pie-eating contests, a grand cherry-themed buffet, and a cherry farmers market. Participants will be able to sample a wide array of cherry-enhanced cuisine and cherry wines from local wineries.

The first few days of the festival feature air shows demonstrating the astonishing flying skills of the U.S. Air Force Thunderbirds. Arrive early and plan to spend much of the day in the same spot.

★ Traverse City Film Festival

The state's premier film event, the **Traverse City Film Festival** (various venues, 231/392-1134, www.traversecityfilmfest.org, $10-75 pp), brings a different slice of Hollywood to northern Michigan—mostly lesser-known films that carry important social messages. Cofounded in 2005 by Academy Award-winning filmmaker Michael Moore, the festival lures celebrities, filmmakers, and cinema buffs in late July or early August. For an entire week, the festival showcases eclectic screenings, informative panel discussions, parties, and live musical performances. Leading Hollywood stars have been known to appear in person.

SHOPPING

Traverse City's main east-west avenue, **Front Street,** is lined with dozens of cafés, galleries, and shops, offering everything from nautical home furnishings to cherry pies. Cobblestone **Union Street** marks Old Town, a growing area of arts and antiques.

If you have a desire for local produce and other hard-to-find items from soaps to soup mixes, browse the **Traverse City Sara Hardy Farmers Market** (www.traversecitymi.gov, 8am-noon Sat. May, 7:30am-noon Sat., 8am-noon Wed. June-Oct.), along the banks of the

1

2

3

CHATEAU
GRAND
TRAVERSE
WINERY • VINEYARDS • INN
ESTABLISHED 1974

Michael Moore's Salute to Film

Perhaps one of Michigan's more eccentric figures, Michael Francis Moore was born in Flint in 1954. After a career in print journalism, Moore turned to filmmaking. His first film, *Roger & Me* (1989), was lauded as a biting indictment of the automotive industry and the start of his politically charged style of filmmaking. In equal measure, he's been called a documentary filmmaker and a propaganda artist. Other films include *The Big One* (1997), an exposé of greedy executives and callous politicians; the Oscar-winning *Bowling for Columbine* (2002), an exploration of the U.S. culture of violence; *Fahrenheit 9/11* (2004), Moore's take on how the Bush administration used the tragic events of 9/11 to push its war agenda; *Sicko* (2007), a comparison of America's health care industry to others around the world; and *Capitalism: A Love Story* (2009), an indictment of corporate interests and how their dogged pursuit of profit has negatively impacted society.

State Theatre

Regardless of the controversial content of his films, Moore's contribution to Michigan's modern culture is undeniable. In 2005, along with photographer John Robert Williams and author Doug Stanton, Moore established the **Traverse City Film Festival** (TCFF, 231/392-1134, www.traversecityfilmfest.org), a charitable, educational organization whose purpose is to preserve one of the country's few native art forms: cinema. The festival, which owns and operates a year-round art-house movie theater in Traverse City, donated to TCFF by local Rotary charities, also lures filmmakers and cinema buffs from around the world to its annual film festival, which usually occurs in late July. This event, which has become one of northern Michigan's biggest attractions, features panel discussions about the filmmaking industry and screenings of a wide selection of movies, including foreign productions, American independent films, documentaries, and classic movies. Films chosen for the TCFF are selected by its board of directors, but submissions sent in by independent filmmakers are considered.

Boardman River, between Union and Cass Streets. You'll find all manner of seasonal vegetables, fruits, and flowers—plus a great selection of muffins.

FOOD

Traverse City is amply supplied with good restaurants, ranging from simple to elegant. **Apache Trout Grill** (13671 S. West Bay Shore Dr., 231/947-7079, www.apachetroutgrill.com, 11am-9pm Mon., 11am-10pm Tues.-Sat., 9am-9pm Sun., $11-28) is a casual spot overlooking the West Arm, featuring fish specialties from the Great Lakes partnered with distinctive sauces. You'll also find steaks, burgers, and ribs.

Sleder's Family Tavern (717 Randolph St., 231/947-9213, www.sleders.com, 11am-10pm Mon.-Sat., noon-10pm Sun., $8-22) has been around since 1882. It's an institution known for its burgers and ribs as well as its gorgeous original mahogany and cherry bar.

Harrington's by the Bay (13890 S. West Bay Shore Dr., 231/421-9393, www.harringtonsbythebay.com, 11am-10pm Sun.-Thurs., 11am-4pm Fri.-Sat., $12-28) emphasizes light dining, offering items like beer-battered portobello fingers and bacon-wrapped shrimp. There are also a few

1: ferris wheel at the National Cherry Festival in Traverse City **2:** the beach at Traverse Bay **3:** vineyards at Chateau Grand Traverse

interesting salad choices, like arugula salad and baby romaine wedge.

For something different, try the Asian-inspired **Red Ginger** (237 E. Front St., 231/944-1733, www.eatatginger.com, 5pm-10pm Mon.-Thurs., 5pm-11pm Fri.-Sat., $13-40). Featuring flavors from Chinese, Thai, Vietnamese, Japanese, and other Asian cuisines, the Red Ginger is easily the best Asian restaurant in northern Michigan. If you go on a Monday, you can enjoy some live jazz while dining on dragon rolls and sake-glazed sea bass.

Trattoria Stella (1200 W. 12th St., 231/929-8989, www.stellatc.com, 11:30am-3pm and 5pm-10pm Mon.-Thurs., 11:30am-3pm and 5pm-11pm Fri.-Sat., 5pm-9pm Sun. $18-38) does the Italian tradition proud with a comprehensive menu that offers pasta, beef, and chicken dishes all prepared with true Mediterranean flair.

On the Old Mission Peninsula, the **Boathouse Restaurant** (14039 Peninsula Dr., 231/223-4030, www.boathouseonwestbay.com, daily from 4pm, $36-68) is one of the region's most highly touted restaurants, with fine diverse cuisine in a nautical atmosphere overlooking the Bowers Harbor marina.

The nearby ★ **Mission Table at Bowers Harbor Inn** (13512 Peninsula Dr., 231/223-4222, www.missiontable.net, 5pm-9pm daily, $18-27) offers elegant dining in an 1880s mansion, complete with a resident ghost and an excellent wine list. Specialties include pan-seared diver scallops and smoked jowl.

ACCOMMODATIONS

The Traverse City area has more than 5,000 guest rooms, everything from inexpensive motels to deluxe resorts. **Traverse City Tourism** (101 W. Grandview Pkwy., 231/947-1120, www.visittraversecity.com) has a good directory and can help you narrow down your choices. In summer months, advance reservations are strongly advised.

Several independent and chain operations line U.S. 31 along East Bay, Traverse City's original tourism stretch, known as the Miracle Mile. Newcomers to the strip include the **Pointes North Beachfront Resort Hotel** (2211 N. U.S. 31, 800/678-1267, www.pointesnorth.com, $190-320 d) with 300 feet of private beach, a waterfront pool, balconies, and in-room mini kitchens. Staying on the other side of U.S. 31 is less costly, and a generous number of public beaches allow easy water access. The **Traverse Bay Inn** (2300 N. U.S. 31, 800/968-2646, www.traversebayhotels.com, $169-249 d) is a tidy and pleasant older motel, with an outdoor hot tub and pool, as well as some updated suites with kitchens and fireplaces. It also allows dogs.

It's not on the water, but the upper floors of the ★ **Park Place Hotel** (300 E. State St., 231/946-5000, www.park-place-hotel.com, $155-289 d) come with incredible views of Grand Traverse Bay. This 1870s downtown landmark was in disrepair in 1989 when the local Rotary club purchased it and invested $10 million in renovations restoring its turn-of-the-20th-century opulence.

The **West Bay Beach—a Delamar Resort** (615 E. Front St., 231/947-3700, https://westbaybeachresorttraversecity.com, $195-275) is a first-class hotel offering a superb view of Grand Traverse Bay and a sandy beach just steps away from the back door. Updated rooms make this a slightly pricey but still worthwhile choice. It's also pet-friendly with some restrictions.

Baymont Inn & Suites (2326 N. U.S. 31, 231/933-4454, www.baymontinns.com, $239-325) offers oversize rooms, a heated indoor pool, and a workout room, and Wi-Fi and breakfast are included. It's conveniently located on U.S. 31 but away from the chaos of downtown, making it easier to get a good night's sleep.

Great Wolf Lodge (3575 N. U.S. 31, 866/478-9653, www.greatwolf.com, $289-390) is the perfect place for families. All rooms are suites of various sizes—but most kids won't spend too much time there. Instead, they'll be splashing around in the massive indoor water park. There's also quality dining and a full schedule of kid-friendly activities.

Just 10 minutes from Traverse City, the pet-friendly year-round **Ellis Lake Resort** (8440 S. U.S. 31, Interlochen, 231/276-9502, www.ellislakeresort.com, $90-160 d) offers comfortable, smoke-free cabins with private baths and fully equipped kitchens. Built in 1939, the cabins are in need of renovation, but most guests appreciate the rustic nature of the place, including the private outdoor yards equipped with picnic tables and campfire pits. Enjoy an outdoor hot tub, a small playground, and a variety of other activities that include croquet, volleyball, hiking, and snowshoeing. There's also a private 70-acre lake with a swimming beach; guests are free to use the resort's canoes, rowboats, and paddleboat, and anglers will appreciate the plentiful stock of bass, perch, bluegill, and pike.

Ranch Rudolf (6841 Brown Bridge Rd., Kingsley, 231/947-9529, www.ranchrudolf.com, $72-175 d) has motel units and a lodge with fireplaces, and it's pet-friendly. The real draw here, however, is the location: 12 miles from Traverse City in the Pere Marquette State Forest on the shores of the Boardman River. There's paddling and fly-fishing right outside the door. Tent and RV sites are also available.

East of Traverse City, golfers and relaxation seekers often flock to the **Grand Traverse Resort and Spa** (100 Grand Traverse Village Blvd., Acme, 231/534-6000 or 800/236-1577, www.grandtraverseresort.com, $209-489 d), a 900-acre spread that offers access to three signature golf courses, three unique restaurants, a sports bar, a wine-tasting room, a luxurious spa, a health club, a private beach, several swimming pools, and a wide range of well-appointed rooms, suites, condominiums, and resort homes. Given such amenities, plus stunning area views and a complimentary shuttle service to the nearby Turtle Creek Casino & Hotel, it's no wonder that the Grand Traverse Resort is also a popular spot for destination weddings.

Camping

You won't find a quiet nature retreat, but if you're looking for clean and convenient camping, then **Traverse City State Park** (1132 N. U.S. 31, 231/922-5270, annual Recreation Passport required: $12 Michigan residents, $34 nonresidents, $9 day pass available to nonresidents only) fits the bill. Just two miles east of downtown, the park has 343 modern campsites (reservations 800/447-2757, www.michigan.gov/dnr, $31) in a suburban atmosphere, grassy with shade trees. A pedestrian overpass crosses busy U.S. 31 to the main feature of the park: a grassy picnic area and a quarter-mile beach on Grand Traverse Bay. Though picturesque, the beach can become unpleasantly jammed on summer weekends.

You'll find more quiet and seclusion at the many rustic campgrounds in the **Pere Marquette State Forest** just a few miles east of town. One to consider is **Arbutus Lake 4** (231/922-5280, $13), with 50 sites on a peaceful chain of lakes. From U.S. 31 near the state park, take Four Mile Road south to North Arbutus Road.

INFORMATION AND SERVICES

For more information, contact the **Traverse City Convention & Visitors Bureau** (101 W. Grandview Pkwy., 231/947-1120, www.visittraversecity.com, 8am-9pm Mon.-Fri., 9am-5pm Sat., noon-6pm Sun.). Stop by the visitors center to pick up maps and brochures, talk to a volunteer about area activities, and check out rotating exhibits that feature the area's culture, history, and environment. You can also consult the **Traverse City Area Chamber of Commerce** (202 E. Grandview Pkwy., 231/947-5075, www.tcchamber.org). For regional news and events, check out the ***Traverse City Record-Eagle*** (www.record-eagle.com) or ***Traverse*** magazine (www.mynorth.com).

To learn more about the Old Mission Peninsula, visit www.oldmission.com. For details about Benzie County, contact the **Benzie County Visitors Bureau** (826 Michigan Ave., Benzonia, 800/882-5801, www.visitbenzie.com, 9am-5pm Mon.-Fri.).

As northwestern Michigan's largest

town, Traverse City offers an assortment of necessary services, including groceries, laundries, and banks. For medical assistance, there's **Munson Healthcare** (www.munsonhealthcare.org), which offers several locations in the area, including **Munson Medical Center** (1105 6th St., Traverse City, 231/935-5000).

GETTING THERE AND AROUND

As with many towns and cities throughout Michigan, there are several ways to reach Traverse City. One option is to fly into **Cherry Capital Airport** (TVC, 727 Fly Don't Dr., Traverse City, 231/947-2250, www.tvcairport.com), about four miles southeast of downtown, which has flights from Detroit and Minneapolis on Delta and from Chicago on American and United. From here, you can hire a car from **Grand Traverse Limousine** (231/946-5466, www.gtlimo.com), a company that provides airport transportation, plus corporate car services and winery/brewery tours. You can also rent a vehicle from one of five national rental car companies at the airport.

Given its location on Grand Traverse Bay, it's also possible to access Traverse City via boat, and both **Greyhound** (231/946-5180 or 800/231-2222, www.greyhound.com) and **Indian Trails** (800/292-3831, www.indiantrails.com) provide regular service to **Traverse City Bus Station** (115 Hall St.). The **Bay Area Transportation Authority** (BATA, 231/941-2324 or 231/778-1025, www.bata.net, one-way $1.50-3 adults, $0.75-1.50 over age 59, students, veterans, active military, and disabled) offers year-round bus service in Grand Traverse and Leelanau Counties. Traverse City is also very bicycle- and pedestrian-friendly.

From Sault Ste. Marie, take I-75, cross the Mackinac Bridge, and follow U.S. 31 to Traverse City; in light traffic, the 160-mile trip will take about three hours. From Detroit, take I-375, I-75, M-72, and U.S. 31; in light traffic, the 256-mile trip will require about four hours. From Chicago, follow I-90 and I-94 through Illinois and Indiana onto I-196/U.S. 31 and I-196, then U.S. 131 toward Cadillac, and M-113 to Traverse City; in light traffic, the 318-mile trip should take less than five hours. En route from Chicago, parts of I-90 and I-94 serve as the Indiana Toll Road.

★ INTERLOCHEN CENTER FOR THE ARTS

South of town, the summertime bustle of Traverse City quickly fades into rolling farmland and woodlots. Incongruously tucked within this rural landscape, 14 miles southwest of Traverse City on M-137, the **Interlochen Center for the Arts** (4000 M-137, Interlochen, 231/276-7200, www.interlochen.org) operates a renowned school on a 1,200-acre campus under a tall canopy of pines. For over 85 years, Interlochen has cultivated a passion for the arts, with year-round programs for adults and a yearly summer camp for young artists, during which nearly 2,500 gifted students come to explore music, dance, theater, film, literature, and visual arts. Audiences can also appreciate Interlochen; throughout the year, this acclaimed institute offers hundreds of concerts, readings, dance and theatrical performances, film screenings, and art exhibitions. Its lineup of musicians and entertainers has always been diverse and impressive, ranging from Itzhak Perlman to the Neville Brothers.

INTERLOCHEN STATE PARK

Not far from the school, 187-acre **Interlochen State Park** (M-137, 231/276-9511, annual Recreation Passport required: $12 Michigan residents, $34 nonresidents, $9 day pass available to nonresidents only) fans out between Green and Duck Lakes, preserving one of the area's few remaining stands of virgin white pine. Thanks to the park's location near Traverse City and Interlochen, its attractive campsites (reservations 800/447-2757, www.michigan.gov/dnr, $23-25), clustered around the lakeshores with many nice lake views, are the main draw. The modern campground, with the bulk of the park's 480 campsites, is on Duck Lake. Several dozen rustic sites are across the park on Green Lake. Both fill up in summer, so reserve ahead.

The Leelanau Peninsula

A ragged land of hills, lakes, and scribbled shoreline straggling northward between Lake Michigan and Grand Traverse Bay, the Leelanau Peninsula has long influenced writers and artists; novelist Jim Harrison, among others, makes his home here. Maybe it's the dramatic dichotomy of the place: On its western shore are the grand dunes, rising directly from the lake's surface; inland is a soft and graceful landscape—a muted palette of red barns, white farmhouses, and rose-colored Queen Annes.

Local lore has it that *leelanau* is a Native American word meaning "land of delights," a description that certainly fits this varied peninsula. In reality, the word was a truncated version of its ancient root, as the area's Ottawa people never used the *l* sound. Henry Schoolcraft, an explorer who mapped the Lake Michigan coast in the 1820s, most likely contrived it, intending to formulate an "Indian-sounding" name.

Leelanau County begins just west of Traverse City, and the county line stretches 30 miles straight west to the Sleeping Bear Dunes and Lake Michigan. Everything above that line is the Leelanau, a 28-mile-long peninsula that includes 98 miles of Great Lakes shoreline, 142 inland lakes and ponds, 58 miles of streams, and numerous award-winning wineries. Roads twist along with the contours of the hills and wander in unpredictable directions, revealing the occasional farm stand. As local author Bill Mulligan has noted, "The meandering expanse of water, woods, and sand of Leelanau is a nice counterweight to the exuberance of Traverse City." Take your time and meander.

★ SLEEPING BEAR DUNES NATIONAL LAKESHORE

Glaciers and a millennium of wind and water sculpted the Sleeping Bear Dunes, rimming this corner of Michigan with a crust of sand and gravel. Classic beach dunes line the southern part of the national lakeshore, created by the prevailing west winds carrying sand to low-lying shores.

Claiming center stage are the immense pyramids of sand spiking up from the very edge of Lake Michigan and climbing at a seemingly impossible angle toward the sky. At their highest, the perched dunes once topped out at 600 feet. Today, Sleeping Bear measures closer to 400 feet, still the largest freshwater dune in the world. It sounds cliché, but words really can't describe the Sleeping Bear Dunes. They can be a sunny, friendly playground with squealing children tumbling down the Dune Climb, or lunar and desolate, a bleak desert on a January day. They can be pale and white-hot at noon, then glow in peaches and pinks like white wine at sunset.

The **Sleeping Bear Dunes National Lakeshore** (9922 Front St., Empire, 231/326-4700, www.nps.gov/slbe, visitors center 8am-6pm daily Memorial Day-Columbus Day, 8:30am-4pm daily Columbus Day-Memorial Day, dunes 24 hours daily, $15 cars, $10 motorcycles, $7 individuals, under age 16 free), established in 1977, encompasses nearly 72,000 acres, including 35 miles of Lake Michigan shoreline, North and South Manitou Islands, lakes, rivers, beech and maple forest, waving dune grasses, and those unforgettable mountains of sand. It's truly a magnificent landscape, unlike anything else.

The Leelanau Peninsula

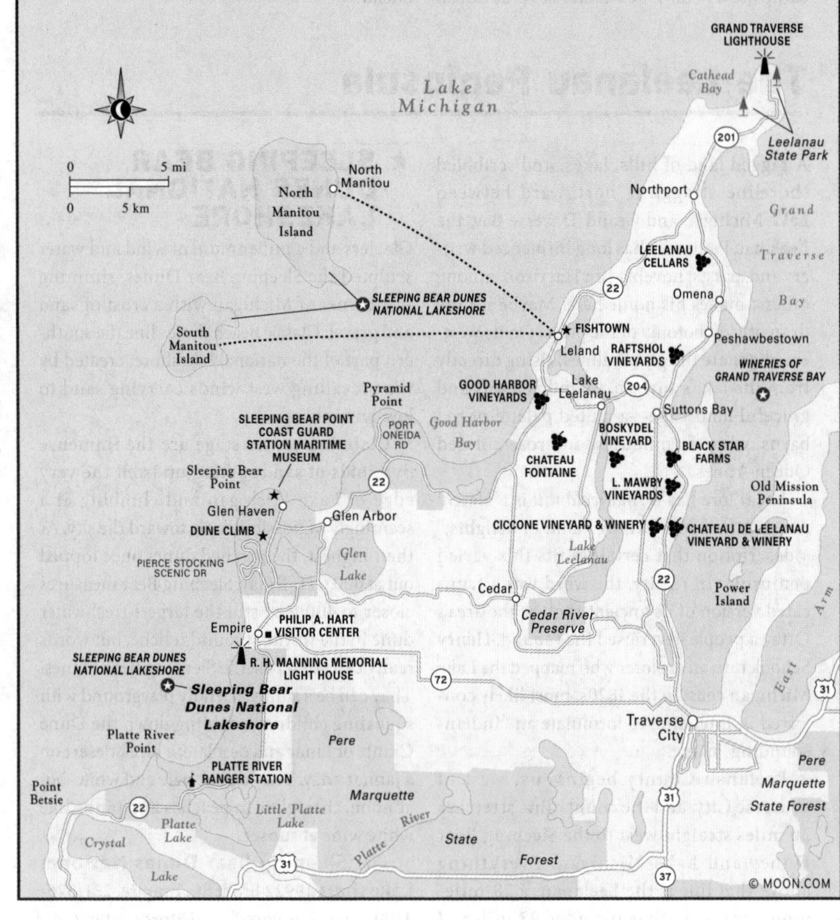

Empire Area

Situated beside Lake Michigan, Empire is home to the state's newest lighthouse, the cylindrical **Robert Manning Memorial Lighthouse,** erected in 1991 to honor a longtime resident. South of Empire, the **Empire Bluff Trail** winds through the forest before entering a clearing for a dramatic vantage point of the big dunes some five miles north. In 0.75 miles, the trail dead-ends at a high bluff overlooking water so clear that schools of big lake trout can often be seen. Farther south, **Platte River Point** provides the perfect setting for viewing the expansive lake, a sandy spot bordered by Lake Michigan and the mouth of the Platte River. Rent an inner tube from **Riverside Canoe Trips** (5042 Scenic Hwy., Honor, 231/325-5622, www.canoemichigan.com, 8am-7pm daily) on M-22 at the Platte River Bridge and enjoy the popular sport of launching in the river and shooting out into the lake.

Legend of the Sleeping Bear

The Sleeping Bear Dunes offer an unmatched view of Lake Michigan.

According to the Ojibwa people that first inhabited the Great Lakes region, a terrible forest fire once raged along the shores of Lake Michigan in what is now Wisconsin. In an effort to flee the conflagration, a mother bear and her two cubs tried to swim across the enormous lake, toward present-day Michigan. When the mother reached the far shore, she climbed to the top of a bluff to await her cubs, who had grown tired and lagged behind. As she waited, the sands collected around her, creating the Sleeping Bear Dunes. The largest dunes became Sleeping Bear Dunes National Lakeshore in 1977. In the legend the cubs sadly drowned, but the Great Spirit took pity on the grieving mother and raised her children from the depths as North and South Manitou Islands, offshore but also part of the protected national lakeshore.

Pierce Stocking Scenic Drive

"I used to have a recurrent nightmare that there was a big highway across the top of the dunes and at the topmost point, a Holiday Inn," writes Kathleen Stocking in *Letters from the Leelanau*. "Now, except for the Holiday Inn, that prescient dream has materialized."

Ironically, the drive is named for Stocking's father, a lumberman who owned much of the land that is now a national park. For those who didn't grow up with the dunes as our backyard, this 7.4-mile paved loop that winds through the woods and atop a stretch of dunes is no doubt less offensive. In any event, the extremely popular route provides easy access to the scenic overlooks of Glen Lake, the dunes, and Lake Michigan.

The drive offers access to the **Cottonwood Trail,** a 1.5-mile sandy self-guided walk that educates visitors about the ecology and diverse plantlife in the dunes. It also leads you to the **Lake Michigan Overlook,** a platform 450 feet above the water with views stretching to Point Betsie, 15 miles south, and 54 miles across to Wisconsin. The National Park Service discourages it, having seen a number of injuries, but visitors often slide their way down the dune at this point, necessitating a steep, exhausting, and time-consuming climb back up.

The nearby **Dune Climb** is a more manageable 130-foot dune on the lee side of the plateau. It's the perfect place to let kids expend their energy or climb for a fine view of shimmering Glen Lake. Hardier souls can continue on the **Dunes Trail,** a challenging 3.5-mile hike that extends from the Dune Climb across several rugged dunes to the sandy shores of Lake Michigan and back.

Glen Haven Area

In sleepy Glen Haven, the National Park Service operates an interesting museum in the old lifesaving station. In summer months, the **Sleeping Bear Point Coast Guard Station Maritime Museum** (9922 Front St., Empire, 231/326-4700, 11am-5pm daily Memorial Day-Labor Day, free) depicts the work of the U.S. Lifesaving Service, which merged with the Revenue Cutter Service in 1915 to form the U.S. Coast Guard. Exhibits include lifesaving boats and the cannon used to shoot lifelines out to the sinking vessels, while video programs illustrate the drill and the rigorous life the crews led. Some 50 ships wrecked along this passage between the mainland and the nearby Manitou Islands, one of the busiest routes on the Great Lakes in the mid-19th century, since it offered a convenient shortcut between Mackinac Island and Chicago. The station originally sat a few miles west at Sleeping Bear Point, but was moved here in 1931 when the ever-expanding dunes threatened to bury it.

East on M-109, **Glen Arbor** occupies a small patch of private real estate completely surrounded by the national lakeshore, Lake Michigan, and Glen Lake. It caters to visitors with mostly tasteful galleries and craft shops, and also has a grocery for replenishing picnic supplies. Cherry lovers shouldn't miss **Cherry Republic** (6026 S. Lake St., 800/206-6949, www.cherryrepublic.com, 9am-9pm daily), which bills itself as "the largest exclusive retailer of cherry products in the United States." You'll find examples of all things cherry-related—cherry baked goods, cherry sodas, chocolate-covered cherries, cherry salsas, and cherry jam.

Near Glen Arbor, the **Pyramid Point** hiking trail is a hilly 2.7-mile loop that leads to the park's northernmost point, with a high lookout over Lake Michigan and Sleeping Bear Bay. To reach the trailhead, take M-22 three miles east of Glen Arbor to Port Oneida Road.

North and South Manitou Islands

Lying about 17 miles off the mainland, the Manitous comprise more than 20,000 acres of once developed land that has largely been reclaimed by nature and is now managed as part of Sleeping Bear Dunes National Lakeshore. South Manitou is the smaller (5,260 acres) and more accessible of the two, serviced by passenger ferry from Leland daily in summer months. The same ferry also stops at North Manitou five times a week in July and August, less frequently in spring and fall. The trip to either island takes about 90 minutes. No cars, bikes, or pets are permitted. For schedule information and reservations, contact **Manitou Island Transit** (Leland, 231/256-9061, https://manitoutransit.com, round-trip $42 adults, $21 under age 13). The islands have potable water at a few locations, but no other services. Hikers should bring all other needed provisions with them.

South Manitou Island was first settled in the 1830s. Islanders made a living by farming and logging, supplying food and fuel to the wood-burning steamers that traveled through the busy Manitou Passage. Isolated from alien pollens, South Manitou also proved the perfect place to produce crops and experiment with hybrid seeds, and was soon highly respected in agricultural circles. A South Manitou rye crop won first prize in an international exposition in 1920; by the 1940s, most of Michigan's bean crop came from South Manitou seed. By the 1960s, though, the island had become mostly a collection of summer cottages, and, a decade later, the National Park Service began buying up the land for the national lakeshore.

Nearby, the 1872 **South Manitou Island Lighthouse** (www.nps.gov/slbe/planyourvisit/smilighthouse.htm) is open on summer afternoons, allowing you to scale the 100-foot tower.

Hikers and backpackers will want to go farther afield. The island has 10 miles of marked hiking trails leading to some interesting sights. If day hikers maintain a steady pace, they'll be able to finish the six-mile round-trip, visit the wreck of the ***Francisco Morazan,*** and still make the afternoon ferry. Like many ships that failed to navigate the tricky Manitou Passage, this Liberian freighter ran aground in 1960. Its battered skeleton lies largely above the water's surface, just a few hundred yards offshore.

Nearby, a side trail winds through a grove of virgin cedars, some more than 500 years old. Deemed too isolated to log, the slow-growing trees are the largest of their kind left in North America, some measuring more than 15 feet around and nearly 90 feet tall. A half mile to the west, there are 300-foot perched dunes, the state's remotest, similar to those on the mainland.

To properly enjoy all the island has to offer, you need to spend more than an afternoon. Camping is permitted only at three rustic campsites, and reservations (231/326-5134, www.nps.gov/slbe) are required.

Like South Manitou, **North Manitou Island** was once a farming and logging community, then a summer colony. Acquired by the National Park Service in 1984, it still contains some parcels of private property. Otherwise, this large island is even less developed than its southern neighbor. Those who come here do so to camp, hike, and explore the abandoned buildings.

North Manitou receives far fewer visitors than South Manitou—until fall hunting season arrives. Nine deer were introduced here in the 1920s in the hopes of developing a herd large enough to hunt, which turned out to be highly successful. By 1981, more than 2,000 deer roamed the island, decimating the vegetation to the point of giving island's forests an "open park-like appearance," according to the National Park Service. Today, it manages the herd by issuing hunting permits.

North Manitou has only one water source and one small rustic campground near the ferry dock; backcountry camping is permitted throughout the island's public property. Backcountry permits (free) are required.

LELAND TO NORTHPORT

The restored **Fishtown** at Leland's harbor is probably one of the most photographed spots in all of Michigan, a collection of 19th-century

climbers at Sleeping Bear Dunes

weathered gray fish shanties lined up on the docks. Whether you find it charming or offensive probably reflects your attitudes about development. For many Leelanau residents, commercialized Leland is a sad commentary on how tourism is erasing a simpler lifestyle.

Leland was a diverse industrial center in the mid-1800s, with two sawmills, a gristmill, an iron smelter, and a flourishing commercial fishing trade. By the early 1900s, eight fisheries were operating here. Where the Carp River flows into Lake Michigan, they built shanties along the docks, which they used to store ice, repair nets, and house equipment. Once common in ports all over the Great Lakes, most of these complexes completely disappeared when commercial fishing declined in the mid-20th century.

In Leland, happily, the shanties remain. **Carlson's Fishery** (205 W. River, 231/256-9801, www.carlsonsfish.com, 10am-4pm Mon.-Thurs., 10am-5pm Fri.-Sun., early Apr.-early Dec.) still operates here, with its sturdy snub-nosed boats tied up to the pier and a shop that sells fresh fillets and smoked trout out of a long deli case. Most of the other shanties now house gift shops and galleries, and the fishing nets dry in the sun solely for the amusement of the summer visitors.

Though it has a touristy side, Leland also has a paradoxically authentic feel. The combination of the two makes the town irresistibly attractive. The Carp River rolls by, where you can gaze down at the steelhead schooling in the waters. And whether or not you care for the shops, appreciate the fact that no one tore down these storied old buildings.

East of Leland is lengthy Lake Leelanau. Popular with anglers, it is also a good spot for paddlers, especially at the **Cedar River Preserve** (Leelanau Conservancy, 231/256-9665, http://leelanauconservancy.org) along its southern shore, part of the Pere Marquette State Forest. Launch a canoe partway up the eastern shore, where Lake Leelanau Road intersects Bingham Road.

North of Leland, handsome **Peterson Park** sits high atop a bluff overlooking Lake Michigan, with picnic tables, a playground, and a great vantage point for the area's renowned sunsets. A steep staircase leads to a rocky beach, a good spot to hunt for Petoskey stones. Take M-201 to Peterson Park Road and turn left. For swimming, **Christmas Cove** offers a perfect arc of sugary sand beach near the tip of the peninsula. To find it, follow M-201 north from Northport; just after it joins

rustic Fishtown building in Leland's harbor

County Road 640, turn left on Kilcherman Road, which leads to Christmas Cove Road.

With a fine horseshoe harbor in the protected waters of Grand Traverse Bay, it's not surprising that **Northport** was one of the first spots settled on the Leelanau. Roman Catholic missionaries established a village there in 1849, bringing with them several area Ottawa families they had successfully converted to Christianity. Within 20 years, Northport was the county seat, overseeing a population of 2,500, and had a thriving commercial fishing industry. At the turn of the 20th century, it built an elaborate resort hotel with room for 250 guests; within five years, the uninsured building burned to the ground. Today, Northport is popular with pleasure boaters, who still appreciate its snug harbor, and shoppers, who cruise its charming downtown, a row of revamped 1860s buildings filled with eclectic antiques and clothing shops.

LEELANAU STATE PARK

Split into two units at the tip of the Leelanau Peninsula, the 1,350-acre **Leelanau State Park** (15310 N. Lighthouse Point Rd., Northport, 231/386-5422 summer, 231/922-5270 winter, annual Recreation Passport required: $12 Michigan residents, $34 nonresidents, $9 day pass available to nonresidents only) is a wonderful surprise. While the northern unit, with its lighthouse and campground, is very popular, most visitors tend to ignore its southern portion—meaning you can often have its lovely beaches and trails to yourself.

In the southern unit, low dunes and more than a mile of sand beach curve along Cathead Bay. It's a one-mile walk from the parking area through maple and beech forest to get to the water, so it seldom draws a crowd. The park's 8.5 miles of walking trails radiate out from the same parking area. The **Mud Lake Tour** circles a wetland area and small lake, a good choice in spring and fall when waterfowl migrate through the area. The **Lake Michigan Trail** leads to the water, but don't skip the short side trail to the overlook—a stairway climbs up a dune for a breathtaking view of North Manitou Island. To reach the southern unit, follow County Road 629 north and turn left just after Woolsey Airport.

Five miles north, the **Grand Traverse Lighthouse** (15500 N. Lighthouse Point Rd., Northport, 231/386-7195, www.grandtraverselighthouse.com, 10am-5pm daily June-Aug., noon-4pm daily May and Sept.-Oct., $5 adults, $2 children) presides over the park's northern unit at the peninsula's tip. Built in 1858, the pretty white brick tower looks woefully small for the huge expanse of water that surrounds it, which prompted the Coast Guard to decommission it in 1972 and replace it with a more pedestrian—but taller—steel tower down on the beach. Today, visitors can stroll through the on-site museum or climb the tower when the lighthouse is open.

SUTTONS BAY

Once a town largely inhabited by immigrant laborers from the fruit orchards, Suttons Bay has gotten fancier and wealthier along with the rest of the Leelanau Peninsula. With mechanization and the corresponding reduced need for labor, the desirable real estate—on Grand Traverse Bay, just 12 miles from Traverse City—was just too good to leave alone. These days, Suttons Bay has almost become a suburb of Traverse City. Residents have worked hard to maintain the community's own personality, though, with colorfully painted storefronts and old-fashioned red telephone booths along St. Joseph's Avenue (M-22). Suttons Bay's downtown boasts a restored movie theater, all manner of galleries and boutiques, and some of the best restaurants in the Grand Traverse region.

★ WINERIES

As on the Old Mission Peninsula, the surrounding waters of Lake Michigan have a moderating effect on the Leelanau Peninsula, providing a surprisingly conducive climate for growing cherries, apples, peaches, and wine grapes. Slow-changing lake temperatures offer consistently moderate temperatures during the growing season; come winter, they insulate the delicate trees and vines from killing deep freezes.

Michigan leads the nation in cherry production, and the Leelanau accounts for a full quarter of that crop. And while Michigan's grape harvest isn't yet ready to challenge California's, a few of its wines have been. Leelanau and Old Mission Peninsula wineries regularly produce award-winning vintages, especially the chardonnays and rieslings that do particularly well in this climate. Serious vintners let their product speak for itself to win over new converts every year. Some 25 wineries now make their home on the Leelanau Peninsula, and most offer both tours and tastings. For the latest information about this winemaking region, consult the **Leelanau Peninsula Vintner's Association** (www.lpwines.com).

Leelanau Cellars

Leelanau Cellars (7161 N. West Bay Shore Dr., Omena, 231/386-5201, www.leelanaucellars.com, 10am-6pm Mon.-Wed., 10am-8pm Thurs.-Sat, noon-6pm Sun.) is the largest winery on the peninsula, producing 65,000 gallons of vinifera, hybrid, and fruit wines each year. Highest honors go to its Tall Ship chardonnay.

L. Mawby Vineyards

L. Mawby Vineyards (4519 S. Elm Valley Rd., Suttons Bay, 231/271-3522, www.lmawby.com, noon-6pm Mon.-Sat., noon-5pm Sun. May-Oct., noon-5pm Wed.-Sun. Nov.-Apr.) is one of the region's smallest wineries—with a big reputation, especially for its sparkling wines and oak-barrel fermented dry whites. Larry Mawby produces about 3,000 cases a year, with a goal to "keep things small enough to do what I want to do—make great wine with minimal intervention." He brings a creative flair to the winemaking business, evidenced in the artful wine labels designed by his wife, artist Peggy Core. From Suttons Bay, follow County Road 633 south to Elm Valley Road.

Good Harbor Vineyards

Some consider Bruce Simpson's dry white chardonnay and pinot gris the finest wines to come out of the Traverse Bay region. An informative self-guided tour at **Good Harbor Vineyards** (34 S. Manitou Trail, 231/256-7165, www.goodharbor.com, 11am-6pm Mon.-Sat., noon-5pm Sun. June-Oct., 11am-5pm Mon.-Sat., noon-5pm Sun. May and Nov., noon-5pm Fri.-Sat. Dec.-Apr.), three miles south of Leland on M-22 in Lake Leelanau, explains the sophisticated process.

Chateau Fontaine Vineyards & Winery

Stop by **Chateau Fontaine Vineyards & Winery** (2290 S. French Rd., Lake Leelanau, 231/256-0000, www.chateaufontaine.com, noon-5pm Mon.-Fri., 11am-6pm Sat. May-Nov.), a onetime potato farm and cow pasture now transformed into 30 acres of grapevines. They produce chardonnay, pinot gris, and Woodland White, among others.

Black Star Farms

In Suttons Bay, you'll find **Black Star Farms** (10844 E. Revold Rd., 231/944-1270, www.blackstarfarms.com, 10am-6pm Mon.-Thurs., 10am-8pm Fri.-Sat., noon-5pm Sun. May-Nov.), billed as "an agricultural destination." This fascinating winery, distillery, creamery, and farmers market also offers a welcoming tasting room and a luxurious bed-and-breakfast.

More Wineries

Take special note of several other locales in Suttons Bay, including **Raftshol Vineyards** (1865 N. West Bay Shore Dr., 231/271-5650, https://raftshol.com, 11am-6pm daily May-Dec., noon-5pm daily Jan.-Apr.), a former dairy enterprise and cherry orchard that now produces over 1,000 cases of Bordeaux varietal red wines annually.

Owned by a cardiologist with a special interest in Michigan's agriculture, **Chateau de Leelanau Vineyard & Winery** (5048 S. West Bay Shore Dr., 231/271-8888, www.chateaudeleelanau.com, noon-5pm Mon., by appointment, Tues.-Thurs., 11am-6pm Sat.-Sun.) presents a tasting room and retail store not far from Grand Traverse Bay.

Established in 1996, the **Ciccone Vineyard & Winery** (10343 Hilltop Rd., 231/271-5553, www.cicconevineyard.com, 11am-6pm daily May-Nov., noon-5pm daily Dec.-Apr.) is a Tuscan-inspired winery and tasting room. For $5 you can purchase a Ciccone wineglass and up to five tastings of the vintner's choice.

DIVING

The waters around North Manitou Island, South Manitou Island, and the Sleeping Bear Dunes are rife with historic dock ruins and shipwrecks, making the **Manitou Passage Underwater Preserve** a fascinating place for scuba divers. Besides the popular *Francisco Morazan* wreck near the south end of South Manitou Island, divers can enjoy exploring wrecks including the *Walter L. Frost,* a wooden steamer that ran aground in 1905, only to be further wrecked in 1960 when the *Morazan* landed on top of it. For more information, contact the **Michigan Underwater Preserve Council** (800/970-8717, www.michiganpreserves.org).

EVENTS

The Leelanau Peninsula is home to a myriad of art festivals, culinary events, and seasonal gatherings. One curious event occurs in September the weekend after Labor Day, the annual **Harvest Stompede Vineyard Run & Walk,** which features a race through Leelanau's vineyards as well as a tour of area wineries. During the weekend, visitors are able to sample wines, gourmet pastas, and other delicacies. For more information, consult the **Leelanau Peninsula Vintner's Association** (www.lpwines.com).

FOOD AND ACCOMMODATIONS

In Leland, a couple of restaurants overlook the river and Fishtown, including ★ **The Cove** (111 River St., 231/256-9834, www.thecoveleland.com, 11am-9pm daily, $9-34), featuring seafood chowder, fish stew, and fresh fish specials. A block or two farther upstream, across M-22, the main street, **The Bluebird Restaurant & Bar** (102 River St., 231/256-9081, http://bluebirdleland.com, 11:30am-1am Mon.-Sat., 10am-11:30pm Sun., closed Mon. fall and winter, $12-33) is a well-known dinner spot, with reasonably priced seafood and meat dishes, homemade soups, and an excellent wine list. Meanwhile, Lake Leelanau is home to **Dick's Pour House** (103 W. Philip St., 231/256-9912, www.dickspourhouse.com, noon-10pm Sun., 11:30am-10pm Mon.-Thurs., 11:30am-11pm Fri.-Sat. summer, 11:30am-8pm Sun.-Thurs., 11:30am-9pm Fri.-Sat. winter, $8-26), where you can sample pizza, sandwiches, soups, pies, and a Friday fish fry.

If your budget won't allow a stay at ★ **Black Star Farms** (10844 E. Revold Rd., Suttons Bay, 231/944-1271, www.blackstarfarms.com, $220-425 d)—a winery, creamery, market, and luxurious B&B—you'll be happy to know that the region also accommodates campers. The rustic campground at **Leelanau State Park** (15310 N. Lighthouse Point Rd., Northport, 231/386-5422 summer, 231/922-5270 winter, annual Recreation Passport required: $12 Michigan residents, $34 nonresidents, $9 day pass available to nonresidents only) has 52 rustic sites ($13), with several right along the water and several more with water views. Though the campground is extremely popular in summer, most sites offer some seclusion.

INFORMATION AND SERVICES

For more information about the Leelanau Peninsula, contact the **Traverse City Convention & Visitors Bureau** (101 W. Grandview Pkwy., 231/947-1120, www.visittraversecity.com, 8am-9pm Mon.-Fri.,

9am-5pm Sat., noon-6pm Sun.). You can also consult the **Leelanau Peninsula Chamber of Commerce** (10781 E. Cherry Bend Rd. Leelanau Studios, Studio 1, Traverse City, 231/252-2880, www.leelanauchamber.com), **Leelanau Communications** (113 N. Main, Leland, 231/409-0396, www.leelanau.com), **Leland Michigan Chamber of Commerce** (231/866-1133, www.lelandmi.com), and **Suttons Bay Area Chamber of Commerce** (231/271-5077, www.suttonsbayarea.com).

If you require other services while traveling across the Leelanau Peninsula, nearby Traverse City offers everything you might need, from groceries to hospitals.

GETTING THERE AND AROUND

The nearest scheduled flights are at **Cherry Capital Airport** (TVC, 727 Fly Don't Dr., Traverse City, 231/947-2250, www.tvcairport.com), and **Greyhound** (231/946-5180 or 800/231-2222, www.greyhound.com) and **Indian Trails** (800/292-3831, www.indiantrails.com) buses stop at the **Traverse City Bus Station** (115 Hall St.). From Traverse City, you can rent a vehicle and head west on M-72 to Empire and Sleeping Bear Dunes National Lakeshore; the 24-mile trip usually takes about 30 minutes. From Traverse City, you can also explore the wineries of the Leelanau Peninsula by heading north on M-22, which traces the perimeter of the peninsula, passing through towns like Suttons Bay, Northport, Leland, Glen Arbor, and Empire. It takes about 42 minutes to cover the 29 miles between Traverse City and Northport via M-22. You can also utilize the **Bay Area Transportation Authority** (BATA, 231/941-2324 or 231/778-1025, www.bata.net, one-way $1.50-3 adults, $0.75-1.50 over age 59, students, active military, and disabled) to navigate the peninsula.

Charlevoix and Vicinity

Woodland people were likely the first to arrive in present-day Charlevoix (SHAR-luh-voy), settling along the Lake Michigan shores some 4,000 years ago, but a French missionary, Pierre François-Xavier de Charlevoix, gave the town its name when he traveled through the region in the early 1700s, surreptitiously searching for the fabled Northwest Passage while avoiding the British.

Nestled between Grand Traverse Bay and Little Traverse Bay, Charlevoix has natural assets that make it an ideal vacation spot. Along with the inherent appeal of Lake Michigan, Charlevoix also abuts its lovely namesake lake, a clear, wishbone-shaped estuary that draws anglers and boaters. This is lake country, river country, trout-fishing country, and the boyhood summer home of Ernest Hemingway, whose family spent the warm-weather months on nearby Walloon Lake. Just a few miles from the crowds that annually descend on Charlevoix, much of Charlevoix County maintains a much slower pace, the kind of atmosphere that inspires drifting downstream in a canoe, casting a line from a quiet bank, or pedaling the two-lane highways that twist through the region.

Beaver Island, accessible by ferry or plane from Charlevoix, is a place to find even greater solitude. Originally settled by the Irish, it became a Mormon stronghold in the 1840s, ruled by a self-proclaimed king who was eventually assassinated by two of his followers. Things are considerably calmer on the island today, a sandy, wooded retreat with an Irish flavor and a decidedly somnolent air. Like much of the region, it's just the place to spark creativity, as it did for Hemingway.

SIGHTS

Downtown

"Charlevoix the Beautiful," they call this

nautical town of 3,000, wedged on an isthmus between Lake Michigan and Round Lake, which opens to the much larger Lake Charlevoix. With flowers flanking Bridge Street (U.S. 31), a walkway along the Pine River linking the lakes, gleaming yachts with clanging halyards, screeching gulls, and nautically themed shops, Charlevoix is lovely.

Since downtown Charlevoix tends to be crowded on most summer days, it's best to park your car and walk. This is a town meant for strolling, and nearly all its sights can best be enjoyed on foot.

Bridge Street is Charlevoix's main drag, lined with restaurants, galleries, gift shops, and 50,000 petunias planted by volunteers each spring and watered by volunteers with a donated tank truck. For a free directory, stop by **Visit Charlevoix** (109 Mason St., 231/547-2101 or 800/367-8557, www.visitcharlevoix.com).

Toward the north end of the shopping district, a drawbridge rises on the half hour to allow tall-masted boats to transit the **Pine River Channel** from Lake Michigan to Round Lake, essentially a yacht basin that connects to much larger Lake Charlevoix. A lovely walkway lit with Victorian-style lamps lines both sides of the channel between Bridge Street and Lake Michigan. Follow the north side to reach the long pier that extends out into Lake Michigan. Michigan Avenue parallels the lakeshore, where stately old homes preside over the waterfront.

Follow the south side of the walkway to the **South Pierhead Lighthouse** and **Lake Michigan Beach,** with fine white sand, changing rooms, a playground, and a picnic area. The woods behind the beach have some short walking trails. Cross the street that parallels the beach, Park Avenue, to check out the peculiar elfin **architecture of Earl Young** scattered throughout this pleasant neighborhood. Young, a local real estate agent and self-taught home designer, constructed or remodeled two dozen homes in the 1930s and '40s, many in the triangular block bounded by Park Avenue, Clinton Street, and Grant Street. Young used natural materials like enormous lake boulders to build his odd mushroom-shaped homes, topping them with curved cedar-shake roofs. They're intermingled amid the Victorians, giving the neighborhood an almost surreal look.

Young was also selected to design the Weathervane Terrace Inn and Stafford's Weathervane Restaurant along the channel. Rock walls and massive fireplaces characterize

the Thatch House, one of Earl Young's architectural oddities

the designs; the restaurant's fireplace features a nine-ton keystone shaped like the state of Michigan. You can get a map directing you to Young-designed homes from **Visit Charlevoix** (109 Mason St., 231/547-2101 or 800/367-8557, www.visitcharlevoix.com).

On the east side of Bridge Street, **East Park** fronts the bustling marina and city docks on Round Lake, which is a fun spot to grab a sandwich and watch the boats. Nearby is **John Cross Fisheries** (209 Belvedere Ave., 231/547-2532, 9am-5pm Mon.-Sat., 9am-4pm Sun.), one of the last commercial fisheries in the area. It sells fresh walleye, perch, lake trout, and whitefish, which it also supplies to local restaurants. You can also buy smoked whitefish or trout by the chunk.

For a different sort of sightseeing experience, head east from town along M-66 and make a stop at **Castle Farms** (5052 M-66, 231/237-0884, www.castlefarms.com, 10am-6pm Sun.-Fri., 10am-2pm Sat., May-June and Sept.-Oct., 9am-6pm Sun.-Thurs., 9am-4pm Fri., 9am-2pm Sat., July-Aug., 10am-4pm Mon.-Sat. Nov.-Apr, self-guided tours $15 adults, $14 seniors 65 and over, $13 military with ID, $3 children ages 3-12). The structure certainly lives up to its name. In 1917 Chicago businessman Albert Loeb purchased 1800 acres just west of Charlevoix. Soon after construction began on a duplicate structure to serve as the summer residence for Loeb and his family. He also began a working dairy farm on-site which operated until 1927. Subsequently abandoned, the property was revived beginning in the early 1960s. Different portions of the building were gradually restored. Today, beautiful Castle Farms functions as a popular wedding destination, but also as a tourist site. Visitors are welcome to take a self-guided tour, visit the on-site winery, or just contemplate the beauty of the impeccably maintained grounds, which include a butterfly garden, the body and spirit garden and labyrinth, and the king's grand courtyard.

Northern Charlevoix

Around the southern end of Round Lake, the grounds of the century-old **Belvedere Club** spread across a high hill, overlooking both Round Lake and Lake Charlevoix. Founded by Baptists from Kalamazoo in the 1870s, the Belvedere Club was planned as a summer resort community, mirroring the Methodists' successful Bay View resort near Petoskey. Wealthy vacationers built summer homes in the opulent fashion of the day, with verandas, dormers, and gabled roofs. Today, many of the homes are occupied in summer by the grandchildren and great-grandchildren of the original owners. Though the streets through still-private Belvedere are closed in July and August, you can get a glimpse of the neighborhood from Ferry Avenue along Lake Charlevoix.

Inspired by the Belvedere Club, the First Congregational Church of Chicago formed a similar community on the north side of the Pine River Channel. As with the Belvedere, the **Chicago Club** is closed to the public, although its elaborate Victorians can be seen from East Dixon Avenue. The road also leads to **Depot Beach,** a popular swimming beach, playground, and picnic area on Lake Charlevoix.

North of the city pier is Mt. McSauba Recreation Area, a municipal ski facility. At its northern end, Mt. McSauba shares a boundary with the **North Point Nature Preserve** (Mt. McSauba Rd. and Pleasant St., 231/347-0991, www.landtrust.org). The 27-acre preserve was purchased with funds raised by the people of Charlevoix, with help from the Michigan Natural Resources Trust Fund. Today it offers several steep nature trails through hardwood forest and a pretty stretch of fairly secluded sand, home to threatened plant species like Pitcher's thistle. To reach the preserve, take U.S. 31 north to Mercer Road, turn left onto Mt. McSauba Road, and turn right before the dirt road. The preserve is on the left. For more information, contact the **Little Traverse Conservancy** (3264 Powell Rd., Harbor Springs, 231/347-0991, www.landtrust.org).

RECREATION

Hiking and Biking

The **Little Traverse Wheelway** extends for approximately 29 miles from Charlevoix to Harbor Springs. The trail is ideal for hiking, jogging, bicycling, and inline skating. Horses and snowmobiles are not permitted. The trail begins at the intersection of Division and Mt. McSauba Roads on the north side of Charlevoix.

Boating

Situated between Lake Michigan and several other inland lakes, Charlevoix is truly a boater's paradise, with three principal centers for boating: the Jordan River, Lake Charlevoix, and, of course, Lake Michigan, which has several access sites along the coast. Boaters and canoeists can access the Jordan River in East Jordan at Old State Road, Webster's Bridge, and Roger's Bridge. Lake Charlevoix presents lovely swimming beaches and several access points for boaters and anglers. Pleasure cruisers can view several sights along the Lake Charlevoix shoreline, from some of the area's most beautiful homes to an old shipwreck at Oyster Bay.

Skiing

About half of a mile north of the city pier lies the **Mt. McSauba Recreation Area** (231/547-3267, www.cityofcharlevoix.org/331/Mt-McSauba, 5pm-9pm Mon., Thurs.-Fri., 11am-4pm Sat., noon-4pm Sun., $15 Mon.-Fri., $18 Sat.-Sun.), one of the state's few municipal ski facilities. Overlooking Lake Michigan, it lures downhill and cross-country skiers. Other popular wintertime activities here include snowboarding, snowshoeing, sledding, and ice-skating. The groomed 1.2-mile cross-country trail is lit at night.

CHARLEVOIX VENETIAN FESTIVAL

Like several other communities along the Lake Michigan coast, Charlevoix presents its own **Venetian Festival** (231/547-3872, www.venetianfestival.com, free) in summer. Begun in 1930 as a simple candlelight boat parade, Charlevoix's version has grown to be the highlight of the season. Usually held during the third week of July, the seven-day event offers daily activities such as concerts and athletic competitions within the town's waterfront parks, in Round Lake Harbor, and on Lake Charlevoix, attracting tens of thousands of visitors. The event culminates in a beautiful Venetian Boat Parade on Round Lake, followed by a spectacular fireworks display.

SHOPPING

Charlevoix's quaint downtown district offers its share of equally quaint shops. For unique children's clothing, check out **Ga Ga For Kids** (323 Bridge St., 231/547-1600, www.gagaforkids.com, 10am-5:30pm Mon.-Sat., 11am-4pm Sun.). Exuding a "shop around the corner" feeling, the **Round Lake Bookstore** (216 Bridge St., 231/547-2699, 10am-5:30pm Mon.-Sat., 10am-4pm Sun.) offers a great sampling of works by regional and national authors.

FOOD

The ★ **Stafford's Weathervane Restaurant** (106 Pine River Ln., 231/547-4311, www.staffords.com, 11am-10pm daily, $13-35) is one of Charlevoix's best restaurants in terms of both food and location. Affiliated with the Stafford restaurants of Petoskey, it specializes in planked whitefish and steaks and overlooks the Pine River Channel. Outside seating is available for lunch and dinner. **Terry's** (101 Antrim St., 231/547-2799, www.terrysofcharlevoix.com, 5pm-close daily, $23-42) has a strong seafood emphasis, and is especially noted for its fresh walleye and whitefish.

ACCOMMODATIONS

Due to Charlevoix's popularity, especially during the summer months, it's essential to make advance room reservations. Charlevoix has a great variety of lodging possibilities, from basic motels on U.S. 31 to upscale condos along the waterfront.

The **Edgewater Inn** (100 Michigan Ave., 231/547-6044, www.edgewater-charlevoix.com, $89-459 d) has suites on Round Lake and amenities like an indoor-outdoor pool and full kitchen facilities. The ★ **Weathervane Terrace Inn & Suites** (111 Pine River Ln., 231/547-9955, www.weathervane-chx.com, $215-399 d) is directly on the Pine River channel, offering an outdoor pool and hot tub as well as views of Lake Michigan and Round Lake. The inn is the only AAA Diamond hotel in Charlevoix. The **Charlevoix Inn & Suites** (800 Petoskey Ave., 231/547-0300, www.charlevoixinnandsuites.com, $159-229 d) offers less expensive accommodations, with an indoor pool and proximity to Lake Charlevoix beaches.

INFORMATION AND SERVICES

For more information about the area, contact the **Charlevoix Area Chamber of Commerce** (109 Mason St., 231/547-2101, www.charlevoix.org, 9am-5pm Mon.-Fri.), **Visit Charlevoix** (109 Mason St., 231/547-2101 or 800/367-8557, www.visitcharlevoix.com), or **Petoskey Area Visitors Bureau** (401 E. Mitchell St., 231/348-2755 or 800/845-2828, www.petoskeyarea.com, 8am-4pm Mon.-Fri.). For local news and events, consult the ***Charlevoix Courier*** (www.petoskeynews.com/charlevoix).

Charlevoix may be a small town, but it has pharmacies, banks, and other essential services. For medical services, go to the **Munson Healthcare Charlevoix Hospital** (14700 Lakeshore Dr., 231/547-4024, www.munsonhealthcare.org).

GETTING THERE AND AROUND

It's possible to fly into **Cherry Capital Airport** (TVC, 727 Fly Don't Dr., Traverse City, 231/947-2250, www.tvcairport.com) or **Pellston Regional Airport** (PLN, 1395 U.S. 31, Pellston, 231/539-8441 or 231/539-8442, www.pellstonairport.com) and rent a vehicle. From the Traverse City airport, take County Road 620, 3 Mile Road, and U.S. 31 to Charlevoix; in light traffic, the 48-mile trip usually takes about 55 minutes. From the Pellston airport, take U.S. 31 south along the coast to Charlevoix; in light traffic, the 36-mile trip should take about 47 minutes.

Both **Greyhound** (800/231-2222, www.greyhound.com) and **Indian Trails** (800/292-3831, www.indiantrails.com) buses stop at the **Beaver Island Boat Company** (103 Bridge Park Dr., 231/547-2311 or 888/446-4095, www.bibco.com) in downtown Charlevoix. With several marinas in the area, it's also possible to arrive in Charlevoix by boat.

A car is the ideal way to explore the surrounding towns and lakes. From Sault Ste. Marie, take I-75, cross the Mackinac Bridge, and take U.S. 31 to Charlevoix, a 110-mile trip that normally takes about 2 hours. From Detroit, follow I-375, I-75, M-32, M-66, and U.S. 31; in light traffic, the 274-mile trip will require about 4.25 hours. Once you reach Charlevoix, you can easily get around town by car or by bike, or on foot.

FISHERMAN'S ISLAND STATE PARK

Five miles south of Charlevoix off U.S. 31, **Fisherman's Island State Park** (16480 Bells Bay Rd., 231/547-6641, annual Recreation Passport required: $12 Michigan residents, $34 nonresidents, $9 day pass available to nonresidents only) is a 10-acre offshore island; most visitors come to enjoy its five miles of lakeshore and wooded dunes. With long stretches of soft sand and exceptionally clear water, it's a particularly good spot to hunt for Petoskey stones.

There's evidence that Woodland people inhabited Fisherman's Island more than 1,000 years ago. Today, the small island is inhabited only by fauna. The state established the park on the island and nearby shoreline in 1978. Wading or swimming across is not recommended, since a strong current often rushes between the island and mainland.

The park is nearly divided in two by a parcel of private property in the middle. The northern portion is the more popular of the two state park sections, with five miles of hiking trails, an attractive day-use area, and 81 rustic campsites (reservations 800/447-2757, www.michigan.gov/dnr, $13). Most are private sites in the woods near the water. Reserve early, and you may get one of the dozen or so sites right on the beach.

To reach the day-use area, hike the marked trail along the dune ridge, or drive south on the park road past the campgrounds. It has grills, picnic tables, outhouses, and a trail leading across bubbling Inwood Creek to the beach. On a clear day, you can see the tip of the Leelanau Peninsula from this fine stretch of beach, and you'll often be treated to a spectacular sunset. For real solitude, access the southern end of the park from the town of Norwood, 11 miles south on U.S. 31. Follow signs to Norwood Township Park on the shoreline, then trace the double-track into the state park. (Driving is not recommended after a rainfall.) You're likely to have the beach and old truck trails all to yourself.

LAKE CHARLEVOIX

Horton Bay

Several authors and artists have roots in northern Michigan, but none more celebrated than Ernest Hemingway. He spent his childhood summers at the family cottage on nearby Walloon Lake, fished the waters of Lake Charlevoix, hunted on the point at Horton Bay, and once escaped a game warden by fleeing across the lake's north arm to the point between the arms, now known as Hemingway Point.

The tiny town of Horton Bay, on Boyne City Road about 10 miles east of Charlevoix, played a special role in Hemingway's life. He spent many a summer afternoon on the front steps of the classic false-front white-clapboard general store, which he describes in his short story "Up in Michigan." For his Nick Adams short stories, he also drew on many of the surrounding places. Later, he married his first wife, Hadley Richardson, at Horton Bay's Congregational Church.

Today, the **Horton Bay General Store** (5115 Boyne City Rd., 231/582-7827, www.hortonbaygeneralstore.com, 8am-2pm Wed.-Sun., tapas 6pm-9pm Fri.-Sat., $9-18) is preserved more as a shrine to Hemingway than a store and eatery—light on foodstuffs but heavy on Hemingway nostalgia. Built in 1876, the cavernous building is filled with Hemingway photos, novels, and even a copy of his 1922 marriage certificate. Over time the store has continued to evolve. Currently there's a bed-and-breakfast upstairs and a tavern in the rear of the store. Lunch is served daily at the counter, which is complemented by a traditional soda fountain. But it's the charming old building itself that draws you in. Steeped in literary history, its inviting front porch is still a great place to while away a summer afternoon.

Boyne City

At the foot of Lake Charlevoix, pleasant and relaxing Boyne City was once a loud industrial town. In the 19th century, Boyne City thrived as a regional logging center, with 90 miles of railroad track linking the town to the surrounding logging camps and feeding its hungry sawmills. Tanneries also became big business at the turn of the 20th century, using bark from the hemlock tree to tan leather. One Boyne City tannery produced six million pounds of shoe leather annually.

Boyne City has done a fine job preserving some of its historic buildings, with a main street that looks like it could be in the Wild West. The best example is the **Wolverine-Dilworth Inn** (300 Water St. 231/582-7388), a 1911 landmark and former hotel boasting a spacious veranda, a terrazzo tile lobby with a fireplace, and a saloon-style dining room.

Boyne Mountain

Six miles southeast of Boyne City in Boyne Falls, Everett Kircher carved out his own piece of history at **Boyne Mountain** (1 Boyne Mountain Rd., Boyne Falls, 231/549-6000 or 800/462-6963, www.boyne.com). A Studebaker dealer from the Detroit area,

Kircher figured out that Detroit's booming auto industry would create considerable wealth for a number of Michigan residents, and many would be looking for a place to vacation. He obtained some farmland near Boyne Falls and proceeded to develop the area's first downhill ski resort. Boyne Mountain opened in 1947.

Over the years, the visionary Kircher became known for "firsts"—the Midwest's first chairlift in 1948, the nation's first freestyle skiing exhibition in 1961, the world's first quad chairlift in 1967, the state's first high-speed quad in 1990, and the nation's first six-person chair in 1992. Kircher was the first to perfect artificial snowmaking, and Boyne's patented snow guns are used at resorts all over the world. Olympic ski planners still contact Boyne for snowmaking consultation.

Even in his 80s, Everett Kircher would come to Boyne headquarters in Boyne Falls nearly every day, overseeing a privately held ski and golf enterprise that seems to grow exponentially every year. In the tightly consolidated ski industry, Boyne is a player: It owns three impressive ski resorts in Michigan. The company also caters to golfers during the warm-weather months, with its spectacular Bay Harbor development near Petoskey.

By those standards, Boyne Mountain seems almost quaint, but is nonetheless an extremely popular resort in summer and winter. The ski area offers over 40 runs, including the Disciples Ridge area, which features some of the steepest pitches in the state. The property also has over 20 miles of groomed and tracked trails for cross-country skiing, which double as mountain biking trails. Each summer two 18-hole golf courses help fill Boyne Mountain's 600-plus hotel rooms.

Jordan River

The Jordan River, which empties into Lake Charlevoix's south arm, was a source of Ernest Hemingway's inspiration. A visit today will engender the same sense of peace and serenity that once moved the famous author. Look for the small wooden canoe signs that signify access points, like the one along Alba Road near the Charlevoix-Antrim county line. Here, the Jordan rolls silently northward, resembling the pale brown of institutional coffee, framed by weeping willows and grassy banks. Anglers are loath to advertise it, but the Jordan is regarded as one of the finest trout streams in the state.

The Jordan River valley cuts a wide swath through the landscape south of Lake Charlevoix, and nowhere is the view more dramatic than from **Dead Man's Hill,** off U.S. 131 south of Boyne Falls. Two miles south of M-32 West, watch for Dead Man's Hill Road; turn west and travel 1.5 miles or so to the end. Here, the flat country lane suddenly falls away to reveal a marvelous valley more than 1,000 feet below: The Jordan straggles through a woodland of pines interspersed with beech and maple, reaching out across the lowlands like spider veins.

The morbid name is in reference to Stanley Graczyk, a 21-year-old logger who, in 1910, mistakenly drove his team of horses up the hill and right over the edge. Dead Man's Hill is also the trailhead for the **Jordan River Pathway,** which loops 18 miles through the valley floor. There's a marked 3-mile loop as well. Maps are available at the trailhead.

Ironton Ferry

Up M-66, the tiny **Ironton Ferry** (9800 Ferry Rd., East Jordan, 231/547-7244, 6:30am-10:50pm daily, $3 vehicles, $0.50 pedestrians) allows passengers to transit from Ironton across the narrows of Lake Charlevoix's south arm to Hemingway Point—a distance of about 100 yards. The ferry made the "Ripley's Believe It or Not" newspaper feature, noting that its captain traveled more than 15,000 miles without ever being more than 1,000 feet from home. It is efficient: The *Charlevoix* takes just two minutes to follow its cable to the far shore, and just a little over four minutes to unload, reload, and be back again—but saves a 15-mile trip around the south arm of the lake. People have found it to be a worthwhile service since 1876.

ELLSWORTH AND VICINITY

Eleven miles south of Charlevoix on County Road 65, Ellsworth wouldn't appear on the map but for very notable exceptions: The Rowe Inn Restaurant and Tapawingo. These two restaurants have drawn rave reviews in national publications like *Gourmet* and *Wine Spectator*. Unfortunately, a poor economic climate forced Tapawingo to close its doors in 2009, but **The Rowe Inn** (6303 E. Jordan Rd., 231/588-7351 or 866/432-5873, www.roweinn.com, 5pm-close Mon.-Sat., noon-5pm Sun. $20-41) remains. With a rather rustic decor and one-of-a-kind entrées like Roasted Maple Leaf Farms Duck Breast, The Rowe has attracted quite a following. Its distinctive menu—thick with rich local ingredients like duck, trout, morels, and fresh berries—and the largest and most outstanding wine cellar in Michigan have earned it a spot among the nation's top restaurants.

Shanty Creek

If you're looking for a year-round destination that accommodates a yen for golfing, hiking, biking, winter sports, and much more, consider visiting **Shanty Creek Resorts** (1 Shanty Creek Rd., Bellaire, 866/695-5010, www.shantycreek.com), a half hour's drive south of Charlevoix. Separated into three villages—Cedar River, Schuss, and Summit—this enormous 4,500-acre swath of land features several dining, lodging, and spa options, three award-winning golf courses, numerous downhill skiing runs, and a fantastic trail network for cross-country skiers and mountain bikers.

The main draw here is **golf** (Apr.-Oct., $25-39 pp). Summit Village, the newly renovated hotel and conference center, has two favored courses: The Legend, designed by Arnold Palmer and named the best course in the Midwest by readers of *Golf Magazine*, and the more wide-open Summit Golf Course, the resort's original. In addition, Summit Village boasts heated indoor and outdoor pools, a spa and fitness center, and a **downhill ski area** with a dozen slopes.

Five minutes away, Schuss Mountain offers more advanced skiing, with 37 runs, three terrain parks, and seven lifts. Its Bavarian-style base area is smaller, with a scattering of villas and condos. This village also has its share of other diversions, including the challenging Schuss Mountain Golf Course, set amid abundant wetlands and rolling hills.

The newest resort, Cedar River Village, houses 14 condos, over 70 luxurious suites, two restaurants, and Cedar River Golf Course, situated amid verdant hills and peaceful waters. Between the three resorts, over 13 miles of groomed and tracked **cross-country trails** wind through hilly terrain and hardwood forest. In summer, many of those same trails become prime **mountain biking routes.** The network includes beginner to expert trails, some made even more difficult by the area's sandy terrain.

BEAVER ISLAND

Traveling to Beaver Island is slow, rather expensive, and there isn't much to do when you get there. Life here ticks along at a rather sleepy, predictable pace: The bank opens every Tuesday 9am-1pm. The ferry brings the mail. When Island Airways arrives from Charlevoix, people departing pretty much know those arriving. Though it ranks as the largest island in Michigan—13 miles long and 6 miles wide—you won't find any towns outside the port of St. James, only simple cottages and 100 miles of sandy roads.

On the other hand, if the inherent isolation and somnolent pace appeal to you, Beaver Island might merit a visit. Stranded 18 miles from the nearest Lower Peninsula shoreline, Beaver Island is the remotest inhabited island in the Great Lakes, offering what may be a quintessential glimpse of island life: unhurried, unbothered, unaffected by whim and fashion. You make your own entertainment here, and it can be delightful. Bike a quiet road to an even quieter beach. Explore the

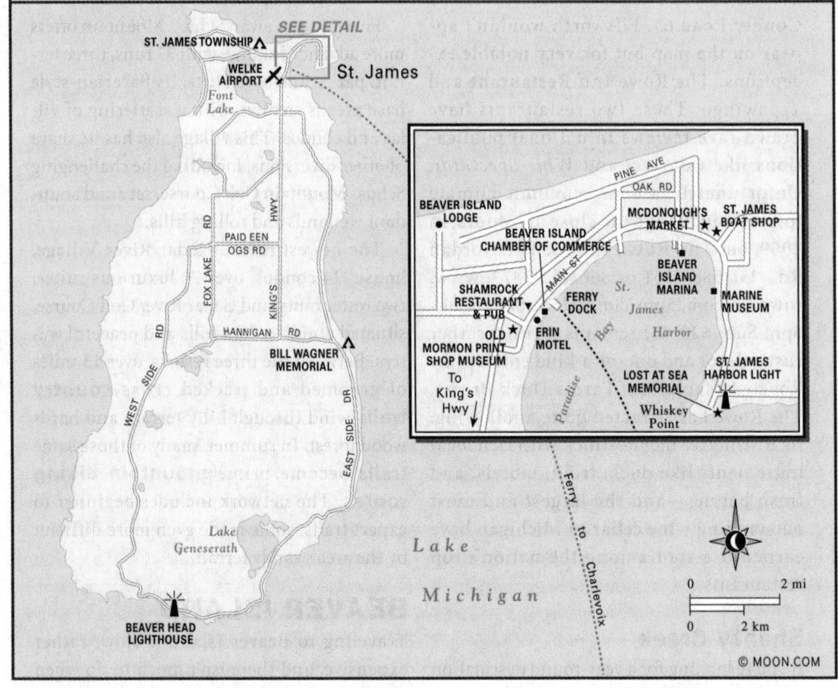

island's quirky history at a couple of terrific little museums. Enjoy a cup of coffee while listening to locals discuss island politics, or paddle a kayak to another island in the Beaver archipelago.

Sights

Beaver Island activity centers around St. James on hook-shaped Beaver Harbor, which many locals still call by its 19th-century name, Paradise Bay. This is where the ferry lands, and where you'll find the sum of the island's commercial development. Everything in St. James is within walking distance.

You can pick up much of the island's colorful history and character without ever leaving the harbor. The **Shamrock Restaurant & Pub** (26245 Main St., 231/448-2278, www.shamrockbarrestaurant.com, 11am-9pm daily, $12-23) is the most popular spot in town for a burger, beer, and island news. At the **St. James Boat Shop** (38230 Michigan, 231/838-2883, www.stjamesboatshop.com), Bill Freese builds gorgeous wood-strip canoes and kayaks, along with beautiful handmade wooden buckets.

From the boat shop, it's just a short walk to Whiskey Point, the **Lost at Sea Memorial,** and the **St. James Harbor Light,** marking the entrance to this well-protected natural harbor. The 19th-century light was staffed for years by Beaver Island native Elizabeth Whitney Williams, the only female lightkeeper on the Great Lakes.

The southern half of the island has far more public land, much of it a state wildlife research area. It has several small lakes, bogs, unimproved roads, and trails that are fun to explore, especially if you have a mountain bike. Fish in **Lake Geneserath,** swim at several sandy beaches on the southern shore, or check out the **Beaver Head Lighthouse** near the island's southern tip, a beautiful cream brick house and tower built in 1858, one of the oldest on all the Great Lakes. Back in the 1920s, thrill-seekers from Charlevoix drove across the thick lake ice, headed for Beaver Island. When a thick fog left them completely disoriented, the keeper guided them to safety with the light's fog signal.

If you plan to explore Beaver Island on your own, pick up two maps in St. James first: the comprehensive island map available at **McDonough's Market** (38240 Michigan Ave., 231/448-2733, www.mcdonoughsmarket.com) and a small history map, available at the chamber of commerce. It points out several noteworthy attractions that you can seek out on your own.

Kayaking

Eleven other islands are scattered around Beaver's northern half, an inviting archipelago for sea kayakers. The islands range in distance from Garden (2 miles away) to Gull (11 miles). Garden, practically due north from St. James, is probably the most intriguing for paddlers, with several protected bays and inlets. High Island, four miles west, has bluffs along the western shore rising to 240 feet. Most of High and Garden Islands are public land, part of the **Beaver Islands State Wildlife Research Area.** Some of the smaller islands are privately owned or otherwise off-limits to preserve nesting sites. For more information, contact the **Gaylord DNR Operations Service Center** (Wildlife Office, 1732 W. M-32, Gaylord, 989/732-3541, www.michigan.gov/dnr).

Accommodations

There are several motels, lodges, B&Bs, and cabins for rent on the island. Near the ferry dock, the **Erin Motel** (231/448-2240, www.erinmotel.com, $83-120 d) overlooks the water with a sand beach. It's also pet-friendly. The **Beaver Island Lodge** (231/448-2396, www.beaverislandlodge.com, $100-285 d) sits along a secluded stretch of beach west of town, with nice rooms and an on-site restaurant.

The island has two rustic campgrounds, with pit toilets and water, both on the lakeshore. The **St. James Township Campground** is on the north side of the island one mile from town and has 12 sites. The **Bill Wagner Memorial Campground,** with 22 sites, is along the east shore, seven miles south of town. Both cost $12 and aren't reservable. There are two grocery stores and a handful of restaurants on the island.

Information and Services

For information about Beaver Island's services, businesses, and lodging options, contact **Discover Beaver Island** (231/448-2505, www.beaverisland.org). For local news and events, consult the monthly ***Beaver Beacon*** (www.beaverbeacon.com).

Getting There and Around

Commercial transportation to Beaver Island is available only from Charlevoix, about 32 miles away. The **Beaver Island Boat Company** (103 Bridge Park Dr., 231/547-2311 or 888/446-4095, www.beaverislandboatcompany.com, one-way $27.50-32.50 adults, $15-20 ages 5-12, under age 5 free, $25 canoes or kayaks, $12 bicycles, rates vary for pets and vehicles) makes scheduled trips April-December, with two trips daily during most of the summer. It takes a little over two hours each way, and the 95-foot-long *Beaver Islander* or 130-foot-long *Emerald Isle* can be a rough ride in choppy waters. Reservations are recommended for passengers and required for autos. If you take the first ferry in the morning, you can make Beaver Island a day trip of six hours or so, returning on the late afternoon ferry. Of course, the time constraints of a day trip will limit you to exploring just a small portion of the island.

Island Airways (111 Airport Dr., 800/524-6895, www.islandairways.com, one-way $55 adults, $52 over age 64, $41 ages 2-9, under age 2 and small pets free, $31 large pets, $20 bicycles), meanwhile, provides daily air service from Charlevoix in a small 10-seater.

The flight takes about 20 minutes, and reservations are required.

It's probably not necessary to have a car on Beaver Island. Though the island is quite large and has more than 100 miles of roads, downtown St. James is ideal for walking and biking. In addition, many accommodations provide transportation from the dock or airport; if there's something specific you want to see, such as the lighthouse on the southern shore, you can usually rent a vehicle for about $55 daily, or $40 for four hours from **Gordon's Auto Rentals and Clinic** (231/448-2438, www.beaverisland.org/transportation/gordons-auto-rentals-and-clinic/), but be sure to reserve ahead of time.

Petoskey and Vicinity

Petoskey (puh-TOS-kee) was originally settled by the Ottawa people in the 1700s and takes its name from a local Native American merchant called Petosega. Offering bountiful fishing and hunting, the region was a desirable place to live. In the 1800s, the federal government negotiated more equitably with local Ottawa and Ojibwa communities than it did elsewhere; tribes were given the first choice of land (despite it already being in their possession) until 1875. European settlers began arriving in the 1850s, establishing logging operations along the Bear River, the name the town used until 1873. With a sawmill, a lime quarry, and other enterprises along the river and Little Traverse Bay, Bear River quickly became an industrial town, complete with buzzing saws and belching smoke.

But changes began with the arrival of the railroad in 1873. Lured north by the beautiful Lake Michigan waters and the cool northern air, new residents began migrating to Petoskey, gradually converting its industrial squalor to an elegant summer getaway. The artesian springs that bubbled throughout town and their "health-giving waters" only encouraged Petoskey's growth. By the turn of the 20th century, Petoskey's center was filled with fine shops and 13 grand resort hotels like the Arlington—surpassed in size only by the rival Grand Hotel on Mackinac Island. Unfortunately, most of Petoskey's grand

downtown Petoskey

resorts burned to the ground in the early 1900s, with only the Perry Hotel remaining, owing to its brick construction.

Thankfully, several other historic buildings survive, as the city realized early on the value of protecting them. From its well-preserved Gaslight District to the entire Victorian neighborhood of Bay View, Petoskey maintains the charm of the grand resort era. The natural resources that attracted those first summer visitors have lost none of their appeal, drawing a steady stream of anglers, boaters, shoppers, golfers, and skiers. To date Petoskey has successfully balanced the need for tourism with the importance of preserving its history. In 1996 the National Trust for Historic Preservation listed Petoskey as one of 10 national historic treasures most worthy of safeguarding, cautioning that "retail, roadway, and residential sprawl threaten the town's historic character and pastoral setting."

SIGHTS

Gaslight District

Though growth does threaten Petoskey—busy U.S. 31 slices right between downtown and the waterfront—the town remains a charming destination for vacationers, with a downtown made for strolling. The Gaslight District anchors the business district, an eight-block area of well-preserved Victorian brick storefronts filled with shops and restaurants that has drawn shoppers since the early 1900s. A low-interest loan program sponsored by the regional chamber of commerce encourages owners to preserve and maintain their properties. Centered around Lake and Howard Streets, the district mixes upscale boutiques with bookstores, art galleries, antiques haunts, and souvenir shops.

Crooked Tree Arts Center

If you enjoy strolling through art galleries, Petoskey is an optimal destination. Despite its relatively small size, the Gaslight District boasts several worthy choices. One such option is the **Crooked Tree Arts Center** (CTAC, 461 E. Mitchell St., 231/347-4337, www.crookedtree.org, 9am-5pm Mon.-Tues. and Thurs.-Fri., 10am-5pm Wed. and Sat., noon-5pm Sun., free). The CTAC was founded in 1971 to bring culture to northern Michiganians and support local and regional artists. In 1978 a former United Methodist Church in central Petoskey became CTAC's official home, and today the multicolored building is hard to ignore. The artistic and educational activities conducted include dance

an old cannon in Pennsylvania Park, in Petosky's Gaslight District

and visual arts classes, wine-tasting events, live concerts, and theatrical performances. Visitors are welcome to wander through the galleries of rotating exhibits by Michigan-based artists. Recent exhibits have showcased Robert de Jonge's images of the state's scenic shorelines and a colorful collection of children's book illustrations.

Little Traverse History Museum

Near the intersection of Petoskey and Bay Streets, follow the pedestrian tunnel under U.S. 31 to **Bayfront Park,** which merges with **Sunset Park** to the east, offering a vast green space along the waterfront. Once the center of Petoskey's sawmill operations, this beautifully improved area now comprises a marina, a walkway along the Bear River, one of the area's historic mineral springs, and the fine **Little Traverse History Museum** (231/347-2620, www.petoskeymuseum.org, 10am-4pm Mon.-Sat. Memorial Day-mid-Oct., $3 adults, under age 11 free) in the restored rail depot.

Perhaps the museum's most popular display is the collection of Ernest Hemingway memorabilia. Hemingway's family began vacationing on nearby Walloon Lake when the writer was just a boy, and the family still owns property there. After he was injured in World War I, Hemingway recuperated in Petoskey, living in a rooming house at the corner of State and Woodland Streets from 1919 to 1920. Here, he gathered material and began drafting *Torrents of Spring,* which alludes to several Petoskey locations. The museum's display includes first editions of that classic novel as well as *For Whom the Bell Tolls* and *A Farewell to Arms.*

Hemingway overshadows Petoskey's other famous author, Bruce Catton, who won a Pulitzer Prize in 1954 for his Civil War account *A Stillness at Appomattox.* Fortunately, the Little Traverse History Museum gives him due recognition.

Near the museum, you can pick up the **Top of Michigan Trail,** a 15-mile paved off-road path that stretches from Bay Harbor through Petoskey to Harbor Springs. Several other trails radiate off this route, creating a network of 180 miles of multiuse recreation pathways between Charlevoix and Mackinaw City. Trail maps are available at the Petoskey Area Visitors Bureau.

WINERY

The arc of northern Michigan wineries doesn't end in the Traverse City area. Just south of town, you'll find the **Mackinaw Trail Winery** (3423 U.S. 131, Petoskey, 231/487-1910, www.mackinawtrailwinery.com, 10am-10pm Mon.-Sat., noon-10pm Sun. May-Oct.). A family-owned business, Mackinaw Trail includes a 15-acre vineyard and a state-of-the-art facility. The winery has won over 50 medals and six best-in-class awards. There's also a brewery on-site.

RECREATION

Golf

While the area around Traverse City and Charlevoix boasts several terrific courses, the Petoskey-Harbor Springs area has no shortage of great golf either. Several lodgings even offer packages and will reserve tee times.

Best known are the four courses at **Boyne Highlands Resort** (600 Highland Dr., 231/526-3000 or 800/462-6963, www.boyne.com, daily May-Oct., $54-145 pp), a ski and golf resort a few miles north of Harbor Springs: The Moor, the Donald Ross Memorial, The Heather, and the Arthur Hills. *Golf Magazine* considers The Heather course, designed by Robert Trent Jones, one of the top courses in the country, with sculpted bunkers and water hazards (and sophisticated global positioning systems on the carts to feed yardage information). The Ross Memorial course is a perennial favorite. It recreates several of the most famous holes throughout the world designed by Ross, considered by many to be the father of golf course architecture.

Boyne also operates the **Crooked Tree Golf Club** (Bay Harbor, 231/439-4030 or 800/462-6963, www.boyne.com, $42-75 pp), a British-style course overlooking

Little Traverse Bay near Petoskey. In Harbor Springs, the **Harbor Point Golf Course** (8475 S. Lake Shore Dr., 231/526-2951, www.harborpointgolfclub.com, $60 pp with cart) had been an exclusive private club since 1896; it's now open to the public in the spring and fall months and considered a favorite walking course by *Golf Digest*.

Near Burt Lake in Brutus, **Hidden River Golf and Casting Club** (7688 Maple River Rd., 231/529-4653, www.hiddenriver.com, daily Apr.-Oct., $59-99 pp) offers classic "up north" scenery, with tall stands of pine and hardwoods and the meandering Maple River; this resort is also popular for fly-fishing.

Winter Activities

Nub's Nob (500 Nubs Nob Rd., Harbor Springs, 231/526-2131, www.nubsnob.com, $45-74 pp) often gets overshadowed by Boyne, but it has its own loyal following. The wooded slopes, well protected from cold winter winds, are best known for short and steep faces like Twilight Zone and Scarface, but its 23 trails and 427-foot vertical drop also have plenty of beginner and intermediate terrain.

ENTERTAINMENT

Just outside town, the **Odawa Casino Resort** (1760 Lears Rd., 877/442-6464, www.odawacasino.com, 24 hours daily) is a 300,000-square-foot entertainment complex with gaming, restaurants, and a theater that books big-name talent on a regular basis. They also have the O zone, a state-of-the-art nightclub.

SHOPPING

Petoskey's delightful Gaslight District offers a wide assortment of shops. **American Spoon** (411 E. Lake St., 231/347-1739, www.spoon.com, 10am-9pm daily) sells a variety of delicious jams, sauces, and more, all made from local produce and other fresh ingredients. Check out the adjacent café for tasty sandwiches made with their sauces. **McLean & Eakin Booksellers** (307 E. Lake St., 231/347-1180, www.mcleanandeakin.com, 9am-8pm Mon.-Sat., 10am-5pm Sun.) occupies an esteemed place—that of the traditional independent bookstore with a knowledgeable staff and an encyclopedic inventory. The store offers an eclectic selection of titles and regularly hosts educational and literary events, especially during the summer months. For a broad shopping experience within one store, visit **Cutler's** (216 Howard St., 231/347-0341, www.cutlersonline.com, 9:30am-6pm, Mon.-Sat., 12:30pm-4pm Sun.). Here you'll find an array of fine items for the home and kitchen. The adjacent woman's store offers an assortment of updated classic fashions.

FOOD

Petoskey offers a superb array of dining options, especially in the downtown area. Since 1875, the historic **City Park Grill** (432 E. Lake St., 231/347-0101, www.cityparkgrill.com, 11:30am-9pm Sun.-Thurs., 11:30am-10pm Fri.-Sat., bar closes later, $10-35) has lured residents and visitors alike despite several transformations over the years. Today patrons come for the happy hour specials and live weekend music in the adjacent bar, plus an eclectic restaurant menu that includes shellfish chowder, jambalaya, almond crusted whitefish, Mediterranean linguine, and filet mignon with blue cheese sauce.

For a more upscale dining experience, try **Chandler's** (215 Howard St., 231/347-2981, www.chandlersarestaurant.com, 11am-11pm, Mon.-Fri., 8am-11pm Sat.-Sun., $25-45). The sophisticated menu is very eclectic, including north Atlantic halibut with parmesan and mascarpone risotto and White Marble Farms pork chop.

ACCOMMODATIONS

Petoskey has an enormous assortment of lodgings, from basic motels along U.S. 31 to resort complexes to condo units that are especially convenient for families or groups.

Unless you're on a tight budget, opt for a stay at the lemon chiffon-colored ★ **Stafford's Perry Hotel** (100 Lewis St., 231/347-4000, www.staffords.com, $159-319 d), which overlooks Little Traverse Bay and dates back to 1899. Today, it's run by successful local innkeeper and restaurateur Stafford Smith, who has done a wonderful job of updating the venerable old building while retaining every bit of its charm. Rates are reasonable for such a treasure. The Perry also features three separate dining choices.

The **Terrace Inn** (1549 Glendale, 231/347-2410, www.theterraceinn.com, $139-199 d) provides an elegant bed-and-breakfast experience in a turn-of-the-20th-century building. A good choice among the area's chain offerings is the **Econo Lodge South** (1859 S. U.S. 131, 231/348-3324, www.choicehotels.com, $139-150 d).

INFORMATION AND SERVICES

For more information, contact the **Petoskey Area Visitors Bureau** (401 E. Mitchell St., 231/348-2755 or 800/845-2828, www.petoskeyarea.com, 8am-4pm Mon.-Fri.) or **Petoskey Regional Chamber of Commerce** (401 E. Mitchell St., 231/347-4150, www.petoskeychamber.com). For local news and events, consult the ***Petoskey News-Review*** (www.petoskeynews.com).

Though it's a relatively small town, Petoskey still has its share of necessary services such as pharmacies. For banking needs, both **Chase** (www.chase.com) and **Fifth Third Bank** (www.53.com) have several branches in Petoskey. For medical services, there is **McLaren Northern Michigan Hospital** (416 Connable Ave., 800/248-6777, www.mclaren.org).

GETTING THERE AND AROUND

Given its position on Little Traverse Bay, the city of Petoskey (www.petoskey.us) operates a public marina that includes transient dockage. By bus, both **Greyhound** (231/439-0747 or 800/231-2222, www.greyhound.com) and **Indian Trails** (800/292-3831, www.indiantrails.com) make regular stops at North Central Michigan College (1525 Howard St.). **Pellston Regional Airport** (PLN, 1395 U.S. 31, Pellston, 231/539-8441 or 231/539-8442, www.pellstonairport.com), northeast of Petoskey, offers commuter service from Detroit on Delta. **Cherry Capital Airport** (TVC, 727 Fly Don't Dr., Traverse City, 231/947-2250, www.tvcairport.com), in Traverse City, offers commuter service from Detroit and Minneapolis on Delta and from Chicago on United and American. You can rent a vehicle at either airport. From the Pellston airport, on U.S. 31 in light traffic, the 20-mile trip to Petoskey should take about 28 minutes. From the Traverse City airport, take County Road 620, 3 Mile Road, and U.S. 31 to Petoskey; in light traffic, the 65-mile trip usually takes about 80 minutes.

A car is the ideal way to explore the surrounding towns and lakes. From Sault Ste. Marie, take I-75, cross the Mackinac Bridge, and follow U.S. 31 to Petoskey, a 93-mile trip that takes about 1.75 hours. From Detroit, follow I-375, I-75, M-32, U.S. 131, and U.S. 31 toward downtown Petoskey; in light traffic, the 268-mile trip will require about 4 hours. No matter how you reach Petoskey, though, you can easily get around town by car or by bike, or on foot.

LITTLE TRAVERSE BAY

North of the Leelanau Peninsula and just half an hour south of the Straits of Mackinac, Little Traverse Bay cuts a nine-mile swath eastward, forming a picture-perfect bay ringed by bluffs, fine sand, and well-protected harbors. Well-known Petoskey, with its historic downtown Gaslight District, sits at the foot of the bay, justifiably drawing many of the area's visitors, but golfers, skiers, anglers, and wanderers will find plenty to enjoy in this appealing and compact region.

LAKE MICHIGAN SHORE

Bay Harbor

A couple of miles west of downtown Petoskey, Bay Harbor represents the nation's largest land reclamation project, a stunning example of what foresight and $100 million can accomplish. Stretching five miles along the shore of Little Traverse Bay and encompassing more than 1,100 acres, this beautiful piece of real estate spent its last life as a cement plant. When the plant closed in 1981, it left behind a scarred, barren landscape that sat untouched for a decade.

With the combined resources of a large utility company and ski industry giant Boyne, Bay Harbor has emerged as one of the nation's most spectacular resort communities. The **Bay Harbor Yacht Club** overlooks a deep-water port (the old quarry) with nearly 500 slips, including 120 for public transient use. An equestrian club provides entertainment, and multimillion-dollar homes dot the property. Public parks buffer Bay Harbor on both sides.

Acclaimed golf designer Arthur Hills has created **The Links, The Preserve,** and **The Quarry golf courses** (5800 Coastal Ridge Dr., 231/439-4085, www.bayharborgolf.com, $115 and up pp), 27 holes that ramble atop 160-foot bluffs, over natural sand dunes, and along the shore for more than two miles. Eight holes hug the water—more than at Pebble Beach. Completed in 1998, it was almost immediately named the eighth best public course in the nation by *Golf Magazine*.

Bay View

Adjacent to Petoskey on the east side of town, Bay View looks like a Hollywood set for a Victorian romance. This amazing community includes 430 Victorian homes, most built before the 1900s. All are on the National Register of Historic Places and represent the largest single collection of historic homes in the country.

Bay View was founded by the Methodist Church in 1875 as a summer-only religious retreat that took some inspiration from the Chautauqua movement in the East. Summers at Bay View were filled with lectures, recitals, craft classes, and religious programs. Over the years, speakers included such notable names as Booker T. Washington, Helen Keller, and William Jennings Bryan.

Originally a tent community, Bay View's canvas lodgings were slowly replaced by Victorian cottages, many with grand views of Little Traverse Bay. Bay View residents were not exceptionally wealthy, which is reflected in the size of the homes. Houses of all shapes and floor plans line up in tidy rows in a shady parklike campus. Residents owned their cottages but leased the land from the Methodist Church.

Today, Bay View remains a quiet enclave, still hosting a full roster of courses, concerts, and other events. While many residents are descendants of Bay View's founding families, the religious focus is much less pronounced. The greatest emphasis now is on carefully preserving Bay View's historical architecture. Even minor renovations require approval by the Bay View Association. For a true taste of another era, plan a stroll or a bike ride through this calm, gentle place.

Petoskey State Park

Just beyond Bay View, **Petoskey State Park** (2475 M-119, Petoskey, 231/347-2311, annual Recreation Passport required: $12 Michigan residents, $34 nonresidents, $9 day pass available to nonresidents only) bends along the east end of Little Traverse Bay. Though quite small at 300 acres, the park nonetheless offers a nice slice of nature between the summertime bustle of Petoskey and Harbor Springs. Its main attraction is its mile-long beach, with soft sand and enough rocks to keep people on the hunt for Petoskey stones. (The coral pattern appears most clearly when wet, so dip a promising-looking stone in the water.) The beach has great views of Petoskey and Harbor Springs and can yield some terrific sunsets.

Climb the 0.7-mile **Old Baldy Trail** for an even better view from the top of a dune. The park's only other hiking trail, the **Portage Trail,** is an easy 2.8-mile loop that winds south to a little inland lake. It's groomed in winter for cross-country skiing.

Nearly 200 modern campsites (reservations 800/447-2757, www.michigan.gov/dnr, $34-37), mostly wooded with good privacy, are

Petoskey Stones

Michigan's official state stone isn't really a stone at all, but a piece of fossilized coral more than 350 million years old. Coral reefs once thrived in the warm seas that covered northern Michigan from Grand Traverse Bay to Alpena on present-day Lake Huron. Petoskey stones are characterized by the distinct honeycomb pattern that covers them. The stones are so commonplace they have little value, but are prized nonetheless by rock enthusiasts or anyone looking for a local souvenir.

When dry, Petoskey stones often look like ordinary stones, typically with a dusty gray-brown hue. Their unique pattern, however, becomes more apparent when wet and especially when polished. Since the stones are quite soft, locals suggest polishing them by hand with 220-grit wet sandpaper, then repeating the process with 400-grit and 600-grit sandpaper. Rock tumblers are not recommended.

Petoskey stones can be found along public beaches almost anywhere in the Traverse Bay region. Some of the more productive spots include Fisherman's Island State Park south of Charlevoix and Petoskey State Park on Little Traverse Bay. You can also find Petoskey stones at area gift shops in the northwestern part of the Lower Peninsula—polished up and often crafted into jewelry.

hidden behind a series of small dunes. Sites along the southern loop are closer to the bay, with a few prime (though more public) sites right on the water.

Harbor Springs

Just north of Petoskey State Park, U.S. 31 veers inland toward Mackinaw City and the straits. To stay along the water, turn west on M-119, which follows the curve of Little Traverse Bay and traces the Lower Peninsula's final stretch of Lake Michigan shoreline.

Harbor Springs represents the quintessential summer resort getaway. A genteel community on the north side of Little Traverse Bay, it features a deep clear harbor tucked against a high wooded bluff, ringed with grand estates, white church spires, and a marina with gleaming yachts bobbing at anchor. Harbor Springs, in fact, has the deepest natural harbor on all of the Great Lakes, which made it a natural stopping point for the large passenger steamers of the early 1900s. Several artesian wells added to its appeal as a popular destination for those seeking healthful air and water. Wealthy industrialist families like the Fords and the Gambles took a liking to Harbor Springs and created a number of exclusive resort communities like Harbor Point and Wequetonsing, where crisp white mansions flank emerald lawns.

Those old-money communities still thrive, inhabited by younger generations of Fords and Gambles. Harbor Point remains the more exclusive of the two, with homes valued at over $10 million. Entrances and exits are by foot or carriage only; cars are banned from the point. You can walk, bike, or drive through Wequetonsing (WEE-kwee to the locals), where homes have names like Summer Set and Brookside, and long lines of Adirondack chairs on the porches.

It all makes for an interesting diversity, where the wealthy, vacationing families and the hired help all mingle in the delightfully tidy downtown. Not surprisingly, Harbor Springs has no strip malls, no sprawl, and no franchise signs.

Shopping is a popular pastime in Harbor Springs, which hosts an appealing mix of galleries, tony boutiques, and distinctive handmade crafts. Start your exploring at Main and State Streets. Also check out the **Harbor Springs History Museum** (349 E. Main St., 231/526-9771, www.harborspringshistory.org, 11am-3pm Tues.-Sat., by donation), which uses photographs, artifacts, and hands-on activities to explore the area's history, from the influence of the Odawa people to the emergence of the ski industry. Here you'll also learn about famous former residents such as Andrew J. Blackbird, an Odawa chief who lived here in the mid-1800s. The town's first postmaster, Blackbird wrote books about Native American languages and legends.

The harbor front is a natural place for strolling, with ample benches and a swimming beach at **Zorn Park** near the west end. The **Thorne Swift Nature Preserve** (231/347-0991 or 231/526-6401, www.landtrust.org) offers a quiet 300-foot sand beach and dune observation deck with a wonderful bay view. Other trails wind through cedar lowlands, with trees canted and curved at crazy angles, and marked with interpretive signs. A protected holding of the very active Little Traverse Conservancy, Thorne Swift has a naturalist on duty daily Memorial Day-Labor Day. Choose a breezy day to visit, as bugs can be onerous during summer months. To reach the preserve from Harbor Springs, head northwest on M-119 for 3.8 miles and then follow Lower Shore Drive for 0.5 miles. The preserve sign is on the left.

★ Tunnel of Trees

The stretch of M-119 from Harbor Springs to Cross Village is considered one of the prettiest drives in the country. The narrow lane twists and turns as it follows Lake Michigan from high atop a bluff with furtive views of the water and the Beaver Island archipelago. Yet it's the trees that take top billing, arching overhead to form a sun-dappled tunnel. The effect is spectacular on autumn afternoons, when the fiery oranges and bronzes glow in the angled sunlight like hot coals.

In spring, trilliums form a blanket of white on the forest floor. Spring also offers a few more deep-blue glimpses of the lake, since the trees usually are not fully leafed out until late May. Any season is a good time to spot wildlife. One trip up the relentlessly winding road you'll spot deer, wild turkeys, and a number of grouse.

Try to bike or drive this road during the week, or at least early or late in the day, when traffic should be lighter. The combination of narrow blacktop, blind curves, the absence of shoulders, and abundant wildlife requires keeping a close eye on the road. The more cars, the less scenery you can enjoy.

Legs Inn

Even if you're well-traveled, it's doubtful you've ever encountered anything like the **Legs Inn** (6425 N. Lake Shore Dr., Cross Village, 231/526-2281, www.legsinn.com, noon-9pm daily, $14-25). Part restaurant, part eclectic folk art display, this is a weird and fascinating place to explore. Outside is strange enough: a roadside building with a facade of fieldstone, accented with bizarre-looking totems and carved wooden legs spiking from the roof—hence the name.

The interior is even more compelling: the bar a dark and mysterious den crammed with twisted driftwood, roots, and stumps turned into cocktail tables. Seemingly every square inch has been carved into fanciful shapes, weird faces, and indescribable animals—and more and more seem to appear as your eyes adjust to the darkness. The theme carries through to the dining rooms, though not with such intensity. These areas are brighter and warmer, with picture windows overlooking gardens and distant views of Lake Michigan.

Legs Inn was created by Stanley Smolak, a Polish immigrant who moved to Cross Village from Chicago in the 1920s. He became enamored with the land and its indigenous people. He befriended the local Ottawa communities still thriving here in the 1920s and was so accepted into their culture that they gave him the Ottawa name of Chief White Cloud. Inspired by their art, he began carving. Soon, word of his restaurant and his relations with the Ottawa made Smolak a celebrity back in Poland.

With its eccentric decor, it's easy to overlook the food at the Legs Inn, which offers a wonderful array of Polish cooking, with rich soups, thick stews, and popular Polish specialties like pierogi. Even the drinks menu offers Polish vodkas and Polish meads, the latter made from honey and fruit juices. The cuisine is authentic—many of the cook staff are

Legs Inn
OPEN
INQUIRE WITHIN
1
2

immigrants themselves. They'll feed you like long-lost relatives.

Sturgeon Bay

M-119 ends at Cross Village, but continue northeast on Scenic Route 1 along Sturgeon Bay to reach **Bliss Township Park,** with low dunes and a pretty sand beach, great for swimming and sunsets. Far enough away from Petoskey and the Straits of Mackinac, it rarely draws a crowd.

Sturgeon Bay also offers the best big-water windsurfing in the area, with an easy shore break and generally warmer water than Little Traverse Bay. Bliss Township Park is a wonderful launch. A second launch is about a mile north of the township beach, just where the road makes a hard right. Beware of poison ivy. Advanced sailors looking for big waves should visit the boat launch in Cross Village, where they appear during westerly and northerly winds.

Wilderness State Park

North of Cross Village near the top of the "mitten," Waugoshance Point stretches west out into Lake Michigan and dribbles off into a series of islands. This is the spectacular setting for **Wilderness State Park** (903 Wilderness Park Dr., Carp Lake, 231/436-5381, annual Recreation Passport required: $12 Michigan residents, $34 nonresidents, $9 day pass available to nonresidents only), the second-largest state park in the Lower Peninsula. Aptly named, it occupies more than 7,500 acres of largely undeveloped land, including more than 26 miles of Lake Michigan shoreline. Despite siting just 15 minutes away from the Straits of Mackinac, it offers remarkable solitude.

Wilderness State Park is one of the nesting sites of the endangered piping plover. When the birds are nesting in late spring and early summer, part of the point is closed to visitors. About 100 other bird species also nest or migrate through the park, making it a favorite of bird-watchers. Anglers gather here, too, with notable bass fishing especially in the grassy beds along the southern shore of the point. The park has a boat launch near the campgrounds and day-use area.

The park offers a wide range of topography, with sandy beaches and rocky limestone ledges along the shore. Inland, 12 miles of old truck trails wind through cedars, pines, and birches. A gravel road leads toward the end of the point, open to autos. To hike there, you can follow the northern shoreline for two miles, unless the endangered piping plovers are nesting. Depending on weather conditions and water depths, it's often possible to wade to Temperance Island—a fun adventure.

Wilderness State Park has two large campgrounds with 250 sites, five rustic cabins, and 24-bunk lodges ($16-74) for rent. The Lakeshore Campground sits on Big Stone Bay in an open grassy setting, with several sites right along the water. Just across the park road, the Pines Campground has more shaded and private sites.

1: Legs Inn in Cross Village **2:** the Tunnel of Trees

Mackinac Island and Northeast Michigan

Commonly called the Sunrise Side, the northeastern part of Michigan's Lower Peninsula is perhaps its most underappreciated portion of the state—which is a shame given its abundance of untamed beauty. Of course, year-round residents and seasonal vacationers value the tranquility of this less traveled place, so most are grateful that development has been slower here than in other parts of Michigan.

The area's remarkable woods—including sizable Hartwick Pines State Park—lure a wide array of recreation seekers, from hikers in summer to hunters in winter, while the region's many lakes, such as Higgins south of Grayling, attract anglers, boaters, and canoeists. Wildlife enthusiasts also relish northeast Michigan—common sights include

Highlights

Look for ★ to find recommended sights, activities, dining, and lodging.

★ **Colonial Michilimackinac State Historic Park:** See costumed soldiers, traders, and homesteaders demonstrate skills of the late 18th century (page 262).

★ **Grand Hotel:** Opened in 1887, this timeless piece of history boasts the world's longest porch and a guest list that's included at least five presidents (page 269).

★ **Diving in Thunder Bay:** Scuba divers will discover a wealth of artifacts in this marine sanctuary. "Shipwreck Alley" is the resting place of more than 80 unfortunate vessels (page 282).

★ **Canoeing on the Au Sable River:** This picturesque river is home to North America's longest nonstop canoe marathon (page 285).

★ **Houghton and Higgins Lakes:** Two of the state's largest inland lakes offer seven swimming beaches for boating in summer and wintertime ice fishing (page 289).

★ **Golf in Gaylord:** Choose from several championship courses with challenging holes, scenic views, and fine lodgings (page 293).

★ **Hartwick Pines State Park:** Visit the state's largest remaining stand of virgin white pines. View forestry exhibits, experience a former logging camp, explore trails, and observe wildlife (page 297).

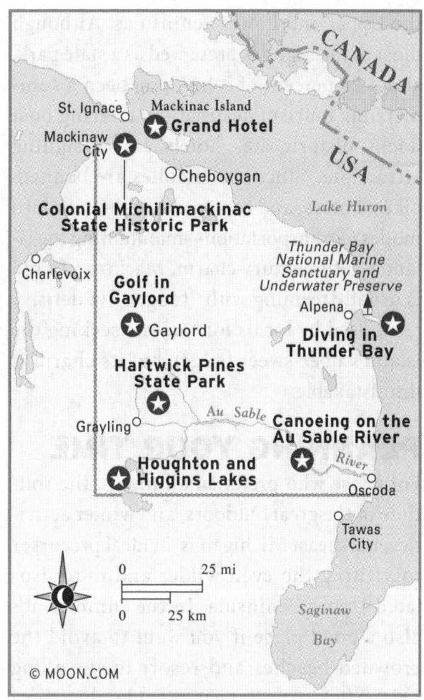

foxes scurrying amid the underbrush, curious deer running along country roads, bald eagles circling above the coves, and majestic elk stalking through Pigeon River Country State Forest, home to the largest free-roaming elk herd east of the Mississippi River.

A superb way to experience the hinterlands of northeast Michigan is via the 22-mile River Road Scenic Byway, showcasing the high cliffs, white pines, and wooded lakes of the Au Sable River Valley. Meanwhile, the Sunrise Side Coastal Highway (U.S. 23) stretches for 200 miles along the Lake Huron shore, from Standish to the Mackinac Bridge. Along the way, motorists can experience quaint coastal towns, inviting beaches, and scenic lighthouses. These stunning drives are especially wonderful in the fall, when the trees are ablaze with spectacular colors.

Situated just north of the mainland lies Mackinac Island, a nostalgic haven between the Upper and Lower Peninsulas. Although most of the island is preserved as a state park, about 20 percent of it has long been a summertime tourism destination, offering boat docks, historic sites, hotels, and intriguing attractions. Since automobiles are banned, bikes, horses, and carriages are the standard modes of transportation—maintaining the island's 19th-century charm. Mackinac Island is usually teeming with "fudgies" (a derisive term used by locals for tourists seeking the island's über-sweet fudge), but its charm is unmistakable.

PLANNING YOUR TIME

For those who prefer small towns, the solitude of the great outdoors, and winter activities, northeast Michigan is an ideal precursor to visiting the even wilder and more isolated Upper Peninsula. In the summer, it's also a good place if you want to avoid the crowded beaches and resort towns along Lake Michigan. Expect considerable company, however, in this area's championship golf courses, near the inland lakes on summer weekends, and especially on Mackinac Island.

To take in the highlights of northeast Michigan, you'll need a minimum of three days, including a day trip to Mackinac Island. A whole week will give you a better chance to tour the historic coastline and explore the interior's impressive forests and lakes.

Two main roads cut through the Huron shore region. U.S. 23 hugs the coastline from Standish to the Straits of Mackinac, offering vistas and villages along the way. I-75 is the quicker, though less scenic, route, heading north from Bay City, through Grayling and Gaylord, to the Mackinac Bridge. For those not driving to northeast Michigan, consider taking a Greyhound bus to towns like Cheboygan, Rogers City, Alpena, Tawas City, Grayling, and Gaylord. It's also possible to fly into the Pellston and Alpena County Regional Airports, both via Delta. If you plan on exploring several areas of the region, it's advisable to rent a vehicle.

For more information about northeast Michigan, consult **Pure Michigan** (Michigan Economic Development Corporation, 300 N. Washington Square, Lansing, 888/784-7328, www.michigan.org).

HISTORY

In appearance, northeast Michigan has come nearly full circle in 200 years. Its first inhabitants were Native Americans, who kept the land much as they found it until the Europeans arrived in the 17th century. Before the rush of settlers to Michigan in the 1830s, more than 13 million of the state's 37 million acres were covered with white pine. These majestic trees thrived in sandy soil, grew up to 200 feet tall, and could live an incredible 500 years. By 1900, however, all that was left of these once awe-inspiring forests were stumps. In 1909, the federal government established the Huron National Forest, the first of many such preserves that sought to repair decades

Previous: Shepler's is one of the ferry lines serving Mackinac Island; Mackinac Island and Bridge; a church on Mackinac Island.

Mackinac Island and Northeast Michigan

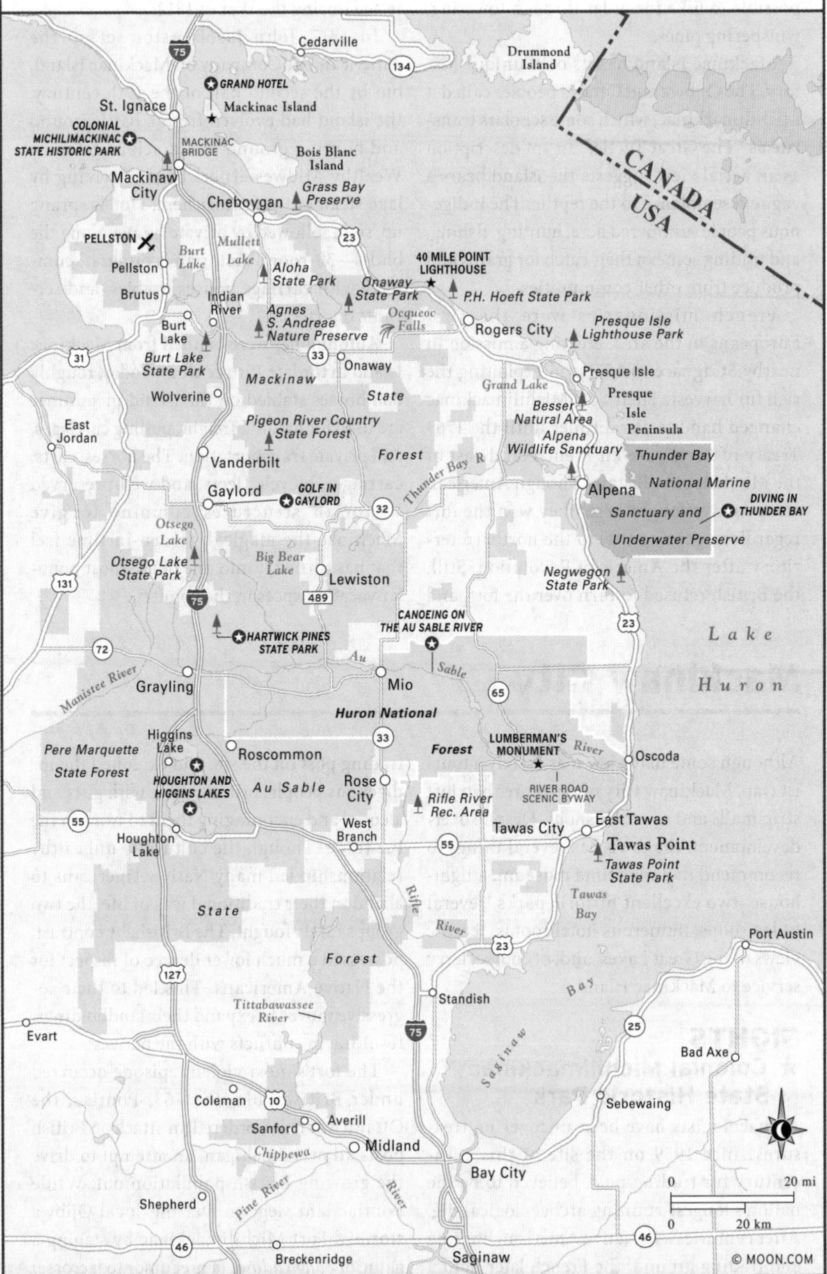

of damage. More than a century later, much of this region is once again forested, and it's possible to hike for miles through towering, whispering pines.

Mackinac Island has its own unique history. The Ojibwa and Ottawa peoples called it Michilimackinac, which some scholars translate as "The Great Turtle," an apt description as an aerial view suggests the island bears a vague resemblance to the reptile. The indigenous people summered here, hunting, fishing, and trading some of their catch for grains and produce from other communities.

French missionaries were the first Europeans in the area, erecting a mission in nearby St. Ignace in 1671 and exploiting the rich fur harvest. Their Fort Michilimackinac changed hands several times until the 1763 Treaty of Paris gave all French land east of the Mississippi to Britain. Though American troops never fought here, they won the fort regardless, gaining title to the northern territory after the American Revolution. Still, the British refused to turn over the fort, and much of lower Michigan, including Detroit, until 1796. The territory was once again contested during the War of 1812.

In 1817, John Jacob Astor set up the American Fur Company on Mackinac Island, but by the second half of the 19th century, the island had evolved from a battleground and hunting ground to a gracious getaway. Wealthy Midwesterners began arriving by lake steamer to summer here. Hotels sprang up, soon followed by private homes along the bluffs—30-room Victorian "cottages," complete with carriage houses, stables, and servants quarters.

Automobiles were banned from Mackinac Island in the late 19th century. Today, roughly 600 horses stabled on the island in summer are used for hauling freight, pulling carriages, and private transportation. The horses, carts, carriages, bicycle fleets, and well-preserved Victorian structures combine to give Mackinac the magical, frozen-in-time feel that has turned it into one of the most popular vacation spots in the country.

Mackinaw City

Although some may view it as merely a tourist trap, Mackinaw City offers more than just strip malls and souvenir shops. Despite overdevelopment, the town has several things to recommend it: a maritime museum, a lighthouse, two excellent historic parks, several fudge shops, numerous hotel rooms, terrific views of the Great Lakes, and, of course, ferry service to Mackinac Island.

SIGHTS

★ Colonial Michilimackinac State Historic Park

Archaeologists have been uncovering treasures since 1959 on the site of this 18th-century fur trading post, believed to be the nation's longest-running archaeological dig. After centuries as a Native American hunting and trading ground, the French later built a trading post on the site and exploited the indigenous people, bribing them with gifts and alcohol and encouraging them to work in the fur trade. Though the culturally unhealthy relationship led many Native Americans to abandon their traditional way of life, the two groups rarely fought. The British, by contrast, possessed a much lower degree of respect for the Native Americans. This led to their aggressive moves to expand their landholdings, resulting in conflicts with the natives.

The fort's most violent episode occurred under British rule. In 1763, Pontiac, the Ottawa war chief, ordered an attack on British posts all over Michigan, an attempt to drive the growing British population out. While Pontiac laid siege to Detroit, local Ojibwa stormed Fort Michilimackinac by staging a game of *baaga'adowe* (a precursor to lacrosse) as a ruse to gain entry. The ensuing attack killed most of the British. The invaders held the fort for close to a year before negotiating a settlement with British authorities.

Today, **Colonial Michilimackinac State Historic Park** (102 W. Straits Ave., 231/436-4100, www.mackinacparks.com, 9am-6pm daily June-Aug., 9am-4pm daily May and Sept.-early Oct., $12.50 adults, $7.50 ages 5-17) just west of the Mackinac Bridge portrays the lives of both the Native Americans and European settlers, with costumed interpreters reenacting daily life at a Native American encampment and a stockade fort. Displays include many of the artifacts unearthed by archaeologists. Interpreters demonstrate various crafts and skills, from cooking and weaving to cleaning weapons. Don't miss the underground archaeological tunnel exhibit, "Treasures from the Sand."

Historic Mill Creek Discovery Park

Today, this exceptionally pretty glen and rushing stream creates a pleasant oasis for visitors, but it was once an innovative industrial site. When the British made plans to move from Fort Michilimackinac to Mackinac Island for security, Scotsman Robert Campbell recognized their imminent need for lumber. He purchased 640 acres of the land around the only waterway in the area with enough flow to power a sawmill. He built the mill in 1790 and later added a blacksmith shop and gristmill.

The site was no longer profitable when the fort ceased operation, so it was abandoned in the mid-1800s. Since the 1970s, archaeologists and historians have worked together to recreate the water-powered sawmill on its original site. Today, visitors to the 625-acre **Historic Mill Creek Discovery Park** (9001 U.S. 23, 231/436-4100, www.mackinacparks.com, 9am-5pm daily June-Aug., 9am-4pm daily May, 11am-4pm Mon.-Fri., 9am-4pm Sat.-Sun. Sept., $9.50 adults, $6.50 ages 5-17) can see the splashing waterwheel in action and visit the orientation center, which has an audiovisual presentation and displays on other artifacts uncovered during the dig. Make sure to walk the park's 1.5 miles of trails, which wind along the creek and millpond, rising up to scenic overlooks with views of the straits and Mackinac Island.

Old Mackinac Point Lighthouse

Sited on a point just east of the Mackinac Bridge, this 1892 cream-brick light guided ships through the busy Straits of Mackinac for nearly 70 years. When the Mackinac Bridge with its higher illumination was completed in 1957, the light became obsolete. Today, the charming **Old Mackinac Point Lighthouse** (9am-5pm daily June-Aug., 9am-4pm daily May and Sept.-early Oct., $8.50 adults, $5.50 ages 5-17), topped with a cherry-red roof, houses a maritime museum, part of Colonial Michilimackinac State Historic Park. A schooner and other ships are docked and on display. The lighthouse grounds serve as their own delightful little park, with impressive views of the Mackinac Bridge as well as picnic tables scattered around a tidy lawn.

Visitors interested in seeing Fort Michilimackinac, Historic Mill Creek Discovery Park, and the Old Mackinac Point Lighthouse can purchase combined tickets at a savings over the individual admission prices. Visit www.mackinacparks.com for details.

From the Old Mackinac Point Lighthouse, you can reach several island and offshore reef lights via boat—though you should take care in these potentially dangerous waters. Two of the most interesting are the 1874 **Spectacle Reef Light**, an impressive example of a monolithic stone lighthouse, and the 1895 **Round Island Light** in the Straits of Mackinac.

Mackinac Bridge Museum

The small but intriguing **Mackinac Bridge Museum** (231 E. Central Ave., 231/436-5534, www.mightymac.org/bridgemuseum.htm, 8am-midnight daily May-Oct., free), above Mama Mia's Pizza, is loaded with information and artifacts on the construction of the

1
2
MACKINAW CROSSINGS
MACKINAW CROSSINGS

$100 million Mackinac Bridge. A very good video documents the bridge's design and construction. For more information about the bridge itself, consult the **Mackinac Bridge Museum** (www.mightymac.org/bridgemuseum.htm).

Lighthouse Tours

Although a self-guided tour of Michigan's lighthouses can be a delightful way to pass a few days in the Great Lakes State, the experience can be even more enlightening with a well-informed guide. Besides shuttling tourists to and from Mackinac Island, **Shepler's Mackinac Island Ferry** (800/828-6157, www.sheplersferry.com) also offers lighthouse cruises ($51.50 adults, $29.50 ages 5-12). Departing from Mackinaw City, these trips guide passengers amid lighthouses and shipwrecks that would be difficult for most to reach otherwise. Along the way, guests are treated to historical tales, which provide informative context for the lighthouses that still stand. The eastbound cruise features offshore lights like Round Island Light and the privately owned Bois Blanc Island Light, while the westbound cruise highlights structures such as the red-and-white-striped White Shoal Light and the 1873 St. Helena Island Lighthouse. There are also extended versions of both cruises: The eastbound ($69 adults, $40.25 ages 5-12) edition adds Skillagalee Lighthouse to the itinerary, while the westbound ($62 adults, $36 ages 5-12) additionally includes Spectacle Reef Lighthouse.

SHOPPING

Although Mackinaw City isn't as high on shoppers' lists as the resort towns along Lake Michigan, it does have its share of worthwhile shops. A pleasant highlight is **Mackinaw Crossings** (248 S. Huron Ave., 231/436-5030, www.mackinawcrossings.com), a tidy open-air collection of restaurants and stores where you can find everything from **Harbor West,** which offers casual resort clothing, to the **Mackinac Bay Build Your Bear,** where children can customize their very own stuffed teddy bears.

1: Old Mackinac Point Lighthouse 2: shopping at Mackinaw Crossings

FOOD AND ACCOMMODATIONS

In between sightseeing and shopping, grab a bite to eat at one of the numerous area restaurants. Step back a couple of centuries at the historic landmark **Dixie Saloon** (401 E. Central Ave., 231/436-5449, www.dixiesaloon.com, 10:30am-2am daily, $11-36). Try the potato-crusted walleye or the fried perch, both locally caught. For something a little more elegant, stop by **The Lighthouse Restaurant** (618 S. Huron Ave., 231/436-5191, www.lighthousemackinaw.com, 4pm-10pm daily, $16-49), with its prime rib, lobster, and excellent wine list.

Since the Straits of Mackinac are a major draw for tourists, Mackinaw City alone has more than 3,000 guest rooms. For a variety of amenities, check out the **Comfort Inn Lakeside** (611 S. Huron Ave., 231/436-5057, www.choicehotels.com, $188-287 d) or the **Ramada Inn Waterfront** (723 S. Huron Ave., 231/436-5055, www.ramadainn.com, $198-278 d). Another fine choice is the **Parkside Inn Bridgeview** (771 N. Huron Ave., 800/827-8301, www.parksideinn.com, $79-189). With a superb view of the Mackinac Bridge, the Parkside offers comfortable rooms, a heated indoor pool, and hot breakfast each morning.

INFORMATION AND SERVICES

For more information, contact the **Mackinaw Area Visitors Bureau** (231/436-5664, www.mackinawcity.com). Mackinaw City has only basic services—a small grocery, a post office, and a 24-hour ATM at **Citizens National Bank** (580 S. Nicolet St., 231/436-5271, www.cnbismybank.com).

GETTING THERE AND AROUND

While Mackinaw City lacks airports, train stations, or bus centers, it's easy to reach the Lower Peninsula's northernmost town. **Pellston Regional Airport** (PLN, 1395 U.S. 31, Pellston, 231/539-8441 or 231/539-8442, www.pellstonairport.com) is a 16-mile, 20-minute drive and has commuter flights from Detroit on Delta. You can rent a vehicle here from Avis or Hertz. With advance reservations, you can also take a **Mackinaw Shuttle** (231/539-7005 or 888/349-8294, www.mackinawshuttle.com) van or shuttle bus from the Pellston Airport to Mackinaw City and other towns in northern Michigan, from Traverse City and Petoskey in the Lower Peninsula to St. Ignace and Sault Ste. Marie in the Upper Peninsula.

Reach Mackinaw City via U.S. 31, I-75, or U.S. 23. From Sault Ste. Marie, take I-75 to St. Ignace, cross the Mackinac Bridge, and follow exit 338 toward U.S. 23; the 59-mile trip typically takes about an hour. From Traverse City, take U.S. 31 to I-75, and follow exit 338 toward South Nicolet Street; without traffic, the 103-mile trip should take two hours. The 289-mile journey from Detroit to Mackinaw City is a direct route via I-75 and usually takes about four hours.

From Chicago, take I-90 and I-94 through Illinois and Indiana to I-196/U.S. 31 and I-196, U.S. 131 County Road 42, M-32, and I-75 to exit 338; in light traffic, the 406-mile trip will require at least six hours. En route from Chicago, parts of I-90 and I-94 serve as the Indiana Toll Road.

Mackinaw City is a fairly small town, so feel free to park your vehicle and stroll the downtown shops and eateries.

Mackinac Island

Linking Lakes Huron and Michigan, the Straits of Mackinac (MAK-i-naw) have been a crossroads of the Great Lakes for hundreds of years, a key waterway for hunting, fishing, trading, and transportation. The four-mile-wide straits also sever Michigan in two, both geographically and culturally. Until the 1950s, the only way across was by ferry, effectively blocking the development of the Upper Peninsula and creating half-day backups at the ferry dock during peak hunting and fishing seasons. Today, the magnificent five-mile-long Mackinac Bridge allows easy transit between the Upper and Lower Peninsulas. But the straits, now a key vacation area for much of the Midwest, continue to lure visitors, and many come specifically for Mackinac Island.

Few other places in Michigan conjure as much history, attention, and affection as the tiny parcel known as Mackinac Island. Over the centuries, the 2,200-acre island has been sacred ground for the Native Americans, an important base for French fur trappers, a fort for British soldiers, a gilded summer retreat for the wealthiest Victorian era industrialists, and a haven for modern-day visitors.

The Victorian era has been beautifully preserved, from the exquisite 1887 Grand Hotel, with its 660-foot-long porch stretching across the hillside, to the clopping of the horse-drawn carriages down the car-free streets. Despite some of the trappings of tourism, Mackinac Island is also irrepressibly charming—Michigan's heirloom jewel. A full 80 percent of the island is a state park, which includes a restored 18th-century fort, undeveloped woodlands, a network of crisscrossing trails, rare wildflowers, and sculpted limestone outcroppings.

Mackinac Island also has far more lodging choices than the famous Grand Hotel, many of which are moderately priced. Plan to spend at least one night, so you have a little time to wander around and get past the cliché. Mackinac doesn't lend itself well to a cursory glance. As the wealthy resort dwellers knew,

Mackinac Island

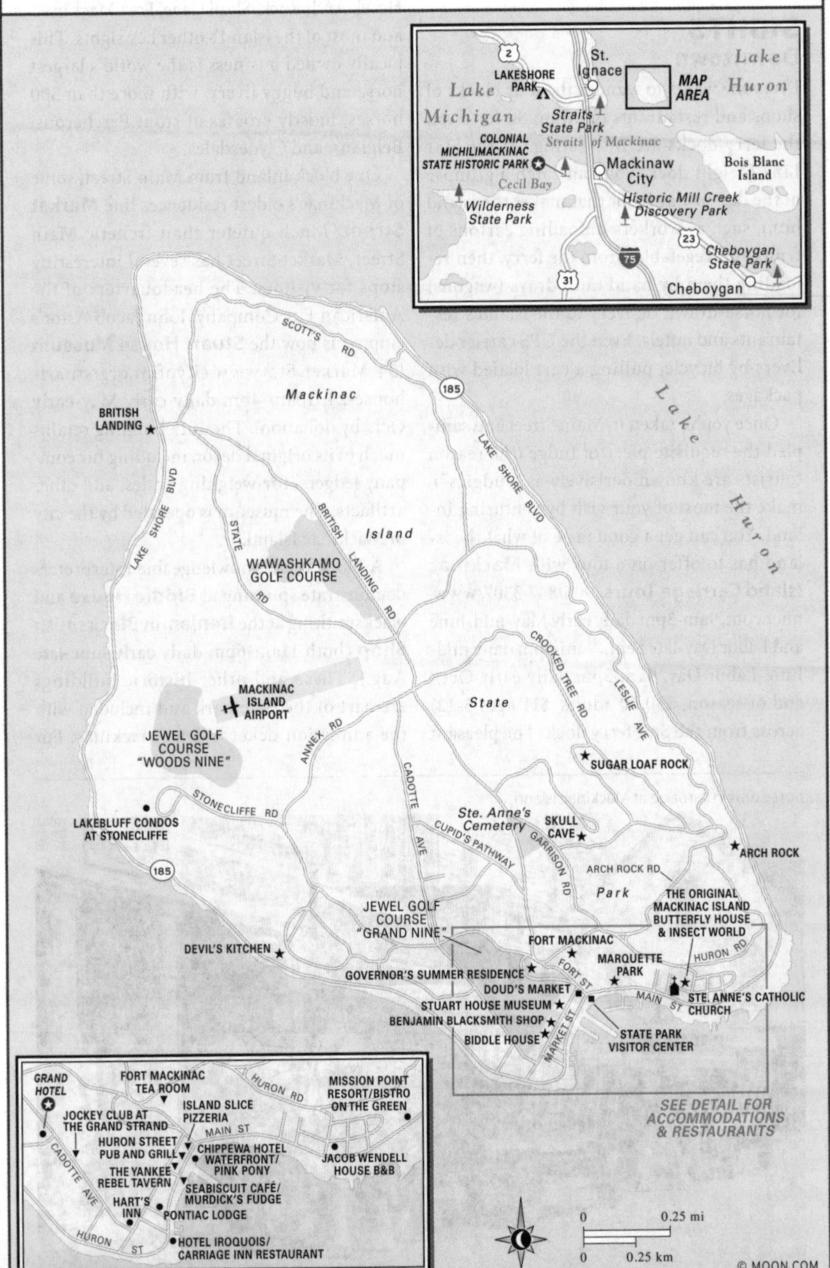

it's a wonderful place to retreat from the ordinary world.

SIGHTS

Downtown

Everyone wants to wander the four blocks of shops and restaurants on Main Street. Even the ferry docks are interesting. At the Star Line Freight dock, you can catch a glimpse of the day-to-day labor that makes the island hum, such as workers unloading cartons of fruits and vegetables from the ferry, then reloading them by hand onto drays (wagons) for horse-drawn delivery to the island's restaurants and hotels. Even the UPS carrier delivers by bicycle, pulling a cart loaded with packages.

Once you've taken in Main Street and sampled the requisite piece of fudge (the reason tourists are known derisively as "fudgies"), make the most of your visit by venturing inland. You can get a good taste of what the island has to offer on a tour with **Mackinac Island Carriage Tours** (906/847-3307, www.mict.com, 9am-3pm daily early May-mid-June and Labor Day-late Sept., 9am-5pm daily mid-June-Labor Day, 9am-2pm daily early Oct.-end of season, $30.50 adults, $11 ages 5-12) across from the Star ferry dock. The pleasant narrated tour takes about two hours, rambling along at a relaxing pace past the Grand Hotel, Arch Rock, Skull Cave, Fort Mackinac, and most of the island's other key sights. This locally owned business is the world's largest horse and buggy livery, with more than 300 horses, mostly crosses of stout Percherons, Belgians, and Clydesdales.

One block inland from Main Street, some of Mackinac's oldest residences line **Market Street.** Much quieter than frenetic Main Street, Market Street has several interesting stops for visitors. The headquarters of the American Fur Company, John Jacob Astor's empire, is now the **Stuart House Museum** (34 Market St., www.cityofmi.org/stuart-house-24, 10am-4pm daily early May-early Oct., by donation). The 1817 building retains much of its original decor, including fur company ledgers, fur-weighing scales, and other artifacts. The museum is operated by the city of Mackinac Island.

A block west, knowledgeable interpreters demonstrate spinning at **Biddle House** and blacksmithing at the **Benjamin Blacksmith Shop** (both 11am-6pm daily early June-late Aug.). These and other historic buildings are part of the state park and included with the admission ticket to Fort Mackinac. For

horse drawn carriage at Mackinac Island

current information, stop by the park visitors center across from Marquette Park on Huron Street, or contact **Mackinac State Historic Parks** (213/436-4100, www.mackinacparks.com, 11am-4pm daily).

From Marquette Park, follow Fort Street up the hill to the **Governor's Residence** at the corner of Fort and East Bluff Road. The state purchased the "cottage" in the 1940s. It is the official summer residence of the governor, though the amount of time actually spent here varies from governor to governor. The house is open for tours on Wednesday mornings. No inside photography is permitted.

Some of the island's more impressive residences line up along **East Bluff.** Wander east from the governor's mansion to see some of these Victorian marvels. Happily, most survived the Depression era, when they could be purchased for pennies on the dollar. Today, they're well cared for, and many are valued in excess of $2 million.

Work your way down one of the sets of public steps to the lakefront. Main Street has become Huron Street here. Continue your walk east, passing smaller, but no less appealing cottages and homes. Many are skirted with geraniums and lilacs, the island's signature flowers. Behind Ste. Anne's Catholic Church, seek out the **Original Mackinac Island Butterfly House & Insect World** (6750 McGulpin St., 906/847-3972, www.originalbutterflyhouse.com, 10am-7pm daily Memorial Day-Labor Day, $12 adults, $8 ages 5-12).

Owner Doug Beardsley once used his greenhouses to grow geraniums for the Grand Hotel and other clients. He relied on biodynamic growing methods, releasing beneficial insects to care for his plants rather than chemical sprays. When economics made his small greenhouse less viable, he continued with his insects. After hearing about a butterfly house in Europe, Beardsley added some different host plants and began ordering pupae from around the world. Now hundreds of butterflies fly freely in his greenhouse atrium, some nearly six inches long. You can observe them up close on walls and plants; if you sit still long enough, they might land on you.

The engaging Beardsley hopes his attraction will help convince gardeners to wean themselves off herbicides and pesticides. He sells helpful insects to control garden pests like aphids and will provide ideas for attracting butterflies to your own garden. Host plants like milkweed and cabbage, where butterflies like to lay their eggs, will work best. "Think of it as planting a caterpillar garden, not a butterfly garden," he says.

★ Grand Hotel

The **Grand Hotel** (286 Grand Ave., 906/847-3331 or 800/334-7263, www.grandhotel.com) has become practically synonymous with Mackinac Island, a gracious edifice built on a truly grand scale. It is the largest summer resort in the world, operating early May-late October. Its famous 660-foot covered front porch is adorned each spring with 2,000 geraniums planted in seven tons of potting soil. Its 11 restaurants and bars serve as many as 4,000 meals a day. Its impeccable grounds offer guests every amenity, from saddle horses to designer golf to swimming in the outdoor pool made famous by the 1940s swimmer and actor Esther Williams, who filmed *This Time for Keeps* here in 1946.

Opulence was the goal of the railroads and steamship lines when they formed a consortium and built the Grand Hotel in 1887, dragging construction materials across the ice by horse and mule. The wealthiest of all Mackinac Island visitors stayed at the Grand Hotel high on a hill overlooking the straits.

Yet unlike other turn-of-the-20th-century resorts that burned to the ground or grew worn and faded, the Grand Hotel has maintained its grace and dignity. It hosts all manner of celebrities and politicians—five U.S. presidents to date—and still offers a sip of the Gilded Age, with high tea in the parlor each afternoon and demitasse served after dinner each evening. Room rates still include a five-course dinner in the soaring main dining room, where the required attire remains jackets with ties for men and skirts, dresses, or pantsuits for women.

The Grand Hotel's polished setting prompted director Jeannot Szwarc to choose it as the location for the 1980 film *Somewhere in Time,* starring Christopher Reeve, Jane Seymour, and Christopher Plummer. Despite limited commercial success and little critical acclaim, the movie has nonetheless developed a huge following; its fan club reunites at the hotel each year in late October.

While room rates at the Grand Hotel are astronomical, they can be a worthwhile splurge if you enjoy this kind of thing—taking high tea, lolling in the beautifully landscaped pool, or dancing to the swing orchestra in the Terrace Room. Nonguests can enter the hotel's public areas and grounds for $10, a fee imposed to thin out the throngs of sightseers more than anything. Highly recommended are a stroll through the grounds, filled with Victorian gardens—24,000 tulips in spring!—and a visit to the elegant Cupola Bar.

Fort Mackinac

At the crest of the bluff, whitewashed **Fort Mackinac** (231/436-4100, 9am-5pm daily early June-Sept. 1, 9:30am-7pm daily early Sept.-early Oct., 9:30am-5pm daily early to late Oct., $13.50 adults, $7.75 ages 6-17) is worth a visit for the views alone, offering the fort's perspective of presiding over downtown, the marina, and Lake Huron. There's also a bevy of other things to see at this military outpost, which the British and Americans struggled over for nearly 40 years.

Along with peering over the parapets, you can wander in and out of 14 buildings within the fort. The barracks, officers' quarters, post hospital, and others are filled with interpretive displays and decorated in period decor. Costumed guides lead reenactments, including musket firings and cannon salutes. A short audiovisual presentation, "The Heritage of Mackinac," shares the fort's basic history.

Mackinac Island State Park

Often overshadowed by other visitor attractions, Mackinac Island's natural history has attracted scientific observation for over 200 years. In the early 19th century, botanists discovered several previously unknown species, including the dwarf lake iris, still common in the Straits of Mackinac region.

Early scientists exploring the area also marveled at the island's distinctive geology, mostly brecciated limestone that has been sculpted by eons of wind and waves. These forces of nature produced some dramatic rock formations, including the inland slab of limestone called **Sugar Loaf Rock,** the lakeside caves of **Devil's Kitchen,** and impressive **Arch Rock,** which rises nearly 150 feet above the eastern shore and is some 50 feet wide.

In recognition of the park's natural curiosities and the growth in tourism, the U.S. government created Mackinac National Park in 1875—following Yellowstone as the nation's second national park. Twenty years later, it was returned to Michigan and became **Mackinac Island State Park** (906/847-3328, www.mackinacparks.com, park 24 hours daily, visitor's center 9am-4pm daily early May-early June and early Sept.-early Oct., 9am-6pm daily early June-Sept. 1., free), Michigan's first state park and one of the very few that does not require a recreation passport or a day pass. For more information about the state park, head to the Mackinac Island Visitor's Center, on the south side of Main Street, across from Marquette Park.

RECREATION

Walk, run, bike, or ride a horse, but make sure you get out of downtown to really see Mackinac Island. You'll be surprised how quickly you can leave any crowds behind as you set out on **M-185,** the road that circles the island for eight miles. Despite the absence of motorized traffic, M-185 is an official state trunk-line highway and part of Michigan's state highway system. It never wanders far from the arresting shoreline and passes many of the island's natural features, all of which are well marked. Traveling clockwise, the first you'll reach is Devil's Kitchen; heading in the

Mackinac's Migrant Wildlife

While the Straits of Mackinac usually serve as a mighty barrier for many of the mammals that dwell on Mackinac Island, Michigan winters can indeed alter the situation, allowing some of the larger mammals, such as wolves, bears, and deer, to reach the mainland via an ice bridge. Unlike what you find in warmer climates, this 2,200-acre island is less isolated. In fact, many of its seasonal visitors are migrant birds, who use this popular migration spot as a resort habitat in spring en route to summer homes in the north.

Although Mackinac Island also attracts seasonal recreationists such as hikers and bikers, bird-watchers are especially fond of this enchanted place. In late April and early May you'll spot golden eagles, bald eagles, and both red-tailed and broad-winged hawks flying overhead. Yellow warblers, American redstarts, and indigo buntings arrive in summer. Along the shoreline, you might also see herrings, cormorants, great blue herons, loons, and Canada geese. Even wintertime guests will be treated to bird sightings: Beautiful snowy owls and great gray owls often fly south from the Arctic to savor the comparatively warmer climate of Mackinac Island.

Some species, however, remain on the island year-round, including cardinals, blue jays, black-capped chickadees, and large red-crested woodpeckers. The difference between them and other native inhabitants is that they're here by choice. They can spread their wings and leave at any time—unlike coyotes, for instance, which must wait for an ice bridge to form before making their escape.

opposite direction, Arch Rock will be your initial destination, the most dramatic of all Mackinac limestone oddities.

About halfway around, on the island's northwestern side lies **British Landing,** where British soldiers invaded in 1812. After hiking across Mackinac's interior, they totally surprised the U.S. garrison at the fort—who were apparently looking the other way—and recaptured the island. Today, the landing is a good spot for a picnic or short break; water and restrooms are available. There's a small **nature center** here, staffed in summer months by a helpful naturalist. Hike the short **nature trail,** which has several interpretive signs as it weaves up a bluff.

British Landing is also a good spot from which to head inland and explore the island's interior. British Landing Road bisects the island and links up with Garrison Road near **Skull Cave,** leading to the fort. It's a hilly, three-mile trip from shore to shore. British Landing Road is considered a major road by Mackinac standards, meaning you'll share it with carriages. Biking or on foot, you'll have endless other options—at last count, Mackinac had some 140 miles of trails and footpaths.

Pick up a free *Mackinac Island Map,* available all over town, and venture off. The map marks the location of old cemeteries, rock formations, and such, but it's even more appealing just to explore the smaller trails on your own and discover pretty, peaceful Mackinac. Everything is well marked, although the compact size of the island makes getting lost unlikely.

NIGHTLIFE

Despite the popularity of its daytime attractions, Mackinac Island also sports an active nightlife scene.

The **Grand Hotel Orchestra,** a five-piece ensemble, takes to the Terrace Room each evening to perform classical standards and popular tunes, perfect for an evening of dancing.

The **Gate House** (1547 Cadotte Ave., 906/847-3772, www.grandhotel.com, 11am-close), an off-site establishment operated by the Grand Hotel, offers late-night dining plus a vast array of beverage choices—creative concoctions like a Coconut Watermelon Mojito

1
SANDERS
2
3
4
ICE CREAM PARLOR

and Electric Lilac Lemonade—plus several of the Grand Hotel's exclusive wines.

Horn's Gaslight Bar (7300 Main St., 906/847-6154, www.hornsbar.com noon-midnight daily) is a great place to enjoy libations while listening and dancing to live music. Local bands representing different musical genres fill the calendar, while every Wednesday is DJ night. A great menu of Southwestern dishes complements the offerings.

The **Mustang Lounge** (1485 Astor St., 906/847-8255, www.mustang-lounge.com, 9am-2am daily) bills itself as the oldest building in Michigan to house a tavern still in operation. It offers 24 varieties of beer and wine, plus a wide assortment of liquor and a powerful jukebox.

Music in the Park (Thurs. June-July) is a series of free outdoor concerts offered in the evening in Marquette Park, weather permitting. The lineup usually includes artists performing folk, soft rock, and classical selections.

SHOPPING

Although shopping isn't a huge activity here, the island does present a few unique browsing options. One noteworthy destination is the **Loon Feather & Balsam Shop** (7427 Main St., 906/847-3591, https://balsamshop.com, 8am-10pm daily May-Nov.). Here you'll find something for almost anyone—Polish pottery, lilac glassware, fishing tackle, and Minnetonka moccasins. Another place is **Giant Turtle Toys of Mackinac Island** (7372 Main St., in the Lilac Tree Courtyard Shops, 906/847-6118, https://greatturtletoys.com, 9am-11pm daily summer), a source for all varieties of toys designed to stimulate kids' imagination and creativity.

FOOD

One of the best dining deals on the island is the ★ **Fort Mackinac Tea Room** (906/847-3328, www.grandhotel.com, 11am-3pm daily June-Sept., $10-15) in the lower level of the officers' quarters within the fort. Surrounded by thick masonry walls, the tearoom serves up both a great atmosphere and delicious food, with good soups, salads, and sandwiches prepared by Grand Hotel chefs. Ask for a spot on the terrace to enjoy the spectacular view.

A more upscale dining option affiliated with the Grand Hotel is **The Jockey Club at the Grand Strand** (1874 Cadotte Ave., 906/847-9212, www.grandhotel.com, 11am-5pm and 5:30pm-9pm daily, $19-58), located near the first tee of The Jewel, one of the hotel's signature golf courses. The menu is classic Americana—lobster and bacon mac and cheese, blue-cheese-crusted petit filet, tempura-fried lobster tails. This is a great destination for a special meal.

Another venue with a view of the links is **Bistro on the Greens** (Mission Point Resort, 6633 Main St., 906/847-3312, www.missionpoint.com, 11am-8pm daily Memorial Day-Labor Day, $12-29), where you'll find an impressive but not overly avant-garde menu. Offerings include tempting choices for lunch and dinner, such as a chicken salad croissant sandwich and grilled lamb chops. There's a fairly extensive list of cocktail choices.

Another tasty downtown option is **The Yankee Rebel Tavern** (1493 Astor St., 906/847-6249, www.yankeerebeltavern.com, 10:30am-midnight daily, $14-37), which serves American-style comfort food, from traditional pot roast to pistachio-encrusted whitefish. Named after the famous underdog horse from 1938, the nearby **Seabiscuit Café** (906/847-3611, www.seabiscuitcafe.com, 7am-2am daily May-Oct., $10-27) prepares some colorfully named appetizers, such as the Painted Pony Macaroni or the War Admiral Hot Wings, plus various salads, sandwiches, and heartier meals ranging from curry chicken to baby back ribs. The restaurant's clever motto is "bet on a good time." Other allusions to the world of horse racing abound.

Billing itself as "the Classic American Pub,"

1: Mackinac Island is motor vehicle-free **2:** the reconstructed Fort Holmes above Fort Mackinac **3:** Arch Rock **4:** the Grand Hotel

the **Huron Street Pub and Grill** (7304 Main St., 906/847-8255, 8am-2am daily, $10-23) is where you'll find all the bases covered—sandwiches like the Huron Street Reuben, dinner choices like backyard barbecue ribs and Lake Superior whitefish, plus the obligatory full bar make this a worthwhile find.

At the Hotel Iroquois, you'll find the **Carriage House Restaurant** (7485 Main St., 906/847-3321, www.iroquoishotel.com, 11am-7pm daily mid-May-mid-Oct., $19-54), the perfect place to dine in elegance while enjoying an unparalleled waterfront view. Entrées include some unusual offerings such as gnocchi with sautéed zucchini and pappardelle pasta puttanesca with artisanal sausage, but you'll also find more familiar classics such as lemon Mediterranean chicken with Italian olives.

A nice casual alternative for lunch is the **Island Slice Pizzeria** (7248 Main St., 906/847-8100, www.islandslicepizzeria.com, 11am-10pm daily Memorial Day-Labor Day, $12-27). Despite the name, the restaurant's offerings also include oven-baked subs, a number of tasty salad choices, plus pizza of all varieties. They offer free delivery on the island.

Of course, everyone has to hit the **Pink Pony** (7221-103 Main St., 906/847-3341, www.chippewahotel.com, 8am-2am daily, $7-32) at least once during a Mackinac visit. In the Chippewa Hotel overlooking the marina, this is the party place for following the famed Port Huron to Mackinac yacht race. The food's terrific, with various omelets for breakfast, delicious salads and sandwiches on the lunch menu, and pasta, steaks, seafood, and ribs for dinner.

Sooner or later, however, you'll succumb to fudge, a visitor's treat since the Victorian era. In fact, a plethora of fudge shops are scattered throughout the downtown shopping area. One of the oldest, **Murdick's Fudge** (7363 Main St., 906/298-0630, www.originalmurdicksfudge.com), established in 1887, has a prime Main Street location, where you can buy a sizable slab to take or mail home, or just a small sliver to nibble during your downtown stroll. Choose from any of dozens of available flavors, including Michigan maple walnut, pumpkin spice, or one of several variations of chocolate.

ACCOMMODATIONS

Along with the ★ **Grand Hotel** (286 Grand Ave., 906/847-3331 or 800/334-7263, www.grandhotel.com, $345-520 pp), there are plenty of grand and graceful places to stay on Mackinac Island. While the rates are higher than on the mainland, don't dismiss staying on Mackinac. Small B&Bs and apartments are often attractive alternatives, with the latter offering good deals for weeklong stays.

The venerable **Chippewa Hotel Waterfront** (7221-103 Main St., 906/847-3341 or 800/241-3341, www.chippewahotel.com, $119-619 d) is a classy and comfortable place in the heart of the island overlooking the marina. The 24-person lakeside hot tub alone may be worth the stay. Meanwhile, the **Hotel Iroquois** (7485 Main St., 906/847-3321, www.iroquoishotel.com, $350-585 d) offers 46 well-appointed guest rooms and suites, including the two-bedroom Lighthouse Suite, which features spectacular views of Round Island Light. Besides private baths, cable television, and complimentary wireless Internet service, this lovely hotel provides direct access to a private sunbathing beach as well as the Carriage House, one of the island's finest restaurants.

One of the more charming and reasonably priced B&Bs on the island is **Hart's Inn at French Lane** (7556 Market St., 906/847-6234, www.hartsmackinac.com, $205-245). Situated away from the "main drag," this is where you can find a comfortable, soothing atmosphere in an elegant setting. Housed in a very old (circa 1830) yet thoroughly updated French-style cottage, each room offers air-conditioning, a private bath, a flat-screen TV, and wireless Internet. A hearty continental breakfast is included, of course.

The **Mission Point Resort** (6633 Main St., 906/847-3312 or 800/833-7711, www.missionpoint.com, $175-599 d) may have

Mackinac's very best location, spread across 18 acres at the island's southeastern tip. Though not from the Victorian era—it was built in the 1950s by the Moral Re-Armament movement, a post-World War II patriotic group—the sprawling bright-white resort is attractive and well-maintained, with beautiful lawns lined with Adirondack chairs. Amenities include an outdoor pool, tennis and volleyball courts, and loads of children's activities.

From May to October, visitors can opt for a stay at the unique **Jacob Wendell House Bed & Breakfast** (231/818-0334, www.jacobwendellhouse.com, May-Oct., $130-315 d), situated on Main Street, within walking distance of the downtown shopping area and marina. Built in 1846, this picturesque Federal-style B&B offers four lovely bedrooms, each of which features a full private bath, plus access to a spacious living room, a formal dining room, and a comfortable kitchen.

If you're looking for a more economical place to stay on the island, the year-round **Pontiac Lodge** (1346 Hoban St., 906/847-3364, www.pontiaclodge.com, $90-425 d) features 11 simply furnished rooms as well as three apartments, ideal for families. Conveniently situated near the ferry dock, this comfortable hotel also boasts an on-site eatery, the Village Inn Restaurant.

For those who love the Mackinac Island experience but crave solitude, try the **LakeBluff Condos at Stonecliffe** (3561 Eckel Dr., 800/699-6927, May-Oct., $165-510). On the island's West Bluff, and far from the souvenir stands and fudge shops, this resort is nonetheless easy walking distance from one of the Grand Hotel's golf courses, the Mackinac Island Airport, and several historical landmarks.

INFORMATION AND SERVICES

For more information, contact the helpful **Mackinac Island Tourism Bureau** (7274 Main St., 877/847-3783, www.mackinacisland.org, 9am-5pm daily) across from the Star ferry dock. You can also consult www.mackinac.com or pick up a copy of the weekly ***Mackinac Island Town Crier*** (www.mackinacislandnews.com).

Mackinac Island offers a limited amount of services, including a few grocery stores and a small police department. For banking needs, stop by the **Central Savings Bank** (21 Hoban St., 906/847-3759, www.centralsavingsbank.com, 9am-4pm Mon.-Fri., 9am-noon Sat. June-Aug.). For medical needs, there is the **Mackinac Island Medical Center** (7474 Market St., 906/847-3582, www.mackinacstraitshealth.org), near Cindy's Riding Stable, which has on-call staff 24 hours daily. Call 911 in an emergency. Ambulance and police vehicles are exceptions to the island's prohibition on motorized transit.

GETTING THERE AND AROUND

Getting There

More than a million people visit Mackinac Island every year, so getting here is easy. One option is to fly into **Pellston Regional Airport** (PLN, 1395 U.S. 31, Pellston, 231/539-8441 or 231/539-8442, www.pellstonairport.com), then either charter a flight to the island through **Great Lakes Air** (906/643-7165, www.greatlakesair.net, one-way from St. Ignace $30, from Cheboygan $50) or use the **Mackinaw Shuttle** (231/539-7005 or 888/349-8294, www.mackinawshuttle.com, rates vary) to reach the ferry docks in Mackinaw City or St. Ignace. You can also reach the ferry docks by private vehicle.

Two ferry services can shuttle you across the Straits of Mackinac in less than 20 minutes, each of which offers departures from both Mackinaw City and St. Ignace: **Shepler's Mackinac Island Ferry** (231/436-5023, 906/643-9440, or 800/828-6157, www.sheplersferry.com, late Apr.-Oct., round-trip $25 adults, $14 ages 5-12, under age 5 free, $10 bikes) and **Star Line** (800/638-9892, www.mackinacferry.com, late Apr.-Oct., round-trip $25 adults, $14 ages 5-12, under age 5 free, $12 bikes).

During the main tourist season—May-October—the lines run several sailings daily. Due to the limited number of sailings, plus the obstacles presented by the winter freeze, you'll find it more challenging to reach Mackinac between November and March.

Ferries deposit you at the southern end of the island, in the heart of the hotels and shops lining Main Street, which follows the curve of the waterfront. It can be a bit chaotic: Dockworkers loading luggage onto pull carts and carriages, flocks of bicyclists dodging horse-drawn buggies, and pedestrians streaming up and down the street eating fudge and window-shopping.

Getting Around

Navigating Mackinac Island is fairly simple, despite the necessity that it be done without a motorized vehicle. One option is to use the horse-drawn taxis, which are available from **Mackinac Island Carriage Tours** (906/847-3323 or 906/847-3307, www.mict.com, $5.50-8 pp, min. of 2, 3 or 4 passengers depending upon the zone) 24 hours daily during the summer months or by appointment November to April. You can easily traverse Mackinac on foot, however, walking and hiking. It's a wonderfully scenic place for casual strolls and all-day hikes.

The island is also a terrific place for cycling. Several bike rental outfits are located downtown; the **Mackinac Island Bike Shop** (906/847-6337, www.bikemackinac.com) rents mountain bikes, cruisers, tandems, and tag-a-longs ($8-10/hr., $44-62/day). All bikes are available in men's and women's styles, and kids' bikes are available, too. It's also possible to rent pet carriers, strollers, electric scooters (a helpful exception to the island's ban on motorized vehicles) and wheelchairs. Rentals also include a helmet, a basket, and a bottle of water. Equipment varies greatly, so look before you pay. If you prefer, you can transport your own bike to the island on the ferry. It's best to choose a hybrid or mountain bike to negotiate most interior trails, and be sure to bring a helmet.

Cheboygan and Vicinity

With a population of 4,800, Cheboygan ranks as one of the largest cities along Lake Huron. While the town offers history buffs a few interesting sites, including a 19th-century opera house, it mainly appeals to outdoor enthusiasts, who venture beyond the city limits to explore surrounding lakes, rivers, and forests. Boaters and anglers especially focus their gaze inland, where a 45-mile-long waterway of rivers and lakes begins at the Lake Huron shore and ends just shy of Lake Michigan's Little Traverse Bay. Cheboygan sits at the mouth of this popular waterway, and enthusiastically welcomes boaters. Hikers, bird-watchers, and other lovers of the outdoors will find plenty of interest.

SIGHTS

Historic Sights and Lighthouses

The **Cheboygan History Center** (427 Court St., 231/627-9597, www.cheboyganhistory.org, 10am-2pm Wed.-Sat. Memorial Day-early Oct., free) was built in 1882 and served as the county jail and local sheriff's home until 1969. The two-story brick structure houses a parlor, kitchen, schoolroom, and bedroom in period style, with an adjacent building that contains logging and marine displays.

The city's **Opera House** (403 N. Huron St., 231/627-5432, www.theoperahouse.org, 10am-4pm daily, $2) once entertained the likes of Mary Pickford and Annie Oakley. Built in 1877, rebuilt after an 1888 fire, then rebuilt again after a 1903 fire, the Victorian-style theater serves as a stage for local entertainment and is open for tours in summer.

From the boardwalk in **Gordon Turner Park** at the northern end of Huron Street, you can gaze out over one of the largest cattail marshes on the Great Lakes. A nesting ground for more than 50 species, it's a favorite of bird-watchers. From the boardwalk and nearby anglers' walkway, you also can see the Mackinac Bridge as well as Round and Bois Blanc Islands. Visitors might also appreciate the quaint 1884 **Cheboygan Crib Light,** an octagonal structure relocated from the mouth of the Cheboygan River to the base of the west breakwater on Lake Huron. Now, the interesting white and red facility (it's termed a "light" as opposed to a "lighthouse" since no keeper ever lived there) is an ideal stop for photographers.

Parks and Preserves

Cheboygan's **Grass Bay Preserve** contains a rare find in the Great Lakes—one of the finest examples of an original interdunal wetland habitat, characterized by beach pools, marshes, flats, and wetlands, all separated by low dunes. Owned by the Nature Conservancy (517/316-0300), this delicate ecosystem comprises a great diversity of plants, including more than 25 species of orchids and 11 types of conifers. Four of the species—dwarf lake iris, Lake Huron tansy, Pitcher's thistle, and Houghton's goldenrod—grow only on the Lake Huron and Lake Michigan shores.

The Nature Conservancy considers Grass Bay its most prized Michigan property. The preserve's original 80 acres have expanded to include more than 830, including a one-mile stretch of Lake Huron shore. From May to September, Grass Bay is noted for its carpet of wildflowers, including lady's slipper, Indian paintbrush, blue harebell, and sundews. The best way to take them all in is from one of the park's two short trails, which wander through an aspen-birch forest and across old shoreline ridges to the beach. Note, however, that this is private—and very fragile—land. Parking can be hard to find—some visitors have used lots on U.S. 23.

RECREATION

For hikers and cross-country skiers, the **Wildwood Hills Pathway** on Wildwood Road in nearby Indian River offers almost complete isolation. Three well-marked trails, ranging four to nine miles in length, take visitors deep into the heart of a northern

Cheboygan Crib Light

Michigan second-growth forest and cross high rolling hills in the Mackinac State Forest just a few miles south of Burt Lake.

Two trailheads on Wildwood Road provide access to the pathway, leading into a dense forest of hardwoods and evergreens. Along the way, the only companions you'll likely have are the wind through the trees, an occasional birdcall, and a curious chipmunk or two. Trail system maps are located at the trailheads and at most major intersections.

The swift and turbulent Pigeon River, designated by the state as a natural river, is the highlight of the **Agnes S. Andreae Nature Preserve.** Located in Indian River, the beautifully secluded 181-acre preserve includes 2,000 feet of Pigeon River frontage. On the river's west side, a lowland stand of cedar bordering the riverbank rises to high bluffs covered with conifers and dense hardwoods. There are more than five miles of trails between both the Andreae and the adjacent Banwell Preserve. Like many other tracts in this undeveloped part of the state, the preserve is owned by the **Little Traverse Conservancy** (3264 Powell Rd., Harbor Springs, 231/347-0991, www.landtrust.org). To find the preserve, get off I-75 at exit 310 near Indian River. Take M-68 east about seven miles until coming to Quarry Road. Turn left and proceed north on Quarry Road for approximately 0.5 mile. Turn left on Dunn Road and continue west for another 0.5 mile.

FOOD AND ACCOMMODATIONS

For good food served up with interesting history, try the **Hack-Ma-Tack Inn & Restaurant** (8131 Beebe Rd., 231/625-2919, www.hackmatackinn.com, 5pm-10pm daily May-mid-Oct., $18-50), housed in a rustic 1894 lodge overlooking the Cheboygan River. Whitefish is the specialty, along with certified black Angus prime rib.

There are several adequate motels in the Cheboygan area, such as the **Best Western River Terrace Motel** (847 S. Main St., 231/627-5688, www.bestwesternmichigan.com, $120-230 d), with most rooms overlooking the Cheboygan River. You can also camp at **Cheboygan State Park** (4490 Beach Rd., 616/627-2811, annual Recreation Passport required: $12 Michigan residents, $34 nonresidents, $9 day pass available to nonresidents only) at one of 78 modern sites ($19-28) along Lake Huron's Duncan Bay. The area is a favorite among anglers, but there's not much in the way of swimming at the campground; instead, head for the park's day-use area, four miles away, which has a sandy beach and bathhouse.

INFORMATION AND SERVICES

For more information, contact the **Cheboygan Area Chamber of Commerce** (124 N. Main St., 800/968-3302, www.cheboygan.com, 9am-5pm Mon.-Fri.). For local news and events, consult the ***Cheboygan Daily Tribune*** (www.cheboygannews.com).

Cheboygan offers most of the services travelers might require, including groceries and banks. For medical assistance, visit **McLaren Northern Michigan-Cheboygan Campus** (748 S. Main St., 800/248-6777, www.mclaren.org).

GETTING THERE AND AROUND

From **Pellston Regional Airport** (PLN, 1395 U.S. 31, Pellston, 231/539-8441 or 231/539-8442, www.pellstonairport.com), you can rent a car, head north on U.S. 31, and take County Road 66 east to Cheboygan. In light traffic, the 20-mile trip should take 24 minutes. You can take a bus directly to the Cheboygan bus stop (309 E. State St.) via **Greyhound** (800/231-2222, www.greyhound.com) or **Indian Trails** (800/292-3831, www.indiantrails.com).

By car, reach Cheboygan via M-27, M-33, or U.S. 23. From Sault Ste. Marie take I-75, cross the Mackinac Bridge, and continue on U.S. 23 south to Cheboygan, a 74-mile trip that usually takes 80 minutes. From Traverse City, take M-72, U.S. 131, County Road 42, M-32, and I-75, then follow Levering Road to

Cheboygan, a 114-mile trip that takes about two hours. Detroit is only four hours away via I-375, I-75, and Levering Road, a 284-mile journey.

THE INLAND WATERWAY

The geography of this region was kind to the early Native Americans and French voyageurs traversing the Lower Peninsula: A chain of lakes and rivers forms a 45-mile water route, very nearly linking Lakes Michigan and Huron. The route was safer and faster than traveling on the big lakes, and certainly beat portaging. Today, the inland waterway remains especially popular for fishing and recreational boating. Narrower portions are dredged to a depth of five feet and a width of 30 feet. Boats up to 30 feet long can join what sometimes looks like a nautical parade.

Burt Lake State Park

Big Burt Lake is the focus of its namesake **Burt Lake State Park** (6635 State Dr., Indian River, 231/238-9392, annual Recreation Passport required: $12 Michigan residents, $34 nonresidents, $9 day pass available to nonresidents only) at its southern end. Anglers flock to this 10-mile-long lake, known as one of the best fishing spots in the state, for panfish, bass, and especially walleye. The park is also popular with swimmers, since it features a soft sand beach that runs the entire length of the park. The park has two boat launches, one next to a popular campground with 375 modern sites ($31). The park offers little in the way of hiking but has an observation tower offering a dramatic view of the lake.

Mullett Lake

Along with neighboring Burt Lake, pretty Mullett Lake is one of the most popular and productive fishing lakes in the state. Anglers vie for walleye and northern pike, but larger stuff lurks down there as well: In 1974, Mullett produced a 193-pound sturgeon, a scaly, long-nosed fish that has evolved little since prehistoric times.

A local mystery involves why a small town on the east end of Mullett Lake was originally named Aloha Depot. Today, it's the site of **Aloha State Park** (231/625-2522, www.michigandnr.com, annual Recreation Passport required: $12 Michigan residents, $34 nonresidents, $9 day pass available to nonresidents only), a small 100-acre site that consists mostly of a boat launch and a 295-site campground ($33). Not especially picturesque by Michigan standards, most sites are relatively open, with only a few directly on the water.

Rogers City to Alpena

Driving along the picturesque Lake Huron shore, you'll encounter a number of sleepy communities, including Rogers City, home to scenic lighthouses, parks, and beaches, and Alpena, a larger city favored by outdoor enthusiasts for its wildlife sanctuary and underwater preserve.

Despite its beautiful beaches, few travelers visit Rogers City, a quiet town of about 2,800, known as home to the world's largest limestone quarry. The Huron shore's limestone was formed by ancient seas that once covered most of the state. Full of coral-forming organisms, they eventually created large limestone deposits, one of which nears the earth's surface in Rogers City. Nearly four miles long and roughly three miles wide, the limestone quarry is expected to produce well into this century.

Protected by the deep curve of Thunder Bay, Alpena is the largest city north of Bay City on the Lake Huron shore, yet it's always been relegated to secondary status.

Part of the reason visitors have overlooked Alpena is because of its relative inaccessibility. More than 70 miles from the nearest interstate highway, it remains an unpretentious working-class town of corner bars and friendly residents. For decades, a diversified group of industries, including paper mills, cement plants, and a training base for the Michigan Air National Guard, all set up shop in town—immunizing it from an over dependence on tourism.

But gradually several of those bread-and-butter industries disappeared, forcing Alpena to promote its assets to attract visitors. And there are many worth promoting, including two lightly visited state parks with several miles of Lake Huron shoreline, a handsome marina, an impressive museum, northern Michigan's only year-round professional theater, and a fascinating underwater preserve containing more than 80 shipwrecks.

SIGHTS

Besser Museum for Northeast Michigan

The excellent **Besser Museum for Northeast Michigan** (491 Johnson St., Alpena, 989/356-2202, www.bessermuseum.org, 10am-5pm Mon.-Sat., noon-4pm Sun., $5 adults, $3 seniors and ages 5-17, under age 5 free) combines art, history, and science on two levels. The museum's highlight is the "Gallery of Early Man," a collection of Great Lakes Native American artifacts considered one of the finest in the country. To the likely embarrassment of archaeologists, the collection, which numbers more than 60,000 pieces, was gathered by Gerald Haltiner, a local state highway worker, and his museum curator son Robert.

The museum purchased the collection from the Haltiners in the 1970s and is working closely with local Native American groups to review its holdings with repatriation in mind. Some of its most intriguing artifacts are the copper items that date back more than 7,000 years, made by people known only as the Copper Culture. The museum's Sky Theater Planetarium, newly renovated and renamed as the digital sky theater, presents rotating shows, many with Native American themes.

Alpena Wildlife Sanctuary

Alpena Wildlife Sanctuary (Wildlife Sanctuary Board, 989/595-3919 or 989/354-1770, www.alpena.mi.us), on U.S. 23 within the Alpena city limits, has been a favorite sanctuary of hikers, paddlers, anglers, and nature lovers since it was established in 1938 by the Michigan Department of Conservation. The 500-acre refuge bordering the Thunder Bay River contains a large expanse of wetlands, an island with fishing platforms, and a viewing platform that overlooks the river. According to the Thunder Bay Audubon Society, more than 130 different species of birds have been spotted here. Year-round residents include Canada geese and mute swans; spring migration brings others, including buffleheads, canvasbacks, and whistling swans.

Lighthouses

Travelers who find the Huron shore mundane in comparison with the state's Lake Michigan shore often change their minds after a visit to the **40 Mile Point Lighthouse.** Seven miles north of Rogers City on U.S. 23, a limitless expanse of blue water sweeps in a 180-degree arc to the horizon. A gently sloping beach proves just right for wading, sandcastle building, and swimming. The 52-foot-tall lighthouse, built in 1897, stands guard as a reminder that Lake Huron can, and often does, turn dangerous. Though not open to the public, it is a favorite of photographers.

Other lighthouses along this stretch include the 1905 **Middle Island Lighthouse** and the 1832 **Thunder Bay Island Light,** both accessible via boat. In Alpena, you won't need a vessel to view the 1914 **Alpena Light,** a skeletal red structure near the Thunder Bay River.

Beaches and Parks

Many rate **P. H. Hoeft State Park** (U.S. 23 N., Rogers City, 989/734-2543, annual Recreation Passport required: $12 Michigan residents, $34 nonresidents, $9 day pass available to nonresidents only) as the most beautiful state park along Michigan's Lake Huron shore. It's easy to see why; with a mile-long swath of soft, white sand, low rolling dunes, and a mixed hardwood-conifer forest, it offers a breathtaking, simple beauty. Surprisingly, it's also one of the least visited state parks in the Lower Peninsula. Even the 144-site modern campground ($34), set against mature pines and hardwoods with plenty of shade and privacy, sits half empty most of the time. Head directly for sites 1-33 just a few steps from the beach. One cabin and four rent-a-tents are also available.

Behind the park's picnic area is an almost totally undeveloped area, with dunes and woods that abound in wildlife and vegetation. Naturalists can search for the more than 40 species of wildflowers that grow here, including many rare orchids and irises. More than four miles of trails loop through the area for hikers and cross-country skiers.

From Rogers City, it's 11 miles west on M-68 to the Lower Peninsula's only major waterfall. **Ocqueoc Falls** (the name means "sacred water") are a series of two- to six-foot drops. The falls are within the **Ocqueoc Falls Bicentennial Pathway,** which is part of P. H. Hoeft State Park. The picturesque site is a favorite of picnickers, sunbathers, and swimmers. A seven-mile trail for hikers and cross-country skiers starts next to the falls.

Just a few hundred yards away, the Bicentennial Pathway, created in 1976, loops through the deep woods and over the gently rolling hills of the Mackinaw State Forest. The pathway's three loops measure 3 miles, 4 miles, and 6.5 miles and are well used by hikers. Bed down at the **Ocqueoc Falls State Forest Campground** (reservations 800/447-2757, www.michigan.gov/dnr, $27-39), across M-68.

Just north of Rogers City on U.S. 23, **Seagull Point Park** (193 E. Michigan Ave.) draws visitors to its beautiful beach curved like a scimitar. A wide band of soft sand and a gradual slope into Lake Huron create a perfect spot for beachcombers, sunbathers, and families. Behind the beach, a two-mile-long interpretive trail winds through a series of low dunes, with signs along the route that identify the area's natural history and accompanying flora and fauna. Near the park, the **Herman Vogler Conservation Area** (240 W. Erie St., Rogers City, 989/734-4000, www.piconservation.org/herman-vogler-conservation-area.html) provides a quiet, car-free place on the Trout River. Five miles of nature trails are open to cross-country skiing in the winter.

Negwegon State Park (Ossineke, 989/724-5126, annual Recreation Passport required: $12 Michigan residents, $34 nonresidents, $9 day pass available to nonresidents only) is a carefully guarded secret among outdoor lovers. What exactly are they hiding? Some of the most beautiful and most isolated beaches on Lake Huron. The 2,469-acre park's shoreline stretches for more than six miles, a lovely string of bays and coves.

Named after Chippewa chief Negwegon, the park also offers three hiking trails named after Native American nations: the Algonquin, Chippewa, and Potawatomi. The 10 miles of trails skirt the shoreline and loop through a heavily wooded interior. A serene retreat, this isolated park offers natural beauty to hikers and backpackers willing to trade convenience for quiet, contemplative walks along eight miles of Lake Huron shoreline. There are no camping or picnic facilities in Negwegon State Park.

Between Negwegon State Park and the considerably smaller **Harrisville State Park** (248 State Park Rd., Harrisville, 989/724-5126, annual Recreation Passport required: $12 Michigan residents, $34 nonresidents, $9 day pass available to nonresidents only) is one of several lighthouses along the Lake Huron shore. The gleaming white **Sturgeon Point Lighthouse** (765/465-3984, www.alconahistoricalsociety.com, 11am-4pm Sat.-Sun and holidays, Memorial Day-Labor Day, free), built in 1869, is active and still maintained by the U.S. Coast Guard—both as a lighthouse and a maritime museum. The grounds are open to the public year-round.

★ DIVING IN THUNDER BAY

Divers have their own sanctuary just off the Alpena shore. Here, the **Thunder Bay National Marine Sanctuary and Underwater Preserve** thrills divers with its clear waters, interesting underwater limestone formations, and a number of shipwrecks. During the 19th and much of the 20th century, the area's rocky islands and hazardous shoals proved treacherous for mariners. The preserve protects some 80 shipwrecks, 14 of which can be explored with the help of a wreck diving charter. Among the most popular are the *Nordmeer,* a German steel steamer that sank in 1966, and the *Montana,* a 235-foot steamer that burned and sank in 1914. **Thunder Bay Scuba** (413 S. Ripley Blvd., Alpena, 989/356-6228, www.tbscuba.com, 9am-5:30pm Mon.-Fri. year-round, 10am-2pm Sat.-Sun. summer) offers charter diving services (about $59/day), departing from Alpena's city marina.

The state established the Thunder Bay National Marine Sanctuary and Underwater Preserve—more than 288 protected miles in all—in 1981, largely to prohibit divers from removing artifacts from the site. In October 2000, the state preserve was also designated a national marine sanctuary, status that grants it federal funding and additional resources for scientific and archaeological study. For more information, contact the **Michigan Underwater Preserve Council** (231/818-8159 or 800/970-8717, www.michiganpreserves.org).

FOOD AND ACCOMMODATIONS

Lodging choices are fairly limited in Rogers City. The best place in town, and the only place with an indoor pool, is the 43-room **Driftwood Motel** (540 W. 3rd St., 989/734-4777, www.driftwoodmotelrc.com, $90-129 d), which overlooks Lake Huron. For a good hot meal, stop into the **Lighthouse Restaurant** (377 N. 3rd St., 989/734-4858, 11am-10pm Mon.-Wed., 11am-midnight Thurs.-Sat., 9am-10pm Sun., $8-15) and select from a lengthy menu offering freshly caught lake fish, steaks, burgers, and pizza. A full bar is also available.

Food from Asia is unusual for northern Michigan. But Rogers City is home to **Chee Peng Chinese and Thai Restaurant** (119 N. Third St., 989/734-2775, 11am-8pm Tues.-Sat., noon-8pm Sun., $7-11). The menu includes the typical almond boneless and lemon chicken, but also becomes a bit more adventurous with Thai entrées such as *pad see-iew* (stir-fried rice noodles with eggs, broccoli, and pea pods in Thai coconut milk sauce) and *pad pung karee* (mushrooms, bamboo shoots, water chestnuts, pea pods, carrots, and onions in a coconut milk sauce).

Hotels and restaurants in Alpena have an unmistakably nostalgic feel, as if you've been transported back to the 1950s or '60s. Chief among them are the **40 Winks Motel** (1021 S. State Ave., 989/354-5622, www.40winksmotel.com, $63-68 d), with simple rooms opposite Lake Huron.

INFORMATION AND SERVICES

For more information, contact the **Rogers City Chamber of Commerce** (292 S. Bradley Hwy., Rogers City, 989/734-2535, www.rogerscityareachamber.com, 9am-3pm Mon.-Fri.) or the **Alpena Area Convention and Visitors Bureau** (235 W. Chisholm St., Alpena, 800/425-7362, www.visitalpena.com). For local news, check out ***Presque Isle County Advance*** (www.piadvance.com) or ***Alpena News*** (www.thealpenanews.com).

Between Rogers City and Alpena, you're likely to find the services you need, from groceries and pharmacies to banks. For medical issues, consult **MidMichigan Medical Center** (1501 W. Chisholm St., Alpena, 989/356-7000, www.midmichigan.org).

GETTING THERE AND AROUND

Delta has commuter flights between Detroit and the **Alpena County Regional Airport**

(APN, 1617 Airport Rd., Alpena, 989/354-2907, www.alpenaairport.com), where you can either hail a cab or rent a car. From the airport, Rogers City is a 37-mile trip that will take about 44 minutes. Both **Greyhound** (989/734-4903 or 800/231-2222, www.greyhound.com) and **Indian Trails** (800/292-3831, www.indiantrails.com) buses stop in Rogers City (285 S. Bradley Hwy.) as well as Alpena (1141 N. U.S. 23).

From I-75, M-68 leads to Rogers City and M-32 to Alpena. Both towns can also be accessed via U.S. 23 along the coast. From Sault Ste. Marie, take I-75, cross the Mackinac Bridge, and follow U.S. 23 to Rogers City, a 115-mile trip that takes about two hours. From Traverse City, take M-72, M-66/U.S. 131, Mancelona Road, Old State Road, Meridian Line Road, and M-32 to Alpena, a 128-mile trip that takes 2.5 hours. From Detroit, take I-375, I-75, and U.S. 23, following the Sunrise Side Coastal Highway to Alpena; in light traffic, the 243-mile trip takes less than four hours.

PRESQUE ISLE

It would be easy to pass the Presque Isle peninsula and never know it was there, but that would be a mistake. This almost completely undiscovered resort area, off the beaten path between Rogers City and Alpena, features two jewels, both worth driving out of the way to see.

On a map, the peninsula looks like a beckoning finger (in French *presqu'île* means "almost an island"—a peninsula). Two classic lighthouses perch at the tip of the strangely shaped peninsula, including the tallest lighthouse on the Great Lakes.

Inside the **Old Presque Isle Lighthouse Complex** (5295 E. Grand Lake Rd., 989/595-6979 or 989/595-5419, www.presqueislelighthouses.org, 10am-5pm Mon.-Fri. late May-mid-June and Labor Day-Oct., 10am-5pm daily, mid-June through Labor Day, by donation), which consists of a light tower and a nearby keeper's dwelling, exhibits and displays relate the history of Great Lakes shipping and light-keeping. Artifacts and antiques include wooden doors from a shipwreck and an old pump organ visitors can play. Built in 1840, the lighthouse was used for 30 years until it was replaced by a new light a mile north. Few other lighthouses offer a more dramatic view. From the parapet surrounding the lantern room, a trip up the two-story tower's winding steps will yield a breathtaking visual reward.

The **New Presque Isle Lighthouse and Museum** (4500 E. Grand Lake Rd., 989/595-5419 or 989/595-9917, www.presqueislelighthouses.org, 10am-5pm Mon.-Fri. late May-mid-June and Labor Day-Oct, 10am-5pm daily, mid-June through Labor Day, by donation) dates to 1870. Trees had grown to obscure the older, shorter lighthouse; the "new" one stretches to 113 feet, the tallest on the Great Lakes. In the middle of 100-acre **Presque Isle Lighthouse Park,** the tower and restored lightkeeper's house look much as they did more than a century ago. On special occasions, a caretaker—a descendant of generations of Great Lakes sailors—plays the part of a turn-of-the-20th-century lightkeeper.

The park's fine nature trails begin at the lighthouse and circle the peninsula's tip. The trails border rugged shoreline then weave in and out of evergreens and hardwoods before reaching the peninsula's tip and a sweeping view of Lake Huron from a rocky beach.

Besser Natural Area, now part of **Rockport State Recreation Area** (annual Recreation Passport required: $12 Michigan residents, $34 nonresidents, $9 day pass available to nonresidents only), offers an intriguing mix of attractions: nearly a mile of wild undeveloped Lake Huron shoreline, a ghost town, a sunken ship, and one of the few remaining stands of virgin white pine left in the state. Reach the 134-acre preserve by taking Grand Lake Road six miles southeast of Presque Isle. For more information, contact **Harrisville State Park** (989/724-5126).

The boom-and-bust logging industry both created and destroyed the ghost town of Bell, which once included a school, a sawmill, a store, a saloon, and several houses during the 1880s. A one-mile self-guided trail leads through a magnificent stand of virgin white pines and passes the ghost town and a tiny inland lagoon, the graveyard for an unnamed small vessel. Halfway along the trail, a plaque honors Jesse Besser, who donated this land to the state in 1966 as a memorial to Michigan's lumber workers. The trail continues through a dark cedar forest before emerging on Lake Huron's shore.

Oscoda to West Branch

Farther along the Lake Huron shore, several towns serve as gateways to an array of priceless outdoor gems, including Oscoda, popular among canoeists, and Tawas City, a favorite among bird-watchers.

Oscoda sits at the mouth of the Au Sable River, famed as a trout stream and navigable by canoe as far as Grayling and Roscommon. The waterway played a prominent part in the state's early pine logging days. At its most populous, the city swelled to more than 23,000, and the river was filled with pine logs on their way to the sawmills. Nature put an abrupt end to the city's logging boom in 1911 when a forest fire swept through, reducing the city's heyday to ashes. The current population is roughly 900.

As for Tawas City, its name derives from Ottawas, an important Chippewa chief who is honored at several spots along this stretch of Lake Huron shore. The twin settlements of Tawas City and East Tawas straddle the Tawas River, which empties into Tawas Bay, formed by a crooked finger of land called Tawas Point.

Today, local festivals, such as February's Perchville USA, reveal the area's popularity with anglers. Visitors can watch the boat-filled bay in Tawas Point State Park, which occupies the fishhook-shaped Tawas Point. It's a favorite of naturalists as much for the ever-changing landscape created by wind and waves during annual winter storms as for some of the best bird-watching in the state.

West of Tawas City, West Branch is a small town with quaint Victorian-style architecture, a downtown shopping district, and an outlet mall. It's also not far from a popular recreation area, the Huron National Forest, and the road to Houghton and Higgins Lakes.

SIGHTS

Beaches and Parks

Opposite the large beach on the shore of Tawas Bay, part of 183-acre **Tawas Point State Park** (686 Tawas Beach Rd., East Tawas, 989/362-5041, daily, annual Recreation Passport required: $12 Michigan residents, $34 nonresidents, $9 day pass available to nonresidents only), the white Victorian-style 1876 **Tawas Point Lighthouse** is undoubtedly the park's most photographed feature and a favorite among lovers of these classic lights. One of the state's best-maintained lighthouses, it is open for guided tours for $5 May-October. Not far away, bird-watchers gather at the day-use area and nature trail. A checklist of birds spotted in the park lists more than 250, with 31 species of warblers and 17 species of waterfowl.

In summer, swimmers favor this park for its white sand and warm shallow waters. Anglers and hikers also appreciate Tawas Point. Here, you'll also find a playground, a picnic area, public restrooms, a spacious campground ($29), and gorgeous sunsets.

From the state park, history buffs can take a self-guided 68-mile driving tour amid key historical, natural, and cultural features west of the park, including the site of a 1984 forest fire, a 1,000-acre marsh that nurtures deer and other wildlife, the 1917 Foote Dam, a former Air Force base, and the Lumberman's Monument, a bronze statue erected in 1931 on the high scenic banks of the Au Sable River. Dedicated to the pioneer spirit and efforts of Michigan lumber workers, the monument isn't far from a visitors center, whose exhibits relate to Michigan's logging era. For more information, pick up brochures at the park office.

At the park office you can also learn more about the **Highbanks Trail,** a seven-mile ungroomed route about 14 miles west of Oscoda that traces the bluffs along the southern shore of the Au Sable River and offers scenic views of the popular canoeing waterway and surrounding wildlife. This hiking trail, which is free and favored by cross-country skiers in winter, also provides access to sites like the 14-foot-tall Lumberman's Monument and the Canoers Memorial, erected in 1950 to honor marathon canoe racing.

Rifle River Recreation Area

Inner tubes seem to be the transportation option of choice on the slow-moving Rifle River, which meanders from the **Rifle River Recreation Area** (2550 E. Rose City Rd., Lupton, 989/473-2258, annual Recreation Passport required: $12 Michigan residents, $34 nonresidents, $9 day pass available to nonresidents only), about 15 miles northeast of West Branch, to Saginaw Bay, some 90 miles south. Paddlers shouldn't overlook the Rifle, though, since it flows through Devoe Lake, one of five paddle-only lakes in this spacious preserve.

The 4,449 acres that now make up the Rifle River Recreation Area were once part of the private hunting preserve of H. M. Jewett, an early auto industry tycoon. Today, most of the visitors who are hoping to leave with a catch are bagging bass and other varieties of fish.

The recreation area includes several miles of paved and packed dirt trails that cross one-lane bridges, circle forest fringed lakes, and lead up several high hills that reveal vistas of tangled stands of cedar. For a great view, head for **Ridge Road,** a dirt track that passes over the park's highest elevations. Hikers can follow 14 miles of picturesque trails that cut through some of the park's most breathtaking terrain.

Visitors can stay at a choice of on-site accommodations, including both rustic and modern campsites as well as five frontier-style cabins, all located in secluded areas far from campgrounds and day-trippers. The cabins have vault toilets, hand-pumped water, and only basic furnishings. In winter, the park is a popular spot for cross-country skiing, ice fishing, and snowmobiling.

★ CANOEING ON THE AU SABLE RIVER

While anglers often try their luck on the Au Sable, paddlers may appreciate the river even more. The **Au Sable River Canoe Marathon** (www.ausablecanoemarathon.org), held the last weekend in July each year, starts in Grayling and ends in Oscoda. For canoe rentals, try **Oscoda Canoe Rental** (678 W. River Rd., 989/739-9040, www.oscodacanoe.com, 8am-4pm daily, $25-45 pp).

Trips on the ***Au Sable River Queen*** (1775 W. River Rd., Oscoda, 989/739-7351, 10am-3pm daily, $16 adults, $8 children, under age 3 free) depart from Foote Dam daily in season. The tours are especially popular during fall colors, and reservations are advised.

SHOPPING

Shopping isn't why most people travel to the southern reaches of northeast Michigan, but not all the attractions in this area are of the natural kind. In a seemingly unlikely place, the **Outlets at West Branch** (2990 Cook Rd., West Branch, 989/345-2594, www.westbranchoutlet.com, 10am-9pm Mon.-Sat., 11am-6pm Sun.) offers an enormous variety of mainstream shopping choices, including a Coach Factory Outlet and an Eddie Bauer outlet store. The mall is east of I-75.

FOOD AND ACCOMMODATIONS

While you won't find any gourmet establishments in the area, the restaurants here offer

Paddling Tips

Paddling throughout Michigan can be a rewarding experience, but it can also be dangerous if you're ill prepared. High winds and strong currents can make paddling conditions challenging. No matter what your experience level, follow these guidelines:

- Ensure that you've had proper instruction for the vessel that you plan to use.
- Check the daily weather forecast, especially predicted wind speeds, beforehand.
- Be aware of currents and water levels; under normal circumstances, you should allow for a minimum paddling time of two miles per hour.
- Inform someone on shore of your plans, especially your intended destination and expected return time; leave a float plan with a responsible individual, place a copy of the plan in a visible spot in your vehicle, and contact the onshore person when you do return.
- Arrange to have a vehicle and dry clothes waiting at your take-out point.
- Secure a spare paddle to your vessel.
- Place your keys, identification, money, and other valuables in a waterproof bag and secure the bag to the vessel.
- Apply sunscreen, even on cloudy days, and insect repellent.
- Wear appropriate clothing for weather and water conditions.
- Have a readily accessible personal flotation device (PFD) with attached whistle for each occupant; children under six must wear PFDs at all times.
- Bring plenty of food and drinking water (one gallon pp per day) in unbreakable watertight containers.
- Bring a cell phone in case of an emergency, but be aware that reception can be sporadic in the backcountry and offshore.
- Pack up all trash and store it on board until you can dispose of it properly at trip's end.
- Leave all historical resources, plants, birds, and marine creatures as you find them.
- Respect all wildlife; do not approach, harass, or feed any animals that you see.
- Be considerate of anglers and other paddlers, avoid crossing fishing lines, and stay to the right of motorboats.

good, basic food in generous portions. One option is **Wiltse's Brew Pub and Family Restaurant** (5606 N. Hwy. F41, Oscoda, 989/739-2231, www.wiltsebrewpub.com, 10:30am-10pm Mon.-Fri., 8am-9pm Sat.-Sun., $12-27), where you can order a homemade beer to go with the chicken dishes and steaks cut to order.

The **Camp Inn Lodge** (3111 N. U.S. 23, Oscoda, 989/739-2021, www.campinnlodge.com, $75-168 d) offers standard motel rooms and cottages near Lake Huron. Another choice is the **Lake Trail Resort** (5000 N. U.S. 23, Oscoda, 989/739-2096, https://laketrailresort.com, $56-116), which also has rustic cabins for weekly rental during July and August.

In West Branch, stay at the **LogHaven Bed and Breakfast** (1550 McGregor Rd., 989/685-3527, www.loghavenbbb.com, $155-175 d), where you'll find comfortable rooms, private baths, hearty country-style breakfasts,

- If you plan to camp, be sure to select a durable surface away from the water, and minimize the impact from campfires, if allowed.

Besides the items already mentioned, bring the following essentials with you:

- an anchor (if you plan to snorkel or camp) and rope
- area maps and NOAA nautical charts
- a bilge pump and sponge
- binoculars
- a camera and extra batteries
- a compass or GPS receiver
- duct tape
- extra waterproof bags
- a first-aid kit
- a pocketknife or multipurpose tool
- a repair kit
- signaling devices such as a flashlight, flare, mirror, or air horn
- sunglasses
- 360-degree light for operating your vessel at night
- towels, extra clothing, and extra shoes in a waterproof bag
- VHF or weather radio
- a wide-brimmed hat

For more information about canoeing and kayaking in Michigan, including paddling destinations and outfitters, consult the **Michigan Department of Natural Resources** (DNR, Parks and Recreation Division, 517/284-7275, www.michigan.gov/dnr) and the **Michigan Association of Paddlesport Providers** (MAPP, www.michigancanoe.com), or visit www.canoeingmichiganrivers.com.

and a place to stable horses. It's a perfect home base for exploring the area's hiking, horseback riding, snowmobiling, and cross-country skiing trails.

Michigan's state parks offer consistently good campgrounds. **Tawas Point State Park** (686 Tawas Beach Rd., East Tawas, 989/362-5041, annual Recreation Passport required: $12 Michigan residents, $34 nonresidents, $9 day pass available to nonresidents only) is no exception, with 210 campsites ($31) and a large sand beach.

INFORMATION AND SERVICES

For more information, contact the **Oscoda Area Convention & Visitors Bureau** (989/739-0900, www.oscoda.com), **Oscoda-AuSable Chamber of Commerce** (4440 N. U.S. 23, Oscoda, 989/739-7322, www.oscodachamber.com), **Tawas Bay Tourist & Convention Bureau** (877/868-2927, www.tawasbay.com), **Tawas Area Chamber of Commerce** (228 Newman St., East Tawas, 989/362-8643, www.tawas.com), or **West**

Branch Visitors Bureau (422 W. Houghton Ave., West Branch, 989/345-2821, www.visitwestbranch.com).

Services in these smaller towns are limited, although basics like groceries and banks are simple to find. For medical issues, consult **Ascension St. Joseph Health System** (200 Hemlock, Tawas City, 989/846-4521, https://healthcare.ascension.org).

GETTING THERE AND AROUND

Despite the remoteness of Oscoda, Tawas City, and West Branch, it's not hard to reach this part of northeastern Michigan. **Alpena County Regional Airport** (APN, 1617 Airport Rd., Alpena, 989/354-2907, www.alpenaairport.com) has commuter flights from Detroit. In a rented car, take M-32 to U.S. 23 to Oscoda, a 54-mile trip that usually takes about an hour. **MBS International Airport** (MBS, 8500 Garfield Rd., Freeland, 989/695-5555, www.mbsairport.org) has commuter flights from Detroit, Chicago, and Minneapolis; from the airport to West Branch is a 64-mile drive that takes about an hour.

Both **Greyhound** (800/231-2222, www.greyhound.com) and **Indian Trails** (800/292-3831, www.indiantrails.com) provide bus service to Tawas City (1020 W. Lake St., 989/362-6120) between West Branch and Oscoda, as well as **Standish** (220 E. Cedar St., 989/846-4613), 27 miles southeast of West Branch via I-75 and 36 miles southwest of Tawas City via U.S. 23.

The easiest way to get around this spread-out region is by car. From Detroit to West Branch, take I-375, I-75, and M-55; in light traffic, the 165-mile trip takes about 2.5 hours. From Sault Ste. Marie, take I-75, cross the Mackinac Bridge, and follow M-55, a 183-mile trip to West Branch that takes 2.75 hours. From West Branch, M-55 leads directly to Tawas City, a 37-mile trip that takes 45 minutes, and from Tawas City, continue to Oscoda via U.S. 23, a 16-mile trip that will take about 20 minutes.

HURON NATIONAL FOREST

Oscoda is also known as the gateway to the **Huron National Forest** (Huron Shores Ranger Station, 5761 N. Skeel Rd., 989/739-0728, www.fs.usda.gov/hmnf), which covers most of the acreage between Oscoda to the east and Grayling to the west. Together, the Manistee National Forest in the western part of the state and the Huron National Forest cover more than 950,000 acres in the northern part of the Lower Peninsula. The scenic Au Sable River flows through the Huron National Forest and was once used to float logs to the sawmills in East Tawas and Oscoda; it is now very popular with paddlers.

The national forest is favored by a wide range of outdoor enthusiasts, including morel mushroom hunters who visit in the spring, and backpackers, swimmers, and cross-country skiers. Trout fishing is a good bet in most lakes and streams, as well as in the legendary Au Sable River.

The forest's famous **River Road Scenic Byway** runs 22 miles along the southern bank of the Au Sable. The byway passes some of the most spectacular scenery in the eastern Lower Peninsula and provides stunning vistas of tree-banked reservoirs and views of wildlife that include everything from bald eagles to spawning salmon. Along the way, you'll also pass the **Lumberman's Monument,** a nine-foot bronze statue that depicts the area's early loggers and overlooks the river valley 10 miles northwest of East Tawas. A visitors center here houses interpretive displays that explore the logging legacy. Just a short walk away, a cliff plummets in a near-vertical 160-foot drop to the Au Sable River. It offers jaw-dropping views of the valley and marks the beginning of the **Stairway to Discovery,** an unusual interpretive nature trail that descends 260 steps to the river and earns distinction as the nation's only nature trail located entirely on a staircase.

Also in the national forest, the **Tuttle Marsh Wildlife Management Area,** about seven miles west of Au Sable, was created in the spring of 1990 as a cooperative effort by the U.S. Forest Service, the state's Department of Natural Resources, and Ducks Unlimited. Once an area filled with mundane shrubs and scattered patches of grass, the wetlands now attract a significant number of migrating waterfowl, shorebirds, and sandhill cranes, as well as muskrats, minks, beavers, and bald eagles.

Backpackers looking for a wilderness camping experience should try the **Hoist Lakes Trail System.** Backcountry camping is allowed just about anywhere in this large, rugged area of more than 10,000 acres. Nearly 20 miles of trails (for hiking only) wander through second-growth forest over gently rolling wooded terrain, around marshes, past beaver floodings, and across streams. The forest teems with deer, bears, coyotes, foxes, owls, hawks, and songbirds, along with turkeys, woodcocks, grouse, and other game birds. Fishing includes good numbers of bass and panfish. The 6.1-mile **Reid Lake Foot Travel Area** marks another great hiking area surrounded by some of the forest's most imposing hardwoods.

About 10 miles west of East Tawas, the **Corsair Trail System** bills itself as "Michigan's Cross-Country Ski Capital," but it is equally popular with hikers and backpackers. Also part of the Huron National Forest, the well-marked trail system (groomed in winter) includes more than 15 loops totaling 44 miles. One writer described this sprawling complex as "a web spun by a spider high on LSD." Choose your own adventure, from a short jaunt along Silver Creek to a two-day trek through the entire system.

Full of rolling hills, deep glacial potholes, and a beautiful hardwood forest, the **Island Lake Recreation Area** offers a quiet and beautiful alternative to the more heavily used recreation areas. You'll find it seven miles north of Rose City via M-33 and County Road 486. Out of the way and relatively small, it hides a swimming beach, a 17-site campground, and a 65-acre lake that supports perch, bluegills, and large- and smallmouth bass. A self-guiding nature trail explains the area's natural history and notes points of interest along the way.

★ HOUGHTON AND HIGGINS LAKES

Near the southern end of northeast Michigan, in Roscommon County, are two of the state's largest inland lakes—22,000-acre Houghton Lake and 10,200-acre Higgins Lake—both of which entice anglers, boaters, canoeists, swimmers, hikers, and campers during the summer months. In winter, this area is also popular among hunters, ice fishers, and cross-country skiers.

Beaches

Both lakes offer a number of terrific beaches. On Higgins Lake is the **North Higgins Lake State Park Day-Use Area,** on North Higgins Lake Drive, and the **South Higgins Lake State Park Day-Use Area,** on County Road 100. Each offers a sandy swimming beach, a bathhouse, a playground, picnic shelters, and a boat launch. You'll need an annual Recreation Passport ($12 Michigan residents, $34 nonresidents, $9 day pass available to nonresidents only) in order to utilize either of these beaches.

Meanwhile, on Houghton Lake is the **Roscommon Township Beach** (Sanford St.), which has a pleasant sandy beach on the south shore, ideal for swimmers of all ages. The area also offers a sheltered picnic area, a small playground, and restrooms.

Boating and Fishing

Houghton and Higgins Lakes are both well known among boaters, canoeists, and anglers. Together, the two enormous lakes offer a dozen launch sites and tons of water to explore. Several facilities rent pontoon and fishing boats; check out **Houghton Lake Marina** (13710 W. Shore Dr., 989/387-4978, 9am-5pm Mon.-Sat., 10am-2pm Sun.) to drift around the lake, savor the sunshine, or try your luck at snagging bass, bluegill, walleye, and pike.

Rebuilding America: The Civilian Conservation Corps

By 1933, the United States had sunk to the lowest point of the Great Depression. One after another, factories and businesses shut down. Lines at soup kitchens reached around city blocks. Nearly 14 million Americans were unemployed.

Along with an economy in ruin, President Franklin D. Roosevelt saw the natural environment in a state of decay as well. While virgin forests had once covered 800 million acres of the United States, old-growth forests had dwindled to just 100 million acres. Erosion had decimated more than 100 million acres of the nation's tillable land and was accelerating at an alarming rate.

In March 1933, Roosevelt asked Congress to authorize the creation of the Civilian Conservation Corps (CCC). A New Deal program, the proposed corps would recruit 250,000 unemployed, unmarried young men to work on federal and state-owned land for "the prevention of forest fires, floods, and soil erosion, plant, pest, and disease control."

The Labor Department would recruit the young men while the War Department would run the program, providing housing, clothing, and food in work camps, and paying them a $30 monthly stipend—$25 of which had to be sent home to their families. The Departments of Agriculture and the Interior planned the work projects, which included reforesting cutover land, preventing fires, developing state parks, and building dams, bridges, and roads. Along with the fieldwork, education was a major feature of the CCC. Camps helped members obtain their high school diplomas and provided supplemental training in at least 30 vocations.

The program was not without controversy. Some criticized the cost; others balked at the idea of military control over labor, comparing it to fascism. Still others contended young men should be with their families, or, as Michigan congressman Fred Crawford suggested, at work in farm fields rather than in "some camp in the woods to participate in a face-lifting operation on Mother Earth."

Fortunately, Roosevelt saw it differently. By implementing the CCC, he leveraged two invaluable resources—the nation's young men and its land—to work together for their mutual benefit. In his message to Congress, Roosevelt declared that "we face a future of soil erosion and timber famine" and that the CCC would "conserve our precious national resources" and "pay dividends to the present and future generations."

The legislation easily passed, and Roosevelt's goal of recruiting some 250,000 workers was

Food and Accommodations

After a long day of boating, fishing, swimming, or exploring the area, satisfy your hunger at the nearby **Buccilli's Pizza** (2949 W. Houghton Lake Dr., Houghton Lake, 989/366-5374, www.buccillispizza.com, 11am-10pm daily, $7-19), which offers tasty pizza for dine-in, takeout, or delivery.

You'll find a decent variety of lodgings in the area, including chain hotels. The **American Inn and Suites** (200 Cloverleaf Ln., Houghton Lake, 989/422-7829, http://americaninnsuitesmi.com, $75-145 d) and the **Lakeside Resort and Conference Center** (100 Clearview Dr., Houghton Lake, 989/422-4000, http://lakesideresortandconferencecenter.com, $169-350 d) each offer terrific access to the lakes as well as numerous water-related amenities, such as canoeing packages and watercraft rentals. At the Lakeside Resort, you'll find the Blue Bayou Restaurant and Lounge, with a deck bar that overlooks the majestic lake.

Houghton and Higgins Lakes both have numerous campgrounds, some catering to RVs, others allowing both tent and RV camping. On Houghton Lake, you'll find the **Houghton Lake Travel Park Campground** (370 Cloverleaf Ln., Houghton Lake, 989/422-3931, www.houghtonlaketravelparkcampground.com, Apr.-Oct., $30-47), which has something for everyone. On Higgins Lake, check out the **Higgins Lake KOA** (3800 W. Federal

met and ultimately exceeded. On April 17, 1933, the nation's first CCC camp opened in the George Washington National Forest in Virginia. By July 1, there were 250,000 men at work in more than 1,460 camps—the fastest large-scale mobilization of men in U.S. history until that time, including World War I. By 1935 "Roosevelt's Tree Army" had ballooned to more than 500,000 workers.

Fruits of the CCC's labor remain throughout Michigan and the Great Lakes region. CCC workers eradicated white pine blister rust in Minnesota, built fire towers and fire roads in Wisconsin, and improved hundreds of miles of fishing streams in Michigan. They built park shelters in Ohio, campgrounds in Indiana, and trails in Illinois. They planted thousands of acres of trees, fought countless wildfires, and built hundreds of bridges and buildings. They even moved moose from Isle Royale to the Upper Peninsula for wildlife studies.

CCC memorial

By 1936, the CCC was above reproach, supported by more than 80 percent of Americans and even endorsed by Roosevelt's political opponents. With the bombing of Pearl Harbor in 1941, however, the nation soon had a more pressing duty for its young men. The nation's entry into World War II, along with an improving economy, meant the 1942 disbanding of the CCC. But its legacy, like the trees it planted, continues to grow in our nation's parks and forests.

The **Civilian Conservation Corps Museum** (11747 N. Higgins Lake Dr., Roscommon), is dedicated to honoring the legacy of the young men who labored so tirelessly for the benefit of Michigan's environment. Currently the museum is under renovation and is expected to reopen to visitors in late 2020.

Hwy., Roscommon, 989/275-8151, www.koa.com, $28-34), which also has yurts, rustic campsites, and deluxe cabins.

Information and Services

For more information about Houghton and Higgins Lakes, contact the **Houghton Lake Area Tourism & Convention Bureau** (9091 W. Lake City Rd., Houghton Lake, 989/422-2002 or 800/676-5330, www.visithoughtonlake.com). Services such as banks and groceries are north via I-75, in Grayling or Gaylord.

Getting There and Around

The easiest way to reach the lakes is by car. From West Branch, take M-55, which hugs the southern shore of Houghton Lake; the 28-mile trip usually takes about 30 minutes. From Grayling, reach North Higgins Lake State Park by heading south on I-75, U.S. 127, and North Higgins Lake Drive, a 13-mile trip that takes about 16 minutes. Once you reach the lakes, you can explore the area via boat or bike or on foot.

Grayling and Gaylord

Neighboring communities along I-75, Gaylord and Grayling are quiet, hospitable communities that wear their local pride on their sleeves.

Gaylord was officially organized in 1875 as Otsego (the current name of the county), a Native American word that means "beautiful lake." Located just north of long, narrow Otsego Lake, Gaylord remains a basically rural village with a year-round population of roughly 3,600. But its gentle, rolling topography and numerous recreation opportunities lure vacationers by the thousands.

Gaylord sits on the highest point in the Lower Peninsula, which inspired the town to morph itself into "the Alpine Village." Its Main Street is decorated with balconies, blossoming window boxes, even a glockenspiel on the Glen's Market grocery store. And while more Polish and German descendants reside here than Swiss, the townspeople happily don dirndls and lederhosen each July during the annual Alpenfest. Some visitors come for the culture, but Gaylord offers plenty of outdoor attractions as well, including world-class golf, accessible inland lakes, and bugling elk.

From Bay City, I-75 cuts across the northeastern part of the state until it bisects the North Country near Grayling, named for the region's once most prolific game fish. Several clean, clear, and immensely popular rivers—most notably, the Au Sable and the Manistee—corkscrew through the region, making Grayling the hub of one of the Lower Peninsula's leading recreational areas. Wanton fishing, and the declining water quality caused by riverbank erosion from logging, combined to make the species extinct by 1930. But although the town's namesake fish may be gone, essential lessons have been learned on protecting species and habitats. Today Grayling offers some of the finest trout fishing in the Midwest and is a key destination for outdoor recreation.

SIGHTS

Call of the Wild Museum

While this unassuming museum has been around for decades, during which the displays haven't changed all that much, the **Call of the Wild Museum** (850 S. Wisconsin Ave., Gaylord, 989/732-4336, www.callofthewildgaylord.com, 9am-9pm daily mid-June-Labor Day, 9:30am-6pm Mon.-Sat., 11am-5pm Sun. Sept.-mid-June, $7.50, adults, $7 seniors 62 and over, $5 ages 5-13) is still a terrific place to take your children. Many of its wildlife displays come packed with audio features, bringing the animals to life. Two projected images of Joseph Bailly help to educate visitors about what life was like in the early 1800s, when Bailly, one of the area's first trappers, originally ventured into northern Michigan.

Otsego Lake State Park

Established in 1920, **Otsego Lake State Park** (7136 Old 27 S., Gaylord, 989/732-5485) is a boating enthusiast's dream. The lake is long and wide, allowing ample room for boats and other water sports. This park has been a popular, family-friendly destination for nine decades.

ALPENFEST

You can't miss the distinctive architecture that's earned Gaylord its "Alpine Village" moniker. To celebrate the community's heritage, part of Main Street is blocked off in the second week of July each year for the annual **Alpenfest** (989/732-6333, www.gaylordalpenfest.com). Established in the mid-1960s, the five-day event features traditional dancing, costumed musicians, yodeling and pie-eating contests, an "Edelweiss" sing-along, and plenty of ethnic food, from sauerkraut to strudel to pasties, in addition to carnival favorites like hot dogs, ice cream, and beer. The open-air "Alpenstrasse" is an

The Tiny Bird with the Huge Following

Kirtland's warbler

Once gravely endangered, **Kirtland's warbler** (also known as a jack pine warbler), has in recent years staged a welcome comeback. While the highest density of warblers, and its prime breeding ground, is the region around the Au Sable River between Grayling and Mio, nests have recently been identified in the Upper Peninsula and northern Wisconsin.

A tiny blue-gray songbird with a yellow breast, Kirtland's warbler winters in the Bahamas, then returns north, where it subsists on insects and blueberries and searches for the proper habitat to suit its picky nesting requirements: young stands of jack pine with small grassy clearings. It builds nests on the low-lying branches of jack pines between 5 and 20 feet high; when the trees get much higher, the warbler abandons them and seeks out younger counterparts.

The bird's precarious plight was a classic case of habitat loss. When forest fires occur naturally, jack pines are one of the first trees to regenerate in burned areas. But decades of logging and fire suppression led to fewer forest fires, which in turn led to fewer young jack pines. To help the warbler, the U.S. Forest Service, the U.S. Fish and Wildlife Service, the Michigan Department of Natural Resources, and other government agencies now do nature's job, cultivating (often through controlled burns), harvesting, and strategic replanting acres of jack pines in the **Kirtland's Warbler Wildlife Management Area.** This is aimed at boosting the supply of young trees suitable for the warblers. Environmentalists also assist the warbler by controlling the region's population of brown-headed cowbirds, which routinely take over warbler nests and outcompete their nest mates for food. Their efforts have succeeded. By 2019 the population was estimated at around 4,600.

Not surprisingly, the bird's breeding grounds are off-limits to the public during the May-August nesting season. From mid-May through late June, however, guided three-hour **tours** (7am daily, $10 pp) are led by the **U.S. Forest Service,** beginning at the Mio Ranger Station (107 McKinley Rd.). From mid-May through early July, the **U.S. Fish and Wildlife Service** and **Michigan Audubon Society** jointly offer guided **tours** (7am Mon.-Fri., 7am and 11am Sat.-Sun. and holidays, free) of the same area, usually departing from the Ramada Inn in Grayling. Of course, actual sightings can't be guaranteed. For more information about the tours, contact the **Forest Service's Mio Ranger Station** (989/826-3252), **Michigan Audubon Society** (517/580-7364), or **Seney National Wildlife Refuge** (906/586-9851).

arts and crafts village showcasing the wares of more than 60 Michigan artists and artisans. The town even makes room for several amusement park rides and carnival games.

RECREATION

★ Golf

Gaylord is perhaps best known for its golf, boasting the largest number of courses in the state: more than 20, with more on the drawing board, ranking it as a premier golf region. Here you'll find the thickest concentration of designer courses anywhere in the United States, including those by some of the best-known architects, such as Robert Trent Jones Sr., Tom Fazio, and Al Watrous.

If you have the time, consider visiting at least three of the area's favored golf courses. Head first to Onaway, on M-68, where you'll find the **Black Lake Golf Club** (2800 Maxon Rd., Onaway, 989/733-4653, www.blacklakegolf.com, daily Apr.-Oct., $60-75 pp with cart). Operated by the United Auto Workers, this magnificent course is part of the union's 1,000-acre family center, which sits astride picturesque Black Lake.

Another winning choice is **Garland Lodge & Resort** (4700 N. Red Oak Rd., Lewiston, 877/442-7526, www.garlandusa.com, daily May-Oct., $80-145 pp). Considered one of the state's most beautiful resorts, Garland offers four magnificent courses amid the woods of northeastern Michigan.

Lastly, schedule a tee time at the lovely **Treetops Resort** (3962 Wilkinson Rd., Gaylord, 989/732-6711 or 888/873-3867, www.treetops.com, daily Apr.-Oct., $55-145 pp). This year-round resort keeps visitors busy with downhill skiing in winter, activities like tennis and biking in summer, and five stunning golf courses.

Hiking and Biking

Popular with equestrians, hikers, cross-country skiers, and snowshoers, the 220-mile **Michigan Shore-to-Shore Riding and Hiking Trail** traverses the entire Lower Peninsula. In this area, it skirts the north end of the George Mason River Retreat Area, passing through pine plantations, stands of hardwood, and along the gentle Au Sable. Other good area access points include the McKinley Trail Camp in Oscoda and across from the Curtisville Store in Glennie.

The rolling terrain of Crawford County makes for some great mountain biking, and even better, the local tourism council actually encourages it—a rare phenomenon. The Grayling Visitors Bureau recommends the following near Grayling: **Michigan Cross-Country Cycle Trail,** a great technical single-track that "goes for miles and miles." Access it where it crosses Military Road, 0.5 miles north of the North Higgins Lake State Park exit off U.S. 27. Also check out the **Hanson Hills Recreation Area** (7601 Old Lake Rd., Grayling, 989/348-9266, www.hansonhills.org, $2 donation), which offers challenging terrain that includes some sandy stretches, and **Wakely Lake,** 10 miles east of Grayling via M-72 and featuring loops of 4.5, 5, and 7 miles. To secure a required parking pass for the Wakely Lake area, contact the **Mio Ranger District** (107 McKinley Rd., Mio, 989/826-3252, www.fs.usda.gov, 8am-4:30pm Mon.-Fri.) of the Huron National Forest.

Closer to Gaylord, the Shingle Mill Pathway links up with the **High Country Pathway,** an 80-mile route that snakes east through state lands in four counties, passing through a wilderness of rolling hills and several creeks feeding the Black River. A side trail leads to Shoepac Lake and the Sinkholes Pathway, where the land is pitted with dry sinkholes and sinkhole lakes, formed when underground limestone caves collapsed.

Elk may be the main attraction at the Pigeon River Country State Forest, but beavers bring visitors to the **Big Bear Lake Nature Pathway,** 17 miles east of Gaylord. Part of the Mackinaw State Forest trail system, the pathway's two loops total just over two miles and lead through a variety of landscape and habitats home to deer, porcupines, woodcocks, waterfowl, and beavers. The shorter 0.8-mile Beaver Lodge Loop circles a pond with an active beaver colony. The longer Eagles Roost Trail carves a wide two-mile loop that threads its way through upland hardwoods and through a dense stand of aspen and an open area carpeted with wildflowers in the summer. Both trails begin and end at the **Big Bear Lake State Forest Campground** (989/732-5485, $15), on the north shore of Big Bear Lake, accessible via Bear Lake Road.

Canoeing

Scenic streams crisscross the forests around Grayling. The Boardman, Manistee, Pine, Rifle, and Au Sable Rivers meander through wetlands, dunes, and tree-covered hills. Canoeing ranks among the area's most popular pastimes, with a number of outfitters, mostly in Grayling, offering adventures on the Au Sable and other area rivers. Even novice paddlers can handle the calm currents of these waterways.

Flowing east from Grayling, the Au Sable

coils through the **Au Sable State Forest.** Designated a state natural river with stretches of the main stream protected as a National Wild and Scenic River, the Au Sable flows past wooded islands and stretches of white sand. At night, paddlers can sleep at one of several state and national forest campgrounds along the banks. For day-trippers, the most popular take-outs are at Stephan Landing (about a 4 hours leisurely paddle from Grayling) and Wakely Landing, a 5.5-hour trip.

Recognized for its excellent trout fishing and often overlooked by paddlers is the Au Sable's South Branch, where you can also launch a boat. You'll find landings at Chase Bridge on the south end and at Smith Bridge, 11 miles north.

The Au Sable, however, can become crowded on hot summer weekends, with raucous groups sometimes floating the river en masse. If you're looking for a party, this is the place, but be aware that local authorities carefully watch for intoxicated paddlers and strictly enforce local laws. Glass containers, kegs, and Styrofoam coolers are prohibited on the Au Sable. If you're looking for a more peaceful experience, depart during the week or arrange to paddle a stretch farther outside Grayling, if an outfitter is amenable. Alternatively, many paddlers find the Manistee River considerably more tranquil. For a complete list of outfitters in the Grayling region, contact the **Grayling Visitors Bureau** (213 N. James St., 989/348-4945 or 800/937-8837, www.grayling-mi.com).

As a testament to its paddling popularity, Grayling is the site of one of the country's few canoeing festivals, the **AuSable River Canoe Marathon** (www.ausablecanoemarathon.org). Held in late July, the 120-mile route runs from Grayling to Oscoda on Lake Huron and ranks as North America's longest and most difficult nonstop canoe race. An estimated 30,000 fans turn out, many following the world-class athletes in the grueling race down the river, which requires some 55,000 paddle strokes and more than 14 hours to complete. It's worth going just to watch the thrilling 9pm shotgun start (the race runs through the night) when more than 50 teams carrying canoes on their heads run through downtown Grayling to the launch site.

Fishing

Fly-fishing enthusiasts from around the country make the pilgrimage to the Au Sable, where the combination of spring-fed water, clean gravel bottoms, and all the right insect hatches make for stellar trout fishing. All along the area's rivers you'll spot anglers standing midstream in hip waders, unfurling a long arc of lemon-colored line across the river with their fly rods or casting from a flat-bottom Au Sable riverboat designed for drifting these shallow waters. Many congregate just east of town in a 10-mile catch-and-release area known as "the holy waters."

While the Grayling Visitors Bureau will help you link up with fishing guides, you can also try your luck from shore. Be sure to obtain a license, available at local shops and gas stations, and check the current fishing regulations first. Both the Manistee and Au Sable Rivers pass through several miles of state and federal lands, so you won't have trouble finding public access.

Farther southeast, the Rifle River and its upper tributaries have earned reputations for yielding good catches of brown, rainbow, and brook trout. Steelhead and chinook salmon are caught on the river's upper reaches, and pike, bass, and panfish are pulled from the dozen or so lakes and ponds in the Rifle River Recreation Area, many of which have public access sites.

Snowmobiling

Gaylord is the crossroads of many snowmobiling trails (www.visitgaylord.com/snowmobile). With over 150 inches of snowfall in an average year, Gaylord is a snowmobiler's dream. Many of the state's best trails either start or pass through the area. If you're looking for a great ride, the **Gaylord-Frederic-Grayling-Blue Bear Loop** will give you a two- to four-day adventure.

FOOD

Gaylord Area

The same Greek American family has been running the **Sugar Bowl** (216 W. Main St., Gaylord, 989/732-5524, www.sugarbowlrestaurantgaylordmi.com, 7am-11pm daily, $12-38) since 1919. Specialties include Lake Superior whitefish, scampi, Athenian chicken, and other favorite ethnic dishes, all prepared on an open hearth. Tip: They serve morel mushroom dishes in season, usually during May. Be sure to check out the vintage photos of historic Gaylord on the walls.

The **Iron Pig Smokehouse** (143 W. Main St., 989/448-2065, www.ironpigsmoke.com, 11am-11pm Mon.-Sat., 11am-10pm Sun., $9-13) is a great place to enjoy hearty barbecue, a style of cuisine that's relatively uncommon in northern Michigan. Offerings include smoked kielbasa and pulled pork.

Gobbler's Famous Turkey Dinners (900 S. Otsego Ave./U.S. 27, Gaylord, 989/732-9005, 11am-9pm daily, $5-14) prepares more than 80,000 pounds of turkey annually and serves it with mashed potatoes, biscuits, gravy, and dressing. The portion sizes are legendary. There's also hand-breaded fresh fish, pizza, and barbecued ribs as alternatives.

Between Gaylord and Lewiston is the single-traffic-light town of Johannesburg, where you'll find ★ **Paul's Pub** (12757 E. M-32, Johannesburg, 989/732-5005, www.paulspubandcatering.com, 11am-10pm Sun.-Thurs., 11am-11pm Fri.-Sat., $7-28), with its wide assortment of beers and the best fried perch in Michigan. They also have an extensive Sunday brunch buffet until 1pm, but try to arrive early. Both Saturday and Sunday are quite busy.

Grayling Area

In downtown Grayling, be sure to visit **Dawson and Stevens** (231 Michigan Ave., Grayling, 989/348-2111, 11am-6pm Sun.-Thurs., 11am-7pm Fri.-Sat., $7-15) for a meal from a 1950s-style diner (think hamburgers, fries, and shakes—plus assorted other soups and sandwiches) and an immersion into what must be one of the largest collection of Coca-Cola memorabilia anywhere, including bottles, caps, vintage advertising posters, and model delivery trucks. Far from your typical lunch stop.

Hungry hunters, paddlers, and bird-watchers head to **Spikes Keg O Nails** (301 N. James St., Grayling, 989/348-7113, www.spikeskegonails.com, 10am-1:30am Mon.-Sat., noon-1:30am Sun., $6-10) for a burger. Try the World Famous Spikeburger, topped with everything. There's also a nice selection of Mexican entrées.

ACCOMMODATIONS

Gaylord Area

The local golf resorts can offer some good package deals, especially for families. ★ **Garland Lodge & Resort** (4700 N. Red Oak Rd., Lewiston, 989/786-2211, www.garlandusa.com, $150-499 d) has several stay-and-play deals where golf is included in the rates. If you're looking for just a simple motel room, you'll find several of the usual chains—Super 8, Days Inn, Comfort Inn—near I-75.

Grayling Area

For paddlers, you can't do better than ★ **Penrod's Au Sable River Resort** (100 Maple St., Grayling, 888/467-4837, www.penrodscanoe.com, $55-103 d, $390-618 w), where small intimate cabins line a peaceful bend in the river. During peak season, the cabins are generally only rented for full-week stays. Penrod's adjacent paddle sports center rents out canoes, kayaks, and mountain bikes and offers shuttle service for river trips. If you care more about location than amenities and are coming to fish, **Gates Au Sable Lodge** (471 Stephan Bridge Rd., Grayling, 989/348-8462, www.gateslodge.com, $70-125 d) has motel-style rooms with a perfect setting right on the banks of the Au Sable. Also right on the Au Sable, **Borchers Au Sable Canoe Livery with Riverside Bed & Breakfast** (101 Maple St., Grayling, 989/348-4921, www.canoeborchers.com, $105-128 d) invites you to slow to the pace of the river on its wrap-around porch.

Camping

Pigeon River Country State Forest (off Sturgeon Valley Rd., 989/983-4101) offers 29 rustic sites ($15) in a nice secluded setting. For waterfront sites, try **Otsego Lake State Park** (7136 Old 27 S., 989/732-5485, annual Recreation Passport required: $12 Michigan residents, $34 nonresidents, $9 day pass available to nonresidents only), with 206 sites ($18-28) on or near Otsego Lake.

You'll find plenty of good-quality inexpensive public campgrounds in the Grayling area. **Hartwick Pines State Park** (4216 Ranger Rd., 989/348-7068, annual Recreation Passport required: $12 Michigan residents, $34 nonresidents, $9 day pass available to nonresidents only) in Grayling offers clean modern sites ($19-29) that fill up fast. You might find a little more solitude and fewer RVs at the **Au Sable State Forest** (5.5 miles east of Grayling via N. Down River Rd., 989/826-3211, annual Recreation Passport required: $12 Michigan residents, $34 nonresidents, $9 day pass available to nonresidents only), which offers several rustic campgrounds ($14).

INFORMATION AND SERVICES

For more information on the Grayling area, contact the **Grayling Visitors Bureau** (213 N. James St., Grayling, 989/348-4945 or 800/937-8837, www.grayling-mi.com, 9am-3pm Mon.-Fri.).

To learn more about the Gaylord area, contact the **Gaylord Area Convention & Tourism Bureau** (101 W. Main St., Gaylord, 989/732-4000, www.gaylordmichigan.net, 8:30am-5pm Mon.-Fri., 9am-2pm Sat.). For local news, consult the ***Gaylord Herald Times*** (www.petoskeynews.com/gaylord).

Grayling has a limited number of services; head north to Gaylord to stock up on supplies. Despite its small size, Gaylord offers a wide range of services, including several banks and gas stations and numerous stores, including Walmart, Home Depot, and Glen's Market. For medical issues, go to **Otsego Memorial Hospital** (825 N. Center Ave., Gaylord, 989/731-2100, www.munsonhealthcare.org).

GETTING THERE AND AROUND

Greyhound (989/348-8682 or 800/231-2222, www.greyhound.com) and **Indian Trails** (800/292-3831, www.indiantrails.com) both provide bus service to Grayling and Gaylord, but most visitors arrive in their own vehicles. The towns, which are both off of I-75, are easy to reach from Detroit (205 miles, 3 hours), Mackinaw City (85 miles, 80 minutes), Traverse City (51 miles, 1 hour), or Chicago (328 miles, 5 hours).

GEORGE MASON RIVER RETREAT AREA

George Mason, an area industrialist, so loved this area that he bequeathed 1,500 acres to the state for its preservation in 1954. About 15 miles east of Grayling on Canoe Harbor Road, the George Mason River Retreat Area is part of the Au Sable State Forest. Subsequent land acquisitions have nearly tripled the size of this natural area, which provides ample opportunity to fish, canoe, or hike for free along a stretch of the South Branch of the Au Sable River. For more information about the George Mason River Retreat Area, open year-round, contact the **Roscommon Field Office** (989/275-4622) of the Michigan Department of Natural Resources (www.michigan.gov/dnr).

★ HARTWICK PINES STATE PARK

The majestic white pine may be the state tree, but few virgin stands remain today. One of the last can be seen at the **Hartwick Pines State Park** (4216 Ranger Rd., 989/348-7068, annual Recreation Passport required: $12 Michigan residents, $34 nonresidents, $9 day pass available to nonresidents only), one of the largest parks in the state. A century ago, more than 13 million of the state's 38 million acres were

Michigan's Elk

A common sight in the Lower Peninsula during much of the 19th century, the eastern elk disappeared from Michigan in the late 1870s. Biologists made several attempts to reintroduce the animal during the early 20th century, but it wasn't until the successful release of seven Rocky Mountain elk in 1918 that the mammals were once again seen regularly in northeastern Michigan.

eastern elk

Wildlife biologists today believe that the region's elk are descendants of those early animals. They roam a 600-square-mile area primarily east and north of Gaylord in Otsego, Cheboygan, Presque Isle, and Montmorency Counties. The heaviest concentration is north of Gaylord in the 95,000-acre **Pigeon River Country State Forest** (9966 Twin Lakes Rd., Vanderbilt, 989/983-4101).

The best way to plan a visit is to stop by the Pigeon River forestry field office off Sturgeon Valley Road. To reach the office from Vanderbilt, drive east on Sturgeon Valley Road about 13 miles (past a prime elk-viewing site), turn left onto Hardwood Lake Road, and continue for about one mile to the office. Although the office hours vary seasonally, the staff, when present, will provide helpful maps and suggest ideal areas and times to spot the elk. Fall rutting season often proves to be the most spectacular, when the bulls throw their heads back and fill the forests with eerie bugling sounds, their distinctive mating call.

covered with the majestic trees, but by the early 1900s more than 160 billion board feet of timber had been harvested. By the 1920s, these once majestic forests were denuded wastelands.

More than 250,000 visitors stroll through the pines annually, marveling at trees that have been here since before the Revolutionary War. Long a popular stop for vacationers heading north, the state park has been improved over the years, with a superb visitors center, a walkway to the pines accessible to wheelchairs and strollers, and a steam sawmill that's part of an extensive logging museum area. The park is also the site of the **Hartwick Pines State Forest Festivals:** four different events held throughout the summer, including **Sawdust Days, Wood Shaving Days, Black Iron Days,** and **Old Time Days.**

The park's **Michigan Forest Visitors Center** boasts a 100-seat auditorium; a 14-minute audiovisual show on "The Forest: Michigan's Renewable Resource," which is presented every 30 minutes; and an exhibit hall that concentrates on forest management. Many of the displays were funded, ironically, by forestry products companies, so don't expect to see a balanced treatment of the environmental effects of logging.

The 49-acre virgin tract of white and red pines is the main attraction. Reaching as high as 10 stories, the majestic trees were slated for cutting in the mid-1890s. Fortunately for posterity, the logging company charged with felling the trees was forced to suspend operations due to economic problems. In 1927, the trees and the surrounding 8,000 acres were purchased from the lumber company and donated to the state for a park.

The self-guided **Old Growth Forest Trail** connects the pines with the visitors center, a 1.25-mile asphalt path that weaves among the regal giants, which includes the Monarch.

Once the tract's largest specimen at 155 feet, a windstorm destroyed the top 40 feet of the now diseased and dying tree. Part of nature's cycle, several other immense white pines tower nearby, ready to take their places in the record books.

While the pines and the museums are the park's dominate features, try not to overlook its other attractions. With more than 9,600 acres, it offers plenty to do besides admire tall trees. Signs and other displays mark the eight-mile **Scenic Drive,** about two miles north of the main entrance, encouraging visitors to explore the woods. Hiking and biking trails include 17 miles of easy trails open to mountain bikes in summer and cross-country skiers in winter. The Au Sable River Trail (no bikes) is one of the loveliest. It crosses the East Branch of the legendary river and passes a rare forest of virgin hemlock, saved from the saw by a sudden drop in the price of its bark, which was once used for tanning leather. The two-mile Mertz Grade Nature Trail loops through the park and past an old logging railroad grade before linking up with the Virgin Pines Trail behind the visitors center.

Open year-round, the park is especially popular in the spring, when wildflowers bloom, and in the early fall, when the colorful hardwoods explode in a riot of fiery reds, yellows, and oranges.

PIGEON RIVER COUNTRY STATE FOREST

With a shaggy chocolate mane and a crown of showy antlers, the eastern elk may be Michigan's most spectacular mammal, sometimes weighing close to 1,000 pounds. Elk are comparatively rare in the Midwest, although approximately 1,000 of the animals—the largest free-roaming herd east of the Mississippi—populate this state forest and the surrounding countryside.

Although its primary draw is the opportunity to spot the elk herd, this 97,000-acre state forest north of Gaylord has miles of hiking trails, good fishing, and scenic rustic campgrounds. The **Shingle Mill Pathway** passes through deep woods and across rolling hilly terrain. Keep an eye out for the forest's other wildlife, which includes bears, coyotes, bobcats, beavers, otters, woodcocks, turkeys, bald eagles, ospreys, loons, and blue herons. For more information on the state forest, stop by the **Pigeon River forestry field office** (off Sturgeon Valley Rd., 989/983-4101).

Eastern Upper Peninsula

The short drive across the Mackinac Bridge from the Lower to the Upper Peninsula can feel like a journey between two disparate countries. Despite sizable towns like St. Ignace and Sault Ste. Marie, the eclectic eastern half of this enormous, sparsely populated peninsula epitomizes the very definition of "wilderness," illustrated by its rushing rivers, thunderous cascades, dramatic cliffs, deserted beaches, and vast tracts of forested terrain.

Although there are several ways to reach the UP, most travelers utilize the "Mighty Mac" bridge, the only vehicular link. From the south, the first stop is St. Ignace, a former fur trading town that now offers a variety of attractions, including an Ojibwa history museum and a casino. Via I-75, the eastern UP's largest city, Sault Ste. Marie, lies only

Highlights

Look for ★ to find recommended sights, activities, dining, and lodging.

★ **Mackinac Bridge:** Once you've crossed the "Mighty Mac," stop in lovely Bridge View Park to snap pictures of this engineering marvel (page 304).

★ **Seul Choix Point Lighthouse:** If you only have time to visit one lighthouse in the Upper Peninsula, head to Seul Choix Point, where you'll find a seasonal museum and a supposedly haunted tower (page 310).

★ **Grand Island National Recreation Area:** Its treasures include sandy beaches, colorful sandstone cliffs, historic lighthouses, and clear, if frigid, waters (page 317).

★ **Miners Castle:** The Pictured Rocks National Lakeshore's most famous formation overlooks the seemingly endless Lake Superior (page 319).

★ **Great Lakes Shipwreck Museum:** See artifacts from "Lake Superior's Shipwreck Coast," such as a bronze bell recovered from the famous *Edmund Fitzgerald* wreck (page 328).

★ **Tahquamenon Falls:** Take a scenic train ride and narrated riverboat cruise to explore one of the largest waterfall systems east of the Mississippi River (page 328).

★ **Soo Locks:** This marvelous structure allows the passage of massive freighters between the Great Lakes, the world's largest waterway traffic system (page 333).

50 miles north. Here, travelers find a unique maritime attraction: the Soo Locks, an engineering marvel that has allowed safe passage for ships transiting from Lake Superior to its lower counterparts for over 160 years.

Those seeking an even more untamed landscape should head west, where over one million acres of protected state and federal land—including the enormous Hiawatha National Forest—await. Every season, adventure seekers are lured to these remote forests and wetlands to share the open space with deer, foxes, black bears, and bald eagles—the true locals of these parts. The peninsula's wild interior, depleted during the 19th-century by an aggressive logging industry, also contains a variety of stunning lakes and waterways. In summer, boaters and anglers flock to the Manistique Lakes, while paddlers relish exploring serpentine rivers like the Two Hearted.

Of course, the most visited areas lie along the coasts. The southern shore, beside Lake Michigan, contains nostalgic towns, sheltered harbors, and historic sites like the haunted Seul Choix Point Lighthouse. The best-known destinations of the northern shore are of the natural variety, such as Pictured Rocks National Lakeshore and Tahquamenon Falls, one of the largest waterfalls east of the Mississippi River. Sadly, the rugged shoreline along Lake Superior is also known as the "Graveyard of the Great Lakes"—an 80-mile stretch that has witnessed the wrecks of more than 300 ships, the memories of which are preserved within the Great Lakes Shipwreck Museum, the Alger Underwater Preserve, and the Whitefish Point Underwater Preserve.

PLANNING YOUR TIME

Airports, bus stations, and public transit systems are few and far between in the Upper Peninsula. While it's possible to reach the eastern half by flying into Escanaba, Marquette, or Sault Ste. Marie, a car is a necessity for exploring. Though not compact, the eastern UP is relatively easy to navigate via its main routes: I-75 between St. Ignace and Canada, U.S. 2 along Lake Michigan, M-28 from I-75 to Munising, and M-123 between I-75, Paradise, and Newberry.

At minimum, you'll need at least four days to visit St. Ignace, Sault Ste. Marie, Pictured Rocks, and the attractions near Whitefish Bay. A week or more is required for die-hard outdoor enthusiasts or those interested in exploring the Lake Michigan shoreline and inland lakes. Crowds are less a concern in the eastern UP, but it is important to pay meticulous attention to the seasons. In general, the UP delivers much harsher weather than Michigan's lower part. Summer here is cooler, especially in the evening, while winter comes earlier, stays longer, and is marked by lower temperatures and higher snow levels.

Pictured Rocks' tourism season, for example, is short. Most of the park's 594,000 annual visitors come in July and August when they're most likely to enjoy daytime temperatures in the 70s. June is quieter, but the blackflies and mosquitoes often aren't worth the trade-off. May and September may be the park's finest months. No matter when you go, though, pack plenty of warm clothes just in case—and note Lake Superior is bone-numbingly cold all year long.

For more information about the communities and attractions within the eastern UP, consult the **Upper Peninsula Travel & Recreation Association** (UPTRA, P.O. Box 400, Iron Mountain, MI 49801, 906/774-5480 or 800/562-7134, www.uptravel.com).

HISTORY

As with other parts of Michigan, the early history of the eastern UP was shaped by Native Americans, the 19th-century logging industry, and the Great Lakes' being a major shipping route. Names like Chippewa County, old logging towns like Blaney Park, and the

Previous: the Pictured Rocks; the Tahquamenon River; a lighthouse on Grand Island.

Eastern Upper Peninsula

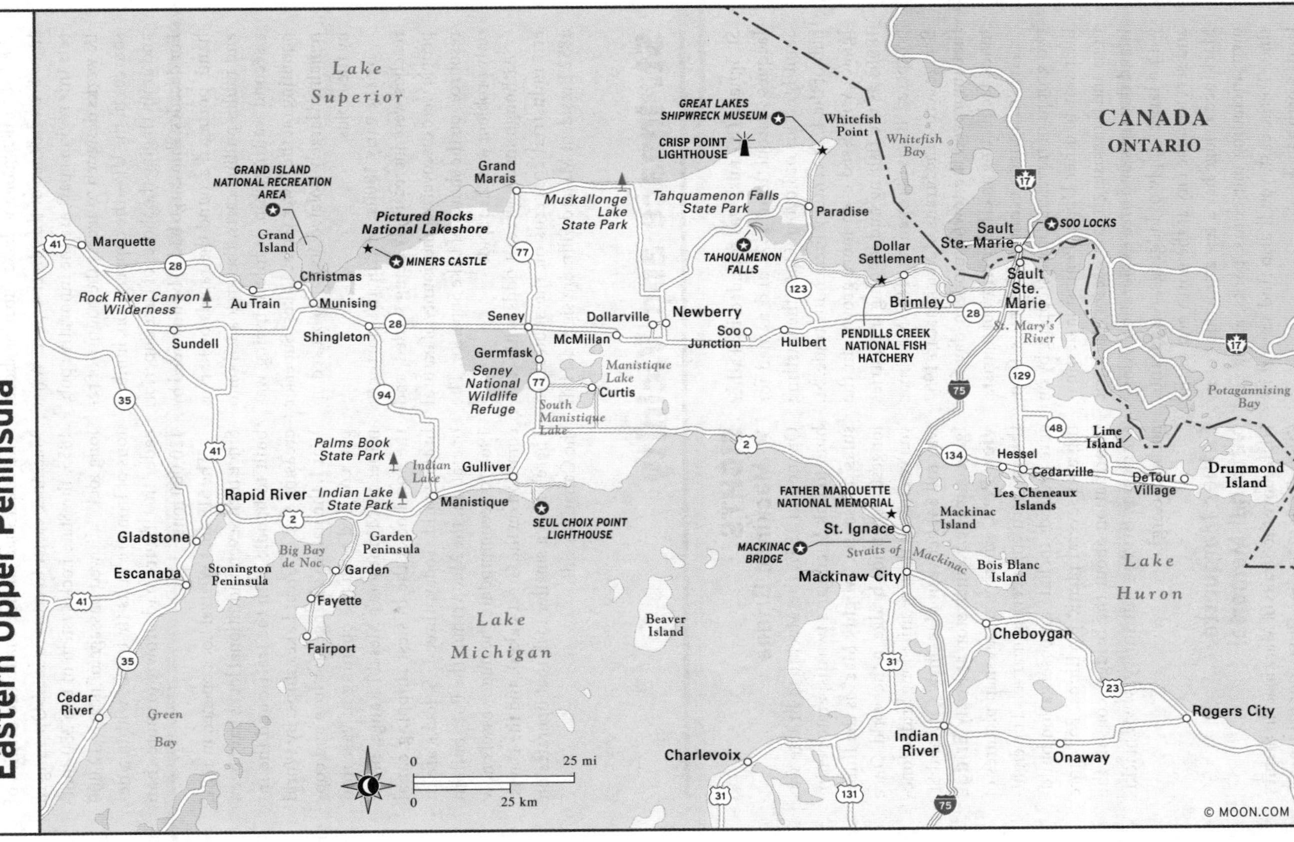

numerous lighthouses and shipwrecks along the Lake Michigan and Lake Superior shorelines are evidence of this diverse past. What sets this region apart are the innovative public works designed to access the bounty of resources in the UP—the copper, iron, lumber, and grain ringing the shores of Lake Superior. For decades, ship cargo had to be unloaded by hand, portaged around the rapids by horses and mules pulling carts, then reloaded onto a second waiting ship. While shipping was booming on the lower Great Lakes, Superior remained largely isolated, its cargo backed up by the rapids.

By the early 1800s, Michigan's northern reaches were increasingly being settled, and people were discovering the bounty of natural resources on the shores of Lake Superior. The only problem was the rapids.

Although locals were at odds with eastern industrial concerns on the subject, in 1852 President Millard Fillmore signed a bill authorizing the first lock at Sault Ste. Marie. The Mackinac Bridge made the Straits of Mackinac easier to cross in 1857. Opening in 1855, the State Lock system of two 350-foot-long locks allowed passage of nearly 12,000 tons of iron ore in its first year; within a decade, that figure had grown to more than 120,000 tons.

The 515-foot Weitzel Lock opened in 1881. Since then several additional locks have been built to handle both the traffic and the increasing size of Great Lakes ships. By World War I, the nation's hunger for iron and copper, coupled with the opening of vast iron mines in Minnesota's Mesabi Range, made the Soo Locks the busiest shipping canal in the world. Today, three U.S. locks are in operation, the MacArthur, the Poe (built in 1968 to accommodate the huge vessels now common on the Great Lakes), and the Davis. There's also a smaller lock that operates on the Canadian side.

St. Ignace and Vicinity

St. Ignace (IG-nus) was founded by Father Jacques Marquette in 1671 and named for Saint Ignatius of Loyola. Once the bustling hub of the 17th-century French fur trade, St. Ignace witnessed even more growth in the 1800s as the fishing and logging industries prospered. It was the opening of the Mackinac Bridge across the Straits of Mackinac in 1957 that improved the town's modern-day fortunes, facilitating an efficient flow of tourists.

The St. Ignace economy benefits from two groups of travelers: those stopping by on their way to other Upper Peninsula destinations and those using it as a base for Mackinac Island day trips and area exploration. Along with a large supply of lodgings, restaurants, and services, the city at the north end of the Mackinac Bridge has a few attractions of its own, including museums, parks, and a casino. To the east, you'll also find several islands worth a look.

SIGHTS

★ Mackinac Bridge

Opened in 1957, the Mackinac Bridge was built to link Michigan's two disparate peninsulas. Presently, "Mighty Mac" is the third-longest suspension bridge in the world. Once you've crossed the five-mile-long bridge (one-way toll $4) between Mackinaw City and St. Ignace, make a quick stop at lovely **Bridge View Park,** where you can snap pictures of this modern engineering marvel. The eight-acre grounds include an observation building and several picnic pavilions. For more information about the bridge, consult the **Mackinac Bridge Authority** (www.mackinacbridge.org).

Father Marquette National Memorial

High above the Straits of Mackinac, in **Straits State Park** (720 Church St., 906/643-8620, annual Recreation Passport required: $12 Michigan residents, $34 nonresidents, $9 day pass available to nonresidents only), east of I-75 and south of U.S. 2, this open-air site commemorates French explorer and Jesuit missionary Jacques Marquette. In the 1660s and 1670s, Marquette paddled through the Great Lakes, establishing dozens of cities, including Sault Ste. Marie and St. Ignace. Marquette later linked up with Louis Joliet and paddled another several thousand miles, making the pair the first European explorers of the Mississippi River. Walking trails at the **Father Marquette National Memorial** (www.michigan.gov/mhc, 8am-10pm daily Apr. 1-late Nov.) feature interpretive signs that discuss Marquette's Great Lakes travels and the impact that geography had on the area's settlement.

Museum of Ojibwa Culture

In contrast to the Father Marquette memorial, the excellent **Museum of Ojibwa Culture** (500 N. State, 906/643-9161, www.museumofojibwaculture.net, 9am-5pm daily Memorial Day-June 30, 9am-8pm daily July 1-Labor Day, 10am-5pm daily Labor Day-Oct. 1, by donation) tells the story of the Ojibwa people and the effect that European explorers had on their culture. Interestingly, the museum is located on the presumed site of Father Marquette's Jesuit mission and grave.

Displays housed in the former Catholic church include artifacts from archaeological digs on the grounds (some dating to 6000 BC), explanations of how the Ojibwa adapted and survived in the area's sometimes harsh climate, and a discussion of how they allied with the French fur traders, though it greatly diminished their traditional way of life. The Huron boardwalk follows the shoreline, with interpretive signs explaining the role of the bay in the area's settlement.

ENTERTAINMENT

St. Ignace might not have the hottest nightlife in Michigan, but you will find at least one round-the-clock entertainment venue. The **Kewadin Casino** (3015 Mackinac Trail, 800/539-2346, www.kewadin.com) promises Las Vegas-style gaming 24 hours daily and top-notch live entertainment on Friday and Saturday nights. Situated on the shores of Lake Huron, the casino resort also offers an 81-room hotel with plenty of amenities. Kewadin runs four other casinos in the eastern Upper Peninsula, in the towns of Hessel, Manistique, Christmas, and Sault Ste. Marie.

The Mackinac Bridge links Michigan's two peninsulas.

FOOD

When you're craving a bite, consider the Kewadin Casino's three dining options: the **Horseshoe Bay Restaurant** (7am-9pm daily, $7-29), **White Tail Sports Bar** (11am-8pm daily, $5-10), and the **Campfire Deli** (11am-midmight Sun.-Thurs., 11am-2am Fri.-Sat.), a great choice for pizza, burgers, and more.

You can also stop by the **Mackinac Grille** (251 S. State St., 906/643-7482, www.mackinacgrill.com, 10:30am-midnight daily, $9-22), where you can sample everything from ribs to burritos or enjoy bourbon planked steak tips.

ACCOMMODATIONS

The St. Ignace area offers plenty of lodgings, from simple motels to full-service resorts. For an inexpensive choice, **Americas Best Value Inns** (1074 N. State St., 906/643-7777, for reservations call 855/680-3243, www.americasbestvalueinn.com, May-Oct., $89-124 d) offers basic rooms at a good value. For something a little fancier, stay at the ★ **Kewadin Casino** (3015 Mackinac Trail, 800/539-2346, www.kewadin.com, $79-149 d), which offers an 81-room hotel, an indoor pool, a fitness center, and a game room. Pets are not allowed.

Camping

The St. Ignace area provides campers lots of options, especially if you want to stay somewhere with some seclusion but still close to the area's many attractions. Just a couple of miles west of the bridge, the **Lakeshore Park Campground** (416 Pointe La Barbe, 906/643-9522, www.lakeshoreparkcampground.com, May 1-Oct. 15, $25-42) has RV sites, tent spaces, and easy access to Lake Michigan. **Straits State Park** (720 Church St., 906/643-8620, annual Recreation Passport required: $12 Michigan residents, $34 nonresidents, $9 day pass available to nonresidents only) may not be particularly peaceful, but the 270 modern and semi-modern sites (reservations 800/447-2757, www.michigan.gov/dnr, $19-31) are clean and convenient. Aim for the nicely wooded sites right on the straits, which offer great views of the bridge. To reach the park, take I-75 to U.S. 2 and exit at Church Street, then follow Church south for half a mile.

INFORMATION AND SERVICES

For more information, contact the **St. Ignace Visitors Bureau** (6 Spring St., Ste. 100, 800/338-6660, www.stignace.com) or the **St. Ignace Chamber of Commerce** (560 N. State St., 906/643-8717, www.saintignace.org). St. Ignace offers numerous services for travelers, from groceries to banks. For medical issues, visit the **Mackinac Straits Hospital** (1140 N. State St., 906/643-8585, http://mackinacstraitshealth.org). The facility is equipped with a 24-hour emergency room.

GETTING THERE AND AROUND

The easiest way to reach St. Ignace is by car. From the Lower Peninsula, simply cross the Mackinac Bridge and you'll find St. Ignace at the northern end of "Mighty Mac." If you're already in the UP, simply head east from Manistique via U.S. 2, an 87-mile trip that will take about 90 minutes, or drive south from Sault Ste. Marie via I-75, a 52-mile trip that takes 53 minutes.

You can come in via **Greyhound** (800/231-2222, www.greyhound.com) or **Indian Trails** (800/292-3831, www.indiantrails.com) buses to the **St. Ignace Bus Station** (700 U.S. 2, 906/643-1531), or fly into one of several regional airports, where you can rent a vehicle from a national chain. From **Pellston Regional Airport** (PLN, 1395 U.S. 31, Pellston, 231/539-8441 or 231/539-8442, www.pellstonairport.com) in the Lower Peninsula, take U.S. 31 and I-75 across the Mackinac Bridge, a 22-mile trip that takes 30 minutes. In the Upper Peninsula, you can fly into **Chippewa County International Airport** (CIU, 5019 W. Airport Dr., Kincheloe, 906/495-5631, www.airciu.com), near Sault Ste. Marie, and drive I-75 South to St. Ignace, a

36-mile trip that normally takes about 37 minutes. From **Sawyer International Airport** (MQT, 125 G Ave., Gwinn, 906/346-3308, www.sawyerairport.com), near Marquette, follow M-94, M-28, M-77, and U.S. 2 for a 157-mile trip running three hours.

LAKE HURON SHORE

East of I-75, the Upper Peninsula narrows into a series of peninsulas, points, and islands. The area functions at a quiet, slow pace—the kind of place where casual cycling, beachcombing, and picnicking mark a summer day, even though there are few true destinations. The area is often overlooked by guidebooks—which is just fine with the locals and summer cottage owners.

M-134 between I-75 and Drummond Island is a lovely and peaceful stretch of highway. The road hugs the Lake Huron shore, past coastal villages, rocky bays, and pine-studded islands. **DeTour Village** marks both the end of the road and the UP mainland. This small village has long served an important navigational role for ships heading up and down the St. Mary's River. Many squeeze through DeTour Passage here between the point and Drummond Island. They make a turn, or detour, to chart a course down the St. Mary's and westward to the Straits of Mackinac or farther downstream to Detroit. DeTour Village has been guiding ships with a navigational light since as far back as 1848. It remains a pleasant place to watch the ship traffic.

Les Cheneaux Islands

The name of Les Cheneaux Islands (lay shen-O), commonly known as "The Snows," comes from the French and translates to "The Channels." The islands, most of them long, narrow, and shaped like shards of glass, number 36, some of which are uninhabited. They lie splintered just off the UP's southeastern shore, forming a maze of calm channels and protected bays in northern Lake Huron. Not surprisingly, this area is a delight for boaters. Tall sailboats, classic cabin cruisers, and simple canoes all share these waters.

The best way to experience Les Cheneaux, of course, is to get out on the water. Aside from the pretty wooded islands themselves, part of the fun is eyeing the beautiful old boathouses that dot the shorelines, especially on Marquette Island. If you have access to a craft, you'll find launches in Hessel and Cedarville, the only two towns in the area. Though the waters are protected and normally quite safe, be sure to bring a chart or at least a map provided by local businesses. Newcomers can find the various bays, channels, and points to be quite confusing.

It might seem almost natural, given the strong boating tradition of this area, that the community is home to a higshly regarded school of boat construction. Housed in a handsome boathouse-style building, the **Great Lakes Boat Building School** (485 S. Meridian St., Cedarville, 906/484-1081, www.glbbs.org) teaches students the art of traditional wooden boat construction. The intensive 12-month program covers carpentry, mechanical systems, and more. This fascinating school offers free public tours (10am and 2pm) for an excellent way to learn about the area's nautical traditions. The 1.5-hour tour is led by a senior faculty member and offers visitors the opportunity to see students at work. The guide is happy to field questions, which tend to be numerous.

Drummond Island

Drummond Island, just across from De Tour Village, is the largest U.S. island in the Great Lakes. About 66 percent of the land is state-owned, with the rest the property of summer residents, who swell the island's population to about 5,000 in July and August. But they seem almost invisible. Life in this fishing-oriented place is focused along the shore, relatively hidden from the island's few roads.

With sandy beaches, inland lakes, cedar swamps, hardwood forests, and open meadows, Drummond Island is home to remarkably diverse animal and plant habitats. Loons, bobcats, moose, and wolves all roam here, and various orchid species grow wild on the island. Biking is a fun way to explore Drummond, since M-134 dissolves into a variety of double-tracks and, eventually, single-tracks. Kayaking is even more exciting. The fjord-like bays and 150 miles of ragged shoreline make this a magical place to paddle.

The universal appeal of golf extends to Drummond Island. **The Rock Golf Course** (Drummond Island Resort and Conference Center, 33494 S. Maxton Rd., 906/999-6343, www.drummondisland.com, daily Apr.-Oct., $45-75 pp with cart) is a spectacular designer course completed in 1990 as part of a venue for corporate retreats. The first-rate facility makes fine use of the natural environment, with holes weaving through woods and limestone outcroppings. Seeing an occasional deer wander across the course is not uncommon.

Accommodations and Camping

Along the Lake Huron shore near Cedarville, **Spring Lodge & Cottages** (916 Park Ave., Cedarville, 906/484-2282 or 800/480-2165, www.springlodge.com, May-Oct., $675-1,295 weekly for a family of 4) is a resort in a wonderful location in the heart of Les Cheneaux. Large and well-maintained grounds house cottages, most overlooking the water. Boat rentals are available. In nearby Hessel, you can stay at year-round ★ **Hessel on the Lake** (210 Island View Rd., 906/484-1463, www.hesselonthelake.com, $150-285 d), which offers 10 fully equipped cottages; weekly rates are available.

Stay in luxury at the **Drummond Island Resort and Conference Center** (33494 S. Maxton Rd., Drummond Island, 800/999-6343, www.drummondisland.com, $130-175 d), a grandiose retreat with handsome log lodge rooms and several private cottages. Guests have access to tennis courts, a restaurant, and a golf course.

The island's best camping is at **Drummond Island Township Park** (906/493-5245 or 800/737-8666, $31-38), about six miles from the ferry dock. This rustic campground contains 46 pretty RV and tent sites tucked in the woods on Potagannissing Bay. Many of the sites have electric service; other amenities include picnic tables, firepits, outhouses, water wells, a sandy beach, and a boat ramp.

Information and Services

For more information about the Lake Huron shore, contact the **DeTour Area Chamber of Commerce** (DeTour Village, 906/297-5987, www.detourvillage.org), **Les Cheneaux**

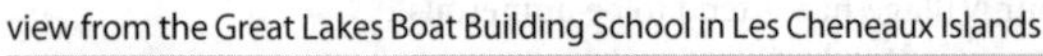

view from the Great Lakes Boat Building School in Les Cheneaux Islands

The Moose Capital of Michigan

Northeast of the Manistique Lakes and Seney National Wildlife Refuge is the village of Newberry, a gateway town to the impressive Tahquamenon Falls. Surrounded by acres of state and national forestland, Newberry serves as a strategic home base for outdoor recreation, but the town has another claim to fame: In 2002, Michigan's state legislature designated Newberry the official "Moose Capital of Michigan." There are more moose sightings in Luce County than in any other place in the state.

While the majestic moose tends to be an elusive creature, your chances of seeing one in the wild are fairly high in the Newberry area. Remember to keep your distance, snap photos from afar, and report any moose sightings to the **Newberry Area Chamber of Commerce** (P.O. Box 308, Newberry, MI 49868, 906/293-5562 or 800/831-7292, www.newberrychamber.net, 9:30am-4:30pm Mon.-Fri.), located just south of the intersection of M-28 and M-123.

Islands Chamber of Commerce (Cedarville, 906/484-3935, www.lescheneaux.net), and the **Drummond Island Tourism Association** (Drummond Island, 906/493-5245, www.visitdrummondisland.com).

Services are limited here; head south to St. Ignace for groceries and other needs. For medical issues, visit the **Mackinac Straits Hospital & Health Center** (1140 N. State St., 906/643-8585, http://mackinacstraitshealth.org).

Getting There and Around

From St. Ignace, you can reach Les Cheneaux Islands driving north on I-75 and then east on M-134 to Hessel, where you'll need a private boat to access this cluster of small islands; the 29-mile trip between St. Ignace and Hessel will take about half an hour. To reach Drummond Island from St. Ignace, take I-75, M-134, and drive through Hessel, continuing another 27 miles (30 minutes) to DeTour Village, where you can board the **Drummond Island Ferry** (906/322-5511, www.eupta.net/ferry-system, from DeTour Village 6:40am-5:40am daily, from Drummond Island 6:10am-5:10am daily, $2 adults, $1 over age 64 and students). The ferry accommodates motorcycles, cars, motor homes, off-road vehicles, and snowmobiles. Consult the EUPTA site for complete rates.

Manistique Area

Four factors created the logging legacy that once dominated the southern reaches of the UP: vast stands of timber, wide rivers for transporting logs, well-protected harbors, and a building frenzy that began in southern Great Lakes ports like Detroit and stretched west across the treeless prairie. Devastating clear-cuts and diminished demand ended the region's logging boom by the early 20th century, but those well-protected ports and deep harbors still serve the area as busy shipping centers and enviable fishing waters.

These destinations can be accessed via U.S. 2, which traces the incomparable Lake Michigan shore west of St. Ignace. One such town, Manistique, sits at the mouth of the winding Manistique River, which twists through Lake Superior State Forest and the Seney National Wildlife Refuge before emptying into Lake Michigan. A community of about 3,000, Manistique offers proximity to historic sites and swimming beaches, and serves as an ideal home base for anglers, boaters, hikers, and other recreationists.

DOWNTOWN MANISTIQUE

Manistique presents a few curiosities for history buffs. The **siphon bridge,** built across the Manistique River in 1919, is a strange engineering feat, partially supported by the water underneath it. In fact, the roadway sits four feet below water level. Its construction was prompted by a paper mill just upstream, which needed to dam the river for its water needs, thus raising the river.

Also interesting is the historic **Manistique Water Tower,** a fancy neoclassical brick structure built in 1922, now serving as the town's landmark. From the boardwalk, strollers can view the vivid red **Manistique East Breakwater Light,** constructed in 1916. It was automated in 1969 and remains operational today.

★ SEUL CHOIX POINT LIGHTHOUSE

East of Gulliver, a road leads you down to a point and this 1895 light, a worthwhile detour. Pronounced "sis SHWA" or "sel SHWA"—French for "Only Choice"—the **Seul Choix Point Lighthouse** (672 N. West Gulliver Lake Rd., 906/283-3183, www.greatlakelighthouse.com, 10am-6pm daily Memorial Day-mid-Oct., by donation) sits at the end of a finger of land that once offered Native Americans and French fur traders the only choice for hiding from storms along this stretch of Lake Michigan shoreline.

The Gulliver Historical Society has done an outstanding job restoring this 1895 lighthouse and creating a maritime museum in the fog signal building. It includes an admirable scale model of the structure, made by hand with thousands of miniature bricks. Visitors may climb the tower to enjoy breathtaking views of much of northern Lake Michigan. You'll have a good chance of seeing ship traffic, since Port Inland, just to the east, is a major commercial port. The tower holds another curiosity. Over the years, visitors and employees have reported odd occurrences at the lighthouse complex, such as phantom footsteps, unexplained smells such as cigar smoke, and misplaced items. Some believe that the spirit of a former lighthouse keeper is still in residence.

To reach Seul Choix from Manistique, follow U.S. 2 for 12.6 miles to Gulliver, then go south on County Road 432 for 4.3 miles, and south on County Road 431 (Seul Choix Rd.) for 4.1 miles to the lighthouse. The 21-mile trip takes about 43 minutes.

THE BAYS DE NOC

At Green Bay's northern end, two large peninsulas—Stonington and Garden—hang down from the UP, forming Little Bay de Noc and Big Bay de Noc. More than 200 miles of wonderfully protected and undulating shoreline, combined with the region's temperate climate, make for outstanding fishing for northern pike, perch, lake salmon, rainbow trout, smallmouth bass, and walleye.

Stonington Peninsula

The quiet Stonington Peninsula is largely ignored by travelers, as it lacks accessible sand beaches or commercial attractions. It's a peaceful place, with smooth slabs of bedrock shoreline and sunny meadows that have reclaimed abandoned farmland. To explore the 15-mile-long peninsula, follow U.S. 2 west of Manistique and turn south on County Road 513 or County Road 511. The Hiawatha National Forest manages a nice stretch of shoreline along the peninsula's west side, with numerous hiking trails.

The peninsula preserves several stands of old-growth hemlocks, hardwoods, and pines. One of the most notable examples is now protected as the **Squaw Creek Old Growth Area,** part of the Hiawatha National Forest. Though not virgin timber, loggers in the 19th century practiced selective cutting, quite unusual at the time, and left behind several large, now huge, trees. Trails are few—just a couple of abandoned logging roads open only to foot traffic. Walking is easy, however, since the high shade canopy created by the trees crowds out the underbrush usually found in the woods.

The peninsula is also an excellent spot for bird-watchers, since the Stonington is a favorite migration stopping point for songbirds. Watch the water's edge for great blue herons. These grand birds stand straight and motionless in the water for several minutes, then quickly snatch unsuspecting fish out of the shallows.

Garden Peninsula

Like Stonington Peninsula, Garden Peninsula is a quiet, peaceful point of land, filled with little-used roads perfect for biking as well as a handful of sleepy farms and orchards. The main artery down the peninsula is M-183, accessed from U.S. 2. As it traces the eastern shore of Big Bay de Noc, M-183 passes through the tiny hamlet of Garden. Along with a few shops, it's home to a commercial fishery at the end of Little Harbor Road, where you can buy fresh catch.

By far the peninsula's most notable attraction is the 711-acre **Fayette Historic State Park** (13700 13.25 Ln., 906/644-2603, annual Recreation Passport required: $12 Michigan residents, $34 nonresidents, $9 day pass available to nonresidents only). If you have time for just one stop in this part of the UP, make it this outstanding state park. Once the site of a large smelting operation, Fayette's limestone furnaces converted raw iron ore from UP mines into pig iron that was loaded onto barges bound for Escanaba. In the 1880s, stinky, industrial Fayette boasted a population of 500, and its loud, hot blast furnaces cranked away seven days a week. By 1891, nearby forests that fueled the furnace were all but depleted, while more efficient steelmaking methods were developed. The furnaces shut down, and the town died with it.

Nearly a century later, Fayette was reborn as a wonderfully restored historic site and state park, surely one of the nation's most scenic ghost towns, its dozen limestone buildings tucked along the sheer white bluffs and deep, clear waters of Snail Shell Harbor. Start at the visitors center, which gives a good historical overview and features a helpful scale model of the village. You can wander in and out of the hotel, opera house, homes, and other buildings, some intact, some just partially—but all thoroughly preserved.

MANISTIQUE LAKES

Near the convergence of County Roads H-33 and H-42, the town of Curtis serves as the base camp for the Manistique Lakes area. Three lakes—North Manistique, Big Manistique, and South Manistique—combine to offer almost 16,000 acres of shallow, warm waters that are extremely popular with boaters, swimmers, and anglers. Big Manistique, one of the largest lakes in the UP, is just 5-10 feet deep, and best known for its perch and bass fishing. To reach the town of Curtis from Manistique, take U.S. 2 East for 30.6 miles, turn left onto Manistique Lakes Road (County Rd. H-33), and head north for 7.4 miles to Main Street. In light traffic, the 38-mile trip should take about 50 minutes. For more information, contact the **Manistique Lakes Area Tourism Bureau** (800/860-3819, www.curtismi.com).

THE FOX RIVER

In 1919, Ernest Hemingway stepped off a train in Seney, asked for directions to a good trout stream, and was directed up an old railroad grade to the east branch of the Fox. While it's impossible to corroborate this claim, Hemingway's UP travels did result in "Big Two-Hearted River," his Nick Adams tale about fishing on what was really the Fox. (The Big Two Hearted actually flows about 25 miles to the northeast.) Consequently, the Fox has always carried a special cachet in the UP and among trout fishers.

The **Fox River Pathway** was no doubt prompted by perennial interest in Hemingway's river. The route stretches 27 miles north from Seney to just shy of Pictured Rocks National Lakeshore and, by UP standards, is less than noteworthy. Its most appealing stretch—especially for anglers looking

1
2

for fishing access—is the southern end, where the trail parallels the main river for 10 miles. Farther north, it follows the Little Fox and the west branch. Heading north, the trail traverses the Kingston Plains, where loggers left behind "stump prairies." Markers along the route provide information about the area's logging history.

SENEY NATIONAL WILDLIFE REFUGE

Seney was a center of activity in the 1880s, both in and out of the woods. Situated along a railroad siding and the shores of the Fox River—used to transport the logs—it became an important transit point. The local economy also revolved around drinking, prostitution, and gambling, and Seney was sensationalized in the national press, revealing a level of debauchery reminiscent of towns in the Wild West.

The problem was that Seney never had the huge fertile forests so common elsewhere in Michigan. Glaciers scrubbed this swath of the central UP flat, creating a patchwork of rivers, wetlands, and rocky, sandy soil. The red and white pines that did grow here were leveled in just a few short years. Optimistic farmers followed the quickly departed loggers. Yet their hopes were soon dashed by the area's poor soils and cold climate, and they too departed almost as quickly as they had come.

Eventually, humans began to help this beleaguered land. The immense **Seney National Wildlife Refuge** (www.fws.gov/refuge/seney) now manages and protects almost 150 square miles of virgin wilderness immediately west of M-77, restoring the wetlands with an intricate series of dikes and control ponds in what began as a Civilian Conservation Corps project in the 1930s. While people on foot or bike can access much of this preserve via an extensive network of maintenance roads, the sanctuary offers plenty of seclusion for its inhabitants. More than 200 species of birds and nearly 50 species of mammals have been recorded here, including bald eagles, trumpeter swans, loons, and even the occasional moose or wolf. Whether you're a dedicated bird-watcher or a casual observer, Seney is a wonderful place to get into a fascinating array of wildlife.

Start your tour at the **visitors center** (906/586-9851, 9am-5pm daily May 15-Oct. 20), five miles south of the town of Seney on M-77. A 15-minute audiovisual program, interactive exhibits, and printed materials give you a good overview of what you can look for in the refuge. From the center, the 1.2-mile **Pine Ridge Nature Trail** allows for a quick foray into wetland habitat. For visitors unable to walk or pedal this type of distance, the refuge offers the **Marshland Wildlife Drive,** a seven-mile one-way route accessible by car from May 15 to October 20. The drive passes through wetlands and forests and offers an exceptional opportunity to view wildlife.

Biking

Many visitors to Seney never get out of their cars and beyond the Marshland Drive, which is a shame. A bicycle is the best way to experience Seney. Bikes are welcome on more than 100 miles of gravel and dirt maintenance roads, which are closed to all motorized traffic except refuge vehicles. A bike allows you to cover considerable ground and is sufficiently quiet so as to not disturb the wildlife. There's also a magical quality about spinning down a gravel road amid chirping and twittering, with nothing but waving grasses and glinting ponds surrounding you for miles. No off-road riding is permitted in the refuge.

ACCOMMODATIONS

While chain hotels are becoming more and more dominant, several nice independent motels still operate along U.S. 2. One example is the **Star Motel** (1142 E. Lakeshore Dr., Manistique, 906/341-5363, $68-78 d). A mile east of Manistique on U.S. 2, this tidy, vintage 1950s-era motel has large rooms, dedicated

1: Seul Choix Point Lighthouse **2:** crystal clear springs flowing into Indian Lake

owners, and a nice setting on the lake. It also allows well behaved dogs.

The gracious **Celibeth House Bed & Breakfast** (4446N Hwy., Blaney Park, 906/283-3409, www.celibethhousebnb.com, $80-125 d), once a lumber baron's home, is a fine out-of-the-way relaxation spot or a good base for day trips to Pictured Rocks National Lakeshore, Seney National Wildlife Refuge, Lake Michigan beaches, and more. Explore the inn's grounds, which cover 85 acres and include a small lake, beaver ponds, woods, and meadows. A horde of hummingbirds frequenting the backyard feeders guarantees a wildlife encounter.

Camping

Camping is readily available at dozens of rustic campgrounds within the **Hiawatha National Forest** (2727 N. Lincoln Rd., Escanaba, 906/786-4062, www.fs.usda.gov/hiawatha, $12-18). A particularly nice one is the very secluded—and difficult to reach—Portage Bay campground on Garden Peninsula's eastern shore. It's southeast of Garden, at the end of Portage Bay Road.

INFORMATION AND SERVICES

For more information about the area around Manistique and Seney, contact the **Manistique Tourism Council** (800/342-4282, www.visitmanistique.com), **Bays de Noc Convention and Visitors Bureau** (230 Ludington St., Escanaba, 906/789-7862, www.visitescanaba.com), and **Manistique Lakes Area Tourism Bureau** (Curtis, 800/860-3819, www.curtismi.com). For services like banks and groceries, Manistique is the most convenient choice, though you'll find a better selection in major towns like Marquette, Escanaba, and Sault Ste. Marie.

GETTING THERE AND AROUND

The closest airport to this region is **Delta County Airport** (ESC, 3300 Airport Rd., Escanaba, 906/786-4902, www.deltacountymi.org), with limited Delta flights. **Sawyer International Airport** (MQT, 125 G Ave., Gwinn, 906/346-3308, www.sawyerairport.com) is near Marquette. Rent a vehicle at either airport from a national chain. From the Sawyer airport, reach Manistique via M-94, U.S. 41, and U.S. 2, an 83-mile trip that will take 90 minutes. From St. Ignace, reach Manistique directly via U.S. 2, an 87-mile trip that will take 90 minutes. From Manistique, drive to the town of Seney—which lies between the Fox River, Seney National Wildlife Refuge, and Manistique Lakes—via U.S. 2, M-77, and M-28, a 40-mile trip that will take 45 minutes. As with most towns in the UP, Manistique and Seney are both easily navigable by foot, bike, or car.

Munising Area

When it comes to enticing visitors, nature dealt Munising, situated on the UP's northern coast, a royal flush. The town of 2,330 curves around the belly of protected Munising Bay. The Grand Island National Recreation Area looms just offshore in expansive Lake Superior. Pictured Rocks National Lakeshore begins at the edge of town and stretches east for over 40 miles. The Hiawatha National Forest is to the south and west. The city of Munising serves as an access point for many of these attractions. M-28 leads to the heart of town, where you'll find restaurants, independent motels, and the ferry dock for cruises to Pictured Rocks.

SIGHTS

Historic Sites

A perennial favorite for visitors to the Munising area is the marvelous two-hour

Glass Bottom Shipwreck Tours (1204 Commercial St., 906/387-4477, www.shipwrecktours.com, $34 adults, $31 over age 61, $12 ages 6-12, $1 age 5 and under, operates from Memorial Day until mid-Oct., cruise times vary based on customer demand). Pete Lindquist, an experienced local who also operates a dive charter, came up with the idea of installing viewing wells in the hulls of a couple of tour boats, so even nondivers can marvel at the area's shallow-water shipwrecks.

The view through the 8- to 10-foot-long windows is truly remarkable. The boat glides directly over shipwrecks, some in as little as 28 feet of water. They fill the viewing windows like historic paintings, perfectly visible in the clear Lake Superior water and looking close enough to touch. On the *Bermuda,* you can easily make out deck lines, hatches, and even piles of iron ore lying on the deck. Weather permitting, the tour visits three shipwrecks, dating from 1860 to 1926. Along the way, Lindquist's knowledgeable crew also shares history and points out features (including the wooden East Channel Light) along the shore of Grand Island.

Waterfalls

Numerous waterfalls are located in the Munising area, many of which are easy to reach. The **Munising Visitors Bureau** (422 E. Munising Ave., 906/387-2138, www.munising.org) prints a waterfall map that will direct you to most of them. Nearby Pictured Rocks National Lakeshore also has several notable falls.

The Tannery Creek spills over **Olson Falls** and **Memorial Falls** right on the northeast edge of town. Follow County Road H-58 (Washington St.) northeast from town, and watch for a small wooden staircase on the right side of the road, across from the road to Sand Point and the National Park Service headquarters. Parking is prohibited alongside the road, so you'll need to park in Munising or Pictured Rocks National Lakeshore and access the site by foot or bike. Climb the stairs and follow the trail through a small canyon to Olson. To reach Memorial Falls, it's easiest to return to County Road H-58, turn right on Nestor Street, and follow the signs.

Right on the outskirts of town, M-28 leads east to **Horseshoe Falls** (turn east on Prospect St.) and **Alger Falls,** which spills down along the highway. The impressive **Wagner Falls** is right in the same area, just off M-94 near the junction of M-94 and M-28. It's a well-marked spot, operated by the state

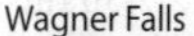

Wagner Falls

park system as a scenic site. Though it feels secluded, 20-foot Wagner Falls is just a few minutes' walk from the parking area. Continue up the streamside trail past the main falls to a second cascade. Wagner Falls offers some of the most stunning photo opportunities in the Upper Peninsula.

About 20 miles west of Munising, wonderful **Laughing Whitefish Falls** has also been protected as a state park scenic site. Here, water plunges 30 feet over hard dolomite rock ledges, then continues rolling and frothing at least twice that far to the bottom of a gorge. To reach Laughing Whitefish Falls, follow M-94 west from Munising to the small town of Sundell, then head north on Dorsey Road for 2.5 miles.

DIVING

When loggers were felling the vast stands of pine across the central Upper Peninsula in the 1800s, Munising grew into a busy port, with schooners carrying loads of timber to the growing cities of the southern Great Lakes and iron ore to an ever-growing number of factories. Yet the narrow and shoal-filled passage between the mainland and Grand Island, and along the Pictured Rocks shoreline, was the downfall of many ships; their skeletons litter the lakebed here.

The **Alger Underwater Preserve** covers 113 square miles, from just west of Grand Island to Au Sable Point near the east end of Pictured Rocks National Lakeshore. Nearly a dozen wrecks lie here, well preserved in Lake Superior's cold, fresh water. Some wrecks, like the 19th-century *Bermuda* and the 145-foot *Smith Moore,* lie upright and nearly intact. The Alger Underwater Preserve marks many of the dive sites with buoys and helps ensure that they will be protected from looters. Removing or disturbing artifacts within an underwater preserve is a felony under Michigan law.

Several factors combine to make the Alger Underwater Preserve one of the finest sport-diving locations in the Midwest. There are several wrecks concentrated in one area; the salt-free water keeps them from deteriorating; many wrecks are at very shallow depths, as little as 20 feet; visibility is excellent, usually a minimum of 25 feet and sometimes twice that; and Grand Island helps moderate the water temperatures. "It's one of the best wreck diving sites for beginners that I can imagine," notes Pete Lindquist, who operates a dive charter in Munising.

Just offshore from the Munising High School, an **underwater museum** among dock ruins includes underwater signs that interpret large maritime artifacts. The Alger Underwater Preserve also attracts divers for its sea caves in about 20 feet of water, where sandstone cliffs have been eroded by wave action. To arrange a dive charter, contact **Lake Superior Shipwreck Diving** (1204 Commercial St., Munising, 906/387-4477, www.shipwrecktours.com). Open Water certification is required.

SHOPPING

While most snowshoes today are made of aluminum, they can't compare to the traditional white ash and rawhide versions. In **Shingleton,** 25 miles west of Seney on M-28, workers at **Iverson Snowshoe & Furniture** (E12559 Mill St., 906/452-6370, www.iversonssnowshoes.com, 7:30am-3:30pm Mon.-Fri.) shape by hand strips of local ash into those classic snowshoe frames. Iversons also makes rustic furniture and trout fishing nets. You can purchase their wares at their shop and can also order online via their website.

FOOD

For a town on the edge of a national park that presumably gets a fair amount of tourist traffic, Munising has surprisingly little in the way of dining. **Muldoon's Pasties & Gifts** (1246 W. M-28, 906/387-5880, www.muldoonspasties.com, 10am-6pm daily) is the best spot in town for a fresh, authentic taste of this UP classic potpie-type meal.

ACCOMMODATIONS

The **Sunset Motel on the Bay** (1315 Bay St., 906/387-4574, www.sunsetmotelonthebay.com, $149-229 d) has a great location right on Munising Bay at the east end of town. Some rooms have kitchenettes. Unlike most commercial strips, the one along M-28 on Munising's near east side is still within walking distance of downtown and the waterfront. Among chain offerings, the **AmericInn by Wyndham** (9926 M-28, Wetmore, 906/387-2000, www.americinn.com, $155-199 d) always ranks among the best.

Camping

For ultimate convenience but with a sense of seclusion, the Hiawatha National Forest's **Bay Furnace** (906/786-4062, www.fs.usda.gov/hiawatha, $14-21) is a good choice. Just west of Munising, north of M-28, it offers 50 rustic sites with a very nice setting next to Lake Superior and overlooking Grand Island. Some sites almost have their own private stretch of beach, and a short cross-country ski trail at the campground's north end gives campers some welcome buffer space.

INFORMATION AND SERVICES

For more information, contact the **Munising Visitors Bureau** (422 E. Munising Ave., 906/387-2138, www.munising.org). Although you'll find a limited amount of supplies in Munising, you might want to head west to Marquette for a wider range of services.

GETTING THERE AND AROUND

To reach Munising, you can fly into **Sawyer International Airport** (MQT, 125 G Ave., Gwinn, 906/346-3308, www.sawyerairport.com), with limited flights from Detroit and Chicago on Delta and American Eagle. You can then rent a vehicle from one of the major rental agencies, head west on M-94 and M-28, a 42-mile trip that will take about 50 minutes. If you're already across the Upper Peninsula, access Munising from Marquette via M-28, a 43-mile trip that will take 50 minutes. From Sault Ste. Marie, take I-75 south to exit 386, and then follow M-28 to Munising, a 122-mile trip that will take 2.25 hours.

★ GRAND ISLAND NATIONAL RECREATION AREA

Though it's just a 10-minute ferry ride from Munising, the surrounding Lake Superior waters effectively isolate Grand Island. For decades the 13,000-acre, largely wooded island

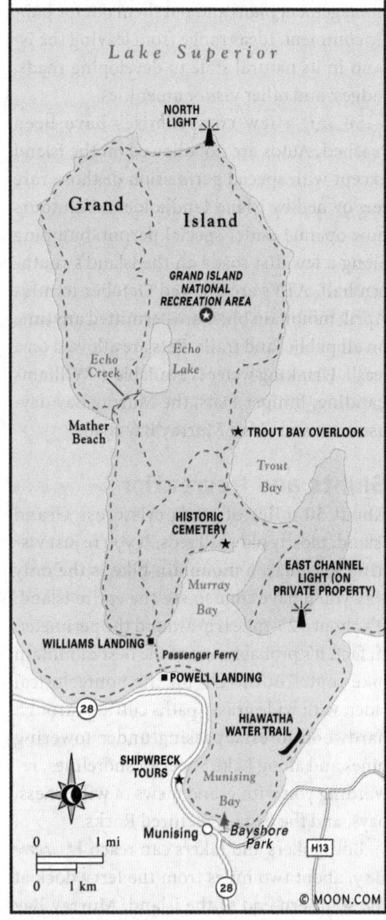

was maintained as a private hunting playground for executives and stockholders of the Cleveland Cliffs Iron Company. In 1989 the U.S. Forest Service purchased all but 40 acres of Grand Island and made it an appendage of the Hiawatha National Forest. Except for those few patches of private property, the entire island—almost the size of Manhattan—is available for hiking, beachcombing, mountain biking, and camping.

With its status as a national recreation area, Grand Island will likely see more development than the rest of the Hiawatha National Forest. Since 1989, the Forest Service has generated mountains of paperwork developing various management plans and put them out for public comment. Ideas range from leaving the island in its natural state to developing roads, lodges, and other visitor amenities.

So far, a few compromises have been reached. Autos are not allowed on the island except with special permission or those rare few owned by island landholders. Van tours now operate under special permit, bumping along a few dirt roads on the island's southern half. ATVs are allowed October to mid-April; mountain bikes are permitted anytime on all public land trails. Pets are allowed on a leash. Drinking water is available at Williams Landing, Juniper Flats, the Murray Bay day-use area, and along Murray Bay road.

Sights and Recreation

About 50 miles of trails crisscross Grand Island, mostly old roadbeds. If you're just visiting for a day, a mountain bike is the only way you'll have time to see the entire island: It's about a 23-mile trip around the perimeter. In fact, it's probably one of the best mountain bike routes in the UP for the nontechnical rider, with wide grassy paths cutting through hardwood forests, passing under towering pines and along Lake Superior shorelines, rewarding you with grand views of wilderness, bays, and the distant Pictured Rocks.

Both hikers and bikers can reach **Murray Bay,** about two miles from the ferry dock at the southern end of the island. Murray Bay has a nice day-use area and a sand beach nestled in a grove of pines. There are also two campsites here, but the location near the ferry dock means you'll have less privacy than elsewhere on the island.

Of special interest is the **historic cemetery,** where you can examine the gravestones of various shipwreck victims and the island's first nonnative settlers. Grand Island had long been a summering ground for the Ojibwa people when Abraham Williams arrived in the 1840s to establish a trading post. He raised a family and died on the island, in 1873, at the then-amazing age of 81. Today, only the descendants of Williams and their spouses can be interred there.

North of Murray Bay, the island sprouts a tombolo off its southeastern corner known as "the thumb." This landmass wraps north and forms **Trout Bay,** a lovely spot ringed with honey-hued beaches and sandstone cliffs. Watch for the low profile of loons bobbing in calm waters. Trout Bay is home to the island's four other developed campsites, which are known for their exceptional beauty.

Camping

There are no reservations, fees, or permits required for camping on Grand Island. The island has two designated campgrounds at Murray Bay (two sites) and Trout Bay (four sites), offering the relative luxury of pit toilets and fire rings. Backcountry camping is permitted throughout the island as long as you stay off the tombolo and private property, and no closer than 100 feet from lakes, streams, cliffs, trails, roads, and natural research areas. No ground fires are permitted. Drinking water is available at Williams Landing, Juniper Flats, the Murray Bay day-use area, and along Murray Bay road.

Information

For more information about Grand Island, contact the **Munising Ranger District** (Hiawatha National Forest, 400 E. Munising Ave., 906/387-3700).

Getting There and Around

A **passenger ferry** (906/387-3503, www.grandislandup.com, times vary Memorial Day-early Oct., $20 adults, $15 ages 6-12, $8 bikes) travels from Munising to Grand Island. In addition to the ferry ticket, there is a $5 per person charge levied by the Hiawatha National Forest. The ferry's departure point is about two miles west of central Munising near Powell Point. Follow M-28 West and watch for the signs. During the peak season (mid-June-mid-Sept.), the ferry runs each hour on the hour from 9am until 6pm. Even if you're planning just a day trip, you'd be wise to pack warm clothing. Rough weather can cancel ferry service at any time. Similarly, hikers and cyclists have been known to lose track of time and miss the last ferry. There is a ship-to-shore radio at Williams Landing in the event of an emergency.

Pictured Rocks National Lakeshore

Lake Superior takes center stage at this National Park Service property, just 3 miles wide but spanning more than 40 miles along the magnificent lake, from Munising to Grand Marais. Pictured Rocks derives its name from the sandstone bluffs that rise 200 feet directly from the water's surface. Washed in shades of pink, red, and green due to the mineral-rich water that seeps from the rock, these famous bluffs extend for more than 15 miles, at times sculpted into caves, arches, and castle-like turrets. The national lakeshore also features a lesser-known but equally spectacular stretch of shoreline called the Grand Sable Banks, where 200-foot-high sand dunes are hemmed by a 12-mile ribbon of sand and pebble beach. You'll also find lakes, forest trails, waterfalls, a lighthouse, and other historic attractions—plenty of reasons to put Pictured Rocks at the top of the list for anyone visiting the eastern UP.

SIGHTS

Munising Falls

Just inside the park's western boundary, a short trail leads to 50-foot Munising Falls, which spills into a narrow gorge before emptying into Lake Superior's Munising Bay. The highlight of this spot used to be the trail that led hikers behind the falls, but erosion problems prompted its closure. It's still worth a stop here, though, for the falls and the adjacent **interpretive center,** which offers a glimpse of this peaceful area's history, home to a belching pig-iron furnace in the 1860s. Munising Falls also marks the west trailhead for the **Lakeshore Trail,** a 43-mile segment of the North Country National Scenic Trail, which spans seven states from New York to North Dakota. The Lakeshore Trail runs the length of the Pictured Rocks National Lakeshore—predictably, never far from the water's edge. The park's eastern trailhead lies near Sable Falls.

Past Munising Falls, the paved access road ends at **Sand Point,** site of the national lakeshore headquarters. While the headquarters primarily houses offices and not visitor services, it also displays some interesting Coast Guard and shipwreck artifacts on its grounds. Sand Point has a small beach and a boat ramp, a good spot to launch a small craft for exploring nearby Grand Island.

★ Miners Castle

The sandstone cliffs five miles northeast of Munising Falls are known as Miners Castle, for the turret-like shape caused by wind and wave erosion. The nine-story-high rock formation is impressive and ranks as one of the park's most popular attractions, despite a 2006 collapse of one of the signature turrets. Boardwalks and steps lead to two viewing platforms out on the rock, where you can peer down into the crystalline waters of Lake Superior. If that moves you to do a little

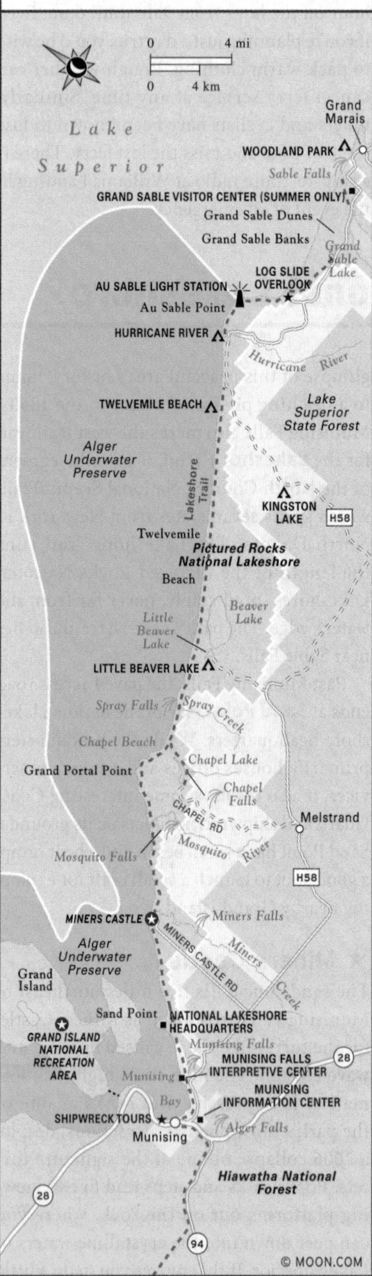

beachcombing and wading, a nearby trail leads down some steps through the pines to **Miners Beach.**

To reach Miners Castle, follow County Road H-58 east from Munising to the well-marked turnoff for Miners Castle Road. Before you reach the Miners Castle formation itself, you'll see another sign on Miners Castle Road directing you to **Miners Falls.** It's a one-mile walk to this pleasant cascade, where Miners Creek tumbles 40 feet over a rocky escarpment.

Chapel Basin Area

Continuing northeast on County Road H-58, the next auto-accessible route into the heart of the park is at Melstrand, where the gravel and dirt Chapel Road bumps six miles toward the shore and another park highlight, the Chapel Basin area. Park here and find plenty to entertain you for a day or a weekend: three waterfalls, a deep inland lake, Lake Superior beaches, and a good hiking loop.

Chapel Falls is the key attraction, as evidenced by the wide paved pathway that leads 1.5 miles to the falls. Amid a pale birch forest, frothing water drops like a horsetail some 90 feet into a gorge and onto Chapel Lake. Continue past the falls to reach **Chapel Beach** in another 1.75 miles, where you'll find a backcountry campground. From here, you can turn right to Chapel Rock and follow the **Lakeshore Trail** 1.5 miles to **Spray Falls,** one of the least visited and loveliest waterfalls in the park, where Spray Creek drops over the sandstone cliffs right into Lake Superior.

If you turn left instead of right at Chapel Beach, you can make a **10-mile loop** around Chapel Basin. Along the way, you'll pass **Grand Portal Point**—another significant Pictured Rocks landmark—before returning to the parking area. Don't leave Chapel Basin without a visit to **Mosquito Falls,** a little farther inland off Chapel Road. The Mosquito River spills over a series of ledges, creating an accessible waterfall that's calm enough for wading and soaking fatigued feet. A trail leads

The Facts About Pictured Rocks

Pictured Rocks

Encompassing more than 73,000 acres in Michigan's Upper Peninsula, **Pictured Rocks National Lakeshore** extends for 42 miles along the southern shore of Lake Superior. It was designated a Michigan state historic site in February 1965, only to be upgraded to the country's first national lakeshore in October 1966. Since then, visitation has steadily increased. Today the park welcomes more than 500,000 visitors annually. Here are some other fun facts about Pictured Rocks:

- Pictured Rocks National Lakeshore was named for the varied hues observed in the sandstone cliffs alongside Lake Superior. Caused by mineral seepage, these colors range from red and orange (iron) to green and blue (copper) to black (manganese) and white (lime).
- In modern times, no pictographs or petroglyphs have been spotted within the park's 42 miles of Lake Superior shoreline. Because the sandstone bedrock here is relatively soft and prone to large collapses, it's unlikely that any rock paintings or carvings would have survived.
- During the summer months, temperatures are commonly in the 70s and 80s Fahrenheit, though 90-degree days are possible. In the winter, temperatures are usually below freezing.
- Blackfly season generally runs mid-May-mid-June. However, other biting insects, such as mosquitoes, deerflies, horseflies, and stable flies, can also be an issue during the summer, so be sure to bring insect repellent and protective clothing.
- While the peak color season is hard to predict, fall colors are usually at their most vibrant in late September or early October. If you hope to see them, plan your visit for the earlier end of the season; the longer you wait, the more probable it is that heavy rainfall or unexpected winds will dislodge many of the leaves.
- Pets must be kept on six-foot leashes at all times and are only permitted in designated areas, such as picnic areas, drive-in campgrounds, and certain other spots, such as Sand Point and Miners Beach; they are not allowed in the backcountry.
- Although small backpacking stoves may be used at individual campsites, campfires are only permitted in the community metal fire rings within certain campgrounds. They are forbidden in the Mosquito River and Chapel Beach campgrounds. Where allowed, fires must be small, use only dead fallen wood, and doused before the site is abandoned.
- Cell phone service is not available throughout much of the park.
- Visitors may hand-pick, for personal use only, any wild blueberries, mushrooms, apples, and other native fruits and berries found in the park; there is, however, a limit of one gallon per person for all but the apples, of which each person can gather up to five gallons per week.

If you're curious about other aspects of the park, including the rules pertaining to visitors, contact the headquarters of **Pictured Rocks National Lakeshore** (N8391 Sand Point Rd., P.O. Box 40, Munising, MI 49862, 906/387-2607, www.nps.gov/piro).

to various sections of the falls and links up with the Lakeshore Trail.

Beaver Lake

Near the center of the park, 800-acre Beaver Lake is the largest inland lake in Pictured Rocks. Anglers are drawn to the lake and the tributaries that feed it, especially for trout. Little Beaver Lake, connected by a small channel, has a boat launch. Boats are limited to 10 horsepower or less, making this a pleasant waterway for paddlers. Little Beaver has one of the park's three auto-accessible campgrounds, with eight sites available on a first-come, first-served basis. Be aware that wetlands cover much of the land between Beaver Lake and Lake Superior, so insects can be a problem, especially in June and early July.

Two good hiking trails leave from the campground. The short and pleasant 0.7-mile **White Pine Trail** is a self-guided nature trail that circles through a 300-year-old pine forest. The 5-mile **Beaver Basin Loop Trail** makes a lap around Little Beaver and Big Beaver Lakes, then follows the Lake Superior shore past sea caves cut by the lake's pounding waves. Boardwalks skirt the wetlands before returning to the trailhead.

Twelvemile Beach

An icon near the Twelvemile Beach campground says it all: Indicating that this is a permitted beach area, it shows a swimmer not in the usual "crawl" position, but with water lapping at the ankles. In other words, the water here is extremely cold. Swim if you dare, but wading is more realistic.

This is what keeps Twelvemile Beach the pristine ribbon of sand that it is. The colder waters keep away all but the most enthusiastic lovers of nature, making it a place where you can stroll for hours with only the company of peregrine falcons, bald eagles, and deer wandering down for a drink. You may even see the occasional black bear snorting around in the sand.

The **Twelvemile Beach campground** is easy to reach, just a short drive off County Road H-58 through a pretty birch forest. Many of the 37 campsites string out along a bluff over the beach—come midweek, or early on Saturday, which is often a turnover day, for one of the choice spots. Some are larger than the average suburban lot and undoubtedly have a better view. Well-placed stairs deposit campers and picnickers at lake level. The campground also has a nice day-use area at its east end.

Five miles farther up the beach (or County Rd. H-58) lies the auto-accessible **Hurricane River campground,** where the Hurricane River spills into Lake Superior.

Au Sable Point

It's a 1.5-mile walk along the Lakeshore Trail from the Hurricane River campground to the **Au Sable Light Station** at Au Sable Point. Built in 1874, the 87-foot brick lighthouse and its keepers provided decades of reliable service—warning ships away from the rocky shoals that extend out for nearly a mile and create shallows of just 6 to 30 feet. Nonetheless, at least 10 steamers were wrecked here. As you walk the trail from the campground, look for parts of the shipwrecks just offshore, often poking out of the sand bottom and easily visible in the gin-clear water. The light was automated in 1958 and recently restored.

Grand Sable Dunes

Just east of Au Sable Point, the **Log Slide Overlook** marks the spot of a once busy logging operation. In the late 1800s, loggers used this high point—some 300 feet above Lake Superior—to send freshly cut logs down to the water's edge, where they were loaded on Great Lakes schooners. Today, you can stand on a platform and simply marvel at the view, with the lighthouse to your left, the great dunes to your right, and the brilliant blue of the big lake filling the horizon. If you're in the mood

1: Miners Castle **2:** Miners Falls **3:** view of Pictured Rocks from the water

for some exercise, the two-mile stretch of the **North Country National Scenic Trail** from the Log Slide to the Au Sable Light Station is one of the park's most scenic hikes.

The Grand Sable Banks and Dunes (*grand sable* is French for "big sands") stretch for nearly five miles from the overlook, glacial banks of gravel supporting the huge mounds of sand. They are magnificent when viewed from a distance—glowing gold and rising up abruptly from the cobalt waters of Lake Superior. In many areas, especially near the overlook, the dunes are free of grasses and plants, so you can frolic around on them without fear of damaging fragile plantlife or causing erosion. Though park officials discourage it for safety reasons, no one will stop you from sliding down the slope. Be aware, though, that the climb back up takes much longer than the way down.

Most people choose to explore the dunes from the eastern end. Near the Grand Sable Visitors Center, a trail winds across the top of the dunes, where fragile marram grass, beach pea, and sand cherry cling to the sand (be careful to stay on the trail here). Interpretive signs discuss the plants' tenuous hold on the environment. The trail to **Sable Falls** also leaves from the visitors center, a 0.5-mile walk largely composed of steps. As you work your way downhill, you'll be treated to several views of this exceptionally picturesque cascade, which drops in tiers through a narrow canyon and out to a rocky Lake Superior beach. Across County Road H-58, the sandy shores and often warm waters of **Grand Sable Lake** make this a wonderful spot for a swim or a picnic.

Grand Marais

Though not part of Pictured Rocks National Lakeshore, the hamlet of Grand Marais marks the park's eastern boundary and is an excellent jumping-off point for a visit to the national lakeshore. This sleepy village, which has a slightly New England feel, is worth a visit of its own for its simple windswept beauty. With an outstanding natural harbor—somewhat rare on Lake Superior's southern shore—Grand Marais was originally settled by fishers. Loggers soon followed, when sawmills were built here in the 1860s and'70s to handle the logging that went on just south of here.

Today, commercial fishing remains a viable economic activity, albeit an increasingly difficult one. Fortunately, tourism has filled the void. The downtown huddles around the harbor, a good spot for kayakers to play in the surf on a north or east wind. The town also offers arts and crafts shops and a handful of clean, inexpensive motels and restaurants.

TOP EXPERIENCE

SCENIC CRUISE

Since the cliffs of Pictured Rocks face Lake Superior, the only way to see them is from the water. **Pictured Rocks Cruises** (100 City Park Dr., Munising, 8am-closing mid-May-mid-Oct., $38-45 adults, $10 ages 6-12, $1 age 5 and under) has three exciting options: the classic (daytime cruise), the sunset cruise, and the Spray Falls cruise, which offers an up close view of the Spray Falls—a 70-foot drop of cascading water flowing into the lake. Be sure to have your camera ready.

KAYAKING

For paddlers, the optimal way to experience the grandeur of this shoreline is in a sea kayak. The importance of safety cannot be overemphasized, however. Only experienced paddlers should venture out on their own, and only in a closed cockpit (meaning no canoes) and after scrupulously monitoring weather conditions. Paddlers can get themselves into serious trouble along Pictured Rocks, caught in sudden summer squalls along the 15-mile rock wall with no refuge. That said, sea kayaking along Pictured Rocks ranks as one of the finest paddles on all the Great Lakes.

Kayak rentals and longer trips to Grand Island and Isle Royale are available, and **Great Northern Adventures** (906/225-8687, www.greatnorthernadventures.com)

also offers guided paddling trips, from one-day excursions along Pictured Rocks to multiday trips that combine kayaking with hiking and mountain biking on nearby Grand Island.

FOOD

Grand Marais has a couple of good finds in the food department, both right downtown on County Road H-77. The **Sportsman's Restaurant** (N14260 Lake Ave., 906/494-2800, 8am-10pm Mon.-Sat., 8am-9pm Sun., $8-25) is more distinctive than its name suggests, with good fish dishes, salads, and homemade soups as well as plenty of burgers and steaks.

★ **Lake Superior Brewing Company** (14283 Lake Ave., 906/494-2337, www.lakesuperiorbrewing.com, 9am-2am daily, $7-28) does the microbrewery tradition proud, with homemade brews like Sandstone Pale Ale and Granite Brown, as well as sandwiches, soups, and great homemade pizzas.

ACCOMMODATIONS

Open year-round, the smoke-free **Beach Park Motel** (E21795 Randolph St., Grand Marais, 906/494-2681 or 906/250-7985, http://beachparkmotel.com, $96 d) offers 14 large rooms, all of which have full baths, cable television, wireless Internet access, microwaves, small refrigerators, and waterfront views. Guests can also partake of the free continental breakfasts during peak season. In addition, pets are welcome for an extra $10 fee. Also, the motel is situated a block east of County Road H-77 on Randolph, which means that it's within easy walking distance to the beach and everything else in town.

East of County Road H-77 on Wilson Street, **The Voyageurs Motel** (906/494-2389, www.voyageursmotelmi.com, $80-130 d) sits atop a ridge overlooking Grand Marais Harbor. Nice rooms with minifridges and a sauna and whirlpool facility make this a good choice.

Camping

Pictured Rocks has three auto-accessible campgrounds ($13)—Beaver Lake, Twelvemile Beach, and Hurricane River—with water and pit toilets. Reservations are not possible. Backcountry camping is permitted only at designated hike-in sites, mostly along the Lakeshore Trail. A $15 permit is required, good for 1-6 campers, and for any number of nights. Most sites do not have water or toilets. Camping is also available in Munising, Grand Marais, and the Lake Superior State Forest, which borders Pictured Rocks to the south.

INFORMATION AND SERVICES

Contact the **Pictured Rocks National Lakeshore headquarters** (906/387-2607, www.nps.gov/piro, 8am-4:30pm Mon.-Fri.). Pictured Rocks also operates several visitors centers, including seasonal ones near Miners Castle and Grand Sable Dunes. Stop at one of these centers before beginning your trip—they have rangers on duty, excellent maps, informative displays, and historical information that will enhance your visit. Some also contain small bookstores.

GETTING THERE AND AROUND

County Road H-58 provides access to the park, winding roughly along the park's southern boundary for 49 miles and linking Munising and Grand Marais. A large stretch of the road—from Beaver Lake to the Grand Sable Dunes—is unpaved and can deteriorate after cold or rainy weather. Be careful to plan your time accordingly—it's an 80-minute trip from one end of the park to the other.

Lake Superior Shore

Traveling east from Pictured Rocks National Lakeshore, you leave behind the grand bluffs, enormous dunes, and well-marked attractions for a decidedly different landscape. Like many UP roads, the sometimes paved, often gravel County Road H-58 winds through the trees, giving few clues as to what lies beyond the pines and hardwoods. This is where the land flattens out—presenting a far less dramatic topography than nearby Pictured Rocks. This inescapable contrast prompts many a visitor to bypass the area, which is good news for those looking for solitude, since these woods conceal little-used hiking trails, scenic paddling rivers, undeveloped stretches of Lake Superior shoreline, and all kinds of secluded lakes and campsites known only to regulars. Continuing along the meandering county roads will bring you to Whitefish Bay and some of the UP's more popular sights, including towering waterfalls and a shipwreck museum.

SIGHTS

Lake Superior State Forest

County Road H-58 passes largely through state forest land, which encompasses much of the Lake Superior shoreline, extends six or seven miles inland in many places, and serves as a buffer zone protecting Pictured Rocks. Several other truck trails lead off gravel County Road H-58, sandy roads that are usually well marked at intersections and quite navigable. They can be confusing, however, so venture onto them with a good map or GPS device.

Muskallonge Lake State Park

Wedged on a 0.25-mile strip of land between Lake Superior and Muskallonge Lake, **Muskallonge Lake State Park** (30042 County Rd. 407, Newberry, 906/658-3338, annual Recreation Passport required: $12 Michigan residents, $34 nonresidents, $9 day pass available to nonresidents only) occupies the site of the old Deer Park township, once home to a sawmill, a hotel, and undoubtedly a saloon or two. Today a few fishing resorts represent the only commerce in this remote area, 18 miles east of Grand Marais.

Water is the draw here. The park's two miles of Lake Superior frontage is wonderfully secluded, with low, grass-covered dunes stretching off to the east and west and no visible development in either direction. It offers peace, quiet, and good rockhounding, especially for agates. Muskallonge Lake is stocked by the Department of Natural Resources and provides good fishing opportunities for northern pike, walleye, smallmouth bass, and perch. Because the lake is relatively shallow, it warms up enough for comfortable swimming—a rarity in much of the UP, which accounts for this park's somewhat surprising popularity in summer.

Crisp Point Lighthouse

One of the state's most obscure lighthouses sits on a tiny arc of land 14 miles west of Whitefish Point. The 58-foot **Crisp Point Lighthouse** occupies an isolated, unbroken stretch of Lake Superior shoreline. The light is about nine miles east of the mouth of the Two Hearted River. Reach it from the west on County Road 412, or from the east via the Farm Truck Road truck trail off M-123.

Though the light was automated decades ago, the handsome 1904 tower and adjacent home still stand. In recent years efforts have been made to restore the structure. The **Crisp Point Lighthouse Historical Society** (http://crisppointlighthouse.org/) operates a visitors center during the summer that offers tours of the lighthouse. Getting there, however, can be a challenge; you'll need a map and a 4WD vehicle. But do not attempt the last two miles if the ground is wet.

The Memory and the Mystery of the *Edmund Fitzgerald*

recovered bell from the *Edmund Fitzgerald*

In early November 1975, the 729-foot lake carrier *Edmund Fitzgerald* departed Superior, Wisconsin, loaded with 26,000 tons of taconite pellets, bound for the port of Detroit and the area steel mills. Launched in 1958, the *Fitzgerald* had a long and profitable record as flagship of the Columbia Line of the Oglebay Norton Corp., with whom Northwestern Mutual Life Insurance, the ship's owner, had contracted. This was to be one of the last trips across Lake Superior before the shipping lanes and Soo Locks shut down for the season.

The *Fitzgerald* had rounded the Keweenaw Peninsula when, at dusk on November 10, one of the worst storms in 30 years besieged Lake Superior. Winds howled at 90 miles an hour, whipping the inland sea into 30-foot swells. The *Fitzgerald* was prepared for bad weather from the northeast, as Superior was notorious for its November gales. Like the captain of the 767-foot *Arthur M. Anderson* traveling nearby, the captain of the *Fitzgerald* had chosen to follow a more protected route across the lake, some 20-40 miles farther north than usual.

Just 10 miles apart, the two captains had been in intermittent visual and radio contact, discussing the perilous weather, which had dangerously shifted from northeast to northwest. At 7:10pm the *Fitzgerald* captain radioed, "We are holding our own." Then abruptly, at 7:15, radio contact was lost. Turning to his radar, the captain of the *Anderson* was shocked to see the *Fitzgerald* had completely vanished from the screen. The 729-foot lake carrier and all 29 hands disappeared without transmitting a distress call.

When the storm cleared, the *Edmund Fitzgerald* was found in 530 feet of water, just 17 miles from the shelter of Whitefish Bay. The wreck lay at the bottom severed in two pieces some 170 feet apart. Debris was scattered over three acres, evidence of the force with which the massive hull hit bottom. Many believe the *Fitzgerald* went bow first, which would have meant nearly 200 feet of the ship was towering over the water's surface at impact.

But after more than 40 years, an exhaustive Coast Guard investigation, and several dives to the site, crucial questions about the incident will most likely never be answered. Of the many theories put forth, the Coast Guard postulates that the ship took on water through leaking hatches, then developed a list, and was swamped by the storm's huge waves. Others believe that, outside the normal shipping lane, the vessel scraped bottom on uncharted shoals. Still others believe the warm taconite pellets weakened the structure of the ship, causing it to snap in two when caught between two particularly enormous waves. It's also possible that elements from each of these scenarios contributed to the ship's demise.

Each November the victims of the disaster, along with those of other maritime tragedies, are remembered at Mariners Church in Detroit during the Great Lakes Memorial Service. The church is referenced by folk singer Gordon Lightfoot in his iconic song "The Wreck of the Edmund Fitzgerald" which he refers to as "the Maritime Sailors Cathedral."

The ship was named after the chairman of the Northwestern Mutual Insurance Company, which commissioned it as an investment in 1957. At its 1958 christening, Fitzgerald's wife experienced difficulty breaking the champagne bottle, ultimately having to make three attempts—considered a harbinger of bad luck in nautical lore.

For further details about this tragedy, or to view the bronze bell recovered from the *Fitzgerald* shipwreck, visit the seasonal **Great Lakes Shipwreck Museum** (18335 N. Whitefish Point Rd., Paradise, 888/492-3747, www.shipwreckmuseum.com, 10am-6pm daily May 1-Oct. 31, $13 adults, $9 ages 5-17, under age 5 free).

Whitefish Point

"The searchers all say they'd have made Whitefish Bay if they'd put 15 more miles behind her." Singer-songwriter Gordon Lightfoot immortalized the ill-fated ore carrier *Edmund Fitzgerald* for the world, but locals here need no reminders. Less than 20 miles from Whitefish Point and the safety of Whitefish Bay, the huge laker and all 29 hands on board succumbed to a fierce November squall in 1975.

On Lake Superior—the largest and fiercest of the Great Lakes—northwest storms can build over 200 miles of cold open water. They unleash their full fury on the 80-mile stretch of water from Grand Marais to Whitefish Point (hence the nickname, the "Graveyard of the Great Lakes"). Whitefish Point has long served as a beacon for mariners, a narrow finger of land reaching toward Ontario and forming the protected waters of Whitefish Bay, one of the few safe havens on the big lake.

★ Great Lakes Shipwreck Museum

To commemorate the many ships that failed to round that point of safety, Whitefish Point is now the home of the **Great Lakes Shipwreck Museum** (18335 N. Whitefish Point Rd., Paradise, 888/492-3747, www.shipwreckmuseum.com, 10am-6pm daily May-Oct., $13 adults, $9 ages 5-17, under age 5 free). With dim lighting and appropriately haunting music, this compact museum traces the history of Great Lakes commerce and the disasters that sometimes accompanied it. Several shipwrecks are chronicled here, each with a scale model, photos or drawings, artifacts from the wreck, and a description of how and why it went down. Most compelling is the *Edmund Fitzgerald* display, complete with a life preserver and the ship's huge bell, recovered in a 1994 expedition led by museum founder Tom Farnquist, an accomplished diver and underwater photographer.

Housed in the former Coast Guard station, the museum also includes the restored lightkeeper's home, a theater showing an excellent short film about the *Fitzgerald* dive, and an interesting gift shop with nautical charts, prints, books, and more. To reach it, take M-123 to Paradise and follow Whitefish Point Road 11 miles north. The museum alone makes this out-of-the-way point a worthy detour.

Whitefish Point Light Station

Whitefish Point first beamed a warning light in 1849 and has done so ever since, making it the oldest operating light station on Lake Superior. Marking the bay's entry, the Whitefish Point Light Station is a utilitarian 80-foot steel structure supported by a framework of steel girders. Though it looks relatively modern, the light actually dates to 1902. The redundant design was considered an extraordinary engineering experiment at the time, but one deemed necessary to withstand the gales that frequently batter this exposed landscape. It was automated in 1970 and continues to serve the ships of Lake Superior.

Oswald's Bear Ranch

For a fun and family-friendly experience, head over to **Oswald's Bear Ranch** (13814 County Rd. 407 [H-37], www.oswaldbearranch.com, 9:30am-5pm daily Fri. before Memorial Day-Labor Day, 9:30am-4pm daily Sept., $20/vehicle or $10 for solo visitor) just north of Newberry. Oswald's is a place where you can see 40 black bears up close and personal in secure enclosures surrounded by dense woods. A special experience is the opportunity to feed jelly to a cub while having your picture taken. This is a place to make treasured memories.

★ Tahquamenon Falls

West of Newberry, the headwaters of the Tahquamenon River bubble up from underground and begin a gentle roll through stands of pine and vast wetlands. Rambling and twisting northeast through Luce County, the river grows wide and majestic by the time it enters its namesake state park. Then, with

1: a bear at Oswald's Bear Ranch **2:** lighthouse at Whitefish Bay **3:** Tahquamenon Falls

1
2
3

the roar of a freight train and the power of a fire hose, it suddenly plummets over a 50-foot drop, creating a golden fountain of water 200 feet wide.

As much as 50,000 gallons of water per second gush over the Upper Tahquamenon, making it the second-largest falls by volume east of the Mississippi, second only to Niagara. Adding to Tahquamenon's majesty are its distinctive colors— bright white foam from the water's high salt content and bronze headwaters from the tannic acid of decaying cedars and hemlocks that line its banks. The water's distinctive hue has earned Tahquamenon the nickname "the root beer falls."

Accessing Tahquamenon Falls is easy, since both the Upper Falls and Lower Falls lie within **Tahquamenon Falls State Park** (41382 W. M-123, Paradise, 906/492-3415, annual Recreation Passport required: $12 Michigan residents, $34 nonresidents, $9 day pass available to nonresidents only), which has provided short well-marked paths to prime viewing sites. At the Upper Falls, follow the trail to the right and down the 94 steps to an observation deck, which brings you so close you can feel the falls' thundering power and the cool mist on your face. The view provides a dual glimpse of the placid waters above, contrasted with the furious frothing below. Four miles downstream, accessible via the **Tahquamenon River Trail,** the Lower Falls plunge over a series of cascades. The best vantage point is from a small island mid-river; a state park concessionaire rents out canoes and rowboats to make the short crossing.

With the dramatic centerpiece of Tahquamenon Falls, it's easy to overlook the rest of this nearly 50,000-acre state park, Michigan's second-largest. In sharp contrast to the often frenzied crowds at the falls (more than half a million people per year, the greatest of any UP state park), the vast majority of the park remains peaceful, etched with 25 miles of little-used hiking trails. From the Upper Falls, the Giant Pines Loop passes through a stand of white pines before crossing M-123. Once on the north side of the highway, link up with the Clark Lake Loop, a 5.6-mile hike that traces the southern shoreline of the shallow lake.

The final 16 miles of the Tahquamenon River wind through the park, spilling into Lake Superior's Whitefish Bay at its eastern terminus. Fishing for muskie and walleye is especially good in the pools below the Lower Falls. Another option is to join the fleet of runabouts and anglers in waders near the mouth of the river, where trout often school.

It's possible to paddle nearly all 94 miles of the Tahquamenon. A popular put-in is off County Road 415 north of McMillan, but you'll start off through several bug-infested miles of wetlands. A better choice is about 10 miles downstream, off County Road 405 at Dollarville, where you can also avoid portaging around the Dollarville Dam. Beyond Newberry, you'll be treated to a pristine paddle, since no roads come anywhere near the river. Watch the banks for bears, deer, and other wildlife. Naturally, you'll have to portage around the falls, but then you can follow the river to its mouth without any other interruptions.

TAHQUAMENON FALLS TOURS

For another look at the river and falls, you may want to plan a day for the **Tahquamenon Train and Riverboat Trip** (Soo Junction, 906/876-2311, www.trainandboattours.com, mid-June-early-Oct., $47 adults, $43 over age 61, $25 ages 3-15, children under age 3 free). Departing from Soo Junction near Newberry (watch for a sign on M-28), a narrow-gauge train chugs its way five miles along an old logging route, through roadless spruce and maple forest, tamarack lowlands, and peat bogs. In about half an hour, the train sighs to a stop deep in the woods at the Tahquamenon's banks. Here you'll transfer to a large tour boat and cruise downstream nearly two hours toward the falls. Just as the river begins to roil and boil, the boat docks on the south shore, and guests walk the last half mile to the falls. The tour returns to Soo Junction via the same route.

Curley Lewis Memorial Highway

This twisting, scenic road, also called Lakeshore Drive, follows the curve of Lake Superior's Whitefish Bay from M-123 east 20 miles to Sault Ste. Marie. It's almost an attraction in itself, passing through the Hiawatha National Forest, offering plenty of water views and a handful of worthwhile stops.

Pendills Creek National Fish Hatchery

Four miles west of tiny Dollar Settlement, the federally run **Pendills Creek Fish Hatchery** (21990 W. Trout Ln., Brimley, 906/437-5231, www.fws.gov/midwest, 7am-3pm Mon.-Fri., free) raises thousands of trout to replenish stock in Lakes Superior, Michigan, and Huron. Visitors can wander around the tanks to peer down at the hundreds of wriggling trout fry (the raceways are covered to protect against birds and other predators) and the breeder trout that weigh in at 15 pounds or more.

Point Iroquois Light Station and Museum

Continuing east, don't miss a chance to climb the tower at the **Point Iroquois Light Station** (906/437-5272, 9am-5pm Tues.-Sat., noon-5pm Sun. mid-May-mid-Oct., free), where Whitefish Bay narrows into the St. Mary's River. Since 1855, a beacon here has helped guide ships through this extremely difficult passage, where reefs lurk near the Canadian shore and the rock walls of Point Iroquois threaten the U.S. side. In 1870, the original wooden light tower was replaced with the present one, a classic white-painted brick structure. A keeper's home was added in 1902.

With fewer and fewer lighthouses open to the public, it's fun to climb the iron spiral staircase for a freighter captain's view of the river, the bay, and frequent shipping traffic. Stop in the adjacent lightkeeper's home, where the local historical society has restored some of the rooms to illustrate the life of a lightkeeper; other rooms feature displays and old photos. The lighthouse and adjacent beach are now part of the Hiawatha National Forest, which should help ensure continued protection.

Mission Hill Overlook

This is the kind of road where every view is better than the last. As the highway curves south, watch for the turnoff to the west marking this terrific overlook. Drive up the sand and gravel road for grand sweeping views of the river and bay, Ontario's Laurentian Mountains, the cityscape of Sault Ste. Marie, freighters that look like toy ships, the Point Iroquois Light, and, just below, Spectacle Lake.

RECREATION

Bird-Watching

A needed resting spot for birds migrating across Lake Superior, **Whitefish Point** is a bird-watcher's dream. Beginning with the hawk migration from April to late fall, the point attracts an amazing variety of birds. Eagles, loons, songbirds, waterfowl, owls, and some unusual Arctic species like arctic loons and arctic terns all pass through, some 300 in all. Even if you're not a birding enthusiast, plan to spend some time at this lovely point, where you can wander the sand beaches, watch the birds, and keep an eye out for the ones that pass quite close to shore as they round the point. Bring along binoculars and a jacket.

Canoeing

The Two Hearted River is fine for canoeing—clean and clear and usually quite mellow—except in spring when, depending on snowmelt, the flow can intensify considerably. A state-designated wilderness river, the Two Hearted winds through pine and hardwood forest. The only signs of civilization you're likely to see are a handful of cottages at the river's mouth. It offers plenty of low banks and sandbars, so picnic spots are easy to find. The Two Hearted is also a widely regarded blue-ribbon trout stream, so be prepared for plenty of anglers when the season opens in April.

Put in at the High Bridge State Forest Campground on County Road 407 (Deer Park Rd.) for a 23-mile trip to the mouth. You'll find two state forest campgrounds and other camping sites along the route. Alternatively, you can hook up with **Two Hearted Canoe Trips** (County Rd. 423, Newberry, 906/658-3357), an outfitter based at the Rainbow Lodge at the river's mouth. It operates trips ranging from a couple of hours to three days. A popular half-day trip departs from the Reed and Green Bridge (east of Muskallonge Lake State Park on County Rd. 410) and takes out at Lake Superior.

Diving

For experienced divers, the **Whitefish Point Underwater Preserve** (www.michiganpreserves.org) offers a fantastic array of wrecks—18 steamers and schooners littered all around the point. (The *Edmund Fitzgerald* is not among them.) Good visibility is a hallmark of this 376-acre preserve. Most wrecks lie in deep water, though, 40 to 270 feet, and in an area with few protected harbors. Needless to say, only very experienced divers and boaters should consider this spot. For information on area dive services, contact the **Experience Michigan's Paradise** (906/492-3927, www.michiganparadise.com).

ACCOMMODATIONS

While there are plenty of chain hotels, the area also has some smaller, more interesting lodgings. **Curley's Paradise Motel** (M-123, Whitefish Point, 906/492-3445, www.superiorsights.com/curleys, $75-179 d) has nice standard rooms as well as cottages and a single-family home for rent. To the south, you'll find the **Evening Star Motel** (7475 M-123, Newberry, 906/293-8342, www.theeveningstarmotel.com, $63-108 d), which boasts 40 clean rooms, some with kitchenettes. The property also has an indoor heated pool. Among chain lodgings, the **Magnuson Grand Hotel** (8122 N. M-123, Paradise, 906/492-3770, www.magnusongrandlakefront.com, $206-230 d) in Paradise offers perhaps the best accommodations in the area. Many rooms offer impressive views of Whitefish Bay, and rates include a premium breakfast each morning.

Camping

There are many campgrounds along the Lake Superior shoreline, including the **Mouth of the Two Hearted River State Forest Campground** (906/492-3415, www.michigandnr.com, $15), where you'll find rustic sites in the state forest. You can also pitch your tent at the **High Bridge State Forest Campground** (906/658-3338, www.michigandnr.com, $15), only 10 miles from Pine Stump and 24 miles from Newberry.

INFORMATION AND SERVICES

For more information about the Lake Superior shore, consult the **Upper Peninsula Travel & Recreation Association** (UPTRA, P.O. Box 400, Iron Mountain, MI 49801, 906/774-5480 or 800/562-7134, www.uptravel.com). If you require services like banks, groceries, and medical care, consider heading to more sizable towns like St. Ignace or Sault Ste. Marie.

GETTING THERE AND AROUND

Although you can certainly hike, bike, and go horseback riding in the Upper Peninsula, the best way to traverse this part of the eastern UP is by car. From Munising, head east on County Road H-58, which leads to several smaller roads. To reach the eastern part of this shoreline, take M-123 north from Newberry to Paradise, a 37-mile trip that takes 41 minutes.

Sault Ste. Marie and Vicinity

The second-largest city in the Upper Peninsula, historic Sault Ste. Marie (population 14,200) serves as a striking contrast to the surrounding hinterlands of northern Michigan. It's well worth a visit, especially to view the boat traffic through the famous Soo Locks that link Lakes Superior and Huron. At the foot of Whitefish Bay, mighty Lake Superior narrows to its terminus at the St. Mary's River, its sole connection to the lower Great Lakes. With Lake Superior's surface at an elevation 21 feet higher than that of Lake Huron, the St. Mary's provides the natural transition—a series of falls and rapids near Sault Ste. Marie. *Sault,* pronounced "soo," and often spelled that way as a nickname, means "falling water," a name given by early French explorers.

The Sault Ste. Marie area was first settled by the Ojibwa people in the 1500s, who called it *Baawitigong.* After discovering a rich supply of whitefish in the turbulent waters, they established a permanent settlement along the shore. The Ojibwa lived here for more than 300 years, but the combination of warring Iroquois—forced west by European immigrants—and the rapidly expanding European settlement, founded in 1668, eventually drove the Ojibwa from the region.

While in town, you might consider crossing the river into Canada, where you'll find Sault Ste. Marie's considerably larger namesake city.

SIGHTS

★ Soo Locks

Nearly every visitor to the Soo makes a pilgrimage to the locks, right in the heart of town at the end of Ashmun Street (Business I-75). The city has wisely dressed up this area with lovely **Brady Park.** Blue freighter signs mark the **Locks Park Walkway,** which wanders along Water Street and is dotted with interpretive plaques that share the city's history.

For visitors and pedestrians, the centerpiece of town is **Soo Locks Park,** a traditional, formal commons maintained by the U.S. Army Corps of Engineers. The Corps manages the locks as well as a **visitors center** (Portage Ave., 906/932-1472, 9am-9pm daily mid-May-mid-Oct., free), next to a raised **viewing platform** that lets you see this engineering marvel in action. A stop at the visitors center will provide a good introduction. Here, a moving model shows how the locks raise and lower ships by opening and closing the gates of a lock chamber and allowing water to rush in or out. No pumps are required; the power of gravity allows the water to seek the correct level. Other displays explain the construction of the locks. Knowledgeable staff with a PA system, along with video cameras upriver, announce approaching vessels. In the summer months, ships generally transit through the locks at a rate of one per hour. The visitors center will have the day's shipping schedule, but be aware that times can change depending on weather conditions and other factors.

It's easy to spend an hour or two watching the ships as they pass through the locks with seemingly just inches to spare. Summer evenings are especially pleasant, when you're likely to have the platform to yourself to watch the illuminated ships. Occasionally a "saltie," an oceangoing vessel, will transit through the locks. Overall, the three most plentiful Great Lakes shipments are iron ore (for steelmaking), limestone (a purifying agent for steelmaking, also used in construction and papermaking), and coal (for power plants).

The locks and viewing platform are open throughout the Great Lakes shipping season, which runs March 25 to January 15. Those dates, however, may be impacted by the buildup of ice on Lake Superior. During the winter months, the locks shut down for maintenance.

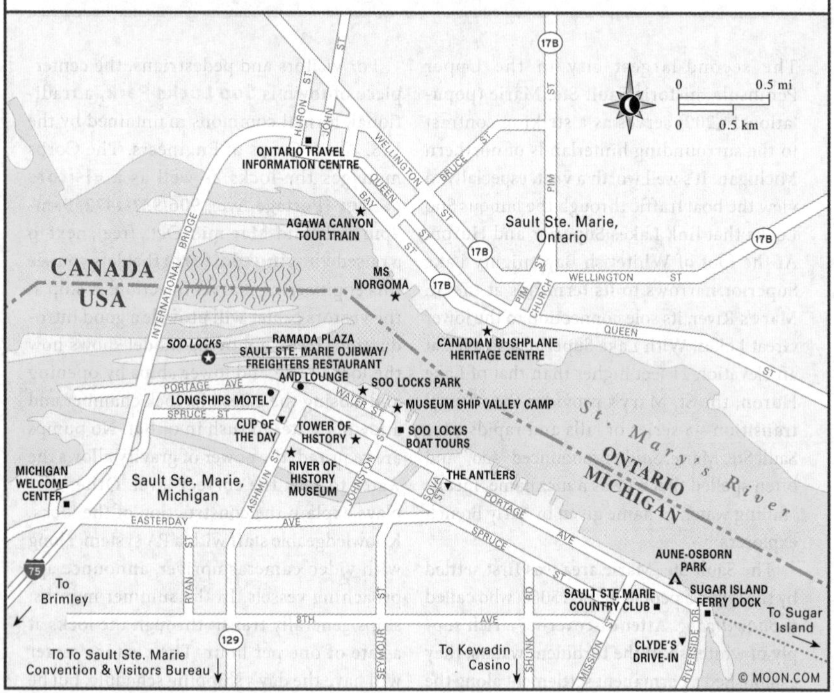

SOO LOCKS BOAT TOURS

After viewing the locks, you can "lock through" yourself on one of these extremely popular tours. The two-hour trip takes you through both the American and Canadian locks and travels along both cities' waterfronts. At busy times, you'll be in the midst of freighter traffic, dwarfed by their enormous steel hulls. The large passenger boats have both heated and open deck areas. The **Soo Locks Boat Tours** (1157 E. Portage Ave. or 515 E. Portage Ave., 906/632-6301, www.soolocks.com, times vary, from 10am daily early May-mid-Oct., $31 adults, $12 ages 5-16) frequency of sailings varies, with the most in midsummer.

The company offers several other cruise options, including themed dinner, luncheon, fireworks, and lighthouses cruises. Visit the website for full details.

Other Downtown Attractions

After watching the big Great Lakes boats, the **Museum Ship *Valley Camp*** (501 E. Water St., 906/632-3658, www.saulthistoricsites.com, hours vary, $14.50 adults, $7.25 ages 5-17) gives you a chance to see what it was like to live and work aboard a giant steamer. This 550-foot steamship logged more than a million miles on the Great Lakes, hauling ore, coal, and stone from 1907 to the mid-1970s. It is now permanently docked five blocks east of the Soo Locks. Visitors can tour the pilothouse, engine room, main deck, crew quarters, coal bunker, and more. Throughout, the ship has a number of aquariums and maritime displays. Most popular: a display on the sinking of the *Edmund Fitzgerald*, including two tattered lifeboats found empty and drifting on the lake. Make sure to stop at the museum shop, housed in a separate building next to the parking lot, which has an excellent selection of maritime books and videos.

Like many observation towers, the **Tower of History** (326 E. Portage Ave., 906/632-3658, www.saulthistoricsites.com, 10am-5pm Mon.-Sat., noon-5pm Sun. mid-May-June and Sept.-Oct., 9:30am-5:30pm Mon.-Sat., 10am-5pm Sun. July-Aug., $7.50 adults, $3.75 ages 5-17, under age 5 free), which lies a few blocks east of the Soo Locks, doesn't quite blend with the landscape. Though it's essentially a stark 21-story concrete monolith, the tower presents a wonderful 360-degree view of the twin Soos, St. Mary's River, Lake Superior, and the forests rolling off in the distance. During clear weather, the view can encompass up to 1,200 square miles. Enjoy the vistas from an open-air deck; just remember to bring a jacket. The tower also includes a few small exhibit areas and a theater showing documentary videos. Happily, the tower is equipped with an elevator.

The **River of History Museum** (531 Ashmun St., 906/632-1999 or 906/632-3658, 11am-5pm Mon.-Sat. mid-May-early-Oct., $7 adults, $3.50 ages 5-17) uses the St. Mary's River as the framework for telling the story of the region's history. Life-size dioramas depict Native Americans spearfishing in the rapids and a French fur trapper's cabin, among others. The museum incorporates lots of sound in its displays: dripping ice from melting glaciers, roaring rapids, and Ojibwa elders passing down legends.

I-500 SNOWMOBILE RACE

Founded in 1969, the **International 500 Snowmobile Race** (906/635-1500, www.i-500.com) has become one of the world's largest and longest snowmobile races. Usually held in early February (with associated festivities beginning in late January) this annual event lures thousands of snowmobilers to Sault Ste. Marie, where they speed around a one-mile oval course, competing against one another for a purse of some $40,000. Visitors relish this frenzied and unusual spectacle.

FOOD

Start your day at **Cup of the Day** (406 Ashmun St., 906/635-7272, www.cupoftheday.com, 7:15am-5pm Mon. and Fri., 7:15am-6pm Tues.-Thurs., 8:15am-3pm Sat., $4-8) for good coffee drinks, a juice bar, plus deli sandwiches and salads at lunchtime. In the Ramada Plaza Ojibway hotel, ★ **Freighters Restaurant** (240 W. Portage Ave., 906/632-4100, https://

the Soo Locks allow ships to transit between Lakes Superior and Huron

ojibwayhotel.com/dining, 7am-9pm daily, $8-42) offers a wall of glass overlooking the locks and a very nice menu featuring steaks and seafood, especially local fish. Freighters is also a great spot for breakfast and lunch.

ACCOMMODATIONS

Now part of the Ramada chain, the rather plush ★ **Ramada Plaza Sault Ste. Marie Ojibway** (240 W. Portage Ave., 906/632-4100, https://ojibwayhotel.com, $143-259 d) has the nicest accommodations in town—and the best location, overlooking the St. Mary's River and the locks. Ask for an upper-level north-facing room. The elegant 1928 building has been well restored, with large rooms, an indoor pool, a whirlpool, and the Freighters restaurant. Ask about packages for a better deal.

For the same good location for less money, try the **Longships Motel** (427 W. Portage Ave., 888/690-2422 or 906/632-2422, www.longshipsmotel.com, $85-107 d), a clean and comfortable independent motel with a choice location across from Soo Locks Park. There are several chain hotels near I-75, but none are near the locks or other downtown walking attractions.

Camping

Right in Sault Ste. Marie, there's a modern, 65-site municipal campground at **Aune-Osborn Park** (1225 Riverside Ave., 906/632-3268, mid-May-mid-Oct., $25-33) on the St. Mary's River near the Sugar Island ferry dock. Just east of Brimley, **Brimley State Park** (9200 W. 6 Mile Rd., 906/248-3422, annual Recreation Passport required: $12 Michigan residents, $34 nonresidents, $9 day pass available to nonresidents only) offers about a mile of sandy Lake Superior beach and a large modern campground ($25-27) but little else. It is, however, a good choice for anyone looking for an easy place to set up camp to enjoy the Soo and other nearby attractions. This is a popular park, so consider making reservations (800/447-2757) if you're aiming for a summer weekend.

INFORMATION AND SERVICES

For more information, contact the **Sault Ste. Marie Convention & Visitors Bureau** (225 E. Portage St., 906/632-3366, www.saultstemarie.com). For local news, consult the ***Sault Ste. Marie Evening News*** (www.sooeveningnews.com).

The Sault Ste. Marie area offers its share of services, including banks, groceries, and more.

GETTING THERE AND AROUND

While it's possible to fly into **Sault Ste. Marie Airport** (YAM, 475 Airport Rd., Sault Ste. Marie, Canada, 705/779-3031, www.saultairport.com) in Ontario, Canada, and cross the **International Bridge** (www.saultbridge.com, $4/C$5.30 passenger vehicles and motorcycles, $6-8/C$7.95-10.60 vehicles with trailers, $10/C$8.60 RVs) to Sault Ste. Marie, Michigan, many travelers may prefer to fly into the Upper Peninsula's **Chippewa County International Airport** (CIU, 5019 W. Airport Dr., Kincheloe, 906/495-5631, www.airciu.com), a 21-mile drive to Sault Ste. Marie that takes about 25 minutes.

Greyhound (800/231-2222, www.greyhound.com) and **Indian Trails** (800/292-3831, www.indiantrails.com) buses both stop regularly at the **Eastern Upper Peninsula Transportation Authority** (EUPTA, 4001 I-75 Business Spur, 906/632-2898, www.eupta.net, 7am-4pm Mon.-Fri.).

From the Lower Peninsula, head north on I-75, cross the Mackinac Bridge, and continue 51 miles north of St. Ignace. The drive from Chicago to Sault Ste. Marie is 463 miles and seven hours on I-90, I-94, I-196, U.S. 131, M-32, and I-75; you'll encounter toll booths on I-90 and I-94 through Indiana, as well as to cross the Mackinac Bridge.

Once you reach Sault Ste. Marie you'll be able to easily walk, bike, and drive around the city. The **Soo Line Taxi** company (906/440-5161) offers transport from the Kewadin

Casino to area hotels and other points in the greater Sault Ste. Marie area.

SAULT STE. MARIE, ONTARIO

Just across the International Bridge is the Soo's sister city in Canada, also named Sault Ste. Marie (population 73,300). The larger of the two, Sault Ste. Marie, Ontario, is home to a huge steel plant and a paper company. In addition to heavy industry, the city also has a great deal to offer visitors. Downtown, a lovely **boardwalk** rambles along the river for about a mile, beginning at the bridge and extending east past fishing platforms, shops, and the MS *Norgoma,* the last passenger ferry built for the Great Lakes, now a museum. On Wednesday and Saturday there's a farmers market near the tented pavilion.

One of the most popular attractions is the **Agawa Canyon Tour Train** (129 Bay St., 800/242-9287, www.agawatrain.com, times vary, C$100.88 adults, C$91.15 seniors, C$54.87 ages 2-18, under age 2 free—during peak fall color season, mid Sept.-mid Oct, fares are C$121.24 for all ages), a seven-hour round-trip through the scenic wooded gorge of the Agawa Canyon. The daylong tour includes a two-hour stopover in the canyon, where you can hike to lookouts, visit waterfalls, wander along the river, or just hang out in the grassy picnic area. The train trip is even more popular in the fall foliage season, and in winter, when it is known as the Snow Train. During these months, the two-hour layover is eliminated.

Reach Ontario via the three-mile-long **International Bridge** (www.saultbridge.com, $4/C$5.30 passenger vehicles and motorcycles, $6-8/C$7.95-10.60 vehicles with trailers, $10/C$8.60 RVs). Keep in mind that U.S. citizens must confirm both proof of identity and proof of citizenship (a passport, or a driver's license with a birth certificate) to enter Canada. Returning to the United States requires a valid passport or enhanced driver's license.

Information

For more information about Sault Ste. Marie, Ontario, contact **Tourism Sault Ste. Marie** (800/461-6020, www.saulttourism.com).

Western Upper Peninsula

Town names throughout the western half of the Upper Peninsula reveal the region's multilayered history. Mohawk and Menominee refer to the Native American nations that once dwelled in these remote lands. Other names are in the language of the Chippewa people, such as Escanaba ("Flat Rock"), Negaunee ("Pioneer"), and Ishpeming ("High Ground"). Still others highlight mining, as in Copper Harbor, Ironwood, Iron Mountain, and Mineral Hills, vestiges of the ore operations thriving here from the mid-19th to the early 20th centuries. Other place-names reflect the arrival of the Europeans, including Marquette, Houghton, and Schoolcraft.

The economic heyday of the western UP was the latter half of the 19th century. The Copper Rush of 1840 eventually yielded an

Highlights

Look for ★ to find recommended sights, activities, dining, and lodging.

★ **Boat Tours of Isle Royale:** Cruise around this isolated archipelago, taking in sights like the Rock Harbor Lighthouse, the Edisen Fishery, Pine Mountain, and Lookout Louise (page 344).

★ **Fort Wilkins Historic State Park:** Explore a restored 1844 military outpost, view one of the oldest lighthouses on Lake Superior, and watch costumed interpreters demonstrate Keweenaw Peninsula history (page 350).

★ **Quincy Mine:** Venture into this former copper mine, once one of the world's richest (page 353).

★ **Porcupine Mountains Wilderness State Park:** Explore towering trees, secluded lakes, wild rivers, and the amazing view from the Lake of the Clouds Overlook (page 358).

★ **Downhill Skiing in the Ironwood Area:** Three solid ski resorts offer plenty of snow-covered slopes (page 364).

★ **Iron County Historical Museum:** See wildlife art, early mining equipment, a former mining site, and several old log cabins (page 366).

astonishing 10 times the mineral wealth of California's better-known gold rush. The discovery of iron four years later produced even more prosperity. Thousands of eager immigrants flocked to the area, resulting in the construction of numerous cities and the creation of millionaires virtually overnight. Timber also emerged as a major industry. Following a decline in the 20th century, only remnants of this mineral-rich past remain—enormous mansions, abandoned mines, ghost towns, and occasional cave-ins beneath homes and streets.

In many respects, the wilderness has reclaimed the land, much of which has been preserved in regional, state, and national parks and forests, including the Porcupine Mountains Wilderness State Park and Ottawa National Forest. Here there are miles of hiking, mountain biking, and cross-country skiing trails. The chance of seeing moose, timber wolves, and black bears is high, the peak summer sun might not set until 11pm, and cell phone coverage is spotty.

While tourism has never reached the level of the Lower Peninsula, it seems that every year more people are discovering this region's unspoiled beauty and cultural attractions, including several in and around Marquette, the UP's largest city. For those seeking solitude, history, and challenging winters, this far corner of the Great Lakes State is the ideal destination.

PLANNING YOUR TIME

The western Upper Peninsula is even more sparsely populated than the eastern half, especially when considering places like isolated Isle Royale, the Keweenaw Peninsula, and the stretch between Escanaba and Menominee. The easiest way to traverse this vast region is by car, but to intimately experience the virgin wilderness, canoes, bikes, boats, horses, or your own feet will sometimes be necessary.

Major highways that cross this region from Wisconsin, are U.S. 2 and U.S. 51 to Ironwood, U.S. 45 to Watersmeet, U.S. 141 to Iron Mountain, and U.S. 41 to Menominee. From the Mackinac Bridge, drive west on U.S. 2 to Escanaba or north on I-75 and M-28 to Marquette. U.S. 41 and M-26 can guide you onto and up the Keweenaw Peninsula, from which ferries and small planes can transport you to Isle Royale.

Although much of the western UP remains unspoiled wilderness, with few sizable towns, it is possible to reach this part of Michigan by Greyhound, which serves towns that include Hancock, Ironwood, Iron River, Iron Mountain, Escanaba, and Marquette. The region's primary airport is Sawyer International Airport, south of Marquette, served by Delta and American Eagle. Smaller airports also operate at Houghton, Ironwood, and Escanaba.

Still, the relative difficulty of reaching the western UP translates to fewer visitors—which is ideal for those do come. With its vast array of diversions, your personal interests will determine when you decide to visit and how long you plan to stay. If you intend to take in the highlights of Isle Royale, the Keweenaw Peninsula, and Marquette, three days should be sufficient. A week or more is necessary for those who appreciate the great outdoors; visitors can spend at least three days exploring Isle Royale alone.

During your visit to the western UP, you should keep time zones in mind. While most of the Upper Peninsula, like all of the Lower Peninsula, is in the eastern time zone, the four counties bordering Wisconsin—Gogebic, Iron, Dickinson, and Menominee—lie one hour earlier, in the central time zone.

For more information about this area, consult the **Western UP Convention & Visitor Bureau** (P.O. Box 706, Ironwood, MI 49938, 906/932-4850 or 800/522-5657, www.explorewesternup.com).

Previous: Lake of the Clouds; Lift Bridge connecting Houghton and Hancock; downtown Calumet.

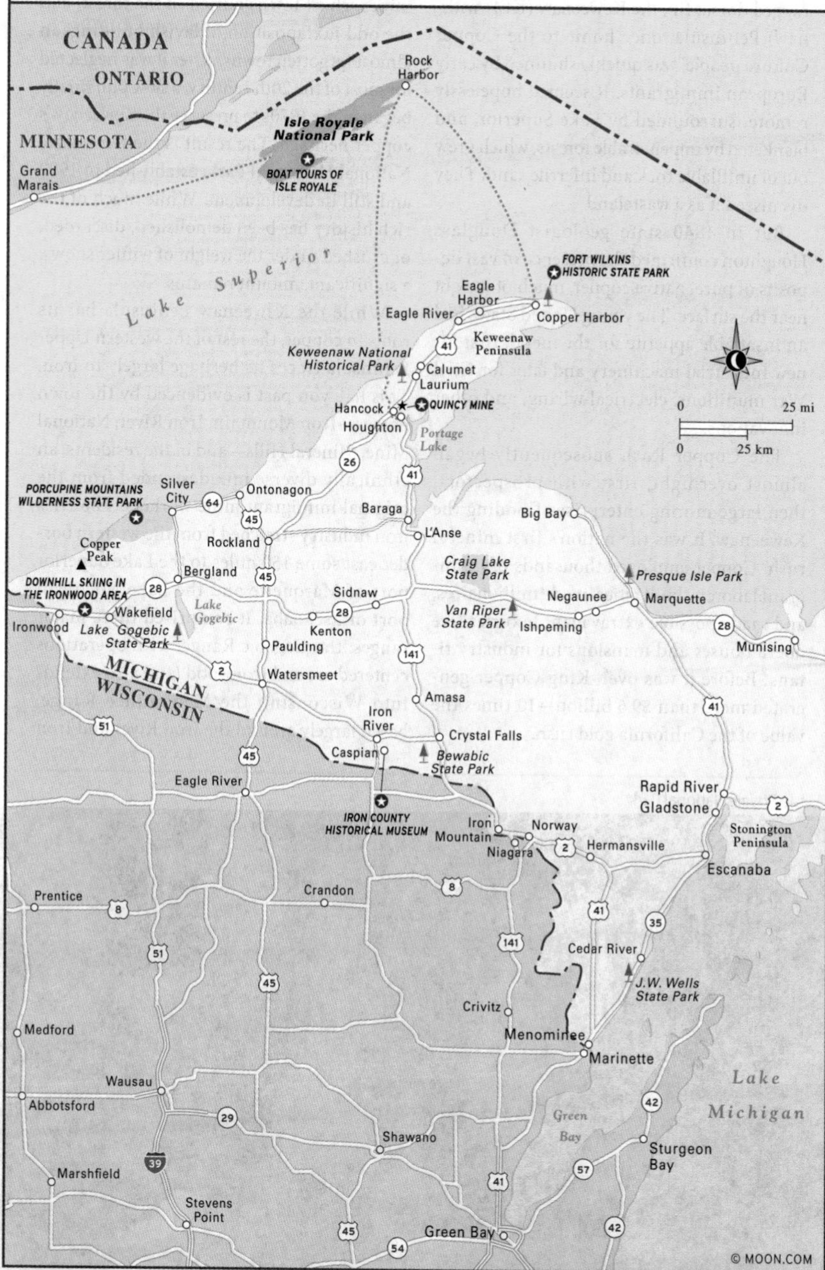
Western Upper Peninsula
CANADA
ONTARIO
MINNESOTA
Rock Harbor
Isle Royale National Park
BOAT TOURS OF ISLE ROYALE
Grand Marais
Lake Superior
FORT WILKINS HISTORIC STATE PARK
Eagle Harbor
Copper Harbor
Eagle River
Keweenaw Peninsula
Keweenaw National Historical Park
Calumet
Laurium
Hancock
QUINCY MINE
Houghton
Portage Lake
0
25 mi
0
25 km
PORCUPINE MOUNTAINS WILDERNESS STATE PARK
Silver City
Ontonagon
Baraga
Big Bay
L'Anse
Rockland
Copper Peak
DOWNHILL SKIING IN THE IRONWOOD AREA
Bergland
Craig Lake State Park
Presque Isle Park
Lake Gogebic
Sidnaw
Negaunee
Marquette
Ironwood
Wakefield
Lake Gogebic State Park
Kenton
Van Riper State Park
Ishpeming
Munising
Paulding
Watersmeet
MICHIGAN
WISCONSIN
Amasa
Iron River
Crystal Falls
Caspian
Bewabic State Park
Eagle River
IRON COUNTY HISTORICAL MUSEUM
Rapid River
Gladstone
Stonington Peninsula
Iron Mountain
Norway
Niagara
Hermansville
Escanaba
Prentice
Crandon
Cedar River
J.W. Wells State Park
Crivitz
Medford
Menominee
Marinette
Wausau
Abbotsford
Lake Michigan
Green Bay
Shawano
Sturgeon Bay
Marshfield
Stevens Point
Green Bay
© MOON.COM

HISTORY

Off the back of the Upper Peninsula like a ragged dorsal fin, the Keweenaw (KEE-wuh-naw) Peninsula, once home to the Copper Culture people, was quickly shunned by early European immigrants. It seemed hopelessly remote, surrounded by Lake Superior, and blanketed by impenetrable forests, which grew out of untillable rock and infertile sand. They dismissed it as a wasteland.

But in 1840 state geologist Douglass Houghton confirmed the presence of vast deposits of pure, native copper, much of it right near the surface. The young United States had an insatiable appetite for the metal, first for new industrial machinery and later for Civil War munitions, electrical wiring, and other innovations.

The Copper Rush subsequently began almost overnight, first with prospectors, then large mining enterprises flooding the Keweenaw. It was the nation's first mineral rush. Copper employed thousands of immigrant laborers, built cities, made millionaires, and made possible extravagant luxuries like opera houses and mansions for industry titans. Before it was over, King Copper generated more than $9.6 billion—10 times the value of the California gold rush.

The Keweenaw's copper legacy still looms large, but in an eerie sort of way: abandoned mines, ghost towns buried in the forest, and the odd juxtaposition of lavish buildings in almost forgotten towns. After it was neglected for most of the 20th century, a slow pull finally began in the 1970s to preserve the Keweenaw's copper heritage. The result is the Keweenaw National Historical Park, established in 1992 and still in development. While much of the rich history has been demolished, discarded, or crushed under the weight of winter snows, a significant amount remains.

While the Keweenaw Peninsula has its roots in copper, the rest of the western Upper Peninsula traces its heritage largely to iron. This halcyon past is evidenced by the town names—Iron Mountain, Iron River, National Mine, Mineral Hills—and in the residents, an ethnically diverse mix descended from the original immigrant mine workers. The UP's iron industry stretched from the western border east some 150 miles to the Lake Superior port of Marquette and the Lake Michigan port of Escanaba. It comprised three major ranges: the Gogebic Range, with operations centered around Ironwood (and also extends into Wisconsin); the Menominee Range, based largely around the Iron River and Iron

Isle Royale National Park

Mountain areas; and the Marquette Range, encompassing Marquette and the Ishpeming-Negaunee area.

Federal surveyors first discovered iron ore in 1844 near present-day Iron River as they surveyed this strange landmass, recently acquired by Michigan. Their compasses swung wildly near Negaunee, where iron ore was so plentiful it was visible even on the surface, intertwined in the roots of a fallen tree. That tree is the official symbol of the city of Negaunee, which itself became linked inextricably with the rise and fall of the iron ore industry.

Aside from a handful of small mining operations, the Upper Peninsula's iron resources remained largely untapped for several decades, until the railroads reached the area. In the 1870s the first major mines started in the Menominee Range. A few years later, the Gogebic Range opened. Many of the early mines were open-pit affairs, but soon the need for iron ore drove miners underground. Today communities like Ishpeming sit atop swiss cheese-like earth riddled with shafts; tracts of land occasionally sink, leaving tilted houses.

World War II created an insatiable demand for iron and drove area mines to peak production, pushing some to depletion. By the 1960s and '70s, the western UP iron ranges had grown quiet after shipping out nearly two billion tons of ore. All the underground iron mines in the UP had closed by 1978, hurt by foreign steelmakers and the use of more plastics in manufacturing.

Isle Royale National Park

Isolated in the vast waters of Lake Superior, Isle Royale is perhaps the model of what a national park is supposed to be—wild, rugged, and remote. The 45-mile-long island's only contact with the outside world is via satellite phone or ship-to-shore radio. One of the least visited parks in the national park system, Isle Royale's yearly attendance is less than a single weekend's worth at Yellowstone.

Civilization on Isle Royale is concentrated in two small developments at opposite ends of the island. Windigo, to the southwest, includes an information center, a grocery, and a marina. Rock Harbor, near the northeast end, offers the same, plus a no-frills lodge and restaurant across from the ferry dock and a handful of cabins overlooking finger-like Tobin Harbor. The rest of the island is backcountry, 210 square miles of forested foot trails, rocky bluffs, quiet lakes, and wilderness campsites.

Those who make the trek by boat or seaplane to Isle Royale come primarily to hike its 165 miles of trails, fish its 46 inland lakes, and paddle its sawtoothed shoreline. Wildlife viewing is popular, especially for spotting moose, which originally swam across to the island from Ontario several decades back. Eastern timber wolves later followed their prey across on the pack ice. But wolf sightings on the island are low, as the wolf population had been all but decimated due to inbreeding. Recently, the National Park Service partnered with the Ontario Ministry of Natural Resources and Energy to repopulate the island with wolves. Eleven animals (seven males and four females) were relocated from Ontario's mainland. Two others had been brought over in 2018, bringing the estimated current total to 15. According to the National Park Service, the new arrivals are adjusting well to their unfamiliar surroundings and expected to soon begin breeding.

Hikers have a good chance of spotting a moose, which often feed in ponds and lowlands or along inland lakeshores. Hidden Lake, across Tobin Harbor south of Lookout Louise, is an exceptionally good spot, since moose have a taste for its mineral licks. If you're lucky enough to come upon a moose,

Isle Royale

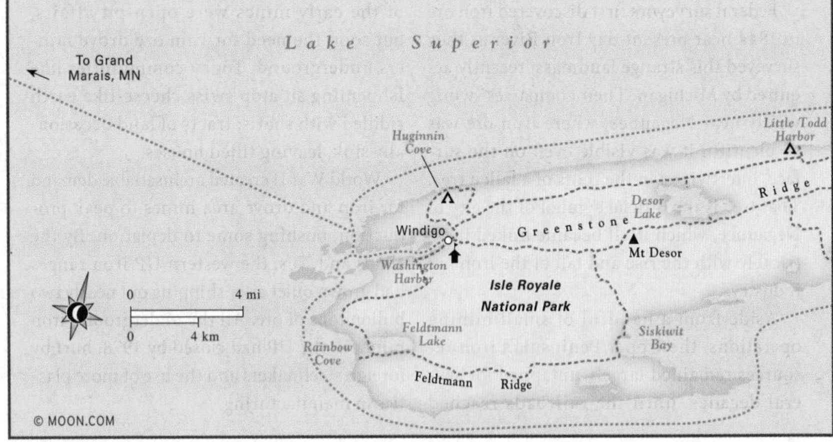

give it a very wide berth. Although they look cartoonish and friendly, moose can be exceptionally dangerous if approached—especially cows with calves or males during the fall rutting season—and are capable of inflicting lethal blows with their hooves.

Despite its name, which implies singularity, Isle Royale National Park actually consists of an archipelago of some 400 islands, all of them remnants of the same landmass. More than 80 percent of the national park lies underwater, beneath shallow ponds, bogs, inland lakes, and the clear, cold water of Lake Superior.

While many national parks struggle with their fate as islands of wilderness surrounded by a more developed world, Isle Royale has the advantage of a much larger, natural buffer zone protecting it from outside encroachment. As a result, it is one of the most closely managed holdings in the national park system. This presents some unique opportunities for protecting the wilderness. Isle Royale is one of the few parks that regulates the number of visitors. Though logistics have done a sufficient job of keeping numbers down thus far, the National Park Service only has to cut back on ferry service or the number of campsites to alter the flow. Limited access also allows the National Park Service to enforce rules more effectively. The National Park Service also takes great pains to preserve its backcountry solitude, with a park brochure reminding hikers to "refrain from loud conversation," "avoid songfests," and "select equipment of subtle natural tones rather than conspicuous colorful gear."

★ BOAT TOURS

The park service shuttles visitors to various island attractions on its 25-passenger **MV *Sandy*** (906/482-0984, www.nps.gov/isro, June-early Sept., $17-49.50 adults, $17-28 children under age 12). The *Sandy* makes several different trips in season. One four-mile boat ride takes passengers to the Hidden Lake Trailhead, where they're asked to debark and are then guided on a two-mile round-trip past Hidden Lake, up 320 feet to **Lookout Louise.** From here, visitors can view the southern shore of Canada and the northern shore of Isle Royale.

Another trip heads across the mouth of Moskey Basin to the historic fishery of Peter and Laura Edisen, restored to show what life was like for the commercial fisheries that once

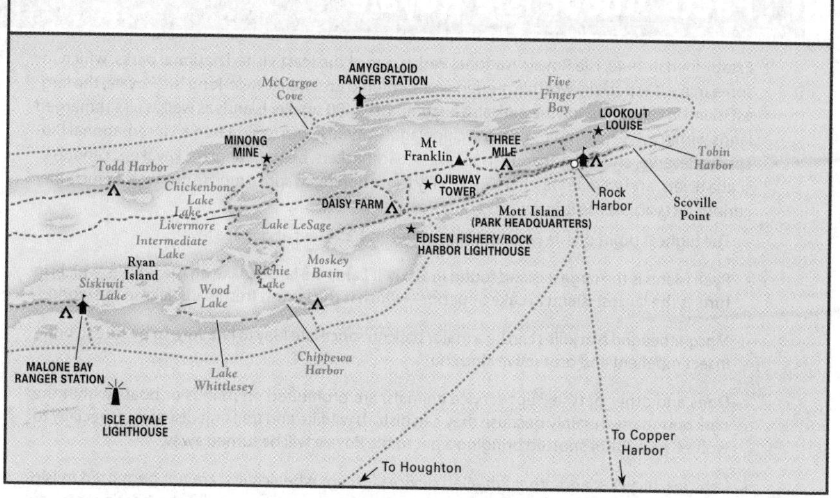

thrived on the island. From **Edisen Fishery,** it's a short 0.25-mile walk to the stout and simple **Rock Harbor Lighthouse,** a white edifice built in 1855 to guide ships to Isle Royale's then-busy copper ports.

Other tours feature out-of-the-way destinations such as the Passage Island Lighthouse and Raspberry Island. History buffs will especially enjoy these tours. Besides viewing the Rock Harbor Lighthouse, you can also select a tour to see the historic Minong Mine, and the site of the *Monarch* shipwreck.

RECREATION

Hiking

Several day hikes are doable if you choose to "motel camp" in Rock Harbor. Don't miss **Scoville Point,** a 4.2-mile loop with interpretive signs that traces a rocky finger of land east of Rock Harbor. Another popular short hike is the 3.8-mile loop to **Suzy's Cave,** formed by the wave action of a once much deeper Lake Superior. **Lookout Louise,** north of Tobin Harbor, offers one of the island's most spectacular views, looking out over its ragged northeastern shoreline. If you have access to a canoe, it's a short paddle plus a two-mile hike. Without a canoe, it's a fine hike along lovely Tobin Harbor and the eastern end of the Greenstone Ridge, but you'll need to retrace your steps to return to Rock Harbor, about a 20-mile round-trip trek.

For another all-day hike, follow the Lake Superior shoreline to the Daisy Farm campground and the Ojibway Trail, which heads north and brings you to the **Ojibway Tower,** an air-monitoring station. The tower marks the highest spot on the eastern end of the island, and you can climb its steps (but not enter the tower room) for an unmatched view of the island's interior lakes and bays on both the north and south sides of the island. Travel back via the Greenstone Ridge and along Tobin Harbor for a varied 18-mile hike that will take you through blueberry patches, wildflower meadows, and serene shorelines. For a similar but shorter hike of about 10 miles, turn north at the Three Mile campground to ascend Mount Franklin, another high point on the Greenstone Ridge.

Canoeing

For paddlers, Isle Royale is a dream destination, a nook-and-cranny wilderness of rocky islands, secluded coves, and quiet bays interrupted only by the low call of the loon.

Facts About Isle Royale

Established in 1940, Isle Royale National Park is one of the least visited national parks, which for some make it especially worth experiencing. Centered around 45-mile-long Isle Royale, the largest island in Lake Superior, the park also encompasses 400 smaller islands as well as all submerged lands within a 4.5-mile radius of the archipelago. In 1980 it was designated an International Biosphere Reserve, and today it appeals to hikers, backpackers, boaters, anglers, kayakers, canoeists, scuba divers, and wildlife watchers, especially those hoping to spot a moose or a wolf. Some other curious facts about Isle Royale:

- The highest point on Isle Royale is Mount Desor, 1,394 feet above sea level.
- Ryan Island is the largest island found in Siskiwit Lake, the largest lake on Isle Royale, which, in turn, is the largest island in Lake Superior—which is the largest freshwater lake in the world.
- Mosquitoes and blackflies can be a major park nuisance late May to late July, so be sure to bring insect repellent and protective clothing.
- Dogs and other pets (except service animals) are prohibited on islands or boats within the park boundaries, mainly because they can disturb wildlife and transmit diseases, especially to wolves. Any visitor spotted bringing a pet to Isle Royale will be turned away.
- Vehicles, bicycles, and other wheeled devices (except wheelchairs) are not permitted in Isle Royale National Park; the only approved modes of transportation are hiking, boating, canoeing, and kayaking.
- Visitors must avoid disturbing wild animals at all times. Observing or photographing them must be done from a safe distance through the use of binoculars or zoom lenses.

If you're curious about other aspects of the park, including the rules pertaining to visitors, contact the headquarters of **Isle Royale National Park** (800 E. Lakeshore Dr., Houghton, 906/482-0984, www.nps.gov/isro).

First-time visitors can't do better than the **Five Fingers,** the collection of fjord-like harbors and rocky promontories on the east end of the island. Not only is it well protected (except from northeasterlies), it offers some of the finest and most characteristic Isle Royale scenery and solitude. Though Isle Royale is generally better suited to kayaks, open canoes can handle these waters in calm weather.

For kayaks, the entire island offers paddling opportunities, though some areas require long stretches of paddling without good shoreline access. Note that open water passages on Lake Superior are recommended only for experienced paddlers and should never be attempted in an open boat like a canoe. Capsizing in Lake Superior can be a life-threatening experience: Water temperatures in the 40s mean hypothermia can occur in minutes. There are several outlets where you can rent canoes, 14-foot fishing boats, and outboard motors at both Windigo and Rock Harbor.

FOOD AND ACCOMMODATIONS

Rock Harbor's **Lighthouse Restaurant** (7am-11am, noon-1:30pm, and 5:30pm-7:30pm daily late May-early Sept., $10-35) serves meals that taste like a gourmet feast after a week of camping fare. The on-site **Greenstone Grill** (7am-11pm daily late May-early Sept., $5-13) is also a good option for hungry hikers; the fare there consists of burgers, sandwiches, pizza, and a wide assortment of regional beer and wine. Meanwhile, the **Marina Store** (9am-5pm daily) in Rock Harbor carries a good supply of food, camping supplies, fuel, and other travel essentials.

Rely on it only for items you forgot to pack, as the store can be very expensive.

Those just looking for a quiet island stay and some swell day hikes can set up a base in comfort at the **Rock Harbor Lodge** (906/337-4993 May-Sept., 866/644-2003 Oct.-Apr., http://rockharborlodge.com, Memorial Day-Labor Day, $237-271 d). Lodge rooms are basic motel-style accommodations, but they sit right at the water's edge with a glorious view of nearby islands and the open waters of Lake Superior. Guests also have use of an adjacent day lodge with a comfortable wood-burning fireplace. Nearby housekeeping cottages have small kitchens, one double bed, and one bunk bed. You can call about reservations year-round, but the lodge is only open Memorial Day-Labor Day. Reservations are a must.

Camping

If you want to see more of the island, camping is the way to do it. Rustic campsites are located throughout Isle Royale, with three types of sites available: tent sites for 1-3 tents, group sites for parties of 7-10, and three-sided shelters that hold up to 6. You must obtain a free camping permit from the Windigo Ranger Station when you arrive, outlining your itinerary, but you can't make reservations. All sites are available on a first-come, first-served basis. Should you reach a site at the end of the day and find it occupied (this can happen within a day's hike from Rock Harbor, especially in August), the unwritten rules say double up. No one expects you to hike off into the dwindling light to the next campsite.

INFORMATION AND SERVICES

For general information about the park, including camping and transportation options, contact **Isle Royale National Park** (906/482-0984 or 906/482-0986, www.nps.gov/isro). You'll find few services and no cell phone reception on the islands, so be sure to stock up on supplies in Houghton or Copper Harbor before heading to Isle Royale.

Isle Royale was one of the first national parks to charge a park user fee. Daily fees are $7 per person per day, free for children under age 12. If you're traveling to the island by ferry or seaplane, the concessionaire will collect your fee. If you're traveling by private boat, you can pay at the ranger station at Windigo or Rock Harbor, or at the **Houghton Visitor Center** (800 E. Lakeshore Dr., 906/482-0984, 8am-6pm Mon.-Fri., 10am-6pm Sat. June-mid-Sept., 8am-4pm Mon.-Fri. mid-Sept.-May) prior to your departure. Also, remember that Isle Royale is one of the few national parks to close during the winter, November to mid-April. This is due to the extreme weather conditions and for wildlife protection and visitor safety.

GETTING THERE AND AROUND

Your options for accessing Isle Royale are seaplane, ferry, or personal boat. The National Park Service operates the largest ferry, the 165-foot MV ***Ranger III***. Usually operating from the end of May to mid-September, it departs from Houghton twice a week, at 9am on Tuesday and Friday, on the six-hour passage to Rock Harbor (one-way $55-70 adults, $35 ages 7-11, under age 7 free), and makes the return trip to Houghton at 9am on Wednesday and Saturday. It costs extra to transport canoes, kayaks, boats, and outboard motors. Make reservations through the national park (906/482-0984, www.nps.gov/isro).

A faster but more expensive boat, the 65-foot MV ***Voyageur II*** travels from Grand Portage, Minnesota, to Windigo in two hours, then continues on to Rock Harbor (one-way $86 adults, $78 children under age 16). On its way to Rock Harbor, it circumnavigates the island, offering drop-off and pickup service along the way, making for a slow but interesting trip. For additional fees, it can also carry canoes, kayaks, bikes, and extra gear or luggage. Schedule of sailings varies. Check the website for complete details. Make arrangements through **Grand Portage-Isle Royale Transportation Line** (218/475-0024

May-Oct., 651/653-5872 Nov.-Apr., www.isleroyaleboats.com) and ask about interisland trip rates; remember that you'll also have to pay a daily user fee ($7 adults, under age 12 free) to access the national park.

Seaplane service from Houghton is the most expensive but quickest way to reach Isle Royale, though the 35-minute flight is often delayed by wind and fog. Service by **Isle Royale Seaplanes** (906/483-4991, www.isleroyaleseaplanes.com) runs mid-May to mid-September. The plane flies daily between the **Hancock Portage Canal Seaplane Base** (21125 Royce Rd., Hancock) and the protected bays at Windigo and Rock Harbor. It can carry up to four passengers (round-trip $330 pp, one-way $230 pp, under age 1 free), plus their luggage. Service is also offered from Grand Marais, Minnesota, to Windigo (round-trip $290 pp, one-way $200 pp) and Rock Harbor (round-trip $380 pp, one-way $260 pp). Flights depart from the **Grand Marais/Cook County Seaplane Base** (123 Airport Rd., Grand Marais, MN, 218/387-3024). Note that you won't be able to bring stove fuel on board, though you can purchase it at one of the park stores on the island. Reservations are required for these flights, and the rates do not include the daily user fee ($7 adults, children under age 12 free) required to access the national park.

Once you've arrived in Isle Royale National Park, you'll have little choice regarding transportation. For most visitors, hiking or kayaking are the only modes of getting around the islands.

The Keweenaw Peninsula

South of Isle Royale, the enormous Keweenaw Peninsula juts out from the northern coast of the Upper Peninsula.

The Keweenaw is home to some of the Midwest's most distinctive geology and oldest exposed rock. Part of the Precambrian Canadian Shield, the peninsula was created more than two billion years ago by spewing volcanoes and colliding continents. Much later, about 1.2 billion years ago, the hardened crust broke apart, and more lava began seeping out through fissures, forming basalt bedrock. For hundreds of years, the basalt piled up thicker and thicker; while groundwater percolated in, filling the bubbles and cracks with minerals and establishing the Keweenaw's vast deposits of copper.

Eventually, the basalt layers sank, forming a basin surrounded by tilted, uplifted rock: the Keweenaw Mountain Range, a spine that runs the length of the peninsula and across Isle Royale. Consequently, the basalt found throughout the Keweenaw is possibly the oldest exposed volcanic rock on earth.

Though the Keweenaw's variety of minerals is not particularly vast, it contains some unusual gemstones in substantial quantity. Rockhounds seek out three in particular: porcelaneous datolite, mohawkite, and chlorastrolite. Chlorastrolite is more commonly known as the Isle Royale greenstone, a tortoiseshell-patterned rock rarely found elsewhere. The peninsula's beaches are also a good place to hunt for agates, thomsonite, epidote, zeolites, red feldspar, and more. Area mineral shops are excellent sources for guidebooks and hunting tips. You'll also find several former mining towns, a few inland lakes, and Keweenaw National Historical Park, comprising numerous historic attractions.

COPPER HARBOR AND VICINITY

Wedged between Lake Superior to the north and long, lovely and tranquil Lake Fanny Hooe to the south, Copper Harbor marks the end of the road in the Keweenaw Peninsula. Even U.S. 41 stops here, circling in a loop some 1,990 miles from its other terminus in Miami. The tip of the peninsula draws people

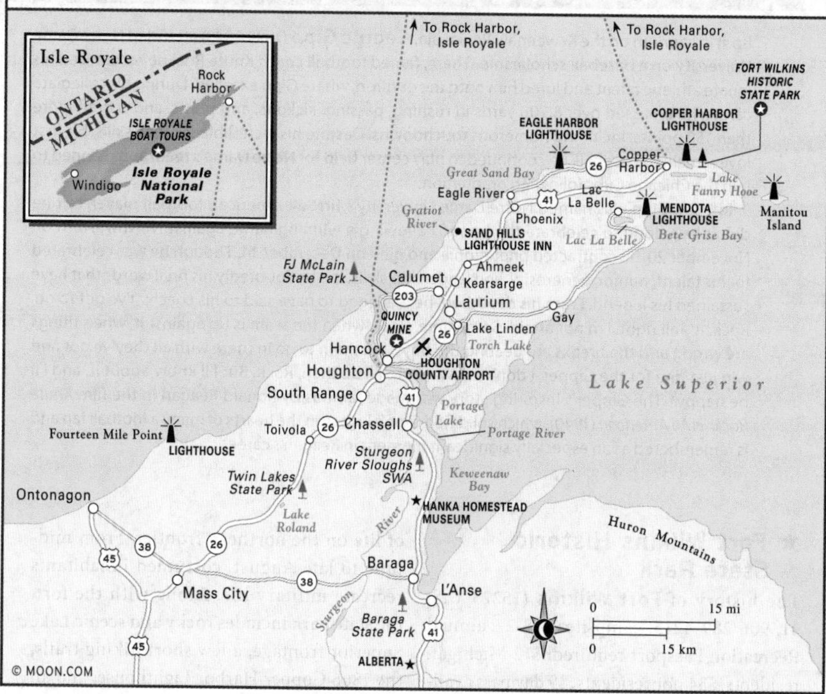

precisely because it is the end of the road, and when they get there, they discover one of the Upper Peninsula's most scenic natural areas and one of its most appealing little towns.

Downtown

Tiny Copper Harbor, population 108, offers more than you might expect from its size. For some unusual shopping, check out the locally made copper plates, bowls, vases, and jewelry at **Studio 41** (260 4th St., 906/289-4808, www.studio41copper.com, 10am-6pm Mon.-Sat.). Rockhounds, meanwhile, will appreciate **Swede's Gift Shop** (260 3rd St., 906/289-4596, 9am-6pm daily May-Oct.), which offers a nice selection of local minerals, plus handcrafted jewelry, paintings, copper artwork, and Scandinavian gifts. Another very unique store is the **Laughing Loon** (242 1st St., 906/289-4813, www.thelaughingloononline.com, 11am-6pm daily). If there's only one gift shop in the whole Upper Peninsula to stop at, this is the one. It showcases handcrafted items of all sorts—wind chimes, wall hangings, and books and artwork by local artists are just some of the cool things you'll find here.

In downtown Copper Harbor, you'll also find a year-round grocery, the **Gas Lite General Store** (39 Gratiot St., 906/289-4652, daily), which packs a lot into a small space. Although the prices may run a bit higher than in other parts of Michigan, it's a convenient and friendly place to stock up on a variety of supplies, from beer and produce to area maps and fishing licenses—everything you might need for a campout, a cabin stay, or a trip to Isle Royale.

The Gipper of Laurium

Born in Laurium on the Keweenaw Peninsula, **George Gipp** (1895-1920) attended Notre Dame University on a baseball scholarship. There, famed football coach Knute Rockne recognized his innate athletic talent and lured him onto the gridiron, where Gipp excelled. During his collegiate career, he amassed over 8,200 yards in rushing, passing, kickoffs, and punts, and scored more than 150 points, including numerous touchdowns. Despite his incredible football skills, his first love remained baseball; he continued to play center field for Notre Dame's team and planned to join the Chicago Cubs following graduation.

In 1920, Gipp was named Notre Dame University's first all-American football player, but he didn't have long to celebrate the honor. Following a winning game against Northwestern on November 20, he contracted pneumonia and died on December 14. Though he was celebrated for his talent, humor, generosity, and leadership skills, it is undoubtedly his final words that have sustained his legend. From his deathbed, he is alleged to have said to his coach: "I've got to go, Rock. It's all right. I'm not afraid. Some time, Rock, when the team is up against it, when things are wrong and the breaks are beating the boys, tell them to go in there with all they've got and win just one for the Gipper. I don't know where I'll be then, Rock. But I'll know about it, and I'll be happy." The Gipper's inspiring story was made famous by Ronald Reagan in the film *Knute Rockne: All American* (1940), which solidified Gipp's legacy in the hearts of many a football fan and is remembered as an especially significant moment in Reagan's career.

★ Fort Wilkins Historic State Park

The history of **Fort Wilkins** (15223 U.S. 41, 906/289-4215, campsites $18-27, annual Recreation Passport required: $12 Michigan residents, $34 nonresidents, $9 day pass available to nonresidents only) reads like one of those excessive military spending stories of the 20th century. With miners pouring north during the Copper Rush, the federal government feared fighting would erupt between miners and the local Native Americans and ordered the construction of a garrisoned fort. In 1844 they sent more than 100 troops, who built barracks, a mess hall, a hospital, and other buildings behind a tall stockade fence, then hunkered down to fend off the fighting. However, no fighting ever broke out, and winters proved long, cold, and desolate. By the following year, half the troops were pulled out and sent south, where the country faced the threat of war with Mexico. By 1846, the rest were gone.

Today, Fort Wilkins stands as one of a few wooden forts remaining east of the Mississippi, with 16 whitewashed buildings wonderfully restored and filled with exhibits of life on the northern frontier. From mid-June to late August, costumed inhabitants recreate military life. Along with the fort, the state park includes rocky and scenic Lake Superior frontage, a few short hiking trails, the 1866 Copper Harbor Lighthouse, and an excellent campground on Lake Fanny Hooe.

Brockway Mountain Drive

Dubbed the most beautiful road in Michigan, this 10-mile route traces the spine of a high ridge between Copper Harbor and Eagle Harbor. Rising 735 feet above Lake Superior, it is the highest paved road between the Rockies and the Allegheny Mountains. A parking area midway allows you to stop and soak in the panorama of Lake Superior and the rolling forests of the Keweenaw, a breathtaking vista no matter how many times you've seen it. Watch for ravens, bald eagles, and peregrine falcons—which sometimes soar below you. Traveling west to east, the end of the drive is marked by a picture-postcard shot of Copper Harbor, tucked between Lake Superior and Lake Fanny Hooe. From this drive, you might catch a glimpse of the 1871 **Eagle Harbor Lighthouse** (906/289-4990, www.

keweenawhistory.org, 10am-5pm daily mid June-late Aug., $5 adults, children free), now site of a maritime museum operated by the Keweenaw County Historical Society.

CALUMET

At the height of the Keweenaw's copper mining glory, the Calumet and Hecla Consolidated Copper Company, operating largely in Calumet, proved the grandest operation of all. At the turn of the 20th century, C&H employed some 11,000 workers who extracted more than 1.5 billion tons of copper from a web of mines tunneled under Calumet. Striking red sandstone buildings with elaborate cornices lined the 12-square-block downtown, filled with elegant shops, soaring churches, some 70 saloons, and even a lavish theater that attracted the nation's leading vaudeville stars. The city buzzed day and night—both above and belowground. After the mines were depleted, Calumet did little to economically diversify. As a result, today the town remains largely frozen in time; a marvel of architecture from the early twentieth century and the primary reason for the area earning national historical park status.

Downtown Calumet

Thanks to the national historical park and renewed civic pride, downtown Calumet looks more historically authentic each day. Ugly 1960s facades have been removed from the elegant sandstone and brick buildings, and new money is coming in to further restore and preserve them. To appreciate this architectural bonanza, stop by the **Keweenaw Convention & Visitors Bureau** (56638 Calumet Ave., 906/337-4579, www.keweenaw.info, 9am-5pm Mon.-Fri.) to pick up a walking-tour guide. A few stops of particular note: The **Union Building** (5th St. and Red Jacket Rd.) was home to one of the area's first banks in 1888 and still retains its original decorative metal cornice. **Shute's Bar** (322 6th St.) looks fairly mundane on the outside, but the interior preserves ornate plaster ceilings and a magnificent backbar with a stained-glass canopy. The **Red Jacket Town Hall and Opera House,** now called the **Historic Calumet Theatre** (340 6th St., 906/337-2610, www.calumettheatre.com), is the pride of the community. The theater portion, added in 1898 as the first municipally owned theater in the country, was a showy extravagance with its plaster rococo in cream, crimson, green, and gilt. And its electric lights were a rarity for the era.

Coppertown USA

The mine's pattern shop, where wooden patterns were made as molds for machine parts, now serves as the home of **Coppertown Mining Museum** (25815 Red Jacket Rd., 906/337-4354, 11am-4pm Mon.-Sat. June-Sept., $4 adults, $2 ages 6-18, active duty military and children under 5 free), a privately run museum and national park-cooperating site that traces the region's copper industry. It includes a number of artifacts, a display of area minerals, a replica of a mining captain's office, a diorama of Native American mining, and more. Another plus—the exhibits are designed to allow for close examination.

HOUGHTON AND HANCOCK

Residents of Lower Michigan may be surprised to learn that the state actually has a northern version of Ann Arbor—the quintessential college town. Houghton, and the adjacent city of Hancock, not only offer great sporting diversions, they boast a quirky ethnic flair, streets lined with beautifully preserved early-1900s buildings, and an intellectual atmosphere characteristic of a center of academia.

Houghton (population 7,700) and Hancock (population 4,600) face each other across the Portage Waterway, with homes and churches built on 500-foot bluffs. Streets (especially on the Hancock side), can be downright unnerving, rivaling those in San Francisco for pitch. The Portage Waterway effectively slices the Keweenaw in two, a 21-mile passage that saves boaters the 100-mile trip around the peninsula.

1
2

An unusual lift bridge links Houghton and Hancock, its huge center section rising like an elevator to let water traffic pass. Today, the Portage Waterway largely serves pleasure boaters and the 165-foot *Ranger III,* the ferry that transports hikers to Isle Royale National Park, 70 miles northwest. Houghton and Hancock are gateways to the Keweenaw and Isle Royale—but visitors just passing through will miss an appealing slice of the region.

Downtown

You can conduct your own historic walking tour of Houghton by strolling down **Shelden Avenue,** the city's main street. Tall facades of brick and red sandstone line the street, like the **Douglass House Hotel** (517 Shelden Ave.), built in 1901 as a luxury hotel and dining establishment for travelers through the Portage Waterway. An addition in 1902 completed the lavish building you see today. The **Finnish-American Heritage Center** (435 Quincy St., 906/487-7302, 8am-4:30pm daily, free), affiliated with Finlandia University, maintains a public gallery that features Finnish artists as well as archives of the area's Finnish settlement.

★ Quincy Mine

Just north of Hancock, the mammoth shaft house of the **Quincy Mine** (49750 U.S. 41, 906/482-3101, www.quincymine.com, 9:30am-5pm Fri.-Sun. late Apr.-May, 9:30am-5pm daily June-mid-Oct., group tours by appointment mid-Oct.-Apr., $12-22 adults, $12-25 over age 54, $5-10 ages 6-12, under age 6 free) dominates the skyline. The Quincy ranked as one of the world's richest copper mines in the late 1800s, producing over a billion pounds of copper. Today, a few of its buildings still stand, and the land beneath it remains stitched with the shafts that stretched more than 1.5 miles deep—an amazing 92 levels—and 2 miles wide.

1: Fort Wilkins on Lake Fanny Hooe **2:** wooden ore cars in front of the Quincy Mine Hoist House in Keweenaw National Historical Park

From the hoist house, the tour starts with a rather dramatic ride in a glass-enclosed tram down the side of a steep hill. Views of the Houghton and Hancock skylines are stunning as the tram descends to an entrance to the mine at Level 7. A tractor carries you a few thousand feet inside, where guides demonstrate mining techniques and give you a feel for what it was like to work deep inside the earth in a drippy, damp environment with only hand tools and candles.

BARAGA AND L'ANSE

While the town of L'Anse continues to suffer from a stuttering economy, the Keweenaw Bay Indian Community is on the upswing. Ojibwa leaders here were among the first to profit from treaty rights that allow them to establish gaming on their land along Keweenaw Bay. Today the popular **Ojibwa Casino and Resort** (16449 Michigan Ave., Baraga, 906/353-6333, www.ojibwacasino.com) in Baraga generates millions of dollars in revenue and feeds much needed tax dollars into the local economy. Other Native American communities have followed suit and opened successful casinos throughout the UP and much of the Lower Peninsula. Consequently, indigenous communities now wield considerable influence in the region.

On a more traditional note, the Ojibwa also host a colorful **powwow** each July, a traditional celebration of dancing and drumming. On the eastern shore of Keweenaw Bay, north of L'Anse, you can visit an Ojibwa burial ground from the mid-1800s, with spirit houses marking graves. These small shelters held offerings of food, provisions to help sustain the soul on its journey to the afterlife.

KEWEENAW NATIONAL HISTORICAL PARK

The **Keweenaw National Historical Park** (headquarters at 25970 Red Jacket Rd., Calumet, 906/337-3168, www.nps.gov/kewe, 9am-5pm Mon.-Fri.) is not so much a place on a map but a place in time. The state's newest property under the authority of the National

Park Service, it was established in 1992 "to commemorate the heritage of copper mining on the Keweenaw Peninsula—its mines, its machinery, and its people."

Rather than an area with simply defined boundaries, the Keweenaw National Historical Park comprises attractions throughout the Keweenaw. Two units anchor the park—the Quincy Unit at the Quincy Mine in Hancock and the Calumet Unit in historic downtown Calumet—but some of this land remains under private ownership. The National Park Service holds a limited amount of land to preserve key sites and conduct interpretive activities. In addition, the park has designated partner sites (known as Keweenaw Heritage Sites) throughout the peninsula, including mine tours and museums. These sites are privately owned, but benefit from increased visibility and federal funds.

GHOST TOWNS

Ghost towns litter the Keweenaw, faded testaments to the boom-and-bust days of copper. The ruins of old mines and stamping plants (facilities that separated copper from rock) line M-26 between Hancock and Calumet. The gray piles of residue are mine tailings or stamping-plant leftovers called stamp sand. Several bona fide ghost towns hide in the woods, especially between Calumet and Copper Harbor. At **Central** (watch for the small brown sign on U.S. 41 about 11 miles north of Mohawk), an exceptionally rich mine produced nearly $10 million by 1898; the surrounding town grew to 1,200. Today, nature has all but reclaimed Central, with just a few clapboard houses creaking in the breeze. Turn right near the top of the hill for a look at the mine ruins and rows of house foundations. Exercise care while walking.

Just south of Copper Harbor on U.S. 41, another sign announces your "arrival" in **Mandan,** directing you down a dirt road disappearing into birches. Follow it south for about 50 yards and homes suddenly erupt out of the woods, lined up in a tidy row. Mandan was the last stop on a trolley line from Hancock.

RECREATION

Anglers and hunters increasingly find themselves sharing the backwoods and waters with hikers, mountain bikers, and paddlers.

Hiking and Biking

Mountain bikers new to the area can hardly believe the wealth of terrific trails in the Keweenaw, literally hundreds of miles of old mining and logging roads, overgrown double-track routes, and technical single-track. They loop through towering pines to backwoods waterfalls, to otherwise inaccessible Lake Superior shorelines, even past ghost towns now buried deep in the woods. Note that trails may peter out or come to a sudden and unexpected dead end.

Vast tracts of land in the Keweenaw are privately owned by large corporations—some mining firms but mostly paper companies. In exchange for a break in state taxes, the companies allow public use of the land for recreation, including hiking, fishing, and mountain biking. Still, for liability reasons, some outfitters and bike shops are loath to hand out maps or recommend these lands for riding. If you ask, though, most bike shops tend to be quite helpful about suggesting trails, especially the **Keweenaw Adventure Company** (155 Gratiot St., Copper Harbor, 906/289-4303, www.keweenawadventure.com), a company that began in 1994 and now helps to organize the annual **Copper Harbor Trails Fest** (www.copperharbortrails.org), a mountain biking race in late summer.

Canoeing and Kayaking

This sport is at its finest in the Keweenaw, where you have plenty of islands, rock formations, and wilderness coastlines to explore. The **Keweenaw Adventure Company** (155 Gratiot St., Copper Harbor, 906/289-4303, www.keweenawadventure.com) rents out kayaks, guides trips, and offers lessons. Beginners should try the 2.5-hour introductory paddle, which includes novice instruction on land and a fine little trip around the harbor and along the Lake Superior shoreline. The Keweenaw Adventure Company also offers some daylong trips around the peninsula—to Horseshoe Harbor, Agate Harbor, and the mouth of the Montreal River—as scheduling permits.

Rivers in the Keweenaw tend to be cold, so white-water kayaking is limited, although it may vary after a rainfall. Sea kayaking, on the other hand, is outstanding, the perfect way to access bluffs, caves, sea stacks, and rocky islands all along the Lake Superior shoreline. The **Keweenaw Water Trail** provides a mapped passageway of more than 100 miles through the Portage Waterway and along the Lake Superior shore, indicating accommodations, campgrounds, launches, and more. For more information and to purchase a water trail map, contact the **Keweenaw Convention and Visitors Bureau** (906/337-4579 or 800/338-7982, www.keweenaw.info). Isle Royale makes for an excellent paddling destination, and the ferries will transport kayaks and canoes for an additional fee. Canoeing is popular on inland lakes, but for safety reasons open boats are not recommended on Lake Superior.

Diving

The cold, clear freshwater of Lake Superior offers outstanding visibility for divers. Though there isn't much to look at in the way of plant and animal life—the cold waters make for a pretty sterile environment—there's plenty of entertainment in the form of interesting underwater geologic formations and shipwrecks.

Ships have been running aground for well over a hundred years near the Keweenaw Peninsula, which poses a considerable navigational hazard. Within the 103-square-mile **Keweenaw Underwater Preserve,** divers can explore the *Tioga,* a freighter that ran aground near Eagle River in 1919, and the *City of St. Joseph,* which met her fate north of Eagle Harbor in 1942. Both ships lie in less than 40 feet of water, with large sections of the hull, deck machinery, and other artifacts clearly visible.

One of the Upper Peninsula's oldest shipwrecks, the *John Jacob Astor,* lies just offshore from Copper Harbor, near the Fort Wilkins State Park Lighthouse Overlook. An Underwater Trail marks the location of the rudder, anchor, and other remnants of the *Astor,* which sank in 1844. For more information, contact the **Michigan Underwater Preserve Council** (MUPC, 231/818-8159 or 800/970-8717, www.michiganpreserves.org).

Winter Activities

A giant snow gauge on U.S. 41 south of Phoenix proudly marks the Keweenaw's record snowfall, a staggering 390.4 inches in the winter of 1977-1978. It wasn't an aberration; the surrounding waters of Lake Superior routinely generate colossal lake-effect snows, often exceeding 300 inches. These massive accumulations, combined with the remarkable local terrain, makes the Keweenaw a haven for snowmobilers, skiers, and snowshoers. Downhill skiers can check out Michigan's most challenging terrain at **Mount Bohemia** (6532 Lac La Belle Rd., 906/360-7240, www.mtbohemia.com, 10:30am-4:30pm Mon.-Fri., 9:30am-5pm Sat.-Sun., lift tickets $73) near Lac La Belle. Although lodging is available at the resort year-round, weather conditions determine the actual skiing season, which usually begins in early December.

FESTIVALS AND EVENTS

Despite its relative isolation from the rest of Michigan, the Keweenaw Peninsula plays host to numerous events and celebrations throughout the year. In winter, residents honor the frigid temperatures with ice-fishing derbies, cross-country skiing races, a winter carnival on the campus of Michigan Technological University, and **Heikinpäivä,** a Finnish American festival that takes place around January 19 every year, mainly in Houghton. Presenting traditional Finnish crafts, music, cuisine, and more, this annual event honors the Finnish culture that helped build this area and remains a significant part of its culture today. In Hancock alone, 40 percent of the population still claims Finnish ancestry.

Of course, the milder months are even busier on the Keweenaw Peninsula. Between May's **International Migratory Bird Day Festival** (www.birdday.org) in Copper Harbor and the **Houghton County Fair** (www.houghtoncountyfair.com) in late August, you'll surely find things to do on the Keweenaw throughout the summer. Of course, besides bike races, art fairs, and heritage events, one of the most popular annual events is Houghton's **Bridgefest** (906/482-5240, www.bridgefestfun.com), a mid-June celebration of the Portage Lake Lift Bridge—or perhaps just an excuse for the community to enjoy live concerts, sporting events, boat tours, arts and crafts exhibits, fireworks displays, and a seafood festival, where even live lobster is part of the fun.

FOOD

The **Pines Restaurant** (174 Gratiot St., Copper Harbor, 906/289-4222, www.pinesresort.net, 8am-9pm daily, $8-19), a small café, is an unbeatably warm and inviting place complete with knotty pine, a stone hearth, and good basic northern Michigan fare—burgers, hearty sandwiches, and a delicious turkey dinner served on Sunday. Get a booth by a window and take in a true "up north" experience. The adjacent **Zik's Bar** (906/289-4222, 10:30am-close daily) is popular with Copper Harbor locals.

Fitzgerald's Restaurant (5033 Front St., Eagle Harbor, 906/337-0666, www.fitzgeralds-mi.com, 3pm-9pm Mon.-Thurs., noon-9pm Fri-Sat. early May-late Oct., $9-30) in the Eagle River Inn offers upscale dining overlooking Lake Superior. The menu features black Angus steaks, fresh fish and seafood, inventive vegetarian dishes, plus Southern-style barbecue prepared on a wood-fired smoker. You'll also find a comprehensive wine list and several selections of beer on tap.

Combine a college town with a large multiethnic population and you'll conjure up a good range of eating options in the Houghton-Hancock area. One great choice is the **Ambassador Restaurant** (126 Shelden Ave., Houghton, 906/482-5054, www.theambassadorhoughton.com, 11am-10:30pm Mon.-Thurs., 11am-midnight Fri.-Sat., 4:30pm-10:30pm Sun., $10-17), which specializes in pastas, pizzas, and almost any sort of sandwich you can conceive of, like the Yodeler (corned beef with shredded lettuce and sliced tomatoes with a zesty dressing) and the three-cheese submarine, in 8-, 16-, and 24-inch versions.

Another noteworthy choice is **The Hut Inn** (58542 Wolverine St./U.S. 41, Calumet, 906/337-1133, www.hutinn.com, 11am-9pm Sun.-Thurs., 11am-10pm Fri.-Sat., $11-33). Situated in a building resembling a Frank Lloyd Wright structure, The Hut offers a quiet setting for a relaxing meal after a long day's drive. Pastas, chicken dishes, and a selection of outstanding steaks make a stop here well worth it.

ACCOMMODATIONS

Located high on a ridge above Copper Harbor and overlooking Lake Fanny Hooe, the log lodge and cabins of the ★ **Keweenaw Mountain Lodge** (14252 U.S. 41, Copper Harbor, 906/289-4403, www.atthelodge.com, early May-late Oct., $155-235 d) were built as a WPA project in 1934. Take advantage of breakfast, lunch, and dinner in the grand dining lodge as well as the scenic nine-hole golf course. The helpful staff can arrange hiking, biking, bird-watching, kayaking, charter fishing, and lighthouse excursions. Reservations at the resort can be difficult to obtain. Try to book a private log cabin, equipped with a fireplace and, in some cases, a whirlpool bath, rather than one of the eight less-inspired hotel rooms, which were added much later than the other buildings.

The no-frills rooms at the **King Copper Motel** (447 Brockway Ave., Copper Harbor, 906/289-4214, www.kingcoppermotel.com, $103-129 d) come with great views of the harbor. Just a few steps from the ferry dock, this is a perfect spot for a warm shower and a real bed after a week of hiking on Isle Royale.

For a truly unforgettable experience, consider spending the night at the ★ **Sand Hills Lighthouse Inn** (5 Mile Point Rd., Ahmeek, 906/337-1744, www.sandhillslighthouseinn.com, $185-260 d), a beautifully preserved (and recently restored) lighthouse constructed in 1917 and now serving as a year-round Victorian-style bed-and-breakfast. Listed on the National Register of Historic Places, this romantic spot offers eight lovely rooms, each with a king or queen bed and private bath. Two of the chambers even have whirlpool bathtubs and a balcony overlooking Lake Superior.

The **Wonderland Motel and Cabins** (55821 Lake Linden Ave., Laurium, 906/337-4511, $67-108 d) offers decent budget-friendly accommodations complete with kitchens in the cabins.

Carla's Lake Shore Motel (14258 U.S. 41, Baraga, 906/353-6256, www.carlasinn.com, $65-85 d) has clean, inexpensive rooms with a view of Keweenaw Bay. It's also dog-friendly.

Camping

Fort Wilkins Historic State Park (15223 U.S. 41, Copper Harbor, 906/289-4215, reservations 800/447-2757, annual Recreation Passport required: $12 Michigan residents, $34 nonresidents, $9 day pass available to nonresidents only) has 159 modern sites ($17-27) in two campgrounds, both on Lake Fanny Hooe. Many sites sit along the water and offer excellent privacy.

West of Ahmeek, the **Sunset Bay RV Resort & Campground** (2701 Sunset Bay Beach Rd., Eagle River, 906/337-2494 June-Oct., 941/232-4832 Nov.-May, www.sunsetbay.com, $25-35) offers a fine view of the sunset from your tent flap. Many of its 11 tent sites and 23 RV spaces sit on Lake Superior. Two cabins, modern restrooms, a laundry and dump station, a nice swimming beach, a small boat launch, several hiking trails, and wireless Internet access are also available.

Keep in mind that many locals simply head out into the woods on weekends and set up camp near a favorite stretch of beach or river. If you choose to do the same, respect "No Trespassing" signs and observe backcountry camping practices, such as burying waste, hanging packs, and so on.

Sunsets get top billing at **McLain State Park** (18350 M-203, Hancock, 906/482-0278, reservations 800/447-2757, annual Recreation Passport required: $12 Michigan residents, $34 nonresidents, $9 day pass available to nonresidents only), where the sky often glows in peaches and pinks before the sun melts into Lake Superior. As at most Michigan state parks, the campsites ($17-27) and cabins ($65) are fine, and many come with those waterfront views. Follow M-203 seven miles north of Hancock.

INFORMATION AND SERVICES

For more information about the Keweenaw Peninsula, including attractions and lodging, contact the **Keweenaw Convention & Visitors Bureau** (56638 Calumet Ave., Calumet, 906/337-4579, www.keweenaw.info, 9am-5pm Mon.-Fri.) or **Keweenaw Peninsula Chamber of Commerce** (902 College Ave., Houghton, 906/482-5240, www.keweenaw.org, 9am-6pm Mon.-Fri.). If you're interested in the local news, consult the daily ***Mining Gazette*** (www.mininggazette.com).

The twin towns of Houghton and Hancock represent the area's largest population center, where you'll find most essential services, like medical care and public transportation. They also serve as the unofficial gateway to the upper Keweenaw. For medical assistance, visit **UP Health System—Portage** (921 W, Sharon Ave., Houghton, 906/483-1777, and 56720 Calumet Ave., Calumet, 906/482-1177, www.portagehealth.org). There are also facilities in Hancock and Lake Linden.

GETTING THERE AND AROUND

Bus service can be spotty throughout the Upper Peninsula, but particularly in the Keweenaw Peninsula; nevertheless, both **Greyhound** (800/231-2222, www.greyhound.com) and **Indian Trails** (800/292-3831, www.indiantrails.com) stop in Hancock (125 Quincy St., 906/483-0093) and L'Anse (102 N. Main St., 906/524-6400).

Flying into **Houghton County Memorial Airport** (CMX, 23810 Airpark Blvd., Calumet, 906/482-3970, www.houghtoncounty.org), with flights from Chicago, can be expensive. At **Sawyer International Airport** (MQT, 125 G Ave., Gwinn, 906/346-3308, www.sawyerairport.com), 108 miles from Houghton near Marquette, you can rent a vehicle and head to the Keweenaw Peninsula via U.S. 41/M-28.

By car, the two main routes around the Keweenaw Peninsula are U.S. 41 and M-26. Many secondary roads in the Keweenaw are dirt or gravel. For traveling across old logging roads and other minor routes, a four-wheel-drive vehicle is strongly recommended. From Marquette, it normally takes 75 minutes to cover the 68 miles on U.S. 41 to L'Anse, 80 minutes to traverse the 72 miles to Baraga, almost 2 hours to travel the 100 miles to Houghton and Hancock, over 2 hours for the 112-mile trip to Calumet, and roughly 2.75 hours to reach Copper Harbor, 146 miles northwest of Marquette.

Ontonagon to Ironwood

From Ontonagon to Ironwood, once thriving mining communities, is some of the most untamed wilderness in Michigan. This western edge of the Upper Peninsula is definitely a recreationist's dream, favored for fishing, canoeing, hunting, hiking, and snowmobiling.

Beginning each November, Lake Superior snows inundate the region, which is marketed to downhill skiers throughout the Midwest as "Big Snow Country." When the snow melts, however, a beautiful landscape emerges—inland lakes and rivers for fishing and paddling plus hundreds of miles of national forest trails for hiking and biking.

ONTONAGON

The Ontonagon Boulder was pried from its namesake riverbank a few miles upstream from the Lake Superior shoreline community of Ontonagon. Today, the two-ton mass of native copper resides at the Smithsonian, while Ontonagon's mining legacy is celebrated in local museums.

Learn about Ontonagon's heyday at the worthwhile **Ontonagon Historical Museum** (422 River St., 906/884-6165, www.ontonagonmuseum.org, 10am-4pm Tues.-Sat. May-Oct., 10am-4pm Thur.-Sat. Nov.-Apr., by donation), a lavender building on M-38, downtown's main street. The historical society's biggest project these days has been restoring the 1866 **Ontonagon Light,** which replaced one of Lake Superior's first lighthouses, built in 1853. Tours of the lighthouse are offered from May-Oct. at 11am, 1:30pm, and 3:30pm Mon.-Sat. and 11am and 1:30pm Sun.

★ PORCUPINE MOUNTAINS WILDERNESS STATE PARK

Anchored along the Lake Superior shore in the northwest corner of the UP, **Porcupine Mountains Wilderness State Park** (33303 Headquarters Rd., Ontonagon, 906/885-5275, annual Recreation Passport required: $12 Michigan residents, $34 nonresidents, $9 day pass available to nonresidents only) covers 59,020 acres, the largest in Michigan's excellent state park system. The U.S. Department of the Interior considered the Porcupine

Mountains for a national park in the 1940s, but they were quickly preserved as a state park in 1945 when loggers threatened their virgin timber before the federal government could take action.

Some years ago, the pitted and rugged landscape of low mountains and tall pines reminded locals of the silhouette of a porcupine. The name stuck, and today the area is endearingly dubbed "the Porkies." It's a destination for casual hikers and hard-core backpackers, with 90-plus miles of well-marked, well-maintained trails.

In this case, bigger also means better. The park preserves the largest tract of virgin hardwoods between the Rockies and Adirondacks and vast stands of virgin hemlock and pine, along with secluded lakes, wild rivers, and some of the Midwest's highest peaks (Summit Peak tops out at 1,958 feet). The Porkies truly provide a sense of wilderness and serenity, an escape from the civilized world.

Hiking

Many park visitors head immediately for the justly famous **Lake of the Clouds Overlook.** From the parking lot at the end of M-107, it's just a few steps to the overlook, where the placid lake slices a long sliver of blue through a thick mat of jade forest hundreds of feet below. The view is the stuff postcards are made of and probably the most photographed scene in the UP.

The overlook also serves as the trailhead for some of the park's most rugged and scenic routes. To properly soak in the Lake of the Clouds view, hike the aptly named **Escarpment Trail,** which winds east and skims over Cloud Peak and Cuyahoga Peak. Bordered by a sheer cliff, the four-mile trail is considered by many to be the most beautiful in the park. Allow ample time to stop and enjoy the shimmering lake and valley floor spreading out around you. If you're fortunate enough to visit in the fall, the vista of color is beyond breathtaking.

Long before the Porcupine Mountains were preserved for their virgin timber and natural beauty, miners harvested the rich minerals buried in their bedrock. At the east end of the park, the **Union Mine Trail** provides a glimpse into the 1840s, when the Porkies pulsed with the excitement of the area's copper rush. Marked with white mine shovels to indicate points of interest, this self-guided interpretive trail forms a one-mile loop along the spring-fed Union River and the site of an old copper mine, now largely swallowed by

Porcupine Mountains Wilderness State Park

nature. In the shadow of lofty hemlocks, you'll see how miners tunneled shafts into the riverbank, and learn about their life in the wilderness—still untamed today.

In winter, the park's many hiking trails double as cross-country skiing trails. Be careful on the higher ones: On days when the strong north wind is blowing, you'll feel the extreme cold.

Camping

Campers have their choice of two campgrounds ($19-22), both with a number of sites overlooking Lake Superior: **Union Bay** (with full hookups and modern restrooms), at the east end of the park, or rustic **Presque Isle** (no hookups), near the mouth of the Presque Isle River on the park's western edge. In addition, three rustic campgrounds (called "outposts") with three to eight sites each are off the South Boundary Road, accessible by car, but with no facilities. They tend to offer more privacy than the regular campgrounds.

As another option, the park has 19 hike-in rustic **cabins** ($73). These are great retreats after a day on the trail. They come with two to eight bunks, mattresses, a woodstove, basic utensils, and protection from the elements, but no electricity or running water. Bring your own stove for cooking. Cabins situated on inland lakes even come with a rowboat, so you can finish the day with a lazy drift across the water. Three **yurts** ($66) and a lodge are also available. **Reservations** (800/447-2757) at any of these can be made as much as a year in advance. Reserving early is a good idea, as the demand is always quite high.

Information

Start your visit at the park's **visitors center** at the junction of M-107 and South Boundary Road. Rangers on duty can provide you with maps and suggest trails. A gift shop has topographic maps and a good selection of nature guidebooks.

Getting There and Around

Two roads lead to Porcupine Mountains Wilderness State Park, the headquarters of which lies about 58 miles northeast of Ironwood. From Wakefield, drive north on County Road 519, which leads to the park's western edge and the Presque Isle River Area, a 17-mile trip that will take you about half an hour. From Bergland, reach the park headquarters via M-64 through Ottawa National Forest; arriving at Lake Superior, the road converges with M-107 near the park's eastern boundary. Turn left onto M-107 toward the park headquarters, or continue toward the Lake of the Clouds Scenic Area; the 30-mile trip between Bergland and the park headquarters takes 40 minutes. South Boundary Road connects County Road 519 and M-64 along the southern edge of the park.

OTTAWA NATIONAL FOREST

Although backpackers could get lost amid the deep woods of Ottawa, and anglers favor Lake Gogebic east of Ironwood, visitors should be sure to visit the **Sturgeon River Gorge Wilderness Area.** The Sturgeon River, a federally designated Wild and Scenic River, travels a circuitous route through much of Baraga County before emptying into Portage Lake near Chassell. One of three wilderness areas within the national forest, the Sturgeon River Gorge Wilderness protects 14,000 acres that surround this river and its tributaries. The highlight is west of U.S. 41 and south of M-38, where the river cuts and tumbles through a magnificent 300-foot gorge. To reach it, follow Forest Road 2200 north from Sidnaw. Follow signs onto Forest Road 2270 to reach a parking area and foot trail that winds down about 0.5 miles to a cascade and the river. Continue west from the parking area on Forest Road 2270 to reach Silver Mountain, with stone steps that lead to a remarkable valley view. In autumn you'll see a fiery display by an abundant maple forest.

The U.S. Forest Service has marked only a few trails within the wilderness area, which appeals to those who love the backcountry. Several grown-over logging roads wind

A Dynasty of Pine

In the mid-1800s, a young and growing United States suddenly had an insatiable appetite for lumber. Settlers, moving west into the treeless plains, needed lumber to build their new towns; burgeoning cities needed it to build more homes and businesses; and railroads also needed lumber as they laid mile after mile of track to link the ever-expanding nation. To satisfy these needs, Michigan's natural resources proved the perfect solution. Immense white pines and other conifers grew thick and tall across the Upper Peninsula and more than half of the Lower Peninsula. Rivers honeycombed through these vast forests, providing a route to the Great Lakes, which in turn connected the northern wilderness to Detroit, Chicago, and other railroad centers in the south.

Around 1850, logging camps began springing up deep in the woods, from the western UP to the shores of Lake Huron. Young men streamed north, some of them farm laborers looking for winter wages, others newly arrived immigrants. The lumberjacks worked by hand, with ax and saw, tree after tree, acre after acre. The logging camps operated primarily in the winter months, when it was easier to transport the huge logs. Workers hauled the logs from the woods to the river's edge, branded the ends with the lumber company's mark, and stacked them there until spring.

In spring, when the ice melted, the colorful and chaotic log drives began. Thousands of logs were shoved into northern rivers, guided downstream by daredevil workers, known as river pigs, who danced across the dangerous mass of moving wood using hooks, poles, and sometimes dynamite to dislodge logjams. It was the most dangerous job in the trade; with one misstep, river pigs could end up crushed between tons of logs or trapped underwater.

Once at the mills, the jumble of logs was sorted according to the mill owners' marks and floated into mill storage ponds. From there, buzzing sawmills sliced the logs into lumber and loaded them onto lumber schooners—and later, barges and steamers—headed primarily to Chicago, the nation's largest lumber market and railroad hub.

In its heyday, the logging industry generated billions of feet of lumber and billions of dollars. Lumber companies made all sorts of proclamations: Michigan mills asserted that they produced enough lumber to lay an inch-thick plank across the state. Success stories were everywhere. A sawmill in Hermansville, Michigan, came up with the idea of tongue-and-groove flooring and quickly became the largest flooring plant in the country, crafting the floors for the Mormon Temple in Salt Lake City and the main lodge at Yellowstone National Park. Timber barons' homes were marvels of hand-carved mahogany, gold-leaf inlay, and cut-crystal chandeliers.

But the era lasted less than 50 years. By 1900 nearly all the big trees were gone, a scorched and denuded landscape of stump prairies left in their place. When farmers were able to convert some of the southernmost pineries into useful cropland, ambitious entrepreneurs sought to do the same in the north. A newspaper publisher in Menominee, Michigan, extolled the virtues of the Upper Peninsula's cutover land for farming or ranching. "No matter where the first Garden of Eden was located," he proclaimed, "the present one is in the Upper Peninsula."

Thousands of hardworking people were lured north by the promise of cheap land in exchange for the backbreaking labor of removing pine stumps and tilling the soil. But by the late 1920s, their work proved futile. Nearly half the UP was tax-delinquent cutover land; most farms and ranches had failed. The stock market had crashed, and the nation's economy was in shambles.

The federal government took a different approach. In 1911 it established the first national forests in Michigan and Wisconsin, setting aside land and creating tree nurseries as a first step in reestablishing the Midwest's great forests. The Civilian Conservation Corps, established in 1933, continued the reforestation efforts, planting trees, fighting fires, and nursing the remaining great forests back to health.

Although we can never recreate the magnificent old-growth forests of yesteryear, pines once again stretch skyward across Michigan. Logging continues, though usually with sophisticated forest management and reforestation practices that help ensure the livelihood of the state's important lumber and paper industries. A few stands of virgin old-growth timber remain, giving us an awe-inspiring glimpse of a lost Michigan landscape.

through the area for hikers who want to explore on their own, for which a topographic map is an absolute necessity. Camping is permitted throughout the wilderness, where you'll find a number of choice spots.

Information

To make sense of what the Ottawa has to offer, start with a map. You can pick up a small brochure or large topographic map at **Ottawa National Forest Headquarters** (E6248 U.S. 2, Ironwood, 906/932-1330, 9am-6pm Mon.-Fri.). Other district offices, in Ontonagon and Watersmeet, may have maps and brochures, but budget cuts have forced them to curtail other visitor services.

IRONWOOD AREA

With mammoth Lake Superior providing the requisite moisture, the northwestern corner of the UP isn't exaggerating when it markets itself as "Big Snow Country." Cool air moving across the warmer waters of Lake Superior creates lake-effect snow when it hits land, generating an average of 200 inches per season. This combines nicely with the area's rugged hills, home to some of the region's largest downhill ski resorts. As a result, the western UP, especially around Ironwood, is one of the Upper Peninsula's more heavily marketed tourism areas, luring sizable crowds of skiers up I-39/U.S. 51 every weekend from Wisconsin, Detroit, and Chicago.

Cross-country skiers and, increasingly, snowshoers also take advantage of the abundant snows. Gogebic County has more dedicated Nordic skiing resorts than anywhere else in the Upper Peninsula, and the Ottawa National Forest offers a dizzying array of terrain for those seeking solitude. The UP never overlooks snowmobiling, and you'll see plenty of trucks pulling snowmobiles; snowmobile routes radiating out from Lake Gogebic are especially popular. To avoid them, ask state park or national forest officials about the proximity of snowmobiling trails from where you plan to set out.

Follow M-505 north from Ironwood to reach **Little Girl's Point,** an area favorite. Perched high on a bluff over Lake Superior, this county park features a sand beach, a boat launch, picnic tables, grills, and fantastic views—the Porcupine Mountains to the east, the Apostle Islands to the west.

From Little Girl's Point, continue west on M-505 to reach **Superior Falls.** The rushing Montreal River puts on its final spectacular show here, plummeting more than 40 feet, then squeezing through a narrow gorge before spilling into Lake Superior a short distance away. You can also reach it by taking U.S. 2 about 11 miles west from Ironwood and turning north on WIS-122; you'll travel through Wisconsin and back into Michigan in the process. In about 4.8 miles, watch for a small brown sign that directs you west into a small parking area near a Northern States Power substation. From here, it's a short walk to the falls. You can also continue down the path past the falls to Lake Superior, a fine sunset spot.

SYLVANIA WILDERNESS AND RECREATION AREA

Sylvania protects its assets well—36 crystalline glacial lakes hidden among thick stands of massive old-growth trees. For anglers who dream of landing that once-in-a-lifetime smallmouth bass, for paddlers who yearn to glide across deep, quiet waters and along untrammeled shoreline, for hikers who wish to travel under a towering canopy of trees and hear nothing more than the haunting whistle of a loon, Sylvania can be a truly magical place.

One of three wilderness areas within the national forest, Sylvania stretches across 18,300 acres near Watersmeet, an area roughly bounded by U.S. 2 to the north, U.S. 45 to the east, and the Wisconsin border to the south. The adjacent Sylvania Recreation Area acts as a buffer, an additional 3,000 acres of lakes and woodlands with a few developed services, like a drive-in campground, a nice beach, flush toilets, and running water.

Once viewed as just another tract of good

timber, Sylvania's fate turned in the late 1890s, when a lumberman who purchased 80 acres near the south end of Clark Lake decided it was too beautiful to cut, and instead kept it as his personal fishing retreat. He invited his wealthy friends—some of them executives of U.S. Steel—who were also captivated by the land. Together, they purchased several thousand additional acres and formed the private Sylvania Club.

Begin a trip to Sylvania with a call or visit to the **Ottawa Visitors Center** (906/358-4724, 10am-4pm Wed.-Sat.), at the intersection of U.S. 2 and U.S. 45 in Watersmeet. The staff can help with maps, regulations, campsite reservations, and other information. Sylvania's rules can be quite unique—especially fishing regulations—so take time to ask questions and read through the materials the rangers provide. To reach Sylvania, follow U.S. 2 west about four miles from the visitors center and turn south on Thousand Island Lake Road. Travel about four miles, following signs to reach the entrance building. All visitors are required to register on arrival.

The entrance is in the recreation area, near the drive-in campground on Clark Lake. If you intend to travel into the wilderness area, plan on treating your own water; you'll find water pumps only in the recreation area. Propane cookstoves are strongly encouraged to lessen the number of feet tramping through the forest in search of dead wood. During summer months, make sure you also have ample insect repellent or, better yet, a head net to combat mosquitoes and blackflies.

RECREATION

Biking

There are many tantalizing mountain biking opportunities in the western Upper Peninsula: 200 miles of trails in three networks with routes ranging from the tamest gravel roads to single-track trails deep in the woods. As a bonus, many link up with waterfalls, remote lakes, and historical features.

Near Marenisco in Gogebic County, the **Pomeroy/Henry Lake network** offers 100 miles of gentle rides on wide gravel roads around a national forest area peppered with small lakes. It's a good choice for families. The **Ehlco network,** just south of the Porcupine Mountains Wilderness State Park, includes single-track deep in the forest, plus grass and dirt paths. Arguably the best of the three is the one outside the national forest: the **Iron County system.** Trails radiating out of Hurley lead past waterfalls, large flowages,

kayaking in the Sylvania Wilderness and Recreation Area

and old mining relics like the Plummer headframe near Pence. Good interpretive signs help make sense of historic sites. Routes in this system range from gravel roads to terrific single-track, though maps may be unclear as to which is which.

Canoeing and Kayaking

Seven major river systems flow within the forest, a staggering 1,000 miles of navigable waters for paddlers. Congress has designated more than 300 of those miles as Wild and Scenic or recreational rivers, leaving them largely in their pristine state. In general, rivers like the Ontonagon and Presque Isle offer quiet water in their southern reaches, winding through relatively flat woodlands. North of M-28, they begin a more rugged descent through hills and bluffs, requiring higher skills and boats appropriate for white water. For strong paddlers with good white-water skills, these rivers offer some of the finest paddling in the Midwest.

Of course, all of this can change depending on rainfall, the amount of springtime snowmelt, and the time of year. Rivers that normally flow gently can be torrents in the spring. Always check with U.S. Forest Service officials, such as the supervisor's office of the **Ottawa National Forest** (E6248 U.S. 2, Ironwood, 906/932-1330, www.fs.usda.gov), before setting out. For maps, brochures, and permits, you can also stop by a district ranger office, such as the **Ontonagon Ranger District** (1209 Rockland Rd., Ontonagon, 906/884-2085).

★ Downhill Skiing

The area's three major downhill ski resorts—Big Powderhorn, Blackjack, and Indianhead—line up conveniently along a short stretch of U.S. 2 just east of Ironwood. All welcome downhill skiers and snowboarders.

Heading east from Ironwood, the first resort you'll reach is **Big Powderhorn Mountain** (N11375 Powderhorn Rd., Bessemer, 906/932-4838, www.bigpowderhorn.net, lift tickets $69 adult, $56 ages 10-17, $44 ages 7-9, $56 seniors 65-74). Powderhorn's 33 downhill runs wrap across two faces, with 700 feet of vertical drop and nine double chairlifts. Perhaps more than the others, Big Powderhorn Mountain caters to families with affordable lift tickets, mostly tame runs, and plenty of ski-in, ski-out lodgings bordering its slopes.

Also in Bessemer, the smaller **Blackjack Ski Resort** (N11251 Blackjack Rd., 800/346-3426, www.bigsnow.com, lift tickets $60-65, $52 ages 10-17 and seniors 65 and over), with 20 trails, carves out a niche in the market by making the most of its terrain. Cameron Run and Spillway are often left ungroomed and offer up good bump skiing, and it's arguably the best resort around for snowboarders, with the area's best half-pipe and a great terrain park on Broad Ax.

A few more miles down the road brings you to Blackjack's sister property, **Indianhead Mountain Resort** (500 Indianhead Rd., Wakefield, 800/346-3426, www.bigsnow.com, lift tickets $60-65, $52 seniors 65 and over and ages 10-17), the area's largest resort with 638 feet of vertical, nine chairlifts, two T-bars, and 29 runs. Indianhead offers some of the region's most challenging, although overly groomed, skiing, and pleasant runs that wind for more than a mile through the woods.

Cross-Country Skiing

Active Backwoods Retreats (E5299 W. Pioneer Rd., 906/932-3502, www.abrski.com, $14 adults, $10 ages 11-17, $6 under age 11) grooms 25 miles of trails for skating and striding on hundreds of acres of private land three miles south of Ironwood. A warming hut, lessons, and rentals are available.

Between Ironwood and Bessemer, take Section 12 Road north from U.S. 2 to reach **Wolverine Nordic Trails** (5851 Sunset Rd., Ironwood, 906/932-0347, www.wolverinenordic.com $10 suggested donation). Situated on private land and maintained by volunteers, its 9.3 miles of groomed trails wind through the hilly country south of the Big Powderhorn ski area. You can, in fact, ride one of Big Powderhorn's chairlifts ($10 pp) to access the network. Otherwise, begin at the lot with the warming hut on Sunset Road off Section 12 Road. Donations boxes are spaced throughout the trail. Funds are used for trail grooming and facility maintenance.

FOOD

If you get hungry while exploring the area, head to Ontonagon, where you'll find **Syl's Café** (713 River, 906/884-2522, 7am-9pm daily, $7-16), a classic small-town café with some of the best pasties around. Their breakfasts are so big you may not need to eat for the rest of the day. In Ironwood, you'll spot what looks like a classic corner tavern, but **Don & GG's** (1300 E. Cloverland Dr., 906/932-2312, 11am-9pm Mon.-Thurs., 11am-10pm Fri.-Sat., $9-19) might surprise you with its vegetarian dishes and smoked trout salad. Don't worry—you can still get burgers and chicken dinners.

ACCOMMODATIONS

There are a number of motels along M-64 between Silver City and Ontonagon. Many are plain, somewhat tired, but adequate mom-and-pop-type places—spartan but just fine after a long day outdoors. One chain offering that is particularly welcoming is **AmericInn by Wyndham** (120 Lincoln Ave./M-64, Silver City, 906/885-5311, www.wyndhamhotels.com/americinn, $157-200 d), where you'll find clean accommodations and a hearty breakfast each morning.

You'll also find a large selection of independent motels along U.S. 2, many of which have great deals and clean and comfortable if simple rooms. A good choice is the **Classic Motor Inn** (1200 E. Cloverland Dr./U.S. 2, Ironwood, 906/932-2000, www.westernup.com/sandpiper, $79-110 d). Reserve well ahead of time during ski season. Meanwhile, the larger area ski resorts offer slope-side or near slope-side accommodations, ranging from dormitories to simple motel rooms to deluxe condominiums. The ★ **Indianhead Mountain Resort** (500 Indianhead Rd., Wakefield, 800/346-3426, www.bigsnow.com, $135-499 d) offers some of the nicest rooms and condos, and close to what you might find at an upscale resort in the Rockies.

Camping

The **Ottawa National Forest** (E6248 U.S. 2, Ironwood, 906/932-1330, www.fs.usda.gov, free-$17) maintains 27 vehicle-accessible campgrounds, all with tent pads, fire grates, and toilet facilities. Many are located along rivers and lakes. Most tend to be quite rustic and secluded, with the exception of Black River Harbor, Sylvania, and Bobcat Lake. A few, like Black River Harbor, require a fee and allow reservations.

INFORMATION AND SERVICES

While many of the area's small communities have chambers of commerce that can help with lodging and other services, the most comprehensive source of tourism information is the **Western UP Convention & Visitor Bureau** (405 Lake St., Ironwood, 906/932-4850 or 800/522-5657, www.explorewesternup.com). If you need more specific details, you can also consult the **Ontonagon County Chamber of Commerce** (Ontonagon, 906/884-4735, www.ontonagonmi.org), **Lake Gogebic Area Chamber of Commerce** (Bergland, 888/464-3242, www.lakegogebicarea.com), and **Ironwood Area Chamber of Commerce** (150 N. Lowell St., Ironwood, 906/932-1122, www.ironwoodchamber.org).

Since most towns in this part of the UP offer limited services, such as local banks and small groceries, it's best to stop first in larger towns like Marquette and Escanaba. There, you'll find a better selection of supplies and services before venturing into the western wilderness.

GETTING THERE AND AROUND

Although the western UP has a couple of small airports in Calumet and Escanaba, both of which offer commuter flights on United or Delta, most air travelers use **Sawyer**

International Airport (MQT, 125 G Ave., Gwinn, 906/346-3308, www.sawyerairport.com) near Marquette. From there, you can rent a vehicle and head west to Ontonagon, a 122-mile trip that will take you 2.25 hours. From the Sawyer airport to Ironwood is a 154-mile drive that takes 3 hours.

Beyond area airports, **Greyhound** (800/231-2222, www.greyhound.com) and **Indian Trails** (800/292-3831, www.indiantrails.com) both offer limited bus service to Ironwood (235 E. McLeod Ave., 906/932-0346). The easiest way to visit the region, however, is by car. From Sault Ste. Marie, drive south on I-75, M-28, and M-38 to Ontonagon; the 278-mile trip should take about 5 hours. From St. Ignace, reach Ironwood by heading west on U.S. 2, M-77, M-28, and U.S. 2; the 306-mile trip usually takes about 5.5 hours.

Iron River to Iron Mountain

The Menominee Range is an anomaly in the Upper Peninsula, the only area not close to one of the Great Lakes. Roughly encompassing Iron, Dickinson, and Menominee Counties (all in the central time zone), as well as the southern reaches of Baraga County, it is a land of deep forests and thousands of inland lakes.

Travelers tend to pass right though the region, which admittedly doesn't look like much from U.S. 2, the main thoroughfare. But that thin strip of development masks an astounding volume of untrammeled wilderness. Wolves thrive here without any human assistance because the region provides exactly the habitat they need: large tracts of land not sliced up by roads and plenty of large prey in the region's abundant white-tailed deer.

Iron County's population centers around **Iron River** and **Crystal Falls,** the picturesque county seat 15 miles east. Both retain their small-town charm. The heart of Dickinson County is **Iron Mountain.** Iron River and Iron Mountain, both former iron-mining centers, now offer visitors several historical museums, a couple of downhill ski slopes, and areas ideal for anglers, canoeists, and kayakers.

SIGHTS

★ Iron County Historical Museum

You won't find a lot of dramatic lighting and fancy display cases at the **Iron County Historical Museum** (100 Brady Ave., off M-189, Caspian, 906/265-2617, www.ironcountyhistoricalmuseum.org, 10am-2pm Sun.-Wed., 10am-6pm Thurs.-Sat. mid-May-Sept. 1, by appointment Sept.-Apr., $10 adults, $5 ages 5-18, under age 5 free), two miles south of U.S. 2. What you will find is an appealing and eclectic blend of local history and culture at this rambling, funky, homegrown museum on the site of the productive Caspian iron mine—whose rusting headframe still looms over the complex; it runs largely on donated money and time. In the main museum building, displays cover everything from Native American history to logging, mining, and sporting equipment and kitchenware from the early 1900s. The perennial favorite is the mechanized iron mine and railroad model. For $0.05, a miniature ore skip hauls rocks to the surface and loads them on the railroad. Outside, several relocated buildings occupy the grounds, including a streetcar barn and the streetcar that once traveled between the mines in Caspian and Iron River.

Bewabic State Park

A small but pleasant chain of lakes is the highlight of **Bewabic State Park** (720 Idlewild Rd., Crystal Falls, 906/875-3324, annual Recreation Passport required: $12 Michigan residents, $34 nonresidents, $9 day pass available to nonresidents only) five miles west of Crystal Falls. Boaters can put in at the first of the Fortune Lakes and make their way to Fourth Lake, an easy day's paddling adventure. Though First Lake can be somewhat congested on summer weekends, the waters get quieter and downright pristine as you proceed down the chain. Most of the shoreline is dotted with cottages, though you can camp on public land bordering Third Lake. Fishing for perch and bass is best on First Lake, the largest (192 acres) and deepest (72 feet). Paddlers can escape fishing boats by passing under the low U.S. 2 bridge to Mud Lake. The park itself has a modern 137-site campground ($13-27) with good privacy, a small stretch of sandy beach, tennis courts, and other amenities. For reservations, call 800/447-2757.

Iron Mountain

Iron Mountain was first settled in about 1880 and reached its heyday soon after, when vast deposits of iron were discovered underfoot. The Chapin Mine—located near present-day U.S. 2 and Kent Avenue on the north end of downtown—helped boost the town's population to almost 8,000 by 1890. Italian immigrants led the melting pot mix working at the Chapin Mine, and Italian neighborhoods still thrive around the old mine on Iron Mountain's north side—as evidenced by the tempting array of Italian restaurants and corner markets.

The long-abandoned Chapin Mine still serves an important role, this time as a magnet for brown bats. An estimated two million bats winter in the shaft, protected from predators yet able to enter and exit freely, thanks to bat-friendly grates installed at the mine entrance. As the weather turns cool in September, the bats congregate all around Iron Mountain before retreating to the mine, an amazing sight.

While iron mining seems to dominate the city's psyche, Henry Ford added to the economic mix in the 1920s, when he bought up huge tracts of nearby forest and built his first company sawmill on land southwest of town. Soon Ford's Kingsford empire included the main plant for making floorboards for the Model T, residential developments for workers, an airport, a refinery, even a plant to make the newly conceived charcoal briquettes. All of the operations eventually closed or were sold off, including the briquette plant, which relocated to Oakland, California.

Iron Mountain's Chapin Mine once led Menominee Range mining production, but it was also one of the wettest mines ever worked. In 1893, an immense steam-operated pump was put to work, a 54-foot-high, 725-ton behemoth—the largest in the world at the time. Though electric pumps replaced it just 20 years later, the pump survives intact at the **Cornish Pump and Mining Museum** (300 Kent St., Iron Mountain, 906/774-1086, www.menomineemuseum.com, 11am-3pm Tues.-Fri., 10am-2pm Sat. June-Labor Day, $5, adults, $4.50 seniors, $3 ages 10-18, children under age 10 free). Along with the impressive pump, this comprehensive museum includes a good-size collection of mining equipment, photos, and clothing as well as a small theater. The adjacent World War II Glider Museum contains arguably the most compelling display of all, the story of the World War II gliders built by Henry Ford's nearby Kingsford plant, used to quietly deploy troops behind enemy lines.

FOOD AND ACCOMMODATIONS

The namesake of **Alice's** (402 W. Adams St., Iron River, 906/265-4764, http://alicesironriver.com, 4:30pm-9pm Tues.-Sun., $10-29) produces Italian specialties just as her immigrant mother did before her, with homemade ravioli and other pasta dishes, gnocchi, and soups.

Italian is the way to go if you've decided to eat out in Iron Mountain. Homemade ravioli, slow-roasted pork, Italian sausage, Roma red sauce—you'll find it all in the town's unassuming Italian eateries. **Bimbo's Wine Press** (314 E. Main St., Iron Mountain, 906/774-8420, 11am-2am daily, $7-21) serves delicious Italian sandwiches like *porchetta* for incredibly reasonable prices. There's also a full bar.

The ★ **Lakeshore Motel** (1257 Lalley Rd., Iron River, 906/265-3611, www.lakeshoremotelicelake.com, $55-100 d) sits on the edge of spring-fed Ice Lake (on U.S. 2, just east of downtown Iron River), with tidy motel rooms, some with kitchenette units. This is a great find, complete with a sandy beach and boat launch.

In Iron Mountain, the **Pine Mountain Resort** (N3332 Pine Mountain Rd., Iron Mountain, 906/774-2747, www.pinemountainresort.com, $119-300 d), now part of the Trademark Collection by Wyndham, anchors a full-service ski and golf resort on the northwest side of town, complete with a dining room, an indoor pool, an outdoor pool, a sauna, tennis courts, and trails ideal for hiking and mountain biking. Choose from standard lodge rooms or condominiums.

INFORMATION AND SERVICES

For more information about the area, contact the **Iron County Chamber of Commerce** (50 E. Genesee St., Iron River, 906/265-3822, www.iron.org, 9am-5pm Mon.-Fri.), **Iron County Lodging Association** (906/265-3611, www.ironcountylodging.com), or **Tourism Association of the Dickinson County Area** (333 S. Stephenson Ave., Ste. 202, Iron Mountain, 800/236-2447, www.ironmountain.org). Remember that unlike most of Michigan, both Iron and Dickinson Counties are situated in the central time zone.

While the towns in this part of the UP offer limited services, such as local banks and small groceries, stop first in larger towns like Marquette and Escanaba, where you'll find a better selection of supplies and services before venturing into the western wilderness.

GETTING THERE AND AROUND

Although the western UP has small airports in Calumet and Escanaba, both with commuter flights on United or Delta, most travelers use **Sawyer International Airport** (MQT, 125 G Ave., Gwinn, 906/346-3308, www.sawyerairport.com) near Marquette. From there, you can rent a vehicle and head to Iron River, a 96-mile trip that takes 2 hours. From the Sawyer airport, reach Iron Mountain in 87 miles, a drive of 1.75 hours.

Greyhound (800/231-2222, www.greyhound.com) offers limited bus service to Iron River (211 E. Cayuga St.) and Iron Mountain (710 Norway St., 906/774-0266). **Indian Trails** (800/292-3831, www.indiantrails.com) buses also stop in Iron River (239 W. Adams St.) and Iron Mountain (710 Norway St., 906/774-0266). By car, both Iron River and Iron Mountain are situated along U.S. 2, easily reached from other parts of the Upper Peninsula. From St. Ignace, access Iron River by driving west on U.S. 2 for 149 miles, turning right onto M-69 and continuing for about 65 miles, and again following U.S. 2 for 15 miles; the 229-mile trip will take 4.25 hours. From Ironwood, you can reach Iron Mountain via U.S. 2, which briefly passes through Wisconsin; the 127-mile trip will take about 2.25 hours.

Menominee to Escanaba

Spiking south like a canine tooth between Wisconsin and the waters of Green Bay, the triangle of land that forms Menominee County and southern Delta County has been dubbed the peninsula's "banana belt"—owing to its distinction as having the UP's most temperate climate because of the relatively warm waters of protected Green Bay and the lightest snowfall in the entire UP. Just 50 inches of snow a year falls in this area, a quarter of what the rest of the Upper Peninsula typically receives. M-35 traces the shore of Green Bay from Menominee, a handsome community near the Wisconsin border, to Escanaba, a sizable town by UP standards, which features a downtown district of shops, restaurants, and historic structures.

SIGHTS

Menominee

The Menominee River spills into Green Bay between the twin cities of Marinette, Wisconsin, and Menominee, Michigan, once the region's richest lumber ports. The bustling business district centers on 1st Street along the waterfront. Fortunately, most of the late 19th-century brick and sandstone buildings remain intact, and renovation and restoration are underway on many. You can explore the **historic district,** guided by a walking tour brochure available at the **Spies Public Library** (940 1st St.). Its 1905 beaux arts facade makes it one of Menominee's most beautiful buildings, and it features prominently on the tour. Also, a growing number of shops and restaurants along 1st Street are adding new life to this already pleasant area.

The waterfront district is home to bayside parks, easily accessible on foot. **Victory Park** stretches along the water between 6th and 10th Avenues, flanked by a new marina and a band shell that hosts summer concerts on Tuesday and Thursday evenings. For a longer walk or bike ride, head south along the water to the **Tourist Park** swimming beach. Farther south, the **Menominee North Pier Light** marks the entrance to Menominee Harbor with a beacon at the end of the rocky breakwater.

Escanaba and Gladstone

Considered large for the area, Escanaba and neighboring Gladstone, just a few miles north, are home to some 17,480 people, serving as the industrial and commercial center for the south-central Upper Peninsula. The natural deepwater port gave Escanaba its start during the Civil War, when a hastily built rail line linked the iron mines in Negaunee with the port to bring coveted raw materials to the weapons makers and railroad builders of the Union army. Today, Escanaba's modern ore port still ships iron, now in the form of iron-clay taconite pellets, to steelmakers in Indiana, Ohio, and southern Michigan.

Downtown Escanaba focuses on Ludington Street, an east-west route that runs from M-35 to the waterfront. The town's landmark is the **House of Ludington,** a grand old Queen Anne resort hotel built in 1865 with an imposing facade that anchors the downtown.

At the foot of Ludington Street, lovely **Ludington Park** offers paved pathways along the water and to a small island (in-line skates permitted), interpretive signs explaining local history, a band shell that hosts concerts on Wednesday evenings in summer, a playground, a beach, tennis courts, and a boat launch. One of the park's most popular attractions is the **Sand Point Lighthouse** (16 Water Plant Rd., 906/789-6790, www.deltahistorical.org, 11am-4pm daily Memorial Day-Labor Day, $5 pp), an 1867 brick light that was restored and reopened as a museum in 1990 by the Delta County Historical Society. In the 1940s, the Coast Guard remodeled the obsolete light for staff housing, removing the lantern room and the top 10 feet of the tower.

1
UNDERGROUND TOURS
MOTORCYCLES
Welcome
2
3
LIQUOR
LUMBERJACK TAVERN
ANATOMY
OF A MURDER
LUNCH
DINNER
THE OUTPOST

WINERY

It might surprise some visitors to the Upper Peninsula that Michigan's ever-expanding wine industry extends into the state's northern tier. In Bark River, just a short drive west of Escanaba, you'll find the **Northern Sun Winery** (983 10th Rd., Bark River, 906/399-9212, www.northernsunwinery.com, 11am-6pm Thurs.-Sat., 1pm-6pm Wed. and Sun. May-Dec., 1pm-5:30pm Fri.-Sat. Jan.-Apr.). The winemakers have worked with researchers to develop especially hardy grapes that stand up to the Upper Peninsula's harsh winters. The result is a unique combination of wines that celebrate the region, including the Marquette, a product that carries the scent of cherry, spice, and black currant.

ACCOMMODATIONS

A typical string of chain motels runs along H-35 between Escanaba and Gladstone, but some nice family-owned operations are still holding their own along the waterfront. The **Terrace Bay Hotel** (7146 P Rd., Gladstone, 906/786-7554, www.terracebayhotel.com, $104-203 d) on Little Bay de Noc between Escanaba and Gladstone offers an array of stylish, contemporary rooms and suites with great bay views. The 200-acre resort complex includes an 18-hole golf course, indoor and outdoor pools, tennis courts, a game room, and more. To find Terrace Bay, watch for the signs on U.S. 41 south of Gladstone.

INFORMATION AND SERVICES

For general information, visit the large and comprehensive **Michigan Welcome Center** (906/863-6496, www.michigan.gov/mdot, 8am-4:30pm daily May-Oct., 8am-4:30pm Tues.-Sat. Nov.-Apr.) in Menominee. The picturesque log building is on U.S. 41 near the state line, just north of the bridge. For more specific details about the region, consult **Visit Escanaba** (230 Ludington St., Escanaba, 906/789-7862, www.visitescanaba.com) or the **Delta Chamber of Commerce** (230 Ludington St., Escanaba, 906/786-2192, www.deltami.org, 9am-5pm Mon.-Fri.). Remember that Menominee County is in the central time zone, like neighboring Wisconsin. When crossing into Delta County, you enter the eastern time zone.

Escanaba offers some services for travelers, but you'll find more in the way of supplies farther north in Marquette. For medical assistance, visit the **OSF St. Francis Hospital** (3401 Ludington St., Escanaba, 906/786-3311, www.osfhelathcare.org).

GETTING THERE AND AROUND

The closest airport to this region is **Delta County Airport** (ESC, 3300 Airport Rd., Escanaba, 906/786-4902, www.deltacountymi.org), which has flights from Detroit on Delta. **Greyhound** (906/789-7030 or 800/231-2222, www.greyhound.com) and **Indian Trails** (800/292-3831, www.indiantrails.com) both provide limited bus service to Escanaba's **Delta Area Transit Authority** (DATA, 2901 N. 27th Ave., Escanaba, 906/786-1186, www.databus.org).

The easiest way to visit Menominee and Delta Counties is by car. From St. Ignace, take U.S. 2 directly west to Escanaba, a 142-mile trip that takes 2.5 hours. Reach Escanaba from Marquette on M-28, U.S. 41, and U.S. 2/U.S. 41; the 67-mile trip takes 75 minutes. From Escanaba, access Menominee via M-35, a 55-mile trip that takes about an hour.

Once you arrive in the region, a car is a necessity to travel all but the shortest of distances, but walking and biking are certainly viable options in Escanaba, Gladstone, Menominee, and other small towns. Bus service is provided by DATA (www.databus.org, one-way $2-10 adults, half fare for seniors 60 and over, students, and disabled, under age 5 free with a paying adult). There are routes in Escanaba and Gladstone, and some routes run up to 30 miles beyond the limits of both towns. For these distances, fares are higher.

1: Big John greets visitors to Iron Mountain **2:** downtown Crystal Falls **3:** Lumberjack Tavern in Big Bay, the setting of *Anatomy of a Murder*

Marquette and Vicinity

With 21,500 year-round residents, Marquette is the largest city in Michigan's Upper Peninsula, tucked in a well-protected natural harbor midway across the UP's northern shore. It grew and still thrives as an important Lake Superior port for the iron ore industry and as the UP's center of commerce, government, and education. Marquette is definitely worth a visit, whether you plan to explore the historic architecture of its waterfront district or rest up before heading into the rugged hills, forests, and rivers just beyond the city limits.

SIGHTS

Third Street, running north-south, and Washington Street, running east-west, represent Marquette's main streets; where they meet is the heart of the shopping and historic district, a good spot to begin exploration of downtown. Buildings like the 1902 **Marquette County Courthouse** (3rd St. and W. Baraga Ave.) and the 1927 **MFC First National Bank** (101 W. Washington St.) showcase the city's affinity for **neoclassical and beaux arts architecture.** Step inside the courthouse for a better look, and take a few moments to savor the sumptuous building, which makes considerable use of marble, mahogany and stained glass. The second-floor courtroom is especially opulent and features a dramatic copper dome with clerestory windows.

Stop and look at the display about Michigan Supreme Court justice and author John Voelker. Better known by his pen name, Robert Traver, the Ishpeming native wrote *Anatomy of a Murder,* a novel based on an actual murder that took place in nearby Big Bay in the 1950s. Later made into a feature film starring Jimmy Stewart, scenes from the popular 1959 movie were filmed here and in Big Bay. Voelker also wrote other novels and books devoted to fishing.

The **Marquette Regional History Center** (145 W. Spring St., 906/226-3571, www.marquettecohistory.org, 10am-5pm Mon.-Tues. and Thurs.-Fri., 10am-8pm Wed., 10am-3pm Sat., $7 adults, $6 seniors, $3 students, $2 under age 13) features artifacts from prehistoric to contemporary times and is overseen by the oldest historical society in the UP.

Another highlight here is the **Marquette Maritime Museum** (300 Lakeshore Blvd., 906/226-2006, http://mqtmaritimemuseum.com, 11am-4pm Tues.-Sun. mid-May-mid-Oct., $7 adults, $12 with the lighthouse, $3 under age 13, $5 with the lighthouse), which preserves the city's maritime history and honors its submarine veterans with exhibits such as a lighthouse lens collection and a silent service memorial. The museum also offers tours of the 1866 **Marquette Harbor Lighthouse** ($7 adults, $12 with the museum, $3 under age 13, $5 with the museum).

RECREATION

Hiking and Biking

A thumb of land thrust out into the big lake, **Presque Isle Park,** about four miles north of downtown, off Lakeshore Boulevard, is a microcosm of the area's beauty: rocky red bluffs, tall pines, and lovely Lake Superior vistas. You can drive through the 323-acre park, but a better option is to get out and stroll or ski along its many trails. Watch for albino deer (white-tailed deer lacking pigment), which survive in this protected setting. Near the park's entrance is a playground, a picnic area, tennis courts, a marina, and a good spot from which to watch the huge 800-foot freighters arrive at the towering railroad ore dock. Also at the entrance of the park, you can pick up the **Marquette Bicycle Path,** a paved route that hugs the shoreline all the way to Harvey and offers access to downtown and the Northern Michigan University campus.

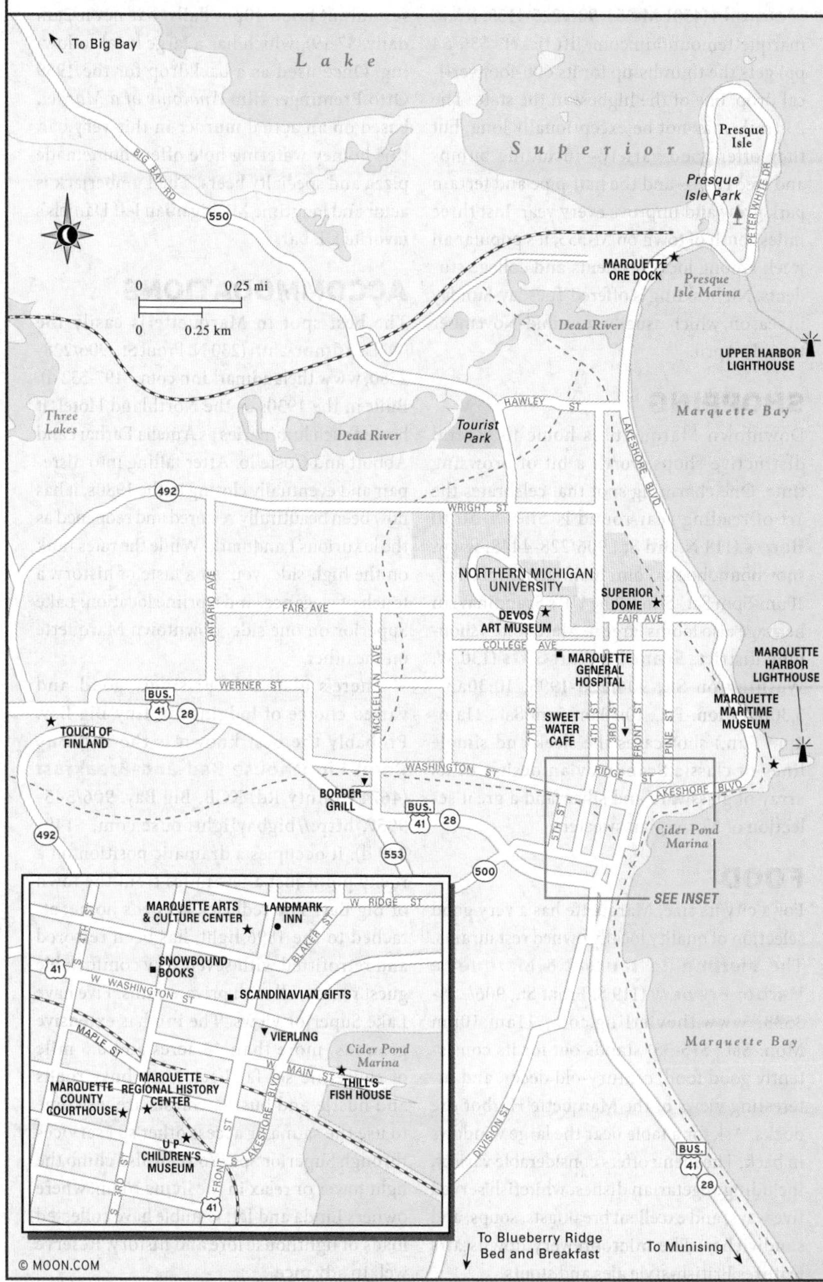
Marquette
To Big Bay
Lake
Superior
BIG BAY RD
550
Presque Isle
Presque Isle Park
PETER WHITE DR
MARQUETTE ORE DOCK
Presque Isle Marina
0
0.25 mi
0
0.25 km
Dead River
UPPER HARBOR LIGHTHOUSE
HAWLEY ST
Marquette Bay
Three Lakes
Dead River
Tourist Park
LAKESHORE BLVD
492
WRIGHT ST
NORTHERN MICHIGAN UNIVERSITY
SUPERIOR DOME
ONTARIO AVE
FAIR AVE
DEVOS ART MUSEUM
COLLEGE AVE
MARQUETTE GENERAL HOSPITAL
MARQUETTE HARBOR LIGHTHOUSE
MCCLELLAN AVE
WERNER ST
BUS. 41
28
TOUCH OF FINLAND
7TH ST
SWEET WATER CAFE
4TH ST
3RD ST
FRONT ST
PINE ST
MARQUETTE MARITIME MUSEUM
WASHINGTON ST
RIDGE ST
BORDER GRILL
5TH ST
Cider Pond Marina
492
553
500
SEE INSET
W RIDGE ST
MARQUETTE ARTS & CULTURE CENTER
LANDMARK INN
BLAKER ST
SNOWBOUND BOOKS
W WASHINGTON ST
SCANDINAVIAN GIFTS
MAPLE ST
VIERLING
Cider Pond Marina
W MAIN ST
THILL'S FISH HOUSE
MARQUETTE COUNTY COURTHOUSE
MARQUETTE REGIONAL HISTORY CENTER
U P CHILDREN'S MUSEUM
S LAKESHORE BLVD
S FRONT ST
S 3RD ST
Marquette Bay
DIVISION ST
To Blueberry Ridge Bed and Breakfast
To Munising

Skiing

Among skiers and snowboarders, **Marquette Mountain** (4501 M-553, 906/225-1155, www.marquettemountain.com, lift tickets $36-54 pp) gets the thumbs-up for its 600-foot vertical drop, one of the highest in the state. The 23 trails may not be exceptionally long, but they offer good variety—including bumps and tree runs—and the half-pipe and terrain park grow and improve every year. Just three miles south of town on M-553, it's popular all week among local residents and college students. Night skiing is offered Tuesday-Sunday in season, which usually runs mid-November to early April.

SHOPPING

Downtown Marquette is home to several distinctive shops worth a bit of browsing time. One charming spot that celebrates the art of reading year-round is **Snowbound Books** (118 N. 3rd St., 906/228-4448, www.snowboundbooks.com, 10am-7pm Mon.-Fri., 10am-5pm Sat.-Sun.). The UP's Scandinavian heritage also looms large in Marquette's shopping district. **Scandinavian Gifts** (130 W. Washington St., 906/225-1993, 10:30am-5:30pm Mon.-Fri., 10:30am-5pm Sat., 11am-4pm Sun.) showcases the sleek and simple lines of classic Scandinavian design in its array of glassware and silver and a great selection of Norwegian sweaters.

FOOD

For a city its size, Marquette has a very good selection of quality locally owned restaurants. The **Vierling Restaurant & Marquette Harbor Brewery** (119 S. Front St., 906/228-3533, www.thevierling.com, 11am-10pm Mon.-Sat., $15-35) stands out for its consistently good food, century-old decor, and interesting views of the Marquette Harbor ore docks. Ask for a table near the large windows in back. The menu offers considerable variety, including vegetarian dishes, whitefish served five ways, and excellent breakfasts, soups, and sandwiches. The microbrewery downstairs features British-style ales and stouts.

In Big Bay, stop by the **Lumberjack Tavern** (202 Bensinger St., 906/345-9912, restaurant noon-10pm daily, bar noon-2am daily, $7-19), which has a large local following. Once used as a backdrop for the 1959 Otto Preminger film *Anatomy of a Murder,* based on an actual murder in this very bar, this homey watering hole offers homemade pizza and specialty beers. The Lumberjack is actor and longtime Michiganian Jeff Daniels's favorite UP bar.

ACCOMMODATIONS

The best spot in Marquette is easily the ★ **Landmark Inn** (230 N. Front St., 906/228-2580, www.thelandmarkinn.com, $197-332 d). Built in the 1930s as the Northland Hotel, it hosted such luminaries as Amelia Earhart and Abbott and Costello. After falling into disrepair and eventually closing in the 1980s, it has now been beautifully restored and reopened as the luxurious Landmark. While the rates rank on the high side, you get a taste of history, a touch of elegance, and a prime location: Lake Superior on one side, downtown Marquette on the other.

There's also a surprisingly good and varied choice of lodgings in tiny Big Bay. Probably the best known is the **Big Bay Point Lighthouse Bed-and-Breakfast** (4674 County Rd. KCB, Big Bay, 906/345-9957, http://bigbaylighthouse.com, $149-229 d). It occupies a dramatic position on a rocky point just a few miles from the town of Big Bay. The redbrick keeper's home, attached to the 1896 light, has been restored and retrofitted with seven very comfortable guest rooms, all with private baths. Five have Lake Superior views. The inn has extensive grounds, more than 43 acres and 0.5 mile of shoreline set far back from busy roads and hustle and bustle. Guests are welcome to use the sauna or access other spa services through Superior Spa. You can also climb the light tower or relax in the living room, where owners Linda and Jeff Gamble have collected loads of lighthouse lore and history. Reserve well in advance.

North Country National Scenic Trail

When completed, the 4,600-mile North Country National Scenic Trail will be the longest continuous off-road hiking trail in the United States. Eventually, it will link communities, forests, and prairies across New York, Pennsylvania, Ohio, Michigan, Wisconsin, Minnesota, and North Dakota. Much of the trail is already open to hikers, cross-country skiers, and other nonmotorized recreationists, though access to bikers and equestrians depends on the land management guidelines of each section. In general, the trail is open at all times and during all seasons, although regional and seasonal closures can occur at the discretion of local landowners and land managers.

Not surprisingly, the Great Lakes State contains the longest stretches of the North Country Trail, linking Michigan's southern border to Wisconsin along the western Upper Peninsula. The complete Michigan segment traverses the Heartland, the Grand Traverse Bay region, the Mackinac Bridge, Pictured Rocks National Lakeshore, Marquette, and three national forests. Maps are available from the **North Country Trail Association** (229 E. Main St., Lowell, 866/445-3628, www.northcountrytrail.org), and although there's no specific fee for using the trail, recreationists may need to secure backcountry permits in areas like Pictured Rocks National Lakeshore or pay entrance fees in places like Wilderness State Park near Petoskey.

The Mackinac Bridge can only be crossed on foot during the famous Labor Day Bridge Walk; otherwise, hikers on the trail (which does include the bridge) must use an alternate mode to cover the span. The **Mackinac Bridge Authority** (N 415 I-75, St. Ignace, www.mackinacbridge.org) will transport hikers (and bikers) in MBA vehicles for a fee of $3.50 per person ($5 for bikes).

For more information about the trail, consult the **National Park Service** (North Country National Scenic Trail, P.O. Box 288, Lowell, MI 49331, 616/340-2004, www.nps.gov/noco), **Michigan Department of Natural Resources** (Forest Resources, P.O. Box 30452, Lansing, MI 48909, 517/284-5900, www.michigan.gov/dnr), or the three units of the **U.S. Forest Service** (www.fs.fed.us): **Huron-Manistee National Forests** (1755 S. Mitchell St., Cadillac, 231/775-2421 or 800/821-6263), **Hiawatha National Forest** (820 Rains Dr., Gladstone, 906/428-5800), and **Ottawa National Forest** (E6248 U.S. 2, Ironwood, 906/932-1330).

Camping

Van Riper State Park (851 County Road AKE, Champion, 906/339-4461, annual Recreation Passport required: $12 Michigan residents, $34 nonresidents, $9 day pass available to nonresidents only) offers 187 easily accessible modern and rustic campsites ($24-30) within earshot of U.S. 41. The 1,044-acre park also has several hiking and cross-country skiing trails as well as a fine sand beach along Lake Michigamme, which is considerably warmer than Lake Superior. Make reservations (800/447-2757, www.michigan.gov/dnr) well in advance.

INFORMATION AND SERVICES

For more information about Marquette and its surrounding areas, contact **Travel Marquette** (117 W. Washington St., 906/228-7749, www.travelmarquettemichigan.com, 9am-5pm daily). For local news, refer to the ***Mining Journal*** (www.miningjournal.net).

As the largest city in the UP, Marquette has a wide array of banks, groceries, pharmacies, gas stations, and other necessary services. For medical assistance, contact the **UP Health System** (850 W. Baraga Ave., 906/449-3000, www.mgh.org). Remember that Marquette is located in the eastern time zone.

GETTING THERE AND AROUND

As the Upper Peninsula's largest city, Marquette is one of the easiest places to reach in the western UP. **Sawyer International Airport** (MQT, 125 G Ave., Gwinn, 906/346-3308, www.sawyerairport.com) has direct flights from Chicago and

Detroit. Rent a vehicle from one of several major rental agencies and head north on M-553 to Marquette, an 18-mile trip that takes 25 minutes. **Greyhound** (800/231-2222, www.greyhound.com) and **Indian Trails** (800/292-3831, www.indiantrails.com) both offer bus service to Marquette (1325 Commerce Dr., 906/228-8393).

Most travelers drive to the city. From Sault Ste. Marie, take I-75 and M-28, a 165-mile trip that takes three hours. From Detroit, drive north on I-75, cross the Mackinac Bridge, and follow U.S. 2, M-77, and M-28 to Marquette; in light traffic, the 455-mile trip will take seven hours. From Chicago, take I-90 and I-94, I-43 and WIS-172 in Wisconsin, enter Michigan on U.S. 41, and take M-35, U.S. 2, and U.S. 41 to Marquette; the 383-mile trip takes less than 6.5 hours. I-94 is a toll road in Indiana.

Once you've reached Marquette, you'll easily be able to walk, bike, and drive around the city. Park your car and use the Marquette Transit Authority, known colloquially as **Marq-Tran** (906/225-1112, www.marqtran.com, 6:15am-7pm Mon.-Fri., 7am-7pm Sat., 7:30am-4:15pm Sun., one-way $2.60 adults, $1.30 students, seniors, and disabled), which provides wheelchair-accessible service to destinations throughout Marquette County, including Negaunee and Ishpeming, every day of the year.

NEGAUNEE AND ISHPEMING

These twin towns 15 miles west of Marquette represent the heart of the iron range. One of the Upper Peninsula's earliest iron mines, the Jackson Mine, opened here in 1847; the nearby Tilden Mine marks the lone vestige of the mining era, as it's the last iron mine operating in the range.

Ishpeming and Negaunee faded with the glory days of mining. The economy never recovered from the closing of most of the area mines in the 1960s, and the once vital downtowns were further displaced by the commercial strips along U.S. 41, which passes north of the towns. But anyone who enjoys the area's local history will find Ishpeming and Negaunee intriguing, with their leftover ornate storefronts, ramshackle antiques shops, and fenced-off cave-in areas—where the land has succumbed to the stress from mining.

Sights

One of the finest museums in the Upper

Washington Street in Marquette

Peninsula, the state-run **Michigan Iron Industry Museum** (73 Forge Rd., Negaunee, 906/475-7857, 9:30am-4:30pm daily May-Oct., 9:30am-4pm Wed.-Fri. and 1st Sat. of each month Nov.-Apr., free) is well worth the short detour off U.S. 41 to its picturesque location along the Carp River. The spot wasn't chosen for its scenery; it marks the site of one of the area's earliest iron forges, built in 1848. This small facility packs a lot of information and well-done displays into a single exhibit hall. It tells the story of Michigan's $48 billion iron mining and smelting industry, which dwarfed the California gold rush ($955 million), Michigan's lucrative logging industry ($4.4 billion), and even Michigan's venerable copper mining ($9.6 billion). You'll learn how iron prompted the development of dozens of port towns and the giant 1,000-foot ore freighters that now ply the Great Lakes. The "Technology Timeline" traces the evolution of exploration, working conditions, and mining methods.

Few people think of Ishpeming as the center of the U.S. ski industry, but America's interest in the sport first originated in northern Michigan. Upper Peninsula residents—many of them Scandinavian immigrants—established the Ishpeming Ski Club in 1887, one of the oldest continuously operating clubs in the nation, and organized the country's first ski jumping competition in 1888. Everett Kircher, visionary founder of Michigan's Boyne Mountain resort, invented the first successful snowmaking machine. Kircher's legacy was the reason Ishpeming was chosen as the site of the **U.S. Ski and Snowboard Hall of Fame and Museum** (610 Palms Ave., 906/485-6323, www.skihall.com, 10am-5pm Mon.-Sat., $5 adults, $3 students through college, under age 12 free). This is the sport's official hall of fame.

The museum, on U.S. 41 between 2nd and 3rd Streets, covers the sport from its earliest origins, beginning with a replica of a 4,000-year-old ski and pole found in Sweden. Most interesting are the displays of early ski equipment, including early poles, which often doubled as weapons; the evolution of chairlifts; and an account of the skiing soldiers of the 10th Mountain Division, who played an important role in the mountains of Italy during World War II. The Hall of Fame plaques offer insightful short biographies of those who shaped the sport, from racers to resort owners.

Recreation

In summer, the entire area is part of the comprehensive **Range Mountain Bike Trail System,** with more than 25 miles of trails stretching from Teal Lake to Lake Sally, south of Suicide Bowl. Routes are covered in the *Marquette Region Hike and Bike Trail Guide*, available from local shops, or contact **Travel Marquette** (117 W. Washington St., Marquette, 906/228-7749, www.travelmarquettemichigan.com, 9am-5pm daily).

Down Wind Sports (514 N. 3rd St., Marquette, 906/226-7112, www.downwindsports.com, 10am-7pm Mon.-Fri. 10am-5pm Sat., 11am-3pm Sun.) is a great local source for information on mountain biking, white-water kayaking, sea kayaking, rock climbing, and more. The shop also hosts weekly climbing outings, mountain bike rides, and river trips in the summer months. Down Wind sells a full line of sporting equipment, including kayaks, skis, and snowshoes, and has rentals available.

THE HURON MOUNTAINS

Ask 10 people where the Huron Mountains begin and end and you'll get 10 different answers. But everyone will agree that the 1,000 square miles of terrain fall within the vague boundaries of Lake Superior to the north and east and U.S. 41 to the south and west. Mount Arvon, about 15 miles due east of L'Anse, tops out at 1,979 feet, the highest point in the state.

On a map you'll see it's an intriguing parcel of land, virtually devoid of towns and roads. What the Huron Mountains do have, however, are peaks and valleys, virgin white pine forests, hundreds of lakes, waterfalls that don't appear on maps, the headwaters of several classic wilderness rivers, far more wildlife than people, and utter silence. Even by UP standards, it's a rugged place.

The area's preservation wasn't the result of happy accident. Beginning around the 1880s, the Huron Mountains became the wilderness retreat of choice for several millionaire industrialists. Cyrus McCormick, head of the lucrative farm-implement company that would become International Harvester, amassed a huge wilderness estate around White Deer Lake, now part of the Ottawa National Forest's McCormick Tract Wilderness Area. Frederick Miller of Miller Brewing owned his piece of wilderness at Craig Lake, now a wilderness state park. Dozens of others owned camps at the Huron Mountain Club, an organization so exclusive that even Henry Ford was turned down for membership when he first applied. The members easily had enough clout to stop construction of a road that was to link L'Anse with Big Bay—County Road 550 abruptly ends west of Big Bay at a gate and security guard house.

Today the 25,000-acre enclave is owned mostly by the descendants of those original members. Though locals grumble about the lack of access to the property, the Huron Mountain Club has proved to be an exceptional steward of the land. It has kept away the loggers, miners, and developers, leaving what some consider the most magnificent wilderness remaining in the Midwest. Within its boundaries lie towering virgin pines, blue-ribbon trout streams, and pristine lakes. Happily, not all of the land is privately held; much of the Huron Mountains wilderness is public land.

Big Bay Area

Many people approach the Huron Mountains from the east, where County Road 550 climbs 30 miles out of Marquette to the tiny town of Big Bay (population 270). Sited above Lake Independence and within minutes of Lake Superior, Big Bay is sandwiched between wilderness and inland sea. The town has swung from prosperity to near ghost-town status more than once, first as a bustling logging outpost, then as one of Henry Ford's company towns, home to busy sawmills. More recently, residents joke about how the local bank, well aware of the town's volatile economy, was loath to loan money to town businesses—an overly conservative stance that proved to be the bank's undoing. While the town's 20 businesses thrived, the bank closed down. Visitors now frequent Big Bay for its Huron Mountains access, Lake Superior harbor, Lake Independence fishing, and unique lodgings.

McCormick Wilderness

Once the private wilderness retreat of Cyrus McCormick, whose father invented the reaping machine, this 27-square-mile tract of wilderness was willed to the U.S. Forest Service by his family in 1967. Today it remains in pristine wilderness condition—remote, undeveloped, and largely unused. In other words, it's perfect for backcountry hiking and camping. No-trace camping is permitted throughout the wilderness area. For more information, contact the **Ottawa National Forest Ranger District** (4810 E. M-28, Kenton, 906/852-3500, 9am-5pm daily).

To access the McCormick Tract, follow U.S. 41/M-28 west from Marquette about 50 miles to Champion. Just after you cross the Peshekee River, follow the first paved road north. This is County Road 607, also called the Peshekee Grade or the Huron Bay Grade. In about 10 miles, you'll see a sign for Arfelin Lake; take the next road to the right and watch for a sign and small parking area.

Once here, you're on your own to explore this rugged terrain of high hills, rivers, muskeg, and bedrock outcroppings. Don't expect marked and maintained hiking trails. This tract is wild, and with the exception of a well-worn path to White Deer Lake, where the McCormicks' lodge once stood, you'll mostly be traveling cross-country. A compass and topographic map are absolute necessities. Wildlife sightings can be excellent as the state's largest moose herd roams here, which in turn has attracted predators like the elusive gray wolf. You're not likely to see a wolf, but may be treated to its hollow wail at your camp in the evening.

Background

The Landscape

GEOLOGY AND GEOGRAPHY

Ask Michiganians to locate a spot in the Lower Peninsula, and they'll most likely use the palm of their right hand (or the back of their left) as an impromptu map to pinpoint locales. Shaped like a mitten, the Lower Peninsula is 286 miles long and 220 miles across at its widest point, and includes a landmass jutting out into Lake Huron universally identified as "the Thumb."

Geographically, no other state is so distinctly divided. Michigan consists of two separate landmasses—the Lower Peninsula and the

Upper Peninsula—circled by Lakes Michigan, Superior, Huron, and Erie, and connected by the Mackinac Bridge, which spans five miles across the Straits of Mackinac.

The Upper Peninsula, which, at its greatest extent, runs for 215 miles from north to south, shares a border with northeastern Wisconsin, then stretches east for 334 miles between Lakes Superior and Michigan, and ultimately touches a third Great Lake, Huron, before reaching its terminus at Drummond Island.

Even farther north is 46-mile-long Isle Royale, the largest island in Lake Superior and Michigan's northernmost point. The entire Isle Royale archipelago is a national park, the remotest and perhaps the least visited site in the National Park System.

Over a period of several hundred million years, a combination of cataclysmic volcanic eruptions and soupy tropical seas initially formed what is now Michigan. In the northern part of the state, around Lake Superior and northern Lake Huron, erupting volcanoes laid down thick layers of basalt that later tilted and faulted, forming the area's rugged, rocky topography of mountain ranges and steep shorelines.

Farther south, a shallow sea covered the vast Michigan Basin, an area that today overlays the four lower Great Lakes. Over millions of years, sand, shells, and other detritus compacted into thick layers of sedimentary rock—the limestone, dolomite, sandstone, and shale now found along the shores of Lake Michigan.

Much later, powerful glaciers added an indelible touch to the landscape, the most recent occurring some 12,000 years ago. Four separate ice sheets scraped across the region, scouring out depressions that became lakes, lowlands, and ragged shorelines, while at the same time reducing the majesty of the peaks found in the western Upper Peninsula, known today as the Porcupine Mountains. As the ice melted and the glaciers retreated, low-lying areas filled with the runoff to create the modern-day Great Lakes.

Michigan comprises three distinct land regions: the Superior Uplands, Northern Highlands, and Great Lakes Plains. The Superior Uplands span the western two-thirds of the Upper Peninsula, a region formed by ancient volcanic activity. It's a landscape of dramatic beauty, characterized by rugged basalt cliffs and thick boreal forests of fir, spruce, and birch. This portion of Michigan is part of the vast Canadian Shield, a geological region that dips down from the Arctic and includes the northern Great Lakes region and the west side of Hudson Bay, resembling a giant horseshoe. Much of the region occupies an elevation of 1,000 feet or higher, including Michigan's highest natural point, Mount Arvon, which tops out at 1,979 feet. The Superior Uplands contain some of the nation's richest deposits of minerals, especially copper and iron ore.

South of the Superior Uplands lie the Northern Highlands, covering the eastern Upper Peninsula and northern Lower Peninsula. Here, basalt bedrock gives way to sandstone and limestone, and boreal forests segue into pine and hardwoods. Once heavily logged for its vast, valuable stands of white and red pine, the Northern Highlands' natural beauty make it an area prized by recreationists for its woods, water, and wildlife.

The Great Lakes Plains stretch across southern Michigan as well as into southern Wisconsin and northern Ohio. This region was heavily impacted by a series of ice ages and their powerful glaciers, which left behind a flattened landscape of sandy lake beds, wetlands, prairies, and fertile topsoil (believed to have been dragged from points farther north), making it Michigan's primary farming region for a variety of fruit and vegetable crops.

Altogether, Michigan's landmass, including inland lakes, covers 58,530 square miles, making it the second-largest state east of the Mississippi. But it is water that

Previous: the Great Seal of the State of Michigan

Two States in One

Is it a case of sibling rivalry or a marriage of irreconcilable differences? That's what many outsiders may wonder about the Upper and Lower Peninsulas of Michigan, physically separated by a five-mile bridge and often thought to be a world apart. Residents of the Lower Peninsula occasionally dismiss the Upper Peninsula (UP) as a bug-infested backwoods. Not surprisingly, UP residents (who proudly call themselves "Yoopers") find the generalization insulting and hypocritical, especially when seeing the outsiders enjoy the UP's woods, wildlife, and beaches while on vacation.

The fact that the two peninsulas form a single state is actually a historical anomaly. The Michigan Territory acquired the UP as a consolation prize in 1837 with the resolution of the Toledo War.

Both Michigan and Ohio had fought for control of the Toledo Strip, a valuable port on Lake Erie. To earn admission to the Union, the Michigan Territory was forced by Congress to relinquish all rights to the Toledo Strip in exchange for the "barren wasteland" of the Upper Peninsula. Thought of at the time to be useless, the area ultimately produced priceless quantities of iron ore and copper, working in Michigan the economic favor.

Much of the rivalry is good-natured; Yoopers, for instance, joke about blowing up the Mackinac Bridge and display bumper stickers portraying a giant UP with a tiny LP dangling from its eastern end. Yet beneath the humor a kernel of seriousness resides. Upper Peninsula residents sometimes feel shortchanged, in that they pay taxes to a distant state capital and receive little in return—save perhaps for another protected land or wildlife program, of which they already have plenty. Occasionally the passions spark a pseudo-serious drive to secede from Michigan and become the nation's 51st state. Most observers, however, see such a move as highly unlikely.

Members of Da Yoopers, a musical comedy troupe from Ishpeming, indulge in a bit a parody when they sing, "Dear Mr. Governor, you better turn us loose / We asked you for some rest stops, instead you sent us moose / The honeymoon is over, the declaration's written / We'll take what's above the bridge, and you can keep the mitten."

defines Michigan and helps to make it the 11th-largest state. Along with its 3,288-mile shoreline—second only to Alaska—it encompasses more than 11,000 lakes, over 36,000 miles of rivers, and nearly 200 named waterfalls, and boasts 16 federally designated Wild and Scenic Rivers. Each peninsula is also home to a national lakeshore: Pictured Rocks in the Upper and Sleeping Bear Dunes in the Lower.

It's no wonder, then, that many of Michigan's nicknames—the Great Lakes State, Water Wonderland, or the Land of Hiawatha—accurately describe this most beautiful of Midwestern states.

CLIMATE

Contrary to popular beliefs, Michigan's climate does vary, given the wide range of latitude covered by two peninsulas. For most of the Lower Peninsula, however, the presence of the Great Lakes provides a degree of moderation, as the lakes cool the hot summer air and warm the cold winter winds.

Michigan has four distinct seasons. Summers require shorts and T-shirts almost everywhere, except near Lake Superior, where you'll want a sweatshirt handy. July and August temperatures average in the 80s Fahrenheit in the Lower Peninsula and the 70s in the Upper Peninsula. From December through February, afternoon highs generally hover in the 30s in the Lower Peninsula and the 20s (or below) in the UP.

Exceptions to these norms are, however, quite common. You can enjoy springlike skiing conditions in the UP in February or freeze on Thanksgiving in Detroit. You may swelter on a summer hike through the woods, then grab for your fleece on a Great Lakes beach.

The Lake Effect

The Great Lakes act like insulators—slow to warm up, slow to cool down. This provides

Average Temperatures

(High/Low °F)

MONTH	DETROIT	MARQUETTE
January	32/19	25/13
February	35/21	28/14
March	46/29	36/22
April	59/39	47/33
May	70/49	59/43
June	79/60	68/52
July	84/64	74/59
August	81/63	74/59
September	74/55	67/52
October	62/43	54/41
November	49/34	40/29
December	36/24	29/18

optimal temperatures for Michigan's valuable fruit harvest: Lake Michigan moderates springtime temperatures, preventing fruit trees and vines from budding until the threat of frost has passed.

The Great Lakes also have a dramatic effect on snowfall. Dry winter air travels over the Great Lakes as the prevailing western winds, absorbing moisture. When this air hits land, it unloads precipitation in the form of snow. Meteorologists refer to this phenomenon as lake-effect snow, which can be surprisingly localized, and explains why you'll find many of the Lower Peninsula's ski resorts clustered along the Lake Michigan coastline.

The prevailing western breezes also affect water temperatures, most noticeably on Lake Michigan. In summer, the warm surface waters tend to blow right into the sandy beaches along the lake's eastern shoreline. While Lake Michigan is rarely warm enough for swimming on the Wisconsin side, the Michigan coast is generally quite pleasant—as evidenced by the bevy of popular beaches along the shore.

Lake Superior is decidedly different. Temperatures on this deep, huge northern lake never climb out of the 40s, save for the occasional shallow bay. "No one's ever drowned in Lake Superior," a humorous saying goes. "They all die of hypothermia first."

Freshwater freezes faster than saltwater, and the Great Lakes will often freeze over from land to several miles out. The ice usually gets thick enough for brave souls to snowmobile to the islands, especially nearby ones like Mackinac. The commercial shipping season shuts down mid-January to late March, and bad weather can delay it even longer. Commercial freighters can cut through ice up to a foot thick. Anything more massive requires the assistance of the U.S. Coast Guard's icebreaker *Mackinaw,* which is a 240-foot reinforced vessel that was commissioned in June 2006 and named after its famous predecessor.

Michigan Winters

Frequent snow and cold temperatures dominate northern Michigan from Thanksgiving through Easter. If you're looking for a place with guaranteed snow coverage, head to the

Upper Peninsula, which gets blanketed with more than 150 inches annually, and where temperatures are consistently below freezing. While the Detroit area averages about 43 inches of snow a year, frequent temperature spikes result in a typical succession of snowfall and snowmelt cycles each winter.

UP snows are legendary, especially in the Keweenaw Peninsula, where 300-inch winters have been known to occur. Sticking far out into Lake Superior, it really gets nailed with lake-effect snows. In summer, you'll often notice curious elevated pier-like contraptions leading from some houses to the sidewalk—no need to shovel those front walks in winter until there's at least 24 inches on the ground. Ladders nailed to roofs are there for a reason, too. When accumulated snows threaten to collapse the roof, the ladders give a foothold from which to clear off the stuff.

It's essential to keep in mind the windchill factor, which is the combined impact of cold temperatures and wind speed. If it's 5°F outside, a 15-mph wind will make it feel like -25°F. Besides being exceedingly uncomfortable, a high windchill elevates the risk for frostbite and hypothermia. Weather forecasts generally warn about the windchill factor. Remember to consider both the temperature and wind speed when dressing for the outdoors.

Despite these concerns, many people welcome Michigan's winter, which accounts for a significant piece of the state's tourism economy. Few other areas in the Midwest can offer as reliable a season for skiing, snowboarding, snowmobiling, ice fishing, ice-skating, and snowshoeing.

Plants and Animals

TREES AND PLANTS

There's a reason that the white pine is the state tree: Vast stands of it once covered the northern portions of the state, making Michigan the nation's leading lumber center. Michigan pine largely rebuilt Chicago after the Great Fire and supplied a hungry nation as it expanded westward across the treeless plains.

Today, a few tracts of virgin white pine, red pine, and cedar remain in Michigan, magnificent species scraping the sky several stories overhead. Much of Michigan's original prime logging land is now second-growth pines, many now approaching the height of their ancestors. Today's logging operations still clear-cut, but in much smaller sections, and are increasingly turning to selective cutting methods.

Along with pines in the north, much of the state is covered in hardwoods, especially oak, maple, aspen, and birch. Since Michigan has few native prairies, except in the southwestern corner of the state, many of its plant species are woodland varieties, including columbine, iris, aster, blazing star, various berries, and several species of orchids. Along the coastal dunes, milkweed and wormwood thrive.

MAMMALS AND BIRDS

Though it's called the Wolverine State, there's no evidence of a significant population of the mammal in Michigan in over 200 years. In 2004, however, a wolverine was seen and photographed near Bad Axe in the Thumb area. Wildlife biologists were uncertain as to its origin and failed to locate any additional specimens.

The state's time-honored nickname may have originated from early fur traders, who brought wolverine pelts to Michigan's numerous trading posts.

With more than half the state forested, Michigan harbors significant numbers of red foxes, skunks, squirrels, badgers, raccoons, porcupines, minks, muskrats, bats, and other small mammals. The state has a huge—and problematic—population of white-tailed deer throughout various areas and a very healthy number of black bears in its northern reaches. Elk can be found in the northeastern portion of the Lower Peninsula, the result of a successful reintroduction program. Wolves, moose, bobcats, and cougars live in secluded areas of the UP.

Some 300 kinds of birds also live in the state, including such notable species as bald eagles, peregrine falcons, loons, swans, herons, and dozens of songbirds. Hunting is popular for game birds, such as ducks, geese, grouse, and pheasant. Michigan lies on a major migratory pathway, so it offers excellent bird-watching in spring and fall. Of special note is the hawk migration, as thousands fly between the southern Lower Peninsula and Canada.

REPTILES, AMPHIBIANS, AND FISH

The backwoods and lakeshores of Michigan are rife with reptiles and amphibians, including numerous varieties of toads, frogs, salamanders, and snakes.

Fortunately, only one venomous snake makes its habitat in Michigan, the eastern massasauga rattlesnake. The massasauga inhabits a wide swath of the country, from the desert Southwest stretching northeast to include much of the upper Midwest, including all of Michigan's Lower Peninsula and parts of southwestern Ontario. The snake can be identified by blotches of dark gray or brown on the top of its back, which gradually becoming smaller on it sides. The massasauga is regarded as shy and known to attack only when provoked; reports of humans being bitten are very rare. Although it is a venomous snake, the only deaths associated with a bite are of victims who did not seek proper treatment. It's recommended to avoid hiking in areas of low visibility to keep from accidentally stepping on one.

With so much water, fish thrive in both the Great Lakes and inland waters. Though commercial fishing has decreased dramatically in the last few decades—the result of overfishing and the accidental introduction of the lamprey eel and zebra mussel—sportfishing remains popular on the Great Lakes. Chinook and coho salmon, steelhead, and lake and brown trout remain plentiful. On inland waters, walleye and yellow perch are prized for flavor, while muskie and northern pike are considered top sport fish. Bass and trout can also be found in inland lakes. Additionally, Michigan has several blue-ribbon streams, especially near Traverse City and Grayling in the Lower Peninsula, and in the eastern UP.

INSECTS AND ARACHNIDS

While parts of Michigan lie along the migratory route of the stunning monarch butterfly, the state also has its share of bothersome insects. The first hatch of mosquitoes usually occurs in early June, depending on local weather conditions. Unless they're carrying a harmful disease like the West Nile virus, they won't seriously injure you, but their sting will cause a small itchy lump. Most populous in woods and low-lying wet areas, and most active at dusk, mosquitoes can persist all summer, but tend to be less of a problem as the season wears on, especially if conditions are dry.

The best way to avoid mosquitoes is to stay in a breeze and wear long pants and long sleeves. While repellent with diethyltoluamide (DEET) is said to be effective, studies have linked it to various health problems. If you choose to use repellent, be sure to wash your hands carefully before eating, and read the label warnings, especially before applying it on small children.

Blackflies can be an equally obnoxious travel companion. Like mosquitoes, blackflies don't usually pose any health risk but have a nasty bite—somewhere between a mosquito bite and a bee sting on the pain scale. Blackflies look like houseflies, only larger. They tend to be worst in the deep woods and in early summer. UP blackflies can be the stuff of legend; anyone planning time in the

Threatened Plants of the Great Lakes

In the summer, Michigan's forests, riverbanks, and beaches are rife with native ferns, weeds, and wildflowers. While some of these vibrant landscapes remain relatively intact, others have long suffered from human encroachment. As a result, the following endemic plants are at risk for extinction, due to habitat loss or destruction:

- **American hart's-tongue fern**—once prevalent throughout the UP's Hiawatha National Forest, now threatened by development, recreational activities, and former logging and quarrying practices
- **Dwarf lake iris**—once prevalent throughout the UP's Hiawatha National Forest and along the northern shores of Lakes Michigan and Huron, now threatened by development, off-road vehicle use, and tourism
- **Eastern prairie fringed orchid**—once prevalent throughout Michigan's prairies and wetlands, now threatened by agricultural practices
- **Houghton's goldenrod**—once prevalent along the sandy shores of Lakes Michigan and Huron, now threatened by human coastal activities
- **Lakeside daisy**—once prevalent in the UP's Hiawatha National Forest, now threatened by limestone quarrying
- **Michigan monkey-flower**—once prevalent along Michigan's streams and lakeshores, now endangered by recreational and residential development
- **Pitcher's thistle**—once prevalent amid Michigan's coastal dunes, now threatened by development, road construction, and recreational activities

While enjoying Michigan's great outdoors, take care not to disturb these and other precious natural resources. For further information, consult the **U.S. Fish and Wildlife Service** (www.fws.gov) or **The Nature Conservancy** (www.nature.org).

backcountry there would be wise to carry the strongest repellent that they can find and pack a head net, too.

The wilds of Michigan are also favored by a variety of beetles, including the multicolored Asian lady beetle, which was imported in the early 20th century to control other insects. You might also encounter spiders on your hikes through the Great Lakes State. Be especially careful of the black widow and the extremely rare brown recluse; the bites of both are poisonous and painful.

REINTRODUCTION PROGRAMS

Michigan has had great success with reintroducing two large mammals to the state. The eastern elk, once common in Michigan, had disappeared from the state by 1875. In 1918, state officials relocated seven Rocky Mountain elk near Wolverine, in Cheboygan County in the northeastern Lower Peninsula. Today more than 900 of the animals roam the woods and meadows of a four-county area. The largest concentration lies within the Pigeon River Country State Forest near Vanderbilt.

In the mid-1980s, moose were reintroduced to a remote area south of the UP's Huron Mountains, where officials released a total of 59 from Ontario, Canada, in two separate operations. The innovative method of their reintroduction was especially interesting: Wildlife biologists airlifted the moose one by one in a sling dangling beneath a helicopter to a base camp, after which they were trucked 600 miles to the Huron Mountains. Van Riper State Park near Champion has an interesting display with photos of the noteworthy "moose lifts." The effort proved successful. Today, an estimated 430 moose roam the western UP, while approximately 100 inhabit the eastern half.

ENDANGERED SPECIES

According to the latest review by the Michigan Department of Natural Resources (DNR), Michigan is home to roughly 130 threatened or endangered animals and insects, and more than 275 plant species. The **U.S. Fish and Wildlife Service** (www.fws.gov) operates an ongoing recovery program designed to revive their numbers in order to maintain a healthy ecosystem.

The resurgence of the gray wolf in the Upper Peninsula is an example of the success brought by federal protection. In 2012, years of conservation efforts under the federal Endangered Species Act allowed populations to sufficiently recover for the FWS to delist the animal. For a time, proposals were floated that would allow the hunting of gray wolves to resume. Complaints lodged by the Humane Society and other groups prompted a federal court to relist the gray wolf in December 2014. This move came despite the strong desires of many UP residents, who have long pleaded for management efforts, including the use of lethal control against problem wolves, particularly those found on their properties.

History

MICHIGAN'S INDIGENOUS PEOPLES

Buried under layers of glacial ice until about 10,000 years ago, the land that is now Michigan was inhospitable to many of the indigenous cultures that thrived in much of the Midwest, including the Paleo and Archaic cultures. Some of the first recorded signs of civilization can be found in the Upper Peninsula's Keweenaw Peninsula, where the Copper Culture people of about 5000-500 BC left evidence of their skill as prehistoric miners, devising ways to extract copper from bedrock and fashioning it into tools. Archaeologists believe that they may have been the world's earliest toolmakers.

Later, the Algonquin people migrated to the Great Lakes region from the banks of the St. Lawrence Seaway, probably after AD 1000. The Algonquins later split into three groups: the Ottawa (or Odawa), the Ojibwa (or Chippewa), and the Potawatomi. Together, they called themselves the Anishinabe ("first people") and named their new land *Michi Gami* ("large lake"). In and around the Great Lakes, they found the state's abundant wildlife—including fish, white-tailed deer, moose, elk, and black bear—and rich natural resources that for centuries provided for their needs.

The three groups coexisted peacefully, each moving to a different area. The Ottawa settled around Sault Ste. Marie, the Straits of Mackinac, and the Leelanau Peninsula; the Ojibwa moved west, along the shores of Lake Superior; and the Potawatomi headed south, to the southern half of the Lower Peninsula. They communicated regularly, and their peaceable relationship proved valuable when others came to their lands. Together, they successfully fought off the warring Iroquois, who came from the east in the 1600s, and presented themselves as a strong and unified people when the Europeans arrived.

FRENCH SETTLERS

Étienne Brulé, the first European to arrive in what is now Michigan in 1615, was more interested in exploiting the land than worshipping it. Brulé was sent by Samuel de Champlain, lieutenant governor of New France, who hoped to find copper and a shortcut to Asia. Brulé sent back reports describing the land's untamed beauty and strange new flora and fauna. Other opportunists soon followed. Some were after Michigan's rich supply of

Pontiac: Hero of the Ottawa

The son of an Ojibwa mother and Ottawa father, Pontiac (1720-1769) eventually became the chief of the Ottawa, Ojibwa, and Potawatomi peoples in the Great Lakes region. He is best known for organizing the most powerful coalition in Native American history.

During the French and Indian War (1754-1763), Native Americans joined the French in their battles against the British over land claims in North America. Nonetheless, the British were able to drive the French out of their most lucrative fur trading areas. In early 1763, Pontiac organized a Detroit-area conference for the many nations of the Great Lakes and Ohio Valley and convinced them to join together to fend off the British. The far-reaching alliance was a remarkable achievement, considering how widespread and disparate the indigenous people were at the time.

Pontiac's diplomatic skills were matched by his military ones. In 1763, Pontiac's forces seized every British post between the Straits of Mackinac and western New York, save for two. The fort at Detroit proved their downfall. While some accounts claim Pontiac's plan to capture Detroit was exposed by a mixed-race woman, his men did besiege the fort for five months, withdrawing only when the French cut off their supplies. Pontiac and his people retreated to their hunting grounds and eventually signed a peace treaty with the British at Detroit in 1765.

Despite pressure from the French to renew warfare, Pontiac lived among the British peacefully until 1769, when he was mysteriously killed in Illinois by a Native American reportedly bribed by a British trader.

furs, others after the souls of what they saw as a godless land. Among the most famous of these early explorers was Father Jacques Marquette, who established the state's first permanent settlement at Sault Ste. Marie in 1668 and a second outpost at the straits of Michilimackinac in 1671. The French *coureurs de bois*, a loose term for unlicensed traders, provided a sharp contrast to the priests and nobility. Rugged individualists, they lived among the Native Americans, respected their customs, and hunted the region's rich stores of game.

Few efforts were made to establish a permanent settlement until 1696, when Antoine de la Mothe Cadillac (born Antoine Laumet) convinced France's Louis XIV that the area was under threat from the British, who were forming alliances with the Native Americans, and that it would be a strategic stronghold for the French crown.

The king sent Cadillac and a 100-strong passel of priests, soldiers, and settlers to establish a more strategically located settlement in 1701. After building Fort Pontchartrain de Detroit, Cadillac persuaded several Native American communities to form a sort of coalition with his forces and build settlements near the fort. Within a short time, thousands of Native Americans and several hundred French families lived in the surrounding area, many establishing narrow "ribbon farms" along the Detroit River. Known as *la ville détroit* ("the village at the strait"), Detroit soon became an important trading post and strategic base for the area's continued settlement. Today, Detroit remains one of the oldest settlements in the Midwest.

BRITISH SETTLERS

The area wasn't peaceful for long. As the fur trade became more lucrative, animosity between the British and French peaked, resulting in the French and Indian War of the mid-1700s. The war ended with the 1763 Treaty of Paris, which terminated the 145-year era of French colonialism and ushered in British rule. Skirmishes continued, though, especially around the Straits of Mackinac. Today museums and historic state parks in the area chronicle the events.

While the French had treated the Native Americans with a certain amount of respect, the British allied themselves with Native

American nations that were traditional enemies of those indigenous to the area. The British actively discouraged settlement of the state's interior to protect their rich fur empire. In 1783, after the American Revolutionary War had ended, the 1783 Treaty of Paris passed the lands to the newly independent United States.

STATEHOOD

The 1825 opening of New York's Erie Canal, which connected Albany on the Hudson River to Buffalo on Lake Erie, created a new water route that enabled the descendants of European settlers on the East Coast to move westward and settle in the Michigan Territory. From 1820 to 1830, the population more than tripled to just over 31,000. In January 1837, the burgeoning territory was awarded statehood, making Michigan the 26th state in the Union.

By 1840, Michigan's population had grown to 200,000. Early industries included farming and agriculture, with lumber becoming a hugely successful enterprise in the later part of the century. Altogether, more than 160 billion feet of pine were cut and hauled from Michigan's north woods by the 1890s—enough to build 10 million six-room houses. While the southern part of the state gradually grew more civilized, the north woods were long filled with wild and rollicking logging camps.

INDIAN REMOVAL ACT

In one of the saddest chapters in our nation's history, President Andrew Jackson signed the Indian Removal Act in 1830, giving the U.S. government permission to "trade" Native American lands east of the Mississippi for unspecified lands out west. The federal government claimed it was for their own protection, predicting—correctly—that settlers would continue to surge into their homelands in the name of frontier expansion.

The Native Americans, of course, had no interest in leaving what had been their homeland for centuries. Communities in northern Michigan were largely ignored by the federal Indian Bureau at first, most likely because the government found their lands undesirable at the time. However, the Potawatomi, who lived on valuable farmland in southern Michigan, were forcibly removed. By the mid-1800s, treaties legally took away more and more Native American land in both the Upper and Lower Peninsulas and established many of the reservations that exist today.

The new state government, however, did treat the indigenous people with a modicum of decency. In 1850, Native Americans were given the right to vote and even run for office in counties where the population was predominantly Native American—a concession unheard of elsewhere for many years.

THE COPPER RUSH

In 1840, state geologist Douglass Houghton confirmed the presence of copper in the Upper Peninsula's Keweenaw Peninsula—vast deposits of pure native copper, much of it right near the surface. The United States acquired the western half of the UP and its mineral rights from the Ojibwa in 1842 as prospectors began flooding toward the wild and remote Keweenaw. The young country had an insatiable appetite for the metal, first for new industrial machinery and, later, for Civil War hardware, electrical wiring, and other innovations.

The copper rush began almost overnight, first with prospectors, then with large mining enterprises swarming the Keweenaw. Lucky prospectors secured deck space on Great Lakes vessels, sailing up Lakes Huron and Michigan, then along the southern shore of Lake Superior. But hundreds of others straggled through the roadless wilderness, trudging overland through northern Wisconsin by snowshoe or following rivers through thick forests to reach the fabled riches. It was the nation's first mineral rush. Copper employed thousands of immigrant laborers, built cities, made millionaires, and prompted extravagant luxuries like opera houses and mansions. The net value of the Upper Peninsula's copper deposits is hard to overstate. Ultimately, it exceeded that of the California gold rush tenfold.

The entire nation turned to the Keweenaw for its copper. From 1845 to 1895, the Keweenaw Peninsula produced 75 percent of U.S. copper; during the Civil War, it produced 90 percent. More than 400 mining companies operated in the Keweenaw over the course of the 19th century, and the resulting demand for labor drew immigrants from more than 30 countries—most notably the British Isles and Scandinavia. With multiple cultures sharing the same mine shafts and communities, Copper Country served as one of the nation's first true melting pots.

By the mid-20th century, however, many of the mines were depleted. With little economic diversity, the area fell into decline, leaving behind tattered houses and empty streets.

THE 20TH CENTURY AND THE RISE OF THE AUTOMOBILE

In the early 1900s, industrial giants like Kellogg and Dow were getting their start, giving rise to industries that continue to flourish today. Yet no innovation had as much influence on the state or the nation as the automobile, initially termed the "horseless carriage." Born shortly after the turn of the 20th century, the industry experienced phenomenal growth, ultimately producing behemoths like Ford, Chrysler, and General Motors. As the entire nation grew dependent on their products, the powerful Big Three automakers altered the character of Michigan—and the nation—forever.

With the auto industry came thousands of high-paying jobs and an improved standard of living. Henry Ford's revolutionary $5-a-day wage attracted workers from across the country and around the world, making Detroit one of the country's richest melting pots. Agricultural workers from the Deep South, looking for a better wage, came north to work in the gleaming new factories. Many were African Americans, an influx that created Detroit's largest ethnic group.

As time passed, changing working conditions and a lack of employee representation in the auto factories spurred another American invention: the labor movement and the rise of unions.

1930-1960

While labor and craft unions existed in Michigan since before statehood, few were very organized until the 1930s. A number of factors contributed to their growth, including auto industry automation, the uncertainties of the Great Depression, and the pro-labor political environment ushered in by the New Deal. The most famous confrontation between labor and management was the 1936 sit-down strike in Flint, which led to General Motors accepting the United Auto Workers as the sole bargaining agent for its employees.

Following the economic despair of the Depression and the shortages of World War II, the 1950s were an era of great growth and prosperity. Only Florida and California attracted more people during the decade. The increase in the number of school-age children led to a considerable expansion of the state's K-12 education system and the founding of new community colleges and other facilities of higher education. In the early 1950s the Mackinac Bridge Authority was formed and tasked with constructing a link between the Upper and Lower Peninsulas. Construction on one of the largest and most innovative engineering projects in the country began in 1954. After more than three years of perilous labor over the turbulent Straits of Mackinac, the "Big Mac" opened to the public on November 1, 1957, bringing together the two disparate halves of the state.

THE CIVIL RIGHTS ERA

Racial tensions have occasionally erupted into violence throughout Michigan's history, particularly during the 1960s. In 1967, growing tensions between Detroit's African American community (at that point comprising some 30 percent of the city's population) and the overwhelmingly white police force came to a head. During the early morning hours of Sunday,

July 23, a police raid on a "blind pig"—an after-hours drinking establishment—touched off several days of civil unrest, which included considerable burning and looting. Before national guard and federal troops restored order, 43 people had been killed, nearly 1,200 injured, and over 7,200 arrested. Damage to property topped $50 million. This tragic event came just days after a similar insurrection in Newark, New Jersey, and was just one of several violent episodes of the era.

In some ways, the city of Detroit and the state of Michigan are still affected by those impactful events. While the makeshift yellow fences that bordered riot sites have long been replaced by new development throughout the city, racial segregation and the exodus of the middle class have only accelerated over the succeeding decades. Race relations are an ongoing front-burner issue in Detroit, which today is one of the most racially divided metropolitan areas in the nation.

CONTEMPORARY TIMES

Along with healing racial wounds, Michigan faces other challenges in the coming years. The state must wrestle with an increasingly poor urban population, growing concern with quality of life, and an overdependence on the ever-fluctuating fortunes of the automobile industry—even with the 2009 bailout by the federal government.

On the positive side, one of Michigan's enduring strengths is its abundant natural resources, including one of the nation's largest forest areas and a staggering supply of freshwater—a commodity that may ultimately prove more valuable than oil. With a 19th-century history of land scarred from clear-cutting virgin forests and poorly executed mining practices, one hopes that Michigan has learned some lessons. Only time will tell if the state chooses to protect or exploit its considerable assets—both human and natural.

Government and Economy

GOVERNMENT

During the 19th century and the early decades of the 20th century, Michigan remained a reliable stronghold of the Republican Party. In 1854 the first official meeting of the GOP was held in Jackson, at a site showcased today by a Michigan Historical Marker. Beginning in the Depression era, however, the Democratic Party began making major inroads in the state.

Labor union leadership, including the powerful United Auto Workers, became much more active in postwar politics, reflecting the union's interest in larger social issues and quality of life outside the workplace. The voting power of African Americans, whose population had more than doubled between 1940 and 1950, also helped strengthen the Democratic Party when it became an early supporter of the civil rights cause. In 1948, Democrat G. Mennen Williams won the first of what would be six two-year terms as Michigan's governor.

Beginning in the 1950s and continuing through today, Michigan politics has been largely bipartisan. Among recent Michigan politicians in the spotlight was Governor Jennifer M. Granholm, a Democrat who became the state's first female governor in 2002, following Republican John Engler's 12-year administration. As governor, Granholm worked to diversify Michigan's economy, expand educational opportunities for residents, and create universal access to affordable health care. Part of President Barack Obama's economic advisory team, Granholm was briefly considered for appointment to the U.S. Supreme Court in 2009.

In 2010 Republican Rick Snyder, a venture capitalist from Ann Arbor, was elected Granholm's successor. Since then, Snyder has garnered mixed reactions from Michiganians, particularly due to controversial measures like the 2011 Public Employee Domestic Partner Benefit Restriction Act, which prevents the same sex domestic partners of local and state government employees from receiving health benefits, and the 2012 Employee Free Choice Act, which provides that payment of union dues cannot be required as a condition of employment.

Another noteworthy figure is former Detroit mayor Dennis Archer, a Democrat and former Michigan Supreme Court justice, who took over from controversial mayor Coleman Young, also a Democrat, in 1994. While Young was best known for antagonizing the suburbs and championing the rights of urban African Americans, Archer proved to be much more of a peacemaker, striving to mend the seemingly insurmountable rift between the predominantly black city and its predominantly white suburbs. Archer declined to run for reelection in 2001, opting to return to private life.

The early years of the 21st century were accompanied by wide-scale political corruption in Detroit. Kwame Kilpatrick, who served as mayor from 2002 until 2008, became embroiled in two major scandals, one of which led to his 2013 conviction on federal racketeering charges. In 2013 Mike Duggan was elected mayor and has presided over an unprecedented wave of investment and development in the downtown and midtown areas. At this writing, all signs point to this trend continuing.

ECONOMY

Despite its patchwork of farm and field, Michigan remains a highly industrialized state. Manufacturing is a leading industry, followed by tourism and agriculture.

For almost two centuries, Michigan has been a mirror of the country's great industrial transition. As the state's economy has evolved from agriculture and fur trading to metals, logging, and, finally, automobile manufacturing, the state has ridden a roller coaster that shows no signs of stopping.

In fact, the ups and downs affecting the state's economic fortunes are nothing new. Like the auto industry, which has experienced both wild success and dismal failure, so it was with the mining era in the Upper Peninsula, which left a legacy of fantastic wealth juxtaposed with depressed towns huddled around depleted mines. In the 1880s, just before the birth of the automobile, many Detroit residents thought that the city had already seen its greatest growth. Little did they know that in the city's workshops and laboratories, inventors were talking about a revolution.

Industry

Most Americans today need only look in their garages or on their kitchen tables to find evidence of Michigan's diversified economy. While a variety of businesses call Michigan home, the state will always be associated with the automobile industry. Michigan's largest town, nicknamed the "Motor City," and most of the state's economy are driven by the most enduring of American inventions.

With $5-a-day wages and innovative automated assembly lines, Henry Ford revolutionized the industrial world with his "horseless carriage." Today, the Detroit Three—Ford, Chrysler, and General Motors—maintain world headquarters in metropolitan Detroit. The automakers in turn spawned hundreds of supplier businesses and legions of millionaires.

Outside Detroit, industries are more varied. To the west, Battle Creek is the cereal capital of the country, a place where the Kellogg family pioneered their new breakfast food at the Battle Creek Sanitarium. Grand Rapids has long been associated with the furniture industry. Midland is the historic home of Dow Chemical Company. Fremont, a small town in western lower Michigan, is home to Gerber, one of the world's best-known baby food companies. Other Michigan concerns include nonelectric machinery, appliances, pharmaceuticals, and lumber.

Agriculture

Beyond the larger cities, however, agriculture dominates. Farming remains an important presence in the state, with approximately 56,000 farms occupying a total of 10 million acres. Crops vary from asparagus to strawberries. The state ranks first in the nation in the production of tart cherries, dry black beans, blueberries, pickling cucumbers, geraniums, and petunias.

Other principal crops include hay, oats, corn, rye, potatoes, soybeans, carrots, celery, wheat, and sugar beets. The western side of the state, which enjoys warmer temperatures provided by Lake Michigan, is known as the Fruit Belt and has made the state a leading producer of apples, plums, peaches, and sweet cherries. The area has also proven surprisingly hospitable for wine grapes, and Michigan's winemaking industry continues to surprise fans with its award-winning and ever-improving vintages. Rounding out the state's wide range of agricultural products are fresh market and processing vegetables, mushrooms, potted eastern lilies, spearmint, milk, eggs, and poultry.

Logging and Mining

Farther north, the Upper Peninsula's economy was long based on logging and mining. Great fortunes were made in logging in the late 1800s, as Michigan's vast stands of virgin timber produced enough wood to lay an inch-thick plank across the state—with enough left over to cover Rhode Island as well. It can be difficult to grasp the riches of Michigan's copper and iron mining industries, each of which dwarfed the California gold rush. Michigan produced more than $9.6 billion in copper and a staggering $48 billion in iron, compared with $955 million from the gold rush. The riches and the miners gradually disappeared as the most accessible deposits were exhausted and global competition began to play a role. By the mid-1990s, nearly all the UP's mines had shut down.

Tourism

Since the UP's former industries collapsed, the area has relied largely on tourism to maintain its sputtering economy, luring many visitors with its unsurpassed rugged beauty. Today, tourism is one of Michigan's largest income producers, accounting for over $17 billion in annual revenues and more than 150,000 jobs statewide. At one time, tourism was focused on the summer months, when beaches, festivals, and resort towns in the Lower Peninsula were most popular. Nowadays, however, the state is a four-season destination, attracting anglers in spring, hunters in autumn, and all manner of skiers, snowmobilers, and skaters in winter.

Shipping and Fishing

Just as semis rumble down the interstate highways, commercial ships transport commodities across the Great Lakes. Officially designated the nation's "Fourth Seacoast" by Congress in 1970, the Great Lakes serve as an essential transportation artery for the nation's commerce. Approximately 125 million tons of cargo travel across the lakes each year on U.S.-flagged ships alone. Without this vital supply line, many of the nation's largest industries, including Michigan's auto manufacturing, could not survive.

With its hundreds of miles of Great Lakes shoreline and dozens of deepwater ports, Michigan is a key player in the Great Lakes transportation network. What's more, the Soo Locks that link Lakes Superior and Huron at Sault Ste. Marie rank as the largest and busiest lock system in the world.

Iron ore forms the foundation of the Great Lakes trade. In Upper Peninsula ports like Escanaba and Marquette, huge lake carriers as long as 1,000 feet load iron ore from nearby mines, then transport it to steelmaking centers in the southern Great Lakes, where the steel is used by heavy manufacturers like Detroit's auto industry.

Heavy manufacturing also drives much of the demand for the second-largest cargo, limestone, which is used as a purifying agent

Henry Ford's Complex Legacy

Industrialist, billionaire, folk hero, preservationist, social engineer—these and many other labels exemplify Henry Ford's status as one of the most influential and complex Americans of the 20th century. While many schoolchildren learn the story of Ford's early adaptation of the assembly line and the affordably priced Model T it spawned, most know little else of the automaker who rose from rural Dearborn, Michigan, to become one of the world's richest and most powerful men.

Ford was born in 1863 on a prosperous farm in what is now a Detroit suburb. His was a typical rural 19th-century childhood, including endless chores and long lessons in a one-room school. From an early age, he was fascinated by all things mechanical. He loved tinkering with watches and was enamored after seeing his first steam engine at the age of 12. Four years later, he moved to Detroit to serve as a machinist's apprentice. At 18 he accepted an engineer position at the Edison Illuminating Company. In 1893 he was promoted to chief engineer and began tinkering with a crude iron contraption in his spare time—an internal combustion engine he engineered following the examples of Europeans Karl Benz and Etienne Lenoir.

In 1894, Ford began work on his first automobile, the Quadricycle, in a small workshop behind his home. Two years later, he took it for its first test run and sold it for $200, later buying it back as a souvenir. By 1898, he'd quit his job at Edison to devote himself full-time to his dream of producing automobiles.

His first business venture, the Detroit Automobile Company, lasted just a year and was dissolved in 1901. His next effort fared only a little better, with Ford resigning in 1902 as president of the Henry Ford Company, which, under Henry Leland's leadership, developed into the Cadillac Motor Company.

Ford finally hit pay dirt with the Ford Motor Company, which he established in 1903 at age 40. The inexpensive, two-cylinder Model A and Model C sold so fast that, by 1905, the company was forced to move out of its original factory into larger quarters. Ford succeeded, in part, because he viewed the automobile not as a luxury but as a tool that could ease the burden of everyday people. He strove to make his products as inexpensive as possible, believing that a low price tag and prompt service would please his customers more than flashy trim.

The car that put America on wheels was Ford's legendary Model T, which became the nation's workhorse. Ford's obsession with improving the efficiency of his factory allowed him to lower the price to just $260 by 1925, causing sales to continue to climb. At its peak, more than 15 million cars were produced.

In 1914, Ford made yet another contribution: a profit-sharing plan that more than doubled the

in steelmaking. The construction, chemical, and paper industries also rely on limestone, of which Michigan has considerable deposits. The limestone quarry in Rogers City, northwest of Alpena, ranks as the largest in the world.

Great Lakes shipping is impacted by the growing amount of foreign-produced goods. Increased imports of consumer items such as refrigerators and automobiles result in a decrease in domestic steel production, which in turn reduces the need for iron ore shipments. In addition, alternative transportation networks such as trains and trucks compete with shipping for some commodities. But despite these issues, shipping has continued to be a stable industry for Michigan, although its ongoing success may be threatened by two other factors: low water levels and the state's relatively new ballast water discharge regulations intended to stop the spread of invasive aquatic species.

salaries of his workers to $5 per day. Begun with the intention of reducing Ford's turnover and training costs, the move also made him a national hero. People flocked to Detroit from around the world to work in his plants.

But by 1918, Ford had become bored with the company and turned to other interests, including a failed attempt to end World War I and an unsuccessful bid for the U.S. Senate. Though his engineering skills were untouchable, Ford enacted other policies that reflected his many eccentricities. His company's Sociological Department, established to monitor the conduct of workers, invaded the privacy of their homes. And beginning in 1920 Ford directed the *Dearborn Independent,* a local newspaper he had purchased, to run a series of rabidly anti-Semitic articles.

Ford's views grew increasingly rigid as he aged. Despite the fact that his $5-a-day plan had made him a working-class hero, he voiced violent opposition to the formation of labor unions, going so far as to employ a network of spies in his plants with the purpose of suppressing any unionization effort—using force if necessary. This caused widespread unrest among his employees. In 1941, Ford Motor Company became the last of the major auto companies to recognize the United Auto Workers, after years of vigorous resistance.

Since Ford, who died in 1947, amassed such enormous fame and wealth, it has been incorrectly assumed that he was the first to build a gas-powered car in the U.S. That distinction actually belongs to George B. Selden of Rochester, New York, who applied for the first patent in 1879, the same year that Ford left the family farm.

While Ford is perhaps the best known of Michigan's auto pioneers, other figures played key roles. Charles B. King, an engineer, drove the first gas-powered horseless carriage through the streets of Detroit in 1896, six months before Ford. That same year, Ransom Olds of Oldsmobile fame drove a gas-powered vehicle through downtown Lansing. A successful industrialist, Olds developed a steam-powered experimental vehicle as early as 1887. He made his greatest mark, however, in 1900 when he invented a tiny motorized buggy known as the Curved Dash runabout. Other key figures include John Dodge, Billy Durant, Charles Mott, and Alfred Sloan Jr., all of whom played crucial, if lesser known, parts in the history of the automobile.

Of today's Detroit Three—Ford, General Motors, and Chrysler—Ford is the only one still partially owned by its founding family. Henry Ford was always at the center of his company, and his descendants remain involved today. William Clay Ford Jr., one of his great-grandsons, was named board chairman in 1999, the first Ford to hold the title in over 15 years. Today, following a five-year stint as Ford's chief executive officer, he serves as the company's executive chairman.

People and Culture

While the Algonquins were the land's first inhabitants, today's Michiganians are a diverse population. The French empire builders were the first Europeans to arrive, and in due time, the British replaced them. Early American settlers included a large group of Yankees from western New York and New England. During the 19th century, European immigrants, including Finns, Swedes, Italians, and the Cornish, arrived seeking a better life, many toiling in Upper Peninsula mines and lumber camps. Germans, Irish, and Dutch migrants settled in the cities and the rich agricultural lands to the south. Later, the automobile industry attracted large numbers of immigrants from southern and eastern Europe, joined later by an influx of arrivals from the American South. Between 1850 and 1900, the state's population increased by more than 600 percent.

Today, Michigan's residents number just under 9.9 million, making it the tenth most populous state in the United States. The vast majority of the state's residents live in the southern third of the Lower Peninsula, mostly near major cities. The three counties of the greater Detroit area—Wayne, Oakland, and Macomb—contain almost 40 percent of Michigan's total population.

NATIVE AMERICANS

In most books about Michigan history, the land's first inhabitants are given little more than a cursory nod, a line or two that identifies the approximately 100,000 early Native Americans as belonging to the nations of the Three Fires—the Ojibwa, Ottawa, and Potawatomi—collectively known as the Anishinabe people. During the 1700s, other nations also migrated to Michigan, including the Huron people, also known as the Wyandotte, who came to southeastern Michigan from Ontario; the Sauk, who lived in the Saginaw River Valley; the Miami, who lived along the St. Joseph River; and the Menominee, who lived in parts of the Upper Peninsula.

The fact that Native Americans get little more than a footnote in many history books reflects a cultural ignorance throughout the nation. One of the few state museums to devote any space to the subject is the excellent Grand Rapids Public Museum, where a fine permanent exhibit ("Anishinabek: The People of This Place") traces the story of the Native Americans of western Michigan. While many communities were being removed from their lands to reservations in Kansas and Oklahoma during the 1880s, Michigan's Anishinabe used skillful negotiation and hard work to remain in their homeland. Through video interviews, photographs borrowed from local families, and hundreds of artifacts, including clothing, tools, and decorative arts, the exhibition tells of the high price they paid to remain residents of the state and of the ongoing struggle to preserve and protect their heritage in an ever-changing modern society.

Today, Michigan is home to one of the largest Native American populations in the country, estimated at 59,300, though it's hard to determine an exact figure, since the label "Native American" can be defined in more than one way—by political, ethnic, or cultural criteria. Depending on the method used, Michigan may have the largest Native American population east of the Mississippi, and only a small percentage live on reservations. As with the state's general population, the majority of Michigan's Native Americans reside near Detroit and Grand Rapids.

There are a number of reservations in the state, including federally recognized lands near Ontonagon, Baraga, L'Anse, Watersmeet, Wilson, Brimley, Sault Ste. Marie, Petoskey, Suttons Bay, Manistee, Mount Pleasant, Fulton, and Dowagiac. Some are authorized to operate their own courts, which exercise exclusive jurisdiction over certain laws and civil matters involving Native Americans and events that occur on their reservations. In addition, Native American councils throughout the state provide a variety of outreach services, economic development initiatives, and cultural activities.

Many reservations have cultural centers, while many tribes host powwows and festivals. As a means of economic support, some operate casinos open to the public. For details, check with local tourism bureaus or inquire at tribal headquarters, which are prominent buildings on most reservations.

IMMIGRANTS

Traveling Michigan's numerous rivers as early as the 1600s, the French fur traders, missionaries, and voyageurs were the area's first nonnative settlers, establishing posts in far-flung areas across the state. The majority of European immigrants, however, didn't arrive until the early 1800s. Expatriate New Englanders first came in the 1830s, acquiring large tracts of land in the state's southern counties. An ever-increasing flow of settlers followed over the next two decades in response to famines in Europe.

During the late 19th and early 20th centuries, refugees from at least 40 countries arrived in record numbers. Among them were Germans, still the largest ethnic group in

Michigan. In the early 1830s the first families settled the Ann Arbor area and the Saginaw River Valley town of Frankenmuth—now a major tourist destination, famous for its Bavarian festivals and all-you-can-eat chicken dinners.

Other early immigrants included Dutch, Irish, and Poles, who continue to make up large chunks of the state's population. Concentrations of Dutch can still be found in Holland, a western city along Lake Michigan, where the tulip festival is one of the state's largest tourist attractions. Poles can be found throughout the state, most notably in Hamtramck, an enclave city surrounded by Detroit. Not far away, Irish arrivals settled Detroit's charming Corktown, the city's oldest neighborhood and the former home of the Detroit Tigers.

By the beginning of the 20th century, a new wave of immigrants poured into the state from southern and eastern Europe, including Austria, Hungary, Italy, and the Balkans. Their arrival coincided with Detroit's newest industry, and thousands of them went to work in the auto factories. More recent migrations included Africans, Asians, Latinos, and Middle Eastern immigrants.

Today, African Americans make up one of the most influential ethnic groups in Michigan, especially in Detroit. While the majority of African Americans came from the South to work in the auto industry, there has been an African American presence in the state since Jean de Sable traded furs in the 1600s.

From the 1830s to the onset of the Civil War, Michigan played an important role in the Underground Railroad, helping enslaved people escape north to Canada. Many escapees stayed in Michigan, mostly in the Lower Peninsula's southwestern corner, where they started their own farms in towns like Benton Harbor. In the 20th century, a much larger number of African Americans arrived after 1910, leaving families in the Deep South to find better jobs in Detroit's factories.

One of the state's newest waves of immigrants has been from the Arab world, including Iraq, Jordan, Lebanon, and Syria. Today, Michigan has one of the nation's largest groups of Arabic people, living in cities such as Dearborn and Southfield, where it's not unusual to see storefront signs in Arabic and women wearing the hijab, the head covering encouraged by Islamic teachings.

The immigrants of the Upper Peninsula vary greatly from those of the Lower Peninsula. The iron and copper mines lured many from Sweden, Finland, Italy, and England with promises of steady work and decent wages, despite difficult job conditions. Swedes and Finns in particular took to the UP, at home with the area's woods and rushing rivers. Finnish names, foods, and the ubiquitous sauna can be found throughout the Keweenaw Peninsula, and Hancock remains largely Finnish, down to its street signs. Farther south, in Detroit, Finnish architect Eliel Saarinen designed much of the Cranbrook campus, a group of highly regarded private schools, a graduate school of visual arts, and a science museum near Detroit.

Arts and Entertainment

FINE ARTS

While state tourism boosters have long sung the praises of Michigan's legendary sand and surf, in recent years they've begun to promote the state's cultural riches. The majority of the arts scene is concentrated in its larger cities, including Detroit, Grand Rapids, and Traverse City. Yet the arts also thrive from Kalamazoo to Kalkaska—both mainstream and underground cultures that survive with little public support. The neighboring towns of Saugatuck and Douglas, for example, rely heavily on arts-related tourism; their downtown streets virtually teem with art galleries.

In Detroit's Cultural Center, the Detroit Institute of Arts is considered one of the country's top art museums, adjacent to the College for Creative Studies, a school dedicated to the visual arts, with a special emphasis on automotive design. Also nearby is the main Detroit Public Library, cornerstone of the nation's fourth-largest public library system. In nearby Bloomfield Hills, you'll find Cranbrook, an educational community that includes the legendary Cranbrook Academy of Art. Throughout its history, Cranbrook has hosted several famous artists as faculty, including Harry Bertoia, Charles Eames, and Carl Milles. Beyond the Detroit area, notable art museums include the University of Michigan Museum of Art in Ann Arbor, a city known for its galleries and excellent summertime art fair; the Flint Institute of Arts, which ranks second in size and scope only to the Detroit Institute of Arts; and the new Eli and Edythe Broad Art Museum at Michigan State University in East Lansing, noted for collections that span more than 5,000 years of art and history. In addition, the Marshall M. Fredericks Sculpture Museum, part of Saginaw Valley State University, contains one of the state's finest sculpture collections.

MUSEUMS

The Henry Ford, in Dearborn, ranks among the state's top tourism draws. It includes the Henry Ford Museum, which pays homage to the tradition of American innovation by displaying a collection of Americana, including classic cars, vintage household items, and exhibits depicting everyday life throughout the nation's history. The museum also houses unique historical items, including a Dunlop Broadside copy of the Declaration of Independence (one of only some 200 known to have been produced), the chair Abraham Lincoln was shot in, plus the presidential limousine John F. Kennedy rode in the day of his assassination. Adjacent Greenfield Village is another component of The Henry Ford. The village is an assemblage of 83 historic buildings, including Thomas Edison's Menlo Park laboratory and Noah Webster's home, where he wrote the first American dictionary, and the Firestone Farm, an actual working farm that produces food for the museum and village and is centered around a 19th-century farmhouse moved to Dearborn from Columbiana, Ohio.

Detroit's Charles H. Wright Museum of African American History, meanwhile, is the largest of its kind in the world, filled with dramatic visual arts and historic artifacts that document the African American experience from the era of slavery to emancipation and to the civil rights movement.

Not surprisingly, a number of the state's museums cover the lore and legends of the Great Lakes and the state's maritime industry. Belle Isle State Park, Detroit's 980-acre urban park, is home to the Dossin Great Lakes Museum, which includes a full-size freighter pilothouse and a massive anchor from the *Edmund Fitzgerald*, the Great Lakes ship that sank mysteriously on Lake Superior in 1975.

In South Haven, the Michigan Maritime Museum traces the state's history from

Native Americans to the 19th century, when huge freighters crossed Lake Michigan and the state's tourism industry began in earnest. In the Upper Peninsula, more stories can be found at Whitefish Point's Great Lakes Shipwreck Museum, which tells the haunting tales of the numerous ships that met their match in the area's frigid, turbulent waters. Also in the UP, the U.S. Ski and Snowboard Hall of Fame and Museum in Ishpeming chronicles both sports, while neighboring Negaunee is home to the Michigan Iron Industry Museum, an excellent state-run facility on the site of one of Michigan's first iron forges.

LITERATURE

While most out-of-towners know about the famous musicians that come from Detroit, few are perhaps aware of the many notable writers who have called the Great Lakes State home, including novelists Ernest Hemingway, Joyce Carol Oates, Elmore Leonard, and L. Frank Baum, author of *The Wonderful Wizard of Oz*. Some authors were born here, including Detroit's Judith Guest, Petoskey's Bruce Catton, Kalamazoo's Edna Ferber, Port Huron's Terry McMillan, and Grayling's Jim Harrison, whose first collection of novellas, *Legends of the Fall*, inspired an Academy Award-winning film. Meanwhile, Pulitzer Prize-winning poet Theodore Roethke was born in Saginaw, and former judge John D. Voelker, who wrote *Anatomy of a Murder* under his pen name, Robert Traver, spent his formative years in Ishpeming. Voelker's novel was based on an actual murder in Big Bay, a small town in the Upper Peninsula, and was later made into an Oscar-nominated movie starring Jimmy Stewart, Lee Remick, and Ben Gazzara.

PERFORMING ARTS

Detroit's Theater District is second only to Broadway in the number of available seats, with performances ranging from cutting-edge productions to the classics. Queen of the venues is the 5,000-seat Fox Theatre, a gloriously gaudy 1920s-era theater that defied the odds to survive until its 1987 restoration by Little Caesars magnate Mike Ilitch. Other Theater District highlights include the Music Hall Center for the Performing Arts and the restored Detroit Opera House. Cities north of Detroit offer their own impressive performance venues, most notably the Whiting in Flint. Even farther north, in Cheboygan, the historic Opera House was once a stop for luminaries such as Mary Pickford and Annie Oakley.

Detroit is one of the few large cities without a resident dance company. Ballets from around the world, however, stop at the city's restored opera house, which sells out regularly, but you'll find modern dance performances at university venues in Ann Arbor and East Lansing. Elsewhere in the state, dance events are held throughout the summer season.

MUSIC

While Michigan has spawned numerous musicians—including Aretha Franklin, the queen of soul, and Madonna, the queen of pop—American music has never been the same since Berry Gordy Jr. started a small recording studio in the early 1960s, giving birth to the Motown Sound. Soon, this fresh, exciting creation was known worldwide, made famous by local talents like Smokey Robinson, Mary Wells, Diana Ross, Marvin Gaye, Gladys Knight, Stevie Wonder, and countless more. Their stories are told in the Motown Museum, also known as Hitsville USA, where displays include everything from the legendary Studio A to flashy Supremes and Temptations costumes.

Classical fans flock to Saginaw's Temple Theatre, where the Saginaw Bay Symphony Orchestra regularly performs, or to Detroit's Orchestra Hall (and the adjoining Max M. Fisher Music Center), home to the 125-year-old Detroit Symphony Orchestra. Almost as old is the award-winning Grand Rapids Symphony, founded in 1930 and now featuring a wide array of classical and pops concerts.

Here you'll also find the impressive Grand Rapids Youth Symphony. Farther north, the Traverse Symphony Orchestra is one of the region's premier ensembles.

The lands around Traverse City and the Lake Michigan shore provide inspiration for the 1,200-acre Interlochen Center for the Arts, a music academy and arts camp founded in 1928. During the summer, students from around the world come to practice and perform in a variety of open-air concerts, most of which are open to the public. Music lovers can also attend live performances, including musicals, throughout the year.

If you're an alternative music fan, plenty of options exist in lower Michigan. In the Detroit area, bands favor Saint Andrew's Hall and the Royal Oak Music Theatre, both known for their warm receptions to cutting-edge artists. Meanwhile, well-known folk artists usually add the Hill Auditorium or Power Center in Ann Arbor to their list of dates, and fans of blues and jazz can find several hangouts in downtown Detroit.

CINEMA

Film entertainers have also impacted Michigan. Jeff Daniels had made his mark on both Hollywood and Broadway, but prefers to live in tiny Chelsea, a village west of Ann Arbor, where the actor, director, and singer founded the acclaimed Purple Rose Theatre Company, named after a Woody Allen film in which he starred. Other successful filmmakers and performers from the Great Lakes State include producer Jerry Bruckheimer, directors Sam Raimi and Francis Ford Coppola, and actors Ellen Burstyn, Gilda Radner, Lily Tomlin, Timothy Busfield, Tom Selleck, Ernie Hudson, Tom Skerritt, J. K. Simmons, Lee Majors, George Peppard, and Piper Laurie, among others.

NIGHTLIFE

Michigan's larger cities have a full plate of nightlife options. On most nights and every weekend, you can choose from blues, jazz, alternative, rock, country, and everything in between. In Detroit, check out the free *Metro Times*, an alternative weekly that provides comprehensive entertainment listings. Another good bet is the entertainment section of the *Detroit Free Press*, which lists city events as well as dates throughout the state. Beyond Detroit, nightlife varies, but almost universally gears up in the summer season.

NATIVE AMERICAN GAMING AND DETROIT CASINOS

As sovereign lands, Native American reservations are legally allowed to offer casino gambling that otherwise exists only in downtown Detroit. Michigan's first Native American-run casino opened in 1984. The Kings Club Casino in Bay Mills, since replaced by the Bay Mills Resort & Casinos, had just 15 blackjack tables and one dice table in a 2,400-square-foot room in the community center. While it wasn't Las Vegas, visitors quickly displayed their love of gambling, pouring millions of dollars into casino coffers, beginning a trend that has expanded ever since.

There are roughly 25 Native American casinos in Michigan, ranging from small simple gambling halls to glitzy showplaces like Leelanau Sands in Peshawbestown. Many are open 24 hours daily and have become enormous tourism draws.

By the early 1990s, the state of Michigan wanted a share of the bounty. In September 1993, Governor John Engler passed the first of several Tribal State Gaming Compacts, giving the state 8 percent of all net income derived from games of chance. While providing the state government with easy cash, the success of the casinos has also given new power and influence to Native American governments.

Other groups were soon eager to seize a piece of this largesse. In 1996, Michigan voters approved a controversial referendum permitting up to three non-Native American casinos within Detroit. After years of controversy, three casinos have opened in the Motor City: the MGM Grand Detroit, The MotorCity Casino Hotel, and Greektown Casino-Hotel.

Given the competition from Detroit, many

of the Native American-owned facilities have expanded. Soaring Eagle, in Mount Pleasant, added a 514-room luxury hotel. The Kewadin complex in Sault Ste. Marie houses an incredible 1,500-seat performance venue. Not surprisingly, even more Native American communities, many of whom live at or near the poverty level, are seeking to open casinos.

While the pros and cons of gambling are subject to ongoing debate, there's no arguing the positive economic effect gaming has had on the reservations. Gambling provides jobs and funds schools, health care facilities, and cultural centers. It's also not easy to overlook the economic benefits provided to those outside the Native American communities, in the form of jobs for the building trades and the tourism industry.

FAIRS AND FESTIVALS

Given the down-to-earth Midwestern atmosphere that permeates the state of Michigan, it's no wonder that fairs and festivals, especially family-friendly ones, are exceedingly popular. Most major towns and small villages celebrate their unique culture with annual events from music festivals to county fairs. While the summer months, in particular, are rife with such celebrations—from Traverse City's National Cherry Festival in July to the Detroit area's Woodward Dream Cruise in August—winter is not without its share of fun. Frankenmuth, for one, offers Zehnder's Snowfest in January, while Sault Ste. Marie hosts the I-500, the world's oldest snowmobile race, in late January or early February.

Essentials

Transportation

GETTING THERE

While international visitors will most likely arrive in Michigan by air or by crossing the land border from Canada, domestic travelers can reach the Great Lakes State by air, water, rail, or road. To determine the best method, consider your budget and intended destinations first.

Air

Detroit Metropolitan-Wayne County Airport (DTW, I-94 and Merriman Rd., Detroit, 734/247-7678, www.metroairport.com), locally

known as the Detroit Metro Airport, is the state's largest and busiest, served by 13 major airlines, including **Delta** (800/221-1212, www.delta.com), **American** (800/433-7300, www.aa.com), **Southwest** (800/435-9792, www.southwest.com), and **United** (800/864-8331, www.united.com). It's also possible to reach many of Michigan's regional airports on scheduled flights, including **Alpena County Regional** (APN, Alpena), **Bishop International** (FNT, Flint), **Capital Region International** (LAN, Lansing), **Cherry Capital** (TVC, Traverse City), **Chippewa County International** (CIU, near Sault Ste. Marie), **Delta County** (ESC, Escanaba), **Gerald R. Ford International** (GRR, Grand Rapids), **Kalamazoo/Battle Creek International** (AZO, Kalamazoo), **MBS International** (MBS, Freeland), **Pellston Regional** (PLN, near Petoskey), and **Sawyer International** (MQT, near Marquette). For a flight to Canada, United can take you to both Sault Ste. Marie and Windsor. **Air Canada** (888/247-2262, www.aircanada.com) also provides service to these and other Canadian destinations as well as flights into Detroit Metro Airport.

Boat

Given Michigan's long shoreline and many dock and marina facilities, it's no surprise that many visitors arrive via boat. The Parks and Recreation Division of Michigan's Department of Natural Resources operates a network of over 90 protected public mooring facilities (fees vary) along the Great Lakes, a "marine highway" that ensures boaters are never far from a safe harbor. For a free copy of *The Handbook of Michigan Boating Laws and Responsibilities,* contact the **Michigan Department of Natural Resources** (Parks and Recreation Division, Mason Bldg., 3rd fl., P.O. Box 30257, Lansing, MI 48909, 517/284-7275, www.michigan.gov/dnr) or download the inexpensive Kindle edition from Amazon.com.

The **SS *Badger*** (Lake Michigan Car Ferry, 701 Maritime Dr., Ludington, 920/684-0888 or 800/841-4243, www.ssbadger.com) is the only remaining passenger steamship on the Great Lakes. The 410-foot-long ship carries up to 600 passengers and 180 vehicles across Lake Michigan from Manitowoc, Wisconsin, to Ludington, Michigan. The enjoyable four-hour passage spares travelers from a congested auto trip through Chicago or a lengthy drive across the Upper Peninsula.

Built in 1952, the SS *Badger* was one of seven railroad and passenger ferries crossing Lake Michigan; you can still see the railroad tracks that lead into the car deck. The *Badger* marked the end of an era; ferries were to the Great Lakes what steamboats were to the Mississippi. Today, it's the only ferry of its kind, and it's been quite inventive in its effort to stay relevant. Although it also transports loaded trucks and occasional business travelers, tourism is its bread and butter. The ship is comfortably outfitted with tables, chairs, a theater showing free movies, a cafeteria and snack bar, a gift shop, a video arcade, and small staterooms ($49 one-way). Equipped with twin berths, these are well worth it if you hope to catch some sleep. There's ample deck space and chaise lounges, if it's warm enough, and the crew even hosts children's activities, bingo, and interactive games. Satellite television and wireless Internet access are also available.

The *Badger* sails daily mid-May through mid-October. It departs Ludington at 9am eastern time and Manitowoc at 2pm central time from the beginning of the season to early June and from early September to the end of the season. From early June to early September, it offers two round-trip passages daily: one leaves Ludington at 9am eastern that arrives in Manitowoc at noon central. The ship then departs Manitowoc at 2pm

Previous: sunset over Lake Superior.

central and arrives in Ludington at 7pm eastern. The evening sailing departs Ludington at 8:45pm eastern and arrives in Manitowoc at 11:45pm central. The return trip departs Manitowoc at 1:30am central and arrives in Ludington at 6:30am eastern. Total sailing time is approximately four hours. Rates are $72 one-way, $131 round-trip adults; $67 and $124 over age 64; $27 and $44 ages 5-15; under age 5 free; $72 one-way for cars, vans, and pickups; $39 one-way for motorcycles; and $6 one-way for bicycles. There is a $7-per-foot charge for motor homes and an $86 one-way fee for pickup campers. Pets must remain in your vehicle or in a ventilated kennel (which you must provide) on the car deck, which *is not* recommended during the hot summer months. For security reasons, you cannot access your vehicle during the crossing. Reservations are strongly recommended.

Train

Amtrak (800/872-7245, www.amtrak.com), which has a hub in Chicago, runs three regular routes through the southern part of Michigan's Lower Peninsula. One Michigan route, the *Pere Marquette,* travels from Chicago through St. Joseph and Holland to Grand Rapids. A second route, the *Blue Water,* travels from Chicago to Kalamazoo, Battle Creek, East Lansing, Flint, Lapeer, and Port Huron. A third Chicago train, the *Wolverine,* splits at Battle Creek and heads for Jackson, Ann Arbor, Dearborn, Detroit, Royal Oak, Troy, and Pontiac. From Windsor and Sarnia, the Canadian cities adjacent to Detroit and Port Huron, respectively, you can take **VIA Rail Canada** (888/842-7245, www.viarail.ca) to Toronto, Vancouver, and 450 other destinations throughout Canada.

Bus

Both **Greyhound** (800/231-2222, www.greyhound.com) and **Indian Trails** (800/292-3831, www.indiantrails.com) operate in most major Michigan cities and plenty of smaller ones. It can be an inexpensive, but slow way to travel. Traveling from Chicago to Marquette, for example, takes over 10 hours but costs less than $100.

Car

A dozen major interstates and highways make it efficient to travel around Michigan by car. I-75 stretches from the state's southern border at Toledo through Detroit and all the way north across the Mackinac Bridge to Sault Ste. Marie. I-69 loops up the middle of the Lower Peninsula along an arc from Indianapolis through Lansing, then continues east to Flint and Port Huron. I-94 from Chicago traverses the southern tier of the state to Detroit and continues to Port Huron. From I-94 just east of Benton Harbor, I-196 extends north along Lake Michigan and over to Grand Rapids, where I-96 heads east to Lansing and Detroit.

Major highways include U.S. 31, which heads north from Indiana, follows the Lake Michigan shore as a major four-lane highway to Ludington, becomes a smaller two-lane road to Traverse City and Petoskey, and merges with I-75 just south of the Mackinac Bridge. U.S. 131, at first a small road near the southern border, becomes a major highway south of Kalamazoo, linking it to Grand Rapids, Cadillac, and Petoskey. U.S. 127, which also begins as a small road near the southern border, heads north from Jackson to Lansing, connecting with I-75 south of Grayling. U.S. 23, which extends north from Toledo, passes through Ann Arbor, merges with I-75 in Flint, and splits off near Standish, becoming the Sunrise Side Coastal Highway, a scenic route that traces the Lake Huron shore all the way to Mackinaw City.

Two main east-west routes traverse the Upper Peninsula (UP). M-28 is the northern route, starting at I-75 near the hamlet of Dafter and passing through Munising and Marquette. U.S. 2 is the southern route, starting in St. Ignace, passing through Escanaba, and heading west to Ironwood. Several north-south highways link the two. If you're traveling all the way from the UP's eastern end to Ironwood, M-28 is usually faster.

GETTING AROUND

Air

Regional airports pepper the state; even the Upper Peninsula has a number of options, including Delta County Airport (ESC) near Escanaba, a stop for Delta Air Lines. It's therefore easy, though often expensive, to fly from one end of Michigan to the other.

It's also possible to charter small planes to some of the more popular islands. **Great Lakes Air** (906/643-7165, www.greatlakesair.net, $30 adults, $16 ages 4-12, under age 4 free, one way), for example, flies from St. Ignace to Mackinac Island, while **Isle Royale Seaplanes** (906/483-4991, www.isleroyaleseaplanes.com, mid-May-mid-Sept., $230 pp one-way, $330 pp round-trip, under age 2 free) provides the only air transportation to Isle Royale National Park, with scheduled trips between Hancock (from the Portage Canal Seaplane Base, 21125 Royce Rd.) and the protected bays at Windigo and Rock Harbor. Reservations are required.

Boat

Surrounded by four Great Lakes and filled with thousands of inland lakes and rivers, Michigan is a popular place for water-based travel during the summer. Visitors will find many pleasure cruises throughout the state, including **Saugatuck Boat Cruises** (716 Water St., Saugatuck, 269/857-4261, www.saugatuckboatcruises.com, hours vary May-Oct., $27 adults, $15 ages 3-12, under age 3 free), offering trips of Saugatuck Harbor and the Kalamazoo River aboard the ***Star of Saugatuck II***, and the ***Bavarian Belle*** (866/808-2628, www.bavarianbelle.com, from 11am daily early May-mid-Oct., $12 adults, $4 age 12 and under), which tours the Cass River in Frankenmuth.

To reach the islands that surround Michigan, boating is usually the best option. The **Beaver Island Boat Company** (231/547-2311 or 888/446-4095, www.bibco.com, hours vary Apr.-Dec., $27.50-32.50 adults, $15-20 ages 5-12, under age 5 free, rates vary for pets and vehicles) links Charlevoix to Beaver Island, while **Shepler's Mackinac Island Ferry** (231/436-5023 or 800/828-6157, www.sheplersferry.com, late Apr.-Oct., $25 adults, $14 ages 5-12, under age 5 free) connects St. Ignace and Mackinaw City to Mackinac Island. **Plaunt Transportation** (231/627-2354 or 888/752-8687, www.bbiferry.com, hours vary daily May-Nov., $18.50 adults, $13 ages 5-11, under age 5 free, rates vary for vehicles) provides service from Cheboygan to Bois Blanc Island, and the **Isle Royale Line** (906/289-4437, www.isleroyale.com, mid-May-Sept., round-trip $124-136 adults, $94-100 under age 12, $60 canoe or kayak) operates between Copper Harbor and Rock Harbor on Isle Royale.

Train

Besides Amtrak, which links several cities in Michigan's Lower Peninsula, the state boasts several authentic train tours. In the Upper Peninsula, the **Tahquamenon Falls Wilderness Excursion** (906/876-2311 or 888/778-7246, www.superiorsights.com/toonerville, hours vary mid-June-early Oct., $47 adults, $43 over age 61, $25 ages 4-15, under age 4 free) leads visitors on a scenic round-trip tour via riverboat and the Toonerville Trolley, a narrow-gauge railroad in operation since the late 1920s. In the Lower Peninsula, the **Southern Michigan Railroad** (517/456-7677 or 734/396-0416, www.southernmichiganrailroad.com, hours vary mid-May-Dec., round-trip $13.60 adults, $11.50 over age 64, $9.40 ages 2-12, under age 2 free) offers seasonal and holiday train tours between Clinton and Tecumseh.

Bus

Most of Michigan's major towns and regions offer a public bus system. The **Detroit Department of Transportation** (DDOT, 313/933-1300 or 888/336-8287, www.detroitmi.gov/ddot) services the city proper, while **SMART** (866/962-5515, www.smartbus.org) covers the suburban communities. Outstate areas are served by **Thumb Area Transit** (TAT, 989/269-2121 or

800/322-1125, www.tatbus.com), Lansing's **Capital Area Transportation Authority** (CATA, 517/394-1000, www.cata.org), the **Ann Arbor Transportation Authority** (734/996-0400 or 734/973-6500, www.theride.org), the **Muskegon Area Transit System** (MATS, 231/724-6420, www.matsbus.com), Traverse City's **Bay Area Transportation Authority** (BATA, 231/941-2324 or 231/778-1025, www.bata.net), and the **Marquette Transit Authority** (906/225-1112, www.marqtran.com).

Car

In Michigan, the birthplace of the automobile, the car is the preferred method of travel. This is never more apparent than on Friday afternoons from May to October, when it seems half of the state's southern residents leave home to head "up north." Though it's best to avoid northbound highways on Friday and southbound roads on Sunday, Michigan—a state of remarkable diversity—is worthy of a road trip.

Roads here are plentiful. Along with interstates and federal highways, the state is crisscrossed with state highways, marked on road maps by a circled number; on signposts, the number is enclosed by a diamond. In conversation, they are preceded by an "M," as in, "Follow M-28 west to Marquette." County roads are marked with rectangles on most road maps. The state also has several toll bridges, including the Mackinac Bridge between Mackinaw City and St. Ignace, and the three international bridges and one tunnel that link Canada to the cities of Detroit, Port Huron, and Sault Ste. Marie.

When planning a route in the Upper Peninsula, consult your map legend regarding road surfaces. All state and federal highways are paved and well maintained, as are most county roads and many secondary roads, but gravel and dirt roads can make for very slow going. For road construction updates, consult the **Michigan Department of Transportation** (State Transportation Bldg., 425 W. Ottawa St., Lansing, MI 48909, 517/373-2090, www.michigan.gov/mdot).

Michigan law requires all drivers, front-seat passengers, and children ages 8 to 15 to wear seat belts. Children younger than 8 or shorter than 4 foot 9 must be properly buckled in a car seat or booster seat. All motorists must yield to emergency vehicles. In addition, drivers must always stop at railroad crossings when the lights are flashing or the crossing gates have been activated. Remember that littering is illegal on state and federal highways. Speed limits on interstate, federal, and Michigan highways vary between 55 and 75 mph; on most county roads it's 55 mph. Although motorcyclists are strongly encouraged to wear helmets at all times, their use is no longer required by Michigan law.

TAXI AND SHUTTLE

Most of Michigan's major cities have taxi and shuttle services. Unless you're at an airport, you'll need to call ahead to arrange a ride. From the Detroit Metropolitan-Wayne County Airport, contact **Checker Cab** (313/963-7000, www.checkerdetroit.com) or **Metro Airport Taxi** (248/214-6823, www.metrotaxidetroit.com). Other services include Marquette's **Checker Transport** (906/226-7777, www.checkertransport.com) and **Up North Rides** (231/350-1248 www.upnorthrides.com), which serves the Petoskey, Bay Harbor, and Harbor Springs area.

RENTAL CAR

Rental cars are available at most commercial airports around the state. In most cities you'll find popular names like **Alamo** (888/233-8749, www.alamo.com), **Avis** (800/633-3469, www.avis.com), **Budget** (800/218-7992, www.budget.com), **Enterprise** (800/261-7331, www.enterprise.com), **Hertz** (800/654-3131, www.hertz.com), and **National** (877/222-9058, www.nationalcar.com). Reservations are strongly recommended; big cities do a huge volume, and small locales don't keep many cars on the lot. If you plan to explore the Upper Peninsula, ask about the company's

Mileage Between Cities

Comprising two large peninsulas, Michigan is a bigger place than it appears on many maps. It can be deceptively far from point A to point B, especially if point A is, say, Kalamazoo and point B is Copper Harbor, which lies 590 miles to the north. To put it into perspective, traveling roughly the same distance from Kalamazoo would take you to Kansas City or Washington, D.C. So, while traveling across Michigan, consider these distances. Note that the estimated driving times presume light to moderate traffic.

DISTANCE FROM DETROIT TO:

- Bay City: 115 miles (1.75 hours)
- Benton Harbor: 186 miles (2.75 hours)
- Copper Harbor: 600 miles (9.75 hours)
- Grand Rapids: 158 miles (2.5 hours)
- Mackinaw City: 289 miles (4 hours)
- Marquette: 455 miles (7 hours)
- Sault Ste. Marie: 345 miles (5 hours)
- Traverse City: 256 miles (4 hours)

DISTANCE FROM MARQUETTE TO:

- Grayling: 251 miles (4.25 hours)
- Ironwood: 145 miles (2.75 hours)
- Lansing: 396 miles (6.25 hours)
- Muskegon: 409 miles (7 hours)
- Petoskey: 202 miles (3.75 hours)
- Port Huron: 456 miles (7.25 hours)
- Saginaw: 356 miles (5.75 hours)
- St. Ignace: 162 miles (3 hours)

DISTANCE FROM CHICAGO TO:

- Detroit: 283 miles (4.25 hours)
- Flint: 274 miles (4 hours)
- Gaylord: 349 miles (5.25 hours)
- Kalamazoo: 147 miles (2.25 hours)
- Marquette: 383 miles (6.5 hours)
- Saugatuck: 141 miles (2.25 hours)
- Sault Ste. Marie: 463 miles (7 hours)
- Traverse City: 318 miles (5 hours)

policies regarding off-road driving. Many forbid you to leave the pavement, which can curtail your access to a lot of UP sights. If you're definitely planning to go off-road, consider renting a sport utility vehicle, which has a higher clearance.

RV

Traversing Michigan via RV can be a wonderful way to see the state's diverse attractions. If you don't have a motor home or trailer of your own, you can easily rent one from various locations. For more information about RV rentals, contact **General RV Center** (888/436-7578, www.generalrv.com) or **Cruise America** (800/671-8042, www.cruiseamerica.com). For a list of Michigan's campgrounds and RV parks, consult the **Michigan Association of Recreation Vehicles and Campgrounds** (MARVAC, 2222 Association Dr., Okemos, 517/349-8881, www.marvac.org) or **Association of RV Parks and Campgrounds Michigan** (ARVC, 4696 Orchard Manor Blvd., Ste. 11, Bay City, 989/619-2608, www.michcampgrounds.com).

Winter Driving

Michigan roads are generally well maintained in winter, plowed free of snow, then salted or sanded. (Salt does a better job of melting, while sand is less destructive to the environment.) During or immediately after a snowstorm, though, it's best to exercise extra caution, as it's often difficult for road crews to keep up with conditions. County and city crews have a well-established hierarchy, first taking care of interstates, state highways, major thoroughfares, and roads to schools and hospitals, then addressing less vital routes. In the Upper Peninsula, many small roads are considered seasonal, which means they're not plowed or patrolled in winter. To check winter driving conditions before you travel, consult the **Michigan State Police** (333 S. Grand Ave., Lansing, MI 48909, 517/332-2521 or 800/525-5555, www.michigan.gov/msp).

If you're not used to driving in snow, don't learn on the road in a Michigan snowstorm. Drive slowly, allow sufficient room between you and the car in front of you, and remember that it may take longer to stop than you're accustomed to. Tap your brakes lightly in succession to come to a stop; never stomp on them, or you'll send your car into a "doughnut." If you have antilock brakes, apply steady pressure and let the system's computer do the work.

Chains or studded tires are not permitted on Michigan roads. Many residents do switch to snow tires, which have a heavier tread and are made of softer rubber, enabling them to better grip snow-covered roads. If you have a rear-wheel-drive car, adding weight to the back end can greatly improve traction. Bags of sand or salt work well, and sand can be used if you get stuck.

Ice is considerably more dangerous than snow, since it provides even less traction and stopping ability. Especially beware of black ice—seemingly wet pavement that is actually glare ice. Watch for icy roads as rain turns to snow (called freezing rain), especially on bridges, where the cold air circulating above and below the road will cause it to freeze first. Ice also forms when a great number of cars drive over a snowy surface (like a heavily traveled interstate), pressing it down into a super slick hardpack. On four-lane roads, the left lane usually looks snowier but may be less icy and, therefore, less slippery.

Equip your vehicle with a shovel, sand or cat litter, and boots in case you get stuck. If that happens, throw the sand or cat litter under the front tires for a front-wheel-drive car, the rear tires on a rear-wheel-drive car. Keep the tires straight and slowly apply the gas. Flooring it will only spin you deeper. Gently rocking the car forward and back, especially if you have someone who can push, works best.

Pack an emergency kit and make sure your car is in good mechanical condition before embarking on your journey; check your batteries, fluids, and tire pressure. Keep a flashlight with fresh batteries, flares, blankets, extra clothing, and a first-aid kit in your vehicle in case you have to spend the night in your car. It could save your life. Help may not always be on the way, especially in rural areas. If you spy a car hung up on a snowbank or in a ditch, try to offer a push or a ride to town (as long as your personal safety isn't in doubt).

Deer Crossings

Michigan's deer population numbers around two million, posing a significant threat to drivers. Thousands contribute to automobile accidents each year, some of them fatal. Deer behave erratically and will dart in front of your car with no warning. Be particularly alert at dawn and dusk, when they are most active, and during the fall hunting season, when they're highly unpredictable. Yellow-and-black "leaping deer" signs warn motorists of roadways where crossings are common, but they can occur virtually anywhere.

Deer may come from the woods or an open field, seemingly out of nowhere. If you see deer by the side of the road, slow down and get ready to stop. If you see a deer cross ahead of you, also slow down—where there's one deer, there are usually several. If you do hit a deer, notify the nearest law enforcement office immediately.

Visas and Officialdom

International travelers need to understand current U.S. policies before arriving in Michigan. With border crossings to Canada in Detroit, Port Huron, and Sault Ste. Marie, it's helpful for all visitors to know the ins and outs of traveling between the two nations.

PASSPORTS AND VISAS

International travelers are required to show a valid passport upon entering the United States. Meanwhile, most citizens from Canada, Bermuda, and the 37 countries that are part of the Visa Waiver Program (VWP)—including France, Italy, Australia, Japan, and the United Kingdom—are allowed to stay in Michigan without a visa for up to 90 days. Since January 2009 VMP participants have been required to apply to the Electronic System for Travel Authorization (ESTA) for approval to travel to the United States; as of September 2010, this formerly free system now costs $14 per registration application or renewal. In addition, VMP travelers must present a digital or biometric passport. These documents resemble traditional passports but carry an embedded electronic microchip containing biometric information that can be used to identify the holder's identity. All other temporary international travelers are required to secure a nonimmigrant visa before entering Michigan. For more information, consult the **U.S. Department of State's Bureau of Consular Affairs** (202/663-1225, http://travel.state.gov).

U.S. citizens who are residents of Michigan, Minnesota, New York, Vermont, or Washington, and Canadians who reside in British Columbia, Manitoba, Ontario, or Quebec are eligible to apply for an **Enhanced Driver's License** from their state or province. This document will serve the functions of a regular driver's license and provide some of the features of traditional passports, including allowing transit between the U.S. and Canada, as authorized by the Western Hemisphere Travel Initiative. Enhanced licenses are not valid for international air travel.

With child abductions on the rise, border officials are especially concerned about protecting minors. If you're traveling with children, you must bring proper identification for them as well, such as a birth certificate, certificate of naturalization (if the child is foreign born), or passport. If the children are not your own, you must also provide written permission from a parent or legal guardian. If you are divorced or separated and traveling with your children, you must provide a copy of the legal custody agreement. For more information, consult **American Consular Services** (http://canada.usembassy.gov/consular_services.html).

Non-U.S. citizens must also have a valid passport. If you're a citizen of a non-EU country, you may also need a visa (obtained in advance from the Canadian Consulate). U.S. resident aliens will be asked to show a green card. For more information, consult the **Canada Border Services Agency** (www.cbsa-asfc.gc.ca).

CUSTOMS

Upon entering the United States, international travelers must declare any dollar amount over $10,000 as well as the value of any articles that will remain in the country, including gifts. A duty will be assessed for all imported goods; visitors are usually granted a $100 exemption. Illegal drugs, obscene items, and toxic substances are generally prohibited. In order to protect U.S. agriculture, customs officials will confiscate certain produce, plants, seeds, nuts, meat, and other potentially dangerous biological products. For more information, consult the **U.S. Department of Homeland Security's U.S. Customs and Border Protection** (202/325-8000, www.cbp.gov).

EMBASSIES AND CONSULATES

Embassies for nations with which the United States has diplomatic relations are located in Washington, D.C. In addition, some nations have consular offices in major cities. Two are in the GM Renaissance Center, including **Canada** (600 Renaissance Center, Ste. 1100, 313/567-2340, www.detroit.gc.ca, 8:30am-4:30pm Mon.-Fri.) and **Japan** (400 Renaissance Center, Ste. 1600, 313/567-0120, www.detroit.us.emb-japan.go.jp, 9:15am-11:45am and 1pm-4:30pm Mon.-Fri.). Other consulates in the Detroit area include **Iraq** (16445 W. 12 Mile Rd., Southfield, 248/423-1250, www.iraqiembassy.us, 9am-4pm Mon.-Fri.), **Italy** (Buhl Bldg., 535 Griswold St., Ste. 1840, Detroit, 9am-noon Mon.-Tues. and Thurs.-Fri., 9am-noon and 2pm-4pm Wed.), **Lebanon** (1000 Town Center Suite 2450, Southfield, 248/945-3511, www.lebanonconsulategdetroit.org, 9am-3pm Mon.-Fri.), **North Macedonia** (2000 Town Center, Ste. 1130, Southfield, 248/354-5537 or 248/354-5537, www.mfa.gov.mk), and **Mexico** (1403 E. 12 Mile Rd. Bldg. E, Madison Heights, 248/336-0320, www.consulmex2sre.gob.mx/detroit).

Additional consulates are nearby in Chicago, including those of the **United Kingdom** (625 N. Michigan Ave., Ste. 2200, 312/970-3800, http://ukinusa.fco.gov.uk, by appt.), **France** (205 N. Michigan Ave., Ste. 3700, 312/327-5200, www.consulfrance-chicago.org, 9am-12:30pm Mon.-Thurs., 8:30am-12:30pm Fri.), and **Germany** (676 N. Michigan Ave., Ste. 3200, 312/202-0480, www.germany.info, 8am-4:45pm Mon.-Thurs., 8am-noon Fri.). For a more comprehensive list of the foreign embassies and consulates in the United States, consult the **University of Michigan's International Center** (www.internationalcenter.umich.edu), specifically the "Travel Abroad Basics" section of the center's comprehensive website.

UNITED STATES-CANADA BORDER

At one time, U.S. citizens were subject to only cursory screening when crossing the Canadian border. Given today's heightened sensitivities, however, Americans must now show either a valid U.S. passport or a certified birth certificate with photo identification (such as a driver's license) to enter Canada. Bear in mind, however, that a valid U.S. passport or Enhanced Driver's License is necessary to return to the United States—a birth certificate won't suffice. Unless you have a criminal record or are suspected of transporting contraband, you'll probably just be asked about the purpose of your visit, then allowed to proceed. Pets require proof of proper vaccinations; plants and animal products will be confiscated. In addition, you must declare any alcohol or tobacco products, which may be taxed depending on the quantity. Obscene materials, illegal drugs, and most weapons are prohibited from entering Canada.

There are four **toll crossings** connecting Michigan and Ontario: the Ambassador Bridge from Detroit to Windsor (www.ambassadorbridge.com, $5/C$6.25 passenger vehicles and motorcycles); the Detroit-Windsor Tunnel (www.dwtunnel.com, Detroit to Windsor $5/C$6.25 passenger and commercial vehicles, Windsor to Detroit $4.50/C$4.75 passenger and commercial vehicles, motorcycles prohibited); the Blue Water Bridge from Port Huron to Sarnia (www.michigan.gov/mdot, $3/C$4 passenger vehicles); and the Sault Ste. Marie International Bridge from Sault Ste. Marie to Sault Ste. Marie, Ontario (www.michigan.gov/mdot, $4/C$5.30 passenger vehicles, $8/C$10.60 vehicles with 2 axle trailers, $6.50/C$8.70 recreational vehicles). If you arrive by plane or boat, you're required to check in at the nearest customs station immediately upon arrival.

Sports and Recreation

GOLF

As it turns out, northern Michigan has the perfect climate for growing turf and a diverse terrain of hills and water views that make for great golf courses. Over the last few decades, golf course architects have built a number of nationally ranked courses, including several with professional names like Arnold Palmer, Robert Trent Jones, and Jack Nicklaus attached.

Traverse City, Mackinac Island, and Oscoda on Lake Huron form a golden triangle of northern Lower Peninsula golf courses where you'll find award winners like the Bear at the Grand Traverse Resort and Spa near Traverse City, Cedar River at Shanty Creek Resorts in Bellaire, Signature at the Treetops Resort near Gaylord, and Fountains at the Garland Lodge & Resort in Lewiston. Outside this zone are plenty of other well-kept and challenging courses. In the Upper Peninsula, Drummond Island, Mackinac Island, and Marquette are home to some of the best. For more information, consult the **Golf Association of Michigan** (GAM, 24116 Research Dr., Farmington Hills, 248/478-9242, www.gam.org), peruse ***Michigan Golf*** (www.michigangolfmagazine.com) or **Pure Michigan** (800/644-2489, www.michigan.org/golf), or visit www.michigangolf.com.

NATIONAL PARKS AND FORESTS

Michigan is home to national parks and national historical parks, national lakeshores, national forests, and national wildlife refuges in both peninsulas. Save for key attractions like waterfalls or beaches, national forests are often overlooked as destinations, but they offer a remarkable range of activities for outdoor enthusiasts. Hiking trails tend to be little used, and campsites are more secluded, more rustic, and usually less crowded than in other places. Mountain biking, which is often forbidden on national park trails, is permitted on miles and miles of federal forestland, and inland lakes, which can be difficult to reach with a boat trailer, are often ideal for those looking for a quiet paddling experience.

The national forests also cover an astounding amount of real estate. The **Ottawa National Forest** in the western UP contains nearly one million acres, while the **Hiawatha National Forest,** in two units in the eastern UP, adds another 895,000 acres. In the Lower Peninsula, the **Manistee National Forest** stretches from Cadillac to just north of Muskegon, an area of more than 540,000 acres, while the **Huron National Forest** covers roughly 439,000 acres in the northeastern section, encompassing lightly developed rivers like the Au Sable.

State Park Explorer Program

Every summer, campers and day-use visitors can participate in the State Park Explorer Program at 44 of Michigan's state parks and recreation areas. Equipped with field guides and hands-on materials, expert rangers and volunteers lead informal programs, nature hikes, and nighttime activities that feature each region's unique natural, cultural, and historical resources. These free programs, which are designed for children and adults alike, focus on a wide assortment of topics, including insects, frogs, birds, mammals, carnivorous plants, forests, ponds, and constellations.

Participating locales range from Van Riper State Park in the Upper Peninsula, where visitors can learn about native dragonflies, owls, black bears, wolves, and moose, to Warren Dunes State Park along Lake Michigan's southeastern shore, where guides explore coastal tides and the area's fossils, birds, and wildflowers. For program details and schedules, consult the **Michigan Department of Natural Resources** (www.michigan.gov/dnr).

For information about hiking, camping, paddling, and other activities, contact the **U.S. Forest Service** (202/205-1680, www.fs.fed.us) or each forest's headquarters: **Ottawa National Forest** (E6248 U.S. 2, Ironwood, 906/932-1330), **Hiawatha National Forest** (2727 N. Lincoln Rd., Escanaba, 906/786-4062), and **Huron-Manistee National Forests** (1755 S. Mitchell St., Cadillac, 231/775-2421 or 800/821-6263). For more information about Michigan's national lakeshores, consult the **National Park Service** (202/208-3818, www.nps.gov); for wildlife refuges, contact the **U.S. Fish and Wildlife Service** (800/344-9453, www.fws.gov/refuges).

STATE PARKS AND FORESTS

State Parks

Michigan has an outstanding state park system. Well-planned and well-maintained, the parks showcase some of the state's most diverse and most beautiful land. Some state parks, like those along Lake Michigan, were clearly set aside for public access, while others preserve historic sites and state jewels like Mackinac Island and the Porcupine Mountains.

Currently, Michigan has more than 100 state parks and recreation areas, covering roughly 285,000 acres. The **Michigan Department of Natural Resources** (Parks and Recreation Division, Mason Bldg., 3rd fl., Lansing, 517/284-7275, www.michigan.gov/dnr) publishes a handy brochure that includes regional maps and charts listing each park's amenities.

Michigan residents can purchase, at the time of their vehicle plate registration, a **Recreation Passport** (www.michigan.gov/recreationpassport, $12 vehicles, $6 motorcycles), which allows access to all state parks, recreation areas, and boat launches during the period of the vehicle registration. The passport may also be purchased at the entrance to any state park for an additional $5 convenience fee. For nonresidents, every entering vehicle, despite the number of passengers, must also have an annual Recreation Passport ($34); otherwise, you'll have to pay a day pass fee ($9) for any state park or recreation area that charges such fees.

State Forests

Like national forests, state forests are a hidden gem for anyone looking for a quiet corner in the wild. Much of the state's forestland was acquired by foreclosure during the Depression when its owners couldn't pay the property taxes. The original owners' loss was the public's gain—much of the property is exceptional, comprising rivers, waterfalls, lakes, beaches, and woodlands. Altogether, Michigan's state forests encompass 3.9 million acres, the largest such system in the nation.

In the Lower Peninsula, you'll find **Pere Marquette State Forest** south of Traverse City, **Mackinaw State Forest** between Gaylord and Mackinaw City, and **Au Sable State Forest** between Grayling and Midland. In the Upper Peninsula, you can explore **Lake Superior State Forest** in the eastern half, **Escanaba River State Forest** in the central part, and **Copper Country State Forest** on the western side. For more information, contact the **Michigan Department of Natural Resources** (517/284-7275, www.michigan.gov/dnr), and, for a nonrefundable $8 fee, you can make a camping reservation (800/447-2757, www.midnrreservations.com) at any state forest campground.

HIKING AND HORSEBACK RIDING

Given its bounty of national parks and lakeshores, federal and state forests, state parks, and whatever county land is set aside for public use, Michigan has almost unlimited offerings for hikers, especially in the Upper Peninsula. Where you go depends on your taste.

For backpackers, **Isle Royale National Park** in Lake Superior is an outstanding choice, free of roads and other development. Rustic campsites along the way allow you to walk across the 45-mile-long island; water taxi services can ferry you back to your starting point. **Porcupine Mountains Wilderness State Park** in the western UP also offers great backpacking in only a *slightly* less remote location. The park's rugged backcountry environment is not what's normally associated with a state park.

Michigan also has a number of linear hiking trails, like the 220-mile-long **Michigan Shore-to-Shore Trail,** a hiking and horseback riding trail that stretches from Empire on Lake Michigan to Oscoda on Lake Huron. For those seeking a real adventure, the **North Country National Scenic Trail** (www.northcountrytrail.org) traverses both the Upper and Lower Peninsulas as part of a 4,600-mile-long national trail that stretches from New York to North Dakota. In Michigan, hikers will encounter a wide array of sights along this trail, from the Fort Custer National Cemetery near Battle Creek to the cliffs of Pictured Rocks National Lakeshore to the trees of Ottawa National Forest.

For more information about hiking and horseback riding trails in Michigan, contact the **Michigan Trail Riders Association, Inc.** (MTRA, 5806 E. State Rd., Hale, 989/473-3205, www.mtra.org).

BIKING

With its rolling topography, stunning shorelines, and ample country roads, Michigan makes for a great biking destination. Some favorite areas for road riding include the wine country region near South Haven and the lovely Leelanau Peninsula. For more information about suggested routes and bicycle tours, check with local tourism bureaus or consult the **League of Michigan Bicyclists** (LMB, 416 S. Cedar St., Ste. A, Lansing, 517/334-9100 or 888/642-4537, www.lmb.org), **Michigan Mountain Biking Association** (MMBA, www.mmba.org), or **Michigan Trails & Greenways Alliance** (MTGA, P.O. Box 27187, Lansing, MI 48909, 517/485-6022, www.michigantrails.org).

Michigan leads the nation in the number of rails-to-trails, with over 50 old railroad beds converted into multiuse trails. For more information, consult the **Rails-to-Trails Conservancy** (202/331-9696, www.railstotrails.org).

Unlike much of the Midwest, Michigan is kind to mountain bikers. Good technical mountain biking can be found in many state and national forests, and ski resorts in the Lower Peninsula have wisely courted mountain bikers by maintaining their cross-country trail networks for biking in the warm months.

As for the Upper Peninsula, you can pretty much consider it a giant mountain biking park. Between the national and state forests, you'll find more miles than you could ever ride, in addition to hundreds of miles of old logging roads. The off-road trails in places like the Keweenaw and the Huron Mountains are the best you'll find between the Rockies and the Appalachians, with a unique Michigan perk: an array of stunning Great Lakes views.

BIRD-WATCHING

Given Michigan's myriad forests, prairies, lakes, rivers, marshes, and beaches, it's no wonder that the state is rife with hundreds of avian species, including songbirds, raptors, shorebirds, and waterfowl. It's also no wonder, therefore, that bird-watchers are drawn to Michigan, especially in the spring and fall.

In Saginaw, the **Shiawassee National Wildlife Refuge** (www.fws.gov/midwest/shiawassee), which hosts over 270 bird species annually, provides trails, observation platforms, and bird species lists, while the **Whitefish Point Bird Observatory** (www.wpbo.org) near Paradise offers field trips for bird-watchers of all skill levels. For more information about Michigan's birds as well as birding tours and festivals, visit www.michiganbirding.com or consult **Michigan Audubon** (P.O. Box 15249, Lansing, MI 48901, 517/580-7364, www.michiganaudubon.org).

HUNTING

With its plentiful populations of deer, ducks, pheasants, turkeys, and other game, Michigan is an especially popular hunting destination. Even black bears and elk can be legally hunted here. Hunting seasons, license requirements, and regulations vary depending upon the animal and region, so it's important to do your research ahead of time. For example, white-tailed deer, the state game mammal, can be hunted with bows October 1 through mid-November and during December; firearms can only be used mid- to late November and in December. In addition, the types of firearms allowed vary between different regions of the state.

For up-to-date regulations and to apply for specific licenses, consult the **Michigan Department of Natural Resources** (517/284-7275, www.michigan.gov/dnr). For a trove of hunting related articles, visit www.michigan-sportsman.com.

BOATING AND FISHING

Boating

Boating is an exceedingly popular summer pastime in Michigan. Boaters cruise from port to port on the Great Lakes, sail around large bays like Grand Traverse and isolated areas like Beaver Island, water-ski on thousands of inland lakes, paddle the state's white-water rivers and quiet waters, cruise the inland waterway through Cheboygan County, and fish just about everywhere.

In popular tourism areas, small watercraft like canoes and fishing boats are readily available for rental. For more information, contact the local chamber of commerce or tourism bureau in the area that you plan to visit. For larger watercraft, such as sailboats, contact the **Michigan Charter Boat Association** (MCBA, 800/622-2971, www.michiganchar-terboats.com).

If you plan to bring your own boat, consult the **Michigan Department of Natural Resources** (517/284-7275, www.michigan.gov/dnr), which provides maps, a listing of public marinas and harbors, a handbook of boating laws, and a harbor reservation system. State law requires that all boaters must carry a Coast Guard-approved life jacket—known as a personal flotation device (PFD)—for each person on board, regardless of the type of boat.

Canoeing and Kayaking

Michigan is a paddler's dream. You can canoe down several National Wild and Scenic Rivers, surf waves along Lake Michigan's shoreline, sea kayak along Pictured Rocks or Isle Royale, or partake in white-water rafting. For less strenuous paddling, the Au Sable River is a perennial favorite, stretching from Grayling to Lake Huron. In late July, it's even the site of the annual 120-mile **Au Sable River Canoe Marathon** (www.ausablecanoemarathon.org), which usually runs from Grayling to Oscoda.

Also in the northeastern Lower Peninsula is the less-crowded Rifle River, east of West Branch. Other popular paddling rivers include the Platte and Betsie Rivers south of Traverse City and the Sturgeon River in the Upper Peninsula. The UP also has several notable white-water rivers, including the beautiful Presque Isle River and the Ontonagon, both of which are designated wild and scenic rivers. For more information on paddling destinations and liveries, consult the **Michigan Association of Paddlesport Providers** (MAPP, www.michigancanoe.com).

Fishing

Fishing is a deeply ingrained Michigan tradition. It's a highly versatile activity, ranging from fly-fishing along a pristine stream in summer to hanging out in an ice-fishing shanty, watching a Lions-Packers game on a portable TV. The quantity of Michigan blue-ribbon trout streams is unrivaled anywhere east of Montana—enough clear, swift, and rocky waters to keep you busy for weeks on end. Most of the best are in the eastern UP (the Fox) and the northern parts of the Lower Peninsula (the Jordan and Boardman).

Fishing charters on the Great Lakes allow the angler to go after big chinook salmon, coho salmon, and lake trout. Lake Michigan's Little Bay de Noc arguably offers the finest walleye fishing in the state, if not in all the Great Lakes. In addition, thousands of inland lakes are habitats for walleye, northern pike, muskie, bass, and perch. Some of the most popular spots are the lakes around Cadillac and Indian River in the Lower Peninsula and the Manistique Lakes chain and huge Lake Gogebic in the UP.

But to avoid the crowds and the whine of outboard motors, it's best to head for any of the dozens of small lakes in the UP's Ottawa and Hiawatha National Forests, which are peaceful, harder to access, and teeming with fish. Some, like the 34 lakes of the Sylvania Wilderness and Recreation Area near Watersmeet, have special fishing regulations, so check with authorities. All Michigan waters require a valid Michigan fishing license. For fishing information, contact the **Michigan Department of Natural Resources** (Fisheries Division, P.O. Box 30446, Lansing, MI 48909, 517/284-7275, www.michigan.gov/dnr). For additional information about fish species, fishing reports, river guides, and charters in your area, contact the **Michigan Charter Boat Association** (MCBA, 800/622-2971, www.michigancharterboats.com).

DIVING

Over a century ago, the Great Lakes were like today's interstate highways—the fastest and most efficient way to get around. Commodities such as lumber and iron ore were hauled from the forests and mines to Great Lakes ports; passengers from urban areas traveled north by steamship to enjoy the fresh cool air of the secluded resorts.

Of course, the Great Lakes were also known for shallow reefs and violent storms, which led to hundreds of shipwrecks. Moreover, the fresh, cold barnacle-free waters kept those shipwrecks from decaying. Many of them sit on the lake floor, undisturbed and virtually unchanged.

Today, divers enjoy exploring the mysteries of these wrecks. Michigan has set aside 14 areas where shipwrecks are particularly prevalent as underwater preserves, protecting their historical significance and mapping them for divers. Collectively, they cover 2,300 square miles of Great Lakes bottomland—an area roughly the size of Delaware. Underwater preserves are located off Isle Royale, the Keweenaw Peninsula, Marquette, Munising, and Whitefish Point on Lake Superior; in the DeTour Passage where the St. Mary's River meets Lake Huron; near Port Austin and Port Sanilac on Lake Huron; and around Grand Traverse Bay, along the Manitou Passage, and beside the western and southwestern shores on Lake Michigan.

Most of the popular dive sites are marked with buoys in summer by volunteers of the

Safety Tips for Underwater Enthusiasts

Safety is an essential aspect of proper underwater diving. The Great Lakes are unpredictable; storms and heavy seas can arise without warning. Here are several precautions:

- Check weather conditions before venturing out, as strong winds and rough seas can create unsafe conditions.
- Make sure that you've had proper scuba diving instruction.
- When in doubt as to your abilities, don't hesitate to hire a dive charter operator.
- Always tell someone on land where you're planning to go and when you intend to return.
- Apply ample waterproof sunscreen and invest in a full wetsuit or dry suit.
- Make sure that your mask and flippers fit properly, and check that you have all necessary equipment, such as weights and air tanks.
- If you find it difficult to walk on the boat while wearing flippers, carry them into the water before putting them on.
- Never dive without displaying a proper red and white diver-down flag on your vessel, and always remove said flag when all divers have returned to the boat.
- Boats should stay at least 300 feet from diver-down flags in open water and at least 100 feet from flags in rivers and inlets; if you cannot maintain such distance, slow down to an idle speed when passing other divers.
- Always dive with a companion, and try to stay together.
- Plan your entry and exit points before jumping into the water.
- Swim into the current upon entering the water and then ride the current back to your exit point.

Michigan Underwater Preserve Council (560 N. State St., St. Ignace, 800/970-8717, www.michiganpreserves.org), which also produces an informative booklet biannually. All the preserves are served by diving charters, which can be found through the **Michigan Charter Boat Association** (MCBA, 800/622-2971, www.michigancharterboats.com). For more information, please contact the chamber of commerce or tourism bureau near the preserve that you want to visit.

Scuba divers should take care not to remove or disturb any underwater artifacts, which is a felony under Michigan law. If you have any information about the theft of underwater artifacts, don't hesitate to report such violations to the **Michigan Department of Natural Resources** (517/284-7275, www.michigan.gov/dnr).

BEACHES AND SWIMMING

For a state nearly surrounded by water, Michigan is not lacking for beaches. Public access is excellent. State parks and forests alone provide more than 140 miles of Great Lakes frontage; county and local parks offer countless more.

The Lake Michigan shore of the Lower Peninsula gets most of the attention; along this Gold Coast, a wide, soft ribbon of sand stretches from the Indiana state line over 200 miles north to the tip of the Leelanau Peninsula, the longest freshwater beach in the world. With the prevailing western winds carrying warm surface water to these shores, Gold Coast beaches are comfortable for summertime bathing too. High dunes rise along stretches of the Gold Coast,

- Don't touch aquatic life.
- Look above the water occasionally to ensure that you haven't drifted too far from the boat; try to stay within 300 feet of the diver-down flag when in open water and within 100 feet when in a river or inlet.
- If you have a diving emergency, dial 911 from your cell phone or use a VHF radio to signal a "MAYDAY."

A helpful saying to remember is "Dive ALIVE," with the letters in *ALIVE* standing for:

- **Air:** Monitor your air supply, always surface with at least 500 psi, and practice out-of-air procedures.
- **Lead Weights:** Wear only enough weight to achieve proper buoyancy, and know how to release your own and your buddy's weight systems.
- **Inspection:** Inspect your gear before every dive trip, replace missing or worn gear, replace batteries in any electronics, and have regulators serviced annually.
- **Verification:** Verify your dive skills, and review your dive plan, signals, and lost-buddy procedures with your diving companion.
- **Escape:** Always dive with surface signaling devices; if you become entangled, remain calm and do what you can to free yourself; if you're lost on the surface, inflate your buoyancy compensation device (BCD), remain calm, maintain your position if possible, and try to attract others' attention.

For more safety tips, consult area diving operators or the **Michigan Underwater Preserve Council** (MUPC, 800/970-8717, www.michiganpreserves.org).

including **Sleeping Bear Dunes National Lakeshore,** west of Traverse City.

The eastern side of the Lower Peninsula, bordered by Lake Huron, also has fine sand beaches curving along the Sunrise Shore. **Tawas Point State Park,** near Tawas City, is noted for its pure white sand. The Huron shore is also famous for its many lighthouses, which at one time were necessary to signal mariners traveling near this low-lying shore.

The beaches of the Upper Peninsula have a decidedly different character—often wild and windswept, rocky and remote. Striped cliffs rise directly from Lake Superior at **Pictured Rocks National Lakeshore;** nearby, the **Grand Sable Dunes** provide enough sand to thrill even the most devoted beachcomber. You probably won't see many people here, but you may glimpse a deer or a black bear headed to the water's edge for a drink—or a bald eagle overhead eyeing the water for a fish. While these beaches are perfect for long, sandy walks, only a hardy few actually swim in Lake Superior—the water temperature rarely climbs out of the 40s. On a sweltering summer day, however, a Lake Superior beach can be a refreshing place to simply lay out. The gentle breeze coming off the water acts as a natural air-conditioner.

The UP's southern shore is on Lake Michigan, a winding coastline filled with bays and inlets. A favorite of anglers, it also has some good beaches—if you know where to look. Public access is a little more difficult. The best spots are along U.S. 2 from Naubinway to the Straits of Mackinac, where rest stops and county parks point you toward nice sandy beaches hidden behind the pines. You'll find another good stretch along Green Bay between Menominee and Escanaba, where several county parks feature good swimming beaches.

WINTER ACTIVITIES

The Great Lakes churn out plentiful lake-effect snowfalls, which fall onto some of the Midwest's hilliest terrain, and make Michigan the top ski destination in the region. While no peak in the state qualifies as mountainous, ski resorts do an admirable job of working with the natural terrain, carving out 600-foot vertical drops and runs that weave through the pines or offer jaw dropping views of the Great Lakes.

Though downhill ski areas can be found throughout the state, the highest concentration is in two primary areas: the western UP from Ironwood to the Porcupine Mountains, and the northwest corner of the Lower Peninsula, from south of Traverse City to just north of Petoskey.

Cross-country skiers have more options. Garland Lodge & Resort, near Lewiston, pampers guests with a beautiful log lodge hidden away in the northeastern Lower Peninsula, surrounded by miles of groomed Nordic trails. In fact, Michigan has several privately run Nordic trail systems. Many of the downhill resorts, such as Crystal Mountain in Thompsonville and Shanty Creek in Bellaire, also have notable Nordic trails. The national lakeshores and many state parks groom trails for skiing, while the state and national forests offer virtually limitless opportunities for backcountry skiing.

Other popular wintertime activities include snowboarding, snowshoeing, snowmobiling, ice-skating, ice fishing, and dogsledding. For more information about Michigan's winter sports, consult the **Michigan Snowsports Industries Association** (MSIA, 7164 Deer Lake Court, Clarkston, 248/620-4448, www.goskimichigan.com) and **Pure Michigan** (888/784-7328, www.michigan.org).

Food and Drink

REGIONAL CUISINE

Short of the few annual powwows held around the state, there's no place to sample the staples of the region's original Native American inhabitants. But the ethnic heritage of Michigan's immigrants is well represented, with the state's diversity reflected in its cuisine.

In Detroit, you can feast on *saganaki* in **Greektown** (www.greektowndetroit.org) and soul food in **Bricktown.** In the southwest Detroit neighborhood known as **Mexicantown** (www.mexicantown.com), busy restaurants stay open until 2am to serve the hungry mole and margarita fans waiting up to two hours for a table. Not far away is **Hamtramck** (www.hamtramck.com), a Polish enclave within Detroit city limits known for traditional kielbasa and pierogi. On Fat Tuesday, the day before the beginning of Lent, Roman Catholic Detroiters of all ethnicities line up at the glass-fronted bakeries to buy up *paczki,* fresh jelly doughnuts. A little farther west, **Dearborn** is home to the largest Arabic communities outside the Middle East. Here, eateries sport signs in English and Arabic and serve up lentil soup, tabbouleh, and *fattoush.*

In **Frankenmuth** (www.frankenmuth.org), a village near Saginaw settled by Germans in the mid-1800s, buses and cars come from miles around for all-you-can-eat chicken and strudel in two cavernous restaurants owned by different branches of the Zehnder family. Made popular by traveling salespeople and Detroit families "out for a drive" in the 1950s, the Bavarian-inspired town has become one of the state's top tourist attractions. In Holland, Dutch food reigns, and flaky pastries are the specialty at the popular Queen's Inn Restaurant at **Neli's Dutch Village** (www.dutchvillage.com).

Fudge and Cherries

Since the 19th century, the regional cuisine of Michigan has been largely influenced by two factors: immigrant cultures and seasonal crops. Visitors interested in international fare can sample Polish pierogi in Hamtramck, Bavarian bratwurst in Frankenmuth, and Cornish pasties throughout the Upper Peninsula. Depending on the season, gourmands can enjoy a wide assortment of homegrown products, from maple syrup to blueberry jam, which can be purchased in various stores throughout the state. In addition, self-pick farms and orchards are abundant in the northern and southwestern portions of the Lower Peninsula; often motorists need only watch for the hand-painted signs along country roads.

Fudge and cherries are two of the state's most popular treats, especially in summer. "Fudgies," as fudge-seeking tourists are often called by Michiganians, flock to the emporiums that dot the northern half of the Lower Peninsula, from Petoskey to Mackinac Island. In July and August, visitors can even watch the fudge-making process in shops like **Doug Murdick's Fudge** (800/238-3432, www.murdicksfudge.com), with locations in Acme and downtown Traverse City.

As for cherries, Traverse City's **National Cherry Festival** (231/947-4230 or 800/968-3380, www.cherryfestival.org) is one of the state's most well-attended summertime events, where connoisseurs can, among other activities, compete in pie-eating and pit-spitting contests. Of course, no visit to the world's largest tart-cherry-growing region would be complete without stopping by the headquarters of **Cherry Republic** (6026 S. Lake St., 800/206-6949, www.cherryrepublic.com) in Glen Arbor, west of Traverse City. Not far from Sleeping Bear Dunes, Cherry Republic boasts everything from cherry wines to cherry-flavored condiments to chocolate-covered cherries.

Throughout the Upper Peninsula, many main street cafés and bakeries serve up the **pasty** (PASS-tee), a potpie creation of beef, potatoes, onions, turnips, and other vegetables. Brought to the UP by Cornish miners, the pasty made for a hearty and filling meal, one that was easy to transport deep into the mine and warm up later with their candles. The same concept works well today if you're headed from town to your campfire.

In Great Lakes ports, you'll often find a commercial fishery operating a small retail store, usually near the waterfront. They often sell both fresh catch and smoked fish. Michigan's abundant fresh fish, from brook trout to walleye are a true delicacy. Smoked fish is superb with a bottle of wine and a Great Lakes sunset.

WINERIES

With temperature extremes moderated by prevailing western winds across Lake Michigan, two areas of the Lower Peninsula have developed into bona fide wine-producing regions. In the southwestern corner and around Grand Traverse Bay, local wineries have won international acclaim with Michigan grapes. White wines like rieslings and chardonnays tend to be their best offerings, but some vintners have had success with reds.

Many Michigan wineries offer free tours and tastings, including **Warner Vineyards** (Paw Paw, 269/657-3165, www.warnerwines.com), **Tabor Hill Winery & Restaurant** (Buchanan, 800/283-3363, www.taborhill.com), and **L. Mawby Vineyards** (Suttons Bay, 231/271-3522, www.lmawby.com). For more information, contact the **Michigan Grape and Wine Industry Council** (517/284-5733, www.michiganwines.com).

BREWERIES

Michigan ranks fifth in the nation for the total number of breweries, with more than 300 independent breweries, microbreweries, and brewpubs. Be sure to sample a few varieties—just remember to enjoy responsibly and do not drink and drive. For more information, consult the **Michigan Brewers Guild**

(225 W. Washtenaw, Ste. C, Lansing, www.mibeer.com).

GROCERIES AND MARKETS

Whether you're traveling via RV or staying in a place with a kitchen, you'll be pleased to know that, despite its acres of rugged countryside and numerous out-of-the-way villages, Michigan has plenty of supermarkets, independent groceries, specialty stores, and farmers markets. So, no matter how long you plan to stay, you'll be able to purchase familiar produce and staples.

You'll find major supermarket chains throughout the Lower Peninsula, including **Meijer** (877/363-4537, www.meijer.com), throughout the southern half. Meijer is also a general retailer offering everything from pet supplies to furniture. Another helpful chain is **Glen's Markets** (800/451-8500, http://glens.spartanstores.com), which you'll find mainly in the northern Lower Peninsula. Independent groceries are fairly common, especially in remoter areas.

If you're hoping to experience Michigan's regional treats and ethnic cuisine, you should visit some of the state's many farmers markets, self-pick farms, and specialty stores—from cheese and sausage shops in Frankenmuth to Traverse City's cherry-related emporiums. For a statewide list of farmers markets, consult the **Michigan Farmers Market Association** (MIFMA, 480 Wilson Rd., Ste. 172, East Lansing, 517/432-3381, www.mifma.org).

Accommodations

Michigan offers a wide range of lodging options, from luxurious resorts to primitive campgrounds. Where you plan to stay, of course, depends on your interests and budget. Though spontaneity can be fun on a vacation, be aware that to ensure availability, reservations may be necessary in advance. Inns and campgrounds can fill up quickly, especially in the summer or during specific annual events. Cost is another factor: By booking in advance, it's also possible to obtain a significantly favorable rate.

While Michigan has plenty of unique lodges and inns, the big hotel and motel chains are also well represented. If you prefer the chains, pick up a copy of the chain's national directory or use its website to find locations, rates, and services. All Michigan lodgings charge 6 percent Michigan sales tax, plus a 6 percent lodging tax. The latter will be reduced to 1.5 percent on July 1, 2020. In addition, some local communities assess an extra local lodging tax, particularly hotels on Mackinac Island. For more information about Michigan's accommodations, consult **The Michigan Travel Companion** (www.yesmichigan.com) or the **Michigan Lodging and Tourism Association** (3815 W. St. Joseph Hwy., Ste. A200, Lansing, 517/267-8989, www.milodging.org).

INDEPENDENT HOTELS AND MOTELS

In the last few decades, the combination of interstate highways, chain lodgings, and America's love of efficiency dealt a fatal blow to hundreds of independently owned motels. The pendulum seems to be swinging the other way, however, and interesting inns and distinctive lodges are cropping up in the most unlikely places. Most are nothing fancy—just simple mom-and-pop motels, the kind of places now romanticized along Route 66.

Independently owned motels never totally disappeared in northern Michigan, especially in the Upper Peninsula. Many UP towns have several, as national chains have stayed away from these remote locations. Some are rundown, but most are clean yet inexpensive, and offer perks that chains might not—allowing pets, for example. Numerous motels are in pedestrian-friendly locations—in small towns or along a waterfront, rather than off a busy highway. Be advised that many accept only cash.

BED-AND-BREAKFASTS

Michigan has hundreds of bed-and-breakfasts. Some are the traditional variety—a spare room or two in someone's quaint old farmhouse—but those have become the exception. Today's B&Bs run the gamut from large inns with pools to renovated lighthouses. For a directory of Michigan's bed-and-breakfasts, contact the **Michigan Lake to Lake Bed-and-Breakfast Association** (6757 Cascade Rd. SE, Ste. 241, Grand Rapids, 888/575-1610, www.laketolake.com).

RESORTS AND LODGES

Many of Michigan's ski resorts double as golf resorts in the summer, ringed with lodging that ranges from motel-style rooms to condo units and town houses with kitchens, which allow you to save considerably on meals. Many also offer amenities like pools, game rooms, and fitness centers, so they can be a particularly good choice for families with active kids. While golf resorts tend to be pricey, ski resorts that don't have the summer golf draw can be great bargains.

For those interested in other activities, like fishing and hunting, Michigan also has a number of seasonal lodges. For information on ski and golf resorts and seasonal lodges, contact **Pure Michigan** (888/784-7328, www.michigan.org).

CABINS AND COTTAGES

A delightful way to experience the rustic beauty of Michigan's varied regions is by staying in a quaint cabin or cottage. Several state parks offer inexpensive lodging in the great outdoors, from furnished cabins at Albert E. Sleeper State Park to tepee rentals at Baraga State Park. Besides cabins, Porcupine Mountains Wilderness State Park also provides basic yurts as well as a historic lodge overlooking Lake Superior. For more information, contact the **Michigan Department of Natural Resources** (517/284-7275, www.michigan.gov/dnr). You can reserve a unit (800/447-2757, www.midnrreservations.com) for a nonrefundable $10 reservation fee. Many of the more popular sites fill up fast, so place your reservation early. The site allows you to do so a full year in advance.

Private cottages, often equipped with comforts like cable television and laundry facilities, are available in resort communities and small towns like Saugatuck, Cadillac, and Petoskey. Whether situated along the beach, beside a golf course, or in the woods, such dwellings can vary in price, size, and amenities, so do your research far in advance. Also keep in mind that reservations are often necessary. For more information about available cabins and cottages throughout the state, consult **The Michigan Travel Companion** (www.yesmichigan.com).

CAMPING

There are several distinctly different styles of camping. You can park an RV next to a pool with a waterslide or pitch a tent in backcountry so remote that you might never see another person. Most people seek something in between. With tens of thousands of campsites, you can probably find something just right.

Most travelers favor the state park campgrounds because they are almost always the nicest ones in the area. Some can get crowded in the summer months. You can reserve a site ahead of time, though specific spots aren't guaranteed, by contacting the **Michigan Department of Natural Resources** (800/447-2757, www.midnrreservations.com) and paying the requisite nonrefundable $10 reservation fee. Many of the more popular sites fill up fast, so place your reservation early. The site allows you to do so a full year in advance.

State and national forests also tend to have nice camping facilities, often more rustic but in appealing out-of-the-way locations. Backcountry camping is permitted in many forests. To reserve a spot in a state forest campground, contact the **Michigan Department of Natural Resources** (800/447-2757, www.midnrreservations.com), and for information about camping in Michigan's national forests, contact **Recreation.gov** (877/444-6777, www.recreation.gov) or the **U.S. Forest Service** (414/297-3600, www.fs.fed.us).

For a complete list of private campgrounds, request a free *Michigan Campground Directory* from the **Association of RV Parks and Campgrounds Michigan** (ARVC, 4696 Orchard Manor Blvd., Ste. 11, Bay City, 989/619-2608, www.michcampgrounds.com) or a free *RV & Campsite* magazine from the **Michigan Association of Recreation Vehicles and Campgrounds** (MARVAC, 2222 Association Dr., Okemos, 517/349-8881, www.marvac.org).

Travel Tips

CONDUCT AND CUSTOMS

Michigan is similar to other Midwestern states in temperament and traditions. While major cities like Detroit and Flint might not follow the general rule, most areas of Michigan, especially smaller towns in the UP and the northern half of the Lower Peninsula, have a down-to-earth wholesome atmosphere. Most residents seem to embrace the values of good education, hard work, and close family ties. As in other U.S. states, more women are working outside the home, whether in the auto plants of southeastern Michigan or the corporations of the Heartland. Traditional gender roles still exist, but those customs are rapidly changing.

Given the state's multiethnic history, reliance on tourism, and proximity to Canada, foreigners and travelers generally feel welcome here. Residents are helpful, hospitable, and forthright. They might use regional language and have unique dialects, especially in ethnic enclaves and in parts of the UP, but politeness and good manners are prevalent. So do as the locals do; be considerate, ask for help when you need it, thank others for their time, and as a courtesy, *always* ask permission before taking a photo.

TRAVELERS WITH DISABILITIES

Thanks to the implementation of the Americans With Disabilities Act, Michigan is very accessible for those with physical limitations. Most welcome centers and rest areas are equipped with features that can accommodate wheelchairs, such as convenient parking spaces, entrance ramps, wide passages, automatic doors, and spacious restrooms. The same can be said for major retail chains, hotel chains, and key attractions, such as the football stadium at the University of Michigan and the Michigan's Adventure amusement park in Muskegon. When in doubt about the possibility of access, call the establishment in question.

TRAVELING WITH CHILDREN

With its multitude of beaches, state parks, museums, and other amusements, Michigan is a very kid-friendly destination. Traveling with children, you'll find lots for them to do. Many restaurants and hotels go out of their way to accommodate young travelers. In Frankenmuth, for instance, **Zehnder's Splash Village Hotel and Waterpark** offers a video arcade, several waterslides, a 24-hour fitness center, and shuttle service to the restaurant.

When traveling with children, supervise them at all times, both to keep them safe and to minimize the possibility of disturbing others. If you decide to venture into Canada, you must have proper identification for them as well as yourself.

TRAVELING WITH PETS

Although pets are prohibited in much of Michigan's national parkland and in most of the state's hotels, restaurants, and stores, many places do welcome them, including highway rest areas. In locations where pets are allowed, it's crucial to understand the relevant rules. Typically you are asked to keep your pets on a leash at all times, walk them in designated areas, control their behavior so as not to disturb or endanger others, and always pick up after them. When in doubt, call ahead to verify the pet policies.

WOMEN TRAVELING ALONE

It's important to take precautions, especially in urban centers like Detroit and Flint. Tell someone back home about your intended travel plans, limit driving to the daytime, and keep close to busy attractions, streets, and campgrounds. Try to stow your money, credit cards, and identification close to your person; big purses make easy targets. If you feel someone is stalking you, find a public place such as a store, tourism bureau, or police station, and don't hesitate to alert the police. Keep the doors to your lodging and vehicle locked at all times.

Before heading out on your trip, be sure to have a cell phone, which can be useful in an emergency. Remember that cell reception is limited or nonexistent in the state's remoter areas, especially parts of the Upper Peninsula.

SENIOR TRAVELERS

Senior travelers should have little trouble getting assistance. For help with directions, there are welcome centers and tourism bureaus throughout the state, plus plenty of locals able to point you in the right direction. In addition, many establishments, especially restaurants, offer discounts to senior travelers. The **National Park Service** (www.nps.gov) offers a lifetime pass ($10) for U.S. citizens and permanent residents over age 61, allowing them and up to four adults free access to national parks and federal lands that charge entrance fees, including national lakeshores.

GAY AND LESBIAN TRAVELERS

Michigan has traditionally been one of the more liberal Midwestern states, especially on the eastern side of the Lower Peninsula, and has evolved with the rest of the nation in recent years in greater tolerance of its gay and lesbian citizens. This courtesy is extended to visitors, although in more conservative communities, old biases persist. Ann Arbor, home to the University of Michigan, and the nearby towns of Chelsea and Ypsilanti stand out as especially LGBTQ-friendly. Along the Southwest Coast, towns like Benton Harbor have a large number of gay-owned vacation homes, and the neighboring villages of Saugatuck and Douglas (www.gaysaugatuck-douglas.com) offer more than 120 LGBTQ-friendly shops, art galleries, restaurants, and lodging options. For more information about related issues, events, and establishments in Michigan, contact the **Pride Source Media Group** (20222 Farmington Rd., Livonia, 734/293-7200, www.pridesource.com), which produces an annual business directory for the state's LGBTQ residents and also puts out a free weekly newspaper, *Between the Lines*, which serves the LGBTQ community.

Health and Safety

Before hitting the road, it's critical that you pack a well-stocked first-aid kit and prepare yourself for the common pitfalls of travel in Michigan.

HEALTH RISKS

Contaminated Water

Although the state's crystal clear streams may look inviting for a drink, don't take the chance. Many of Michigan's most pristine lakes and streams may be tainted with *Giardia lamblia,* an organism that is most commonly transmitted in the feces of beavers, moose, and other mammals. Giardiasis can result in severe stomach cramps, vomiting, and diarrhea. As one Isle Royale ranger once said, "It won't kill you, but it may make you wish you were dead." Chemical treatment with Halizone will not make water safe from giardia; you need a water purifier filtering down to 0.4 microns. Boiling is also effective, but make sure to get the water to a full rolling boil for five minutes. In addition, Isle Royale water may be infected with the hydatid tapeworm, which can also be eradicated by filtering or boiling.

Insects

Wood ticks and deer ticks are found in Michigan woods and grasslands. The larger wood tick, about 0.25 inches long, attaches to the skin and feeds on the person's blood—but is surprisingly harmless. If you find a wood tick on you or your pet, grasp it as close to the head as possible and pull slowly. Be sure not to leave a piece of the insect embedded or it may cause an infection. Ticks are generally attracted to the body's warm areas—such as the scalp, neck, armpits, and genitals. This also applies to dogs. Be sure to check under the collar and all around the ears.

Deer ticks are more dangerous, as they may transmit Lyme disease, a potentially debilitating condition. Lyme disease shows up as a temporary red rash that often resembles a ring slowly expanding outward. As the disease progresses, other symptoms include sore joints, fatigue, and nausea. If left untreated, it can lead to arthritis and severe neurological and cardiac problems. Caught early, it can be treated effectively with antibiotics.

To complicate matters, deer ticks are tiny—scarcely larger than the head of a pin. Like wood ticks, they burrow into the skin, especially in warm places. After hiking, check your own skin and your hiking partners' carefully. If you find one and it's large enough, grasp the tick and pull it off slowly, or use tweezers. If you've been in a tick-infested area, watch for a developing rash within the next week and have anything suspicious promptly looked at by a doctor. Your best defense against ticks is to wear long pants and long sleeves, and cover your skin liberally with a hard-core repellent like those containing DEET.

Dogs are also susceptible to Lyme disease. Check your dog carefully and thoroughly for deer ticks by slowly running your fingers or a comb through the coat to get a look at the skin—a task that requires a lot of patience, both on your part and your dog's. Pay particular attention to the ears, neck, belly, and genitals. Signs that your dog may have acquired Lyme disease include nausea, fatigue, and lameness that may come and go from different joints. If you see potential symptoms, get your pet to a veterinarian immediately. Like humans, dogs respond well to antibiotics if the disease is caught early enough.

There is a canine vaccine for Lyme disease, but veterinarians are divided on how effective it is. At least be aware of the various tick repellent sprays on the market, and be sure to use them before venturing into the deep woods.

Plants

While hiking Michigan's forests, marshes, and beaches, be careful where you step. It's easier than you think to trip on a root or other obstruction. Unless you're certain that you've found a patch of wild blueberries or other recognizable fruit, you should refrain from digesting any tempting berries, flowers, plants, and the like without first consulting local residents or expert field guides.

One plant in Michigan that can be dangerous merely to touch is poison ivy, two primary species of which inhabit all of the Lower Peninsula and much of the Upper. The plant grows close to the ground (often in wet areas) or on the trunks of trees and consists of three tear-shaped leaves. The leaves often have sharp teeth protruding from their tips.

When skin comes in contact with the oily resin secreted by the plant's leaves, it triggers an allergic reaction that results in a red rash characterized by itching, swelling, and blisters. The toxicity is powerful enough that if you were to breathe the fumes from burning poison ivy, an asthmatic response might result. Medical attention is needed if the reaction is severe, the blisters begin oozing pus, or the person experiences a fever of over 100 degrees. Knowing how to identify poison ivy and avoiding it in the first place are clearly the preferable course of action.

Wild Animals

Although black bears seem more frightening, especially when you're deep in the woods, deer are by far the biggest danger—as they cause thousands of collisions a year on Michigan roads. Black bears are found throughout northern Michigan; the Upper Peninsula has an especially large population. They usually live in areas of heavy forest but will routinely wander into open areas in search of food. They're beautiful animals, and you should consider yourself lucky to observe one.

Black bears are generally shy creatures that would prefer to have nothing to do with you. If they hear you coming, they'll run the other way. If you happen to see one before it sees you, leave it an escape route, then clap, yell, or bang pans. Give an especially wide berth to a mother and cubs. There are very few documented cases of black bear aggression against humans, and theories vary on what to do if you should ever find yourself in such a situation. Most behaviorists believe that, unlike grizzlies, black bears will be intimidated by dominance behavior like shouting and waving your arms.

The biggest problems come when bears are lured into populated areas by human carelessness. It's always sad to see a bear relocated from its home territory, but it happens frequently in campgrounds where humans store food or dispose of garbage improperly. If you're car camping, keep all food in your vehicle—with doors and windows closed. If you're tent camping, keep everything in airtight storage containers and suspend the containers on a line between two trees, high enough off the ground and far enough apart to be out of a bear's reach. Latched coolers shoved under a picnic table are not sufficient to repel bears.

Clean pans and utensils immediately after use, dumping water well away from camp, and store them with the food. Never keep any food (even gum) in your tent. Bears have an extremely good sense of smell and may be tempted to join you. Some say cosmetics can also attract them, so play it safe and store your soap and toothpaste with the food. You might want to leave your tent unzipped during the day while you're gone. Bears are curious; if they want to check out your tent, they'll make their own entrance if they can't find one.

If you're at a campground, deposit garbage in the animal-proof refuse containers provided. If you're backcountry camping, pack out all trash. Needless to say, never attempt to feed a bear, no matter how tame it may seem.

Heatstroke

During Michigan summers, hot, sunny days are common, and it's crucial that you prepare for them. Although sunscreen will help to prevent sunburn (which, if experienced often, can cause long-term problems for your skin), you must apply it often and liberally. Prolonged sun exposure, high temperatures, and inadequate water consumption can also

Avoiding Animal Attacks

Porcupines, black bears, moose, gray wolves, and other wild animals roam freely throughout Michigan, so it's quite possible that you might spot them during your travels, especially while exploring the state's vast forests. Although many of these creatures are wary of people, some may be curious. At such times, it might be easy to forget how to handle an encounter with a wild animal. Adhere to the following rules:

- Observe wildlife from a distance; do not follow or approach the animals.
- Never feed wildlife; it can damage their health, alter their natural behavior, and expose them to predators.
- Never taunt or disturb wildlife.
- Protect wildlife by storing your food and trash securely.
- Control pets at all times, or leave them at home.
- Avoid wildlife during sensitive phases, such as mating or nesting seasons.

For more information about respecting wildlife, consult the **Michigan Department of Natural Resources** (517/284-7275, www.michigan.gov/dnr) or contact the Colorado-based **Leave No Trace Center for Outdoor Ethics** (303/442-8222 or 800/332-4100, www.lnt.org).

cause dehydration, which can lead to heat exhaustion—a harmful condition whereby your internal cooling system begins to shut down. Symptoms may include clammy skin, weakness, vomiting, and abnormal body temperature. In such instances, you should lie down in the shade, remove restrictive clothing, and drink some water.

If you do not treat heat exhaustion promptly, your condition can worsen quickly, leading to heatstroke or sunstroke—a dangerous state whereby your internal body temperature starts to rise to a potentially fatal level. Symptoms can include dizziness, vomiting, diarrhea, abnormal breathing and blood pressure, headache, cessation of sweating, and confusion. If any of these occur, seek medical attention immediately. At the first onset of symptoms, your companions should move you into the shade; remove your clothing; lower your body temperature with cool water, damp sheets, or fans; and give you water to drink, if you're able.

Extreme Cold

While winter can be a beautiful time to visit the Great Lakes State, there's no doubt that Michigan winters can be long, hard, and cruel, especially for those unaccustomed to such cold snowy conditions. If you plan to travel here from November to March, be sure to pack plenty of warm clothes, including sweaters, mittens, hats, and waterproof boots. Be prepared to dress in layers (including your feet), as it's always better to remove clothing than to not have enough, especially if you plan to be outside for a while.

One condition to avoid is hypothermia, whereby the body temperature begins to decline to a dangerous level. Being cold and wet for an extended period of time, such as during a snowstorm, can be fatal. Try to keep warm and dry at all times. If you start to shiver, slur your speech, stumble, or feel drowsy, do not fall asleep. Instead, find some shelter, change into dry clothes, try to move around, and eat a quick energy snack.

You should also watch out for frostbite, which can occur when blood vessels near the skin constrict, sending more blood to your vital organs and allowing outer tissues to freeze. The body parts most susceptible are your nose, cheeks, ears, and extremities. Initially, affected areas might tingle, itch, burn, whiten, go numb, or turn cold. Prolonged frostbite could cause swelling, blisters, and, ultimately, blackened skin. Diabetes, alcohol consumption, tobacco use, fatigue, dehydration, high altitude, and improper clothing can all exacerbate the situation. To avoid long-term damage and possible amputation, you should find shelter immediately and warm the affected areas. If your condition is severe, a doctor will need to oversee the rewarming process in order to determine the extent of the damage.

Getting Lost

Part of Michigan's charm is its plethora of untamed backcountry areas and the possibility of exploring them in any season. Losing oneself in such wilderness might sound romantic, but in reality it can be downright deadly, especially during extreme weather. To protect yourself from harmful long-term exposure to the elements, it's crucial to plan your route ahead of time, consult local residents before heading into an isolated area, and inform someone else of your intentions in case you don't return as scheduled. When venturing into the wilderness, it's also advisable to travel in a group of at least four; in an emergency situation, one of you can stay with the afflicted person while the other two seek help.

If you stick to the main highways, you might need little more than a reliable map to navigate Michigan. But if you want to explore the state's remoter areas, it's imperative that you bring a compass and GPS receiver with you. Today's smartphones are often equipped with these features. Be advised, however, that despite improved coverage over the past decade, cell phones still lose connectivity in the Lower Peninsula's northern forests and throughout much of the Upper Peninsula.

MEDICAL SERVICES

Emergency Care

All of Michigan is tied into the **911** emergency system. Dial 911 free from any telephone, including pay phones, to reach an operator who can quickly dispatch local police, fire, or ambulance services. This service also works from cell phones. Be aware, however, that cellular signals can be spotty or nonexistent in rural areas. Much of the Upper Peninsula, including Pictured Rocks National Lakeshore, remains without reliable cellular service.

Hospitals and Pharmacies

If you experience an illness or injury, hospitals and pharmacies are plentiful throughout the state, especially in major cities like Detroit, Flint, Grand Rapids, and Marquette.

Insurance

Insurance is strongly recommended while traveling in Michigan. Whether you're a U.S. citizen driving your own car or an international traveler in a rented RV, you should invest in medical, travel, and auto insurance before embarking on your trip to protect yourself and your assets. If you're driving a rental car, consider the rental company's offer of supplemental insurance.

CRIME

Despite the negative reputation of places like Detroit and Flint, Michigan is a relatively safe place. It might be hard to believe in the modern day, but residents of the northern rural areas rarely lock their doors at night. People here are, for the most part, friendly and helpful. Still, whether you're visiting Detroit or a small town on the Leelanau Peninsula, it's important to take commonsense precautions.

Never leave valuables in plain view on a car seat; secure them in the trunk, where they're invisible to thieves. In an accident on the highway, do not abandon your vehicle, as this may invite would-be thieves. When sightseeing, keep your money and important items hidden on your person; purses and backpacks are much easier to steal. Do not walk alone at night, even in a small town, and try not to travel on the highways after dark. Even if you have AAA roadside assistance, help can be slow to come if you break down on a country road at night.

If you're traveling via RV, do not dry-dock

alone in an isolated place. Try to stay in an RV park, a campground, or, at the very least, a well-lit parking lot. When venturing into the wilderness, try to camp with others. If you do find yourself in trouble, don't hesitate to find a phone and dial **911.** Of course, the time that it takes police and emergency vehicles to reach you will depend on your location, and may take longer in the UP's remoter areas.

Information and Services

MAPS AND VISITOR INFORMATION

For general information on traveling in Michigan, your best source is the state-run **Pure Michigan** (888/784-7328, www.michigan.org, 9am-5pm Mon.-Fri.). Your call will be answered by a live person who can send you brochures and field your questions about festivals, activities, lodgings, and more. You may find it even more convenient to visit the website, which offers a comprehensive database of communities, accommodations, restaurants, and recreation. Be aware that some of the information can be outdated, so always call ahead.

Suggested Maps

Michigan's official state road map is a rarity: unlike most maps, it doesn't relegate the UP to the opposite side. Pick one up at a **Welcome Center** or request one from **Pure Michigan** (888/784-7328, www.michigan.org). **AAA** (800/222-6424, www.aaa.com) also offers a helpful Michigan map ($8 nonmembers, free for members).

For more detail, **DeLorme** (207/847-1165 or 800/642-0970, www.garmin.com) produces the *Michigan Atlas & Gazetteer* ($23), with the state portrayed in 102 large-scale maps. Though the 15-inch-long format is unwieldy for hikers, it's a great resource for planning your trip; it even identifies campgrounds, golf courses, wineries, historic sites, bicycle routes, and other points of interest. You can find it at many Midwestern bookstores and gas stations, or order it online directly from Garmin, DeLorme's parent company.

If you'll be exploring the backcountry, you should invest in an official topographical (topo) map produced by the **U.S. Geological Survey** (888/275-8747, www.usgs.gov). Michigan's national parks and forests have topo maps for sale at their visitors centers or ranger stations. Outside federal lands, you may find them in local outfitter shops. If you can, buy or order one ahead of time through an outfitter or travel store. Once you're in the field, if you can't find the map you need, it may be unavailable.

Welcome Centers

The **Michigan Department of Transportation** (MDOT, 517/373-2090, www.michigan.gov/mdot) operates 14 year-round welcome centers throughout the state. Stocked with maps and brochures, these facilities are staffed with travel counselors who are knowledgeable about the state in general and their region in particular. The centers are marked on the state map and by signs on the nearest highway. Hours vary.

The Lower Peninsula has eight welcome centers: **Clare** (U.S. 10/127, north of town), **Coldwater** (I-69, 6 miles north of the Indiana-Michigan state line), **Detroit** (2835 Bagley St., off I-75), **Dundee** (U.S. 23, 6 miles north of the Ohio-Michigan state line), **Mackinaw City** (Nicolet St., off I-75), **Monroe** (I-75, 10 miles north of the Ohio-Michigan state line), **New Buffalo** (I-94 at the Indiana-Michigan state line), and **Port Huron** (I-69/94, west of the Blue Water Bridge).

The Upper Peninsula has six welcome centers: **Iron Mountain** (U.S. 2/141 downtown), **Ironwood** (U.S. 2 at the Wisconsin-Michigan state line), **Marquette** (U.S. 41/M-28, 2 miles south of town), **Menominee** (U.S. 41 at the Wisconsin-Michigan state line), **Sault Ste. Marie** (I-75, south of the International Bridge), and **St. Ignace** (I-75, north of the Mackinac Bridge).

Regional Tourism Bureaus

All of Michigan's major cities and many of its small towns offer tourism services through area convention and visitors bureaus (CVBs) or chambers of commerce. The state also has several regional tourism offices that cover larger areas.

In the Lower Peninsula, you can contact the **Thumb Area Tourism Council** (TATC, 989/672-0991, www.thumbtourism.org), **Southwestern Michigan Tourist Council** (269/925-6301, www.swmichigan.org), **Michigan Beachtowns Association** (www.beachtowns.org), and **West Michigan Tourist Association** (WMTA, 616/245-2217, www.wmta.org). In the Upper Peninsula, contact the **Western UP Convention & Visitor Bureau** (906/932-4850 or 800/522-5657, www.explorewesternup.com) and **Upper Peninsula Travel & Recreation Association** (UPTRA, 906/774-5480 or 800/562-7134, www.uptravel.com). To reach local tourism offices, consult the **Michigan Association of Convention and Visitor Bureaus** (MACVB, 231/823-0015, www.visitmichigan.org).

COMMUNICATIONS AND MEDIA

Cell Phones

Today, a cell phone is virtually a necessity for travelers. Keep in mind, however, that cellular coverage is not universal in many rural areas, especially the Upper Peninsula.

Media

Most of Michigan's major towns have at least one daily newspaper, from the ***Detroit News*** (www.detnews.com) and the ***Detroit Free Press*** (www.freep.com) to Escanaba's ***Daily Press*** (www.dailypress.net). Some places, such as Detroit and Traverse City, even have their own magazine. Such periodicals are terrific sources of information for festivals, restaurants, sporting events, outdoor activities, and other diversions.

Local television and radio stations, such as Detroit's ABC affiliate WXYZ (www.wxyz.com), are also excellent sources of regional information. Pick up a newspaper in your area for a list of channels.

MONEY

Currency and Credit Cards

Bank debit cards and major credit cards (like Visa and MasterCard) are accepted statewide, even in the smallest towns. In addition, automated teller machines (ATMs) have become more prevalent, allowing travelers to withdraw cash whenever they need it. If you're uncomfortable using ATMs, you'll find banks open during business hours and occasionally on Saturday. However, many self-registration campgrounds, independent motels, eateries, and stores often accept only cash. Never count on getting by with only plastic.

If you're traveling to or from Canada, you'll find currency exchanges at the border and at nearby banks in both countries. Since the exchange rate fluctuates, you should plan to exchange currencies whenever coming or going. For up-to-date exchange rates, consult www.xe.com.

If you're a U.S. resident with Canadian currency left over at the end of a trip, try to end up with bills, not coins. Many banks, especially away from border towns, will exchange only paper money, so you can easily find yourself with $10 or $20 worth of heavy souvenirs.

Sales Tax

In Michigan, most goods and some services, including hotel accommodations, are subject to a 6 percent sales tax. Although there is no additional statewide lodging tax in Michigan, some counties do impose one, including Calhoun, Genesee, Ingham, Kalamazoo, Kent, Muskegon, Saginaw, and Washtenaw. A few municipalities levy a local hotel tax, including Detroit and Mackinac Island.

Tipping

Although the amount of a gratuity depends on the level of service received, general tipping guidelines in Michigan and the United States suggest that restaurant servers, delivery drivers, and bartenders receive 15-20 percent of the pretax bill; taxi, limousine, and shuttle drivers should receive at least 15 percent of the entire fare; valets, porters, and skycaps should receive $2 per vehicle or piece of luggage. You may also choose to tip hotel concierges, restroom and coat-check attendants, spa and salon personnel, musicians and street performers, and other service providers.

It's also worth noting that tour guides, fishing guides, boat captains, and other excursion operators should be tipped as well. No matter how much such tours or trips cost, the gratuity is never included in the rates. While the amount of a tip will depend on the cost, length, and nature of the trip in question—not to mention your satisfaction with the services received—it's generally accepted to tip between 10 and 20 percent of the overall cost of the trip. If a guide or operator makes an exceptional effort, such as unexpectedly extending the length of a trip, then it's recommended that you increase the size of your tip accordingly. Poor tipping could harm your reputation among other guides and operators, while more generous tipping could ensure even better service next time.

WEIGHTS AND MEASURES

Electricity

In Michigan, electrical outlets operate on the North American standard 120 volts, 60 hertz. Coming from Europe, Asia, or a country that operates at 220 or 240 volts, you'll need an adapter to use your electronics or small appliances. Outlets vary between the two-prong and three-prong variety, for which you might also need an adapter, easily purchased in hardware and electronics stores.

Time Zone

Most of Michigan is in the eastern time zone (ET), with the exception of the four Upper Peninsula counties that border Wisconsin: Gogebic, Iron, Dickinson, and Menominee Counties are in the central time zone (CT). Michigan observes daylight saving time between mid-March and early November. Most smartphones and automotive clocks adjust automatically when crossing a time-zone boundary.

Resources

Glossary

The following regional terms and abbreviations will help you navigate your way across the state of Michigan and perhaps better understand its unique people and culture:

Big Mac: a nickname for the Mackinac Bridge, the link between Michigan's Upper and Lower Peninsulas; also called simply "The Bridge" by many residents, especially those who don't live in proximity to the bridges that cross the United States-Canada border

downriver: a reference to the Wayne County suburbs south of Detroit, which front the Detroit River

downstate: a reference to Michigan's Lower Peninsula

D-Town: a nickname for the city of Detroit

eh: a spoken interjection commonly used by Upper Peninsula natives to solicit a response or add emphasis to a statement (e.g., "There's no place like Michigan, eh?")

Eight Mile: Eight Mile Road, the boundary between Detroit and its northern suburbs

fudgies: a nickname for tourists, especially in the northern part of Michigan's Lower Peninsula, which is known for its ubiquitous fudge shops

the LP: a seldom-used abbreviation for Michigan's Lower Peninsula

Michigander: the most frequently used demonym for a Michigan resident

Michiganian: an alternative demonym for a Michigan resident

Mighty Mac: an alternative nickname for the Mackinac Bridge, the link between Michigan's two peninsulas

the Mitten: a commonly used nickname for Michigan's Lower Peninsula

Motor City: a nickname for Detroit that honors the town's rich automotive history

Motown: a record label and musical style that originated in Detroit; also used as a nickname for the city itself

pasty: a handheld pastry filled with meat and vegetables, popular in Michigan's Upper Peninsula

pop: a term that refers to carbonated sodas or soft drinks

the Soo: a commonly used nickname for Sault Ste. Marie, a city in the Upper Peninsula

Spartan: the mascot of Michigan State University in East Lansing

the Thumb: a generally accepted term for the region of Michigan's Lower Peninsula that lies between Saginaw Bay, Lake Huron, and I-75, and that resembles the thumb of a mitten

tip of the Mitten: a reference to the Straits of Mackinac

tip of the Thumb: a reference to the town of Port Austin

Trolls: a nickname used by residents of Michigan's Upper Peninsula to refer to their counterparts in the Lower Peninsula

the UP: a frequently used abbreviation for Michigan's Upper Peninsula

up north: a reference to a place north of wherever one is in Michigan, typically used to refer to the Upper Peninsula or the northern part of the Lower Peninsula by residents of that state's southern tier.

Wolverine: the mascot of the University of Michigan in Ann Arbor

Yooperland: a nickname for Michigan's Upper Peninsula; also called "Da Yoop" or "Yoopsconsin" by UP residents

Yoopers: a nickname for residents of Michigan's Upper Peninsula

Warrior: the mascot of Wayne State University in Detroit

Suggested Reading

FICTION AND PROSE

Catton, Bruce. *Waiting for the Morning Train: An American Boyhood.* Detroit: Wayne State University Press, 1987. Reflecting on his childhood in Benzonia, southwest of Traverse City, a Pulitzer Prize-winning journalist and historian offers a beguiling look at boyhood memories, which segues into more serious discussions about the impact of technology on our society. Catton (1899-1978) originally published this memoir in 1972.

Emerick, Lon L. *The Superior Peninsula: Seasons in the Upper Peninsula of Michigan.* Skandia, MI: North Country Publishing, 1996. A collection of essays and love letters about the biggest of the Great Lakes, categorized by seasons.

Gruley, Bryan. *The Hanging Tree.* New York: Simon & Schuster, 2010. In this follow-up mystery to *Starvation Lake,* small-town newspaper editor Gus Carpenter must struggle, with the help of his old flame, to understand what really happened to Gracie McBride, an apparent suicide victim found dead shortly after returning to her hometown.

Gruley, Bryan. *The Skeleton Box.* New York: Simon & Schuster, 2013. The last of a trilogy that includes *Starvation Lake* (2009) and *The Hanging Tree* (2010), this mystery features small-town newspaper editor Gus Carpenter as he investigates the most difficult story of his life: the murder of his ex-girlfriend's mother, whose body was found in his own mother's house.

Hemingway, Ernest. *The Complete Short Stories of Ernest Hemingway.* New York: Scribner, 1998. Hemingway's works have been published numerous times, but this volume includes his finest Michigan-based short stories: "Up in Michigan," set in Horton Bay, and numerous Nick Adams tales, including "Big Two-Hearted River," about fishing in the Upper Peninsula.

Leonard, Elmore. *Out of Sight.* New York: William Morrow Paperbacks, 2012. Famous for his crime novels, many of which have been turned into films, Leonard tells the story of a career thief and his unlikely relationship with a U.S. marshal, which takes them from Detroit's grittiest streets to its most upscale suburbs.

Steinberg, Michael, ed. *Peninsula: Essays and Memoirs from Michigan.* East Lansing, MI: Michigan State University Press, 2000. An eclectic regional anthology of nearly 40 contemporary essays and memoirs, written by current and former Michiganians, including Jim Harrison and Jack Driscoll. The stories focus on the state's great outdoors and metropolitan areas.

Traver, Robert. *Anatomy of a Murder.* New York: St. Martin's Press, 1983. Originally published in 1958, this popular novel was penned by former Michigan Supreme Court justice and UP resident John D. Voelker (aka Robert Traver), about a lover's triangle murder that took place in nearby Big Bay. It was later made into a noteworthy motion picture.

GEOGRAPHY AND ECOLOGY

Barnes, Burton V., and Warren H. Wagner Jr. *Michigan Trees: A Guide to the Trees of Michigan and the Great Lakes Region*. Ann Arbor, MI: University of Michigan Press, 2004. Originally published in 1913 by different authors, this updated field guide was written by two University of Michigan professors of forestry and botany, respectively.

Blacklock, Craig. *The Lake Superior Images*. Moose Lake, MN: Blacklock Nature Photography, 1998. Blacklock, son of famous nature photographer Les Blacklock, circumnavigated Lake Superior by kayak to capture images for this award-winning book, which surely belongs on every northern coffee table.

Dickmann, Donald I., and Larry A. Leefers. *The Forests of Michigan*. Ann Arbor, MI: University of Michigan Press, 2003. Two forestry professors from Michigan State University examine the natural history, ecology, management, and economic importance of the varied forests that cover roughly half of the state.

Huber, N. King. *The Geologic Story of Isle Royale National Park*. Washington DC: U.S. Department of the Interior Geological Survey, 1983. For a government publication, this is a rather colorfully written study of Isle Royale's distinctive topography, an understanding of which makes an Isle Royale backpacking trip all the more memorable.

Mueller, Bruce, and Kevin Gauthier. *Lake Huron Rock Picker's Guide*. Ann Arbor, MI: University of Michigan Press, 2010. Featuring black-and-white images, this identification guide assists rockhounds along the eastern side of Michigan's Lower Peninsula.

Mueller, Bruce, and Kevin Gauthier. *Lake Superior Rock Picker's Guide*. Ann Arbor, MI: University of Michigan Press, 2007. Besides identifying numerous rocks found along the shores of Lake Superior, this guide also offers helpful advice on where to locate each stone and how to polish what you find.

Peterson, Rolf O. *The Wolves of Isle Royale: A Broken Balance*. Ann Arbor, MI: University of Michigan Press, 2007. In this firsthand study, a wildlife biologist and professor of wildlife ecology scrutinizes the ancient predator-prey relationship between the stealthy Isle Royale wolf and the native moose.

Smith, Gerald R., and Emily Damstra. *Guide to Great Lakes Fishes*. Ann Arbor, MI: University of Michigan Press, 2010. Written by a former University of Michigan professor of ecology and evolutionary biology, this comprehensive guide features informative essays, illustrations, and photographs about more than 60 of the region's most commonly found fish species.

Tekiela, Stan. *Birds of Michigan Field Guide*. Cambridge, MN: Adventure Publications, 2004. With color photographs and an easy-to-use format, the second edition of Tekiela's indispensable field guide can help even amateur bird-watchers observe most of Michigan's native species.

Tekiela, Stan. *Wildflowers of Michigan Field Guide*. Cambridge, MN: Adventure Publications, 2000. As with all of Tekiela's colorful field guides, this one is ideal for both beginners and those familiar with Michigan's varied wildflowers.

Voss, Edward G., and Anton A. Reznicek. *Field Manual of Michigan Flora*. Ann Arbor, MI: University of Michigan Press, 2012. Written by two world-renowned plant curators at the University of Michigan, this incredibly comprehensive, thoroughly updated field guide offers everything that naturalists might want to know about more than 2,700 of Michigan's native and nonnative seed plants.

HISTORY AND CULTURE

Ashlee, Laura Rose, ed. *Traveling Through Time: A Guide to Michigan's Historical Markers.* Ann Arbor, MI: University of Michigan Press, 2005. This revised edition is the definitive, illustrated guide to nearly 1,500 of Michigan's historic sites, found along highways, in storied neighborhoods, and around urban centers.

Carson, David A. *Grit, Noise, and Revolution: The Birth of Detroit Rock 'n' Roll.* Ann Arbor, MI: University of Michigan Press, 2006. A narrative history of the long-haired, hard-rocking musicians who helped to change the face of rock music.

Clifton, James, James McClurken, and George Cornell. *People of the Three Fires: The Ottawa, Potawatomi, and Ojibway of Michigan.* Grand Rapids, MI: Grand Rapids Inner-Tribal Council, 1986. An excellent introduction to these three cultures, not only with an emphasis on history and traditions, but also a solid discussion of modern Native American issues.

Darden, Joe T., Curtis Stokes, and Richard W. Thomas. *The State of Black Michigan, 1967-2007.* East Lansing, MI: Michigan State University Press, 2007. An investigation of how Michigan's black population and its interactions with whites have changed since the insurrection in Detroit during the summer of 1967.

Dempsey, Dave, and Jack Dempsey. *Ink Trails: Michigan's Famous and Forgotten Authors.* East Lansing, MI: Michigan State University Press, 2012. This engaging book explores the secrets and legends surrounding some of Michigan's poets, novelists, and other writers, including those that were born here or found inspiration in the state's varied towns, cities, and landscapes.

Dodge, R. L. *Michigan Ghost Towns of the Lower Peninsula.* Berkeley, CA: Thunder Bay Press, 2002. A compilation of the settlements and communities that have faded into Michigan's history.

Dunbar, Willis F., and George S. May. *Michigan: A History of the Wolverine State.* Grand Rapids, MI: William B. Eerdmans Publishing, 1995. First published in 1965 and since revised, this widely praised comprehensive work covers the rich history of Michigan, from the early days of the first Native American settlers to the political developments of the mid-1990s.

Frimodig, David. *A Most Superior Land: Life in the Upper Peninsula of Michigan.* Lansing, MI: Michigan Department of Natural Resources, 1983. Offering a wealth of historical photos, this wonderful series of short essays and anecdotal tales illustrates the history of the Upper Peninsula.

Gustin, Lawrence R. *Billy Durant: Creator of General Motors.* Ann Arbor, MI: University of Michigan Press, 2008. Initially published in 1973, this well-researched biography explores the man who cofounded General Motors and made Flint one of America's greatest industrial centers.

Jolly, Ron, and Karl Bohnak. *Michigan's Upper Peninsula Almanac.* Ann Arbor, MI: University of Michigan Press, 2009. Authored by a veteran radio broadcaster and a respected meteorologist, this comprehensive almanac offers a bevy of information about the Upper Peninsula, including longtime businesses, popular tourist spots, record snowfalls, curious myths, and much more.

Maki, Craig, and Keith Cady. *Detroit Country Music: Mountaineers, Cowboys, and Rockabillies.* Ann Arbor, MI: University of Michigan Press, 2013. Written by two dedicated musicians, researchers, and radio broadcasters, this groundbreaking book uncovers the musicians, labels, radio programs, and performance venues that nurtured Detroit's little-known but vibrant country and bluegrass music scene.

Stonehouse, Frederick. *The Wreck of the Edmund Fitzgerald*. Gwinn, MI: Avery Color Studios, 2006. Though one of several books covering this famous shipwreck, this particular title is considered by many historians to be the definitive work on the subject, scrutinizing the events leading up to the tragedy and offering various theories about the cause of the ship's demise. Originally published in the mid-1970s, the release of this new edition coincides with the sinking's 30th anniversary.

Taylor, Sprague. *Tahquamenon Country: A Look at Its Past*. Lansing, MI: Historical Society of Michigan, 1991. The history of the people who depended on Michigan's mighty Tahquamenon River, as told by a lifelong resident of the eastern Upper Peninsula.

Thurner, Arthur W. *Strangers and Sojourners: A History of Michigan's Keweenaw Peninsula*. Detroit: Wayne State University Press, 1994. The socioeconomic history of the diverse immigrants who established and sustained the communities of the UP's Keweenaw, Houghton, Baraga, and Ontonagon Counties.

Vachon, Paul. *Detroit: An Illustrated Timeline*. St. Louis: Reedy Press, 2019. A lavishly illustrated coffee table book that presents a series of vignettes, each describing a noteworthy "hinge" moment in Detroit history.

Vachon, Paul. *Forgotten Detroit*. Charleston, SC: Arcadia Publishing, 2009. Through historical photos and engaging narrative, the author relates some of Detroit's lesser-known yet fascinating stories.

Vachon, Paul. *Lost Restaurants of Detroit*. Charleston, SC: The History Press, 2016. A fascinating look back on some of the most storied eateries from Detroit's past, plus several historic venues still in operation.

PARKS AND RECREATION

DuFresne, Jim. *Backpacking in Michigan*. Ann Arbor, MI: University of Michigan Press, 2007. Written by a Michigan native and author of more than 20 wilderness and travel guides, this book features 50 backpacking trails across both peninsulas, plus photographs and detailed maps.

DuFresne, Jim. *The Complete Guide to Michigan Sand Dunes*. Ann Arbor, MI: University of Michigan Press, 2005. In addition to providing a comprehensive explanation of dune formation, this guide offers all the necessary information—including more than 40 detailed maps—for swimmers, picnickers, hikers, skiers, and campers to explore nearly 50 duneland areas, from the remote to the well-known.

DuFresne, Jim. *Isle Royale National Park: Foot Trails & Water Routes*. Clarkston, MI: MichiganTrailMaps.com, 2011. Now in its fourth edition, this is the definitive guide to Isle Royale, filled with practical information about campsites, portages, fishing spots, and more.

DuFresne, Jim. *Michigan's Best Campgrounds: A Guide to the Best 150 Public Campgrounds in the Great Lakes State*. Berkeley, CA: Thunder Bay Press, 2011. In his updated fourth edition, this expert outdoorsman and writer suggests the best campsites for anglers, canoeists, hikers, bikers, and birdwatchers during the state's most popular season, May-October.

Funke, Tom. *Explorer's Guide 50 Hikes in Michigan's Upper Peninsula: Walks, Hikes, and Backpacks from Ironwood to St. Ignace*. Woodstock, VT: The Countryman Press, 2008. This guide features daylong and overnight trips for hikers, backpackers, and other recreationists throughout the Upper Peninsula. Each hike description is accompanied by a detailed topographical map, a difficulty rating, directions to the trailhead, and commentary about any related natural and cultural history.

Hillstrom, Kevin, and Laurie Hillstrom. *Paddling Michigan.* Guilford, CT: The Globe Pequot Press, 2001. An invaluable survey of 70 of Michigan's finest lakes, streams, and coastal waterways, whether known for amazing scenery, historical significance, or marine wildlife and activities. Ideal for canoeists and kayakers of all skill levels, this guide, though outdated, nonetheless contains valuable and detailed maps, preparation advice, seasonal tips, and lists of local paddling organizations.

REGIONAL TRAVEL

Cantor, George. *Explore Michigan: Detroit.* Petoskey, MI: Petoskey CO-PUB, 2005. Cantor, a former media personality and writer for the *Detroit News* who died in 2010, prepared a series of travel and activity guides for key Michigan destinations, including the state's premier city.

Cantor, George. *Explore Michigan: Leelanau.* Petoskey, MI: Petoskey CO-PUB, 2005. Though brief, this guide can definitely assist visitors on their tour of the Leelanau Peninsula, northwest of Traverse City.

Cantor, George. *Explore Michigan: Little Traverse Bay.* Petoskey, MI: Petoskey CO-PUB, 2005. This compact guide explores the restaurants, historic hotels, beaches, and other recreational diversions in and around Petoskey.

Cantor, George. *Explore Michigan: Mackinac.* Petoskey, MI: Petoskey CO-PUB, 2005. As with all of Cantor's compact travel guides, this one offers enough history, photographs, and practical information for any first-time visitor to experience Mackinac Island.

Cantor, George. *Explore Michigan: Traverse City.* Petoskey, MI: Petoskey CO-PUB, 2005. Cantor's comprehensive take on the Traverse City area.

Roach, Jerry, and Barb Roach. *The Ultimate Guide to East Michigan Lighthouses.* Durand, MI: Bugs Publishing, 2007. Rife with stunning images, this guide offers descriptions, directions, historical notes, contact numbers, and area travel information for more than 30 lighthouses along the eastern side of the Lower Peninsula, stretching from the Detroit River Light to the Old Mackinac Point Lighthouse.

Roach, Jerry, and Barb Roach. *The Ultimate Guide to Upper Michigan Lighthouses.* Durand, MI: Bugs Publishing, 2007. This handy guide explores more than 50 of the Upper Peninsula's lighthouses, from the St. Helena Lighthouse to the Wawatam Light. As with their previous lighthouse guides, the authors have included helpful descriptions and directions, historical background notes, colorful photographs, and plenty of travel details, such as contact numbers and information about area events and attractions.

Roach, Jerry, and Barb Roach. *The Ultimate Guide to West Michigan Lighthouses.* Durand, MI: Bugs Publishing, 2007. Filled with winning photographs, this guide (the first in the series of three) offers descriptions, directions, historical notes, contact numbers, and area travel information for more than 30 lighthouses along the western side of the Lower Peninsula, extending from the St. Joseph Pier Lights to McGulpin's Point Light.

Vachon, Paul. *Moon Michigan's Upper Peninsula.* Berkeley, CA: Avalon Travel, 2015. Updated by a Michigan native, this insider's view of the Upper Peninsula invites visitors to explore the forests, waterfalls, former mining towns, and isolated islands that define this one-of-a-kind place.

Suggested Viewing

Michigan has long been a favorite spot for filmmakers and television producers. While Detroit has received most of the screen time, as in television shows like *Hung* (2009-2011), *Detroit 1-8-7* (2010-2011), and *Low Winter Sun* (2013), the wilds of the Upper Peninsula have also served as cinematic backdrop.

Anatomy of a Murder (1959). Written by Wendell Mayes. Directed by Otto Preminger. Starring James Stewart, Ben Gazzara, Lee Remick, and George C. Scott. Based on the famous novel by a former Michigan Supreme Court justice, this engaging courtroom drama focuses on a small-town lawyer struggling to defend his client, a hotheaded army lieutenant arrested for the murder of a bartender who allegedly assaulted his wife. Set in the Upper Peninsula, the film features historic locations like the Marquette County Courthouse, the Ishpeming Carnegie Public Library, and Big Bay's Thunder Bay Inn.

8 Mile (2002). Written by Scott Silver. Directed by Curtis Hanson. Starring Eminem, Kim Basinger, Mekhi Phifer, and Brittany Murphy. During the course of one critical week, a young, angry rapper from the wrong side of Detroit's Eight Mile Road tries to achieve his musical goals while contending with various problems in his life.

Escanaba in da Moonlight (2001). Written and directed by Jeff Daniels, based on the eponymous play. Starring Jeff Daniels and Harve Presnell. In this whimsical comedy about deer hunting season amid the wilds of the Upper Peninsula, a macho man must deal with his eldest son's curse of never having killed a buck of his own.

Gran Torino (2008). Written by Nick Schenk. Directed by Clint Eastwood. Starring Clint Eastwood and Bee Vang. When a young immigrant tries to steal a prized automobile from his prejudiced neighbor—a retired Polish American automobile factory worker, Korean War veteran, and recent widower—the older man attempts to reform the teenager and protect his family from the gang members that infest their Highland Park neighborhood.

Hoffa (1992). Written by David Mamet. Directed by Danny DeVito. Starring Jack Nicholson, Danny DeVito, Armand Assante, and J. T. Walsh. Inspired by legendary labor union leader Jimmy Hoffa, this controversial film follows Hoffa's tumultuous career, from his numerous battles with the RTA and President Roosevelt to his 1975 disappearance.

Out of Sight (1998). Written by Scott Frank. Directed by Steven Soderbergh. Starring George Clooney, Jennifer Lopez, Ving Rhames, Steve Zahn, and Don Cheadle. Based on the eponymous Elmore Leonard novel, this humorous crime thriller follows the unlikely relationship between a career thief and a U.S. marshal, from the sweltering heat of Miami to the bitter cold of Detroit.

Roger & Me (1989). Written and directed by Michael Moore. In the first of several films that have defined Moore's "docuganda" style, the filmmaker tries to confront General Motors CEO Roger Smith about the massive downsizing that contributed to Flint's decline.

Somewhere in Time (1980). Written by Richard Matheson, based on his novel *Bid Time Return*. Directed by Jeannot Szwarc. Starring Christopher Reeve, Jane Seymour, and Christopher Plummer. After meeting an elderly actress who seems to know him from the past, a young Chicago playwright uses self-hypnosis to travel back to the early 1900s, where he embarks upon an ill-fated love affair inside Mackinac Island's Grand Hotel.

Internet Resources

CUISINE AND TRAVEL

Michigan Back Roads

www.michiganbackroads.com

If you enjoy exploring less-traveled destinations, you'll appreciate this website, which offers suggestions on short getaways along Michigan's back roads, where you'll encounter small towns, local inns and shops, historic sites, and other unique locales.

Michigan Cuisine

www.micuisine.com

Ostensibly, the company that runs this website is a graphics design firm for Michigan-based restaurants, but you'll also find regional recipes and cookbook suggestions, plus links to many of the state's eateries, festivals, culinary schools, and food associations.

Michigan Festivals and Events Association

www.mfea.org

Search this website for information about many of Michigan's cultural and community events, from art fairs to corn mazes.

The Michigan Travel Companion

www.yesmichigan.com

Use this comprehensive website to research Michigan's accommodations from motels to resorts. You can browse options by region, city, or type of lodging.

My North

www.mynorth.com

The online home of *Traverse* magazine serves as a useful repository for those eager to explore the northern part of the Lower Peninsula, from Manistee to Mackinac Island. Listed here are recipes as well as details about lodging, dining, events, wineries, outdoor activities, and the arts.

Pure Michigan

www.michigan.org

Michigan's official travel and tourism website offers just about everything you need to know about the state's cities, accommodations, restaurants, casinos, attractions, shops, parks, events, recreational activities, and entertainment venues. Just be aware that some of the information can be out of date, so always call ahead when making travel plans.

Southwestern Michigan Tourist Council

www.swmichigan.org

Travelers hoping to explore the varied beaches, wineries, golf courses, museums, antiques shops, and other attractions in the southwestern corner of Michigan's Lower Peninsula will find plenty of useful information on this website, including details about the area's dining and lodging options.

Thumb Area Tourism Council

www.thumbtourism.org

The TATC website is a helpful resource for those planning a trip to the Thumb. You'll find information about area attractions, parks, beaches, marinas, events, accommodations, historic sites, and more.

Upper Peninsula Travel

www.uptravel.com

Operated by the Upper Peninsula Travel & Recreation Association (UPTRA), this portal offers complete travel and lodging information for the UP, including details about events, activities, restaurants, campgrounds, waterfalls, lighthouses, and other attractions, plus current weather reports.

West Michigan Tourist Association
www.wmta.org
Based in Grand Rapids, the WMTA has been promoting West Michigan—the western half of the Lower Peninsula, from the Indiana border to the Straits of Mackinac—since 1917. The group's website provides a wealth of travel information from events to attractions to accommodations. You can also make reservations, find travel deals and coupons, and peruse maps and suggested itineraries.

GENERAL INFORMATION

Absolute Michigan
www.absolutemichigan.com
As its slogan states, this comprehensive website offers both visitors and residents "all Michigan, all the time"—a collection of links, features, news, and information about everything from wineries and art galleries to historic events and vacation cottages.

MD Travel Health
www.mdtravelhealth.com
Updated daily, this medical website is an excellent resource for travelers. Here, you'll find information about specific destinations, available clinics, infectious diseases, and illness prevention, as well as tailored advice for those with special needs, such as diabetics and pregnant women.

State of Michigan
www.michigan.gov
Michigan's official website offers a wide array of information about the state's economic growth, educational issues, health and safety considerations, environmental resources, and governmental departments. Here, you can check road closures, purchase fishing and hunting licenses, and even learn more about the state's symbols, landmarks, and little-known historical facts.

U.S. Department of State
www.travel.state.gov
Whether or not you're a U.S. citizen, this website, operated by the U.S. Department of State's Bureau of Consular Affairs, will help you travel safely across the United States-Canada border near Detroit, Port Huron, and Sault Ste. Marie. International travelers will also find guidelines for flying into and out of Michigan.

HISTORY AND CULTURE

Historical Society of Michigan
www.hsmichigan.org
This website features a wealth of information related to the preservation of Michigan's history, including comprehensive lists of historic events, local historical organizations, and libraries, plus links to publications like *Michigan History* magazine—the ownership of which was transferred from the state's former Department of History, Arts and Libraries to the Historical Society of Michigan in 2009.

Michigan State University Press
http://msupress.msu.edu
You'll find a number of titles by Michigan-based writers, from statewide economic studies to personal essays about the Great Lakes to historical accounts of Michigan's immigrants, colleges, railroads, and shipwrecks.

University of Michigan Press
www.press.umich.edu
Peruse this website for a wealth of Michigan-related books that shed light on the state's history and culture. Included here are historical accounts, personal memoirs, biographies, and field guides.

Wayne State University Press
www.wsupress.wayne.edu
A publisher that offers a wide assortment of titles, including its Great Lakes Series, which covers Michigan and regional history, Detroit history, and Michigan art and architecture, among many other topics.

PARKS AND RECREATION

Boating Safety Resource Center
www.uscgboating.org
Use this comprehensive website, operated by the U.S. Coast Guard's Boating Safety

Division, to prevent accidents and fatalities while boating in Michigan.

League of Michigan Bicyclists
www.lmb.org

Road and mountain bikers can explore this website for biking routes, clubs, events, and shops throughout the state.

Mackinac State Historic Parks
www.mackinacparks.com

Visitors to Mackinaw City and Mackinac Island should stop here first for information about the area's various historic sites, including details about admission rates, hours of operation, and special events.

Michigan Charter Boat Association
www.michigancharterboats.com

In addition to fish species descriptions and current fishing reports, this website offers access to hundreds of charter fishing boats, river fishing guides, sailing excursions, and diving trips that service the coastal areas and open waters of the Great Lakes and Lake St. Clair.

Michigan Department of Natural Resources
www.michigan.gov/dnr

From this recreation portal, you'll learn most of what you need to know about fishing, hunting, camping, boating, hiking, biking, and snowmobiling in the Great Lakes State. Also included here are maps, publications, and information about law enforcement, forest management, state parks, historic sites, trails, and wildlife.

Michigan Interactive
www.fishweb.com

Besides offering numerous maps and lodging options, this website provides a trove of advice for anglers, boaters, paddlers, hikers, golfers, snowmobilers, off-road enthusiasts, and even mushroom hunters.

Michigan Snowsports Industries Association
www.goskimichigan.com

Skiers and snowboarders should peruse this website for details about Michigan's downhill ski slopes, outfitters, and snow conditions.

Michigan Underwater Preserves
www.michiganpreserves.org

A resource for divers, this website offers advice and information about all of Michigan's underwater preserves, from Isle Royale to Sanilac Shores.

National Park Service
www.nps.gov

The National Park Service provides detailed maps, brochures, and contact information for each of its roughly 400 parks, lakeshores, monuments, recreation areas, and other natural and cultural sites throughout the United States. Use the state-by-state search function to learn more about Michigan's protected places, including Isle Royale National Park, Keweenaw National Historical Park, Pictured Rocks National Lakeshore, Sleeping Bear Dunes National Lakeshore, and Motor Cities National Heritage Area.

National Wild and Scenic Rivers System
www.rivers.gov

Learn more about Michigan's federally designated Wild and Scenic Rivers, from the Au Sable to the Sturgeon.

Sam Crowe's Michigan Birding
www.michiganbirding.com

Visit this website for information about popular bird-watching spots, tours, and festivals throughout Michigan.

U.S. Fish and Wildlife Service
www.fws.gov

You can find useful information about Michigan's endangered species, including the gray wolf and Kirtland's warbler, as well as details regarding the state's wildlife refuges, such as Shiawassee National Wildlife Refuge and Detroit River International Wildlife Refuge.

U.S. Forest Service
www.fs.fed.us

Through this website, you can learn more about Michigan's national forests, from the Upper Peninsula's Hiawatha National Forest to the Lower Peninsula's Huron-Manistee National Forests.

Index

C

H

I

N

O

P

QR

S

T

UV

WXYZ

List of Maps

Photo Credits

All photos © Paul Vachon except page 6 © (top left) Michael Deemer, Dreamstime.com; page 7 © (bottom left) Alicia Hess, Dreamstime.com; page 8 © Baluzek, Dreamstime.com; page 10 © Ehrlif, Dreamstime.com; page 11 © (bottom) Jacob Boomsma, Dreamstime.com; page 12 © (top) Craig Sterken, Dreamstime.com; (bottom) Wavebreakmedia Ltd, Dreamstime.com; page 14 © (top) Foodio, Dreamstime.com; (bottom) Lukas Gojda, Dreamstime.com; page 19 © (bottom) Craig Sterken, Dreamstime.com; page 21 © (bottom) Helgidinson, Dreamstime.com; page 28 © (bottom) Edward Lange, Dreamstime.com; page 30 © Ehrlif, Dreamstime.com; page 34 © Atomazul, Dreamstime.com; page 37 © (top right) Petr Švec, Dreamstime.com; page 42 © (bottom) Roman Halanski Jr., Dreamstime.com; page 50 © (top left) Nyker1, Dreamstime.com; (bottom) Roman Halanski, Dreamstime.com; page 56 © Byelikova, Dreamstime.com; page 61 © Bhofack2, Dreamstime.com; page 67 © (top) Smontgom65, Dreamstime.com; (bottom) Joe Sohm, Dreamstime.com; page 76 © (top left) Aviahuismanphotography, Dreamstime.com; (bottom) Steven Cukrov, Dreamstime.com; page 84 © Paul Brady, Dreamstime.com; page 85 © (top left) Ken Wolter, Dreamstime.com; page 103 © Craig Sterken, Dreamstime.com; page 107 © (top) Smontgom65, Dreamstime.com; (bottom) Smontgom65, Dreamstime.com; page 109 © Lindaparton, Dreamstime.com; page 112 © Lindaparton, Dreamstime.com; page 117 © (top right) Dkklatt, Dreamstime.com; (bottom) Ehrlif, Dreamstime.com; page 122 © Ehrlif, Dreamstime.com; page 133 © Sean Pavone, Dreamstime.com; page 134 © (top left) Mrskmk, Dreamstime.com; (top right) Ffooter, Dreamstime.com; page 139 © (top) Alex Grichenko, Dreamstime.com; page 144 © (top left) Michael Deemer, Dreamstime.com; (top right) Michael Deemer, Dreamstime.com; (bottom) Roberto Galan, Dreamstime.com; page 149 © (top left) Jian Zhang, Dreamstime.com; (top right) Kevin Ruck, Dreamstime.com; page 153 © Jian Zhang, Dreamstime.com; page 155 © Toni Marie Cole, Dreamstime.com; page 157 © Jim Roberts, Dreamstime.com; page 167 © Shriram Patki, Dreamstime.com; page 175 © Susan Sheldon, Dreamstime.com; page 178 © Michigannut, Dreamstime.com; page 183 © (top left) Susan Sheldon, Dreamstime.com; (top right) Kristalwithak, Dreamstime.com; page 194 © (top left) Kenneth Sponsler, Dreamstime.com; (top right) Mark Lucey, Dreamstime.com; (bottom) Kenneth Sponsler, Dreamstime.com; page 201 © Ian Mendel, Dreamstime.com; page 207 © R. Gino Santa Maria, Dreamstime.com; page 208 © WKTV Grand Rapids; page 221 © Gotstock, Dreamstime.com; page 224 © (top left) Kirk Hewlett, Dreamstime.com; (top right) Holly0722, Dreamstime.com; (bottom) Kirk Hewlett, Dreamstime.com; page 234 © Gregory Stawicki, Dreamstime.com; page 249 © Kenneth Sponsler, Dreamstime.com; page 259 © (top left) Rhbabiak13, Dreamstime.com; page 264 © (top) Bambi L. Dingman, Dreamstime.com; (bottom) Picturemakersllc, Dreamstime.com; page 268 © Helgidinson, Dreamstime.com; page 272 © (top) Alexey Stiop, Dreamstime.com; (left middle)Cheri Alguire, Dreamstime.com; (right middle)Shriram Patki, Dreamstime.com; (bottom) Lembi Buchanan, Dreamstime.com; page 277 © Haveseen, Dreamstime.com; page 293 © Fischer0182, Dreamstime.com; page 298 © Le Thuy Do, Dreamstime.com; page 308 © Marysue Ryan, Dreamstime.com; page 312 © (top) Jim Roberts, Dreamstime.com; (bottom) Rhbabiak13, Dreamstime.com; page 329 © (top right) Richardhoeg, Dreamstime.com; (bottom) Steve Lagreca, Dreamstime.com; page 342 © Michael Thompson, Dreamstime.com; page 352 © (top) AngelSchwai, Dreamstime.com; (bottom) Steve Lagreca, Dreamstime.com; page 359 © NatmacStock, Dreamstime.com; page 363 © Steven Prorak, Dreamstime.com; page 376 © Adeliepenguin, Dreamstime.com